Fodor's

HONG KONG

20th Edition

Where to Stay and Eat for All Budgets

Must-See Sights and Local Secrets

Ratings You Can Trust

Fodor's Travel Publications   New York, Toronto, London, Sydney, Auckland
www.fodors.com

FODOR'S HONG KONG

Editors: Laura M. Kidder (lead project editor), Nuha Ansari, Margaret Kelly, Adam Taplin

Editorial Production: Linda K. Schmidt

Editorial Contributors: Joshua Samuel Brown, Hiram Chu, Eva Chui Loiterton, Robin Goldstein, Chris Horton, Victoria Patience, Elyse Singleton, Sofia Suárez

Maps & Illustrations: David Lindroth, *cartographer*; William Wu; with additional cartography provided Henry Columb, Mark Stroud, and Ali Baird, Moon Street Cartography; Bob Blake and Rebecca Baer, *map editors*

Design: Fabrizio La Rocca, *creative director*; Guido Caroti, *art director*; Tina Malaney, Chie Ushio, *designers*; Moon Sun Kim, *cover designer*; Melanie Marin, *senior picture editor*

Production/Manufacturing: Robert B. Shields

Cover Photo (Causeway Bay): So Hing-Keung/Corbis

Twentieth Edition

ISBN 978-1-4000-1718-8

ISSN 1070-6887

SPECIAL SALES

This book is available at special discounts for bulk purchases for sales promotions or premiums. Special editions, including personalized covers, excerpts of existing books, and corporate imprints, can be created in large quantities for special needs. For more information, write to Special Markets/Premium Sales, 1745 Broadway, MD 6-2, New York, New York 10019, or e-mail specialmarkets@randomhouse.com.

AN IMPORTANT TIP & AN INVITATION

Although all prices, opening times, and other details in this book are based on information supplied to us at press time, changes occur all the time in the travel world, and Fodor's cannot accept responsibility for facts that become outdated or for inadvertent errors or omissions. So **always confirm information when it matters,** especially if you're making a detour to visit a specific place. Your experiences—positive and negative—matter to us. If we have missed or misstated something, **please write to us.** We follow up on all suggestions. Contact the Hong Kong editor at editors@fodors.com or c/o Fodor's at 1745 Broadway, New York, NY 10019.

PRINTED IN THE UNITED STATES OF AMERICA

10 9 8 7 6 5 4 3 2

Be a Fodor's Correspondent

Your opinion matters. It matters to us. It matters to your fellow Fodor's travelers, too. And we'd like to hear it. In fact, we *need* to hear it.

When you share your experiences and opinions, you become an active member of the Fodor's community. That means we'll not only use your feedback to make our books better, but we'll publish your names and comments whenever possible. Throughout our guides, look for "Word of Mouth," excerpts of your unvarnished feedback.

Here's how you can help improve Fodor's for all of us.

Tell us when we're right. We rely on local writers to give you an insider's perspective. But our writers and staff editors—who are the best in the business—depend on you. Your positive feedback is a vote to renew our recommendations for the next edition.

Tell us when we're wrong. We're proud that we update most of our guides every year. But we're not perfect. Things change. Hotels cut services. Museums change hours. Charming cafés lose charm. If our writer didn't quite capture the essence of a place, tell us how you'd do it differently. If any of our descriptions are inaccurate or inadequate, we'll incorporate your changes in the next edition and will correct factual errors at fodors.com *immediately.*

Tell us what to include. You probably have had fantastic travel experiences that aren't yet in Fodor's. Why not share them with a community of like-minded travelers? Maybe you chanced upon a beach or bistro or B&B that you don't want to keep to yourself. Tell us why we should include it. And share your discoveries and experiences with everyone directly at fodors.com. Your input may lead us to add a new listing or highlight a place we cover with a "Highly Recommended" star or with our highest rating, "Fodor's Choice."

Give us your opinion instantly at our feedback center at www.fodors.com/feedback. You may also e-mail editors@fodors.com with the subject line "Hong Kong Editor." Or send your nominations, comments, and complaints by mail to Hong Kong Editor, Fodor's, 1745 Broadway, New York, NY 10019.

You and travelers like you are the heart of the Fodor's community. Make our community richer by sharing your experiences. Be a Fodor's correspondent.

Happy traveling!

Tim Jarrell Publisher

CONTENTS

MAPS

HONG KONG IN FOCUS

ABOUT THIS BOOK

Our Ratings

Sometimes you find terrific travel experiences and sometimes they just find you. But usually the burden is on you to select the right combination of experiences. That's where our ratings come in.

As travelers we've all discovered a place so wonderful that its worthiness is obvious. And sometimes that place is so unique that superlatives don't do it justice: you just have to be there to know. These sights, properties, and experiences get our highest rating, **Fodor's Choice,** indicated by orange stars throughout this book.

Black stars highlight sights and properties we deem **Highly Recommended,** places that our writers, editors, and readers praise again and again for consistency and excellence.

By default, there's another category: any place we include in this book is by definition worth your time, unless we say otherwise. And we will.

Disagree with any of our choices? Care to nominate a place or suggest that we rate one more highly? Visit our feedback center at www. fodors.com/feedback.

Budget Well

Hotel and restaurant price categories from ¢ to **$$$$** are defined in the opening pages of each chapter. For attractions, we always give standard adult admission fees; reductions are usually available for children, students, and senior citizens. Want to pay with plastic? **AE, D, DC, MC, V** following restaurant and hotel listings indicate whether American Express, Discover, Diner's Club, MasterCard, and Visa are accepted.

Restaurants

Unless we state otherwise, restaurants are open for lunch and dinner daily. We mention dress only when there's a specific requirement and reservations only when they're essential or not accepted—it's always best to book ahead.

Hotels

Hotels have private bath, phone, TV, and air-conditioning and operate on the European Plan (aka EP, meaning without meals), unless we specify that they use the Continental Plan (CP, with a continental breakfast), Breakfast Plan (BP, with a full breakfast), or Modified American Plan (MAP, with breakfast and dinner) or are all-inclusive (including all meals and most activities). We always

list facilities but not whether you'll be charged an extra fee to use them, so when pricing accommodations, find out what's included.

Many Listings
- ★ Fodor's Choice
- ★ Highly recommended
- ⊠ Physical address
- ✛ Directions
- Ⓕ Mailing address
- ☎ Telephone
- 🖷 Fax
- ⊕ On the Web
- ✑ E-mail
- 🖾 Admission fee
- ☉ Open/closed times
- ► Start of walk/itinerary
- Ⓜ Metro stations
- ▤ Credit cards

Hotels & Restaurants
- 🏨 Hotel
- 🛏 Number of rooms
- ☖ Facilities
- ❑ Meal plans
- ✕ Restaurant
- ☛ Reservations
- 🏠 Dress code
- ☊ Smoking
- Ⓨ BYOB
- ✕🏨 Hotel with restaurant that warrants a visit

Outdoors
- ⚐ Golf
- ⚠ Camping

Other
- ⓒ Family-friendly
- ⓕ Contact information
- ⇨ See also
- ⊠ Branch address
- ☞ Take note

1

Experience Hong Kong

China ferry terminal, Kowloon

WORD OF MOUTH

"We have visited Hong Kong three times, staying a week or two each time. So, all in all, we have spent a good month there. Just know that Hong Kong is a very engaging city. It's so easy to get around and enjoy yourself unassisted."　　　　　—marya

HONG KONG PLANNER

Looks Deceive

Hong Kong is complex. On the surface it seems that every building is a sculpture of glass and steel and every pedestrian is hurrying to a meeting. But look past the shiny new surfaces to the ancient culture that gives the city its exotic flavor and its citizens their unique outlook.

Wording It Right

Try to learn a few basic Cantonese expressions like "*lei-ho*?" ("hi, how are you?") and "*mm-goi sai*" ("thanks very much"). The official languages are English and Cantonese. Mandarin—the language of China—is gaining in popularity both here and in Macau, where the languages are Portuguese and Cantonese.

In hotels, major restaurants, and large stores, almost everyone speaks English. Taxi and bus drivers and staffers in small shops, cafés, and market stalls do not.

Ask for directions from MTR employees or English-speaking policemen, identifiable by the red strips on their epaulettes. Get your concierge to write down your destination in Chinese if you're headed somewhere off the main trail.

Peruse the Web site of the **New Asia Yale in China Chinese Language Centre** (⊕ www.cuhk.edu.hk/clc) at the Chinese University of Hong Kong for language study courses.

Good for Kids

Put the Star Ferry, the Symphony of Lights, the Peak Tram, and a skyscraper climb atop your list. The Hong Kong Heritage Museum has a gallery where 4- to 10-year-olds can dress up in Hakka clothes and reconstruct pottery. Colorful, very hands-on main galleries have plenty for teens.

Ocean Park has a balance of toned-down thrills and high-octane rides, so you could take 3- or 4-year-olds right through to teenagers. A massive aquarium and a giant-panda enclosure round out the offerings. Older kids might enjoy seeing candy-pink dolphins in their natural habitat on a Dolphinwatch half-day trip. If you want even more beasties, tropical birds fill the walk-through Edward Youde Aviary in Hong Kong Park, while a black jaguar is the zoo's most famous resident.

Mallrats can make plenty of like-minded local friends at Times Square, Pacific Place, and Kowloon Tong's Festival Walk, all of which are safe places to wander.

Visitor Information

Swing by the Hong Kong Tourist Board (HKTB) visitor center before even leaving the airport. They publish stacks of helpful free exploring booklets, run a plethora of tours all over the territory (and beyond), and operate a multilingual helpline. Their detailed website is a fabulous resource. If you're planning on visiting several museums in a week, pick up an HKTB Museum Tour Pass, which gets you into several museums and costs HK$30.

Hong Kong Tourist Board (HKTB; ⊠ Hong Kong International Airport, Arrivals Level, Lantau ⊙ Daily 7 AM–11 PM ⊠ Causeway Bay MTR Station, near Exit F, Causeway Bay ⊙ Daily 8–8 ⊠ Star Ferry Concourse, Tsim Sha Tsui, Kowloon ⊙ Daily 8–8 ☎ 2508–1234 (hotline) ⊕ www.discoverhongkong.com).

Navigating

■ Hong Kong's streets seem utterly chaotic, but getting lost in Central is an achievement. If you manage it, get your bearings by looking up: orient yourself using the waterfront TwoIFC skyscraper. In Kowloon, remember where you are in relation to Nathan Road, where the MTR (underground railway) stations are.

■ The MTR, which links most of the areas you'll want to visit, is quick, safe, clean, and very user-friendly. The KCR transit system links Kowloon with areas in the New Territories.

■ Pay with a rechargeable Octopus card. You can use it on the MTR, KCR, buses, trams, the Star Ferry, the Peak Tram—even at the racetrack.

■ It's often not worth taking the MTR for one stop, as stations are close. Walk or take a bus or tram.

■ Most MTR stations have multiple exits, so consult the detailed station maps to determine which exit lets you out closest to your destination.

■ If you're crossing Central, use the covered walkways that link its main buildings, thus avoiding stoplights, exhaust fumes, and weather conditions.

■ On Hong Kong Island, Queen's Road changes its suffix every so often, so you get Queen's Road East, Queen's Road Central, and Queen's Road West. These suffixes, however, don't exactly correspond with the districts, so part of Queen's Road Central is actually in Western. As street numbers start again with each new section, be sure you know which part you're headed for, or better still, the intersecting street. The same goes for Des Voeux Road.

When to Go

Hong Kong's high season, October through late December, sees sunny days and cool, comfortable nights. January, February, and sometimes early March are cool and dank, with long periods of overcast skies and rain. March and April can be either chilly and miserable or sunny and beautiful. By May the temperature is consistently warm and comfortable.

HONG KONG TEMPERATURES

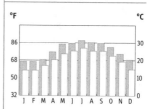

June through September are the cheapest months for one reason: they coincide with the hot, sticky, and very rainy typhoon (hurricane) season. Hong Kong is prepared for blustery assaults; if a big storm approaches, the airwaves crackle with information, and your hotel will post the appropriate signals (a No. 8 signal indicates the worst of winds, and a black warning is the equivalent for rain). This is serious business—bamboo scaffolding can come hurtling through the streets like spears, ships can sink in the harbor, and large areas of the territory can flood. Museums, shops and transport shut down, too.

TOP ATTRACTIONS

The Big Buddha

(A) How did a remote Lantau Island plateau make the city's must-do checklist? It's mostly due to the 242-ton Tian Tan Buddha statue, which sits in the lotus position on a hill next to the Po Lin Buddhist Monastery. Since the statue was built, the Ngong Ping area has gone platinum. Nearby is the Wisdom Path, a beautiful religious walk.

Chi Lin Nunnery

(B) Such a peaceful haven seems unlikely amid New Kowloon's grimy sprawl. Yet when you step over the wooden threshold of the Chi Lin Nunnery, the tower blocks fade away. Its stone-flagged courtyards, wooden halls, and unadorned altars invite reflection.

Dim Sum

(C) As you bite into a moist *siu mai* it dawns on you why everyone says you haven't done dim sum until you've done it in Hong Kong. Fresh, innovative ingredients and devout diners make dim sum places here very different from those in Chinatowns worldwide.

Going Green

(D) Hong Kong and its environs are dotted with golf courses: from the popular (and cheap) Kau Sai Chau public course near Sai Kung town to the popular (and luxe) Mission Hills Golf Club & Resort, the world's largest golf facility, near Shenzhen on the mainland.

Harbor Views

(E) The skyline that launched a thousand postcards. . . . See it on a stroll along the Tsim Sha Tsui waterfront, from a Star Ferry crossing the harbor, or from the breezy viewpoints of Victoria Peak. By day, the skyscrapers glitter. When the sun sets, Hong Kong puts on its neon party gear.

Hong Kong Heritage Museum

(F) How did scattered fishing and farming communities become an iconic metropo-

lis? This beautifully planned museum chronicles Hong Kong's changing face, from village life to booming new towns. An exquisite Chinese art collection and an interactive exhibition on Cantonese Opera are two more reasons to head here.

Horse Racing at Happy Valley

(G) Every year, Hong Kongers gamble over US$10 billion, and the Happy Valley Racetrack is one of their favorite places to do it. As the horses pound along, thousands of punters scream themselves into a frenzy—they're more of a spectacle than the races, truth be told.

Jetfoil Getaway

(H) Ask Hong Kongers about Macau, the former Portuguese colony an hour away by jetfoil, and they'll go on about its good food and wine and its casinos. They may forget to tell you about the old town squares paved in elegant patterns and lined with colonial buildings. They may also neglect to mention the gray-sand beaches.

Markets & Malls

(I) Shopping is a religion here, and with so many retail temples, it's easy to see why. At Kowloon's street markets, clothes, electronics, and souvenirs compete for space with food carts. Exquisite antiques fill windows along Hollywood Road, from Central to Sheung Wan, where herbalists peddle strange-looking remedies. Big-name designers monopolize Central's malls. Prices are more down to earth in Causeway Bay's Times Square mall.

The Trails

(J) Well-maintained trails crisscross Hong Kong's greenery. You can visit the best wilderness areas simply by tackling part of the MacLehose Trail in Sai Kung Country Park. Crossing the Dragon's Back—a Hong Kong Island ridge—leads to unparalleled Southside sea views and the village of Shek O.

FREE THINGS TO DO

It's easy to spend money in the big city: shopping, entrance fees, food, shows, late-night cocktails. But if you'd like to put your wallet away for a while, here are some of our favorite options.

Art
Works by local prodigies adorn the walls of the tony—but free—private galleries in Central, SoHo, and Sheung Wan. Hanart TZ Gallery, Plum Blossoms, and Grotto Fine Art are stalwarts. There's a leafy backdrop for the Sculpture Walk, a collection of 20 works—including an Eduardo Paolozzi—that winds through Kowloon Park. Contemporary sculpture also dots the waterside promenade near the museum of art in Tsim Sha Tsui.

Bright Lights
During the "Symphony of Lights," held at 8 each night, 33 skyscrapers are lit up on cue as a commentator introduces them in time with a musical accompaniment.

Culture Classes
The tourist board runs free classes on feng shui, traditional Chinese medicine, and tea appreciation. A tai ch'i master will put you through the moves in Hong Kong Park Monday and Wednesday through Friday at 8 AM.

Enlightenment
Inner peace is priceless, and though it's customary to make a small donation, all of Hong Kong's temples are free. So are the Tian Tan Buddha and the Wisdom Path on Lantau Island, though you have to pay to get there first.

Junk Rides
There's only one old-fashioned junk still floating round the harbor. Thanks to the tourist board, foreigners can ride the *Duk Ling* for free Thursday afternoon and Saturday morning.

Music
High-quality ensembles perform at "Happy Hour" concerts, Thursday at 6 PM in the Hong Kong Cultural Centre's foyer. Family variety shows with dance, music, and acrobatics take place on Saturday at 2:30 PM. There are also free organ recitals one Saturday a month.

Museums
Plan your cut-price museum marathon for Wednesday, when there's no admission charge at government-run museums. Note that the Hong Kong Tourist Board (HKTB) museum pass gets you into all government-run museums for HK$30. Buy it at participating museums.

Walkabouts
In town, you can take in colonial architecture during an hour-long stroll through Western between the University of Hong Kong and Western Market. Is the weather bad? Try walking through Central without ever leaving a building—the sign of a true Hong Konger. You can also head for the hills outside of town, hiking along the Dragon's Back or to the Lion Rock.

Views
It doesn't cost a cent to ride up to the Bank of China's 43rd-floor observation deck or to visit the Hong Kong Monetary Authority, on the 55th floor of the International Finance Centre, for fabulous harbor views over to Kowloon. Reverse the vista from the Tsim Sha Tsui waterfront promenade, the best place to see the Hong Kong Island skyline.

FEASTS & FÊTES

The loudest and proudest traditional festival, **Chinese New Year** brings Hong Kong to a standstill each year. Shops shut down, and everywhere you look there are red and gold signs, kumquat trees, and pots of yellow chrysanthemums, all considered auspicious. On the first night there's a colorful parade; on the second the crowds ooh and ahh at the no-costs-spared fireworks display over the harbor. (1st day of 1st moon, usually late Jan.–early Feb.)

The Chinese New Year festivities end with the colorful **Spring Lantern Festival.** Hong Kong's green spaces—especially Victoria Park—become a sea of light as people gather with beautifully shaped paper or cellophane lanterns. It's also a day of celebration for couples. (15th day of 1st moon, usually Feb.)

Ancestor-worship is a big part of traditional Chinese religions, and on **Ching Ming** families meet to clean the graves of their departed loved ones. (Apr. 5) Thousands make the yearly trip to Cheung Chau Island for the exuberant **Cheung Chau Bun Festival**, a four-day-long Taoist thanksgiving feast. Sixty-foot towers covered in buns quiver outside Pak Tai Temple, and there's a huge procession of children dressed as gods carried atop tall poles. (8th day of 4th moon, usually May)

The **Dragon Boat Festival** pits long, multi-oared dragon-head boats against one another in races across the harbor. It commemorates the hero Qu Yuan, a poet and scholar who drowned himself in the 3rd century BC to protest government corruption. These days, it's one big harborside party. (5th day of 5th moon, usually June)

There are smoldering piles of paper all over the place during **Hungry Ghosts Festival.** Replicas of houses, cars, and Monopoly-style "hell money" are burned as offerings to the ghosts allowed to wander the earth for these two weeks, when the gates of hell are opened. (15th day of 7th moon, usually Aug.—Sept.)

During the **Mid-Autumn Festival**, crowds gather to share *yue bing* or "moon cakes," which are stuffed with red-bean or lotus-seed paste. These commemorate a 14th-century revolution, when co-conspirators' notes were baked inside them. Colorful paper lanterns fill Hong Kong's parks, and performers dress up for a huge dragon dance in Causeway Bay. (15th day of 8th moon, usually Sept.–Oct.)

ON THE MOVE

The city's transport options are as varied—old and new, fast and slow, land and sea—as they are comprehensive, safe, and easy to use. Some are sights in their own right. There's no train timetable, because they run so frequently. Buses are air-conditioned, have cushioned seating, and are as clean as a whistle. On the seas, enjoy a quick scenic trip across the harbor on the iconic Star Ferries, or take a fast ferry to an outer island or even Macau. For a leisurely ride harking back to the days of old, nothing beats a double-decker tram. So go on: skip taxis and take public.

Double-Decker Trams. Tall, thin, and rumbling, the iconic trams have efficiently, albeit *slowly*, moved passengers across Hong Kong Island since 1904. This is the world's largest fleet of double-deckers still in operation. The beloved trams, which locals call "ding ding" because of the noise the horns make, are a fun and inexpensive way to cruise the island, if you have the time. Enter from the rear, head straight up the narrow staircase, and grab a seat at the very front for the best views. At this height, you can almost reach out and touch the neon signs. One interesting 20-minute journey takes you through Central's forest of skyscrapers east to Wan Chai's wet markets and clothing shops, ending at Southern Playground, where kids play basketball and soccer and the older folk play Chinese checkers. All journeys cost HK$2.

Midlevels Escalator. A practical human mover, this is actually a 1-km-long (½-mi-long) combination of escalators and walkways that provide free, glass-covered transport up or down the steep incline between Central and Midlevels. The effortless trip provides a view of small Chinese shops, a wet market, the Jamia Mosque at Shelley Street, and gleaming residential high-rises. In fact, you're often so close to the apartments that it's impossible to avoid peering in, perhaps on a family having dinner or watching TV. Starting at Staunton Street, the escalator cuts through the fashionable SoHo area, filled with cafés, bars, and boutiques.

Plan to ride the escalators up between 10:20 AM and 11:30 PM. From 6 to 10 AM they move downhill only, so commuters from Midlevels can get to work. After 11:30 PM the escalators shut down, and that equates to a long walk on steep steps. You can get off at any point and explore side streets where vendors sell porcelain, clothes, and antiques (not necessarily authentic). Most buildings have tiny makeshift altars to ancestors, usually made of colorful red paper with gold Chinese characters, with offerings of fruit and incense. ✉ *Enter across from Central Market, at Queen's Rd. Central and Jubilee St., Central* ⊙ *Daily 6 AM–11:30 PM.*

Ngong Ping 360 Skyrail. The breathtaking 3.5-mile (5.7-km) cable-car journey takes you above the Lantau Island's greenery, from Tung Chung to Ngong Ping. During the 25-minute ride, you get a glimpse of the Big Buddha, sitting and smiling peacefully on a mountaintop. ☎ *2109–9898* ⊕ *www.np360.com.hk.* ⊙ *Weekdays*

FLY THE FRIENDLY SKIES

With 1.8 mi (2.9 km) of moving walkways, 14 acres of glass, and around 30 acres of carpeting, the international terminal at Chek Lap Kok Airport is the world's largest. At $20 billion to build, it's also the world's most expensive. A super-efficient express train runs between the city and this modern marvel in 23 minutes.

10–6, weekends 10–6:30 ✉ *HK$58–68 one-way, HK$88–98 round-trip*

Peak Tram. ★ Fodor's Choice Hong Kong is very proud of the fact that its funicular railway is the world's steepest. Before it opened in 1880 the only way to get up Victoria Peak, the highest hill overlooking Hong Kong Harbour, was to walk or take a bumpy ride in a sedan chair on steep steps. You really can't afford to miss the thrilling tram journey. On the way up, grab a seat on the right-hand side for the best views of the harbor and mountains. The trams, which look like old-fashioned trolley cars, are hauled the whole way in seven minutes by cables attached to electric motors. En route to the upper terminal, 1,805 feet above sea level, the cars pass five intermediate stations. At times they seem to travel at an impossibly vertical angle, but don't fret; it's all perfectly safe.

At the top you immediately enter the Peak Tower, a mall full of restaurants, shops, and amusements such as Madame Tussaud's wax museum. There's a viewing platform on the mall's roof. Outside the Peak Tower, another mall faces you. Well-signed nature walks around the Peak are wonderful respites from the commercialism. Bus 15C, an antique double-decker with an open top, shuttles you to the Peak Tram Terminal from Edinburgh Place, next to City Hall. ✉ *Between Garden Rd. and Cotton Tree Dr., Central* ☎ *2522–0922* ⊕ *www.thepeak. com.hk* ✉ *HK$20 one-way, HK$30 round-trip* ☾ *Daily every 15 mins, 7 AM–midnight.*

Star Ferry. ★ Fodor's Choice Since 1898 the ferry pier has been the gateway to the island for people from Kowloon. If it's your first time in the city, you're all but required to cross the harbor and back on the Star Ferry at least once. It's a beautiful, re-

WELL TRAINED

It's fast, reliable, and spotless. It moves 2.4 million people every weekday. Not many cities have a metro system as efficient and rider friendly as Hong Kong's MTR. All signs and maps are in Chinese and English, and the six train lines take you all across Hong Kong Island and the Kowloon Peninsula.

laxing trip on antiquated, characterful vessels. An evening ride is even better, when the city's neon and skyscrapers light up the sky. The distinctive green-and-white vessels are beloved harbor fixtures; many people prefer the gentle, smooth sailing trip to one on the busy MTR. The ferry's home is Pier 7 of the Outlying Islands Ferry Piers.

There are two classes: a first-class ticket (HK$2.20) gives you a seat on the upper deck, with its air-conditioned compartments. Second-class seats (HK$1.70) are on the lower deck and tend to be noisy because they're near the engine room. For very different experiences, try the upper deck one way and the lower deck on the other. ■ TIP➔ **For trips from Central to Tsim Sha Tsui, seats on the eastern side have the best views—the ferries don't turn around, though, so remember to swing the seats so that you face forward.**

Across the way, the pier makes a convenient starting point for any tour of Kowloon. (It also has a bus terminal, which sends buses to all parts of Kowloon and to the New Territories.) As you face the bus station, Ocean Terminal, where luxury cruise ships berth, is on your left; inside this terminal, and in adjacent Harbour City, are miles of air-conditioned shopping arcades. ✉ *Central* ☾ *Daily 6 AM–midnight.*

FENG SHUI STRUCTURES

There's a battle going on in Central, a battle between good and evil forces. Feng shui (pronounced *fung shoy* in Cantonese, *foong shway* in Mandarin, and literally translated as "wind" and "water") is the art of placing objects to bring about yin–yang balance. In the West, feng shui seems like just another interior-design fad; here it's taken very seriously.

One school looks at buildings in relation, say, to mountains or bodies of water. It's ideal, for example, for a building to face out to sea with a mountain behind it. (Is it coincidence that this allows for the best views and breezes?). Another school focuses on shapes in the immediate environment; triangles, for instance, give off bad feng shui. Both schools are concerned with the flow of energy. Entrances are placed to allow positive energy to flow in, and objects such as mirrors are used to deflect negative energy. Cities are often short of such natural feng shui improvers as babbling brooks, but not to worry: a fish tank is a fine alternative.

Case Study 1: Bank of China

Bank of China Tower. In the politics of Hong Kong architecture, the stylish art deco building that served as the old Bank of China headquarters was the first trump:

SAFE NOT SORRY

Nearly all major developers—even multinationals like Disney—consult feng shui masters, if only in deference to local employees. It's estimated that at least 50% of Hong Kongers believe in the power of feng shui to some extent. Better safe than sorry. To learn more, contact the tourist board, which offers weekly feng shui tours.

---

built after World War II, it was 20 feet higher than the adjacent Hongkong & Shanghai Bank (HSBC). In 1985 HSBC finished a steel-and-glass structure that dwarfed the old Bank of China, whose officials in turn commissioned the Chinese-American architect I. M. Pei to build a bigger, better headquarters, which was completed in the early 1990s.

Architectural Assessement: Although it's not as innovative as the HSBC skyscraper, the Bank of China Tower is a masterful, twisting spire of replicating triangles (uh oh). As the first building to break the ridgeline of Victoria Peak, it dominates Hong Kong's landscape and embodies the posthandover balance of power. Its 43rd-floor observation deck also offers panoramic, uncrowded Central views.

Feng Shui Assessment: The tower has some of the worst feng shui in town. Some say that because the building thins at the top, it resembles a screwdriver—one that's drilling the wealth out of Hong Kong; others prefer the metaphor of a knife into the heart of the SAR. The two antennas sticking out of the top are said to resemble the two incense sticks burned for the dead. Circles, which look like coins, bring prosperity. The opposite effect is supposedly caused by the building's triangular angles and sharp edges—indeed, many believe that it has had a negative affect on nearby structures. The Lippo Centre, which faces one of the triangles, was formerly the Bond Centre, owned by disgraced Australian businessman Allen Bond, who was forced to sell the building because of financial troubles. Local gossip has it that Government House—still the residence of colonial governors when the bank was built—was the target of these bad vibes. Indeed, after

the handover, Hong Kong's first chief executive, Tung Chee-Hwa, refused to live there, citing its bad feng shui.

✉ *1 Garden Rd., Central* ☏ *No phone* ☉ *Observation deck: weekdays 8–6, Sat. 9–1* 💲 *Free* Ⓜ *Central MTR, Exit J2.*

Case Study 2: HSBC

Hongkong & Shanghai Bank (HSBC) Main Building. Designed by Sir Norman Foster, the headquarters of Hong Kong's premier bank (it's depicted on most of the territory's paper money) was completed in 1985 at a whopping cost of more than US$1 billion. At a time of insecurity vis-à-vis China, it was a powerful statement that the bank had no intention of taking its money out of the territory.

The two bronze lions outside the building also guarded HSBC's previous headquarters, built in 1935. The one with the gaping mouth is named Stephen, after the Hong Kong branch manager at the time; the other's called Stitt, after the manager in Shanghai. If you look closely, you can see bullet marks in them from the 1941 Battle of Hong Kong.

Architectural Assessment: With its distinctive ladder facade, many consider this building a triumph—a landmark of modern architecture, even. It sits on four props that allow you to walk under it and look up through its glass belly into the soaring atrium within. Even more interesting is Foster's sensitive treatment of high-tech details: the mechanics of everything, from the elevators' gears and pulleys to the electric signs' circuit boards, are visible through smoked glass. Because of all these mechanics, irreverent locals call this the Robot Building. ■ TIP➔ **Computer-controlled glass mirrors—480 of them—change position**

throughout the day to reflect natural light into the bank. You can get an insider perspective by taking the escalators through the public banking hall up to the third-floor atrium.

Feng Shui Assessment: Rumor has it that during construction, the escalators were reset from their original straight position so that they would be at an angle to the entrance. Because evil spirits can only travel in a straight line, this realignment was thought to prevent waterborne spirits from flowing in off Victoria Harbor. The escalators are also believed to resemble two whiskers of a powerful dragon, sucking money into the bank. Atop the building and pointing toward the Bank of China Tower are two metal rods that look like a window-washing apparatus. The rods are a classic feng shui technique designed to deflect the negative energy—in this case, of the Bank of China's dreaded triangles—away and back to its source.

✉ *1 Queen's Rd., across from Statue Sq., Central* 💲 *Free* ☉ *Weekdays 9–5:30, Sat. 9–12:30* Ⓜ *Central MTR, Exit K.*

THE PEAK EXPERIENCE

★ Fodor's Choice **Victoria Peak's** Chinese name, Tai Ping Shan, means Mountain of Great Peace, and it certainly seems to inspire momentary hushed awe in visitors at the viewing point, a few yards left along the road from the tram terminal. Spread below you is a glittering forest of skyscrapers; beyond them the harbor and—on a clear day—Kowloon's eight mountains. On a rainy day wisps of cloud catch on the buildings' pointy tops; at night both sides of the harbor burst into color. Consider having dinner at one of the restaurants near the upper terminus. ■ TIP→ **Forsake all else up here and start your visit with the lookout point: there are a hundred other shopping ops in the world, but few views like this.**

As you step off the Peak Tram, the feeling that you left your stomach somewhere down in Central disappears. The cure? A sharp intake of breath and bout of sighing over the view. Whatever the time, whatever the weather, be it your first visit or your 50th, this is Hong Kong's one unmissable sight. ■ TIP→ **Before buying a return ticket down on the tram, consider taking one of the beautiful low-impact trails back to Central. There are also buses down.**

There are spectacular views in all directions on the **Peak Circle Walk,** an easy-going 2.2 mi (3.5-km) paved trail that starts at the Upper Tram Terminus. Start by heading north along fern-encroached Lugard Road. There's another stunning view of Central from the lookout, 20 minutes along, after which the road snakes west to an intersection with Hatton and Harlech roads. From here Lantau, Lamma, and—on incredibly clear days—Macau come into view. The longer option from here is to wind your way down Hatton to the University of Hong Kong campus in the Western district.

The tacky **Peak Tower** (✉ 128 Peak Rd., Victoria Peak, Central ☎ 2849–7654 🕐 7 AM–midnight) is packed with largely forgettable shops and restaurants. Kids might be persuaded to enjoy the Peak Explorer, a virtual-reality ride through outer space, or the Rise of the Dragon, which takes you on a railcar through a series of animated scenes from Hong Kong's history. There's also a branch of Ripley's Believe It or Not! Odditorium—by the looks on most of the Mainlanders' faces, they've gone with the "not" option. Local heroes Jackie Chan and Michelle Yeoh are some of the famous faces resisting meltdown at Asia's first branch of London's famous wax works, **Madame Tussaud's** (✉ Peak Tower, Level 2, 128 Peak Rd., Victoria Peak, Central ☎ 2849–6966 ⊕ www.madame-tussauds.com ✉ HK$115 🕐 10 AM–10 PM). The usual celebrity suspects—from Beckham to Marilyn—are here. The **Peak Galleria** mall scores high on nothing else but the cheese scale. ■ TIP→ **Bypass the overpriced tourist traps inside and head straight up the escalators to the third-floor viewing gallery, which looks down over the Pok Fu Lam country park and reservoir, and, on a clear day, Aberdeen.**

TO YOUR HEALTH

In recent years Traditional Chinese Medicine (TCM) has caused a lot of holistic hype in the west. Round here, though, it's been going strong for a while—more than 2,000 years, to be precise. Although modern Hong Kongers may see western doctors for serious illnesses, for minor complaints and everyday pick-me-ups they still turn to traditional remedies.

To get to the root of your body's disequilibrium a TCM practitioner takes your pulse in different places and examines your tongue, eyes, and ears, as well as talking to you. Your prescription could include herbal tonics, teas, massage, dietary recommendations, and acupuncture.

Learning to Balance

Taoists believe that the world is made up of two opposing but interdependent forces: negative yin, representing darkness and the female, and positive yang, standing for light and masculinity. Both are essential for good health: when one becomes stronger than the other in the body, we get sick.

Another all-important concept is *chi*, the energy or life force behind most bodily functions. It flows through channels or meridians: if these are blocked, ill health can ensue. Acupuncture along these meridians is a way of putting your chi in order.

It's not all inner peace—to be healthy you have to be in harmony with your environment, too. The Five Elements theory divides up both the universe and the body into different "elemental" categories: water, wood, fire, earth, and metal. Practitioners seek to keep all five elements in balance.

If you don't know your chi from your chin, and you're not sure if you need a dried seahorse or a live snake, head to the **Eu Yan Sang Medical Hall.** Glass cases at this reputable store display reindeer antlers, dried fungi, ginseng, and other medicinal mainstays; English-language cards explain some of the items' uses. Grave but helpful clerks behind hefty wooden counters will happily sell you purported cures for anything from the common cold to impotence (the cure for the latter is usually slices of reindeer antler boiled into tea). ■ TIP→ The Hong Kong Tourism Board runs free introductory classes on Chinese medicine here Wednesday at 2:30 PM. There are other smaller branches all over Hong Kong. From Sheung Wan MTR, walk left along Wing Lok Street, right into Wing Wo Street, then left onto Queen's Road Central. ✉ *152–156 Queen's Rd. Central, Western* ☎ *2544–3870* ⊕ *www.euyansang.com.sg* ☉ *Daily 9–7:30* Ⓜ *Sheung Wan MTR, Exit E2.*

⚠ Chinese medicines aren't regulated by the Hong Kong government. Anything that sounds dubious or dangerous might be just that.

Brush up on traditional treatments at the **Hong Kong Museum of Medical Sciences.** The least morbid and most enlightening exhibits compare Chinese and western medical practices and show Chinese medicines of both animal and plant origin. Elsewhere dusty displays of old medical equipment send macabre thrills up your spine. Reaching this museum is a healthy experience in itself: you pant up several blocks' worth of stairs to the Edwardian building it's in. ■ TIP→ The cheat's way of getting here is on the Midlevels Escalator: alight at Caine Road and walk west four or five blocks to Ladder Street. The museum is just down the first flight of stairs, on the left. ✉ *2 Caine La., Western* ☎ *2549–5123* ⊕ *www.hkmms.org.hk* ✆ *HK$10* ☉ *Tues.–Sat. 10–5, Sun. 1–5.*

TO YOUR HEALTH

Taking the Cure

Therapeutic massages are the specialty at **Charlie's Acupressure and Massage Centre of the Blind** (✉ Canton House, 9th fl., room 903, 54–6 Queen's Rd. Central, Central ☎ 2877–9999). Ballet dancer Rudolf Nureyev was one celebrity who relaxed his overworked muscles here. An hour-long massage costs around HK$250.

The **Hong Kong University Chinese Medicine Clinic and Pharmacy** (✉ Admiralty Centre, 2nd fl., unit 5, Harcourt Rd., Admiralty ☎ 2143–6871 clinic, 2865–0689 master practitioners Ⓜ Admiralty MTR, Exit A) is a training clinic run by the most respected med school in town. It also has master practitioners of acupuncture and orthopedics on hand. Consultations start at HK$100, visits to the masters at HK$300.

Acupuncture, acupressure, and herbal medicine are just some of the offerings at the **Quality Chinese Medical Centre** (✉ Jade Centre, 5th fl., unit A, 98 Wellington St., Central ☎ 2882–1788 ⊕ www.qcmchk.com). Consultations start at HK$65; expect to pay around HK$220 for an acupuncture session.

NO GIN, JUST TONIC

Downing a glass of herbal health tonic is a normal part of many a Hong Konger's day. There are blends for flu, headaches, colds, and coughs. Many stores have English labels, otherwise tell the server your troubles, and he or she will run you off a glass of whatever works best. Most cost HK$6–HK$20 a dose.

Established in 1669, **Tong Ren Tang** (✉ Melbourne Plaza, 2nd fl, Unit B, 33 Queen's Rd. Central, Central ☎ 2868–0609) has long been one of mainland China's best-respected traditional medicine companies. There are consulting rooms and a pharmacy at this branch.

Healthy Ways

★ In colonial times **Bonham Strand,** a curving thoroughfare in the Sheung Wan district, was a major commercial hub. Sadly, its wooden shop fronts are fast falling victim to real estate development. The few that remain are medicinal mother lodes: wood-clad walls are lined with shelves of jars filled with pungent ingredients such as fungi,

SMOOTH MOVES

Tai Chi (A Centuries-Old Art)

Just before dawn you'll see young businesspeople and retirees alike practicing tai chi: slow, steady, flowing movements with moderate postures designed to improve physical and mental well-being. There's no better advertising for tai chi than seeing an octogenarian balance on one leg, with the other outstretched and held high for a long moment before gracefully swinging into yet another pose. Although the health and philosophical aspects of tai chi may be common knowledge, few people know that it's also a subtle, sophisticated, and scientific method of self-defense.

barks, and insects. These are consumed dried and ground up—infused in hot water or tea or taken as powder or pills. West of the intersection with Wing Lok Street, the original facades give way to those with big plate-glass windows displaying bundles of hairy-looking forked yellow roots—this is the heart of the ginseng wholesale trade. Ginseng is a broad-spectrum remedy that's a mainstay of Chinese medicine.

★ A sharp but musty smell fills the air when you turn down **Wing Lok Street or Des Voeux Road West,** Sheung Wan streets renowned for their dried-seafood stores. Out of shop fronts spill sacks filled to bursting with dried and salted fish, seahorses, shrimp, and abalone—a shellfish that is to China what oysters are to the west. The cucumber look-alikes are sea slugs. Foot-wide fungi, gleaming beans, wrinkly red prunes, nuts, and even rosebuds make up the rest of the stock. A grimmer offering lurks behind a few shop windows: highly prized shark's fins, purported to be an aphrodisiac.

At Possession Street, where Queen's Road Central becomes **Queen's Road West,** shop windows display what looks like clumps of fine vermicelli noodles, ranging in color from pale gold to rich chestnut. It's not pasta, though; these are birds' nests, another of Sheung Wan's intriguing specialties. They're used to make a highly prized (and correspondingly expensive) soup that tastes rather disappointingly like egg white.

In herb shops on Queen's Road West beyond the intersection with Hollywood Road, it's a tough call as to who's more wizened: the clerks or the dried goods they sell. Either way, these stores convey the longevity benefits of Chinese medicine. Forget the gleaming teak counters of Central's tony TCM boutiques, here the herbs, dried mushrooms, and other more mysterious ingredients are displayed in plastic jars and burlap sacks.

Don't poke your fingers into the grubby cages outside shops on **Hillier Street:** this is the center of the snake trade. A snake's meat is used in winter soups to ward off colds and its gallbladder reputedly improves vigor and virility.

Tai Chi Masters (AD 1247–New Millennium & Beyond)

Tai chi's founder was Chang San Feng, a Taoist, who was born in AD 1247. One of the greatest masters, however, was Yang Lu Chan (1799–1872), who served as the chief combat instructor to the Imperial Guard during the Ching Dynasty and who was known as Invincible Yang. To follow in their footsteps you must study under an accomplished master, who can demonstrate techniques, identify faults, and create a calming atmosphere. To try tai chi while you're in town, contact the tourist board. There are free classes in Hong Kong Park Monday and Wednesday–Friday at 8 AM.

BEACHES

Surprising as it may seem, Hong Kong has many fantastic beaches with gorgeous views of the sea, dotted with small green islands. In Southside, ever-popular Repulse Bay is a sort of Chinese Coney Island. Just to the south is smaller, less-crowded Deep Water Bay, and farther around is the more intimate South Bay. Turtle Cove is isolated and beautiful, and Shek O's beach has a Mediterranean feel. Day trips to the outlying islands (⇨ Island Hopping) can also include sunbathing time on a clean beach. You can reach most beaches by train, bus, or taxi; the latter will cost HK$150 and up.

The waters off beaches in the New Territories, particularly the Sai Kung Peninsula are crystal clear. Pollution can be a problem on the Southside, though that doesn't deter the thousands who flock seaside for respite from the heat. ■ TIP➜ **Hong Kong's Environmental Protection Department has set some tough guidelines and goals for cleaning up area waters. For more info, including beach-by-beach pollution ratings, check out the EPD's Web site: www.epd.gov.hk/epd.**

Southside

Deep Water Bay. On Island Road, just to the east of Ocean Park and all its amusements, this bay was the setting for the William Holden film *Love Is a Many Splendored Thing* (1955), and its deep coves are still lovely. Near Deep Water Bay are the manicured greens of the Deep Water Bay Golf Course, which is owned by the Hong Kong Golf Club. Not surprisingly, the area has become a multimillionaires' enclave and is home to Hong Kong's richest man, Li Ka-shing, a very private real-estate tycoon.

To rent a speedboat, waterskiing equipment, and the services of a driver, contact the **Waterski Club** (✉ Pier at Deep Water Bay Beach, Deep Water Bay ☎2812–0391) or ask your hotel for the names and numbers of other outfitters. The cost is usually about HK$700 per hour.

From Exchange Square Bus Terminus in Central, take Bus 6, 64, 260, or 6A.

■ TIP➜ **For a scenic route to Deep Water Bay, take Bus 70 from Central's Exchange Square to Aberdeen and change to Bus 73, which passes the beach en route to Stanley.**

Repulse Bay. It's named after the British warship HMS *Repulse* not, as some local wags say, after its slightly murky waters. It was home of the now demolished Repulse Bay Hotel, which gained notoriety in December 1941 when Japanese clambered over the hills behind it, entered its gardens, and overtook the British, who were using the hotel as headquarters. Repulse Bay Verandah Restaurant & Bamboo Bar—a great place for British high tea—is a replica of the eating and drinking establishment that once graced the hotel. High tea costs HK$128 and is served weekdays from 3 to 5:30 and weekends from 3:30 to 5:30. You can also grab a bite at one of several Chinese restaurants and snack kiosks that dot the beach. The Lifesaving Club at the beach's east end resembles a Chinese temple, with large statues of Tin Hau, goddess of the sea, and Kwun Yum, goddess of mercy. △ **If you opt for a meal in a seafood restaurant here or at any beach, note that physicians caution against eating raw shellfish because of hepatitis outbreaks.** *From Exchange Square Bus Terminus in Central, take Bus 6, 6A, 6X, 66, 64, or 260.*

Shek O. This wide beach is almost Mediterranean in appearance with its low-rise houses and shops set prettily on a headland. In Shek O village you can find old mansions, small shops selling inflatable

toys and other beach gear, and a few popular Chinese and Thai restaurants. Follow the curving path from the town square across a footbridge to the "island" of Tai Tau Chau, really a large rock with a lookout over the South China Sea. Little more than a century ago, this open water was ruled by pirates. Also near town is the Shek O Golf and Country Club and the superb Shek O Country Park, with great trails and bird-watching: look for Kentish plovers, reef egrets, and black-headed gulls, as well as the colorful rufus-backed shrike and the ubiquitous chatty bulbul. *From Central, take MTR to Shau Ki Wan, then take Bus 9 to last stop (about 30 min).*

Stanley. Notorious during World War II as the home of Japan's largest POW camps in Hong Kong, Stanley is now known primarily for its market, a great place for deals on knickknacks, ceramics, paintings, casual clothing, and sporting goods—including, ironically enough, snow-skiing gear. The old police station, built in 1859, now houses a restaurant. Past the market, on Stanley Main Street, a strip of restaurants and pubs faces the bay. On the other side of the bay a temple honoring Tin Hau, goddess of the sea, is wedged between giant modern housing estates.

Stanley's wide main beach is the site of the dragon boat races, usually held in June, in which teams paddle out into the sea, turn around, and, at the sound of the gun, race ferociously back to shore. The beach is popular with the windsurfing, waterskiing, and wakeboarding crowd. **Patrick's Water-skiing** (✉ Tai Tam, Stanley ☎ 2813–2372) is run by the friendly, laid-back man himself. Patrick will take you to the best area waters and give you pointers on your technique. The fee—HK$700 per hour—includes a range of equipment.

> ## WINDSURFING
>
> Windsurfing has grown dramatically in popularity since Hong Kong's Lee Lai-shan sailed off with a women's Olympic gold medal at the 1996 Summer Olympic Games in Atlanta, inspiring a generation of youngsters to take up the sport, which is further popularized on ESPN and MTV. Now windsurfing centers at Tai Tam on Hong Kong Island, Sha Ha beach in Sai Kung, and Tung Wan Beach (Lee's home on Cheung Chau Island) will gladly start you on the path to glory with some lessons.

From Exchange Square Bus Terminus in Central, take Bus 6, 6A, 6X, 66, 64, or 260.

The New Territories

Hap Mun Wan. Half Moon Bay is a brilliant, golden sand beach on a grassy island near Sai Kung Town. It's one of the many small beaches among dozens of small islands near Sai Kung that are popular and easy to reach. **Bunn's Divers Institute** (✉ 38–40 Yee Woo St., Causeway Bay ☎ 2574–7951) runs outings for qualified divers to areas like Sai Kung. The cost of a day trip runs HK$700 and includes two sessions, one in the morning and another in the afternoon. Bring your own lunch.

Sampans to Half Moon depart from the Sai Kung waterfront, beside the bus station. If you're sharing a sampan with other passengers, remember the color of the flag on the roof: that's the color you need for your return ferry. Shared sampans cost HK$40. ■ TIP→ To cruise around the harbor, rent a *kaido* (pronounced "guy-doe," one of the small boats run by private operators for about HK$130 round-trip), and stop at tiny Yim Tin Tsai Island, which has a rustic Catholic mis-

Hong Kong Beaches

San Tin

Tai Po

Tolo Harbour

Wu Kai Sha

NEW TERRITORIES

Ha Tsuen

Tai Mong Tsai

Sai Kung — **Sha Ha**

Tuen Mun

Pak Tin

Ho Chung

Hap Mun Wan

Sham Tseng

Tsuen Wan

Port Shelter

Siu Lam

Ma Wan

KOWLOON

Hang Hau

Silverstrand

Lung Ha Wan

♦ **Hong Kong Disney Land**

Discovery Bay

Kowloon Bay

Yau Tong

Junk Bay

Tai Chik Sha

Discovery Bay

Kennedy Town

HONG KONG

HONG KONG ISLAND

TUNG LUNG CHAU

Tung Chung

Mui Wo

PENG CHAU

Silvermine Bay

HEI LING CHAU

Aberdeen

Deep Water Bay

AP LEI CHAU

Shek O

Silvermine Beach

Repulse Bay

Stanley

LANTAU ISLAND

Pui O Wan

CHI MA WAN PENINSULA

Yung Shue Wan

Stanley Bay

Cheung Sha

CHEUNG CHAU

LAMMA ISLAND

Sheung Sze Mun

PO TOI ISLANDS

←TO MACAU

South China Sea

0   4 miles

0   4 kilometers

---

sion church built in 1890. *From Central, take MTR to Choi Hung, then green Minibus 1A to Sai Kung Town.*

Sha Ha. The sand isn't fine and golden, but the main reason people visit this beach is for the windsurfing. Sha Ha's waters are shallow, even far from shore, and ideal for beginning windsurfers. Feeling exhausted after a day out on the water tackling the wind? Grab something to eat at the restaurants and bars that dot the beach. You can take lessons or rent a board at the **Kent Windsurfing Centre** (✉ Sha Ha, Sai Kung. ☎ 9733–1228). Ask for Eddy. *From Central take MTR to Choi Hung, then green Minibus 1A to Sai Kung Town. It's a 10-min walk along shore to Sha Ha.*

Silverstrand. Though a little rocky in spots, it has soft sand and is always crowded on summer weekends. Walk down a steep set

of steps to reach the small stretch of beach where families enjoy all manner of floating beds and tubes in the sea. Despite the heat, barbecuing is a popular beach activity here and elsewhere. The local style is to hold special long forks laden with sausages, chicken, or other meats over the coals. *From Central, take MTR to Diamond Hill, then Bus 91. Alight at big roundabout.*

Lantau Island

An often-overlooked fact is that when visitors arrive, they land on Lantau island—a large stretch of reclaimed land purposely built for the airport called Chep Lap Kok. Twice the size of Hong Kong Island, Lantau is now also home to the giant Tian Tan Buddha, which sits majestically on a hilltop. The Ngong Ping cable car whisks you here in 15 minutes. Also on Lantau is Dis-

neyland, a small version of its American counterparts, and the charming Tai O Fishing Village.

Cheung Sha. Popular Cheung Sha is only a short taxi or bus ride from the Silvermine Bay ferry pier. Its mile-long expanse is excellent for swimming. The Stoep restaurant on the beach serves great Mediterranean and South African fare. Watching the sunset here is a perfect way to end a sun-drenched day. ■ TIP→ **There are only 30 taxis on the entire island, so on weekends, when things get busy, make sure you get one back to the pier by asking the restaurant to get it for you.** *Take ferry from Central's Pier 6 to Mui Wo. Buses meet ferry every half hour on weekdays and Sat.; on Sun., buses leave when full.*

Silvermine Beach. The stretch of beach can be seen from the ferry as you approach the island, though because of its proximity to the pier and other fishing boats, the waters aren't as clean as those at Cheung Sha. You can rent bikes at the Silvermine Beach Hotel and explore the village of Mui Wo. *Take ferry from Central's Pier 6 to Mui Wo. Buses meet ferry every half hour on weekdays and Sat.; on Sun., buses leave when full.*

REGION / BEACH	Travel Time from Central	Peaceful	Swimmable	Lifeguards	Showers/ Restrooms
SOUTHSIDE					
Deep Water Bay	20 mins.	crowded	often	yes	yes
Repulse Bay	30 mins.	crowded	often	yes	yes
South Bay	30 mins.	crowded	yes	yes	yes
Shek O	60 mins	crowded	yes	yes	yes
Stanley	40–45 mins.	crowded	yes	yes	yes
NEW TERRITORIES					
Hap Mun Wan	60–75 mins.	often	yes	yes	yes
Sha Ha	60–75 mins.	often	yes	no	no
Silverstrand	60 mins.	crowded	yes	yes	yes
Clear Water Bay	70–80 mins.	crowded	yes	yes	yes
OUTER ISLANDS					
Cheung Chau: Tung Wan	60–75 mins.	crowded	yes	yes	yes
Lamma: Hung Shing Ye	60–75 mins.	often	yes	yes	yes
Lamma: Lo So Shing	60–75 mins.	often	yes	yes	yes
Lantau: Cheung Sha Wan	60–75 mins.	often	yes	yes	yes
Tap Mun	90–120 mins.	yes	yes	no	no

ISLAND HOPPING

There are 235 so-called Outer Islands, and several of them are great escapes from the city for the waterfront views, some seafood, and a little peace. Island villages are up to speed (to the regret of many, cell phones work), but they run at a humane pace. Hong Kong ferries travel from Central to many of the islands, where beaches are often a short walk from the pier.

Cheung Chau. This small, car-less island southwest of Hong Kong is best known as being the home to windsurfing Olympic gold medalist Lee Lai-shan. At the tip of the beach here is a lovely outdoor restaurant owned by relatives of San-San (as she's affectionately called), who have proudly hung a large framed picture of the athlete in her golden moment. The island community lives mostly on the sandbar that connects the two hilly tips of this dumbbell-shape land mass. It's a one-hour ferry ride from Central's Pier 5 outside Two IFC, and the town harbor is lined with seafood restaurants and shops.

On weekends Tung Wan, Cheung Chau's main beach, is so crowded that its sweep of golden sand is barely visible. At one end of the beach is the Warwick Hotel. Plenty of nearby restaurants offer refreshments, seafood, and shade. There are no private cars allowed on this island, so the air is noticeably clean.

Lamma Island. Lamma is as close to a 1960s bohemian scene as Hong Kong gets—full of laid-back expats driven out of Central by high rents. They've spawned a subculture of vegetarian restaurants, health-food shops, and craft stores. The ferry from Central's Pier 4, in front of Two IFC, to the village of Sok Kwu Wan or to Yung Shue Wan takes about 25 minutes. It doesn't matter which village you go to

first—time spent on beaches near them and on the hour-long walk through rolling green hills between them are what a leisurely afternoon on Lamma is all about.

"Beach" overstates the scale of the sandy strip known as Hung Shing Ye. It's also called Power Station Beach because of the massive power plant visible from it. The view doesn't deter the young locals, who materialize whenever the rays shine down. They even swim here—sometimes. Stay on shore if you see plastic bags or other refuse on the water. Or just head to Yung Shue Wan, the former farming and fishing village that's been an expat enclave since the early 1980s. Main Street is lined with handicraft shops, though the smell of the fish markets is a reminder of Lamma's humbler, less cosmopolitan origins.

Popular with families, Lo So Shing beach is an easy 20- to 30-minute hike on a paved path from Sok Kwu Wan, the smaller and grittier of Lamma's two villages and one that's notable mainly for the string of cavernous seafood restaurants that line the path leading from the pier. ■ TIP→ **If you arrive on foot from Yung Shue Wan, your first glimpse of the bay from the hills will be stunning.**

Ping Chau. Not to be confused with Peng Chau, this 2½ square km (1 square mi) piece of land is in the far northeast of the New Territories, near the mainland coast. It's almost deserted and has a checkered history. Guns and opium were once smuggled from here, and during the Cultural Revolution many mainlanders swam through shark-infested waters in hopes of reaching Ping Chau and the freedom of Hong Kong.

The island's largest village, Sha Tau, is something of a ghost town, with many

cottages boarded up. A large part of the island is country parkland, with footpaths overgrown with orchids, wild mint, and morning glories. At the island's south end are two huge rocks known as the Drum Rocks, or Watchman's Tower Rocks. At the north end is a chunk of land that has broken away from the island; the Chinese say it represents the head of a dragon.

The ferry to Ping Chau departs on weekends at 9 AM and returns only at 5:15 PM. On Saturday there's an extra trip at 3:30 PM. Board the ferry at Ma Liu Shui, near the University KCR stop. Since there's only one daily ferry, be sure to verify the timing with the HKTB before you leave. A round-trip costs HK$80.

Po Toi Island. Three barren little fishing islands, virtually unchanged since medieval times, sit in the extreme southeast of Hong Kong. Only Po Toi Island is inhabited (sort of), with fewer than 100 people. It offers spectacular walks and a fine seafood restaurant. Walk uphill past primitive dwellings, many deserted, to the Tin Hau Temple, or walk east through the hamlet of Wan Tsai, past banana and papaya groves, to some geometric rock carvings, believed to have been carved during the local Bronze Age, about 2,500 years ago.

A trip to the Po Toi Islands is an all-day affair. Ferries leave Aberdeen on Tuesday, Thursday, and weekends at 8 AM and from St. Stephen's Beach in Stanley at 10 or 11:30 AM. Ferries return at 3 and 4:30 PM directly to St. Stephen's Beach, or at 6 PM to Aberdeen via St. Stephen's Beach. A round-trip costs HK$40.

Tap Mun Island. About a 15-minute walk from the Chinese University along Tai Po Road in Sha Tin is the Ma Liu Shui Ferry Pier. This is the starting point for a ferry tour of the harbor and Tap Mun Island, whose east side is home to Tap Mun Cave and some of the territories' best-kept beaches. The ferry makes many stops; if you take the 8:30 AM trip you'll have time to hike around Tap Mun Island and be back in the city by late afternoon. The last ferry returning from the island is at 5:30 PM. A round trip costs HK$32 on weekdays and HK$50 on weekends.

The New Fisherman's Village, on the island's southern side, is populated mainly by Hakka women. About 1 km (½ mi) north, near the western shore, is the ancient village of Tap Mun, where you'll see old women playing mah-jongg. The Tin Hau Temple, dedicated to the goddess of the sea, is less than ½ km (¼ mi) north of the village. It's atop steps that lead down to the harbor; inside are old model junks and, of course, a veiled figure of the goddess.

HAKKA WHO'S WHO

There are around 70 million people of Hakka descent in the world. Famous people of Hakka origin include shoe god Jimmy Choo, actors Leslie Cheung and Chow Yun-Fat, Canto-pop star Leon Lai, and former Canadian governor-general Adrienne Clarkson.

SAIL AWAY: SAMPANS & JUNKS

Named after an English lord, not the Scottish city, the Southside town of Aberdeen (30 minutes from Central via Bus 70 or 91) was once a pirate refuge. After World War II it became commercial as the *tanka* (boat people) attracted visitors to their floating restaurants. In the harbor are some 3,000 junks and sampans, still interspersed with floating restaurants, among them the famous Jumbo Kingdom, its faux-Chinese decorations covered in lights. The tanka still live on houseboats, and though the vessels look picturesque, conditions are depressing.

Elderly women with sea- and sun-weathered skin and croaking voices may invite you aboard a sampan for a harbor ride. It's better to go with one of the licensed operators that depart on 20-minute tours daily from 8 to 6 from the seawall opposite Aberdeen Centre. Tickets are HK$40. A tour lets you see how the fishing community lives and works and how sampans are also homes, sometimes with three generations on one small vessel. Ironically, about 110 yards away are the yachts of the Marina Club and the slightly less exclusive Aberdeen Boat Club.

You can also hire a junk to take you to outer islands: Cheung Chau, Lamma, Lantau, Po Toi, or the islands in Port Shelter, Sai Kung. Sailing on a large (up to 80-feet long), well-varnished, plushly appointed, air-conditioned junk—which can serve as a platform for swimmers and water-skiers—is a unique Hong Kong experience. Many local "weekend admirals" command these floating rumpus rooms, which are also known as "gin junks" because so much alcohol is often consumed aboard them.

Ap Lei Chau Island (Duck's Tongue Island), accessible via sampan or Buses 90B or 91 along the bridge that connects it with Aberdeen, has a yard where junks, yachts, and sampans are built, almost all without formal plans. With 80,000 people living on 1 square km (½ square mi), Ap Lei Chau is the world's most densely populated island.

■ **TIP→** Look to your right when crossing the bridge for a superb view of the harbor and its countless junks.

The ritzy restaurant-bar **aqua luna** (☎ 2116—8821 ⊕ www.aqua.com.hk) is on the *Cheung Po Tsai*, an impressive 28-meter junk named for a pirate and created by an 80-year-old local craftsman. It's slow but impressive, with magnificent red sails. A 45-minute cruise through Victoria Harbour costs HK$150 by day and HK$180 at night. Departures are every hour on the half hour 1:30 PM to 10:30 PM from Tsim Sha Tsui Pier, near the Cultural Centre, and 15 minutes later from Queen's Pier, Central.

The *Duk Ling,* is a fully restored 25-year-old fishing junk whose large sails are a sight to behold. But the best thing about the *Duk Ling* is that a ride won't cost you a dime. The HKTB offers visitors free one-hour sails from Kowloon Pier (Thursday at 2 PM and 4 PM, Saturday at 10 AM and noon) and from Central's Queen's Pier (Thursday at 3 PM and 5 PM, Saturday at 11 AM and 1 PM). Register first at the HKTB offices at the Star Ferry Pier in Tsim Sha Tsui; when you do, bring your passport to prove you're from out of town.

HIKING

Most visitors don't come for the lush lowlands, bamboo and pine forests, rugged mountains with panoramas of the sea, and secluded beaches, but nature is never very far from all the skyscrapers. Truth be told about 40% of Hong Kong is protected in 23 parks, including three marine parks and one marine reserve.

Don't expect to find the wilderness wholly unspoiled, however. Few upland areas escape Hong Kong's relentless plague of hill fires for more than a few years at a time. Some are caused by dried-out vegetation; others erupt from small graveside fires set by locals to clear the land around ancestors' eternal resting spots. Partly because of these fires, most of Hong Kong's forests, except for a few spots in the New Territories, have no obvious wildlife other than birds—and mosquitoes. Bring repellent.

Gear

Necessities include sunglasses or a hat, bottled water, day pack, and sturdy hiking boots. Wear layered clothing; weather tends to be warm during the day and cold toward nightfall. The cliff sides get quite windy. If you need some basics, there are several options.

Although it doesn't sell the same range of equipment, backpacks, and clothes you'd find back home, **Great Outdoor Clothing Company** (⊠ Basement, Silvercord Bldg., 30 Canton Rd., Tsim Sha Tsui, Kowloon ☎ 2730–9009) will do in a pinch. **Timberland** (⊠ Shop 212, Pacific Pl., 88 Queensway, Admiralty ☎ 2868–0845) sells hiking boots, backpacks, and appropriate togs. **World Sports Co. Ltd.** (⊠ 2/F, 83 Fa Yuen St., Mong Kok, Kowloon ☎ 2396–9357) caters to your every outdoor need with a very helpful staff.

Pick up guides such as *Hong Kong Hikes* from any bookstore. You can buy trail maps at the **Government Publications Centre** (⊠ Pacific Pl., Government Office, G/F, 66 Queensway, Admiralty ☎ 2537–1910). Ask for blueprints of the trails and the Countryside Series maps. Note that the HM20C series has handsome four-color maps, but they're not very reliable. The HKTB also provides maps with good walking trails and hikes.

Trails

Fodor's Choice **Dragon's Back.** One of the most popular trails crosses the "rooftop" of Hong Kong Island. Take the Peak Tram from Central up Victoria Peak, and tackle as much or as little of the range as you feel like—there are numerous exits "downhill" to public-transport networks. Surprisingly wild country feels a world away from the urban bustle below, and the panoramas—of Victoria Harbour on one side, and South Island and outlying islands on the other—are spectacular. You can follow the trail all the way to the delightful seaside village of Shek O, where you can relax over an evening dinner before returning to the city by minibus or taxi. The most popular route, and shorter if you're not up for a huge hike, is from Shek O Country Park. Take the MTR from Central to Shaukeiwan, then Bus 9, alight after the first roundabout, near the crematorium. The entire trip takes the better part of an unforgettable day.

Lion Rock. The easiest way to access the trail to Lion Rock, a spectacular summit, is from Kowloon. The hike passes through dense woodland with bamboo groves along the Eagle's Nest Nature Trail and up open slopes to Beacon Hill for 360-degree views over hills and the city. The contrasting vistas of green hills and the cityscape are ex-

HIKING

traordinary. There's a climb up the steep rough track to the top of Lion Rock, a superb vantage point for appreciating Kowloon's setting between hills and sea. The trail ends at Wong Tai Sin Taoist Temple, where you can have your fortune told. To start, catch the MTR to Choi Hung (15 minutes from Tsim Sha Tsui) and a 10-minute taxi ride up Lion Rock. From Wong Tai Sin, return by MTR.

★ Fodor's Choice | MacLehose Trail. Named after a former Hong Kong governor, the 97-km (60-mi) MacLehose is the grueling course for the annual charity event, the MacLehose Trailwalker. Top teams finish the hike in an astonishing 15 hours. Mere mortals should allow three to four days from beginning to end or simply tackle one section or another on a day hike or two.

This isolated trail through the New Territories starts at Tsak Yue Wu, beyond Sai Kung, and circles High Island Reservoir before breaking north. A portion takes you through the Sai Kung Country Park, Hong Kong's most beloved preserve, and up a mountain called Ma On Shan. Turn south for a high-ridge view, and walk through Ma On Shan Country Park. From here walk west along the ridges of the mountains known as the Eight Dragons, which gave Kowloon its name.

After crossing Tai Po Road, the path follows a ridge to the summit of Tai Mo Shan (Big Hat Mountain), which, at 3,140 feet above sea level, is Hong Kong's tallest mountain. On a clear day you can even see the spire of the Bank of China building in Central from here. Continuing west, the trail drops to Tai Lam Reservoir and Tuen Mun, where you can catch public transport back to the city. To reach Tsak Yue Wu, take the MTR to Choi Hung and then Bus 92 or 96R, or Minibus 1 to Sai Kung Town. From Sai Kung Town, take Bus 94 to the country park.

■ TIP→ **An easier way to access Tai Mo Shan is via an old military road. En route you'll see the old British barracks, now occupied by the People's Liberation Army. A lookout about two-thirds of the way up affords views of rolling green hills in the foreground and urban development in the distance. Take the MTR to Tsuen Wan and exit the station at Shiu Wo Street, then catch Minibus 82.**

Wilson Trail. The 78-km (48-mi) long trail runs from Stanley Gap on the south end of Hong Kong Island, through rugged peaks that have a panoramic view of Repulse Bay and the nearby Round and Middle islands, and to Nam Chung in the northeastern New Territories. You have to cross the harbor by MTR at Quarry Bay to complete the entire walk. The trail is smoothed by steps paved with stone, and footbridges aid with steep sections and streams. Clearly marked with signs and information boards, this popular walk is divided into 10 sections, and you can easily take just one or two (figure on three to four hours a section); traversing the whole trail takes about 31 hours.

Section 1, which starts at Stanley Gap Road, is only for the very fit. Much of it requires walking up steep mountain grades. For an easier walk, try Section 7, which begins at Sing Mun Reservoir and takes you along a greenery-filled, fairly level path that winds past the eastern shore of the Sing Mun Reservoir in the New Territories and then descends to Tai Po, where there's a sweeping view of Tolo Harbour. Other sections will take you through the monkey forest at the Kowloon Hill Fitness Trail, over mountains, and past charming Chinese villages.

VERY AMUSING

Given all the malls here, you'd be forgiven for thinking that shopping is all Hong Kongers do for kicks. But there's a different brand of adrenaline on offer at the territory's world-class amusement parks, just a short way from the retail strips. Zoos, an aviary, and a bird garden slow things down a bit.

Thrills & Spills

🕙 **Hong Kong Disneyland.** If you're expecting an Asian take on the Magic Kingdom, think again—this park on Lantau Island is aimed at mainland Chinese hungry for apple-pie Americana. Still, it's as gleaming and polished as all the other Disneys, and it has one big advantage: few visitors, which means short lines. You can go on every ride at least once and see all the attractions in a day. If your kids are theme park–savvy, the incredibly tame rides here won't win their respect. That said, there are loads for little kids. Space Mountain is the only attraction with a height restriction, so there's no ride-exclusion angst for them. ■ TIP➔ Hong Kong Disneyland operates a Fastpass system, which lets you jump the lines at the most popular attractions. Stick your entry ticket into the Fastpass machines at each ride, and you'll be given a time to come back (usually within an hour). You can only have one ride "Fastpass activated" at a time.

You enter right into **Main St., USA,** an area paying tribute to early-20th-century small-town America. Shops—cute though they are—outnumber attractions here, so save lingering for the 3:30 PM parade, which winds up in the Town Square. Sleeping Beauty's castle, with its trademark turrets, is the gateway to faux-medieval **Fantasyland.** Choose from two spin-cycles—the Mad-Hatter's Teacups or Cinderella's Carousel—while you wait for your Winnie-the-Pooh Fastpass time.

Throbbing drums let you know you've hit **Adventureland,** on the park's south side. Landscapers have really run amok at attractions like Tarzan's Treehouse, on an island only accessible by rafts and the Jungle River Cruise. Inspired by the Bogart–Hepburn film *The African Queen,* this canopied boat ride takes you past "ancient" ruins, headhunters, and a volcano. Animated beasties—crocs, snakes, hippos, elephants, partying gorillas—will try to scare or squirt you, egged on by the boat's quipping skipper.

In **Tomorrowland** attractions look more like the *Jetsons* than the future. It's home to rollercoaster-in-the-dark Space Mountain, a humbled version of the original. While you're waiting for your Fastpass time, help Buzz Lightyear blast the daylights out of the evil Zurg, or spin out the wait on the Orbitron's flying saucers. ■ TIP➔ Shade is limited so take the lead from locals and make an umbrella your No. 1 accessory—use it as a parasol if the sun blazes down or the traditional way if it pours.

If you do one show, make it the *Festival of the Lion King.* Give your feet a rest but get your toes tapping with this energetic live performance of the animated film. The one place where Disney meets the East is at ye olde Corner Café. It may seem surreal, but run with it: the congee, curry, sushi, dim sum, stir fries, and kebabs are excellent, as theme-park food goes. If your kids are suspicious of far-flung fare, the Starliner Diner in Tomorrowland does burgers and fries.

The MTR is the quickest way here: take the Tung Chung line to Sunny Bay Station, then change to the Disneyland Resort Line, whose special trains have royal-blue plush seating and Mickey-shape win-

VERY AMUSING

dows. ✉ *Lantau Island* ☎ *1–830—830* ⊕ *www.hongkongdisneyland.com* ✉ *HK$350 weekends, holidays and July and Aug.; HK$295 other days.* ⊙ *Weekdays 10—8, weekends 10–9* Ⓜ *Disneyland Resort Station.*

★ ☺ **Ocean Park.** When it comes to amusement parks, there's no question where Hong Kongers' loyalties lie. This marine-theme park embraces both high- and low-octane buzzes and spectacular zoological attractions; they even breed endangered species here. And there's an educational twist to many of the attractions. The park stretches out over 170 hilly acres, and you can gaze down at much of it from spookily silent cabins of the mile-long cable car that connects the tamer Lowlands area to the action-packed Headland. ■ TIP→ **If all you fancy is roller-coasting, enter the park at the Tai Shue Wan Middle Kingdom entrance, and head straight up the escalator to Adventureland. If you're planning to do everything, start at the main entrance.**

The highlights of the **Lowland Gardens** are the giant pandas, An An and Jia Jia, who lumber fetchingly around their bamboo-filled enclosure. Paths wind to other enclosures, including a cantilevered butterfly house where rare species are bred, and the traditional Chinese architecture of the Goldfish Pagoda. Cross a rickety bridge to the lush undergrowth of the Amazing Amazon: its inhabitants are richly colored birds like toucans and flamingos. The Dino display focuses on such modern "dragons" as the Chinese alligator.

Hong Kong's biggest rollercoaster, the Dragon, is at the **Headland,** where the cable car stops. It might not quite be up to international standards, but it still loops the loops. There's also a Ferris wheel and swinging pirate ship here. If your kids want a ticket to ride but are too small to get past Headland height restrictions, make for the old-school attractions at **Kids World.** There's a carousel as well as kid-size fairground stalls. You can also sneak in some learning at Dolphin University. (The first-ever dolphins born from artificial insemination were born in Ocean Park.)

More than 2,000 fish find their way around the Atoll Reef in **Marine Land.** The 70 inhabitants of the Shark Aquarium look a bit listless, though they may still raise a few hairs on the back of your neck. If you're comfortable with performing animals, head for the Ocean Theatre, where dolphins, orcas, and sea lions clown around with surprising grace. In **Adventureland,** the Wild West–theme Mine Train was designed to feel rickety and screw-loose, which is probably why it rates highest on the scream-o-meter. Expect a light spraying or a heavy drenching at the Raging River: it all depends on your seat (and your luck). Rounding up the adrenaline boosts is the Abyss Turbo Drop, consisting, simply, of a 200-foot vertical plunge. It will definitely give you that sinking feeling.

Ocean Park is 30 minutes from the Admiralty MTR by Bus 620. Buses 70, 75, 90, 97, 260, 6A, 6X, and 29R also run from Central. ✉ *Tai Shue Wan Rd., Aberdeen, Southside* ☎ *2552–0291* ⊕ *www. oceanpark.com.hk* ✉ *HK$185* ⊙ *Tues.– Sun. 10–6.*

Quieter Pursuits

★ ☺ **Bird Garden.** The air fills with warbling and tweeting about a block from this narrow public garden. Around 70 stalls stretch down one side of it, selling all the birds, cages, and accessories a bird owner could need. More gruesome are the

heaving bags of creepy-crawlies—old men tending the stalls lift larvae with chopsticks and pop them into the open mouths of baby birds. Birds are a favorite pet in Hong Kong, especially among the elderly, who often take them out for a "walk" in bamboo cages.

Plenty of free birds also swoop in to gorge on spilled food and commiserate with imprisoned brethren. The garden was built to replace the old, mazelike Bird Market, which was closed down during the worst Bird Flu outbreaks. (Government sanitation programs mean the flu is no longer a threat, though all the vendors here ignore signs warning against contact with birds.) From the MTR station walk east along Prince Edward Road for three short blocks, then turn left onto Sai Yee Street, then right onto Flower Market Road, for an aromatic approach. The bird garden is at the end of this flower-market street. ⊠ *Yuen Po St., Prince Edward, Kowloon* ☎ *Free* ⏲ *Daily 7 AM–8 PM* Ⓜ *Prince Edward, Exit B1.*

Edward Youde Aviary. Fluttering feathers, caws, chirps, and warbles fill your ears as you enter this aviary that's home to more than 600 birds from 150 species. You crisscross a rain-forest environment on timber walkways elevated to canopy level (50 feet). Vibrant flashes of color swoop down or settle in nearby branches. Greedy-mouthed pelicans preen as they bathe in the first-floor stream. The aviary was named for a bird-loving colonial governor and is in the southwest of Hong Kong Park, which you reach by walking up through Pacific Place shopping mall from the Admiralty MTR. ⊠ *Hong Kong Park, 19 Cotton Tree Dr., Admiralty* ☎ *2521–5041* ⊕ *www.lcsd.gov.*

ONLY IF YOU MUST

The highlight of the interactive **Hong Kong Science Museum** (⊠ 2 Science Museum Rd., Tsim Sha Tsui East, Kowloon ☎ 2732-3232 ⊕ www.lcsd.gov.hk) is a series of experiments that test memory and cognitive ability. Yup. That's about it.

Although the **Hong Kong Space Museum** (⊠ 10 Salisbury Rd., Tsim Sha Tsui, Kowloon ☎ 2734-2722 ⊕ www.lcsd.gov.hk) counts an advanced planetarium among its attractions, most American kids will pass on this. The museum seems past its prime. When we visited, several interactive attractions were broken.

hk/parks/hkp ☎ Free ⏲ Daily 9–5 Ⓜ Admiralty MTR, Exit C1.

⏱ **Hong Kong Zoological & Botanical Gardens.** The city has grown around the gardens, which opened in 1864, and though they're watched over by skyscrapers on most sides, a visit to them is still a delightful escape. Paths lined with semitropical trees, shrubs, and flowers wind through cramped zoo enclosures. Sloths, orangutans, pink flamingoes, and a depressed-looking black jaguar are among the 30 represented species. Albany Road slices the park in half: jaguars, birds, and the greenhouse are on the eastern side, the other animals are to the west. A pedestrian underpass connects the two sides. In the very early morning the elderly people practicing tai chi chuan here are inspiring. ⊠ *Upper Albert Rd. opposite Government House; enter on Garden Rd., Central* ☎ *2530–0154* ⊕ *www.lcsd.gov.hk* ☎ *Free* ⏲ *Zoo: daily 6 AM–7 PM. Gardens: daily 6 AM–10 PM.*

CINEMA HONG KONG

Hong Kong is the film capital of Asian martial-arts and triad-theme movies. Unlike the shoot-'em-ups of Hollywood, the camera work in these flicks emphasizes the ricochet choreography of physical combat. You'll see some of the cheesiest, funniest, most artistically and athletically amazing movies ever made if you pop into a local movie theater.

Hong Kong films and actors haven't gone unnoticed in the West. Quentin Tarantino's *Kill Bill* films show obvious influences from Hong Kong cinema as does Ang Lee's critically acclaimed *Crouching Tiger, Hidden Dragon.* Jackie Chan, Jet Li, and Chow Yun-Fat have all found success in Hollywood, and Maggie Cheung won the best actress award at the 2004 Cannes Film Festival for her work in the film *Clean*, directed by Olivier Assayas.

The Classics

Jackie Chan has been called a "physical genius" and "the world's greatest action star." After years of international fame and accolades, this stuntman extraordinaire finally broke into the American market with *Rumble in the Bronx* in the mid-1990s. Two years later, Chan solidified his fame in the West with his first exclusively U.S. production, *Rush Hour.* In Hong Kong he's the man who's guaranteed to draw the crowds every time his latest movie is released. When he's on the silver screen, Hong Kongers know they can kick back and forget about their troubles for a while.

Of course Chan isn't Hong Kong's only martial-arts golden son. Recent heroes include John Woo, director of such bullet-ridden cult classics as *A Better Tomorrow, The Killer*, and *Hard-Boiled.* He was also responsible for launching Chow Yun-Fat's movie career. Chow Yun-Fat, who was born on the small island of Lamma and moved to Hong Kong in 1965, is the ultratough, muscular martial artist who worked with Woo on the action-move classic *A Better Tomorrow.* Both men are also known for the slick Hollywood flick *The Replacement Killers,* which Woo produced and Yun-Fat starred in. But Yun-Fat's name is now most associated with his graceful fighting prowess in Ang Lee's *Crouching Tiger, Hidden Dragon.*

But it was Bruce Lee who broke the ground and still shines as the star to live up to in life and on the screen. Martial artists still talk about Lee and his muscular physique and style. Just after moving to America in the 1960s, Lee was challenged to a fight by Cantonese experts in Oakland's Chinatown because he was teaching Chinese "secrets" to non-Chinese individuals (considered treason among some in the martial-arts community). Lee won the challenge, and students around the world still study such techniques. In part they can thank Lee for their schooling.

Also check out the work of Wong Kar-wai, known as a director of more thoughtful, critically acclaimed, artistic films. His best works include *In the Mood For Love, Chungking Express, Happy Together,* and *Fallen Angels.* Other recommendable films include the *Once Upon a Time in China* trilogy, which stars Jet Li; *The Bride with White Hair,* with Leslie Cheung and Brigitte Lin; the *Swordsman* films; *Chinese Ghost Story; Fist of Legend,* with Jet Li and Michelle Yeoh.

Ang Lee won an Oscar in 2005 for the brilliant, yet controversial *Brokeback Mountain.* His earlier films include *The Wedding Banquet* and *Eat Drink Man Woman.* Even though it takes place on the Main-

Cinema Hong Kong   > 35

land, you shouldn't miss the 1988 classic *The Last Emperor* for its insight into China. *The Joy Luck Club* is also a useful insight into Chinese culture, albeit Chinese-American culture.

A Night at the Movies

If a Jackie Chan or Chow Yun-Fat film is out, nearly every cinema in town will be showing it. Other movies are mostly B-grade, centering on the cops-and-robbers and slapstick genres; locals love these because they star popular (and very attractive) Hong Kong actors. Most local films have English subtitles, but check listings. For show times and theaters, pick up *HK Magazine* and the *South China Morning Post.* Tickets are HK$60—HK$70, depending on screening times; some cinemas have half-price tickets on Tuesday and for shows before noon. Refreshment kiosks sell two varieties of popcorn—the traditional salty type or a chocolate-flavored variety. Among the usual candy offerings and hot dogs, you'll also find Chinese beef jerky and dried squid. (Hey, you're in Hong Kong.) ▣ TIP→ Theaters are notoriously frigid. Bring a sweater, jacket, or, like the locals, a shawl.

★ **Broadway Cinematheque.** The train-station design of this art house has won awards: a departure board displays foreign and independent films (local films are rare). You can read the latest reel-world magazines from around the globe in a mini-library. A shop sells film paraphernalia, and there's a coffee- and snack bar as well. To get here, use the Temple Street exit at the Yau Ma Tei MTR. ⊠ *Prosperous Garden, 3 Public Square St., Yau Ma Tei, Kowloon* ☎ *2388–3188 for ticket reservations* ⊕ *www.cinema.com.hk.*

Cine-Art House. The quaint, two-theater cinema screens art-house and foreign films.

It's old and musty, but it's a mini-institution. Definitely bring your own shawl. There's no refreshment kiosk as food and drink aren't allowed inside. ⊠ *G/F, Sun Hung Kai Centre, 30 Harbour Rd., Wan Chai* ☎ *2317–6666* ⊕ *www.cityline.com.*

★ **Hong Kong Arts Centre Theatre.** It screens the best independent, classic, documentary, animated, and short films, often with themes focusing on a particular country, period, or director. It's not exactly blockbuster popcorn-flick fare; no matter, as food and drink are theater no-no's. ⊠ *2 Harbour Rd., Wan Chai* ☎ *2582–0200* ⊕ *www.hkac.org.hk.*

★ **Palace IFC.** Large, sink-into red leather seats and ushers in tuxedos make this boutique cinema seem more like a Broadway theater than a multiplex. Five screens show new releases, foreign and independent films, and celluloid classics like *Gone With the Wind* and *West Side Story.* Those who get chilled will appreciate the "shawl loan." There's also a bookshop and café, where you can discuss whether Rhett really did give a damn. ⊠ *IFC Mall, 8 Finance St., level 1, Central* ☎ *2388–6268* ⊕ *www. palaceifc.cinema.com.hk.*

UA Cinemas Pacific Place. UA, Hong Kong's largest multiplex chain, screens the latest American blockbusters, the occasional foreign film, and a few local comedies and dramas. The cinemas lack character, but their ushers are extremely helpful, and there's a good selection of refreshments. ⊠ *Pacific Pl., 88 Queensway, Admiralty* ☎ *2317–6666* ⊕ *www.cityline. com.hk.*

OFF TO THE RACES

Even if you're not a gambler, it's worth going to one of Hong Kong's two tracks just to experience the phenomenon. The "sport of kings" is run under a monopoly by the Hong Kong Jockey Club, one of the territory's most powerful entities. It's a multimillion-dollar-a-year business, employing thousands of people and drawing crowds that approach insanity in their eagerness to rid themselves of their hard-earned money. Profits go to charity and community organizations.

The season runs from September through June. Some 65 races are held at one or the other of the two courses—on Saturday or Sunday afternoon at Sha Tin and Wednesday night at Happy Valley—which must rank among the world's great horse-racing experiences.

In the public stands the vibe is electric and loud thanks to feverish gamblers shouting and waving their newspapers madly. Both courses have huge video screens at the finish line so you can see what's happening every foot of the way. ■ TIP→ The HKTB offers track tours that cost HK$550–HK$1,080 and can include transfers, lunch, and tips on picking a winner.

★ Fodor's Choice **Happy Valley Racetrack.** Hong Kong punters are the world's most avid horse-racing fans, and the beloved track in Happy Valley—opened soon after the British first arrived in the territory—is one of their headquarters. The roar of the crowd as the jockeys in bright silk colors race by is a must see. The joy of the Happy Valley track, even for those who aren't into horses, is that it's smack in the middle of the city and surrounded by towering apartment blocks—indeed, people whose balconies hang over the backstretch often have parties on racing days. The track is a five-minute walk from the Causeway Bay MTR. ⊠ *Hong Kong Jockey Club, 1 Sports Rd., Happy Valley* ☎ *2966-8111* ⊕ *www.hkjc.com* ☒ *HK$10.*

★ **Sha Tin Racecourse.** Whether you enter Sha Tin by road or rail, you'll be amazed to find this metropolis in the middle of the New Territories. One of the so-called "new towns," Sha Tin underwent a population explosion starting in the mid-1980s that transformed it from a town of 30,000 to a city of more than a half million. The biggest attraction is the racecourse, which is newer and larger than the one in Happy Valley. In fact it's one of the world's most modern courses and, as such, is the venue for all championship events, including some equestrian events for the 2008 Olympics. The easiest way to get here is by taxi, or you can catch the MTR to Kowloon Tong and transfer to the KCR train, which stops at the Racecourse Station on race days. A walkway from it takes you directly to the track. ⊠ *Tai Po Rd., next to Racecourse KCR station, Sha Tin* ☎ *2966-6520* ☒ *HK$10.*

> ## WORD OF MOUTH
>
> Happy Valley racecourse is right in the city. The museum isn't much, but it's definitely a great place for racing. Sha Tin is an excellent easy-to-reach racecourse **outside town**. If you visit Macau, definitely go to the Macau Jockey Club. I couldn't find any useful handicapping info at Happy Valley. Get the daily paper; the horses' past performances are listed in the sports section.
>
> –mrwunnfl

Hong Kong
Neighborhoods

Midlevels

WORD OF MOUTH

". . . a visit to the Peak, a Star Ferry ride across the harbour, a walk along the Esplanade . . . there's a ton of stuff to do, none of which involves buying copy watches or fake Prada bags or having bad food at a night market."

—Cicerone

TO STAND ON THE TIP OF KOWLOON PENINSULA and look across the harbor to the full expanse of the Hong Kong Island skyline is to see the triumph of ambition over fate. Whereas it took Paris and London 10 to 20 generations and New York 6 to build the spectacular cities seen today, in Hong Kong almost everything you see was built in the time since today's young investment bankers were born.

Hong Kong Island and Kowloon are divided physically and psychologically by Victoria Harbour. On Hong Kong Island, the central city stretches only a few kilometers south into the island before mountains rise up, but the city goes several more kilometers north into Kowloon. In the main districts and neighborhoods, luxury boutiques are a stone's throw from old hawker stalls, and a modern, high-tech horse-racing track isn't far from a temple housing more than 10,000 buddhas.

If you're on Hong Kong Island and feeling a little disoriented, remember that the water is always north; in Kowloon it's always south. Central, Admiralty, and Wan Chai, the island's main business districts, are opposite Tsim Sha Tsui on the Kowloon Peninsula. West of Central are Sheung Wan and the other (mainly residential) neighborhoods that make up Western. Central backs onto the slopes of Victoria Peak, so the districts south of it—the Midlevels and the Peak—look down on it. Causeway Bay, Shau Kei Wan, Quarry Bay, North Point, and Chai Wan East run east along the shore after Wan Chai. Developments on the south side of Hong Kong Island are scattered: the beach towns of Shek O and Stanley sit on two peninsulas on the southeast; industrial Aberdeen and Ap Lei Chau are to the west.

West of Hong Kong Island lie Lamma, Cheung Chau, and Lantau islands. Lantau is connected by a suspension bridge to west Kowloon. More than 200 other islands also belong to Hong Kong.

Kowloon's southern tip is the Tsim Sha Tsui district, which gives way to Jordan, Yau Ma Tei, Mong Kok, and Prince Edward. Northeast are the New Kowloon districts of Kowloon Tong, Kowloon City, and Wong Tai Sin, beyond which lie in the eastern New Territories—mostly made up of mountainous country parks and fishing villages. The Sai Kung Peninsula juts out on the east, and massive Sha Tin New Town is north of New Kowloon, over Lion Rock Mountain. The Kowloon–Canton Railway and a highway run north of this to the Chinese border at Lo Wu.

Industrial Sham Shui Po lies west of Prince Edward, and the urban sprawl continues northwest to New Territories New Town Tsuen Wan. The western New Territories is a mixture of country parks and urban areas.

Hong Kong's older areas—the southern side of Central, for example—show erratic street planning, but the newer developments and reclamations follow something closer to a grid system. Streets are usually numbered odd on one side, even on the other. There's no baseline for street numbers and no block-based numbering system.

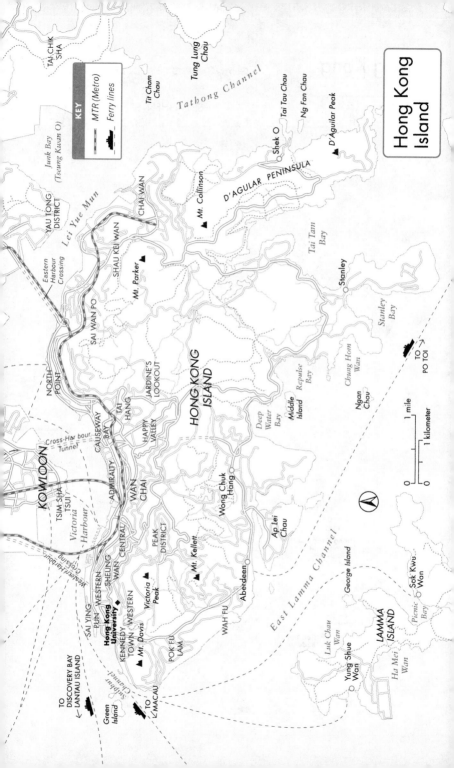

Hong Kong
Island

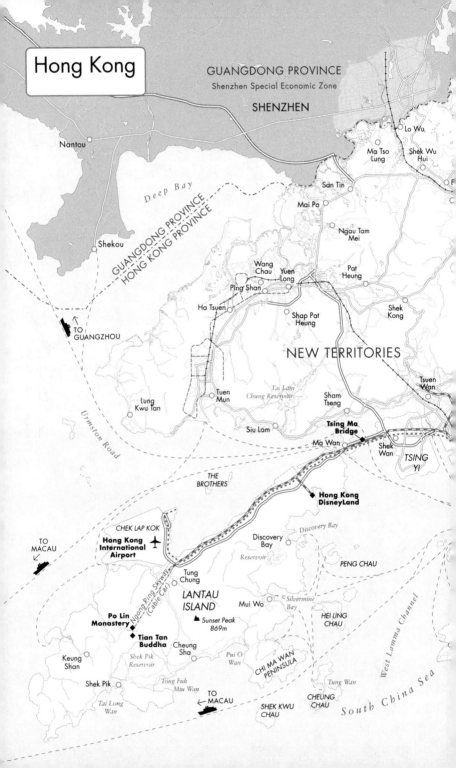

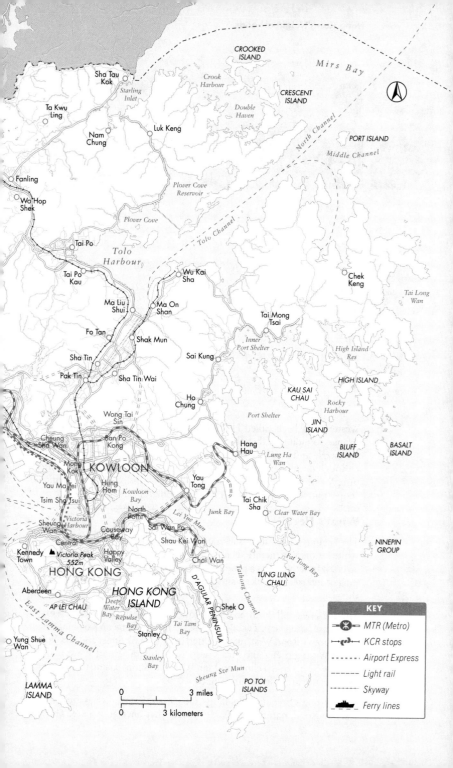

WESTERN

Sightseeing
★ ★ ★

Dining
★ ★

Lodging
★ ★

Shopping
★ ★ ★

Nightlife
★

The old lady faces rows of large glass jars filled with mysterious contents. She waits patiently at the counter, its polished teak worn by generations of hands and elbows. The pharmacist grinds the ingredients—some of herbal origin, others animal—of the tea her doctor has prescribed. Taking two aspirin might be a quicker solution to her backache, but it won't get to the root of the problem. She's been coming here for years. It's worth the wait.

Western has been called Hong Kong's Chinatown, and though it's a strange-sounding epithet, there's a point to it. The area is light-years from the dazzle and bustle of Central, despite being just down the road. And although developers are making short work of the traditional architecture, Western's colonial buildings, rattling trams, old-world medicine shops, and lively markets still recall bygone times.

What's Here

The Sheung Wan district's iconic **Western Market,** a hulking brown-and-white colonial structure, is a good place to get your bearings. Built in 1906, it functioned as a produce market for 83 years. Today it's a shopping center selling trinkets and fabrics—the architecture is what's worth the visit.

Strange smells fill the air in the narrow streets west of the market: many trades are based here. There's Chinese herbal medicine on Ko Shing Street and Queen's Road West; dried seafood on Wing Lok Street and Des Voeux Road West; ginseng and bird's nests on Bonham Strand West; and the engraved seals called chops on Man Wa Lane. Shops selling temple goods like incense are also commonplace.

Hong Kong's best antiques shops and classical-art galleries are on Hollywood Road, named for the Holly trees that once grew here. The farther west you go, the less genuine things get. Porcelain, curios, and not-very-old trinkets masquerading as artifacts make up most of the offerings on Upper Lascar Row, a flea market commonly known as Cat Street. At the corner of Hollywood Road and the long flight of stairs known as Ladder Street, sandalwood smoke floats out of **Man Mo Temple.** Hong Kong's oldest Chinese temple honors the Taoist gods of literature and war. Farther west is Possession Street. A sign here marks where Captain Charles Elliott stepped ashore in 1841 to claim Hong Kong for the British empire. This was once the waterfront, but aggressive reclamation has left it several blocks inland.

The maze of streets west of Man Mo Temple is known as Tai Ping Shan (the Chinese name for Victoria Peak, which towers above it). It's a sleepy area filled with small shops. ■ TIP➡ Food tourists should duck into Sheung Wan Wet Market, at Sai Ying Pun and Centre streets. Cantonese food demands the freshest ingredients, and serious cooks buy them—often still wriggling—at markets like this. One of the city's oldest residential districts, Tai Ping Shan was badly hit by plague outbreaks in the 1890s. You can find out all about these and other medical episodes at the **Hong Kong Museum of Medical Sciences,** at the top of Ladder Street.

The unimaginatively named Midlevels is midway up the hill between Victoria Peak and the Western and Central districts. Running through it is the **Midlevels Escalator,** which connects now-defunct Central Market (at the border of Central and Western) with several main residential roads. Free of charge and protected from the elements, this series of moving walkways makes the uphill journey a cinch. Before 11 AM, they move only downward, carrying yuppies bearing coffee to work.

When all you see from the escalator are hip bars and restaurants, you're in SoHo, the area *so*uth of (i.e., above) *Ho*llywood Road and epicenter of Hong Kong's latest gastro revolution. The Midlevels Escalator goes right by the gray-and-white **Jamia Mosque** on Shelley Street. The original 1840s structure was rebuilt in 1915, and shows its Indian heritage in the perforated arches and decorative facade work. The mosque isn't open to non-Muslims, but it occupies a small verdant enclosure that's a welcome retreat.

It's worth a trip out to the western end of the Midlevels to see the imposing Edwardian buildings, most along Bonham Road, of Hong Kong University, where competition for a place is fierce. The **Hong Kong University Museum & Art Gallery** has excellent Chinese antiquities.

A Perfect Day

From Sheung Wan's markets to the hip international eateries (and drinkeries) of SoHo, Western is a foodie's paradise. Here's how to make a culinary adventure of it.

There's only one breakfast of champs in Hong Kong, and that's dim sum. Head for **Lin Heung Lau Tea House** (⇨ Quick Bites) any time after 10 AM and fill up on things like *ha gau* (steamed shrimp dumplings) and *cha siu bau* (barbecue pork buns), washed down with lots of tea.

GETTING ORIENTED

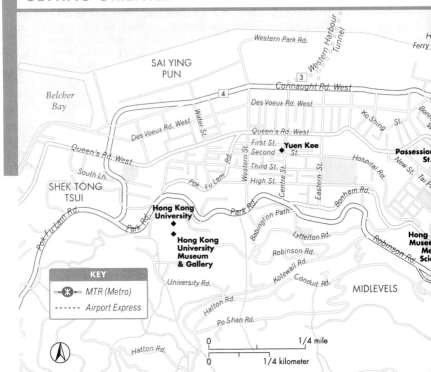

THE TERRITORY

The Midlevels Escalator forms a handy boundary between Western and Central. Several main thoroughfares run parallel to the shore, each farther up the slope: Des Voeux Road (where the trams run), Queen's Road, Hollywood Road (where SoHo starts), and Caine Road (where the Midlevels begin).

As to how far west Western goes, it technically reaches all the way to Kennedy Town, where the tramlines end, but there isn't much worth noting beyond Sheung Wan.

TAKING IT IN

Colonial Architecture. You can see Western's colonial buildings on an hour-long stroll from the University of Hong Kong (take a cab or bus out). East along Bonham Road, which becomes Caine Road, are Victorian apartments. The medical sciences museum is at Ladder Street. Head downstairs, then left onto Hollywood Road to Possession Street. Follow this downhill, doglegging right and left through Bonham Strand, onto Morrison, and to the Western Market.

Traditional Goods. An hour is enough time to wander Sheung Wan's traditional shops. In the morning, when trade's brisk, take the tram to Wilmer Street. Walk a block south and turn left onto Queen's Road West (herbal remedies, temple goods). Walk left for a block at Possession, then loop left through Bonham Strand West (ginseng), right for a block at Des Voeux, then back along Wing Lok (dried seafood). Continue on Bonham Strand (bird's nests), dipping left onto Hillier (snakes) and beyond to Man Wa Lane (chops).

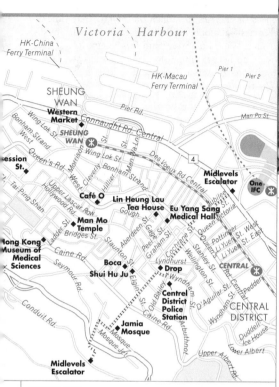

GETTING AROUND

The most atmospheric way to Sheung Wan is on a tram along Des Voeux Road. From Central or Admiralty, this is probably the quickest mode, too: no traffic, no subway lines, or endless underground walks. There are stops every two or three blocks. In addition, the Sheung Wan MTR station brings you within spitting distance of Western Market.

The Macau Ferry Terminal is behind the MTR (use Exit D). **Turbojet** (☎ 2859-3333 ⊕ www.turbojet.com.hk) vessels run every 15–30 minutes round the clock. Crossings take 50 minutes. You can usually buy tickets on the spot (HK$142 weekdays, HK$176 weekends). ■ TIP→ **You need your passport to go to Macau.**

The Midlevels Escalator is fun up as far as SoHo. If you're going farther, take a bus or a cab; the thrill wears off and it can take 20 minutes to reach the top. Buses 3, 40, and 40M run between the university and Jardine House in Central, as does green Minibus 8. Both pass the top of Ladder Street. Expect a taxi from Central to the Midlevels to cost HK$20.

QUICK BITES

Sink into the leather sofas at **Boca** (✉ 65 Peel St., Western ☎ 2548-1717) and watch trendy SoHo go by. Tapas are the specialty: classics like *gambas al ajillo* (garlic prawns) and Hong Kong originals like butterfish in ginger.

Cracked Formica tabletops, cranky waiters, old men reading the newspapers: there's nothing fancy about **Lin Heung Lau Tea House** (✉ 160-164 Wellington St., Sheung Wan, Western ☎ 2544-4556). But it's been doing great dim sum for years, as locals will testify. Tea is brewed in *gai wan* (traditional lidded cups) rather than pots—watch old-timers at the next table to learn how it's done.

Café O (✉ 285 Queen's Rd. Central, Sheung Wan, Western ☎2851-0890) is a Sheung Wan trailblazer. Pizza by the meter is the signature dish, but the mega-breakfasts (served all day) are fierce competition. Fresher-than-fresh juices and smoothies help you keep your energy up.

Get to Sheung Wan Wet Market early to watch expert shoppers in action. Earn their respect by examining fish gills for freshness and picking up a bag of lychees or cherries to munch on the go. Take time to browse the dried delicacies—abalone, bird's nests, sea cucumbers, mushrooms—in shops around Wing Lok Street and Des Voeux Road. You might want to invest in an herbal indigestion cure, just in case. Got a sweet tooth? Try a traditional dessert at **Yuen Kee** (⌧ 32 Centre St., Western ☎ 2548—8687)—the almond soup is divine.

Walk over to Gage Street for a steaming bowl of wonton noodles at any *dai pai doing* (street restaurant). Wander more stalls on chaotic Graham Street—the meat stalls aren't for the fainthearted—then go for some liquid sustenance. Many SoHo bars along the Midlevels Escalator start happy hour at 5 PM. Wind up the day with top-notch Shanghainese, Sichuan, or Cantonese dishes amid lots of lacquered wood at **Shui Hu Ju** (⌧ 68 Peel St., SoHo, Western ☎ 2869–6927).

At a Glance

EXPERIENCES ⇨ Ch. 1

On the Move
Midlevels Escalator

To Your Health
Bonham Strand
Des Voeux Road West
Eu Yang Sang Medical Hall
Hillier Street
Hong Kong Museum of
   Medical Sciences
Queen's Road West
Wing Lok Street

CULTURAL SIGHTS ⇨ Ch. 3

Hong Kong University Museum & Art Gallery
Man Mo Temple

ALSO WORTH NOTING

Jamia Mosque
Macau Ferry Terminal
Soho District

Quick Bites
Boca
Café O
Lin Hueung Lau Tea House
Yuen Kee

SHOPPING ⇨ Ch. 4

Department Store
Wing On

Markets
Western Market
Sheung Wan Wet Market

RESTAURANTS ⇨ Ch. 5

Budget
Katong Laksa

Moderate
Da Ping Huo
Jing Cheng Xiao Chu
Shui Hu Ju
Soho Spice
Yellow Door Kitchen

2

CENTRAL

Sightseeing
★ ★ ★ ★

Dining
★ ★ ★

Lodging
★ ★ ★

Shopping
★ ★ ★ ★

Nightlife
★ ★ ★ ★

The young businessman has loosened his tie and is sipping a pint outside a bar in Lan Kwai Fong. It's Tuesday, but the streets are buzzing with lawyers, traders, and it-girls relaxing after work—or shopping. The man's buddy taps his beer bottle and says, "Drink up, mate." It's not time to go home; rather, they've spotted friends up the hill—this beer is the first of many, and it's time to move on.

Shopping, eating, drinking—Central lives up to its name when it comes to all of these. But it's also Hong Kong's historical heart, packed with architectural reminders of the early colonial days. They're in stark contrast to the soaring masterpieces of modern architecture that the city is famous for. Somehow the mishmash works. With the harbor on one side and Victoria Peak on the other, Central's views—once you get high enough to see them—are unrivaled. It's the liveliest district, packed with people, sights, and life.

What's Here

One building towers above the rest of Central's skyline: Two IFC, or the second tower of the **International Finance Centre.** The tall, tapering structure has been compared to at least one—unprintable—thing; and is topped with a clawlike structure straight out of Thundercats. Designed by Argentine architect Cesar Pelli (of London's Canary Wharf fame), its 88 floors measure a whopping 1,362 feet. Opposite it stands its dinky little brother, the 38-floor One IFC. The massive IFC Mall stretches between the two, and Hong Kong Station is underneath.

Jutting out into the harbor in front of the International Finance Center is the **Outlying Islands Ferry Pier.** Ferries regularly leave from here to Lantau, Lamma, and Cheung Chau islands.

GETTING ORIENTED

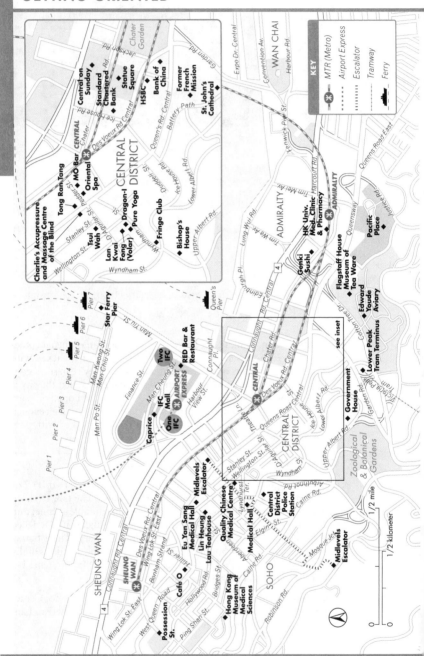

KEY

❋ MTR (Metro)
····· Airport Express
····· Escalator
········ Tramway
▬▬ Ferry

WAN CHAI

CENTRAL DISTRICT

Central on Sunday
Standard Chartered Bank
Statue Square
HSBC
Bank of China
Former French Mission
St. John's Cathedral

Charlie's Accupressure and Massage Centre of the Blind
Tong Ren Tang
MO Bar
Oriental Spa
Dragon-i
Pure Yoga
(Volar)
Lan Kwai Fong
Tsui Wah
Fringe Club
Bishop's House

ADMIRALITY

HK Univ. Med. Clinic & Pharmacy
Genki Sushi
Flagstaff House Museum of Tea Ware
Pacific Place
Edward Youde Aviary
Lower Peak Tram Terminus
Government House

Queen's Pier
Star Ferry Pier
Pier 7
Pier 6
Pier 5
Pier 4
Pier 3
Pier 2
Pier 1

RED Bar & Restaurant
Two IFC
AIRPORT EXPRESS
IFC Mall
One IFC
Caprice

CENTRAL
see inset
CENTRAL DISTRICT

Zoological & Botanical Gardens

SHEUNG WAN

Midlevels Escalator
Eu Yan Sang Medical Hall
Lin Heung Lau Techouse
Quality Chinese Medical Centre
Medical Hall
Central District Police Station
Midlevels Escalator

Café O
Possession St.
Hong Kong Museum of Medical Sciences

SOHO

1/2 mile
1/2 kilometer
0
0

GETTING AROUND

Central MTR station is a mammoth underground warren with a host of far-flung exits. A series of travelators join it with Hong Kong Station, under the IFC Mall, where Tung Chung line and Airport Express trains arrive and depart. Rattling old trams along Des Voeux Road have you at Sheung Wan, Admiralty, and Wan Chai in minutes. They continue to Causeway Bay, Happy Valley, and beyond. Bus routes to and from all over pass through Central's Exchange Square and under the Admiralty Centre in Admiralty.

Star Ferry vessels to Kowloon leave Pier 7 every 6–10 minutes 6:30 AM–11:30 PM; the 7-minute trip costs HK$2.20 (upper deck). Ferries run from the Outlying Islands Ferry Pier, in front of the IFC, every half-hour 6 AM–midnight. **New World First Ferry** (☎ 2131-8181 ⊕ www.nwff.com.hk), goes to Lantau (from Pier 6) and Cheung Chau (Pier 5). Journeys take 30–50 minutes and cost HK$13.40–HK$16.70. **Discovery Bay Transportation Service** (☎ 2987-7351 ⊕ www.hkri.com.hk) has high-speed boats for Lantau every 10–30 minutes from Pier 3. Trips take 25–30 minutes and cost HK$27.

QUICK BITES

At lunch time people flood the cul-de-sac that is, oddly enough, known as Rat Alley (Wing Wah Lane off D'Aguilar Street). Menu-bearing waiters vie for your attention: choose from Thai, Malay, Indian, Chinese, or American places.

No visit to Central is complete without a bowl of noodles at **Tsui Wah** (✉ ground fl., 15-19 Wellington St., Central ☎ 2525-6338) down the hill from Lan Kwai Fong. It's open until 4 AM. Need an instant sushi fix? Pull up a stool at the conveyor belt at **Genki Sushi** (✉ Ground fl., Far East Finance Centre, 16 Harcourt Rd, Admiralty ☎ 2865-2933). There are also sleek hardwood booths and a sashimi menu. Oh, and the bill usually only comes to HK$40–HK$60 per person.

THE TERRITORY

The Midlevels Escalator and Cotton Tree Drive form the boundaries of Central with Western and Admiralty districts, respectively. Streets in the area between Queen's Road Central and the harbor are laid out more or less geometrically. On the south side of Queen's Road, however, is a rabbit-warren of steep lanes. Overhead walkways connect Central's major buildings, an all-weather alternative to the chaotic streets below.

TAKING IT IN

Colonial Central. Former *South China Morning Post* columnist Jason Wordie (☎ 2476-3504 ⊕ www.jasonswalks.com) leads three-hour tours (HK$280) loaded with anecdotes.

The Urban Runway. They say the ability to cross Central without touching street level is the sign of a true Hong Konger. Here's a 30-minute route. Start in the IFC mall; leave by Pret a Manger on the southeast side, turn right into the walkway, pass the General Post Office and Jardine House and into the Armani floor of the Chater Building. The door between Emporio and Fiori leads to Alexandra House—take the stairs left of Dolce and Gabbana and into the Landmark. Turn right after Jimmy Choo, up the stairs past Clarins, and into the Central Building. Cross to the back right of the elevator lobby, through the bridge into the Entertainment Building, which drops you in Lan Kwai Fong. Time your walk to finish at 6 PM–happy hour.

Just behind the IFC is '60s skyscraper **Jardine House,** recognizable by its many round windows. It's home to Jardine, Matheson & Co., the greatest of the old British *hongs* (trading companies) that dominated trade with imperial China. Once an establishment linked to opium trafficking, it's now a respected investment bank.

Arguably the best way to take in Central's architecture isn't on land but arriving from Kowloon on one of the sturdy green-and-white Star Ferries. The view of the skyline isn't bad from the **Central Star Ferry Pier,** either. **Statue Square** is directly to the south. The land it's on was gifted to the public by the Hongkong & Shanghai Bank (HSBC, whose headquarters dominate the southern end), with the proviso that nothing built on it could block the bank's view of the water.

DID YOU KNOW?

Statue Square took its name from bronze figures of British royalty that stood here before the Japanese occupation, when they were removed and melted down. The only figure exempt was stern Sir Thomas Jackson (1841–1915) who looks over the square toward HSBC—he was the chief manager for more than 30 years.

The Victorian–Chinese hybrid building on Statue Square's east side is the Legislative Council Building. Built for the Supreme Court in 1912, it's now home to the 60-member Legislative Council (LegCo). It's often the focus of the demonstrations that have become a fixture of Hong Kong life since 1997. In front of the council building is the Cenotaph, a monument to all who lost their lives in the two world wars.

Along Statue Square's southern end are the three buildings of Hong Kong's note-issuing banks: the art deco former headquarters of the **Bank of China,** the rose-color wedge of the **Standard Chartered Bank,** and the spectacular strut-and-ladder facade of the **HSBC.** The latter is one of the most important buildings in 20th-century architecture; walk under it and look up into the atrium through the curved glass floor, or go inside for a view of the building's mechanics.

Hong Kong's answer to New York's 5th Avenue and London's King's Road are the first few blocks of Chater Road, Des Voeux Road Central, and Queen's Road Central (the thoroughfares that stretch west from Statue Square). Few designers do not have—or do not crave—a boutique in priceless über-posh minimalls like the Landmark, Alexandra House, or the Pedder Building. Within spitting distance, but at the other end of the income scale, are Li Yuen Street East and Li Yuen Street West. Known as the Lanes, they're packed with stalls selling cheap *cheongsams* (sexy, slit-skirt, silk dresses with Mandarin collars) and Hello Kitty merchandise. On the south side of Queen's Road is steep Pottinger Street, a haberdasher's paradise.

In Hong Kong, the word "nightlife" is synonymous with **Lan Kwai Fong,** a few narrow lanes filled with bars and clubs just up the hill from the intersection of Queen's Road Central and Pedder Street. Veering right at the top gets you to Wyndham Street and the start of a series of high-caliber antiques and Oriental-rug shops. The colonial building just after the street becomes Hollywood Road is the **Central District Police Station,** a must-have location in any self-respecting Hong Kong cop movie. It was the neighborhood headquarters from 1864—when part of it was built—through 2004.

Several colonial structures are clustered on Lower Albert Road, which starts at the curving eastern end of Wyndham Street. The brown-and-white brick building on the corner is the Old Dairy Farm Building, built in 1898. Once a big glorified fridge housing a meat and dairy shop, it's now home to the **Fringe Club** arts center and the Foreign Correspondents' Club, the haunt of hard-drinking international journalists. The big gray Victorian building across the road is Bishop's House, official residence of the Anglican bishop since 1851. Lower Albert Road forks in two; the lower branch is Ice House Street, which curves down the hill to Queen's Road. Before the bend is a magnificent balustraded stone staircase that becomes Duddell Street; it's adorned with four old-fashioned gas lamps that have been lighting the way since the late 1870s.

Farther uphill on Central's eastern edge are the **Hong Kong Zoological & Botanical Gardens,** a welcome green breathing space. The handsome white Victorian occupying the land between Upper and Lower Albert roads is **Government House.** Constructed in 1855, it was the official residence of British governors but is shunned by the new chief executives—some say because it has bad feng shui. During the Japanese occupation it was significantly rebuilt, so it exhibits a subtle Japanese influence, particularly in the roof eaves. The gardens are opened to the public once a year in March, when the azaleas bloom.

A peaceful gap in the skyscrapers—on Garden Road and up from Queen's Road Central—accommodates the Anglican **St. John's Cathedral,** a graceful Gothic form. Completed in 1849, it's made of Canton bricks in the shape of a cross. Among the WWII relics it houses are the cathedral doors themselves, made from timber salvaged from British warship HMS *Tamar.*

Victoria Peak soars 1,805 feet above sea level and looks over Central and beyond. Residents here take special pride in the positions to which they have, quite literally, risen; theirs is the island's most exclusive address. The steep tracks up to it starts at the **Peak Tram Terminus,** near St. John's Cathedral on Garden Road.

A narrow tree-lined lane called Battery Path runs uphill parallel to Queen's Road Central behind the HSBC building. The British built it when they arrived in 1841 to move their cannons uphill—hence the name. At the top of Battery Path sits the **Former French Mission Building,** an elegant red-brick building with white stone windows and green shutters. Finished in 1917, it's now home to the Court of Final Appeal.

Central's skyscrapers spill over into Admiralty, the next district east. It's home to **Pacific Place** shopping mall and the 25 green acres of **Hong Kong Park.** Here you'll find the **Flagstaff Museum of Tea Ware,** and the **Edward Youde Aviary.**

A Perfect Day (and Night)

Nine Hours of Luxury

With boutiques, spas, and coffee shops galore, Central has everything you need to be a *tai-tai*—localspeak for ladies who lunch—even if you're a man. There's *so* much more to do than lunch, so take a leaf out of their book and spend some time (and lots of money) on—who else?—yourself.

Start off by harmonizing the inner you with an early-morning yoga class (a trial class is free, or it's HK$800 for a monthlong visitor pass) at **Pure Yoga** (⊠ The Centrium, 16th fl., 60 Wyndham St., Central ☎ 2971–0055 ⊕ www.pure-yoga.com). Then head to the **Oriental Spa** (⊠ Landmark Mandarin Oriental, 15 Queen's Rd. Central ☎ 2132—0011 ⊕ www. mandarinoriental.com/landmark) for the three-hour Urban Retreat package (HK$2,580), which includes a facial, massage, and foot treatment. You need to book a week ahead.

Relaxing is hungry work. But not just anyone should be allowed to prepare your lunch, so book a table at **Caprice** (⊠ 8 Finance St., Central ☎ 3196–8888) in the Four Seasons hotel. It's hard to know whether to gaze at the view of the harbor, the French chandeliers, or the chefs in the open kitchen as they cook up the best French food in town.

What better way to work off lunch than shopping? The Landmark and Chater House are packed with international designers, but don't neglect the Pedder Building where local luxury brands like Shanghai Tang sell made-to-measure Chinese-style suits and cheongsams. Reflect on your busy day over Bellinis at **MO Bar** (⊠ 15 Queen's Road Central, Central ☎ 2132–0077) in the Landmark Oriental.

Ten Hours on the Town

When the neon comes up, office-Central transforms into party-Central. The nights are long and Hong Kongers play hard, but here's a plan guaranteed to earn local party animals' respect.

Boozing is an expensive pastime, so keep costs down with a happy hour bar crawl through Lan Kwai Fong. When the sun's about to set, grab a cab to the IFC Mall and watch the orb descend over the harbor as you sip a quirky cocktail at an open-air table in the **RED Bar + Restaurant** (⊠ Level 4, Two IFC, 8 Finance St., Central ☎ 8129–8882).

Don't worry about losing your momentum by stopping for dinner. Just head to celebrity haunt **dragon i** (⊠ Upper G/F, The Centrium, 60 Wyndham St., Central ☎ 3110–1222), where there's sushi, dim sum, *and* cocktails to nourish you. The giant birdcages are pretty cool, too. Pace yourself at **Drop** (⊠ On Lok Mansion, 39–43 Hollywood Rd., basement [entrance off Cochrane St.], Central ☎ 2543–8856), where the fab cocktails are tempting and the funky sounds are mesmerizing. You could easily overindulge. Be sure to hit ultratrendy club **Volar** (⊠ B/F, 39–44 D'Aguilar St., Central ☎ 2810–1272) for dancing. Stumble out and head to **Tsui Wah** (⇨ Quick Bites) for a restorative 3 AM bowl of noodles.

At a Glance

LANTAU ISLAND

Sightseeing
★ ★ ★ ★

Dining
★

Lodging
★

Shopping
★

Nightlife
★

It's a gray day. As the bus chugs up the narrow road the clouds descend, cloaking all in wispy white. At Ngong Ping, everyone rushes to exit—everyone except two Buddhist monks. They descend last, their crimson and saffron robes splashing color into the mist. The tourist hordes hightail up the stone staircase; the monks remain below. Soon, the clouds part, and the giant bronze Buddha stands out against the sky. Good things come to those who wait.

A decade of manic development has seen Lantau become much more than just "the place where the Buddha is." There's a mini-theme park at Ngong Ping to keep the Buddha company. Not to be outdone, Disney has opened a park and resort on the northeast coast. And, of course, there's the airport, built on a massive north coast reclamation. At 55 square mi, Lantau is almost twice the size of Hong Kong Island, so there's room for all this development—and the laid-back attractions—beaches, fishing villages, and hiking trails—that make the island a great getaway.

What's Here

One of Lantau's main ferry hubs, **Mui Wo,** is a sleepy little town with some good waterfront restaurants. Silvermine Bay Beach, a pleasant sandy stretch is a half mile northeast of the Mui Wo ferry pier. A gentle uphill trail leads to the Silvermine Caves and Waterfall, the small 19th-century mine that gave the bay its English name. The well-signposted walk takes about an hour from Mui Wo and eventually links with the Lantau Trail. Two miles of golden sand 5 mi southwest of Mui Wo make **Cheung Sha Beach,** Hong Kong's longest. It gets breezy here, but that's why windsurfers love it.

The most glorious views of Lantau—and beyond—are from atop Fung Wong Shan, or **Lantau Peak,** but at 3,064 feet it's not for the faint-hearted. It's a strenuous 7½ mi west from Mui Wo, or you can take the easy way by starting at the Po Lin Monastery—still a good two hours.

Tucked away on the west of Lantau is **Tai O,** a fishing village inhabited largely by the tanka (boat people), whose stilt houses have mostly been replaced by government-funded high-rises. Similarly, an old rope-pulled ferry connecting the village proper with a small island has been replaced with a metal bridge. Aging Hakka women, however, haul the ferry back into action on weekends. You can also see salt pans and a 16th-century temple dedicated to Kwan Tai, god of war.

Lantau is connected to the Kowloon Peninsula by the world's longest suspension bridge, the 4,518-foot Tsing Ma Bridge. Airport Express and MTR trains run through its sheltered lower level; a highway runs atop it, with stunning views of the Pearl River delta to the west.

Lantau's most famous resident is a big guy: the **Tian Tan Buddha** is the world's largest seated outdoor bronze Buddha, a string of qualifiers that's practically a mantra in itself. He sits on the Ngong Ping plateau, beside the **Po Lin Monastery,** a onetime haven of peace. You can still find stillness at the nearby **Wisdom Path,** a short hillside walk lined by massive wooden tablets inscribed with parts of a Buddhist sutra (prayer). Ngong Ping is also home to a religious theme park, **Ngong Ping Village,** with interactive exhibits on the Buddha, as well as gift shops and restaurants.

Lantau's northwest coast looks kinda funny thanks to the curiously geometrical bit of land that was reclaimed for the **Hong Kong International Airport.** You might be too dazed to notice when you arrive, but Sir Norman Foster's Y-shape design is an architectural marvel.

Looking at the tower blocks and perfectly planned avenues of **Tung Chung New Town,** home to around 80,000 people, it's hard to imagine that only 15 years ago this was a small village. Over the MTR station is a mall filled with outlet stores for big local brands. All that remains of the old Tung Chung is the hulking granite **Tung Chung Fort** (⊠ Tung Chung Rd., Lantau ☉ Wed.–Mon. 10–5). The first fortification on this spot was built during the Song Dynasty; the current structure dates from 1832.

The latest item on Lantau's laundry list of developments is **Hong Kong Disneyland.** Though it's tame compared to other Magic Kingdoms, it's fast bringing Mai Kei Lao Shui—as the world's most famous mouse is known locally—to a mainland audience.

A Perfect (Sunny) Day

Leave Central on the Mui Wo ferry at around 11 AM—bag a window seat for the views. From Mui Wo Ferry Pier catch Bus 1 or a cab to Che-

GETTING ORIENTED

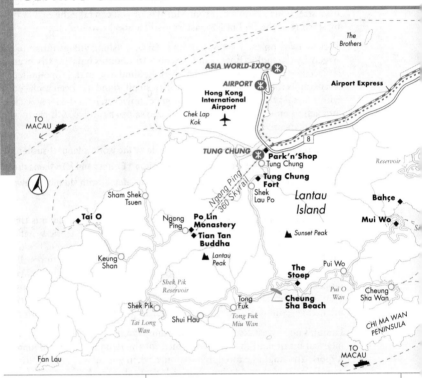

THE TERRITORY	TAKING IT IN
Most Lantau roads lead to Tung Chung, the north shore new town, close to Hong Kong International Airport. It's connected to Kowloon by the lengthy Tsing Ma Bridge, which starts near Hong Kong Disneyland, on Lantau's northeast tip. The Tung Chung Road winds through mountains and connects north Lantau with the southern coast. Here, the South Lantau Road stretches from the town of Mui Wo in the east to Tai O in the west, passing Cheung Sha Beach and Ngong Ping.	Candy-pink dolphins might sound like something Disney cooked up, but Lantau's cutest residents are actually the endangered species *Sousa chinensis*, native to the Pearl River estuary. There's only a thousand left, but ecotourism company **Hong Kong Dolphinwatch** (☎ 2984-1414 ⊕ www.hkdolphinwatch.com) guarantees you a sighting of them on their 2½ hour cruises (HK$320)—or a free second trip. Lantau has some great hiking—friendly guides lead the way at **Walk Hong Kong** (☎ 9187-8641 ⊕ www.walkhongkong.com). Its all-day Lantau trek combines a 2½ hour hike from the Buddha to Tai O village with sightseeing at each end. The HK$600 cost includes transport to and from Central. Make inquiries at least a week ahead. To see Lantau's big sights whistle-stop style, try **Splendid Tours** (☎ 2316-2151 ⊕ www.splendidtours.com). A daylong trip (HK$550) takes in the Tsing Ma Bridge, Cheung Sha Beach, Tai O village, and Ngong Ping.

2

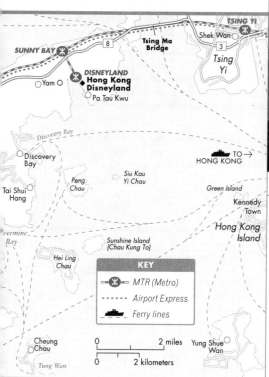

GETTING AROUND

The speediest way to Lantau from Central is the Airport Express, which stops at Tung Chung and the airport—but it'll cost ya (HK$100). Vastly cheaper (HK$26), the MTR's Tung Chung line runs the same route but takes a bit longer. Plan one leg of your trip by ferry—it's a half-hour trip from Central, with great views. **New World First Ferry** (☎ 2131-8181 ⊕ www.nwff.com.hk) vessels to Mui Wo leave every 15 minutes from Central's Pier 6 (HK$11.30–HK$22.20).

Bus routes are winding, and rides can be heart-stopping. There's service every half hour from Tung Chung and Mui Wo to Ngong Ping, more frequently to Tai O. The most direct way to Ngong Ping is the 20-minute trip on the **Ngong Ping 360 Skyrail** (☎ 2109-9898 ⊕ www.np360.com.hk). The cable car runs weekdays 10–6 and weekends 10–6:30; fares are HK$58-$68 one-way and HK$88-98 round-trip.

You can reach Tung Chung by a red taxi from Kowloon or Central, but the long, toll-ridden trip costs HK$340 from Central. Blue taxis travel Lantau (but can't leave it)—but hairpin bends make costs add up.

QUICK BITES

If you're hiking, stop off in Tung Chung for provisions. Deli counters in the huge branch of the local supermarket **Park'n'shop** (⊠ Citygate Mall, Basement, 20 Tat Tung Rd., Lantau) have sushi, sandwiches, salads, baked goods, and precut fruit.

For lunch on Cheung Sha Beach—or on Lantau in general—everyone agrees: **The Stoep** (⊠ 32 Lower Cheung Sha Village Rd., Lantau ☎ 2980-2699) is the place. Its name means "patio," appropriately: tables are outside, facing the beach. It's run by South Africans, and the food's a mix of Mediterranean standards and South African–style barbecued meat—try the mixed grill.

You're spoiled for choice on the Mui Wo waterfront, but cozy Turkish café **Bahçe** (⊠ Shop 19, Ground fl., Mui Wo Centre, Lantau ☎ 2984-0222) is a good bet. You can make a meal out of several *meze* (small snacks)—the flaky filo triangles are delicious—or beef up with a kebab. At night, the place is more like a bar.

ung Sha Beach for an early lunch at Stoep (⇨ Quick Bites) and a stroll on the sands. Bus 2 from here takes you up to Ngong Ping, where you need a good hour or two to visit the Buddha and monastery; more if you plan to tour Ngong Ping Village. Stock up on water here.

There are stunning views from the Wisdom Path. From here, it's an hour's easy hiking to Tung Chung Fort. The well-signposted trail winds down a green valley, passing the occasional stream, several mountains (which you don't have to go up), and the unremarkable Lo Hon Temple. There'll be views of the airport to your left—a reminder of Lantau's changing face.

After a quick visit to the fort, you can walk (or catch a cab) into Tung Chung town center. Refuel with a juice or a coffee at a Citygate Mall café before taking the MTR back to Hong Kong Island.

At a Glance

EXPERIENCES ⇨ Ch. 1
On the Move
Ngong Ping 360 Skyrail

Beaches
Cheung Sha
Silvermine Beach

Hiking
Trail past Shek Pik
  Reservoir
Wisdom Path

Very Amusing
Hong Kong Disneyland

CULTURAL SIGHTS ⇨ Ch. 3
Ngong Ping Village
Po Lin Monastery
Tian Tan Buddha
Wisdom Path

ALSO WORTH NOTING
Lantau Peak
Mui Wo (town)
Hong Kong International
  Airport
Tai O (village)
Tung Chung New Town

Quick Bites
Bahçe
Park 'n' Shop
The Stoep

RESTAURANT ⇨ Ch. 5
Expensive
Crystal Lotus

WAN CHAI, CAUSEWAY BAY & BEYOND

Sightseeing
★ ★ ★

Dining
★ ★ ★ ★

Lodging
★ ★ ★

Shopping
★ ★ ★

Nightlife
★ ★ ★

"Baht! Baht! Baaaahhtttt! Baaaaaaahhhhhhtttt!" the impassioned bettor hollers. The horses pound by, and then it's over. The man curses loudly. He had a couple hundred on horse eight (baht), which came nowhere close. In the paddock behind him, bow-legged jockeys in radioactive-looking silks are showing off horses for the last race. The man wipes his brow, which gleams under the floodlights. One animal catches his eye. There's just time for one last bet. This time he might get lucky.

The Happy Valley races are a vital part of Hong Kong life, so it's only fitting that they're in one of the city's most vital areas. A few blocks back from Wan Chai's new office blocks are crowded alleys where you might stumble across a wet market, a tiny furniture-maker's shop, or an age-old temple. Farther east, Causeway Bay pulses with Hong Kong's best shopping streets and hundreds of restaurants. At night, the whole area comes alive with bars, restaurants, and discos, as well as establishments offering some of Wan Chai's more traditional services (think red lights and photos of semi-naked women outside).

What's Here

Land is so scarce that developers usually only build skyward, but the **Hong Kong Convention & Exhibition Centre** (⊠ 1 Expo Dr., Wan Chai ☎ 2582–8888) is an exception. It sits on a spit of reclaimed land jutting into the harbor. Its curved-glass walls and swooping roof make it look like a tortoise lumbering into the sea or a gull taking flight, depending on whom you ask. Of all the international trade fairs, regional conferences, and other events held here, by far the most famous was the

GETTING ORIENTED

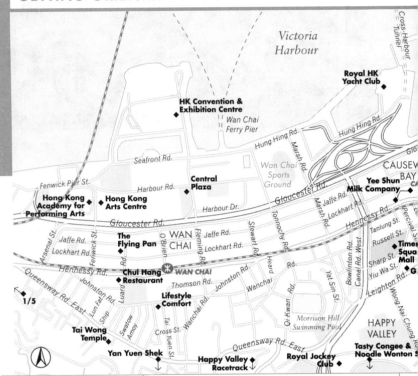

Victoria Harbour

Royal HK Yacht Club

HK Convention & Exhibition Centre

Wan Chai Ferry Pier

Seafront Rd.

Hung Hing Rd.

Hung Hing Rd.

Marsh Rd.

Cross-Harbour Tunnel

Wan Chai Sports Ground

Gloucester Rd.

CAUSEWAY BAY

Fenwick Pier St.

Central Plaza

Harbour Rd.

Hong Kong Academy for Performing Arts

Hong Kong Arts Centre

Harbour Dr.

Gloucester Rd.

Jaffe Rd.

Lockhart Rd.

Yee Shun Milk Company

Hennessy Rd.

Tanlung St.

Russell St.

Jaffe Rd.

Lockhart Rd.

Arsenal St.

Fenwick St.

The Flying Pan

WAN CHAI

Fleming Rd.

O'Brien Rd.

Jaffe Rd.

Lockhart Rd.

Stewart Rd.

Tonnochy Rd.

Heard Rd.

Canal Rd. West

Bowrington Rd.

Sharp St.

Yiu Wa St.

Times Square

G

Hennessy Rd.

Chui Hang Restaurant

WAN CHAI

Thomson Rd.

Johnston Rd.

Wanchai

Rd.

Yat Sin St.

Leighton Rd.

Wong Nai Chung

Queensway Rd. East

Johnston Rd.

Ship St.

Lun Fat St.

Luard Rd.

Swatow St.

Amoy St.

Tai Yuen St.

Cross St.

Wanchai Rd.

Oi Kwan Rd.

Morrison Hill Swimming Pool

HAPPY VALLEY

Lifestyle Comfort

Tai Wong Temple

Yan Yuen Shek

Queensway Rd. East

Happy Valley Racetrack

Royal Jockey Club

Tasty Congee & Noodle Wonton S

1/5

THE TERRITORY

Wan Chai's trams run mostly along Hennessy Road, with a detour along Johnston Road at the neighborhood's western end. Queen's Road East runs parallel to these two streets to the south, and a maze of lanes connect it with Hennessy.

The thoroughfares north of Hennessy—Lockhart, Jaffe, and Gloucester, which is a freeway—are laid out in a grid. Causeway Bay's diagonal roads make it hard to navigate, but it's small; wander around and before long you'll hit something familiar.

TAKING IT IN

Once Upon a Time in the East. There were settlements here long before the British arrived, and the area was strategically important after colonization. Find out about it all from local historian Jason Wordie (☎ 2476–3504 ⊕ www.jasonswalks.com), who runs three tours through Wan Chai, Causeway Bay, and Shau Kei Wan.

A Wan Chai Wander. Rattle to Wan Chai by tram along roads dense with jutting signs, just like in the movies. Get off at Southern Playground, and wander the lanes south of Johnston Road before heading up Luard Road and over walkways to the Hong Kong Academy for Performing Arts and Hong Kong Arts Centre, in adjacent seafront buildings. The convention center is a few minutes away—wander its harbor-side promenade. If you time this part for dusk, Wan Chai's drinking holes will be lighting up as you walk back to the MTR along Fleming Road. Look up at Central Plaza on your right.

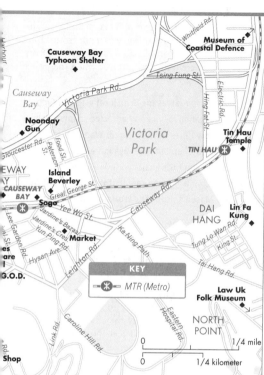

GETTING AROUND

Both Wan Chai and Causeway Bay have their own MTR stops, but a pleasant way to arrive from Central is on the tram along Hennessy Road. All the lines go through Wan Chai, but check the sign at the front if you're going beyond. Some continue to Quarry Bay and North Point, via Causeway Bay, while others go south to Happy Valley.

The underground stations are small labyrinths, so read the signs carefully to find the best exit. Traffic begins to take its toll on journey times farther east—the MTR is a better option for Shau Kei Wan and Chai Wan.

There are Star Ferries between Tsim Sha Tsui and Wan Chai every 10-12 minutes. They leave from the ferry pier just east of the convention center.

Like all of Hong Kong, Wan Chai isn't really dangerous at night, but single women strolling the streets in the wee hours might get unwanted attention from groups of drunk expats or marines. Taxis are a good idea late at night.

QUICK BITES

In a nightspot-packed district, a café serving breakfast round the clock is bound to be a hit. **The Flying Pan Wan Chai** (✉ 3rd fl., 81-85 Lockhart Rd., Wan Chai ☎ 2528-9997) has waffles, blintzes, 16 different omelets, bagels, muffins, grilled sandwiches—the list goes on. Throw in squishy sofas and a jukebox, and it's perfect—be it 3 AM or 3 PM.

Steaming bowls of noodle soup are all that's plunked down on the plastic tables at **Chui Hang Restaurant** (✉ 80 Hennessy Rd., Wan Chai ☎ 2186-8522). If you're only coming once, try a bowl with fish balls; make like other diners and slurp, slurp, slurp.

Yee Shun Milk Company (✉ 506 Lockhart Rd., Causeway Bay ☎ 2591-1837 ✉ 15 Percival St., Causeway Bay ☎ 2576-1828) sounds kooky, but you can't leave Causeway Bay without dessert at this basic diner. The signature dish is steamed milk with ginger juice. Alternatively, there's steamed egg, a local custard.

1997 Handover ceremony. An obelisk commemorates it on the waterfront promenade, which also affords great views of Kowloon.

Outside the center stands the *Golden Bauhinia.* This gleaming sculpture of the Bauhinia flower, Hong Kong's symbol, was a gift from China celebrating the establishment of the Hong Kong SAR in 1997. Dropjawed mainland tourists gather here daily at 7:50 AM, when the police hoist the SAR flag.

DID YOU KNOW?

Wan Chai was once one of the five *wan*—areas the British set aside for Chinese residences—but it developed a reputation for vice and attracted sailors on shore leave during the Vietnam War. How times have changed: Wan Chai is still as risqué an area as Hong Kong has to offer, but that says more about the city's overall respectability than it does about the available indulgences. For all its bars and massage parlors, Wan Chai is now so safe that it seems a pale version of the "Wanch" of Richard Mason's novel *The World of Suzie Wong.*

The western end of Wan Chai's waterfront is home to two of Hong Kong's most important arts venues. Dance, classical music, and opera—be it Chinese or Western—make up the lion's share of performances at the massive **Hong Kong Academy for Performing Arts.** On the other side of Fenwick Street is the lower-key **Hong Kong Arts Centre.**

Clad in reflective gold, silver, and copper-color glass, triangular **Central Plaza**, at Harbour and Flemming roads, is glitzy to the point of tastelessness. On completion in 1992 it was briefly the city's tallest building, but then Two IFC beat it by a mere 130 feet. Note the colorful fluorescent tube lights atop the building; they actually make up a clock so complicated that no one knows how to tell time using it.

Trams clatter along Johnston Road, which is choked with traffic day and night. It's also packed with shops selling food, cell phones, herbal tonic, and bargain-basement clothes. Rattan furniture, curtains, picture frames, paper lanterns, and Chinese calligraphic materials make up the more traditional assortment at Queen's Road East, which runs parallel to Johnston Road. The lanes that stretch between the two roads are also lined with stalls, forming a minimarket of clothing and accessories.

Shoppers crowd the streets of Causeway Bay, the area east of Wan Chai, seven days a week. There are also lots of restaurants and the odd sight. The action happens in a five-block radius of the intersection of Hennessy Road and Percival Street. Ten-story megamall **Times Square** is here, and a couple of blocks south is trendy hotspot Yiu Wa Street, with designer boutiques and bars. Also close are Japanese department store **Sogo** and lifestyle specialists G.O.D. Another of the area's specialties are micromalls of quirky streetwear like **Island Beverley.**

Hong Kong's maritime past and present are much in evidence on Causeway Bay's waterfront. Sampan dwellers and old-fashioned junks once gathered during bad weather in the **Causeway Bay Typhoon Shelter.** Most boat-dwellers have moved to dry land, so these days it's mainly yachts and speedboats that moor here. A few traditional sampans, crewed primarily by elderly toothless women, still ferry owners to their sailboats. Nautical expats gather for drinks at the posh **Royal Hong Kong Yacht Club.** A block farther east stands the **Noonday Gun,** which Noel Coward made famous in his song *Mad Dogs and Englishmen*; it's still fired at noon every day.

DID YOU KNOW?

Opium-smuggling-turned-investment-bank Jardine Matheson once had its warehouses in Causeway Bay. The company moved to Central decades ago, but left a legacy of street names: there's Jardine's Bazaar and Jardine's Crescent, two of Causeway Bay's best shopping streets, and Yee Wo Street with the firm's Chinese name.

Victoria Park, Hong Kong Island's largest park, is a welcome breathing space on the edge of Causeway Bay and bounded by Hing Fat, Gloucester, and Causeway roads. It's beautifully landscaped and has an aviary and recreational facilities for swimming, lawn bowling, tennis, roller-skating—even go-kart racing. At dawn every morning hundreds practice tai chi chuan here. It's also the site of mid-autumn's Lantern Carnival, with the trees a mass of colorful lights. Just before Chinese New Year (late January to early February), the park hosts a huge flower market. On the eve of Chinese New Year, after a traditional family dinner at home, much of Hong Kong happily gathers here to shop and wander until the early hours of the new year.

It's way inland now, but the small **Tin Hau Temple** (⊠ Tin Hau St., Causeway Bay) tucked behind Victoria Park once stood on the waterfront: it honors the Taoist goddess of the sea. Its construction date is unknown, but the temple bell was made in 1747.

High above Wan Chai halfway to Victoria Peak, is the suggestively shaped monolith known as **Yan Yuen Shek** (⊠ south of Bowen Rd. between Wan Chai Gap Rd. and Stubbs Rd.), or Lovers' Rock. It's a favorite with local Bridget Joneses, who visit it to burn joss sticks and make offerings in hope of finding a husband. The easiest way up is on Minibus 24A from Admiralty.

The biggest attraction east of Causeway Bay for locals and visitors alike is legendary **Happy Valley Racetrack,** where millions of Hong Kong dollars make their way each year. The races make great nights out on the town.

The island's far eastern districts—Shau Kei Wan, North Point, Quarry Bay, and Chai Wan—are all undeniable parts of the "real" Hong Kong, which means they're full of offices, apartment blocks, and factories. Shau Kei Wan is home to the **Museum of Coastal Defence** (⊠ 175 Tung Hei Rd., Shau Kei Wan, Eastern ☎ 2569–1500 ⊕ http://hk.coastaldefence.museum ⊑ HK$10; free Wed. ☉ Fri.–Tues. 10–5) in the converted Lei Yue Mun Fort. The museum is in the redoubt, a high area of land overlooking the narrowest point of the harbor; you take an elevator and cross an aerial walkway to reach it. As well as the fascinating historical displays indoors, there's a historical trail complete with tunnels, cannons, and observation posts.

In the middle of Chai Wan's high-rises is the **Law Uk Folk Museum,** a tiny traditional village house showing what life was like when this part of town was nothing but fields.

A Perfect Day (and Night)

A Day for Those Who Can't Agree

If your group includes both shopaholics and history buffs, there's no need to squabble: Causeway Bay's the perfect place to divide and conquer. Start the day in perfect harmony with midday dim sum at Cheung's Cuisine on the eighth floor of Times Square shopping mall. The pickings are top-notch, and the sleek booths and silk cushions seem made for lingering—other diners think likewise, so book a table on weekends.

Time to part company. Retail therapists have a whole afternoon to mall- and stall-trawl. Pickings at Times Square Mall are particularly unusual, so don't dawdle too long before rifling the designer rails at Yiu Wa Street, Causeway Bay's hippest address. Afterward check out the weird and wonderful creations at Island Beverley and bargain-hunt along Jardine's Crescent and Jardine's Bazaar.

Meanwhile, the more studious can take the MTR to Chai Wan for a brief visit to Law Uk Folk museum. If boats are your bag, take the MTR or a cab to Shau Kei Wan, where the Museum of Coastal Defence will keep you busy for a good couple of hours. Then a waterfront cab ride brings you to the Royal Hong Kong Yacht Club to check out the rich boys' toys and the Noonday Gun and Typhoon Shelter.

Rendezvous near Times Square, and sweeten things up with a dessert at Hui Lau Shan—nothing beats the sago in mango juice with extra mango. Hours on your feet will have taken their toll, so counter the effects together with a foot massage and back rub (HK$200) at one of the massage places *without* a red light outside—there are lots in the Bartlock Centre at 3 Yiu Wa Street in Causeway Bay.

A Night in the East

When the sun goes down all kinds of other lights fill the sky. In Wan Chai, the neon signs of bars (both reputable and otherwise); on the waterfront, the beams illuminating skyscrapers in the Symphony of Lights; and in Happy Valley, the floodlighting at the racetrack.

If it's race night, grab an early, stabilizing meal around the corner at the **Tasty Congee and Noodle Wonton Shop** (⊠ 21 King Kwong St., Happy Valley, Wan Chai ☎ 2838–3922), a Cantonese restaurant that looks like something from the 1930s. Then, dressed comfortably but chicly, be at the track by 8 for turf 'n' tippling. Take some throat lozenges if you plan to bet—you'll want to scream as loudly as the thousands around you. Wait for the crowds to ease, and then get a cab over to Wan Chai for drinking and dancing. There are plenty of feel-good beery boozers where you know the words to every song—Carnegie's, Delaneys, Joe Banana's, and From Dusk Till Dawn, to name a few. If you fancy something sophisticated, look the part and make your way to **1/5** pronounced "one-fifth" (⌂ 9 Star St., Wan Chai ☎ 2520—2515), where the bestest martinis are shaken to the beats of funk and soul. When you're done? Why, breakfast at the **Flying Pan** (⇨ Quick Bites), of course, no matter the hour.

At a Glance

SOUTHSIDE

Sightseeing
★ ★ ★

Dining
★ ★

Lodging
★

Shopping
★ ★

Nightlife
★

The bus fills with exclamations of *"wah, wah!"* ("wow, wow!") as Southside comes into view, its blue waters sparkling in the sun. After the Aberdeen tunnel, the bus hugs a narrow, windy, mountain road that seems straight out of a TV ad for cars. Indeed, luxury autos race by, as do still more spectacular views. Out to sea, yachts, junks, and speedboats sail between small green islands. All this is just a short way from busy city streets.

For all the unrelenting urbanity of Hong Kong Island's north coast, its south side consists largely of green hills and a few residential areas around picturesque bays. With beautiful sea views, real estate is at a premium; some of Hong Kong's wealthiest residents live in beautiful houses and luxurious apartments here. Southside is a breath of fresh air—literally and figuratively. The people are more relaxed, the pace is slower, and there are lots of sea breezes.

What's Here

On side streets in the town of **Aberdeen** you'll find outdoor barbers at work and any number of dim sum restaurants. You'll also see traditional sights like the Aberdeen Cemetery with its enormous gravestones, and yet another shrine to the goddess of the sea: the Tin Hau Temple. During the Tin Hau Festival in April and May hundreds of boats converge along the shore here.

Aberdeen's harbor contains about 3,000 junks and sampans. Several generations of one family can live on each junk (you may recall when Angelina Jolie's character, Lara Croft, stepped aboard such a boat in *Tomb Raider 2*). This area is also home to the **Jumbo Kingdom** floating restaurant—a riot of neon lights and color (⇨ Quick Bites). A bridge connects Aberdeen with **Ap Lei Chau Island** (Duck's Tongue Island), where boat-builders work in the old way. Unspoiled just a decade ago, Ap Lei Chau is now covered with public housing, private estates, and shopping malls.

Most Hong Kongers have fond childhood memories of **Ocean Park.** It was built by the omnipresent Hong Kong Jockey Club on 170 hilly acres overlooking the sea just east of Aberdeen. Highlights include the giant pandas, An An and Jia Jia; Marine Land's enormous aquarium; Ocean Theatre, where dolphins, seals, and a killer whale perform; and such thrill rides as the gravity-defying Abyss Turbo Drop. Just east of Ocean Park, and the first beach you reach after leaving Central, is the lovely **Deep Water Bay.**

Repulse Bay is home to a landmark apartment building with a hole in it. Following the principles of feng shui, the opening was incorporated into the design so the dragon that lives in the mountains behind can readily drink from the bay. The popular Repulse Bay Verandah Restaurant and Bamboo Bar (⇨ Quick Bites) is a great place for a meal with majestic bay views. The beach is large and wide but be warned: it's the first stop for most visitors. At the beach's east end, huge statues of Tin Hau—Goddess of the Sea and Goddess of Mercy—border on gaudy. In the 1970s, when worshippers were planning to erect just one statue, they worried she'd be lonely, so an additional statue was created to keep her company.

Beyond Deep Water and Repulse bays is the town of **Stanley.** There's great shopping in the renowned at Stanley Market, whether you want casual clothes, sneakers, cheap souvenirs, cheerful bric-a-brac—even snow gear. Stanley's popular and beautiful beaches are the site of the Dragon Boat Races held every June.

DID YOU KNOW?

The Chinese name for Stanley translates as "Red Pole." Depending on who you talk to, it refers to the red flowers on two silk-cotton trees here or to a nearby hill that turns red at sunset, acting as a beacon for sailors. The English name comes from Lord Stanley, a 19th-century British official.

Seaside **Shek O** is Southside's easternmost village. Weekend beachgoers and hikers crowd the Thai restaurant on the left as you enter town. Every shop here sells the same inflatable beach toys—the bigger the better, it seems. Cut through town to a windy road that takes you to the "island" of Tai Tau Chau, really a large rock with a lookout over the South China Sea. Little more than a century ago, this open water was ruled by pirates. You can hike through nearby Shek O Country Park, where the bird-watching is great, in less than two hours.

A Perfect Day (or So)

Grab breakfast at your hotel, and get off from Central to Aberdeen for a sampan ride. Be prepared for the strong smell of drying fish and the noise of boat women shouting over engine noise. Afterward hop a cab or bus for a 10-minute ride to Repulse Bay beach for a swim and some sunbathing.

GETTING ORIENTED

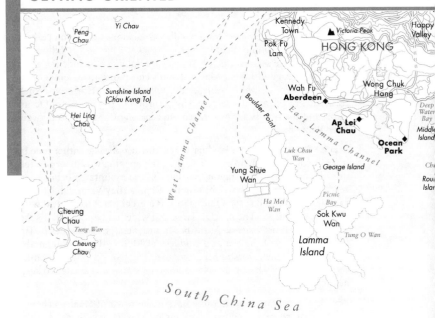

TAKING IT IN	TRANSPORTATION FROM CENTRAL TO . . .
If you travel independently pick one hub and explore in and around it: Aberdeen with its junks and sampans on the southwest coast; Stanley and its market on the south central coast; or, perhaps, Shek O with its beaches and parkland far to the southeast. **Gray Line Tours** (☎ 2368−7111 ⊕ www.grayline.com.hk) has eight-hour, HK$285 day trips (departing at 8 AM) to Ocean Park.	**Aberdeen:** 30 minutes via Bus 70 or 91. (Ap Lei Chau is 15 minutes from Aberdeen on Bus 90B or 91; 10 minutes by sampan). **Deep Water Bay:** 20 minutes via Bus 6, 64, 260, or 6A. **Ocean Park:** 30 minutes via Star Ferry Pier and Bus 629. **Repulse Bay:** 30 minutes via Bus 6, 6A, 6X, 66, 64, or 260. **Shek O:** 50 minutes via MTR to Shau Ki Wan and then Bus 9 to the last stop. **Stanley:** 40 minutes via Bus 6, 6A, 6X, 66, 64, or 260. Note that express buses skip Aberdeen and Deep Water Bay, heading directly to Repulse Bay and Stanley. Buses run less frequently in the evening, so it's more convenient to grab a taxi (they're everywhere).

2

QUICK BITES

In **Stanley Market** there are dozens of cheap local and international eateries along the bustling lanes. For more upscale yet still casual joints, head to Stanley Main Road, where restaurants overlook the bay.

Treat yourself to British high tea at the **Repulse Bay Verandah Restaurant & Bamboo Bar** (✉109 Repulse Bay Rd., Southside ☎2812–2722). Tea is served weekdays from 3 to 5:30, weekends from 3:30 to 5:30, and costs HK$128.

A favorite place for lunch, drinks, or just alfresco lounging is Shek O's **Black Sheep Restaurant** (✉ G/F, 330, Southside, Shek O ☎2809–2021), a small place with an eclectic menu and the kind of relaxed vibe that makes you wonder if you're still in Hong Kong.

The **Top Deck at the Jumbo** (✉ Jumbo Aberdeen Pier, Shum Wan Pier Dr., Wong Chuk Hang, Southside ☎2552–3331) was built on the previously unused upper deck of the Jumbo Kingdom floating restaurant. It's a fantastic alfresco spot on the water, serving international cuisine.

GOLFERS TAKE NOTE

Deep Water Bay is flanked to the north by the **Deep Water Bay Golf Club** (✉19 Island Rd., Deep Water Bay ☎2812–7070 ⊕ www.hkgolfclub.org), which is owned by the Hong Kong Golf Club. The most convenient course to play if you're staying on Hong Kong Island has nine challenging holes. It's a members' club (some of Hong Kong's richest businessmen play here), but it's casual, and visitors with handicap cards are admitted on weekdays from 9 to 2 (call ahead, though).

Greens fees are HK$450 for 18 holes. Club rental will cost you another HK$100; a caddy, still another HK$110. The club also has two restaurants (one serving Chinese fare, the other western dishes), a fitness center, and a swimming pool.

Refuel on the terrace of the Repulse Bay Verandah Restaurant (⇨ Quick Bites), before taking a cab or the bus to Stanley Market, 10 to 15 minutes away. Enjoy sundowners at a restaurant or bar on Stanley's Main Street overlooking the bay. Take a taxi or bus back to Aberdeen for dinner at the Top Deck at the Jumbo Kindom floating restaurant (⇨ Quick Bites).

If you have kids, spend the whole day at Ocean Park. Afterward high tea at the Repulse Bay Verandah Restaurant is a must.

If you only have a half day, take a sampan ride around Aberdeen, followed by a dim sum lunch at the Jumbo Kingdom floating restaurant. Take a taxi to Stanley Market.

At a Glance

EXPERIENCES ⇨ Ch. 1

Beaches
Deep Water Bay
Repulse Bay
Shek O
Stanley

Island Hopping
Cheung Chau
Lamma Island
Po Toi Island

Sail Away: Sampans & Junks
aqua luna
Jumbo Kingdom Floating Restaurant

Hiking
Dragon's Back
Wilson Trail

Very Amusing
Ocean Park
ALSO WORTH NOTING
Aberdeen (town)
Ap Lei Chau (Duck's Tongue Island)

Quick Bites
Black Sheep Restaurant
Repulse Bay Verandah Restaurant

SHOPPING ⇨ Ch. 4
Market
Stanley Village Market

RESTAURANTS ⇨ Ch. 5
Budget
Shek O Chinese & Thailand Seafood Restaurant

Moderate
The Boathouse
El Cid
Han Lok Yuen (Lamma Island)
Jumbo Floating Restaurant
Lucy's
Spices
The Verandah

Expensive
Top Deck (at the Jumbo)

2

KOWLOON

Sightseeing
★ ★ ★

Dining
★ ★ ★ ★

Lodging
★ ★ ★ ★

Shopping
★ ★ ★ ★

Nightlife
★ ★ ★

"Suit, sir? Best tailor in Hong Kong!" calls out a portly vendor as you pass his shop. His last attempt—"Cheapest cashmere in town!"—just reaches you as another man murmurs "Copy watch, copy watch." Half a block on, a middle-age woman shakes out a concertina of photos: "Chanel bag, missy? Gucci, Fendi, Vuitton? Good price." The vendors are discreet and patient. You might walk by, the next person might stop—it's all in a day's work.

There's much more to the Kowloon Peninsula than rock-bottom prices and goods of dubious provenance. Just across the harbor from Central, this piece of Chinese mainland takes its name from the string of mountains that bound it in the north: *gau lung*, "nine dragons" (there are actually eight mountains, the ninth represented the emperor who named them). Island residents rarely venture here—their loss, because Kowloon's dense, gritty urban fabric is the backdrop for Hong Kong's best museums and most interesting spiritual sights. And, of course, there's street upon street of hardcore consumerism in every imaginable guise.

What's Here

One of the best things to see in Tsim Sha Tsui (TST) is, well, Central. There are fabulous cross-harbor views from the **Star Ferry Pier** as well as from the ferries themselves. The sweeping pink-tile **Hong Kong Cultural Centre** and the Former KCR (Kowloon–Canton Railway) Clock Tower are a stone's throw away, the first stop along the breezy pedestrian **TST East Promenade**, which starts here and stretches a couple of miles east. ■ TIP→ **Try to visit the promenade once in the daytime and once at 8 PM for the "Symphony of Lights," a nightly show in which 33 skyscrapers light up on cue as a commentator introduces them in time with a musical accompaniment.**

GETTING ORIENTED

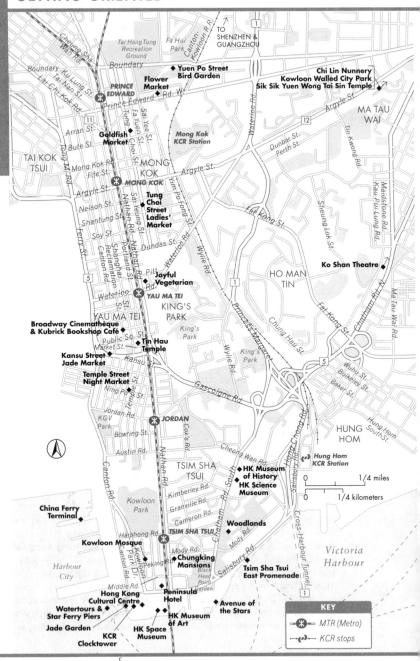

TO SHENZHEN & GUANGZHOU

Tai Hang Tung Recreation Ground

Fa Hui Park

Boundary

Ku Lung St.
Tai Nan St.
Lat Chi Kok Rd.

Boundary

PRINCE EDWARD

Prince Edward Rd. W.

Flower Market

Yuen Po Street Bird Garden

Chi Lin Nunnery
Kowloon Walled City Park
Sik Sik Yuen Wong Tai Sin Temple

MA TAU WAI

Argyle St.

Maidstone Rd.
Kau Pui Lung Rd.

Arran St.

Goldfish Market

Bute St.

Fa Yuen St.
Sai Yee St.
Tung Choi St.

Mong Kok Rd.

TAI KOK TSUI

Fife St.

Mong Kok Rd.

Dunbar St.
Perth St.

Tin Kwong Rd.

MONG KOK

MONG KOK

Argyle St.

Nelson St.

Tung Choi Street Ladies' Market

Shantung St.

Soy St.

Dundas St.

Shanghai St.
Reclamation St.
Portland St.
Canton Rd.
Ferry St.
Nathan Rd.
Sai Yeung Choi St.

Yim Po Fong St.

Fat Kong St.

Sheung Lok St.

HO MAN TIN

Ko Shan Theatre

Fat Kong St.
Chatham Rd.
Ma Tau Wai Rd.

Pitt St.

Joyful Vegetarian

Waterloo Rd.

Wylie Rd.

YAU MA TEI

YAU MA TEI

KING'S PARK

King's Park

Broadway Cinematheque & Kubrick Bookshop Café

Public Sq. St.

Market St.

Tin Hau Temple

King's Park

Princess Margaret Rd.

Chung Hau St.

Wuhu St.
Bulkeley St.
Baker St.

Kansu Street Jade Market

Kansu St.

Temple Street Night Market

Gascoigne Rd.

Wylie Rd.

Ning Po St.

Jordan Rd.

KGV Park

JORDAN

Cox's Rd.

HUNG HOM

Hung Hom South St.

Bowring St.

Austin Rd.

TSIM SHA TSUI

Kimberley Rd.

Cheong Wan Rd.

HK Museum of History

HK Science Museum

Hung Hom KCR Station

China Ferry Terminal

Kowloon Park

Granville Rd.

Cameron Rd.

0   1/4 miles
0   1/4 kilometers

Kowloon Mosque

Haiphong Rd.

TSIM SHA TSUI

Woodlands

Mody Rd.

Victoria Harbour

Harbour City

Peking Rd.

Chungking Mansions

Middle Rd.

Black Head Point Garden

Mody Rd.

Satisbury Rd.

Tsim Sha Tsui East Promenade

Nathan Rd.
Kowloon Park Dr.
Canton Rd.

Chatham Rd. South

Salisbury Rd.

Hong Chong Rd.

Cross-Harbour Tunnel

Hong Kong Cultural Centre

Watertours & Star Ferry Piers

Jade Garden

KCR Clocktower

HK Space Museum

Peninsula Hotel

HK Museum of Art

Avenue of the Stars

Harbour City

KEY	
⊛	MTR (Metro)
⟋	KCR stops

GETTING AROUND

The most romantic way from Hong Kong Island to southern Tsim Sha Tsui (TST) is by Star Ferry. There are crossings from Central every 7–10 minutes and a little less often from Wan Chai.

TST is also accessible by MTR. Underground walkways connect the station with Kowloon-Canton Railway's Tsim Sha Tsui East terminus, where KCR East Rail trains depart every 10–15 minutes for the eastern New Territories. The Kowloon Airport Express station is amid a construction wasteland west of TST. One day it will connect with KCR West Rail; for now hotel shuttles link it to the rest of Kowloon.

The MTR is your best bet for Jordan, Yau Ma Tei, Mong Kok, Kowloon Tong, Lok Fu, and Wong Tai Sin. But you'll need a bus or cab to reach Kowloon Tong from Wong Tai Sin or TST East.

QUICK BITES

Woodlands (✉ Ground fl., Mirror Tower, 61 Mody Rd., Tsim Sha Tsui East, Kowloon ☎ 2369–3718) is a find. Expect fabulous south Indian food—all vegetarian—and fantastic mango lassi. The HK$60 *thalis* (10 tiny curry dishes served with rice and chapatis) are perfect for the indecisive, uninitiated, or just plain greedy.

Arty tomes surround the tables at the **Kubrick Bookshop Café** (✉ Broadway Cinemathèque, 3 Public Square St., Yau Ma Tei, Kowloon ☎ 2384–8925). It's attached to the city's best art-house cinema. Tuck into sandwiches, pasta dishes, and cakes. The coffee's great, too.

Jade Garden (✉ 4th fl., Star House, opposite Star Ferry Concourse, Tsim Sha Tsui, Kowloon ☎ 2730–6888) is a popular dim sum chain. Old ladies push around trolleys stacked high with bamboo steamers, so you can choose whatever looks tasty.

THE TERRITORY

Kowloon's southernmost district is Tsim Sha Tsui (TST), home to the Star Ferry Pier and the Peninsula Hotel. The waterfront extends a few miles to TST East. Shops and hotels line Nathan Road, which runs north from the waterfront through the market districts of Jordan, Yau Ma Tei, and Mong Kok.

New Kowloon is the unofficial name for the sprawl beyond Boundary Street. The district just north is Kowloon Tong. Two spiritual sights—Wong Tai Sin and Lok Fu—are a little farther east. The tongue sticking out into the sea to the south was the runway of the old Kai Tak Airport. Kowloon City is a stone's throw west.

TAKING IT IN

Walk the Talk (✉ HKTB Office, TST Star Ferry Concourse ☎ 2380–7756 ⊕ www.walkthetalk.hk) tours use your mobile phone as an audioguide. The TST tour is packed with serious history punctuated by kooky anecdotes. Kowloon looks great from the harbor, and the **Hong Kong Tourist Board** (HKTB; ✉ TST Star Ferry Concourse ☎ 2508–1234 ⊕ www.discoverhongkong.com) runs cruise combos. The Harbour Lights Cruise leaves before sunset and winds up at Lei Yue Mun, a fishing community in east Kowloon, for a seafood dinner. The Top of the Town tour starts at a revolving restaurant in Wan Chai before heading to Temple Street Market and a nighttime harbor trip. Plain old cruises depart morning, afternoon, and evening.

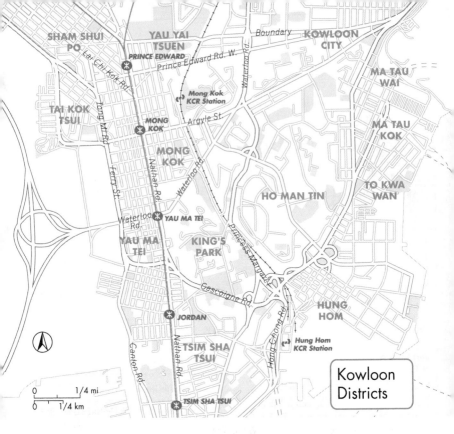

Kowloon
Districts

0   1/4 mi
0   1/4 km

One of the world's best Chinese art collections is inside the tiled cube that is the **Hong Kong Museum of Art.** Looking like an oversize golf ball sliced in half, the **Hong Kong Space Museum** (✉ 10 Salisbury Rd., Tsim Sha Tsui, Kowloon ☎ 2734–2722 ⊕ www.lcsd.gov.hk) stands behind the art museum. Despite many attractions—a planetarium, a solar telescope, an Omnimax theater—it's fairly unremarkable, and children under three aren't allowed. Admission is HK$10; hours are Monday and Wednesday–Friday 1–9, weekends 10–9.

The grand building on the other side of Salisbury Road is the famed **Peninsula Hotel.** The fleet of Rolls-Royce taxis outside indicate the heights of luxury here. You can have tea in the colonnaded lobby and stroll through the shopping arcade. You have to look down to appreciate the **Avenue of the Stars** (✉ TST East Promenade outside New World Renaissance Hotel, Tsim Sha Tsui, Kowloon). Countless local film stars have pawed the wet concrete—you might not recognize their names but it goes to show how big Hong Kong's film industry is.

The area beyond Chatham Road South is known as TST East, reclaimed land that's still taking form and is home to the fascinating **Hong Kong Museum of History.** The **Hong Kong Science Museum** (✉ 2 Science Museum Rd., corner of Cheong Wan Rd. and Chatham Rd., Tsim Sha Tsui East,

Kowloon ☎ 2732–3232 ⊕ www.lcsd.gov.hk) has kid-friendly hands-on exhibits, including an energy machine, a miniature submarine, and cognitive and memory tests. That said, it's more of a rainy-day time-killer than a must-see. Admission is HK$25; hours are Monday to Wednesday (when it's free) and Friday 1–9, weekends 10–9.

Kowloon's famous Nathan Road runs several miles north from Salisbury Road in TST. It's filled with hotels, restaurants, and shops—indeed, retail space is so costly that the southern end is dubbed the Golden Mile. The mile's most famous tower block is ramshackle **Chungking Mansions,** packed with cheap hotels and Indian restaurants. It was the setting for arty local director Wong Kar-Wai's film *Chungking Express.* To the left and right are mazes of narrow streets with even more shops selling jewelry, electronics, clothes, souvenirs, and cosmetics. Skulking individuals chanting "copy watch" and "copy suit" are on every street corner—at least they're honest about the "Rolexes" they sell.

Just behind Nathan Road, at TST's north end, are the 33 acres of **Kowloon Park.** It's crisscrossed by paths and landscaped to within an inch of its life but is still refreshing after all those shops. Hong Kong's largest Islamic worship center, **Kowloon Mosque,** stands in front of the park. The heart of Yau Ma Tei, north of TST, is **Temple Street,** home to Hong Kong's biggest night market. Stalls selling kitsch of all kinds set up in the late afternoon in the blocks north of Public Square Street. Chinese opera performers often give recitals. Fortune-tellers, prostitutes, and street doctors also offer their services here.

Traditional trades are plied on Shanghai Street. There are blocks dominated by tailors or by shops selling Chinese cookware or everything you need to set up a household shrine. Nearby Ning Po Street is known for its paper kites and for the colorful paper and bamboo models of worldly possessions (boats, cars, houses) that are burned at Chinese funerals.

From priceless ornaments to fake pendants, if it's green and shiny it's at the **Kansu Street Jade Market.** Quality and prices at the 450 stalls vary hugely, so if you're not with a jade connoisseur, stick with the cheap and cheerful. Chaotic street markets continue in Mong Kok, technically the last Kowloon district (Boundary Street marks the beginning of the New Territories, though these days the urbanized areas are known as New Kowloon). It's one of the best places to see gritty Hong Kong.

As you head north it's mostly locals browsing the **Tung Choi Street Ladies' Market.** It runs the entire length of the street but is best between Dundas and Argyle. Despite its name, stalls are filled with no-brand clothes and accessories for both sexes. Parallel **Fa Yuen Street** is sneaker central; its sports shops sell some brands you know and lots you don't.

East of Nathan Road, things get back to nature. The few blocks between Prince Edward Road West and Boundary Street are home to a **Flower Market, Goldfish Market,** and the twittering, fluttering **Yuen Po Street Bird Garden.** The vastly varying prices of the flora and fauna on offer are defined not just by their rarity but by how lucky they're thought to be. Arguably Hong Kong's most beautiful park, **Kowloon Walled City Park,** designed in Qing Dynasty style, is near the old Kai Tak Airport, between Tung Tau Tsuen and Tung Tsing roads. Hong Kong's Thai community is based in the streets south of the park, and there are countless hole-in-the-wall Thai restaurants.

DID YOU KNOW?

Only the occasional patch of daylight was visible from the labyrinthine alleys of the Kowloon Walled City, Hong Kong's most notorious slum. Originally a 19th-century Chinese fortress, the city wasn't included in the British lease of the New Territories, thus it remained part of China and out of bounds to the Hong Kong Police. The Triads ruled its unlicensed doctors and dentists, opium dens, brothels, gambling houses, and worse. When it was razed in 1992, there were 50,000 people crammed into a space measuring only 500 by 650 feet.

Two spiritual sights dominate New Kowloon. Exuberant **Sik Sik Yuen Wong Tai Sin Temple** is a Taoist-Buddhist-Confucianist complex filled with noisy worshippers. In Diamond Hill, peace pervades the all-wood **Chi Lin Nunnery,** built in Tang Dynasty style without nails.

Perfect Hours in Kowloon

Only got a couple of hours between meetings? Your kids—or you—haven't got the stamina to keep going all day? Kowloon's fragmented layout means it's perfect for breaking up into short-tour-size chunks. Hardcore sightseeing masochists can lump them all into one tourist feast.

A Few Hours of . . .

. . . the Movies. Start at Chungking Mansions, which starred in the art-house classic *Chungking Express*. It's a short walk to the Avenue of the Stars and the handprints of Jackie Chan and company. From here you'll have a great view of the harbor, which Pierce Brosnan appeared out of in *Die Another Day* (not to be tried on your own; the water is very polluted). On the other side is the IFC building that La Jolie jumped from in *Tomb Raider 2*. Catch the MTR to the Broadway Cinemathèque in Yau Ma Tei for an art flick and a bite at Kubrick Café.

. . . Indulgence. When it comes to luxury, the **Peninsula Hotel** (⊠ Salisbury Rd., Tsim Sha Tsui, Kowloon ☎ 2366–6251 ⊕ www.peninsula. com) is your one-stop shop. Start with afternoon tea in the lobby (HK$340 for two); have a body massage (HK$940) at the spa; buy a dinner outfit at Chanel or Shanghai Tang; take the elevator to 28th-floor Felix for harbor-view cocktails; then book a table downstairs at Gaddi's for a fabulous French dinner. A suite here would be a fitting finish.

. . . Spiritual Stuff. Only one MTR stop apart, Wong Tai Sin Temple and Chi Lin Nunnery are two of Hong Kong's must-do spiritual sights. One's a clattering, chaotic temple-turned-spiritual-mall, the other a peaceful haven. A veggie meal at **Joyful Vegetarian** (⊠ 530 Nathan Rd., Yau Ma Tei, Kowloon ☎ 2780–2230) is in order after. If your soul's still hungry, there's the Tin Hau Temple in Yau Ma Tei; the Shanghai Street altar shops are just up the road.

2

. . . the Old Days. Start at the top by taking a cab or bus to Kowloon City Park, where the old walled city stood: there's a model inside the renovated almshouse. Then take a couple of hours to wise up at the history museum in TST East, before strolling to the old KCR Clock Tower (built in 1915) near the Star Ferry, which has run since 1888.

At a Glance

EXPERIENCES ⇨ Ch. 1
On the Move
Star Ferry

Hiking
Lion Rock

Very Amusing
Bird Garden
Hong Kong Science Museum
Hong Kong Space Museum

Cinema Hong Kong
Broadway Cinematheque

CULTURAL SIGHTS ⇨ Ch. 3
Chi Lin Nunnery
Hong Kong Museum of Art
Hong Kong Museum of History
Sik Sik Yuen Wong Tai Sin Temple
Tin Hau Temple

ALSO WORTH NOTING
Avenue of the Stars
Chungking Mansions
Hong Kong Cultural Centre
Kowloon Park
Kowloon Mosque
Kowloon Walled City Park
Peninsula Hotel
TST East Promenade

Quick Bites
Jade Garden
Joyful Vegetarian
Kubrick Bookshop Café
Woodlands

SHOPPING ⇨ Ch. 4
Department Stores
Chinese Arts & Crafts
Lane Crawford
Marks & Spencer
Seibu
Sincere
Sogo
Yue Hwa Chinese Products Emporium

Malls
Festival Walk
Harbour City (Ocean Terminal, Ocean Centre, Gateway Arcade)
Langham Place
Rise Commerical Building

Markets
Arts & Crafts Fair
Flower Market
Goldfish Market
Kansu Street Jade Market
Ladies' Market
Temple Street Night Market

RESTAURANTS ⇨ Ch. 5
Budget
Best Noodle Restaurant
Guangdong Barbecue Restaurant
Happy Garden Noodle & Congee Kitchen
Hing Fat Restaurant
Kung Tak Lam
Tao Shanghai Noodle
Tso Choi Koon

Moderate
Aqua
Avenue
Café Kool
Great Shanghai Restaurant
Hutong
Lo Chiu Vietnamese Restaurant
Main Street Deli
Spring Deer
Tapas Bar

Expensive
Felix
Morton's of Chicago
Oyster & Wine Bar
Sabatini
SPOON by Alain Ducasse
Steak House
Yan Toh Heen

THE NEW TERRITORIES

Sightseeing
★ ★ ★
Dining
★
Lodging
★
Shopping
★
Nightlife
★

An 80-year-old lady hawks souvenirs outside the centuries-old walled village that's now a museum. Her ancestors once owned the entire area. Walkers young and old trek up Hong Kong's highest mountain—enthusiastic, a spring in their step, and quick to wave. Whether you soak up heritage and culture or sweat it out on trails, the New Territories has the perfect blend of old and the new.

Rustic villages, incense-filled temples, green hiking trails, pristine beaches—the New Territories have a lot to offer. Until a generation ago, the region was mostly farmland with the occasional walled village. Today, thanks to a government housing program that created "new towns" like Sha Tin and Tuen Mun with up to 500,000 residents, parts of the region are more like the rest of Hong Kong. Within its expansive 518 square km (200 square mi), however, you'll still feel far removed from urban congestion and rigor. It's here where you can visit the area's lushest parks and sneak glimpses into traditional rural life in the restored walled villages and ancestral clan halls.

What's Here

Head to Tsuen Wan in the western New Territories to visit **Sam Tung Uk Museum,** which translates to "Three Rows of Dwelling Museum." It's the restoration of walled Hakka village built in 1786. The large front door faces west–southwest, and follows the feng shui principles of placement between mountain and water. In line with the traditional village architecture, rooms extend from a central courtyard. There's also an ancestral hall and an exhibition space with displays of period furniture, handicrafts, and agricultural equipment.

The **Yuen Yuen Institute** (⊠ Lo Wai Village, Tsuen Wan ☎ 2492–2220) is made up of pavilions and prayer halls built in the 1950s to bring together the three streams of Chinese thought: Buddhism (which emphasizes nirvana and physical purity), Taoism (nature and inner peace), and Confucianism (following the practical and philosophical beliefs of Confucius). The main three-tier red pagoda is a copy of the Temple of Heaven in Beijing, and houses 60 statues representing the full cycle of the Chinese calendar—you can look for the one that corresponds to your birth year and make an incense offering. To reach the institute, take the MTR to Tsuen Wan and exit the station at Shiu Wo Street, then catch Minibus 81. Admission is free, and hours are daily 8:30–5

Made of volcanic rock, **Tai Mo Shan**—which means Big Hat Mountain–is Hong Kong's highest point at 3,140 feet. It's in Tai Mo Shan Country Park, north of Tsuen Wan, and is also known as Foggy Mountain as it's covered in clouds almost daily. When the mist—and pollution—clears, the view stretches all the way to Hong Kong Island.

DID YOU
KNOW?

The New Territories got their name when the British acquired this area. Whereas Hong Kong Island and Kowloon were taken outright following the Opium War of 1841, the land that now constitutes the New Territories was handed over much later on a 99-year lease. It was this lease that expired in 1997 and was the catalyst for the return of the entire colony to China.

The huge **Ching Chung Koon Taoist Temple,** adjacent to the Ching Chung LRT station near the town of Tuen Mun in the far western New Territories, has room after room of altars filled with the heady scent of incense burning in bronze holders. On one side of the main entrance is a cast-iron bell with a circumference of about 5 feet—all large monasteries in ancient China rang such bells at daybreak to wake the monks and nuns for a day of work in the rice fields. On the other side of the entrance is a huge drum that was used to call the workers back in the evening. Inside, some rooms are papered with small pictures; people pay the temple to have these photos displayed so they can see their dearly departed as they pray. Colorful plants and flowers, hundreds of dwarf shrubs, ornamental fishponds, and pagodas bedeck the grounds. Take the MTR to Tsuen Wan station and then Bus 66M or 66P to Tuen Mun. Alternatively, you can take the MTR to Kwai Fong Station, then board Bus 58M, alighting at the Tuen Mun Catholic Secondary School. The temple is nearby, but the entrance isn't obvious, so ask for directions.

In the far northern New Territories—just south of Shenzhen—a small unmarked path in the village of Sheung Shui leads to the ancestral hall **Liu Man Shek Tong.** It was built in 1751 and was one of few such halls that survived the Cultural Revolution. A restoration preserved the spectacular original roofs and ornamentation, but substituted concrete walls to take the weight off rickety pillars—at some cost to the site's aesthetic unity, unfortunately. The Liu clan, for whom this hall was built, was obsessed with education: the wood panels hung in the rear hall indicate the education levels achieved by various clan members under the old

GETTING ORIENTED

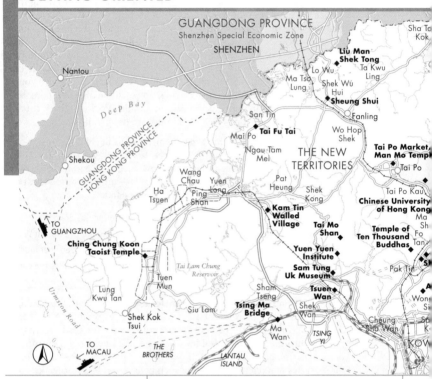

THE TERRITORY	QUICK BITES

The New Territories borders mainland China to the north and Sai Kung Peninsula to the east. Places worth visiting are a fair distance from each other, so day trips here take some planning—and some patience. You're definitely on "the other side," where few people speak English.

It's best to choose two or three sights to visit in a day, allowing 15–30 minutes of travel time between each, depending on whether you're going by bus or taxi.

Sai Kung Town's waterfront has a plethora of outdoor seafood restaurants. If you have a sweet tooth, drop by the famous **Honeymoon Dessert Shop** (✉ G/F, 10C Po Tung Rd., Sai Kung) for such saccharine delights as mango pudding, chilled sago coconut soup, and banana crepes. Go on, you deserve it.

On Castle Peak Road near Tuen Mun, the **Miu Fat Buddhist Monastery** is a popular place for a vegetarian lunch. Dishes have lots of greens, mushrooms, and "meat," which is actually made from rice flour. Lunch is served between noon and 3:30. Take the MTR to Tsuen Wan, then a taxi to the monastery. Alternatively, take the Airport Railway train to Tsing Yi Station and then take Bus 53, 63M, 63X, or 68A.

2

TAKING IT IN

Even if you don't think of yourself as a tour type, the best way to see some of the smaller villages is on one of the Hong Kong Tourist Board's organized tours that loop through the region. The guides are extremely knowledgeable and helpful.

Gray Line Tours (☎ 2207-7235 ⊕ www.grayline.com.hk) has full- and half-day tours that stop at the Yuen Yuen Institute and Tai Mo Shan lookout, among other places. Full-day tours (HK$395, including lunch) depart from Queen's Pier in Central at 8:30 AM and from the YMCA in Tsim Sha Tsui in Kowloon at 9 AM. Half-day tours (HK$295) depart from the same places from 1 PM and 1:30 PM, respectively.

Gray Line's five-hour Heritage Tour (HK$295) takes you to the Man Mo Temple, the Lam Tsuen Wishing Trees, and other cultural sights. Tours depart from the Kowloon Hotel in Tsim Sha Tsui at 8:45 AM Monday, Wednesday, Friday, and Saturday.

KEY

⊗ MTR (Metro)

KCR stops

Light rail

Ferry lines

GETTING AROUND

Between the bus, MTR, and the Kowloon–Canton Railway (KCR), you can get close to many sights. Set off on the MTR from Central to Tsuen Wan; from there, taxis, buses, and minibuses will take you to places such as the Yuen Yuen Institute and Tai Mo Shan. For Sha Tin and other spots in the east, take the MTR to Kowloon Tong; transfer to the KCR to Sha Tin station. To reach the Sai Kung Peninsula, take the MTR from Central to Choi Hung, then the green Minibus 1A to Sai Kung Town.

To tour at your own pace consider hiring a car and driver. **Ace Hire Car** (☎ 2893-0541) charges HK$160 per hour (three-hour minimum). **DCH Transport** (☎ 2768-2977) is HK$280 an hour (three-hour minimum). You can hire a green **New Territories taxi** (☎ 2527-6324 or 2574-7311) for around HK$100. Ask that the driver meet you at a convenient train station.

imperial civil-service-exam system of the Qing Dynasty. Take the KCR to Sheung Shui, then Bus 73K and alight at Sheung Shui Wai on Jockey Club Road. The hall is open Wednesday, Thursday, and weekends 9 to 1 and 2 to 5. Admission is free.

Tai Po, which means "shopping place," more than lives up to its name. In the heart of the region's breadbasket, the town is fast becoming a utilitarian "new town," but its main open-air market is a feast for the eyes, with baskets of lush green vegetables, freshly cut meat hanging from great racks overhead, fish swimming in tanks awaiting selection, and all types of baked and steamed treats. To reach the village, take the KCR to the Tai Po Market stop. Adjacent to the Tai Po market is the 100-year-old **Man Mo Temple**; you'll smell the incense offered by worshippers. The temple is open daily from 9 to 6.

The **Lam Tsuen Wishing Trees,** which were featured in Hong Kong's chapter of *The Amazing Race* TV show, are an important Chinese New Year pilgrimage site. People from throughout Hong Kong come to the two banyan trees to make wishes and offerings. Some people burn joss sticks and incense; others throw an orange—tied to a wish written on a piece of paper—up into a tree (if it catches on a branch the wish will come true). Unfortunately, the weight of the oranges has caused several branches to fall off. People also visit the trees during exam time or when their health or that of a loved one is in jeopardy. Take the KCR train to Tai Po Market train station, then take Bus 64K or 65K, or Minibus 25K.

Whether you enter **Sha Tin** by road or rail, you'll be amazed to find this new town metropolis smack dab in the middle of the New Territories. It's home to the popular **Sha Tin Racecourse,** Hong Kong's largest and a spectacular place to watch a race. Racing season is from September through June. The racecourse has its own stop on the KCR (called "Racecourse"). Sha Tin is also home to the fantastic **Hong Kong Heritage Museum,** devoted to Chinese history, art, and culture. Exhibitions are housed in a five-story building surrounded by a traditional Chinese courtyard.

The **Chinese University of Hong Kong Art Museum** (✉ Tai Po Rd., Sha Tin ☎ 2609–7416 ⊕ www.cuhk.edu.hk/ics/amm ≊ Free), in the Institute of Chinese Studies Building has paintings and calligraphy from the Ming period to modern times. There are also collections of bronze seals, carved jade flowers, and ceramics from South China. Take the KCR to University station, then a campus bus or taxi. The museum is open Monday through Saturday 10 to 4:45 and Sunday 12:30 to 5:30.

The **Temple of Ten Thousand Buddhas** houses, in fact, nearly 13,000 Buddha statues, each in a slightly different pose. It's an impressive feat, which took Shanghai craftsmen 10 years to complete. There are some 500 steps leading to the temple, so bring water.

To the east of Sha Tin, **Sai Kung Peninsula** has a few small towns and Hong Kong's most beloved nature preserve. The hikes through the hills surrounding High Island Reservoir are spectacular, and the beaches are among the territory's cleanest. Seafood restaurants dot the waterfront at Sai Kung town as well as the tiny fishing village of Po Toi O in Clear Water Bay. Take the MTR to Choi Hung and then Bus 92 or 96R, or Minibus 1 to Sai Kung Town. Instead of taking the bus, you can also catch a taxi along Clearwater Bay Road, which will take you into forested areas and land that's only partially developed with Spanish-style villas overlooking the sea. At Sai Kung town, you can rent a sampan that will take you to one of the many islands in the area for a day at the beach. Sai Kung Country Park has several hiking trails that wind through majestic hills overlooking the water. This excursion will take a full day, and you should only go if it's sunny.

Tap Mun Island, also known as Grass Island, makes a great day trip. Most people have a seafood lunch at the restaurant run by Loi Lam, a stocky, vivacious fellow who speaks fluent English with a fantastic accent from Manchester, England. There are a couple of temples and shrines dotting the island, as well as beautiful beaches. A sampan from Wong Shek Pier in Sai Kung Country Park will speed you here.

Two-and-a-Half Perfect Days

Catch the MTR from Central to Tsuen Wan, then take Minibus 81 to Lo Wai Village to reach the Yuen Yuen Institute, the only temple in Hong Kong devoted to all three Chinese religions: Buddhism, Confucianism, and Taoism. For lunch, take a taxi to the Miu Fat Buddhist Monastery, a popular restaurant serving vegetarian dishes. Take a break from the history and culture and walk off the lunch by heading to Tai Mo Shan by taxi, and hike through the country park, experiencing the greener side of Hong Kong.

Alternatively head to Tap Mun Island for a day of sunbathing on a pristine beach, punctuated only by a delicious seafood lunch. You can take the MTR from Central to the Chinese University Station and then walk 15 minutes along Tai Po Road in Sha Tin to the Ma Liu Shui Ferry Pier, where a vessel will take you to the island. Or you can take the MTR from Central to Choi Hung, then Bus 92 or 96R or Minibus 1 to Sai Kung Town. From there, jump in a taxi to Wong Shek Pier in Sai Kung Country Park and then board a sampan for the island.

If you only have half a day to spend in the New Territories, then Sha Tin is the place to be. Take the MTR to Kowloon Tong, then the KCR to Tai Wai to visit the Hong Kong Heritage Museum, dedicated to Chinese history, art, and culture. From here, take a taxi to the Sha Tin KCR station and follow the signs to the Temple of 10,000 Buddhas. Hike up the steps to reach the temple where thousands of gold statues sit in various poses. End the day at Sha Tin Racecourse (via taxi or the KCR to Racecourse Station).

At a Glance

EXPERIENCES ⇨ Ch. 1

Beaches
Hap Mun Wan
Sha Ha
Silverstrand

Island Hopping
Ping Chau
Tap Mun Island

Hiking
MacLehose Trail

Off to the Races
Sha Tin Racecourse

CULTURAL SIGHTS ⇨ Ch. 3
Hong Kong Heritage
  Museum
Pak Tai Temple
Sam Tung Uk Museum

Tai Fu Tai
Temple of Ten Thousand
  Buddhas

ALSO WORTH NOTING
Chinese University of Hong
  Kong Art Museum
Ching Chung Koon Taoist
  Temple
Lam Tusen Wishing Trees
Liu Man Shek Tong
  (ancestral hall)
Man Mo Temple
Sai Kung Peninsula
  (nature preserve)
Tai Mo Shan (Big Hat
  Mountain)
Tai Po (town)
Yuen Yuen Institute
  (prayer halls)

Quick Bites
Honeymoon Dessert
  Shop
Miu Fat Buddhist
  Monastery

SHOPPING ⇨ Ch. 4

Mall
New Town Plaza

RESTAURANTS ⇨ Ch. 5

Budget
Chung Thai Food
  Restaurant & Sea Food

Moderate
Jaspa's
Tung Kee Seafood
  Restaurant

Cultural Sights

Entrance to Wong Tai Sin Temple, Kowloon

WORD OF MOUTH

"The larger-than-life exhibits at the Hong Kong Museum of History will capture the fancy of the most jaded museum goer. Also, the ceramics at the art museum are quite lovely. If you really enjoy museums, though, take the subway to the Hong Kong Heritage Museum in the New Territories, where there aren't so many tourists. My daughter and I went for the Cantonese Opera appreciation class." —marya

By Victoria
Patience

As well as the material wealth you hear so much about, Hong Kong also has abundant cultural riches. Locals may worship the dollar, but they also pay respects to a host of deities in colorful temples. Hong Kong's intriguing history and Chinese art are the fortes of the city's well-curated museums. And though continual redevelopment means most old buildings were demolished years ago, some exquisite traditional constructions—notably temples and villages—remain.

Life as It Was

In a place where "face" is all important, appearances are strangely deceiving. Hong Kong may be a concrete jungle, but it also has lots of green space. Having trouble envisioning life before skyscrapers? Preserved Hakka villages can help as can several museums tracing Hong Kong from rural backwater to pulsating hub.

Art Immersion

Hong Kong is often maligned as a cultural desert. True, New York, London, and Paris have more going on, but they're several times larger than Hong Kong. Keep your expectations reasonable, and stick to the exhibits the city does best. Chinese art, for one: several excellent collections make this one of the best places in the world to experience it, especially since the Cultural Revolution wreaked havoc with such things on the other side of the border.

Sacred Spaces

Hong Kongers are intensely superstitious. Most homes have some kind of household god, and people regularly consult fortune tellers or astrologists. When clinching deals and building skyscrapers, businessmen and architects take numerology and feng shui into account. That said, spirituality is a very down-to-earth affair here. Buddhism, Taoism, and Confucianism are the territory's major religions, and some temples roll them together for worshipping ease. Clattering temple courtyards are the best place to see up close how nothing—and everything—is sacred in Hong Kong.

CHI LIN NUNNERY

✉ 5 Chi Lin Dr., Diamond Hill, Kowloon

☎ 2354-1789

💳 Free

🕐 Nunnery daily 9–4:30, lotus-pond garden daily 7-7

Ⓜ Diamond Hill, Exit C2.

TIPS

■ Left of the Main Hall is a don't-miss hall dedicated to Avalokitesvra, better known in Hong Kong as Kwun Yum, goddess of mercy and child-bearing, among other things. She's one of the few exceptions to the rule that bodhisattvas are represented as asexual beings.

■ Be sure to keep looking up—the lattice-work ceilings and complicated beam systems are among the most beautiful parts of the building.

■ Combine Chi Lin Nunnery with a visit to Sik Sik Yuen Wong Tai Sin Temple, only one MTR stop or a short taxi ride away.

★ Fodor's Choice   🕐 Not a single nail was used to build this nunnery, which dates from 1934. Instead, traditional Tang Dynasty architectural techniques involving wooden dowels and bracket-work hold its 228,000 pieces of timber together. Most of the 15 cedar halls house altars to *bodhisattvas* (someone who has reached enlightenment)—bronze plaques explain each one.

HIGHLIGHTS

Feng Shui principles governed construction. The buildings face south toward the sea, to bring abundance; their back is to the mountain, provider of strength and good energy. The temple's clean lines are a vast departure of most of Hong Kong's colorful religious buildings—here polished wood and gleaming Buddha statues are the only adornments.

The Main Hall is the most imposing—and inspiring—part of the monastery. Overlooking the smaller second courtyard, it honors the first Buddha, known as Sakyamuni. The soaring ceilings are held up by 28 cedar columns, measuring 18 feet each. They also support the roof—no mean feat, given that its traditionally made clay tiles make it weigh 176 tons.

Courtyards and gardens, where frangipani flowers scent the air, run beside the nunnery. The gardens are filled with bonsai trees and artful rockeries. Nature is also present inside: the various halls and galleries all look onto two courtyards filled with geometric lotus ponds and manicured bushes.

HONG KONG HERITAGE MUSEUM

✉ 1 Man Lam Rd., New Territories, Sha Tin

☎ 2180-8188

🌐 hk.heritage.museum

💰 HK$10; free Wed.

🕐 Mon., Wed.–Sat. 10–6, Sun. 10–7

Ⓜ Che Kung or Sha Tin KCR

TIPS

■ Time your arrival to coincide with one of the hourly (on the hour) English-language presentations in the ground-floor Orientation Theater.

■ There's lots of ground to cover: prioritize the New Territories Heritage, the T. T. Tsui Gallery, and the Cantonese Opera Halls, all permanent displays, and do the temporary history and art exhibitions if energy levels permit.

■ Don't miss the opera hall's virtual makeup display, where you get your on-screen face painted like an opera character.

■ The museum is a five-minute signposted walk from Che Kung Temple KCR Station. If the weather's good, walk back along the leafy riverside path that links the museum with the Sha Tin KCR Station, in New Town Plaza mall, 15 minutes away.

★ Fodor's Choice   ☾ This fabulous museum is Hong Kong's largest, yet it still seems a well-kept secret: chances are you'll have most of its 10 massive galleries to yourself. They ring an inner courtyard, which pours light into the lofty entrance hall.

HIGHLIGHTS

The New Territories Heritage Hall is packed with local history—6,000 years of it. See life as it was in beautiful dioramas of traditional villages—one on land, the other on water (with houses-on-stilts). There's also lots of info and artifacts related to religion and festivals. The last gallery documents the rise of massive urban New Towns. There's even a computer game where you can design your own.

In the T. T. Tsui Gallery of Chinese Art exquisite antique Chinese glass, ceramics, and bronzes fill nine hushed second-floor rooms. The curators have gone for quality over quantity. Look for the 4-foot-tall terra-cotta Horse and Rider, a beautiful example of the figures enclosed in tombs in the Han Dynasty (206BC–AD220). The Tibetan religious statues and *thankga* paintings are unique in Hong Kong.

The Cantonese Opera Hall is all singing, all dancing, and utterly hands-on. The symbolic costumes, tradition-bound stories, and stylized acting of Cantonese opera can be impenetrable: the museum provides simple explanations and stacks of artifacts, including century-old sequined costumes that put anything Vegas dreams up to shame.

Kids love the Children's Discovery Gallery, where hands-on activities for 4- to 10-year-olds include dressing up in traditional Hakka gear and putting a broken "archaeological find" back together. The Hong Kong Toy Story, charting more than a century of local toys, brings a whole new dimension to that Made in Hong Kong tag in the toy box.

HONG KONG MUSEUM OF ART

✉ 10 Salisbury Rd., Tsim
   Sha Tsui, Kowloon

☎ 2721–0116

⊕ www.lcsd.gov.hk

💳 HK$10; free Wed.

🕐 Fri. and Sun.–Wed.
   10–6, Sat. 10–8

Ⓜ Tsim Sha Tsui MTR, Exit E

3

TIPS

■ Traditional Chinese landscape paintings are visual
records of real or imagined
journeys—a kind of trave-
logue. Pick a starting point
and try to travel through the
picture, imagining the journey the artist is trying to
convey.

■ There are educational
rooms tucked away on the
eastern side of every floor.
Kids can emboss traditional
motifs on paper or do brass
rubbings; there are also free
gallery worksheets in English. A good selection of reference books makes them
useful learning centers for
adults, too.

■ Guided tours can help you
to understand art forms
you're not familiar with.
There are general museum
tours in English Monday
through Saturday at 11 AM
and 4 PM. Check the Website
for the schedule of more detailed visits to specific galleries—they change every
month.

■ If you prefer to tour alone,
consider an English-lan-
guage audio-guide: it's informative, if a little dry, and
it costs only HK$10.

★ **Fodor's Choice** ☺ An extensive collection of Chinese art is packed inside this boxy tiled building on the Tsim Sha Tsui waterfront in Kowloon. The collections here contain a heady mix of things that make Hong Kong what it is: Ming ceramics, 2,000-year-old calligraphic scrolls, 1,100 works chronicling colonization, kooky contemporary canvases. Thankfully it's organized into thematic galleries with clear, if uninspiring, explanations. Hong Kong's biggest visiting exhibitions are usually held here too. The museum is a few minutes' walk from either the Star Ferry or Tsim Sha Tsui MTR stop.

HIGHLIGHTS

The Chinese Antiquities Gallery is the place to head if Ming's your thing. A series of low-lit rooms on the third floor houses ceramics from Neolithic times through the Qing dynasty. Unusually, they're displayed by motif rather than by period: dragons, phoenixes, lotus flowers, and bats are some of the auspicious designs. Bronzes, jade, lacquerware, textiles, enamel- and glassware complete this collection of decorative art.

In the Chinese Fine Art Gallery you get a great introduction to Chinese brush painting, often difficult for the Western eye to appreciate. Landscape paintings from the 20th-century Guangdong and Lingnan schools form the bulk of the collection, and modern calligraphy also gets a nod.

The Contemporary Hong Kong Art Gallery showcases a mix of traditional Chinese and Western techniques—often in the same work. Paintings account for most of the pieces from the first half of the 20th century, when local artists used the traditional mediums of brush and ink in innovative ways. Western techniques dominate later work, the result of Hong Kong artists spending more time abroad.

TIAN TAN BUDDHA

✉ Ngong Ping, Lantau Island

☎ 2109–9898 to Ngong Ping Village

💲 Buddha: lower podium free, upper podium and museum HK$23 or free with meal ticket. Monastery and path free. Village HK$65. Village and return Skyrail HK$145

🕐 Buddha daily 10–5:30. Monastery and path daily dawn–dusk. Village weekdays 10–6, weekends 10–6:30.

TIPS

■ You can get here on the Ngong Ping 360 Skyrail or via Buses 2 and 23 from Mui Wo and Tung Chung, respectively. To reach Lantau Island from Central take the Airport Express or the MTR to Tung Chung or the New World First Ferry from Pier 6 to Mu Wo.

■ The only way to the upper level, right under the Buddha, is through an underwhelming museum inside the podium. You only get a couple of feet higher up.

■ The booth at the base of the stairs is only for tickets to the museum or for lunch–wandering around the Buddha is free.

■ The monastery's vegetarian restaurant is a clattering canteen with uninspiring fare. Pick up sandwiches at the Citygate Mall, Tung Chung, or eat at a restaurant in Ngong Ping Village.

★ **Fodor's Choice** ☾ Hong Kongers love superlatives, even if making them true requires strings of qualifiers. So the Tian Tan Buddha is the world's largest Buddha—that's seated, located outdoors, and made of bronze. It doesn't need the epithets: its vast silhouette against the sky is impressive. Steep stairs lead to the lower podium, essentially forcing you to stare up at all 242½ tons of Buddha as you ascend. At the top, cool breezes and fantastic views over Lantau Island await.

HIGHLIGHTS

Po Lin Monastery. It's hard to believe today, but from its foundation in 1927 through the early '90s, this monastery was virtually inaccessible by road. These days, it's at the heart of Lantau's biggest attraction. The monastery proper has a gaudy, commercial, orange temple complex. Still, it's the Buddha people come for.

Wisdom Path. This peaceful path runs beside 38 halved tree trunks arranged in an infinity shape on a hillside. Each is carved with Chinese characters that make up the Heart Sutra, a 5th-century Buddhist prayer that expresses the doctrine of emptiness. The idea is to walk around the path—which takes 5 minutes—and reflect. To reach it, follow the signposted trail to the left of the Buddha.

Ngong Ping Village. People were fussing about this attraction before its first stone was laid. Ngong Ping Village is a money-making add-on to the Tian Tan Buddha. Indeed, if a journey here is one of enlightenment, then Nirvana is much easier to reach than previously thought. Walking With Buddha is intended to be an educational stroll through the life of Siddartha Gautama, the first Buddha, but it's more of a multimedia extravaganza that shuns good taste with such kitsch as a self-illuminating Bodhi tree and piped-in incense. No cost has been spared in the dioramas that fill the seven galleries—ironic, given that each represents a stage of the Buddha's path to enlightenment and the eschewing of material wealth.

MORE ON LIFE AS IT WAS

★ **Hong Kong Museum of History.** A whopping HK$156 million went into making this museum engaging and educational. The permanent Hong Kong Story re-creates life as it was rather than simply displaying relics of it: indeed, actual artifacts are few. The museum's forte is clear explanations of spectacular life-size dioramas, which include village houses and a Central shopping street in colonial times. The ground-floor Folk Culture section is a Technicolor introduction to the history and customs of Hong Kong's main ethnic groups: the Punti, Hakka, and Hoklo. Upstairs, gracious stonewalled galleries whirl you through the Opium Wars and the beginnings of colonial Hong Kong. ■ TIP→ **Unless you're with kids who dig models of cavemen and bears, skip the pre-history and dynastic galleries. Reserve energy for the last two galleries: a chilling account of life under Japanese occupation and a colorful look at Hong Kong life in the '60s.**

Budget at least two hours to stroll through—more if you linger in each and every gallery. Pick your way through the gift shop's clutter to find local designer Alan Chan's T-shirts, shot glasses, and notebooks. His retrokitsch aesthetic is based on 1940s cigarette-girl images. To get here from the Tsim Sha Tsui MTR walk along Cameron Road, then left for a block along Chatham Road South. A signposted overpass takes you to the museum. ✉ *100 Chatham Rd. S, Tsim Sha Tsui, Kowloon* ☎ *2724–9042* ● *http://hk.history.museum* ✇ *HK$10; free Wed.* ☉ *Mon. and Wed.–Sat. 10–6, Sun. 10–7* Ⓜ *Tsim Sha Tsui MTR, Exit B2.*

Law Uk Folk Museum. This restored Hakka house was once the home of the Law family, who arrived here from Guangdong in the mid-18th-century. It's the perfect example of a triple-*jian*, double-*lang* residence. Jian are enclosed rooms—here, the bedroom, living room, and workroom at the back. The front storeroom and kitchen are the *lang*, where the walls don't reach up to the roof, and thus allow air in. Although the museum is small, informative texts outside and displays of rural furniture and farm implements inside give a powerful idea of what rural Hong Kong was like. It's definitely worth a trip to bustling industrial Chai Wan, at the eastern end of the MTR, to see it. Photos show what the area looked like in the 1930s—these

THE HAKKA

The Hakka or "guest" people from northeast China first arrived in Hong Kong during a late-17th-century government effort to populate the coast. They fiercely held onto their language and traditions, were dealt the worst lands, and were scorned by the local Punti community. Their farming lifestyle was notoriously tough; women worked the fields as hard as men (leading to a happy side effect of unbound feet). Even today the Hakka have a reputation for being hardworking and conscientious; education and solidarity are also cultural mainstays. In the New Territories you still might see traditionally dressed women in open-crown, broad-brimmed hats, circled by a curtain of black cloth.

days a leafy square is the only reminder of the woodlands and fields that once surrounded this buttermilk-color dwelling. ⊠ *14 Kut Shing St., Chai Wan, Eastern* ☎ *2896–7006* ⊕ *www.lcsd.gov.hk* ✉ *Free* ☉ *Mon.–Wed., Fri., and Sat. 10—6, Sun. 1–6* Ⓜ *Chai Wan, Exit B.*

Sam Tung Uk Museum. A walled Hakka village from 1786 was saved from demolition to create this museum. It's in the middle of industrial Tsuen Wan, in the western New Territories, so its quiet whitewashed courtyards and small interlocking chambers contrast greatly with the nearby residential towers. Hakka villages were built with security in mind, and this one looks more like a single large house than a village. Indeed, most Hakka village names end in *uk,* which literally means "house"—Sam Tung Uk translates as "Three Beam House." Rigid symmetry dictated the village's construction: the ancestral hall and two common chambers form the central axis, which is flanked by the more private areas. The front door is angled to face west–southwest, in keeping with feng shui principles of alignment between mountain and water. Traditional furniture and farm tools are displayed in each room. ■ TIP➡ **Head through the courtyards and start your visit in the exhibition hall at the back, where a display gives helpful background on Hakka culture and preindustrial Tsuen Wan—explanations are sparse elsewhere. You can also try on a Hakka hat.** ⊠ *2 Kwu Uk La., Tsuen Wan, New Territories* ☎ *2411–2001* ✉ *Free* ☉ *Mon. and Wed.–Sun. 9–5* Ⓜ *Tsuen Wan, Exit B3.*

★ **Tai Fu Tai.** It's worth the trek almost to the Chinese border to visit this preserved 1865 home of New Territories merchant and philanthropist Man Ching-luen. The surefire path to becoming a big shot in Imperial China was passing civil service examinations, but few people from Hong Kong—which was Hicksville at the time—made the grade. Man Ching-luen proved the exception in 1875. Congratulatory tablets from the emperor hang in the house's entrance hall. The room layout, beautifully decorated doors, and roof ridges are all characteristic of Qing Dynasty architecture. Stained-glass and roccoco moldings reflect European influences, a result of the British victory over China in the Opium War of 1841. Women could watch guests unobserved from an upper gallery here, which also has an enclosed courtyard for star-gazing, charmingly called a "moon playing chamber." To reach the house, cross over the road outside Sheung Shui KCR station and take Bus 76K toward Yuen Long—alight at San Tin, 5½ km (3 ½ mi) away. The five-minute walk to the mansion is signposted from there. Alternatively, get a taxi from the station—one-way costs HK$35; for under HK$100 the taxi will wait for you and take you back, too. ⊠ *Wing Ping Tsuen, San Tin, New Territories* ⊕ *www.lcsd.gov.hk* ✉ *Free* ☉ *Wed.–Mon. 9–1 and 2–5.*

MORE ART IMMERSION

★ **Hong Kong University Museum & Art Gallery.** Chinese harp music and a faint smell of incense float through its peaceful rooms. The small but excellent collection of Chinese antiquities includes ceramics and bronzes, some dating from 3000 BC; fine paintings; lacquerware; and carvings in jade, stone, and wood. There are some superb ancient pieces: ritual vessels, decorative mirrors, and painted pottery. The museum has the world's largest collection of Nestorian crosses, dating from the Mongol Period (1280–1368). These belonged to a heretical Christian sect who came to China from the Middle East during the Tang Dynasty (618–907).

There are usually two or three well-curated temporary exhibitions on: contemporary artists who work with traditional media often feature. ■ TIP➔ **Don't miss part of the museum: the collection is spread between the T. T. Tsui Building and the Fung Ping Shan Building, which you access via a first-floor footbridge.** The museum is out of the way—20 minutes from Central via Buses 3A or 40 M, or a 15-minute uphill walk from Sheung Wan MTR—but it's a must for the true Chinese-art lover.

MINI-MUSEUMS

In Central, the antiques stores and galleries that pack the curving block of Wyndham Street from, roughly, Lower Albert Road to where Wyndham becomes Hollywood Road are more like miniature museums than shops. Their showrooms—generally open daily 10 to 7—have furniture, art, and artifacts; prices aren't low but they're still less than elsewhere. Shops farther west along Hollywood sell curios masquerading as artifacts. Still farther west, shops and stalls collectively known as Cat Street sell a mix of fake antiques and genuine communist kitsch: this is the place for all those Chairman Mao accessories you always wanted. Note that Cat Street's name is Upper Lascar Row in Sheung Wan.

✉ *94 Bonham Rd., Midlevels, Western* ☎ *2241–5500* ⊕ *www.hku.hk/hkumag* 🖃 *Free* ☉ *Mon.–Sat. 9:30–6, Sun. 1:30–5:30.*

MORE SACRED SPACES

Man Mo Temple. It's believed to be Hong Kong Island's oldest temple, though no one knows exactly when it was built. The consensus is sometime around the arrival of the British in 1841. It's dedicated to the Taoist gods of literature and of war: Man, who wears green, and Mo, dressed in red. A haze of incense fills the small building—you first catch the fragrance a block away. Huge spirals of the stuff coil down from the ceiling, scattering ash on the worshipping old ladies. The temple bell, cast in Canton in 1847, and the drum next to it are sounded to attract the gods' attention when a prayer is being offered—give it a ring to make sure yours are heard. ■ TIP➔ **To check your fortune, stand in front of the altar, select a small bamboo cylinder, and shake it until a stick falls out. The number on the stick corresponds to a written fortune, the English translation of which is in a book that the temple will happily sell you.** ✉ *Hollywood Rd. at Ladder St., Western* ☉ *Daily 8–6* Ⓜ *Sheung Wan, Exit A2.*

Pak Tai Temple. In the 19th-century Cheung Chau Island was a haven for pirates like the notorious Cheung Po Tsai, whose name translates as Cheung Po the Kid and whose treasure cave is reportedly on the island's southwest tip. The temple here is dedicated to Pak Tai, the god of the sea, who is supposed to have rid the island of pirates. He's thanked

Continued on page 100

SPIRITUALITY IN CHINA

Even though it's officially an atheist nation, China has a vibrant religious life. But what are the differences between China's big three faiths of Buddhism, Taoism, and Confucianism? Like much else in the Middle Kingdom, the lines are often blurred.

Walking around the streets of any city in China in the early 21st century, it's hard to believe that only three decades ago the bulk of the Middle Kingdom's centuries-old religious culture was destroyed by revolutionary zealots, and that the few temples, mosques, monasteries, and churches that escaped outright destruction were desecrated and turned into warehouses and factories, or put to other ignoble uses. Those days are long over, and religious life in China has sprung back to life. Even though the official line of the Chinese Communist Party is that the nation is atheist, China is rife with religious diversity.

Perhaps the faith most commonly associated with China is Confucianism, an ethical and philosophical system developed from the teachings of the sage Confucius. Confucianism stresses the importance of relationships in society and of maintaining proper etiquette. These aspects of Confucian thought are associated not merely with China (where its modern-day influence is dubious at best, especially in a crowded subway car), but also with East Asian culture as a whole. Confucianism also places great emphasis on filial piety, the respect that a child should show an elder (or subjects to their ruler). This may account for

(left) Offering up joss sticks.
(below) The Yong he Gong Lama temple in Beijing.

3

Confucianism's status as the most officially tolerated of modern China's faiths.

Taoism is based on the teachings of the *Tao Te Ching*, a treatise written in the 6th century BC, and blends an emphasis on spiritual harmony with that of the individual's duty to society. Taoism and Confucianism are complementary, though to the outsider, the former might seem more steeped in ritual and mysticism. Think of it this way: Taoism is to Confucianism as Catholicism is to Protestantism. Taoism's mystic quality may be why so many westerners come to China to study "the way," as Taoism is sometimes called.

Buddhism came to China from India in the first century AD and quickly became a major force in the Middle Kingdom. The faith is so ingrained here that many Chinese openly scoff at the idea that the Buddha wasn't Chinese. In a nutshell, Buddhism teaches that attachment leads to suffering, and that the best way to alleviate the world's suffering is to purify one's mind, to abstain from evil, and to

Tian Tan, The Temple of Heaven in Beijing.

cultivate good. In China, there are three major schools: the Chinese school, embraced mainly by Han Chinese; the Tibetan school (or Lamaism) as practiced by Tibetans and Mongolians; and Theravada, practiced by the Dai and other ethnic minority groups in the southwest of the country.

TEMPLE FAUX PAS

Chinese worshippers are easygoing. Even at the smallest temple or shrine, they understand that some people will be visitors and not devotees. Temples in China have relaxed dress codes, but you should follow certain rules of decorum.

- You're welcome to burn incense, but it's not required. If you do decide to burn a few joss sticks, take them from the communal pile and be sure to make a small donation. This usually goes to temple upkeep or local charities.

The Buddha

- When burning incense, two sticks signify marriage, and four signify death.

- Respect signs reading NO PHOTO in front of altars and statues. Taoist temples seem particularly sensitive about photo taking. When in doubt, ask.

- Avoid stepping in front of a worshipper at an altar or censer (where incense is burned).

- Speak quietly and silence mobile phones inside of temple grounds.

- Don't touch Buddhist monks of the opposite sex.

- Avoid entering a temple during a ceremony.

TEMPLE OBJECTS

For many, temple visits are among the most culturally edifying parts of a China trip. Large or small, Chinese temples incorporate a variety of objects significant to religious practice.

INCENSE
Incense is the most common item in any Chinese temple. In antiquity, Chinese people burned sacrifices both as an offering and as a way of communicating with spirits through the smoke. This later evolved into a way of showing respect for one's ancestors by burning fragrances that the dearly departed might find particularly pleasing.

BAGUA
Taoist temples will have a bagua: an octagonal diagram pointing toward the eight cardinal directions, each representing different points on the compass, elements in nature, family members, and more esoteric meanings. The bagua is often used in conjunction with a compass to make placement decisions in architectural design and in fortune-telling.

"GHOST MONEY"
Sometimes the spirits need more than sweet-smelling smoke, and this is why many Taoists burn "ghost money" (also known as "hell money"), a scented paper resembling cash. Though once more popular in Taiwan and Hong Kong (and looked upon as a particularly capitalist superstition on the mainland), the burning of ghost money is now gaining ground throughout the country.

CENSER
Every Chinese temple will have a censer in which to place joss sticks, either inside the hall or out front. Larger temples often have a number of them. These large stone or bronze bowls are filled with incense ash from hundreds of joss sticks placed by worshippers. Some incense censers are ornate, with sculpted bronze rising above the bowls.

STATUES
Chinese temples are known for being flexible, and statues of various deities, mythical figures, and multiple interpretations of the Buddha abound. Confucius is usually rendered as a wizened man with a long beard, and Taoist temples have an array of demons and deities.

PRAYER WHEEL
Used primarily by Tibetan Buddhists, the prayer wheel is a beautifully embossed hollow metal cylinder mounted on a wooden handle. Inside the cylinder is a tightly wound scroll printed with a mantra. Devotees believe that the spinning of a prayer wheel is a form of prayer that's just as effective as reciting the sacred texts aloud.

CHINESE ASTROLOGY

According to legend, the King of Jade invited 12 animals to visit him in heaven. As the animals rushed to be the first to arrive, the rat snuck a ride on the ox's back. Just as the ox was about to cross the threshold, the rat jumped past him and arrived first. This is why the rat was given first place in the astrological chart. Find the year you were born to determine what your astrological animal is.

RAT

1924 ▪ 1936 ▪ 1948 ▪ 1960 ▪ 1972 ▪ 1984 ▪ 1996 ▪ 2008

Charming and hardworking, Rats are goal setters and perfectionists. Rats are quick to anger, ambitious, and lovers of gossip.

OX

1925 ▪ 1937 ▪ 1949 ▪ 1961 ▪ 1973 ▪ 1985 ▪ 1997 ▪ 2009

Patient and soft-spoken, Oxen inspire confidence in others. Generally easygoing, they can be remarkably stubborn, and they hate to fail or be opposed.

TIGER

1926 ▪ 1938 ▪ 1950 ▪ 1962 ▪ 1974 ▪ 1986 ▪ 1998 ▪ 2010

Sensitive, and thoughtful, Tigers are capable of great sympathy. Tigers can be short-tempered, and are prone to conflict and indecisiveness.

RABBIT

1927 ▪ 1939 ▪ 1951 ▪ 1963 ▪ 1975 ▪ 1987 ▪ 1999 ▪ 2011

Talented and articulate, Rabbits are virtuous, reserved, and have excellent taste. Though fond of gossip, Rabbits tend to be generally kind and even-tempered.

DRAGON

1928 ▪ 1940 ▪ 1952 ▪ 1964 ▪ 1976 ▪ 1988 ▪ 2000 ▪ 2012

Energetic and excitable, short-tempered and stubborn, Dragons are known for their honesty, bravery, and ability to inspire confidence and trust.

SNAKE

1929 • **1941** • **1953** • **1965** • **1977** • **1989** • **2001** • **2013**

Snakes are deep, possessing great wisdom and saying little. Snakes can often be vain and selfish while retaining sympathy for those less fortunate.

HORSE

1930 • **1942** • **1954** • **1966** • **1978** • **1990** • **2002** • **2014**

Horses are thought to be cheerful and perceptive, impatient and hot-blooded. Horses are independent and rarely listen to advice.

GOAT

1931 • **1943** • **1955** • **1967** • **1979** • **1991** • **2003** • **2015**

Wise, gentle, and compassionate, Goats are elegant and highly accomplished in the arts. Goats can also be shy and pessimistic, and often tend toward timidity.

MONKEY

1932 • **1944** • **1956** • **1968** • **1980** • **1992** • **2004** • **2016**

Clever, skillful, and flexible, Monkeys are thought to be erratic geniuses, able to solve problems with ease. Monkeys are also thought of as impatient and easily discouraged.

ROOSTER

1933 • **1945** • **1957** • **1969** • **1981** • **1993** • **2005** • **2017**

Roosters are capable and talented, and tend to like to keep busy. Roosters are known as overachievers, and are frequently loners.

DOG

1934 • **1946** • **1958** • **1970** • **1982** • **1994** • **2006** • **2018**

Dogs are loyal and honest and know how to keep secrets. They can also be selfish and stubborn.

PIG

1935 • **1947** • **1959** • **1971** • **1983** • **1995** • **2007** • **2019**

Gallant and energetic, Pigs have a tendency to be single-minded and determined. Pigs have great fortitude and honesty, and tend to make friends for life.

during the weeklong, springtime Bun Festival. Expect parades of the island's deities, huge towers of buns, and lots of color. The renovated temple originally dates to 1783: when an image of Pak Tai was brought to appease the spirits of people killed by pirates, thought to be the source of bubonic plague outbreaks. Apparently he did the trick: he remains the island's favorite deity. Beside the main altar are four whalebones from the nearby sea. ■ TIP➡ **Make a full day of your trip to Cheung Chau. It's a gorgeous island with several temples. Kwan Yu Pavilion, the biggest, is dedicated to war god Kwan Tai. There's also a Kwun Yum temple and four shrines honoring sea goddess Tin Hau. A walk takes in most places of worship as well as the pirate cave.**

New World First Ferry sails to Cheung Chau twice hourly from Central Ferry Pier 5. Normal ferries take 50 minutes, fast ones 30. Turn left from Cheung Chau ferry pier and walk ½ km (¼ mi) along waterfront Praya Street, until you see the temple to your right, over a playground. ⊠ *Pak She St., Cheung Chau Island, New Territories* 🎫 *Free* ☉ *Daily 9–5.*

★ **Sik Sik Yuen Wong Tai Sin Temple.** There's a very practical approach to prayer at one of Hong Kong's most exuberant places of worship. Here the territory's three major religions—Taoism, Confucianism, and Buddhism—are all celebrated under the same roof. You'd think that highly ornamental religious buildings would look strange with highly visible vending machines and LCD displays in front of them, but Wong Tai Sin pulls it off in cacophonic style. The temple was established in the early 20th century, on a different site, when two Taoist masters arrived from Guangzhou with the portrait of Wong Tai Sin—a shepherd boy said to have healing powers—that still graces the main altar. In the '30s the temple was moved here; continuous renovations make it impossible to distinguish old from new.

Start at the incense-wreathed main courtyard, where the noise of many people shaking out *chim* (sticks with fortunes written on them) forms a constant rhythmic background. After wandering the halls, take time out in the Good Wish Garden—a peaceful riot of rockery—at the back of the complex. At the base of the complex is a small arcade where soothsayers and palm readers are happy to interpret Wong Tai Sin's predictions for a small fee. At the base of the ramp to the Confucian Hall, look up behind the temple for a view of Lion Rock, a mountain in the shape of a sleeping lion. ■ TIP➡ **If you feel like acquiring a household altar of your own, head**

> **WORD OF MOUTH**
>
> "My husband had his fortune told at the Sik Sik Yuen Wong Tai Sin Temple; a hoot, really. He wanted to know if his college football team, the Miami Hurricanes, would have a winning season. The prediction didn't exactly match his question—something about cooperation or the like—but it was a kitschy, fun thing to do."
>
> –tripgirl

for Shanghai Street in Yau Ma Tei, the Kowloon district north of Tsim Sha Tsui, where religious shops abound. ⊠ *Wong Tai Sin Rd.,, Wong Tai Sin, Kowloon* ☎ *2327–8141* ⊞ *Donations expected. Good Wish Garden: HK$2* ☯ *Daily 7–5:30* Ⓜ *Wong Tai Sin, Exit B2 or B3.*

★ **Temple of Ten Thousand Buddhas.** You climb some 400 steps to reach this temple: but look on the bright side, for each step you get about 32 Buddhas. The uphill path through dense vegetation is lined with life-size golden Buddhas in all kinds of positions. If you're dragging bored kids along, get them to play "Spot the Celebrity Lookalike" on the way. ■ TIP→ **In summer bring water and insect repellent.** Prepare to be dazzled inside the main temple: its walls are stacked with gilded ceramic statuettes. There are actually nearly 13,000 Buddhas here, a few more than the name suggests. They were made by Shanghai craftsmen and have been donated by worshippers since the temple was built in the 1950s. Kwun Yum, goddess of mercy, is one of several deities honored in the crimson-walled courtyard.

Look southwest on a clear day and you can see nearby **Amah Rock,** which resembles a woman with a child on her back. Legend has it that this formation was once a faithful fisherman's wife who climbed the mountain every day to wait for her husband's return, not knowing he'd been drowned. Tin Hau, goddess of the sea, took pity on her and turned her to stone.

The temple is in the foothills of Sha Tin, in the central New Territories. Take Exit B out of the Sha Tin KCR station, walk down the pedestrian ramp, and take the first left onto Pai Tau Street. Keep to the righthand-side of the road and follow it around to the gate where the signposted path starts. ■ TIP→ **Don't be confused by the big white buildings on the left of Pai Tau Road. They are ancestral halls, not the temple.** ⊠ *Off Pai Tau St., Sha Tin,, New Territories* ⊞ *Free* ☯ *Daily 9–5:30* Ⓜ *KCR East Rail: Sha Tin.*

Tin Hau Temple. This incense-filled site is dedicated to Taoist sea goddess Tin Hau, queen of heaven and protector of seafarers. The crowds here testify to her being one of Hong Kong's favorite divine beings—indeed, this is one of around 40 temples dedicated to her. Like all Tin Hau temples, this one once stood on the shore. Kowloon reclamation started in the late 19th

GODS OF WORK & WAR

Different gods often watch over various professions. Man Cheung (Man for short) protects civil servants and those taking exams, for example. Strangely one of the territory's most popular deities is the patron of both policemen and their mafia enemies, the Triads. Kwan Tai is a deified 3rd-century warlord recognized by Buddhists, Taoists, and Confucianists. He's known as the God of War, but he actually promotes the values of brotherhood and loyalty rather than bloodthirstiness. His other names include Guan Yu, Kwan Yu, and Mo.

century, and now the site is more than 3 km (2 mi) from the harbor.

The main altar is hung with gold-embroidered red cloth and usually piled high with offerings. There are also two smaller shrines inside the temple honoring earth god Tou Tei and city god Shing Wong. Both the temple and stalls in the eponymous market outside are fortune-telling hotspots: you may well be encouraged to have a try with the chim. Each stick is numbered, and you shake them in a cardboard tube until one falls out. A fortune-teller asks you your date of birth and makes predictions from the stick based on numerology. Alternatively, you could have a mystically minded bird pick out some fortune cards for you. ■ TIP➔ **It's a good idea to agree on prices first; bargaining with fortune-tellers is common.** ⊠ *Market St.,, Yau Ma Tei, Kowloon* ⊗ *Daily 7–5:30* Ⓜ *Yau Ma Tei, Exit C.*

SEA GODS

Tin Hau, the Taoist Queen of Heaven, is also the goddess of the sea and patroness of seafarers. Her birthday is celebrated at Joss House Bay in Sai Kung in late April or early May. She's also known as Mazu (in Mandarin) and A-ma (in Macau). Pak Tai, the Supreme Emperor of Dark Heaven and the Taoist sea god, is thanked for ridding Cheung Chau Island of pirates during the Bun Festival (usually in May). He's known as Bei Di in Mandarin. Kwun Yum (Guan Yin in Mandarin) is the Buddhist goddess of mercy; she rivals Tin Hau as the protector of sailors and fisherfolk.

Shopping

WORD OF MOUTH

"If you want trinkets, try the Ladies' Market and Temple Street Market in Kowloon—bargain hard! If you want cheap ladies' clothes, Granville Street in Kowloon has cute shops. I don't think bargaining is the done thing here."   —bkkmei

"If I had to choose one mall to shop in, I'd pick Harbour City/Ocean Terminal near the Star Ferry in Tsim Sha Tsui (Kowloon), which has 700 shops, 50 restaurants, and entertainment venues."   —Lia

HONG KONG
SHOPPING PLANNER

Pace Yourself

Shopping streets and malls are packed with people. In summer, pounding the streets weighed down by bags quickly starts to feel like an exercise from *Survivor*. Then, the minute you step into a mall, arctic a/c blasts have you shivering. Dress comfortably, carry a water bottle and light sweater, and stop frequently to rest and refuel.

The Only Way Is Up

With space at a premium, shops and small businesses are tucked into all sorts of places—up the back staircase of a scruffy building, down an alleyway, or on an office tower's 13th floor.

Shopping Tours

Detailed list, limitless credit, and limited time? **Asian Cajun** (☎ 2817–3687 ⊕ www.asiancajun.com) run personalized tours to choice Hong Kong shops, including little-known stores and private dealers. Three-hour excursions run about HK$500, plus transportation costs.

Malls, markets, and outlets are all included in tailor-made tours led by Sandra Haughton's company, **Shopping 4 U.** Book through **Concorde Travel** (☎ 2526–3391 ⊕ www.concordetravel.com). Costs range from HK$350 to HK$500 per person for daylong tours (8- to 10-person minimum).

Best Buys

Brushing Up. Granted, becoming a master brush painter takes years. But calligraphy equipment makes a wonderful display, even if your brushwork doesn't. Boxed sets of bamboo-handled brushes, porcelain inkwells, and smooth inkstones start at HK$200 at Yue Hwa.

Kung-Fu Fighting. You've seen *Enter the Dragon* a hundred times, you've visited all the Bruce Lee locations, you practice your karate chops daily. Time to get the drum cymbal, leather boots, sword, whip, double dagger, studded bracelet, and *kempo* gloves. **Kung Fu Supplies Co.** (⊠ 192 Johnston Rd., Wan Chai ⊕ www.kungfu.com.hk Ⓜ Wan Chai) can kit you out.

On the Table. Remind yourself of all those dim sum meals by dressing up your dining room. Black-lacquer chopsticks and brocade place mats are in street stalls all over. Stanley Market has beautiful appliqué table linen. Department stores like Wing On sell cheap bamboo dim sum baskets—good for cooking or storage.

Opium Den Chic. Silk dressing gowns and basic *cheongsams* (silk dresses with Mandarin collars) are a bargain in markets and at Yue Hwa or Chinese Arts & Crafts. For more luxurious versions, try Shanghai Tang or Blanc de Chine, who also do men's Mao jackets. Get some brocade cushion covers for a matching bedroom.

Seal of Approval. Have your name engraved in Chinese, English, or both on traditional chops (seals). Made of wood, stone, or even jade, they're usually ornately carved, often with animals of the Chinese zodiac. Sets come with a tub of sticky red ink. Man Wa Lane in Sheung Wan is a great place to find them.

Tea for Two. Yixing teapots like those at Fook Ming Tong will melt even coffee-guzzlers' hearts. For the best brews head to Lock Cha Tea Shop. Standard leaves come in pretty tins at local supermarkets like Park 'n' Shop. Yue Hwa does cheap porcelain tea sets. For more information, ⇨ *see* All the Tea in China *in* Chapter 5.

Shop Around

Prices vary hugely. For big items, do research before the trip and then comparison shop in different districts. Ask clerks to record prices on store business cards: it helps you to keep track and ensures you get the quoted rate if you return to buy. Keep expectations realistic. A US$5 (about HK$40) pure silk shirt probably isn't pure silk. That said, it may still be a good shirt at a great price.

Sales

Hong Kongers look forward to the sales like most people look forward to summer vacation. From late December through February and July through September, prices plummet. It may be retail heaven, but it isn't therapy—shoppers all but wrestle bargains from each other at hot sales like Lane Crawford's or Joyce's. Many shops frown on trying things on during sales. Stand your ground, and you'll probably swing a fitting room.

The Perfect Fit

There's no two ways about it: most Americans stand a few inches taller (and wider) than the average Hong Konger. Finding bigger sizes, particularly at cheap shops, can be frustrating. Tailoring—thank goodness it's affordable here—may be the only way to go. Also, cheaper clothes often shrink in the wash; if debating between two sizes, go for the larger one.

Tricks of the Trade

Be wary of absurd discounts designed purely to get you in the door. Product switches are also common—after you've paid, they pack a cheaper model. Avoid electronics shops in Tsim Sha Tsui, whose fearsome reputation is well-earned. Check purchases carefully, ensuring clothes are the size you wanted, jewelry is what you picked, and electronics come with the accessories you paid for. *Always* get an itemized receipt. Without one, forget about getting refunds. Shops displaying the Hong Kong Tourism Board's (HKTB) QUALITY TOURISM SERVICE sticker (an easily recognizable junk boat) are good bets. You can complain about prices or treatment at them to the **HKTB** (☎ 2508–1234). For complaints about all other shops, call the **Hong Kong Consumer Council** (☎ 2929–2222).

Bargaining Power

Prices are always negotiable at markets, and you can expect discounts in small shops, too, especially for electronics or if you buy several things at once. The norm ranges from 10% to 50% off. Be firm and decisive—walking away from a stall can often produce a radical price drop.

Don't let anyone guilt-trip you; rest assured that no Hong Kong salesperson will sell you anything that doesn't cut them a profit.

Faking It

The Hong Kong government has seriously cracked down on designer fakes. Depending on how strict the police are being when you visit, you may not find the choice of knockoffs you were hoping for.

Bear in mind that designer fakes are illegal, and as such you could get into trouble if you get caught with them going through customs.

Cash or Plastic

In spite of the credit-card decals on shop doors (every card you could possibly imagine and more), many smaller stores will insist on cash or add 3% to 5% to the total if you pay by credit card.

If you plan to use plastic, ask if there's a charge before gloating over your "bargain."

By Victoria Patience and Sofia Suárez

They say the only way to get to know a place is to do what the locals do. When in Rome, scoot around on a Vespa and drink espresso. When in Hong Kong, shop. For most people in this city, shopping is a leisure activity in itself, whether that means picking out a four-figure party dress, rifling through bins at an outlet, upgrading a cell phone, or selecting the freshest fish for dinner.

Shopping is so sacred that sales periods are calendar events, and most stores close on just three days a year—Christmas Day and the first two days of Chinese New Year. Imagine that: 362 days of unbridled purchasing. Opening hours are equally conducive to whiling your life away browsing the racks: all shops are open until 7 or 8 PM; many don't close their doors until midnight.

It's true that the days when everything in Hong Kong was mind-bogglingly cheap are over. It *is* still a tax-free port, though, so you can get some good deals. But it isn't just about the savings. Sharp contrasts and the sheer variety of experiences available make shopping here very different from back home.

You might find a bargain or two elbowing your way through a chaotic open-air market filled with haggling vendors selling designer knockoffs, the air reeking of the *chou tofu* ("stinky" tofu) bubbling at a nearby food stand. But then you could find a designer number going for half the usual price in a hushed marble-floor mall, Vivaldi piping through the loudspeaker, the air reeking of designer fragrances worn by fellow shoppers. What's more, in Hong Kong, the two extremes are often within spitting distance of each other.

Needless to say, thanks to travelers like you running out of space in their suitcases, Hong Kong does a roaring trade in luggage. No need to feel guilty, though—shopping here is practically cultural research. All you're doing is seeing what local life is really like.

MAJOR SHOPPING AREAS

Hong Kong Island

Western

The past is very much alive in Western, Hong Kong Island's most traditional neighborhood, and nowhere more than in its shops. Different streets are known as centers for particular trades. Along Hollywood Road, between Sheung Wan and Central, antique Chinese furniture and collectibles fetch high prices in upscale showrooms. You can get similar-looking items half their price (and less than half their age) in Upper Lascar Row, which also does a brisk trade in Communist retro paraphernalia, mah-jongg tiles, and fans.

Man Wa Lane is the place for chops (seals carved in stone with engraved initials). Traditional Chinese medicine is the commercial lifeblood of Sheung Wan proper: ginseng, snake musk, birds' nests, and shark's fins are some of the delicacies available. (For more information, ⇨ To Your Health *in* Chapter 1.) Locals stock up on less exotic household goods at Sincere and Wing On, two of Hong Kong's largest department stores.

Central

New York, London, Paris, Milan . . . Central. When it comes to designer labels, the district's name says it all. Where else can you find a mall with a whole floor dedicated to Armani or calculate the Pradas per square mile? Spacious, golden-hue centers like the IFC Mall, the Landmark, Prince's Building, and the Galleria are the fashion hunting grounds of Hong Kong's well-to-do, and all places to head if your shopping list reads like *Vogue's* directory pages.

Platinum taste but no platinum card? Cut-price designer outlets fill the Pedder Building, also home to iconic local store Shanghai Tang. There's offbeat urban attire—jeans, in particular—at the hip boutiques scattered through Lan Kwai Fong and SoHo. Hong Kong's coolest art galleries are also here, if it's your walls you're looking to dress.

Central may be fashion heaven, but there's an earthier side to it, too. Head out of the air-conditioned malls and down to the stalls on Li Yuen streets East and West for cheap souvenirs like silk dressing gowns. Ribbons, buttons, and sequins come in colors you didn't know existed on steep Pottinger Street, a haberdasher's dream.

Admiralty

Shopping in Admiralty is synonymous with one thing—glitzy Pacific Place Mall. Locals come here for the designer labels, and visitors to stock up on souvenirs at Chinese Arts & Crafts. Elevated walkways connect it to three lesser shopping centers: the Admiralty Centre, Queensway Plaza, and United Centre.

Wan Chai

No malls, no air-conditioning, no Prada—Wan Chai has all these things in its favor when shopping in Central starts to feel a bit samey. Tourists don't shop here much, so you can try out your Cantonese at the rock-bottom no-name outlets on the lanes between Johnston Road and Queen's Road East. Everything from underwear to evening wear is on offer. On Johnston Road shops selling bamboo birdcages and kung fu gear pay homage to Wan Chai's traditional side; the Suzy Wong stereotype lives on in the marine-filled tattoo parlors lining Lockhart Road. Rosewood furniture and camphor-wood chests are two of the specialties of the furniture shops on Queen's Road East and Wan Chai Road, near Admiralty. If this all sounds too traditional, don't despair: techno-happy modern Hong Kong is alive and well at the Wan Chai Computer Centre on Hennessy Road, a collection of dozens of computing outlets.

Causeway Bay

Hong Kong fashionistas hungry for new labels choose Causeway Bay over Central any day. Quirky-but-cool Asian brands that won't arrive stateside for years are the pull at Japanese department store Sogo and micromalls like the Island Beverley. The low-profile storefronts on Yiu Wa Street belie its being *the* hottest address for homegrown clothing and housewares. Similar up-and-coming boutiques are scattered along Vogue Alley, at the intersection of Paterson and Kingston streets. Local shops that have already made their name around here include lifestyle specialists G.O.D., which has a big branch on Leighton Street.

Ten-story megamall Times Square soars behind all this—its mix of designer and midrange gear makes it a good one-stop shop destination. Other good bets for clothing are the big branches of local chains like Giordano on Kai Chui Road. Prices in the stalls and poky shops along Jardine's Crescent and Jardine's Bazaar are unbeatable. Cheap souvenir stalls here are another boon. You can see how real Hong Kongers do their food shopping at the "wet market" (so called because the vendors are perpetually hosing down their produce), at the end of these streets. Locals also head to Hennessy Road for jewelry, watches, luggage, stereos, cameras, and electronic goods.

Southside

Stanley Village Market is the reason most visitors come south. Trawling its crowded lanes for clothes, sportswear, and table linen can take half a day—more if you stop to eat. Classy reproductions of traditional Chinese furniture (with price tags to match) are the main draw at the Repulse Bay's shopping arcade, nearby. Farther west is Ap Lei Chau, a small island known for its designer outlets—the most famous is Joyce. A bridge connects it to Hong Kong Island proper.

Kowloon

Kowloon is home to the famous Nathan Road, where bright neon lights adorn every building. Locals usually don't shop on Nathan Road, and tourists usually get ripped off there. But when it comes to outdoor markets, Kowloon draws locals and in-the-know visitors who are willing to bargain for their bargains. In addition to good sales at outdoor vending areas such as the Temple Street Night Market and the Ladies' Market, cultural shopping experiences abound in places such as the Bird Garden or the Jade Market.

■ TIP→ Visiting all the outdoor markets in Kowloon in one day may be exhausting. You're better off picking three sites you want to spend some time in rather than rushing through them all.

Tsim Sha Tsui

Lighted up in neon and jam-packed with shops, garish Nathan Road is Tsim Sha Tsui's main drag, usually crammed with tourists and sketchy salespeople alike. "What a drag" is the phrase that often comes to mind when shopping here: sky-high prices and shop assistants bent on ripping you off leave you wishing you'd gone elsewhere. Slip down the side streets, though, and things get better. Granville and Cameron roads are home to cheap clothing outlets, while Japanese imports and young designers fill the boutiques at the funky minimall called Rise. Chinese emporiums Yue Hwa and Chinese Arts & Crafts have big branches here—both are great places to stock up on cheap souvenirs.

Although Tsim Sha Tsui is known for its low-end shopping, that doesn't mean luxury goods are out of the picture. The Peninsula Arcade, Joyce, and the vast Harbour City shopping center all have a big-name count fit to rival Central's. One contrast are the shoppers, who tend to be a bit lower key. Bespoke tailoring is another Tsim Sha Tsui specialty— quality varies enormously, so try to choose somewhere well-established, like Sam's (For lots of tips on tailoring, ⇨ It Suits You, *below*).

Jordan, Yau Ma Tei & Mong Kok

The bright-lights-big-city look of Tsim Sha Tsui gives way to housing blocks and tenements hung with aging signs north of Jordan Road. Streets are crowded and traffic is manic, but this down-to-earth chaos is what makes shopping in these north Kowloon neighborhoods rewarding. Well, that and all the bargains at the area's markets. Yau Ma Tei has jade and pearls at Kansu Street; and bric-a-brac and domestic appliances fill atmospheric Temple Street nightly. Farther north are blocks and blocks of brandless clothes and accessories at the Fa Yuen Street Ladies' Market. Parallel Tung Choi Street has cut-price sporting goods. Goldfish, flowers, and birds each have their own dedicated market in Prince Edward, north of Mong Kok. Yue Hwa's five-story Jordan shop is one of the best places in Hong Kong for cheap gifts. The new kid on this particular block is Langham Place shopping mall, slated to transform Mong Kok shopping. So far it's certainly changed the landscape—the tall glass-and-steel building is like nothing else in the neighborhood.

Sham Shui Po

Two stops from Mong Kok on the MTR is Sham Shui Po, a labyrinth of small streets teeming with flea markets and wholesale shops, where you can buy anything from electronics to computers to clothing. The Golden Computer Arcade, stuffed with small computer hard-

---

WORD OF MOUTH

"You can find lots of knockoffs in the Mong Kok area off Nathan Road. They tend not to have the best stuff on display (afraid they will be raided as I have seen done). Just say what you're looking for or show a photo (better yet), and they will bring it to you."   –dperry

ware shops, is favored by local mouse potatoes. Prices are competitive, but parts usually come without a warranty.

New Kowloon & New Territories

The best shopping to be had beyond Boundary Street—the official start of the New Territories—is in malls. Luminous, spacious, and with an excellent selection of shops, Kowloon Tong's Festival Walk is one of the most pleasant such places in town. New Town Plaza in Sha Tin is easily reached by KCR and has some local brands hard to get in Central or Kowloon.

THE STORES

Department Stores

Hong Kong's many Chinese-product stores offer some of the territory's most unusual and spectacular buys—sometimes at better prices than in the rest of China. Whether you're looking for pearls, gold, jade, silk jackets, fur hats, Chinese stationery, or just a pair of chopsticks, you can't go wrong with these stores. Most are open seven days a week but are crowded on sale days and at lunchtime on weekdays. The clerks are expert at packing, shipping, and mailing goods abroad, if not so well schooled in the finer art of pleasant service.

★ **Chinese Arts & Crafts.** Head to this long-established mainland company to blitz through that tiresome list of presents in one fell swoop. It stocks a huge variety of well-priced brocades, silk clothing, carpets, and cheap porcelain. Incongruously scattered throughout the shops are specialty items like large globes with lapis oceans and landmasses inlaid with semi-precious stones for a mere HK$70,000. Other more accessible—and more packable—gifts include appliqué tablecloths and cushion covers or silk dressing gowns. ⊠ *Pacific Place, Admiralty* ☎ *2827–6667 for information* ⊕ *www.chineseartsandcrafts.com.hk* Ⓜ *Admiralty, Exit F* ⊠ *Asia Standard Tower, 59 Queen's Rd. Central, Central* Ⓜ *Central, Exit D2* ⊠ *China Resources Bldg., 26 Harbour Rd., Wan Chai* Ⓜ *Wan Chai, Exit A5* ⊠ *Star House, 3 Salisbury Rd., Tsim Sha Tsui, Kowloon* Ⓜ *Tsim Sha Tsui, Exit F* ⊠ *Nathan Hotel, 378 Nathan Rd., Jordan, Kowloon* Ⓜ *Jordan, Exit B1.*

Harvey Nichols. When this legendary British retailer announced its Hong Kong opening, locals were skeptical, saying nothing would ever live up to the original London store. But Harvey Nicks quickly had them eating their (Phillip Treacy) hats with the sheer volume of hyper-cool labels they stock. The menswear section has been a particularly big hit with local celebs, while local *tai-tais* (ladies who lunch) have declared the fourth-floor restaurant *the* place for mid-shopping-spree coffee breaks. ⊠ *The Landmark, Pedder St. and Des Voeux Rd., Central* ☎ *3695–3388* ⊕ *www.harveynichols.com* Ⓜ *Central, Exit G.*

★ **Lane Crawford.** This prestigious western-style department store has been the favorite of local label-lovers for years—not bad for a brand that started out as a makeshift provisions shop back in 1850. The massive new flagship store in the IFC mall feels like a monument to fashion's biggest names, with exquisitely designed acres divided up into small gallerylike spaces for each designer. The phenomenal brand list includes everything from haute couture through designer denim to Agent Provocateur lingerie. Sales here are more like fashionista wrestling matches, with everyone pushing and shoving to find bargains. ⊠ *Podium 3, IFC Mall, 8 Finance St., Central* ☎ *2118–3388, 2118–7777 Lane Crawford concierge* ⊕ *www.*

TOP SHOPS
Best Upscale Mall: Festival Walk
Biggest Selection Under One Roof: Harbour City
Chinese Chic: Shanghai Tang
Gifts Galore: Yue Hwa
Best Custom Suit: Sam's Tailor
Best Designer Outlet: Joyce Warehouse

4

lanecrawford.com ⊠ *Pacific Place, 88 Queensway, Admiralty* Ⓜ *Admiralty, Exit F* ⊠ *Gateway Mall, 3 Canton Rd., Tsim Sha Tsui, Kowloon* Ⓜ *Tsim Sha Tsui, exit E* ⊠ *Times Square, 1 Matheson St., Causeway Bay* Ⓜ *Causeway Bay, exit A.*

Marks & Spencer. Classic, good-quality clothing is what this British retailer has built an empire on—its underwear, in particular, is viewed as a national treasure. Although basics are on the staid side, the newer Per Una, Autograph, and Limited collections are decidedly trendier. This is one of the few stores in town to stock a full range of sizes. There are branches in many of Hong Kong's malls—most of the shops have a British specialty food section, too. ⊠ *28 Queen's Rd., Central* ☎ *2921–8321* Ⓜ *Central, Exit D1* ⊠ *Times Square, 1 Matheson St., Causeway Bay* Ⓜ *Causeway Bay, Exit A* ⊠ *Harbour City, 5 Canton Rd., Tsim Sha Tsui, Kowloon* Ⓜ *Tsim Sha Tsui, Exit A1.*

Seibu. This Japanese department store is actually owned by local tycoon Dickson Poon, who counts Harvey Nichols among his other possessions. Western ready-to-wear labels make up the bulk of its offerings: expect hip streetwear at the Langham Place and Causeway Bay branches and more professional looks at the Pacific Place branch. This is also home to Japanese houseware shop Loft, and the aptly named Great Food Hall, where homesick expat foodies stock up on imported delicacies. ⊠ *Pacific Place, 88 Queensway, Admiralty* ☎ *2971–3333* Ⓜ *Admiralty, Exit F* ⊠ *G/F, Windsor House, 311 Gloucester Rd., Causeway Bay* Ⓜ *Causeway Bay, Exit E* ⊠ *Langham Place, 8 Argyle St., Mong Kok, Kowloon* Ⓜ *Mong Kok, Exit C3.*

Sincere. Hong Kong's most eclectic department store stocks everything from frying pans to jelly beans. Run by the same family for more than a century, Sincere has several local claims to fame: it was the first store in Hong Kong to give paid days off to employees, the first to hire women in sales positions—beginning with the founder's wife and sister-in-law—and the first to establish a fixed-price policy backed up by the regionally novel idea of issuing receipts. Although you probably won't have heard of its clothes or cosmetic brands, mostly imported from the mainland, you might come across a bargain. ⊠ *173 Des Voeux Rd., Central* ☎ *2544–2688* ⊕ *www.sincere.com.hk* Ⓜ *Sheung Wan, Exit E3* ⊠ *Grand Century Place, Levels 2–3, 193 Prince Edward Rd. W, Prince Edward, Kowloon* Ⓜ *Prince Edward, Exit B2.*

Sogo. A lynchpin of the Causeway Bay shopping scene, Japanese brand Sogo's main branch has 10 floors of clothing, cosmetics, and housewares. There's a dazzling variety of Chinese, Japanese, and international brands—the store is particularly strong on streetwear, makeup, and accessories. The downside is that it's all squeezed into a tiny retail space, which can make shopping here cramped work. The considerably smaller Tsim Sha Tsui branch is in the basement shopping arcade under the Space Museum. ✉ *555 Hennessy Rd., Causeway Bay* ☎ *2833–8338* ⊕ *www.sogo.com.hk* Ⓜ *Causeway Bay, Exit F* ✉ *12 Salisbury Rd., Tsim Sha Tsui, Kowloon* Ⓜ *Tsim Sha Tsui, Exit F.*

Fodor'sChoice

★ **Yue Hwa Chinese Products Emporium.** Its five floors contain Chinese goods, ranging from clothing and housewares through tea and traditional medicine. The logic behind the store's layout is hard to fathom, so go with time to rifle around. As well as the predictable tablecloths, silk pajamas, and chopstick sets, there are cheap 'n' colorful porcelain sets and offbeat local favorites like mini-massage chairs. The top floor is entirely given over to tea—you can pick up a HK$50 packet of leaves or an antique Yixing teapot stretching into the thousands. ✉ *301–309 Nathan Rd., Jordan, Kowloon* ☎ *3511–2222* ⊕ *www.yuehwa.com* Ⓜ *Jordan, Exit A* ✉ *55 Des Voeux Rd., Central* Ⓜ *Central, Exit B* ✉ *1 Kowloon Park Dr., Tsim Sha Tsui, Kowloon* Ⓜ *Tsim Sha Tsui, Exit E.*

Wing On. Great values on household appliances, kitchenware, and crockery have made Wing On a favorite with locals on a budget since it opened in 1907. It also stocks clothes, cosmetics, and sportswear, but don't expect to find big brands (or even brands you know). You *can* count on rock-bottom prices and an-off-the-tourist-trail experience, though. ✉ *211 Des Voeux Rd. Central, Sheung Wan, Western* ☎ *2852–1888* ⊕ *www.wingonet.com* Ⓜ *Sheung Wan, Exit E3* ✉ *Cityplaza, 18 Tai Koo Shing Rd., Tai Koo Shing, Eastern* Ⓜ *Tai Koo Shing, Exit D2.*

Malls & Centers

Cityplaza. An ice-skating rink, a bowling alley, and a multiplex theater are some of the reasons Cityplaza is the city's most popular family mall. So popular, in fact, that it's best to steer clear on weekends, when you have to fight through the crowds. Toys and children's clothing labels are well represented, as are low- to midrange local and international adult brands. There are also branches of Marks & Spencer, local department stores Wing On and UNY, and Log-On, a houseware store owned by local deli chain City'Super. ✉ *18 Tai Koo Shing Rd., Tai Koo Shing, Eastern* ⊕ *www.cityplaza.com.hk* Ⓜ *Taikoo Shing, Exit D2.*

Fodor'sChoice

★ **Festival Walk.** Don't be put off by Festival Walk's location in residential Kowloon Tong—it's 20 minutes from Central on the MTR. Make the effort to get here: Festival Walk has everything from Giordano (Hong Kong's answer to The Gap) to Vivienne Tam. By day the six floors sparkle with sunlight, which filters through the glass roof. Marks & Spencer and Esprit serve as anchors; Armani Exchange and Calvin Klein draw the elite crowds; while Sistyr Moon, Camper, and Agnès b. keep the trend-spotters happy. Hong Kong's best bookstore, Page One, has a big branch downstairs. The mall also has the city's largest ice rink as well as a multiplex cinema, perfect if you're shopping with kids who want a respite from the sometimes scorching hot weather. ⊠ *80 Tat Chee Ave., Kowloon Tong, Kowloon* ⊕ *www.festivalwalk.com.hk* Ⓜ *Kowloon Tong.*

FodorśChoice
★
Harbour City. The four interconnected complexes that make up Harbour City contain almost 700 shops between them—if you can't find it here, it probably doesn't exist. Pick up a map on your way in as it's easy to get lost. **Ocean Terminal,** the largest section, runs along the harbor and is divided thematically, with kidswear and toys on the ground floor, and sports and cosmetics on the first. The top floor is home to white-for streetwear store LCX, which sells brands like ztampz and Super Lovers. Near the Star Ferry pier, the **Marco Polo Hong Kong Hotel Arcade** has branches of the department store Lane Crawford and quirky lifestyle-specialists G.O.D. Louis Vuitton, Prada, and Burberry are some of the posher boutiques that fill the **Ocean Centre** and **Gateway Arcade,** parallel to Canton Road. Most of the complex's restaurants are here, too. A cinema and three hotels round up Harbour City's offerings. ⊠ *Canton Rd., Tsim Sha Tsui, Kowloon* ⊕ *www.harbourcity.com.hk* Ⓜ *Tsim Sha Tsui, Exit E.*

★ **IFC Mall.** The people at the International Finance Centre love superlatives: having made Hong Kong's tallest skyscraper (Two IFC), they built the city's poshest mall under it. A quick glance at the directory—Tiffany, Kate Spade, Prada, Gieves & Hawkes—lets you know that the IFC isn't for the faint of pocket. Designer department store Lane Crawford also has its flagship store here. Even the mall's cinema multiplex is special: the deluxe theaters have super-comfy seats with extra legroom. If you finish your spending spree at sunset, go for a cocktail at RED or Isola, two rooftop bars with fabulous harbor views. The Hong Kong Airport Express station (with in-town check-in service) is under the mall, and the Four Seasons Hotel connects to it. Avoid the mall between 12:30 and 2, when it's flooded with lunching office workers from the two IFC towers. ⊠ *8 Finance St., Central* ⊕ *www.ifc.com.hk* Ⓜ *Hong Kong, Exit A1.*

Island Beverley. This hip micromall played a big part in putting Causeway Bay on the fashion map. Shoe-box-size boutiques fill its four cramped floors—some showcase small local designers, others stock Japanese and Korean brands hard to find overseas. Edgy clubwear competes for the space with cutesy numbers for girls who just don't want to grow up. Indeed, many of the clothes look like they'll only fit local schoolgirls, but not to worry: Island Beverley has a great selection of bags, accessories, and jewelry. ⊠ *1 Great George St., Causeway Bay* Ⓜ *Causeway Bay, Exit E.*

The Landmark. If you haven't got a boutique in the Landmark, you clearly haven't made it in the fashion world, darling. Central's most prestigious shopping site houses Celine, Loewe, Gucci, Joyce Boutique, Hermès, and Harvey Nichols, among others. Even if your credit-card limit isn't up to a spree here, the hushed atrium café is the best place in town to watch well-coiffed tai-tais on the prowl. A pedestrian bridge links the Landmark with shopping arcades in Jardine House, the Prince's Building, the Mandarin Oriental Hotel, and 9 Queen's Road. ⊠ *Pedder St. and Des Voeux Rd., Central* Ⓜ *Central, Exit G.*

Langham Place. This mall's rich brown sandstone stands in stark contrast to the pulsating neon signs and crumbling residential blocks around it. Yet Langham Place has fast become a fixture of Mong Kok's chaotic shopping scene, with nearly 300 shops packed into 15 floors. It's especially popular with hipsters, who come for the local and Japanese labels in offbeat boutiques ranged around a spiral walkway on the 11th and 12th floors. Extra-long escalators—dubbed "Xpresscalators"—whisk you quickly up four levels at a time. The elegant glass-and-steel skyscraper atop the mall is the Langham Place Hotel. ⊠ *8 Argyle St., Mong Kok, Kowloon* ⊕ *www.langhamplace.com.hk* Ⓜ *Mong Kok, Exit C3.*

Lee Gardens One and Two. These two adjacent malls are a firm favorite with local celebrities. They come as much for the mall's low-key atmosphere—a world away from the bustle of Central—as for the clothes. And with so many big names under one small roof—Gucci, Ralph Lauren, Yohji Yamamoto, Jean-Paul Gaultier, and Hermès, to name but a few—who can blame them? The second floor of Lee Gardens Two is taken up with designer kiddie wear. The two buildings, one on either side of Hysan Avenue, are linked by a second-floor footbridge. ⊠ *33 Hysan Ave., Causeway Bay* ⊕ *www.leegardens.com.hk* Ⓜ *Causeway Bay, Exit F.*

New Town Plaza. If you're looking to come down to fashion earth after the designer heaven that is Central, Sha Tin's New Town Plaza is a great bet. Decidedly off the tourist trail, the New Territories' best mall has more than 350 midrange shops and restaurants anchored by Marks & Spencer and Japanese department store Seibu. The usual local suspects abound, but lesser known local brands like Lu Lu Cheung and Pedder Red also have stores. International names like Miss Sixty, French Connection, and Kookai make up the pickings. A huge multiplex cinema draws crowds on weekends. New Town Plaza is also home to two of Hong Kong's kitscher attractions: a musical fountain and Snoopy World, celebrating Schultz's hound. The mall is connected to several other smaller malls and a hotel via a series of walkways and is adjacent to the Sha Tin KCR station. ⊠ *18 Sha Tin Centre St., Sha Tin* ☎ *2699–5992* ⊕ *www.newtownplaza.com.hk* Ⓜ *Sha Tin KCR.*

Pacific Place. Once Hong Kong islands' classiest mall, Pacific Place has since been upstaged by the IFC. Yet it remains popular with well-to-do Hong Kongers, perhaps because it's quieter and more exclusive than most malls. High-end international prêt-à-porter fills most of its four floors and two department stores, Seibu and Lane Crawford, also have branches here. When your bags are weighing you down, sandwiches, sushi, and Starbucks are on hand, as is a multiplex cinema. The Marriott, the Island Shangri-La, and the Conrad hotels are all connected to this plaza. Elevated walkways join Pacific Place with three lesser arcades: the **Admiralty Centre, United Centre,** and **Queensway Plaza.** ⊠ *88 Queensway, Admiralty* ⊕ *www.pacificplace.com.hk* Ⓜ *Admiralty, Exit F.*

★ **Pedder Building.** Although dwarfed by flashy skyscrapers, the Pedder Building is an elegant stone construction housing a mix of outlets and shops with local luxury brands. Shanghai Tang's flagship store takes up the ground floor and basement. Upstairs, Blanc de Chine does clothes in similar styles to Shanghai Tang but in subtler colors. Floors 4, 5, and 6 are packed with small designer outlets, with 30% or more off retail prices. Labels Plus has

Continued on page 120

MARKETS
A GUIDE TO BUYING SILK, PEARLS & POTTERY

Chinese markets are hectic and crowded, but great fun for the savvy shopper. The intensity of the bargaining and the sheer number of goods available are pretty much unsurpassed anywhere else in the world.

Nowadays wealthier Chinese may prefer to flash their cash in department stores and designer boutiques, but generally, markets are still the best places to shop. Teens spend their pocket money at cheap clothing markets. Grandparents, often toting their grandchildren, go to their local neighborhood food market almost daily to pick up fresh items such as tofu, fish, meat, fruit, and vegetables. Markets are also great places to mix with the locals, see the drama of bargaining take place, and watch as the Chinese banter, play with their children, challenge each other to cards, debate, or just lounge.

Some markets have a mishmash of items, whereas others are more specialized, dealing in one particular ware. Markets play an essential part in the everyday life of the Chinese and prices paid are always a great topic of conversation. A compliment on a choice article will often elicit the price paid in reply and a discussion may ensue on where to get the same thing at an even lower cost.

GREAT FINDS

The prices we list below are meant to give you an idea of what you can pay for certain items. Actual post-bargaining prices will of course depend on how well you haggle, while pre-bargaining prices are often based on how much the vendor thinks he or she can get out of you.

PEARLS

Many freshwater pearls are grown in Taihu; seawater pearls come from Japan or the South Seas. Some have been dyed and others mixed with semiprecious stones. Designs can be pretty wild and the clasps are not of very high quality, but necklaces and bracelets are cheap. Post-bargaining, a plain, short strand of pearls should cost around HK$40.

ETHNIC-MINORITY HANDICRAFTS

Brightly colored skirts from the Miao minority and embroidered jackets from the Yunnan area are great boho souvenirs. The heavy, elaborate jewelry could decorate a side table or hang on a wall. Colorful children's shoes are embellished with animal faces and bells. After bargaining, a skirt in the markets should go for between HK$215 to HK$295, and a pair of children's shoes for HK$40 to HK$60.

RETRO

Odd items from the hedonistic '20s to the revolutionary '60s and '70s include treasures like old light fixtures and tin advertising signs. A rare sign such as one banning foreigners from entry may cost as much as HK$9,700, but small items such as teapots can be bought for around HK$240. Retro items are harder to bargain down for than mass-produced items.

MAOMORABILIA

The Chairman's image is readily available on badges, bags, lighters, watches, ad infinitum. Pop-art-like figurines of Mao and his Red Guards clutching red books are kitschy but iconic. For soundbites and quotes from the Great Helmsman, buy the Little Red Book itself. Pre-bargaining, a badge costs HK$25, a bag HK$50, and a ceramic figurine HK$370. Just keep in mind that many posters are fakes.

CERAMICS

Most ceramics you'll find in markets are factory-made, so you probably won't stumble upon a bargain Ming dynasty vase, but ceramics in a variety of colors can be picked up at reasonable prices. Opt for pretty pieces decorated with butterflies, or for the more risqué, copulating couples. A bowl-and-plate set goes for around HK$25, a larger serving plate HK$50.

BIRDCAGES
Wooden birdcages with domed roofs make charming decorations, with or without occupants. They are often seen being carried by old men as they promenade their feathered friends. A pre-bargaining price for a medium-sized wooden cage is around HK$175.

PROPAGANDA AND COMIC BOOKS
Follow the actions of Chinese revolutionary hero, Lei Feng, or look for scenes from Chinese history and lots of *gongfu* (Chinese martial arts) stories. Most titles are in Chinese and often in black and white, but look out for titles like *Tintin and the Blue Lotus*, set in Shanghai and translated into Chinese. You can bargain down to around HK$15 for less popular titles.

SILK
Bolts and bolts of silk brocade with blossoms, butterflies, bamboo, and other patterns dazzle the eye. An enormous range of items made from silk, from purses to slippers to traditional dresses, are available at most markets. Silk brocade costs around HK$35 per meter, a price that is generally only negotiable if you buy large quantities.

JADE
A symbol of purity and beauty for the Chinese, jade comes in a range of colors. Subtle and simple bangles vie for attention with large sculptures on market stalls. A lavender jade Guanyin (Goddess of Mercy) pendant runs at HK$250 and a green jade bangle about HK$275 before bargaining.

MAH-JONGG SETS
The clack-clack of mah-jongg tiles can be heard late into the night on the streets of most cities in summer. Cheap plastic sets go for about HK$50. Far more aesthetically pleasing are ceramic sets in slender drawers of painted cases. These run about HK$245 after bargaining, from a starting price of HK$440. Some sets come with instructions, but if not, instructions for the "game of four winds" can be downloaded in English at www.mahjongg.com.

SHOPPING KNOW-HOW

When to Go
Avoid weekends if you can and try to go early in the morning, from 8AM to 10AM, or at the end of the day just before 6PM. Rainy days are also good bets for avoiding the crowds and getting better prices.

Bringin' Home the Goods
Although that faux-Gucci handbag is tempting, remember that some countries have heavy penalties for the import of counterfeit goods. Likewise, that animal fur may be cheap, but you may get fined a lot more at your home airport than what you paid for it. Counterfeit goods are generally prohibited in the United States, but there's some gray area regarding goods with a "confusingly similar" trademark. Each person is allowed to bring in one such item, as long as it's for personal use and not for resale. For more details, go to the travel section of www.cbp.gov. The HM and Revenue Customs Web site, www.hmrc.gov.uk, has a list of banned and prohibited goods for the United Kingdom.

⚠ The Chinese government has regular and very public crackdowns on fake goods, so that store you went to today may have different items tomorrow. In Shanghai, for example, pressure from the Chinese government and other countries to protect intellectual property rights led to the demise of one of the city's largest and most popular markets, Xiangyang.

BEFORE YOU GO

■ Be prepared to be grabbed, pushed, followed, stared at, and even to have people whispering offers of items to buy in your ear. In China, personal space and privacy are not valued in the same way as in the West, so the invasion of it is common. Move away but remain calm and polite. No one will understand if you get upset anyway.

■ Many Chinese love to touch foreign children, so if you have kids, make sure they're aware of and prepared for this.

■ Keep money and valuables in a safe place. Pickpockets and bag-slashers are becoming common.

■ Pick up a cheap infrared laser pointer to detect counterfeit bills. The light illuminates the hidden anti-counterfeit ultraviolet mark in the real notes.

■ Check for fake items, e.g. silk and pearls.

■ Learn some basic greetings and numbers in Chinese. The local people will really appreciate it.

HOW TO BARGAIN

Successful bargaining requires the dramatic skills of a Hollywood actor. Here's a step-by-step guide to getting the price you want and having fun at the same time.

DO'S	DONT'S

Browsing in a silk shop

Chinese slippers at a ladies' market

DO'S

■ Start by deciding what you're willing to pay for an item.

■ Look at the vendor and point to the item to indicate your interest.

■ The vendor will quote you a price, usually by punching numbers into a calculator and showing it to you.

■ Here, expressions of shock are required from you, which will never be as great as those of the vendor, who will put in an Oscar-worthy performance at your prices.

■ Next it's up to you to punch in a number that's around 75% of the original price—or lower if you feel daring.

■ Pass the calculator back and forth until you meet somewhere in the middle, probably at up to (and sometimes less than) 50% of the original quote.

DONT'S

■ Don't enter into negotiations if you aren't seriously considering the purchase.

■ Don't haggle over small sums of money.

■ If the vendor isn't budging, walk away; he'll likely call you back.

■ It's better to bargain if the vendor is alone. He's unlikely to come down on the price if there's an audience.

■ Saving face is everything in China. Don't belittle or make the vendor angry, and don't get angry yourself.

■ Remain pleasant and smile often.

■ Buying more than one of something gets you a better deal.

■ Dress down and leave your jewelry and watches in the hotel safe on the day you go marketing. You'll get a lower starting price if you don't flash your wealth.

some men's fashions as well as women's daytime separates. La Place has Prada bags and a large selection of Chanel jackets at about 20% off retail. Many discounted items are actually seconds, so look carefully for defects. ⊠ *12 Pedder St., Central* Ⓜ *Central, Exit D1.*

Rise Commercial Building. Many a quirky Hong Kong streetwear trend is born in this fabulous micromall. Don't let its grubby exterior put you off: this arcade is a haven of Asian cool. Japanese designers are particularly well-represented—look out for über-hip brand A Bathing Ape, which does some of the funkiest T-shirts around. Handmade shoes and chunky retro jewelry are other fixtures—and all at bargain prices. ⊠ *5–11 Granville Circuit, off Granville Rd., Tsim Sha Tsui, Kowloon* Ⓜ *Tsim Sha Tsui, Exit B2.*

★ **Times Square.** This gleaming mall packs most of Hong Kong's best-known stores into 12 frenzied floors, organized thematically. Lane Crawford and Marks & Spencer both have big branches here, as does favored local deli City'Super. Cheap local brands like U2 and Baleno are in the basement, giving way to designers like Anna Sui on the second floor, and midrange options like Zara higher up. The sports and outdoors selection is particularly good. An indoor atrium hosts everything from heavy-metal bands to fashion shows to local movie stars; there's also a cinema complex and a dozen or so eateries. The huge Page One bookshop is on the ninth floor. ⊠ *1 Matheson St., Causeway Bay* ⊕ *www.timessquare.com.hk* Ⓜ *Causeway Bay, Exit A.*

Markets

Markets embody some of the best things about Hong Kong shopping—bargains, local color, and buzz. Bargaining is the norm, so take initial asking prices with a grain of salt, and stand your ground. Leave all guilt at home—however low you get the salesperson to go, they'll always come out with a profit.

Famous Cat Street—the curio haunt in Upper Lascar Row, running behind Central and Western—is now full of small, high-quality Chinese antiques shops, but in the street outside you'll still see plenty of hawkers selling inexpensive jewelry, opium pipes, Mao buttons, and assorted paraphernalia.

Cutesy characters like Hello Kitty are plastered over wallets, pencil cases, and a hundred other products in the stalls on Li Yuen Streets East and West, two parallel lanes in Central. Embroidered dressing gowns and cheap watches are also specialties here. Similar goods fill the stands on Wan Chai's Spring Garden Lane, where you can sometimes pick up wicker items, too. Rock-bottom clothing outlets fill the surrounding streets. Over in Mong Kok entire streets have been given over to stalls selling imitation clothing, accessories, and souvenirs.

Each Hong Kong district has an Urban Council–run market selling fruit, vegetables, meat, seafood, and live chickens (squeamish people take note: chickens are slaughtered out in the open here). Surrounding the markets are small stores with every imaginable kitchen and bathroom appliance, as well as clothes and electronics.

Around heavy pedestrian areas you'll find illegal hawkers with a wide variety of cheap goods, but beware—constantly on the lookout for the police, vendors may literally run off with their goods. If so, get out of their way! In summer they often materialize in Tsim Sha Tsui in front of the Hyatt, around Granville and Mody roads, and at the Star Ferry Terminal.

Arts & Crafts Fair. Small stalls from local cottage industries sell handicrafts each Sunday and on public holidays outside the Cultural Centre on the Tsim Sha Tsui waterfront. Portrait artists are at hand to capture your likeness, and there's other artwork, jewelry, clothing, and knick-knacks. Each stall-holder is chosen by a panel of judges who look to promote Hong Kong artists and small businesses. ⊠ *Hong Kong Cultural Centre Piazza, Salisbury Rd., Tsim Sha Tsui, Kowloon* ☉ *Sun. and public holidays 2–7* Ⓜ *Tsim Sha Tsui, Exit E.*

Flower Market. Huge bucketfuls of roses and gerbera spill out onto the sidewalk along Flower Market Road, a collection of street stalls selling cut flowers and potted plants. Delicate orchids and vivid birds of paradise are some of the more exotic blooms. During Chinese New Year there's a roaring trade in narcissi, poinsettias, and bright yellow chrysanthemums, all auspicious flowers. ⊠ *Flower Market Rd., off Prince Edward Rd. W, Mong Kok, Kowloon* ☉ *Daily 7 AM–7:30 PM* Ⓜ *Prince Edward, Exit B1.*

☺ **Goldfish Market.** Goldfish are considered auspicious in Hong Kong (though aquariums have to be positioned in the right place to bring good luck to the family), and this small collection of shops is a favorite local source. Shop fronts are decorated with bag upon bag of glistening, pop-eyed creatures, waiting for someone to take them home. Some of the fishes inside shops are serious rarities and fetch unbelievable prices. ⊠ *Tung Choi St., Mong Kok, Kowloon* ☉ *Daily 10–6* Ⓜ *Mong Kok, Exit B2.*

Jardine's Bazaar and Jardine's Crescent. These two small parallel streets are so crammed with clothing stalls it's difficult to make your way through. Most offer bargains on the usual clothes, children's gear, bags, and cheap souvenirs like chopstick sets. The surrounding boutiques are also worth a look for local and Japanese fashions, though the sizes are small. ⊠ *Jardine's Bazaar, Causeway Bay* ☉ *Daily noon–10 PM* Ⓜ *Causeway Bay, Exit F.*

Kansu Street Jade Market. Jade in every imaginable shade of green, from the milkiest apple-tone to the richest emerald, fills the stalls of this Kowloon market. If you know your stuff and haggle insistently, you can get fabulous bargains. Otherwise stick to cheap trinkets. Some of the so-called "jade" sold here is actually aventurine, bowenite, soapstone, serpentine, and Australian jade—all inferior to the real thing. Strings of freshwater pearls also go for a song, although you may have to have them restrung. ⊠ *Kansu St. off Nathan Rd., Yau Ma Tei, Kowloon* ☉ *Daily 10–4* Ⓜ *Yau Ma Tei, Exit C.*

WORD OF MOUTH

"Let the seller name a price; don't make the first offer. Then start bargaining based on a discount off his price—anywhere from 60% or more. If you're buying a large quantity, get a volume discount. Cash will get a better price than credit card. If you don't get the price you want, walk away; there's another guy at the next stall with basically the same stuff, anyway."

–Cicerone

★ **Ladies' Market.** Block upon block of tightly packed stalls overflow with clothes, bags, and knickknacks along Tung Choi Street in Mong Kok. Despite the name there are clothes for women, men, and children here. Most offerings are imitations or no-name brands; rifle around enough and you can often pick up some cheap 'n' cheerful basics. Haggling is the rule here: a poker face and a little insistence can get you dramatic discounts. At the corner of each block and behind the market are stands and shops selling the street snacks Hong Kongers can't live without. Pick a place where plenty of locals are munching and point at whatever takes your fancy. Parallel **Fa Yuen Street** is Mong Kok's unofficial sportswear market. It's lined with small shops selling cut-price sneakers—some real, others not-so-real. To reach the market, walk two blocks east along Nelson Street from the Mong Kok MTR station. ⊠ *Tung Choi St., Mong Kok, Kowloon* ⊙ *Daily noon–11 PM* Ⓜ *Mong Kok, Exit B2.*

★ **Stanley Village Market.** This was once Hong Kong's most famed bargain trove, but its ever-growing popularity means that Stanley Village Market no longer has the best prices around. Still, you can pick up some good buys in sportswear and casual clothing if you comb through the stalls. Good value linens—especially appliqué tablecloths—also abound. Dozens and dozens of shops line a main street so narrow that awnings from each side meet in the middle, and on busy days your elbows will come in handy. Weekdays are a little more relaxed. One of the best things about Stanley Market is getting here: the winding bus ride from Central (routes 6, 6A, or 260) or Tsim Sha Tsui (route 973) takes you over the top of Hong Kong Island, with fabulous views on the way. ⊠ *Stanley Village, Southside* ⊙ *Daily 11–6.*

★ **Temple Street Night Market.** Each night, as it gets dark, the lamps strung between the stalls of this Yau Ma Tei street market slowly light up, and the air fills with the smells wafting from myriad food carts. Hawkers try to catch your eye by flinging clothes up from their stalls. Cantonese opera competes with pop music, and vendors' cries and shoppers' haggling fills the air. Adding to the color here are the fortune-tellers and the odd magician or acrobat who has set up shop in the street. Granted, neither the clothes nor cheap gadgets on sale here are much to get excited about, but it's the atmosphere people come for—any purchases are a bonus. The market stretches for almost a mile and is one of Hong Kong's liveliest nighttime shopping experiences. ⊠ *Temple St., Mong Kok, Kowloon* Ⓜ *Jordan, Exit A* ⊙ *Daily 5 PM–midnight; best after 8 PM.*

Western Market. This redbrick Victorian in the Sheung Wan district was built in 1906 and was originally used as a produce market. These days the first floor is filled with unmemorable shops selling crafts, toys, jewelry, collectibles; second-floor shops sell a remarkable selection of fabric. A more surreal experience is lunch, dinner, or high tea in the Grand Stage Chinese restaurant and ballroom on the top floor. After a great Chinese meal you can while away the afternoon with the old-timers trotting around the room to a live band belting out the cha-cha and tango. ⊠ *Des Voeux Rd., Western* Ⓜ *Sheung Wan.*

Specialty Shops

Antiques

What could be a better souvenir than an exquisite antique to pass down through the generations? Hong Kong has many reputable dealers with covetable collections of genuine antiques. Still, you'll need to be careful lest that "Ming" vase you bought was actually made in a factory yesterday.

Inspect the piece from every angle, even if it means getting on your hands and knees. Antique furniture fans have no qualms about opening up a piece and asking to see its backside to compare the patina and quality of the woods. Factors that determine value include condition, age, rarity, workmanship, and materials. In-depth knowledge of the item and its history not only safeguards your investment, it also deepens your enjoyment of it for the long term. You'll also be in a better position to buy once you've read up on items that interest you. For example, doing research on Tang horses and camels will reveal that such pieces were damaged in the tombs and rarely come with the original legs.

Be sure to request not only receipts but also certificates of authenticity. For major investments, consider having tests done to verify age. At the end of the day, if something seems too good to be true, it probably is. The best defense is to buy from a reputable dealer. Look for the QUALITY SERVICES TOURISM logo at the door, check the Hong Kong Tourist Board's *A Guide to Quality Shops* or download it from the HKTB Web site for your PDA. *Arts of Asia,* published six times a year, has been a wonderful resource for Asian antiquities collectors since 1970. Its charismatic publisher and editor, Tuyet Nguyet, brings together experts from around the world and shares her unique insights. You can read past articles, buy a subscription, or purchase back issues through the Web site www.artsofasianet.com.

AUCTION HOUSES

The auction scene is filled with record-breaking sales and some of the planet's finest Asian art and antiques. Major houses usually host sales at the Hong Kong Convention and Exhibition Centre in spring and fall. Call them or check their Web sites for full schedules and lot references.

Christie's. Christie's entered the market in 1985. Its respected specialists focus on Asian art and jewelry such as jadeite pieces and watches. Among the art auctions are those devoted to Chinese ceramics; Chinese calligraphy; and classical, modern, and contemporary paintings from China and elsewhere in Asia. ✉ 22/ F, Alexandra House, 18 Chater Rd., Central ☎ 2521–5396 ⊕ www.christies.com Ⓜ Central.

Sotheby's. The respected auction house opened here in 1973. Its teams work with Chinese ceramics, jade carvings, snuff bottles, and

---

LAW ON YOUR SIDE

Although mainland law forbids that any item more than 120 years old leave China, the SAR isn't held to this rule. It's perfectly legal to ship your antique treasures home.

classical and contemporary paintings. The auction house also deals in watches and jewelry, including jadeite and western pieces. ✉ *31/F, Pacific Place, 88 Queensway, Admiralty* ☎ *2524–8121* ⊕ *www.sothebys. com* Ⓜ *Admiralty.*

DEALERS

Altfield Gallery. If only your entire home could be outfitted by Altfield. Established in 1980, the elegant gallery carries exquisite antique Chinese furniture; Asia-related maps and topographical prints; Southeast Asian sculpture and decorative arts from around Asia, including silver artifacts and rugs. ✉ *Prince's Bldg., 10 Chater Rd., Central* ☎ *2537–6370* ⊕ *www.altfield.com.hk* Ⓜ *Central.*

Arch Angel Antiques. Ask for Bonnie Groot, who will enthusiastically and knowledgeably guide you through the three floors of fine ceramics, furniture, ancestor portraits, and more. Across the road, the Groots have opened Arch Angel Art, which specializes in contemporary Vietnamese and Southeast Asian art. ✉ *G/F, 53–55 Hollywood Rd., Central* ☎ *2851–6848* Ⓜ *Central* ✉ *58 Hollywood Rd., Central* Ⓜ *Central.*

China Art. The Chiang family runs this retail and wholesale operation that specializes in craftsman-restored Chinese antiques, especially furniture. The family's honest approach is apparent in its exhibitions and has inspired a coffee table book, *Antiques in the Raw.* ✉ *G/F, 15 Hollywood Rd., Central* ☎ *2234–9924* ⊕ *www.chinaart.com.hk* Ⓜ *Central.*

Chine Gallery. Dealing in antique furniture and rugs from China, and furniture from Japan, this dark, stylish gallery accommodates international clients by coordinating its major exhibitions with the spring and fall auction schedules of Christie's and Sotheby's. ✉ *42A Hollywood Rd., Central* ☎ *2543–0023* ⊕ *www.chinegallery.com* Ⓜ *Central.*

Contes d'Orient. This beautiful showroom displays Chinese antique furniture, scholar's items, and archaeological stone works. Owner Oi Ling Chiang gives frequent talks. Succinct books on collecting by type are also sold here. Sister showroom, **Gallery Oi Ling** (✉ *G/F, 85 Hollywood Rd., Central* ☎ *2964–0554* Ⓜ *Central*), just down the road, sells terracotta, pottery, and bronze antiques. ✉ *G/F, 52 Hollywood Rd., Central* ☎ *2815–9422* ⊕ *www.contesdorient.com* Ⓜ *Central.*

The Green Lantern. Irish expat Olive Dundon has cleverly retained original elements of the former print shop in which her store is housed. With her unique sense of style, Dundon brings together Chinese and Tibetan antiques, contemporary lighting designed in-house, silk soft furnishings, OM Living bed linens, and home accessories. ✉ *72 Peel St., SoHo, Central* ☎ *2526–0277.*

Hanlin Gallery. For Japanese works of art and woodblocks, visit this refined, calm gallery run by specialist Carlos Prata since 1986. His collection and expertise extend to furniture, textiles, silver, and European glass. ✉ *G/F, Wilson House, 19–27 Wyndham St., Central* ☎ *2522–4479* ⊕ *www.hanlingallery.com* Ⓜ *Central.*

Honeychurch Antiques. Highly respected dealers, Lucille and Glenn Vessa (one of the few accredited appraisers here), were the first to set up shop on Hollywood Road. The landscape has changed, but this shop still provides fine Chinese, Japanese, and Southeast Asian antique silver, porcelain, and unaltered furniture. ☒ *G/F, 29 Hollywood Rd., Central* ☎ *2543–2433* Ⓜ *Central.*

Indosiam Rare Books. Yves Azemar indulges his passion for rare books and prints about former French colonies in Asia in this tiny apartment, which he has converted into a library–shop. The French schoolteacher is happy to sit and chat about this fascinating genre—the lectures are never boring. ☒ *1/F, 89 Hollywood Rd., Central* ☎ *2854–2853* Ⓜ *Central.*

Manks Ltd. Inside a historic house surrounded by skyscrapers and high-ways you'll not only find 20th-century decorative arts, European an-tiques, and Scandinavian furniture, but also the delightful Susan Man. Visits to her shop are by appointment only. ☒ *Shop House, 2 Kennedy Terrace, above Kennedy Rd., Midlevels, Western* ☎ *2522–2115* ⊕ *www. manks.com.*

Picture This Gallery. It's a one-of-a-kind source for vintage posters—mainly with travel and movie themes—early photography of Hong Kong and elsewhere in China, antique maps, prints and engravings, antiquarian books, and limited-edition reproductions or works by artists such as Dong Kingman. You might imagine a dusty library, but Christopher Bailey's welcoming gallery is spacious, bright, and organized. ☒ *6/F, Office Tower, 9 Queen's Rd., Central* ☎ *2525–2820* ⊕ *www. picturethiscollection.com* Ⓜ *Central.*

Tào Evolution. Here, old and new objects are among the unusual finds of a pair of designers whose work takes them around the globe. Look for contemporary and tribal art as well as furniture that conveys an eclectic Asian spirit. ☒ *G/F, 58 Peel St., SoHo, Central* ☎ *2530–2102* Ⓜ *Central.*

Teresa Coleman Fine Arts Ltd. You can't miss the spectacular textiles hanging in the window of this busy corner shop. Specialist Teresa Cole-man sells embroidered costumes from the Imperial Court, antique tex-tiles, painted and carved fans, jewelry, lacquered boxes, and engravings and prints. ☒ *79 Wyndham St., Central* ☎ *2526–2450* ⊕ *www. teresacoleman.com* Ⓜ *Central.*

The Tibetan Gallery. At this extension of Teresa Coleman Fine Arts you'll find antique Tibetan *thangkas* (Buddhist paintings), bronzes, textiles, and exquisite rugs. Manager Josephine Chan is also a restoration ex-pert. ☒ *55 Wyndham St., Central* ☎ *2530–4863* ⊕ *www.teresacoleman. com* Ⓜ *Central.*

Wattis Fine Art. Run by affable expert Jonathan Wattis and his wife, Vicky, Wattis Fine Art specializes in antique maps and prints and photographs of Hong Kong, China, and Southeast Asia. ☒ *2/F, 20 Hollywood Rd., Central* ☎ *2524–5302* ⊕ *www.wattis.com.hk.*

Wing Tei. Helpful owner Peter Lee sells wonderful porcelain plates as well as curios, furniture, and wood carvings. ☒ *190–F Hollywood Rd., Central* ☎ *2547–4755* Ⓜ *Central.*

Yue Po Chai Antique Co. One of Hollywood Road's oldest shops is at the Cat Street end, next to Man Mo Temple. Its vast and varied stock in-cludes porcelain, stone carvings, and ceramics. ☒ *G/F, 132–136 Hol-lywood Rd., Central* ☎ *2540–4374* Ⓜ *Central.*

Art

Hong Kong is a hub for contemporary Asian art, particularly that from Hong Kong and mainland China, Indonesia, Vietnam, Thailand, and the Philippines. Although concentrated around the antique dealers on Hollywood Road, art spaces stretch east to Wan Chai, west to Sheung Wan, and well beyond into the New Territories.

Openings take place weekly. A quick reference for what's on, *ArtMap* (⊕ www.artmap.com.hk), is a free monthly distributed in most coffee shops and countless other outlets. *Asian Art News* is a bimonthly magazine with a good guide to what's happening in galleries around the region. It's sold at bigger newsstands for HK$50.

GALLERIES

Alisan Fine Arts. In a quiet corner of the sleek Prince's Building shopping arcade is this established authority on contemporary Chinese artists. Styles range from traditional to modern abstract, and media include oil, acrylic, and Chinese ink. Founded in 1981 by Alice King, this was one of the first galleries in Hong Kong to promote the genre. ⊠ *Prince's Bldg., 10 Chater Rd., Central* ☎ *2526–1091* ⊕ *www.alisan.com.hk* Ⓜ *Central.*

Art Statements Gallery. Set on the charming terraced steps just below Hollywood Road and in the burgeoning Noho area, this gallery makes up for its discreet location with often boundary-pushing works of art by conceptual Asian artists, as well as leading artists from Europe and North America. Since opening the gallery in 2003, founder Dominique Perregaux has brought a fresh perspective to the local art scene. ⊠ *G/F, 5 Mee Lun St., Noho, Central* ☎ *2122–9657* ⊕ *www.artstatements.com* Ⓜ *Central.*

Gaffer Studio Glass. In the city's first gallery specializing in studio glass—which is gaining respect in the collecting world—there's not a floral paperweight in sight. The 4,000-square-foot, natural-light-filled space is a great backdrop for modern sculptures and functional vessel glass works by artists from Southeast Asia, Australia, and the United States. ⊠ *17/F, Hing Wai Centre, 7 Tin Wan Praya Rd., Southside Aberdeen* ☎ *2521–1770* ⊕ *www.gafferstudioglass.com.*

Grotto Fine Art. Director and chief curator Henry Au-yeung writes, curates, and gives lectures on 20th-century Chinese art. His hidden gallery (hence the "grotto" in the name) focuses exclusively on local Chinese artists, with an interest in the newest and most avant-garde works. Look for paintings, sculptures, prints, photography, mixed-media pieces, and conceptual installations. ⊠ *2/F, 31C–D Wyndham St., Central* ☎ *2121–2270* ⊕ *www.grottofineart.com* Ⓜ *Central.*

▪ TIP➔ Galleries can arrange to have your work of art framed or can recommend a reputable framer.

Galerie La Vong. The works of today's leading Vietnamese artists, many of whose creations reveal an intriguing combination of French impressionist and traditional Chinese influences, are the focus here. ⊠ *13/F, 1 Lan Kwai Fong, Central* ☎ *2869–6863* Ⓜ *Central.*

Hanart TZ Gallery. This is a rare opportunity to compare and contrast cutting-edge and experimental art from mainland China, Taiwan, and Hong Kong selected by one of the field's most respected authorities. Unassuming curatorial director, Johnson Chang Tsong-zung, also cofounded the Asia Art Archive, and has curated exhibitions at the São Paolo and Venice biennials. ⊠ *2/F, Henley Bldg., 5 Queen's Rd., Central* ☎ *2526–9019* ⊕ *www.hanart.com* Ⓜ *Central.*

John Batten Gallery. John Batten is the kind of gallery owner who takes the time to talk to you, pulling out catalogs, books, and other materials to illustrate his points. This one-time SoHo pioneer, whose artists hail from around Asia and the Pacific, developed a reputation for solo and group exhibitions with challenging themes. Once an innovator, always an innovator: John closed his gallery space in 2006 and adopted a guerilla approach to exhibiting—that is, temporary shows set up in warehouses, abandoned lots, and the like. Call for details about what's on and where. ☎ *2854–1018* ⊕ *www.johnbattengallery.com.*

Plum Blossoms Gallery. You can't miss this gallery's unique, asymmetrical window. The airy, New York–style space displays groundbreaking contemporary Chinese art alongside ancient Asian textiles and rugs. Ask the refreshingly knowledgeable staff to escort you upstairs to see more. ⊠ *1 Hollywood Rd., Central* ☎ *2521–2189* ⊕ *www.plumblossoms.com* Ⓜ *Central.*

Sandra Walters Consultancy Ltd. Sandra Walters, a longtime figure on the art scene, represents a stable of Asian and international artists encompassing a variety of periods and styles. Make an appointment for her or one of her team to advise you on small to significant investments. ⊠ *501 Hoseinee House, 69 Wyndham St., Central* ☎ *2522–1137* Ⓜ *Central.*

Schoeni Art Gallery. Known for vigorously promoting Chinese art on a global scale, this gallery, founded by Manfred Schoeni in 1992, has represented and supported various artists from mainland China with styles ranging from neorealism to postmodernism. Manfred's daughter Nicole now pinpoints exciting new artists for her prominent clientele. Informative past exhibition catalogs are placed atop Chinese antiques, which are also presented in this huge space. You're likely to pass the Hollywood Road branch first, but Old Baily Street gallery is the better of the two. ⊠ *Upper G/F, 21–31 Old Bailey St., Central* ☎ *2525–5225* ⊕ *www.schoeni.com.hk* Ⓜ *Central.*

Sin Sin Fine Art. Take the escalator up to Prince's Terrace, where you can't miss this corner gallery's large windows or the arresting human form sculpture installed on an outer wall. Inside, works by diverse emerging and established artists from Indonesia, Thailand, mainland China, Hong Kong, and France reveal the aesthetic individuality of the lively Hong Kong designer and entrepreneur, Sin Sin. There are also regular exhibitions and artist talks. An extension, Sin Sin Annex near Cat Street in

Sheung Wan, is a space for more progressive installations, objets, and performance art. ⊠ *G/F, 1 Prince's Terr., Midlevels, Western* ☎ *2858–5072* ⊕ *www.sinsin.com. hk* ⊠ *G/F, 52 Sai St., Sheung Wan, Western.*

10 Chancery Lane Gallery. A visit here takes you behind the historic Central Police Station, where walls facing the gallery's distinctive red door are still topped by broken glass, a common security measure. Since it opened in 2000, the clean, white-walled gallery has focused on emerging artists from all over the world, as well as more established names. Owner-curator Katie de Tilly has a particularly keen eye for photography. ⊠ *G/F, 10 Chancery La., SoHo, Central* ☎ *2810–0065* ⊕ *www.10chancerylanegallery.com* Ⓜ *Central.*

Yan Gallery. This is the place for Hong Kong–based artist Hu Yongkai's charming, slightly cartoonish depictions of Chinese women in traditional settings (you've almost certainly seen fakes in a Stanley Market stall). The gallery, which isn't as stuffy as some and more commercial than others, also represents Bob Yan, whose extremely popular and colorful dog portraits are commissioned by private clients. ⊠ *G/F, 77 Wyndham St. Central* ☎ *2139–2345* ⊕ *www.yangallery.com* Ⓜ *Central.*

Zee Stone Gallery. Massive street-level windows display the decorative kind of paintings we've come to expect from Vietnam, Burma, and China—from photorealistic portraits to abstract landscapes. A visit here provides a view into what's popular with casual collectors. ⊠ *G/F, Yu Yuet Bldg., 43–55 Wyndham St., Central* ☎ *2810–5895* ⊕ *www.zeestone.com* Ⓜ *Central.*

> ### ART CRAWL?
>
> The art world's version of a pub crawl, **Hong Kong Art Walk** (⊕ www.hongkongartwalk.com) is an excellent chance to experience the gallery scene. Held over the course of one evening every March, it gives ticket holders unlimited access to more than 40 galleries where food and drinks donated by neighboring restaurants help create a festive environment. Proceeds go to charity.

Beauty & Cosmetics

World-class shrines to cosmetics have brought almost every European, American, and Japanese beauty line—from drugstore makeup to niche skincare systems—you can think of to Hong Kong. For an overview of what's on offer, just visit a department store like Harvey Nichols or Seibu. At Lane Crawford, customer service—not always Hong Kong's strongest suit—is taken to new levels with a personalized "cosmetic concierge service." Although questionable regulation and typically poor quality make it best to avoid cheap mainland cosmetics, a few local brands do stand out. Discount chains have become so popular, there's at least one in every shopping district. And if all this shopping is tiring you out, retail therapy of another kind is within reach at Hong Kong's pampering spas.

DISCOUNT SHOPS

Sa-Sa Cosmetics. The fuchsia pink signs that announce Hong Kong's best and largest cosmetic discounter will become familiar sights on any

Taking the tram, Victoria Peak.

(top) Star Ferry views are among the best. (bottom) Cantonese opera performers, Hong Kong Heritage Museum.

(top) Tai chi practitioners William Ng and Pandora Wu Ng, Hong Kong Park. (bottom) Real life in the city, Wan Chai shopping street.

One of the world's largest bronze Buddhas sits on a lotus flower at Po Lin Monastery, Lantau Island.

(top left) The Chinese introduced tea to the world; learn all about it at the Flagstaff House Museum of Tea Ware. (top right) *Manpower* sculpture by Rosanna Li, Grotto Fine Art gallery. (bottom) Energy = trams + taxis + neon.

(top) A promenade and lanterns frame the Hong Kong skyline, Avenue of the Stars, Kowloon waterfront. (bottom left) Hakka woman in traditional garb. (bottom right) Shopping is a religion in Hong Kong, and the Pacific Place mall is just one of its many temples.

(top) Po Lin Monastery, Lantau Island. (bottom) Dancing girls with fans.

(top) Who knew there were such beaches here? Sai Kung Peninsula, New Territories. (bottom left) Native son Chow Yun-Fat in *Crouching Tiger, Hidden Dragon*. (bottom right) Rides on the restored *Duk Ling* junk are compliments of the tourist board.

shopping expedition. Look for deals on everything from cheap glittery makeup to sleek designer lines. Fragrances are a particularly good buy; prices are usually even lower than those at airport duty-free shops. ⊠ G/F and 1/F, Sai Yeung Choi St. S, Mong Kok, Kowloon ☎ 2770–1311, 2505–5023 customer service and branch info ⊕ www.sasa.com Ⓜ Mong Kok ⊠ G/F and M/F, Peter Bldg., 62 Queen's Rd. Central, Central Ⓜ Central.

DRUGSTORES

Watsons. The CVS of Hong Kong sells western medicines and health and beauty products, as well as some traditional Chinese products. Some stores also have pharmacies. ⊠ Zone GW (The Gateway), Harbour City, Canton Rd., Tsim Sha Tsui, Kowloon ☎ 2117–1093, 2608–8383 customer service and branch information Ⓜ Tsim Sha Tsui.

Mannings. Like Watsons, you'll find this chain throughout the city. It sells everything from shampoo and lotions to emery boards and cough medicine (western and Chinese brands). Some stores have pharmacies. ⊠ IFC Mall, 8 Finance St., Central ☎ 2523–6706, 2299–3381 for customer service and branch information Ⓜ Central.

HONG KONG GOODIES

Eu Yan Sang. The Sheung Wan area is a quaint and pungent place to shop for traditional Chinese herbs and medicines. But this reliable source—in operation since 1879—is a more straightforward option. ⊠ 152–156 Queens Rd. Central, Western ☎ 2544–3870, 2544–3308 for customer service and branch information ⊕ www.euyansang.com ⊠ G/F, 18 Russell St., Causeway Bay ☎ 2573–2038 Ⓜ Causeway Bay ⊠ G/F, 11–15 Chatham Rd. S, Tsim Sha Tsui, Kowloon Ⓜ Tsim Sha Tsui.

Kwong Sang Hong. This shop carries Hong Kong's first local cosmetics line, also known as Two Girls Brand. The colorful, old-fashioned packaging, which is reminiscent of traditional Chinese medicines, is more remarkable than the products. That said, the line's classics—including hair oil, talcum powder, and face cream—do make lovely gifts. ⊠ Causeway Place, Hong Kong Mansion, 2–10 Great George St., Causeway Bay ☎ 2504–1811 ⊕ www.ksh.com.hk Ⓜ Causeway Bay ⊠ Basement, Silvercord, 30 Canton Rd., Tsim Sha Tsui, Kowloon Ⓜ Tsim Sha Tsui ⊠ Two Girls Kiosk, 1/F Lobby, Dragon Centre, 37k Yen Chow St., Sham Shui Po, Kowloon Ⓜ Sham Shui Po.

Skin Nursery by menthoderm. The unisex skincare line sold here is known for deep-pore cleansing, which tends to be more aggressive in Asia than elsewhere. So what if its natural, concentrated ingredients come from Europe and are blended in a U.S. laboratory? The line's cosmopolitan approach makes it quintessentially HK. Its spacious Skin Nursery also provides facial and body treatments for women and men. ⊠ 3/F, CNAC Group Bldg., 10 Queen's Rd. Central, Central ☎ 2147–3803 ⊕ www.menthoderm.com Ⓜ Central.

Red Earth. No, it's not a candy store. This shop's rainbow confections are actually affordable makeup basics in simple packaging. You'll also find Red Earth products in Esprit stores as well as stand-alone boutiques. ⊠ 2–10 Great George St., Causeway Place, Causeway Bay ☎ 2808–1675, 2700–0202 for customer service and branch information ⊕ www.

redearth.com Ⓜ *Causeway Bay* ✉ *Basement, Kaiseng Comm. Centre, 4–6 Hankow Rd., Tsim Sha Tsui, Kowloon* Ⓜ *Tsim Sha Tsui.*

INTERNATIONAL LINES

FACES. FACES is a sprawling one-stop shop carrying a long list of high-profile and niche beauty brands. It also hosts regular product launches and special presentations by international beauty experts. ✉ *Ocean Terminal, Canton Rd., Tsim Sha Tsui, Kowloon* ☎ *2118–5622* Ⓜ *Tsim Sha Tsui.*

Pure Beauty by Watsons. Developed by one of Hong Kong's oldest drugstores this slick, well-lighted store focuses on "masstige" (mass + prestige) cosmetics and skincare. Like ordinary Watsons stores, Pure Beauty also carries health supplements, professional hair-care products, and fragrances. ✉ *Basement 2, Times Square, 1 Matheson St., Causeway Bay* ☎ *2506–1521* Ⓜ *Causeway Bay.*

SPAS

Hong Kong's mix of western and eastern treatments is unrivaled. You can have a quick manicure or an extravagant spa day; try threading (an ancient hair removal method) or Chinese-method hair. With more treatments for men and treatment rooms for couples, the boys don't need to feel left out, either. Warning: you'll be spoiled for life.

▮ TIP➔ Hotel spas stay open until 10 or 11 PM, a few hours later than the stand-alone establishments, so you can leave your day open for shopping.

Acupressure and Massage Centre of the Blind. Looking for a good massage without all the glitz? Visit these skilled and affordable blind masseurs trained in acupressure, reflexology, and Chinese massage. ✉ *Tung Ming Bldg., 40–42 Des Voeux Rd., Central* ☎ *2810–6666* Ⓜ *Central.*

The Feel Good Factor. It's the perfect place to unwind after antiquing on nearby Hollywood Road. During your pedicure or express manicure, you can sit by the window and watch the world go by or you can choose a cozier, more secluded spot. For facials, massages, waxing, and airbrush tanning, you'll be escorted to inner rooms. ✉ *G/F, Lyndhurst Tower, 1 Lyndhurst Terrace, Central* ☎ *2530–0610* ⊕ *www.feelgoodfactor.com.hk* Ⓜ *Central.*

Four Seasons. Enter via a light wood and stark white hallway into treatment rooms that ooze modern cool. The two-hour, signature Pure Indulgence treatment uses organic

WAX FIGURES

No one likes to contemplate hair removal, especially the dreaded Brazilian wax, but Hong Kong has some true experts in the field. No-nonsense Betty at the **Mandarin Beauty Salon and Barber Shop** (✉ Mandarin Oriental, 5 Connaught Rd., Central Ⓜ Central) has hair-removal techniques that are whispered about in the best of circles. The gentle Helena at the hidden **Beautiful Skin Centre** (✉ Pacific Place, 88 Queensway, Admiralty ☎ 2877–8911 ⊕ www.paua.com.hk Ⓜ Admiralty) uses an ultra-soothing coconut wax to get you bare.

products—it's head-to-toe pampering for your body and your soul. Harbor views and a Japanese garden also help to alter your mood. ⊠ *8 Finance St., Central* ☎ *3196–8888* ⊕ *www.fourseasons.com* Ⓜ *Central.*

★ **Happy Foot Reflexology Center.** Who knew pressure on your big toe could help clear your sinuses? Reflexology is Hong Kong's cheap and cheerful way to relax, and Happy Foot is the legendary place to have it done. The armchairs are comfortable, and the therapists are ex-

perts, but don't expect a luxe experience. Interiors are basic, and you'll share a room with other customers. ⊠ *6/F, 11/F, and 13/F, Jade Centre, 98–102 Wellington St., Central* ☎ *2544–1010* Ⓜ *Central* ⊠ *19/F, Century Square, 1–13 d'Aguilar St., Central* Ⓜ *Central* ⊠ *1/F, Elegance Court, 2–4 Tsoi Tak St., Happy Valley.*

Indulgence. Enter at street level via the calm white, Provençal-style boutique filled with hard-to-find brands for the true beauty addict. Ascend the stairs to check in. You'll be guided farther into the 5,700-square-foot space with rooms for manicures and pedicures, facial and body treatments, and hair styling for men and women. The terrace café has spa cuisine. ⊠ *G/F, 33 Lyndhurst Terrace, Central* ☎ *2815–6600* Ⓜ *Central.*

Fodors Choice **The Oriental Spa.** If you indulge in just one Hong Kong spa treatment,
★ have it here. Designed as a journey from the outer into the inner world, the experience begins on the check-in and fitness floor. You're taken up to the next level and offered a welcome tea, then guided deeper into this haven, where treatments are administered by excellent therapists in serene rooms. Try the signature Time Ritual, a holistic combination of therapies adapted to your specific needs on the day. Treatments here get you access to the vitality pool, the amethyst-crystal steam room, the authentic Turkish hammam, and more. Next door to the Oriental Spa, the legendary **Mandarin Beauty Salon and Barber Shop** (⊠ Mandarin Oriental, 5 Connaught Rd., Central Ⓜ Central) offers traditional favorites. Ask for a famous Shanghainese pedicure with Samuel and his knives (yes, knives!), or see Betty for eyebrow threading. ⊠ *Landmark Mandarin Oriental, 15 Queen's Rd. Central, Central* ☎ *2132–8011* ⊕ *www.mandarinoriental.com* Ⓜ *Central.*

Paul Gerrard Hair and Beauty. Up the copper-gilt stairwell of this old Chinese building on an old Hong Kong–style stepped street, this sophisticated little spa has got it just right. When respected hair stylist, Paul Gerrard, took on an extra floor for facial and body treatments he considered every detail—even the wheels on his carts are soundproof. Sink into a massage chair for a manicure or pedicure, and just relax. ⊠ *1/F, Wah Hing House, 35 Pottinger St., Central* ☎ *2869–4408* ⊕ *www.paulgerrard.com* Ⓜ *Central.*

The Peninsula Spa. Here's another excuse to visit Hong Kong's grand dame hotel—as if you needed one. Even the aromatic hand soaps in the bathrooms soothe the senses at this lavish east-meets-west sanctuary, which has separate facilities for men and women. You'll enjoy Oriental, Ayurvedic, and other therapies in rooms overlooking the harbor. Consider booking a Peninsula Ceremony, a series of holistic treatments chosen for you by a skilled therapist. ⊠ *Salisbury Rd., Tsim Sha Tsui, Kowloon* ☎ *2315–3322* ⊕ *www.peninsula.com* Ⓜ *Tsim Sha Tsui.*

Quality Chinese Medical Centre. Acupuncture looks alarming but is painless. Where better to try it than in China? This reputable center is also a good place to learn more about traditional Chinese medicine and herbal remedies. ⊠ *18/F, Island Beverly, 1 Great George St., Causeway Bay* ☎ *2881–8267* ⊕ *www.qcmchk.com* Ⓜ *Causeway Bay* ⊠ *5/F, Jade Centre, 98 Wellington St., Central* ☎ *2882–1788* Ⓜ *Central.*

Clothing

You've come at a good time. Creativity is on the rise, and new designers and shops are cropping up across the territory. There are countless opportunities to visit out-of-the-way ateliers, meet designers, and even commission one-off pieces that will never go out of style. Brands from around the world converge in this shopping mecca. Some lines, especially those from Japan, might be new discoveries. Others are luxury brands you have at home (you'd be hard-pressed to find a brand that isn't distributed here).

Whether you get a better deal on designer labels is debatable. For now, Hong Kong has no sales tax, which certainly makes a difference on big-ticket items. It also means that prices are the best in Asia and generally lower than in North America (though not necessarily than in Europe). Look for good deals on cashmere, custom-made clothing and accessories, and jewelry.

CASHMERE

In the SAR, you can drape yourself in soft, sumptuous cashmere for a lot less than in other world cities. Chinese department stores carry basic, square-cut cashmere sweaters for men and women at decent prices. That said, cashmere is sold at every price point, so comparison shopping is a must.

■ **TIP→** Remember that pure cashmere comes from a Kashmir goat. If the knit includes wool, silk, or any other material, it's a blend. Also inspect weight (a big price determinate), texture, and weave.

★ **Pearls & Cashmere.** Warehouse prices in chic shopping arcades? It's true. This old Hong Kong favorite is elegantly housed in hotels on both sides of the harbor. In addition to quality men's and women's cashmere sweaters in classic designs and in every color under the sun, they also sell reasonably priced pashminas, gloves, and socks, which make great gifts for men and women. In recent years the brand has developed the more fashion-focused line, BYPAC. ⊠ *Mezzanine, Peninsula Hotel Shopping Arcade, Salisbury Rd., Tsim Sha Tsui, Kowloon* ☎ *2723–8698*

CLOSE UP

The Choice Is Joyce

LOCAL SOCIALITES and couture addicts still thank Joyce Ma, the fairy godmother of luxury retail in Hong Kong, for bringing must-have labels to the city. Others may be catching up, but her Joyce boutiques are still ultrachic havens outfitted with a *Vogue*-worthy wish list of designers and beauty brands.

Joyce Beauty. Love finding unique beauty products from around the world? Then this is the place for you, with cult perfumes, luxurious skin solutions, and new discoveries to be made. Bring your credit card— "bargain" isn't in the vocabulary here. ⊠ *Times Square, 1 Matheson St., Causeway Bay* ☎ *2970-2319* Ⓜ *Causeway Bay* ✉ *G/F, New World Tower, 16-18 Queen's Rd. Central, Central* Ⓜ *Central* ✉ *Lane Crawford, IFC Mall, 8 Finance St., Central* Ⓜ *Central* ✉ *The Gateway, 3-27 Canton Rd., Tsim Sha Tsui, Kowloon* Ⓜ *Tsim Sha Tsui* ✉ *Festival Walk, 80 Tat Chee Ave., Kowloon Tong, Kowloon* Ⓜ *Kowloon Tong.*

Joyce Boutique. Not so much a shop as a fashion institution, Joyce Boutique's hushed interior houses the worship-worthy creations of fashion's greatest gods and goddesses. McCartney, Galliano, Dolce & Gabbana, Prada, Miyake: the stock list is practically a mantra. Joyce sells unique household items, too, so your home can live up to your wardrobe. ⊠ *New World Tower, 16 Queen's Rd., Central* ☎ *2810-1120* ⊕ *www.joyce. com* Ⓜ *Central, Exit G* ✉ *Pacific Place, 88 Queensway, Admiralty* Ⓜ *Admiralty, Exit F* ✉ *Harbour City, Tsim Sha Tsui, Kowloon* Ⓜ *Tsim Sha Tsui, Exit F.*

Joyce Warehouse. Fashionistas who've fallen on hard times can breathe a sigh of relief. Joyce's outlet on Ap Lei Chau, the island offshore from Aberdeen in Southside, stocks last season's duds from the likes of Jil Sander, Armani, Ann Demeulemeester, Costume National, and Missoni. Prices for each garment are reduced by about 10% each month, so the longer the piece stays on the rack, the less it costs. Bus 90B gets you from Exchange Square to Ap Lei Chau in 25 minutes; then hop a taxi for the four-minute taxi ride to Horizon Plaza. ⊠ *21/F, Horizon Plaza, 2 Lee Wing St., Southside* ☎ *2814-8313* ⊙ *Tues.- Sat. 10-6, Sun. noon-6.*

4

⊕ *www.pearlsandcashmere.com* Ⓜ *Tsim Sha Tsui* ✉ *Mezzanine, Mandarin Oriental, 5 Connaught Rd., Central* Ⓜ *Central* ✉ *G/F, New World Centre, 18–24 Salisbury Rd., Tsim Sha Tsui, Kowloon* Ⓜ *Tsim Sha Tsui.*

Dorfit. A longtime cashmere manufacturer and retailer, Dorfit caters to a variety of men's, women's, and children's tastes. Knitwear here comes in pure cashmere as well as blends, so be sure to ask which is which. ▪ TIP→ After visiting the Pedder Building branch of Dorfit be sure to duck into other on-site discount cashmere shops, such as Aptitude Clothing International, and Fabel. ⊠ *6/F, Mary Bldg., 71–77 Peking Rd., Tsim Sha Tsui, Kowloon* ☎ *2312–1013* ⊕ *www.dorfit.com.hk* Ⓜ *Tsim Sha Tsui* ✉ *6/ F, Pedder Bldg., 12 Pedder St., Central* Ⓜ *Central.*

Lung Sang Hong. It's easy to miss this little shop, quite literally set up in a staircase. Although it doesn't sell the cheapest cashmere scarves in town (about HK$1,245–HK$1,400), it has some of the finest, with the quality, diamond weave, and lightness of the fabled "ring pashmina." Men's and women's cashmere knits are also sold here. Ask to go up to the first-floor showroom for more. ⊠ *G/F, 45–47 Stanley Main St., Stanley Market, Stanley, South Side* ☎ *2577–6802 or 9323–2360.*

CHILDREN'S CLOTHES

Several malls have dedicated special sections to western-style children's clothing, accessories, and toys, including: Ocean Terminal in Tsim Sha Tsui, Times Square and Windsor House in Causeway Bay, and Prince's Building in Central. The famous labels are here, but they aren't necessarily priced lower than you'd find at home. Stanley Market and similar shopping streets, however, sell recognizable brands at generous discounts.

For Chinese-style kids' clothing, nothing beats the collection by Shanghai Tang, where the luxury and the prices are both high. Look for acceptable, cheaper alternatives in Chinese department stores or markets such as the Lanes on Li Yuen streets East and West.

Bumps to Babes. It has everything you could possibly need for babies and children, all in one place. In addition to familiar brands of clothing, diapers, toiletries, food, and toys, look for strollers, books, maternity wear, furniture, and more. ⊠ *5/F, Pedder Bldg., 12 Pedder St., Central* ☎ *2522–7112* ⊕ *www.bumpstobabes.com* Ⓜ *Central* ⊠ *21/F, Horizon Plaza, 2 Lee Wing St., Southside, Ap Lei Chau.*

★ **Hoi Yuen Emporium Co.** Of all the cheaper alternatives to Shanghai Tang, this is the best. It has a fantastic selection of Mao collared jackets for boys and girls. Chinese-style onesies come in muted, noncartoonish colors, and cost less than HK$80. ⊠ *Stanley Market, 64 Stanley Main St., South Side, Stanley* ☎ *2813–0470.*

Lace Department Store. You might head straight for the embroidered linens, but back up and review the children's clothing by the door. You've seen these beautiful, traditional, hand-smocked cotton dresses, and baby overalls in elegant European stores, sold at prices to make you faint. Here expect to pay as little as HK$195 to HK$230. As you tour the city, keep an eye out for embroidered linens specialists who carry similar dresses. ⊠ *6/F, Pedder Bldg., 12 Pedder St., Central* ☎ *2523–8162* Ⓜ *Central.*

Marleen Molenaar Sleepwear. When Hong Kong–based Dutch designer and mother Marleen Molenaar discovered how limited her choices were for children's pajamas and sleepwear, she founded her own label. The gorgeous 100% cotton, high-quality classic European collections are sold around the world and through her showroom, by appointment. ⊠ *10/F, Winner Bldg., 27–39 D'Aguilar St., Central* ☎ *2525–9872 or 9162–0350* ⊕ *www.marleenmolenaar.com* Ⓜ *Central.*

Mrs. Chan. One of the top children's clothing stalls in Stanley Market sells everything from play-date clothes to Christmas Day bests. Push your way through the piles and hanging examples of tasteful, brand-name pieces for babies, boys, and girls. Come here first, then do some comparison shopping before pulling out your wallet. ⊠ *Stall opposite Stanley Municipal Services Bldg., 6 Stanley Main St., South Side, Stanley* ☎ *6082–7503.*

Toto. Home-grown, like its founder, Toto makes pretty European design clothing in pure cotton. Apart from its cute angel trademark, the collection has unembellished, white, pink, or blue clothes for babies and children. It's stocked in many Hong Kong maternity wards. ⊠ *Pedder Bldg., 12 Pedder St., Central* ☎ *2869–4668* ⊕ *www.totobaby.com* Ⓜ *Central.*

HONG KONG COUTURE

Hong Kong has a surprising number of talented designers. Although labels like Shanghai Tang and Blanc de Chine have achieved worldwide attention, others are still in the exciting chrysalis stage—which means you can still say you knew them when.

Azalea by i'sis. A fantastic place for hip yet understated dresses and separates that will have everyone asking, "Ooh, where'd you get that?" At first glance, this looks like all the other trendy little boutiques in Causeway Bay, but everything here is just that much better made—and better looking—with a fit that accounts for curves. You can find the same items at select U.S. boutiques, but prices will be 1½ to 2 times what they are here. ⊠ *G/F, Po Foo Bldg., 3–5 Foo Ming St., Causeway Bay* ☎ *2808–4183* Ⓜ *Causeway Bay.*

Barney Cheng. One of Hong Kong's best-known, locally based designers, Barney Cheng creates haute couture designs and prêt-à-porter collections, infusing his glam, often sequined, pieces with wit. When the Kennedy Center in Washington, D.C., hosted an exhibition titled "The New China Chic," Cheng was invited to display his works alongside those by the likes of Vera Wang and Anna Sui. ⊠ *12/F, World Wide Commercial Bldg., 34 Wyndham St., Central* ☎ *2530–2829* ⊕ *www.barneycheng.com* Ⓜ *Central.*

Episode. Locally owned and designed Episode collections focus on accessories and suiting and other elegant clothing for working women and ladies who lunch. Look also for the younger Jessica, the trendy Colour, and the casual Weekend Workshop and Oxygen collections. Though distinct, each collection pays close attention to current trends in the fashion world. ⊠ *B/F, Entertainment Bldg., 30 Queen's Rd. Central, Central* ☎ *2943–2115 customer service* ⊕ *www.toppy.com.hk* Ⓜ *Central* ⊠ *Times Square, 1 Matheson St., Causeway Bay* Ⓜ *Causeway Bay* ⊠ *Gateway Arcade, Harbour City, Canton Rd., Tsim Sha Tsui, Kowloon* Ⓜ *Tsim Sha Tsui.*

Lu Lu Cheung. A fixture on the Hong Kong fashion scene for more than a decade, Lu Lu Cheung's designs ooze comfort and warmth. In both daytime and evening wear, natural fabrics and forms are represented in practical yet imaginative ways. ⊠ *The Landmark, Central* ☎ *2537–7515* ⊕ *www.lulucheung.com.hk* Ⓜ *Central* ⊠ *New Town Plaza, Shatin Centre St., New Territories Shatin* Ⓜ *KCR Shatin.*

Pocket Venus. Hong Kong–based English designer Jane Troughton creates spirited, youthful women's wear with a vintage feel—think exclusive prints and beautiful beading. This charming, by-appointment-only atelier provides the opportunity to not only view the latest collections, seen on countless London celebrities, but also to meet the friendly designer. Her fashions are also sold at Seibu department store, but a trip there is far less entertaining. Following her marriage in a dress of her own her design, Troughton launched a bespoke wedding-gown service. ⊠ *G/F, Koon Nam House, 14 Shing Wong St., SoHo, Central* ☎ *2548–8086* ⊕ *www.pocket-venus.net* Ⓜ *Central.*

Olivia Couture. The surroundings are functional, but the gowns, wedding dresses, and *cheongsams* by local designer Olivia Yip are lavish. With a growing clientele, including socialites looking to stand out, Yip is quietly making a name for herself and her Parisian-influenced pieces. ⊠ *G/F, Bartlock Centre, 3 Yiu Wah St., Causeway Bay* ☎ *2838–6636* ⊕ *www.oliviacouture.com* Ⓜ *Causeway Bay.*

Ranee K. Designer Ranee Kok Chui-Wah's showrooms are scarlet dens cluttered with her one-off dresses and eclectic women's wear that bring new meanings to "when East meets West." Known for her quirky *cheongsams* and dresses, she has also collaborated with brands such as Furla and Shanghai Tang. Special clients and local celebrities enjoy her custom tailoring, too. ⊠ *G/F, 47K Staunton St., SoHo, Central* ☎ *2108–4068* ⊕ *www.raneek.com* Ⓜ *Central* ⊠ *G/F, 62K Leighton Rd., Causeway Bay* Ⓜ *Causeway Bay.*

Sabina Swims. A few minutes' walk from Central, Sabina Swims is in a quaint old building, formerly an art gallery. One of the pioneers in the now burgeoning Noho area, Hong Kong girl Sabina Wong Sutc first opened the boutique as a showroom for her pretty bikinis. Other unique swimwear, accessories, and resort wear brands have since chosen the airy yet discreet space to show their wares. The Sabina Swims collection is cleverly sold as separates because the designer knows that women aren't always the same size on top and on the bottom. There are also matching swimsuits for mother and daughter outings and reversible sun hats in the same materials. ⊠ *1/F, 99F Wellington St., Noho, Central* ☎ *2115–9975* ⊕ *www.sabinaswims.com.*

FodorśChoice   **Shanghai Tang.** In addition to the brilliantly hued—and expensive—dis-
★   plays of silk and cashmere clothing, you'll find custom-made suits starting at around HK$5,000, including fabric from a large selection of Chinese silks. You can also have a *cheongsam* (a sexy slit-skirt silk dress with a Mandarin collar) made for HK$2,500–HK$3,500, including fabric (⇨ *also,* Tailoring, *below*). Ready-to-wear Mandarin suits and unisex kimonos are all in the HK$1,500–HK$2,000 range. Among the Chinese souvenirs are novelty watches with mah-jongg tiles or dim sum instead of numbers. There's a second location inside the Peninsula Hong Kong. ⊠ *12 Pedder St., Central* ☎ *2525–7333* ⊕ *www.shanghaitang. com* Ⓜ *Central* ⊠ *Peninsula Hong Kong, Salisbury Rd., Tsim Sha Tsui, Kowloon* Ⓜ *Tsim Sha Tsui.*

Boutique Alert: Hip

FOR YEARS, fashion cognoscenti and victims alike have relied on **D-mop** (⊕ www.d-mop.com for info and locations) to bring out new generation talent, whatever the cost. **Ztampz** (⊕ www.ztampz.com for info and locations) mixes cartoonish and avant-garde fashion from all over, including up-and-coming designers from Thailand and Japan. Limited edition T-shirts printed with slick simians are what cult Japanese brand **A Bathing Ape** (⊕ www.bape.com for info and locations) built their empire on. True devotees call it "Bape." **Sistyr Moon** (⊠ Festival Walk, 80 Tat Chee Ave., Kowloon Tong, Kowloon Ⓜ Kowloon Tong) shops, including Soul Sistyr and Hysteric Glamour, offer a distinct blend of cute, sexy, rock-chick fashion from Brazil to Australia. When their cool customers become mothers, they can dress the kids at Hysteric Mini.

Siberian Fur Store Ltd. In general, furs sold by reputable Hong Kong deal-ers are the ideal combination of superior quality and low prices. This shop, owned and operated by a prominent local family, is famous for its high quality furs and special attention to design. ⊠ *G/F, 29 Des Voeux Rd. Central, Central* ☎ *2522–1380* Ⓜ *Central* ⊠ *G/F, 21 Chatham Rd. S, Tsim Sha Tsui, Kowloon* Ⓜ *Tsim Sha Tsui.*

★ **Sin Sin Atelier.** Sin Sin represents the best of Hong Kong design. Her con-ceptual, minimalist clothes, jewelry, and accessories retain a Hong Kong character, while drawing from other influences—especially Japan. Yet the pieces are ultimately a unique expression of her ebullient spirit. A regular performer in Hong Kong community theater, Sin Sin prefers to introduce her collections via unusual presentations such as modern dance performances rather than catwalk shows. She also has an art space directly across the road and a fine art gallery up the hill in SoHo. ⊠ *G/F, 52 Sai St., off Hollywood Rd. at Cat St. end, Western* ☎ *2521–0308* ⊕ *www.sinsin.com.hk.*

Sonjia by Sonjia Norman. Walk past a local garage and snoozing dogs in this old-style Hong Kong area to find the low-key atelier of Korean-Eng-lish ex-lawyer Sonjia Norman. The designer, known for her active wear brand, Chibi, has quietly crafted luxurious, one-of-a-kind pieces and mod-ified vintage clothing for years under the Sonjia label. Her clothes are the epitome of understated stealth wealth. ⊠ *G/F, 2 Sun St., Wan Chai* ☎ *2529–6223* ⊕ *www.sonjiaonline.com* Ⓜ *Wan Chai.*

Spy Henry Lau. Local bad boy Henry Lau brings an edgy attitude to his fashion for men and women. Bold and often dark, his clothing and ac-cessories lines are not for the fainthearted. ⊠ *1/F, Cleveland Mansion, 5 Cleveland St., Causeway Bay* ☎ *2317–6928 customer service* ⊕ *www. spyhenrylau.com* Ⓜ *Causeway Bay* ⊠ *Shop C, G/F, 11 Sharp St., Causeway Bay* Ⓜ *Causeway Bay.*

Vivienne Tam. You know when you walk into a Vivienne Tam boutique—the strong Chinese motif prints and modern updates of traditional women's clothing are truly distinct. Don't let the bold ready-to-wear col-lections distract you from the very pretty accessories, which include footwear with Asian embellishments such as jade. Tam is one of the best-known Hong Kong designers and, even though she's now based outside the SAR, the city still claims her as their own. ⊠ *Pacific Place, 88 Queensway, Admiralty* ☎ *2918–0238* ⊕ *www.viviennetam.com* Ⓜ *Admiralty* ⊠ *Harbour City, Canton Rd., Tsim Sha Tsui, Kowloon* Ⓜ *Tsim Sha Tsui* ⊠ *IFC Mall, 8 Finance St., Central* Ⓜ *Central.*

HONG KONG CASUAL

Blue Star. The unbelievably cheap basics in this shop—part of the Giordano family of stores—deliver on the simple motto: "Variety, Efficiency, Economy." Pick up plain, unbranded T-shirts, shorts, and other casual wear. Fashionistas may turn their noses up at the straightforward designs, but Blue Star jeans fit remarkably well for as little as HK$116. ⊠ *G/F, Li Dong Bldg., 7–11 Li Yuen St. E, Central* ☎ *2921–2481, 2786–8295 customer service and branch information* Ⓜ *Central* ⊠ *G/F, Circle Apartment, 13–15 Tai Yuen St., Wan Chai* Ⓜ *Wan Chai* ⊠ *G/F, Golden Crown Court, 66 Nathan Rd., Tsim Sha Tsui, Kowloon* Ⓜ *Tsim Sha Tsui.*

Bossini. A Giordano competitor, Bossini takes a very similar approach to casual clothing, with collections for women, men, and children. Its brand philosophy, "Color Our World," is an indication of the variety on offer. ⊠ *G/F and 1/F, Victoria Heights Bldg., 192–194 Nathan Rd., Tsim Sha Tsui, Kowloon* ☎ *2377—4322* ⊕ *www.bossini.com* Ⓜ *Tsim Sha Tsui* ⊠ *G/F, On Lok Yuen Bldg., 27A Des Voeux Rd., Central* Ⓜ *Central* ⊠ *Times Square, 1 Matheson St., Causeway Bay* Ⓜ *Causeway Bay.*

Crocodile. If this quality weekend wear seems similar to a European label with a similar logo, that's because it is. Nevertheless, the collections for men, women, and children are well made and worth a look. ⊠ *G/F, 50 Connaught Rd., Central* ☎ *2541–5743* ⊕ *www.crocodile.com.hk* Ⓜ *Central* ⊠ *G/F, 527–529 Lockhart Rd., Causeway Bay* Ⓜ *Causeway Bay.*

Giordano. Hong Kong's version of the Gap is the most established and ubiquitous local source of basic T-shirts, jeans, and casual wear. Like its U.S. counterpart, the brand now has a bit more fashion sense and slick ad campaigns, but still offers reasonable prices. A few of its hundreds of stores are listed here, but you'll have no problem finding one on almost every major street. Customer service is generally good, even if the young, energetic staff screeches "hello" then "bye-bye" at every customer in a particularly jarring way. Through the Web site, you can even order custom-made jeans. Diffusion lines include the more sophisticated Giordano Ladies and the even cheaper Blue Star. ⊠ *G/F, Capitol Centre, 5–19 Jardine's Crescent, Causeway Bay* ☎ *2923–7111* ⊕ *www.giordano.com.hk* Ⓜ *Causeway Bay* ⊠ *G/F and M/F, On Lok Yuen Bldg., 27 Des Voeux Rd., Central* Ⓜ *Central* ⊠ *G/F and 1/F., 65–69 Peking Rd., Tsim Sha Tsui, Kowloon* Ⓜ *Tsim Sha Tsui.*

Giordano Ladies. If Giordano is the Gap, Giordano Ladies is the Banana Republic, albeit with a more Zen approach. It's clean-line modern classics in neutral black, gray, white, and beige; each collection is brightened by a single highlight color, red one season, blue the next, and so on. Everything is elegant enough for the office and comfortable enough for the plane. ⊠ *1/F, Capitol Centre, 5–19 Jardine's Cresecent Cause-*

Boutique Alert: Jeans

A CROP OF fun boutiques, many with multiple locations, capitalizes on the world's fascination with high-end denim and contemporary clothing. **Bauhaus** (⊕ www.bauhaus.com.hk for info and locations) sheds light on local youth fashion with an especially strong selection of jeans from around the world. **Indigo** (⊕ www. indigohongkong.com for info and locations) was one of the first to introduce a denim bar, "Jeanuine Experts," to help you find the best fit. They have a good range of sizes, too. Hong Kong's younger generations create their looks with contemporary casual and denim pieces from the immensely popular **I.T** (⊕ www.ithk. com for info and locations) shops, which include I.T, i.t, izzue, b+ab, and double-park.

4

way Bay ☎ *2923–7118* ⊕ *www.giordanoladies.com* Ⓜ *Causeway Bay* ✉ *Man Yee Bldg., 60–68 Des Voeux Rd., Central* Ⓜ *Central* ✉ *1/F, Manson House, 74–78 Nathan Rd., Tsim Sha Tsui, Kowloon* Ⓜ *Tsim Sha Tsui.*

F.C.K (Fashion Community Kitterick). One of the trendiest local chains sells several brands including: Kitterick, Z by Kitterick, Red's, K-2, a.y.k, and the Lab. These are clothes that Hong Kong's brand-conscious youth is happy to wear. ✉ *1/F, Fashion Island, 11 Great George St., Causeway Bay* ☎ *2881–0276* ⊕ *www.kitterick.com.hk* Ⓜ *Causeway Bay.*

Crafts & Curios

China's traditional crafts include lanterns, temple rubbings, screen paintings, paper cuttings (still sold in most stationery shops), bamboo-stemmed brushes and calligraphy accoutrements, and engravings on stone. Although finding them all in one place seems like cheating, Chinese department stores make it easy with entire departments dedicated to Chinese crafts.

Upper Lascar Row, better known as Cat Street, comes at the western end of Hollywood Road, just below Man Mo Temple. Colorful stalls outside small antiques shops sell reproduction ceramics, giant paintbrushes, Communist little red books, and various other old (or old-looking) curios.

Custom-made chops or carved Chinese seals have been ordered on Ma Wa Lane in Sheung Wan since the 1920s. The experts here will give you a Chinese name (be warned, they sometimes have fun with this), and carve it onto your choice of soapstone, ivory, stone, jade, etc., in as little as one hour, giving you time to wander past this interesting area's herbal, snake, and birds' nest shops. These stalls will also print name cards with a bit more lead time (one to seven days).

Amazing Grace. A bazaarlike clutter of handicrafts from around Asia surround you in this store, which first opened in the '70s. Take these Vietnamese silk lanterns, Balinese sarongs, Asian-theme Christmas ornaments, and mirrored Indian accessories out of the muddled context, and they look quite impressive. ⊠ *Star House, 3 Salisbury Rd., Tsim Sha Tsui, Kowloon* ☎ *2730–5455* ⊕ *www.amazinggracehk.com* Ⓜ *Tsim Sha Tsui.*

Good Laque. These elegant lacquerwares make wonderful gifts. The reasonably priced decorative home accessories, tabletop items, and photo albums come in classic red, black, and metallic colors as well as silver or gold. ⊠ *G/F, Stanley Market, 40–42D Stanley Main St., Southside Stanley* ☎ *3106–0163* ⊕ *www.goodlaque.com* ⊠ *16/F Horizon Plaza, 2 Lee Wing St., Southside, Ap Lei Chau.*

★ **Mountain Folkcraft.** A little old-fashioned bell chimes as you open the door to this fantastic old shop filled with handicrafts and antiques from around China. Amid the old treasures, carved woodwork, rugs, and curios, are stunning folk-print fabrics. To reach the store from Queen's Road Central, walk up D'Aguilar Street toward Lan Kwai Fong, then turn right onto Wo On Lane. ⊠ *12 Wo On La., Central* ☎ *2525–3199* Ⓜ *Central.*

The Pottery Workshop. The small gallery in the entrance of this workshop—which holds pottery classes and shows—sells works by local artists, many of whom are also instructors here. Enter on Wyndham Street or through a door inside the Fringe Club. ⊠ *G/F, 2 Lower Albert Rd., Central* ☎ *2525–7949* ⊕ *http://ceramics.com.hk* Ⓜ *Central.*

Sang Woo Loong. At more than 90 years old, Mr. Leung Yau Kam is Hong Kong's oldest lantern maker who has refused to move his workshop across the border like all the others. These intricate, handmade works in paper take fantastical forms such as bright orange goldfish. Their role has changed over his long career from functional to purely decorative, but lanterns are still important in Chinese society. This is especially true during the Mid-Autumn Festival, when children carry their special lanterns outdoors to view the full moon. Ask for one that can pack flat. ⊠ *G/F, 28 Western St., Sai Ying Pun, Western* ☎ *2540–1369.*

Gizmos, Gadgets & Accessories

Variety and novelty—not prices—are the reasons to buy electronic goods and accessories in Hong Kong these days. Products are often launched in this keen, active electronics market before they are in the United States and Europe. The street sweepers may wear old-fashioned rattan Hakka hats, but even they carry cutting-edge, almost impossibly tiny phones. Indeed, cell phones are status symbols—often they're changed seasonally, like fashion accessories.

Broadway. Like its more famous competitor, Fortress, Broadway is a large electronic goods chain. It caters primarily to the local market, so some staff members speak better English than others. Look for familar name brand cameras, computers, sound systems, home appliances, and mobile phones. Just a few of the many shops are listed here. ⊠ *Times Square, 1 Matheson St., Causeway Bay* ☎ *2506–0228* ⊕ *www. ibroadway.com.hk* Ⓜ *Causeway*

WORD OF MOUTH

"If you want [cheap] electronics and are from the United States, shop at home; there are no bargains here." –bkkmei

Boutique Alert: Earthy

Sanskrit (⊕ www.sanskrit.com.hk for info and locations) reflects generations of South Asian influences in Hong Kong, and sells the biggest names in Indian fashion with beautiful, beaded pieces.

Xtreme Green (⊕ www.xtremegreen. com.hk for info and locations) was started by an environmentally concerned group in Hong Kong. They sell top organic and fair trade clothing brands so you can feel virtuous without looking like you've walked off a commune.

4

Bay ✉ *Ocean Centre, Harbour City, Canton Rd., Tsim Sha Tsui, Kowloon* Ⓜ *Tsim Sha Tsui* ✉ *G/F, 48–50 Sai Yeung Choi St. S, Mong Kok, Kowloon* Ⓜ *Mong Kok.*

★ **Fortress.** Part of billionaire Li Ka-shing's empire, the extensive chain of shops sells electronics with warranties—a safety precaution that draws the crowds. It also has good deals on printers and accessories, although selection varies by shop. You can spot a Fortress by looking for the big orange sign. For the full list of shops, visit the Web site. ✉ *Times Square, 1 Matheson St., Causeway Bay* ☎ *2506–0031* ⊕ *www.fortress. com.hk* Ⓜ *Causeway Bay* ✉ *Ocean Centre, Harbour City, Canton Rd., Tsim Sha Tsui, Kowloon* Ⓜ *Tsim Sha Tsui* ✉ *Chung Kiu Commercial Bldg., 47–51 Shan Tung St., Sai Yeung Choi St., Mong Kok, Kowloon* Ⓜ *Mong Kok* ✉ *Lower G/F, Melbourne Plaza, 33 Queen's Rd. Central, Central* Ⓜ *Central.*

CAMERAS

Many of Hong Kong's thousands of camera shops are clustered in the back streets around Nathan Road in Tsim Sha Tsui, and around Stanley Street in Central. (Just remember to follow the guidelines in the "Shop Smart" box, particularly in Tsim Sha Tsui.) There are also secondhand sellers in the market on Ap Liu Street (take the MTR to Sham Shui Po, and exit at Ap Liu Street) and the warren of little shops in Champagne Court (16 Kimberley Road, Tsim Sha Tsui). True aficionados will be able to sort the vintage Hasselblads from the junk.

Delon Photo & Hi-Fi Centre. Longtime residents ask for popular salesman Elmen Sit when they come to Delon. He'll take you through the range carried here. Sit also demystifies various bits of equipment for novices—he'll even tell you what you *don't* need. Prices are good, but not amazingly cheap. ✉ *Ocean Centre, Harbour City, Canton Rd., Tsim Sha Tsui, Kowloon* ☎ *2730–0214* Ⓜ *Tsim Sha Tsui.*

Photo Scientific Appliances. This is where local photographers come for their equipment. Expect good prices on both new and used cameras, lenses, video cameras, and accessories. While you're here, pump the regular customers for insider tips. ✉ *G/F, 6 Stanley St., Central* ☎ *2522–1903* Ⓜ *Central.*

Shop Smart

DO SOME RESEARCH beforehand and know what you want. Then ask lots of questions and compare prices before making a purchase. Stick to shops listed in the HKTB's free *Guide to Quality Shop*. Featured shops usually have the QTS logo on their door or window. Here are a few other considerations:

■ **Be aware of regional differences.** Although technology is moving toward multisystem capabilities, it's not quite there yet. DVDs and players might work in only a specific region. Some recording equipment still works on systems, such as NTSC (United States), PAL (Hong Kong, Australia, Great Britain, most of continental Europe), SECAM (France, Russia). Whenever possible, ask for "region-free." Also, although most electronics now automatically convert between 110 and 220 volts, it's best to ask before you buy.

■ **Check the paperwork.** Reputable dealers should give you a one-year *worldwide* guarantee; however, not all guarantees and warranties cross borders. Make sure you'll have the customer service and assistance you require when you take it back home. Some of the cheapest electronics in Hong Kong are parallel imports, which rarely have international warranties. Also, make sure the instructions are in English.

■ **Never be rushed.** Don't be afraid to walk away, even if a clerk claims an item is the last one in stock. This will give you more bargaining power, as will buying several items at once.

■ **Be wary of "great" deals.** A common ploy is to lure customers in with the promise of a great deal, only to "discover" that item is suddenly out of stock. When you're offered a more expensive alternative, walk away.

■ **Test the equipment.** Be sure that the picture or sound quality is truly good. If a shopkeeper cannot oblige a test-run request, ask him or her to direct you to the manufacturer's showroom.

■ **Watch for hidden fees.** Paying by credit card may increase the final bill by 3% to 5%, even though most card companies prohibit the practice.

■ **Don't fall for the old bait and switch.** Before you leave the store, double-check that you've been given the model you selected and that everything it comes with is there, including all parts, accessories, the warranty card, and your invoice.

William's Photo Supply. For those who prefer to shop in air-conditioned comfort, this reliable dealer is discreetly positioned on an upper floor of the elegant Prince's Building. The selection here caters to both amateur and professional photographers. ⊠ *341 Prince's Bldg., 10 Chater Rd., Central* ☎ *2522–8437* Ⓜ *Central.*

CDS, DVDS & VCDS

If you'd like to stock up on Hong Kong and Asian movies, from the Kung Fu classics of the Shaw Brothers to the latest art house works from mainland China, then you've come to the right place. Love Canto-Pop and

Mando-Pop music? It's here in abundance. If you're hoping to find prices slashed, though, you'll be disappointed.

Small stores in Sham Shui Po, Mong Kok, and Causeway Bay seem promising and cheap, but rarely offer prices much lower than the established shops listed below. They're also known to carry poor quality, pirated copies that look and sound like they were captured by a novice with the family video camera.

Be aware of regional designations for DVDs and players. The United States and Canada are Region 1; the United Kingdom is Region 2. Newer players might be region-free or multiregion, but double-check before you buy. VCDs don't have the picture quality or added features of DVDs, but they're usually region-free and significantly cheaper (about HK$15–HK$45). Just be sure the foreign-language movies have subtitles in English.

CD Warehouse. Though not quite warehouse level, prices here are low enough to compete with the cheap outlets around Causeway Bay and Sham Shiu Po, especially for DVDs and VCDs of the latest movies and TV shows. Music CDs also cost less than at major retailers in Hong Kong, but are not cheaper than in the United States. The catalog includes releases from around Asia and abroad. ⊠ *Basement 2, Times Square, 1 Matheson St., Causeway Bay* ☎ *2506–0621* Ⓜ *Causeway Bay* ⊠ *New Town Plaza, Shatin Centre St., New Territories Shatin* Ⓜ *KCR Shatin.*

HMV. This U.K.-based chain has a wide selection of local and international music covering everything from rap to classical and Canto-Pop to Japanese music. A huge selection of DVDs and VCDs are here as well, ranging from U.S. and international movies and television shows to local movies. VCDs are a lot cheaper than DVDs. International magazines are sold here at the best prices in town, but they still cost a lot more than in their countries of origin. For more locations, check the Web site. ⊠ *G/F and 1/F, HK Pacific Centre, 28 Hankow Rd., Tsim Sha Tsui, Kowloon* ☎ *2302–0122* ⊕ *www.hmv.com.hk* Ⓜ *Tsim Sha Tsui* ⊠ *1/ F, Central Bldg., 1–3 Pedder St., Central* Ⓜ *Central.*

Hong Kong Records. Although this company from way back hasn't updated its look in years, you'll find a good selection of current local and international CDs and DVDs. The lower profile also means prices are sometimes lower than in flashier retailers. ⊠ *Pacific Place, 88 Queensway Admiralty* ☎ *2845–7088* Ⓜ *Admiralty* ⊠ *Festival Walk, 80 Tat Chee Ave., Kowloon Tong, Kowloon* Ⓜ *Kowloon Tong.*

COMPUTERS

Several malls specialize in computers and peripherals. Each mall contains hundreds of shops, ranging from small local enterprises to branches of international brands. Legitimate products sit beside blatant fakes, and the individual shops rarely give out retail phone numbers. The real computer bargains are the generic brands from Asia.

Computer games, which are immensely popular here, average HK$195 to HK$230, and the variety is wide due to the selection of Sony Playstation and Dreamcast imports from Japan. Not all games, however, are compatible with U.S. systems.

■ TIP→ Because they couldn't possibly keep the stock in these miniscule spaces, staffers usually have to fetch the product once you've confirmed interest. They'll ask you to pay beforehand, but don't hand over any money until you've inspected the product.

DG Lifestyle Store. An appointed Apple Center, DG carries Macintosh and iPod products. High-design gadgets, accessories, and software by other brands are add-ons that meld with the sleek Apple design philosophy. ✉ *In Square, Windsor House, 311 Gloucester Rd., Causeway Bay* ☎ *2504–4122* ⊕ *www.dg-lifestyle.com* Ⓜ *Causeway Bay* ✉ *IFC Mall, 8 Finance St., Central* Ⓜ *Central* ✉ *New Town Plaza, Shatin Centre St., New Territories Shatin* Ⓜ *KCR Shatin.*

Golden Computer Arcade. It's the most famous—some would say infamous—computer arcade in town. Know what you want before you go to avoid being dazed by the volume of computer equipment and software. ✉ *146–152 Fuk Wa St., Sham Shui Po, Kowloon* ☎ *2729–7399* ⊕ *www.goldencomputerarcade.org.hk/einfo.htm* Ⓜ *Sham Shui Po.*

Mong Kok Computer Centre. This labyrinth of small shops and narrow corridors is somewhat claustrophobic, but it has many good deals on computers and software. Ask for a warranty, and read it carefully. ✉ *8–8A Nelson St., Mong Kok, Kowloon* Ⓜ *Mong Kok.*

Star Computer City. Right next to the Star Ferry and the Harbour City megamall complex, Star Computer City has one whole floor dedicated to computers. The 2C Software Collection offers a variety of software. Look carefully, and you'll find bargains. ✉ *2/F, Star House, Salisbury Rd., Tsim Sha Tsui, Kowloon* ☎ *2730–4382* Ⓜ *Tsim Sha Tsui.*

Wanchai Computer Centre. You'll find honest-to-goodness bargains on computer goods and accessories in the labyrinth of shops here. And you can negotiate prices. Your computer can be put together by a computer technician in less than a day if you're rushed; otherwise, two days is normal. The starting price is HK$3,100 depending on the hardware, processor, and peripherals you choose. This is a great resource, whether you're a techno-buff who's interested in assembling your own computer (a popular pastime with locals), or a technophobe looking for discounted earphones. ✉ *130 Hennessy Rd., Wan Chai* ☎ *No phone* Ⓜ *Wan Chai.*

★ **Windsor House Computer Plaza.** Clean, wide corridors distinguish this less frantic computer arcade from the others. It has three floors of computer products with a wide selection of Mac and PC computer games, video games, laptops, desktops, and accessories. This is a reputable center with competitive prices. ✉ *10/F–12/F, Windsor House, 311 Gloucester Rd., Causeway Bay* ☎ *2895–6796* Ⓜ *Causeway Bay.*

Home Furnishings

ASIAN-LIFESTYLE STORES

We know you're probably bored with "lifestyle" shopping, but before you start yawning, note the world "Asian" before it here. Over the last decade, Hong Kongers have woken up to the joys of home decor, and they're doing it with pieces inspired by and produced in Asia. Enlightened lifestyle retailers range from cheeky to aloof, affordable to exorbitant—but all have a modern Asian approach.

G.O.D. This lifestyle pioneer plays with ideas, designs, and words with wonderfully imaginative yet functional results. The name is a phonetic play on the Cantonese phrase, "to live better." Its huge product range consists mostly of home furnishings and tableware, though there are some fashion items. Affordable creations, such as red rubber trays for making "double happiness" character ice cubes, Buddha statues irreverently painted in DayGlo tones, and old-fashioned Chinese textiles reimagined in modern settings, are both nostalgic and contemporary. ⊠ *G/F and 1/ F, Leighton Centre, 77 Leighton Rd., entrance on Sharp St. E, Causeway Bay* ☎ *2890–5555* ⊕ *www.god.com.hk* Ⓜ *Causeway Bay* ⊠ *G/F and 1/F, 48 Hollywood Rd., Central* Ⓜ *Central* ⊠ *3/F, Hong Kong Hotel, Harbour City, Canton Rd., Tsim Sha Tsui, Kowloon* Ⓜ *Tsim Sha Tsui* ⊠ *Level 6, Langham Place, 8 Argyle St., Mong Kok, Kowloon* Ⓜ *Mong Kok.*

Inside. Inside takes Asian concepts and motifs and transforms them into its own fresh, contemporary home accessories, soft furnishings, table linens, gifts, and select clothing for adults and children. Made from natural materials and fibers, the products come in signature white and sunbleached tones with a few well-placed highlights and discreet flashes of sparkle. There's a nice balance of luxury and casual items, with prices to match. ⊠ *Prince's Bldg., 10 Chater Rd., Central* ☎ *2537–6298* ⊕ *www.inside.com.hk* Ⓜ *Central* ⊠ *The Repulse Bay, 109 Repulse Bay Rd., South Side* ⊠ *Horizon Plaza, 2 Lee Wing St., South Side, Ap Lei Chau.*

Kou. Socialite and interior designer Louise Kou's lifestyle boutique is a moody mix of dark jewel tones and silver on two floors connected by an internal staircase. Different rooms allow her to showcase chinaware, silverware, lamps, linens, fashion accessories, clothes, lingerie, and unique household items. When Kou can't find what she desires somewhere in the world, she simply has it custom-made. ⊠ *22/F, Fung House, 19–20 Connaught Rd., Central* ☎ *2530–2234* ⊕ *www. kouconcept.com* Ⓜ *Central.*

Muji. Anyone who knows this Japanese brand is always delighted to find one of its stores. And Hong Kong has five of them. The full name is Mujirishi Ryohin (meaning, "no brand quality goods"), which only partly describes the sleek, minimalism of everything from household items and stationery to clothing and simply packaged snacks. Think cardboard beige, clean white, and metal. ⊠ *3F, Lee Theatre Plaza, 99 Percival St. Causeway Bay* ☎ *2808–0622* ⊕ *www.muji.com.hk* ⊠ *Level 7, Langham Place, 8 Argyle St., Mong Kok, Kowloon* Ⓜ *Mong Kok* ⊠ *3/F, Miramar Shopping Centre, 132 Nathan Rd., Tsim Sha Tsui, Kowloon* Ⓜ *Tsim Sha Tsui.*

OVO. Push past heavy, giant doors to enter this atmospheric, high-ceiling showroom, which feels like a cross between a museum and a temple. The fusion and contrasts of east and west permeates every surface of the minimalist furniture, home furnishings, and accessories designed by the in-house team. Items are smart and rarely fussy. Beautiful, unvarnished blocks of wood, for example, are proposed as side tables. ⊠ *G/F, 16 Queen's Rd. E, Wan Chai* ☎ *2526–7226* ⊕ *www.ovo.com.hk* Ⓜ *Admiralty.*

CARPETS & RUGS

You might walk in looking for a carpet, but ask the right questions and you're sure to leave with much more. Many of these merchants share the exotic origins of their stock, especially Pakistan, and some have been here for generations. Consummate salespeople, they're happy to run through the history and different types of old and new rugs from Persia, China, India, Pakistan, and elsewhere. Contemporary designs are a newer category with price tags to rival designer versions sold abroad. Overall, though prices have increased since the late 1990s, carpets are still cheaper in Hong Kong than in Europe and the United States. Note: Americans *are* allowed to import Persian rugs into the United States.

Carpet Buyer. With a modern approach to an age-old business, a son of the Oriental Carpet Trading House family sells high-quality carpets from China, India, and Pakistan at warehouse prices. ⊠ *G/F, Horizon Plaza, 2 Lee Wing St., South Side, Ap Lei Chau* ☎ *2850–5508* ⊕ *www. carpetbuyer.com.*

Mir Oriental Carpets. From a family that has been in the business for five generations, Heena Mir and Shaziya Mir offer great service and a range so large only they could help you through it. They sell Persian, Pakistani, Indian, Afghan, and Russian carpets. The private collection of Persian and Caucasian carpets is on view by appointment only. ⊠ *G/F, 52 Wyndham St., Central* ☎ *2521–5641* ⊕ *www.mirorientalcarpets.com* Ⓜ *Central.*

Oriental Carpet Trading House Ltd. Rizwan Butt keeps extra chairs for customers and friends who stop by to chat about his wide array of rugs and carpets from Iran, Afghanistan, and Russia, among others. With the kind of expertise only gained by growing up in the family business, he's often invited to give lectures on the subject. ⊠ *G/F, 74 Hollywood Rd., Central* ☎ *2523–9502* ⊕ *www.orientalcarpethk.com* Ⓜ *Central.*

Tai Ping Carpets. Headquartered in Hong Kong, Tai Ping is highly regarded for its custom-made rugs and wall-to-wall carpets. They take 2½ to 3 months to make specially ordered carpets; you can specify color, thickness, and even the direction of the weave. Tai Ping's occasional sales are well worth attending; check the classified section of the *South China Morning Post* for dates. ⊠ *Prince's Bldg, 10 Chater Rd., Central* ☎ *2522–7138* ⊕ *www.taipingcarpets.com* Ⓜ *Central.*

Tribal Rugs Ltd. An incongruous sight in an average-looking mall, this shop consists of floor-to-ceiling piles of jewel-tone Afghan, Iranian, Central Asian, and Turkmen rugs; kilims; contemporary Pakistani carpets; and classic Persians. Ask the knowledgable staff for assistance. ⊠ *2/F, Admiralty Centre, 18 Harcourt Rd., Admiralty* ☎ *2529–0576* Ⓜ *Wan Chai.*

CERAMICS

Before you try to board the plane with the new 24-person dinner set or massive planter that you bought for a song, consider all your options. You'll begin to recognize classic Chinese colors and motifs such as blue and white, famille rose, dragons, goldfish, flowers, and even bats—a lucky symbol in the culture. Be sure to ask if any intended tableware is microwave-safe and can be put in the dishwasher, and find out if staffers can arrange shipping for you.

For a full selection of ceramic Chinese tableware, visit the various Chinese department stores, which also have bargains on attractively designed

That's a Wrap

WANDER INTO the pretty Edwardian-style Western Market in Sheung Wan, and you'll find the entire second floor bursting with pure silk shantung, cotton-pique shirting, French lace, silk brocade, velvet, damask, and printed crepe de chine—just some of the exquisite, reasonably priced fabrics available in Hong Kong. Although professional sourcing agents spend most of their time in Sham Shui Po on Kowloon side, Western Market's vast selection is more than adequate. Thai silk costs a bit more here than in Bangkok but is still much cheaper than in the United States or Europe.

Chinese Arts & Crafts and Yue Hwa Chinese Products Emporium have great selections of Chinese brocades and other fabrics. Look also for Chinese hand-embroidered and -appliquéd linen and cotton in Stanley Market. ■ TIP➔ When buying a hand-embroidered item, check that the edges are properly overcast; if not it's probably machine made. You'll be looking for reasons to buy lots of the the blue-and-white, patterned Chinese country fabrics at Mountain Folkcraft. Just check that you can bring your bolts on the plane; shipping may cancel out any discount.

The **Textile Society of Hong Kong** (⊕ www.textilesocietyofhk.org) hosts talks, expeditions, and events to explore all aspects of traditional and contemporary textiles. It counts as its members design professionals, museum curators, collectors, historians, textile conservators, dealers, and craftspeople. Textile Society member Edith Cheung's atelier, **Cloth Haven** (⊠ G/F, 7 Upper Station St., Central ☎ 2546–0378), hosts weaving classes on looms right on the shop floor—amid a mix of textiles, vintage clothing, and design inspirations.

vases, bowls, and table lamps. Inexpensive buys can also be had in the streets of Tsim Sha Tsui, the shopping centers of Tsim Sha Tsui East and Harbour City, the side streets of Western, and the shops along Queen's Road East in Wan Chai.

Lee Fung China Ware Co., Ltd. Friendly service and a decent selection of Chinese and Western-style dinnerware makes this a good one-stop shop, uniquely situated just off the Midlevels Escalator. It also carries vases and antique reproductions. ⊠ G/F, 18 Shelley St., SoHo, Central ☎ 2524–0630 ⊕ www.leefungchina.biz.com.hk.

Overjoy Porcelain. The showroom itself is nothing to write home about, but the service is good and so are the prices on dinnerware, vases, lamp bases, and the like, in traditional patterns. Take the MTR to the Kwai Hing station in the New Territories, then grab a taxi. Or visit the smaller Wan Chai shop. ⊠ 1/F, Block B, Kwai Hing Industrial Bldg., 10–18 Chun Pin St., New Territories, Kwai Chung ☎ 2487–0615 Ⓜ Kwai Hing ⊠ 1/F, Fleet Arcade, Fenwick Pier, 1 Lung King St., Wan Chai Ⓜ Admiralty.

Wah Tung Ceramic Arts. It's a slightly slick but reliable manufacturer and retailer of predominantly handcrafted ceramics that has been in operation since the early days of trade with the West (1863). The overwhelmingly large product line includes antique replicas, vases, dinnerware, figurines, and more—all in classic Chinese motifs. ⊠ *G/F, 59 Hollywood Rd., Central* ☏ *2543–2823* ⊕ *www.wahtungchina.com* Ⓜ *Central* ✉ *14–17/F Grand Marine Ind. Bldg., 3 Yue Fung St., Southside, Aberdeen.*

Jewelry

Visitors from all walks of life come to Hong Kong, and the one thing they all want to buy is jewelry. It is, in fact, the most popular item with foreign shoppers, as evidenced by entire tour buses you'll see idling outside large jewelry chains. Jewelry is not subject to any local tax or duty, which helps keep prices down. Settings for diamonds and other gems also cost less here than in most western cities, though quality engraving services are hard to find. Hong Kong is known as a center for jade jewelry, and has become a trading and distribution center for pearls, too, thanks in part to growth in the Chinese and South Sea pearl industry and the decline of Tahitian pearls. Turnover is fast, competition is fierce, and the selection is fantastic.

∎ TIP→ Some countries charge a great deal more for imported set jewelry than for unset gems, so do check your country's customs regulations to avoid a nasty surprise.

The city is also a leading pure-gold item producer. Hong Kong law requires all jewelers to indicate both the number of carats and the identity of the shop or manufacturer on every gold item displayed or proffered for sale. Make sure these marks are present and that you receive an invoice listing specifics, such as the weight and price of each item. Also, check current gold prices, which many stores display, against the price of the gold item you're thinking of buying.

Main areas for gold jewelry include Yee Wo Street and Hennessy Road (take the MTR to Causeway Bay and use Exit D2) and Nathan Road from Mong Kok to Tsim Sha Tsui (take the MTR to Mong Kok, Yau Ma Tei, Jordan, Tsim Sha Tsui stations). For factory outlets, see the HKTB's *Factory Outlets for Locally Made Fashion and Jewellery.* Consult the **Hong Kong Jewellers' & Goldsmiths' Association** (☏2543–9633 ⊕www.jewelrynet.com/hkjga) for information on the gold jewelry scene.

Brigetta Jewelry. Designer Bridget King makes fresh, contemporary pieces using semiprecious stones, Swarovski crystals, gold vermeil, and sterling silver. She has a keen sense of color and shows considerable restraint, so her pieces tend to look as good with jeans as they do with cocktail dresses. Her shop is open by appointment only. ⊠ *Admiralty Center Tower 1, 18 Harcourt Rd., Admiralty* ☏ *9155–3546* ⊕ *www.brigettajewelry.com.*

Chocolate Rain. The collections—dreamed up by a Hong Kong fine arts graduate—consist of pieces handcrafted of recycled materials, jade, crystals, precious stones, and mother of pearl. The showroom also displays works by the designer's friends, and it doubles as a classroom for jewelry-making courses. ⊠ *G/F, 63 Peel St., SoHo, Central* ☏ *2975–8318* ⊕ *www.chocolaterain.com* Ⓜ *Central.*

Kai-Yin Lo. Kai-Yin Lo is famous for her Asian-inspired jewelry, combining contemporary style with ancient Chinese designs and materials such as jade. When Cartier saw her work in the 1980s, it bought an entire collection. The *International Herald Tribune* has credited her with bridging the gap between fine and fashion jewelry. Lo has since shifted focus to act as a consultant, lecturer, and writer on heritage, art, culture, and philanthropy, but private sales of her jewelry continue by appointment. ☎ 2773–6009 ⊕ *www.kaiyinlo-design.com.*

Jan Logan. This Australian designer has celebrities wearing her youthful yet elegant designs. Pieces contrast cultured, South Sea, and Tahitian pearls with onyx, diamonds, quartz, and other stones. ⊠ *IFC Mall, 8 Finance St., Central* ☎ 2918–4212 ⊕ *www.janlogan.com* Ⓜ *Central.*

Madeleine Thompson. Hong Kong–raised Maddy Thompson is young, talented, amiable, and has the kind of jet-set life that you read about—you know, weekend jaunts to Bangkok, for example, led by fellow partyer Kate Moss, who wears Thompson's jewelry on the streets of London. Thompson uses jade, rose quartz, onyx, and mother of pearl in pieces with Buddhist symbols and other Asian motifs. Look for her works at Lane Crawford in the IFC mall or make an appointment to see them. ☎ 9629–7882 ⊕ *www.madeleine-thompson.com.*

Qeelin. With ancient Chinese culture for inspiration and *In The Mood for Love* actress Maggie Cheung as the muse, something extraordinary was bound to come from Qeelin. Its name was cleverly derived from the Chinese characters for male ("qi") and female ("lin"), and symbolizes harmony, balance, and peace. The restrained beauty and meaningful creations of designer Dennis Chan are exemplified in two main collections: Wulu, a minimalist form representing the mythical gourd as well as the lucky Number 8; and Tien Di, literally "Heaven and Earth," symbolizing everlasting love. Classic gold, platinum, and diamonds mix with colored jades, black diamonds, and unusual materials for a truly unique effect. A sweeter addendum to the collection was added recently in the form of Bo Bo, the panda bear. ⊠ *IFC Mall, 8 Finance St., Central* ☎ 2389–8863 ⊕ *www.qeelin.com* Ⓜ *Central* ⊠ *Peninsula Shopping Arcade, Salisbury Rd., Tsim Sha Tsui, Kowloon* Ⓜ *Tsim Sha Tsui.*

Saturn Essentials. If you're looking for a local artisan, a reasonably priced piece of silver, semiprecious stones, and sometimes even gold jewelry—or you just want a chat with a nice lady—visit Maureen "Mo" Gerrard. Her shop is opposite the wonderful salon of her son, Paul Gerrard (⇨ Spas, *above*). ⊠ *G/F, 36 Pottinger St., Central* ☎ 2537–9335 Ⓜ *Central.*

Tayma Fine Jewellery. Unusual colored "connoisseur" gemstones are set by hand in custom designs by Hong Kong–based jeweler Tayma Page Allies. The collection is designed to bring out the personality of the individual wearer, and includes oversize cocktail rings, distinctive bracelets, pretty earrings, and more. ⊠ *Prince's Bldg., 10 Chater Rd., Central* ☎ 2525–5280 ⊕ *www.taymajewellery.com* Ⓜ *Central.*

WHY PAY RETAIL?

As Central becomes Sheung Wan, a little lane called Wing Kut Street (between Queen's Road Central and Des Voeux Road) is home to costume jewelry showrooms and wholesalers, many of whom accept retail customers and offer bargain-basement prices.

Tina Barrat. This locally based French designer's work has a couture sensibility tempered by playfulness. The recent collection features vintage-look pearl bracelets and necklaces accented by lace and shell flowers. Look for Tina's work at F, a boutique of predominantly Brazilian fashion labels. ✉ *5/F, Hollywood Commercial House, 3 Old Bailey St., Central* ☎ *3102–2060* Ⓜ *Central.*

★ **Sin Sin Atelier.** Everything Sin Sin does is dynamic, exciting, and unique. Her shop is at the far end of Hollywood Road, near the Cat Street Bazaar, where you can glimpse old Hong Kong. Displayed beside clothing inspired by innovative Japanese fashion, is her silver jewelry done in bold, beautiful geometric designs—what she calls "artsy yet wearable." The multitalented Sin Sin also performs Cantonese Opera in venues such as City Hall. ✉ *G/F, 52–53 Sai St., Central* ☎ *2521–0308* ⊕ *www.sinsin. com.hk.*

DIAMONDS

Hong Kong is one of the world's largest diamond-trading centers, and prices are often at least 10% lower than world-market levels. For information or advice contact the **Diamond Federation of Hong Kong, China Ltd.** (☎ 2524–5081 ⊕ www.diamondfederationhk.com).

◼ TIP➔ When buying diamonds, remember the four "C's: color, clarity, carat (size), and cut. Shop only in reputable outlets—those recommended by a local or listed in the HKTB's shopping guide.

King Fook Jewellery. When considering jewelry stores, longevity is a good thing. King Fook has been around since 1949, promising stringent quality control, quality craftsmanship, and professional service. ✉ *G/F, Hong Kong Mansion, 1 Yee Wo St., Causeway Bay* ☎ *2576–1032* ⊕ *www.kingfook.com* Ⓜ *Causeway Bay* ✉ *G/F, 30–32 Des Voeux Rd. Central, Central* Ⓜ *Central* ✉ *G/F, Hotel Miramar Shopping Arcade, 118–130 Nathan Rd., Tsim Sha Tsui Kowloon* Ⓜ *Tsim Sha Tsui.*

Larry Jewellery. This is a long-established source for handcrafted jewelry made from high-grade precious stones. Catering to local tastes since 1967, the traditional company has a new push to attract younger customers. That said, there really is a wide enough range to please most tastes. ✉ *G/F, 72 Queens Rd. Central, Central* ☎ *2521–1268* ⊕ *www. larryjewelry.com* Ⓜ *Central* ✉ *The Landmark, Pedder St. and Des Voeux Rd., Central* Ⓜ *Central* ✉ *Pacific Place, 88 Queensway, Admiralty* Ⓜ *Admiralty* ✉ *G/F, 33 Nathan Rd., Tsim Sha Tsui, Kowloon* Ⓜ *Tsim Sha Tsui.*

Ronald Abram Jewellers. Looking at the rocks in these windows can feel like a visit to a natural history museum. Large white-and-rare-color diamonds sourced from all over the world are a specialty here, but the shop also deals in emeralds, sapphires, and rubies. With years of expertise, Abrams dispenses advice on both the aesthetic merits and the investment potential of each stone or piece of jewelry. ✉ *Mezzanine, Mandarin Oriental, 5 Connaught Rd., Central* ☎ *2810–7677* ⊕ *www. ronaldabram.com* Ⓜ *Central.*

TSL Jewellery. One of the big Hong Kong chains, TSL (Tse Sui Luen) specializes in diamond jewelry and manufactures, retails, and exports its designs. Its range of 100-facet stones includes the Estrella cut, which reflects nine symmetrical hearts and comes with international certification. Although its contemporary designs use platinum settings, TSL also sells pure, bright yellow gold items targeted at Chinese customers. ⊠ *G9–10, Park Lane Shopper's Blvd., Nathan Rd., Tsim Sha Tsui, Kowloon* ☎ *2332–4618* ⊕ *www.tsljewellery.com* Ⓜ *Tsim Sha Tsui* ⊠ *G/F, 35 Queen's Rd. Central, Central* Ⓜ *Central* ⊠ *G/F, 1 Yee Woo St., Causeway Bay* Ⓜ *Causeway Bay.*

Carat. Forget the cheesy cubic zirconium of the past. One look at its stark white showrooms, and you'll see that Carat has mastered the creation and presentation of synthetic gemstones. Hand-assembled in precious-metal settings, the large collection spans various eras of jewelry styles. The second line, Carat Emporium, is inspired by exotic cultures and made with colorful semiprecious stones. ⊠ *G/F, 23 D'Aguilar St., Central* ☎ *2526–9688* ⊕ *www.carat.cc* Ⓜ *Central* ⊠ *IFC Mall, 8 Finance St., Central* Ⓜ *Central.*

JADE

The days of romantic, ocean-crossing quests for treasure may seem long gone (especially when your local store stocks items from Bangkok to Bologna). Yet jade, a wonderful Hong Kong buy, has retained its exoticism. It comes not only in green but also in shades of purple, orange, yellow, brown, white, and violet.

Buying jade is tricky and best done with an expert or trusted merchant. Translucency and evenness of color and texture determine jade's value. Top-quality jade is pure green and very expensive. Yellow-tinged pieces are acceptable, but those with brown or gray are not.

Although you'll see trinkets and figurines purportedly of jade throughout Hong Kong, most are of jadeite jade from Burma. Nephrite jade, not as vibrant or valuable, is also sold. The best jadeite is semitransparent; opaque jadeite with cloudy patches has less value. Be careful not to pay jade prices for green stones such as aventurine, bowenite, soapstone, or serpentine, which can be bleached and impregnated with polymers or dyed to look like rare jade. Many of the pieces for sale at the Kansu Street Jade Market are made of these impostors. That said, there are wonderful finds in the endless sea of stalls brimming with trinkets of every size, shape, and color.

Chinese Arts & Crafts. In direct contrast to the thrill of digging through dusty piles at the open-air Jade Market, the trustworthy Chinese Arts & Crafts department stores provide a clean, air-conditioned environment in which to shop for classic jade jewelry—and the prices reflect that but aren't too outrageous. ⊠ *G/F, Star House, 3 Salisbury Rd., Tsim Sha Tsui, Kowloon* ☎ *2735–4061* ⊕ *www.chineseartsandcrafts.com.hk* Ⓜ *Tsim Sha Tsui.*

> **IT'S GOOD TO BE JADED**
>
> The Chinese believe that jade brings luck, and it's still worn as a charm in amulets or bracelets. A jade bangle is often presented to newborns, and homes are often adorned with jade statues or other carved decorative items.

Chow Sang Sang. Chow Sang Sang has more than 100 shops in greater China. In addition to its contemporary gold, diamond, jade, and wedding collections for the local market, the manufacturer and retailer also sources international brands. ✉ *Silvercord, 30 Canton Rd., Tsim Sha Tsui, Kowloon* ☎ *2735–4622, 2192–3123 customer service and branch information* ⊕ *www.chowsangsang.com* Ⓜ *Tsim Sha Tsui* ✉ *G/F, 74 Queen's Rd. Central, Central* Ⓜ *Central* ✉ *G/F, 525 Hennessy Rd., Causeway Bay* Ⓜ *Causeway Bay.*

Chow Tai Fook. Jade is not the only thing you'll see from this local chain founded in 1929. It also has fine jewelry in diamond, jadeite, ruby, sapphire, emerald, pearl, 18K gold, and more traditional pure gold. ✉ *G/ F, AON China Bldg., 29 Queen's Rd. Central, Central* ☎ *2523–7128, 2526–8649 customer service and branch information* ⊕ *www. chowtaifook.com* Ⓜ *Central* ✉ *Ocean Terminal, Harbour City, Canton Rd., Tsim Sha Tsui, Kowloon* Ⓜ *Tsim Sha Tsui* ✉ *G/F, Chow Tai Fook Centre, 580A Nathan Rd., Mong Kok, Kowloon* Ⓜ *Mong Kok.*

Edward Chiu. Everything about Edward Chiu is *fabulous,* from the flamboyant way he dresses to his high-end jade jewelry. The minimalist, geometric pieces use the entire jade spectrum, from deep greens to surprising lavenders. He's also famous for contrasting black-and-white jade, setting it in precious metals and adding diamond or pearl touches. ✉ *IFC Mall, 8 Finance St., Central* ☎ *2525–2618* ⊕ *www.edwardchiu.com* Ⓜ *Central.*

Wing On Jewelry Ltd. There's a nostalgic charm to the butterflies, birds, and natural forms fashioned from jade, pearls, precious stones, and gold here. Everthing looks like an heirloom inherited from your grandmother. With on-site gemologists and artisans, and a commitment to post-sale service, this store has a long list of repeat customers. If, however, you lean toward Scandinavian aesthetics and clean lines, this probably isn't the place for you. ✉ *146 Johnston Rd., Wan Chai* ☎ *2572–2332* ⊕ *www.wingonjewelry.com.hk* Ⓜ *Wan Chai* ✉ *459 Hennessy Rd., Causeway Bay* Ⓜ *Causeway Bay.*

PEARLS

From lifelong investments handed down for generations to affordable fashion jewelry, pearls are still a good buy in Hong Kong. A symbol of purity and one of the eight jewels in Chinese culture, pearls come in a variety of shades including white, silver white, light pink, darker pink, cream, and yellow. The most coveted are perfectly round, though baroque (asymmetrical), semi-baroque, drop, and oval are also popular.

Cultured pearls are grown in mollusks with a surgically implanted tissue or bead nucleus. Freshwater pearls (grown in a freshwater mollusk) tend to look like rough grains of rice. The larger cultured types grown in the white-lip oyster, about 8mm to 22mm in diameter, are known as South Sea pearls and come in hues from white to darker gold. Tahitian pearls are produced by the black-lip oyster; they come in shades of black and gray, as well as blue, purple, green, orange, and gold.

When shopping for pearls, look at luster, size, color, and surface—judgments that are properly made against a white background in daylight.

(Biting them to test for that authentic gritty texture will not help your chances of a discount.)

■ TIP→ For a better understanding of pearls, consult an expert or take the HKTB's Secrets of Pearl Shopping class, in which you'll learn how to use a pearl grading chart and how to shop with confidence.

Gallery One. This is the next best option for midrange pearls if you can't make it to the Jade Market. Gallery One blends into Hollywood Road's backdrop of trinket-filled storefronts, but its selection of freshwater pearls stands out. Prices are reasonable, and they will string together whichever combination of pearls and semiprecious stones you choose. Gallery One also carries Tibetan and Buddhist beads in wood and amber as well as bronze sculptures. ⊠ *G/F, 31–33 Hollywood Rd., Central* ☎ *2545–6436* ⊕ *www.gallery-one.com.hk* Ⓜ *Central.*

K. S. Sze & Sons. More salon than store, powdered elderly ladies who lunch and casually dressed tourists all come here for the same thing: quality pearls, fine jewelry, and excellent service. In addition to classic styles, K.S. Sze works closely with clients on custom orders. ⊠ *Mezzanine, Mandarin Oriental, 5 Connaught Rd., Central* ☎ *2524–2803* ⊕ *www.kssze. com* Ⓜ *Central.*

Mandarin Australia. These are not your grandmother's pearls. The story goes something like this: a Hong Kong resident and an Australian woman met on a Chinese language course in Beijing and became fast friends. They shared an idea to create young, funky pearl bracelets and necklaces to sell at low prices and, unlike so many of us would-be entrepreneurs, they actually did it. Now sold to retailers on several continents, the collections feature baroque pearls with accents picked up on trips: antique buttons from Shanghai, Murano glass from Venice, turquoise and gold from Istanbul, and silver beads from Mexico. You'll need to make an appointment; ask for Joanna when you call. ☎ *9670–8253.*

Po Kwong Jewellery Ltd. Specializing in strung pearls from Australia and the South Seas, Po Kwong will add clasps to your specifications. They also carry pearl earrings, rings, and pendants. ⊠ *18/F, HK Diamond Exchange Bldg., 8–10 Duddell St., Central* ☎ *2521–4686.*

Sandra Pearls. Without a recommendation like this, you might be wary of the lustrous pearls hanging at this little Jade Market stall. The charming owner, Sandra, does, in fact, sell genuine and reasonable cultured and freshwater pearl necklaces and earrings. Some pieces are made from shell, which Sandra is always quick to point out, and could pass muster among the snobbiest collectors. ⊠ *Stall 381 and Stall 447, Jade Market, Kansu St., Yau Ma Tei, Kowloon* ☎ *9485–2895* Ⓜ *Yau Ma Tei.*

Super Star Jewellery. Discreetly tucked in a corner of Central, Super Star looks like any other small Hong Kong jewelry shop—with walls lined by display cases filled with the usual classic designs (old-fashioned to some) in predominantly gold and precious stones. What makes them stand out are the good prices and personalized service. Their cultured pearls and mixed strands of colored freshwater pearls are not all shown, so ask Lily or one of her colleagues to bring them out. ⊠ *The Galleria, 9 Queen's Rd. Central, Central* ☎ *2521–0507* Ⓜ *Central.*

WATCHES

Street stalls, department stores, and jewelry shops overflow with every variety, style, and brand imaginable, many with irresistible gadgets. Just remember Hong Kong's remarkable talent for imitation. A super-bargain gold "Rolex" may have hidden flaws—cheap local mechanisms, for instance, or "gold" that rusts. Stick to officially appointed dealers carrying the manufacturers' signs if you want to be sure you're getting the real thing.

When buying an expensive watch, check the serial number against the manufacturer's guarantee certificate and ask the salesperson to open the case to check the movement serial number. If the watch has an expensive band, find out whether it comes from the original manufacturer or is locally made, as this will dramatically affect the price (originals are much more expensive). Always obtain a detailed receipt, the manufacturer's guarantee, and a worldwide warranty.

Artland Watch Co Ltd. Elegant but uncomplicated, the interior of this established watch retailer is like its service. The informed staff will guide you through the countless luxury brands on show and in the catalogs from which you can also order. Prices here aren't the best in Hong Kong, but they're still lower than at home. ⊠ *G/F, Mirador Mansion, 54–64B Nathan Rd., Tsim Sha Tsui, Kowloon* ☎ *2366–1074* Ⓜ *Tsim Sha Tsui* ✉ *G/F, New Henry House, 10 Ice House St., Central* Ⓜ *Central.*

City Chain Co. Ltd. With more than 200 shops in Asia and locations all over Hong Kong, City Chain has a wide selection of watches for various budgets, including Swatch, Cyma, and Solvil & Titus. ⊠ *Times Square, 1 Matheson St., Causeway Bay* ☎ *2506–4217* ⊕ *www.citychain.com* Ⓜ *Causeway Bay* ✉ *G/F, Yat Fat Bldg., 44–46 Des Voeux Rd. Central, Central* Ⓜ *Central* ✉ *G/F, 16 Carnarvon Rd., Tsim Sha Tsui, Kowloon* Ⓜ *Tsim Sha Tsui.*

Eldorado Watch Co Ltd. At this deep emporium of watch brands, seek the advice of one of the older staffers who look like they've been there since the British landed. Brands include: Rolex, Patek Philippe, Girard-Perregaux, etc. ⊠ *G/F, Peter Bldg., 58–62 Queen's Rd., Central* ☎ *2522–7155* Ⓜ *Central.*

Elegant Watch & Jewellery Company Limited. With luxury watch collectors in mind, Elegant Watch is an authorized dealer of more than 35 top brands such as Tag Heuer, Breitling, Vacheron Constantin, Seiko, Franck Muller, and more. ⊠ *G/F, Luk Hoi Tong Bldg., 31 Queen's Rd. Central, Central* ☎ *2868–1882* ⊕ *www.elegantwatch.net* ✉ *Times Square, 1 Matheson St., Causeway Bay* Ⓜ *Causeway Bay* ✉ *Ocean Terminal, Harbour City, Canton Rd., Tsim Sha Tsui, Kowloon* Ⓜ *Tsim Sha Tsui,.*

Scorva Ltd. After years of experience in the watch industry, Hong Kong–based Satyajeet Sethi has applied his passion for design to a line of bold luxury timepieces. Made from steel and various precious metals, the watches come in various colors with special details such as chronograph features and diamonds. ⊠ *Hollywood Plaza, 610 Nathan Rd., Mong Kok, Kowloon* ☎ *3690–2760* ⊕ *www.scorva.com.*

Shoes & Bags

Shoes: they fit even when your skinny jeans don't; they're among the first things you look at when sizing someone up; and they captivate people the world over, from dictators' consorts to humble housewives. Hong Kongers are just as obsessed with footwear as the rest of the world. Add to that an obsession with brands and the next it-bag, and you have the makings for an amazing shoe and bag marketplace.

In opulent malls and department stores, designer must-haves seem to have leapt from the pages of fashion magazines onto the shelves. You'd be hard pressed to name an international label not represented here. Hong Kong also has a growing number of local brands that fill the gap between high fashion and cheap market products. Out of Asia, they become exotic objects that only you possess. That said, prices are rarely better than back home, and it's often hard to find shoes above size 8.

The best buys are custom-made. Wong Nai Chung Road, near the racecourse where Causeway Bay meets Happy Valley, has long been the destination for reasonably priced, medium quality shoes. Some shops can whip up an order in five days, though more complicated designs could take three weeks or more. A few stores will arrange delivery by mail, but it's always best to receive orders in person in case of problems.

■ TIP➔ Your feet swell as the day goes on (especially true in Hong Kong, thanks to heat and humidity). It may seem counterintuitive, but try shoes in the afternoon, when your feet are swollen. It's better to have shoes that are loose early in the day and just right later on than to have shoes that are just right early in the day and tight later on.

Hop's Handbag Co. Ltd. Uh-oh. You've over-shopped, and now packing is a problem. Hop over to Hop's for cheap luggage, from generic to name brands such as Samsonite. They also sell lots of handbags: some nameless but acceptable; others, amazing throwbacks to the '80s (and now back in fashion). ✉ G/F, 19 Li Yuen St. E, Central ☎ 2523–3888 Ⓜ Central.

J.J. Partners. A sophisticated choice in Happy Valley. You won't see the men who manage this store flipping through the pages of Vogue, but the selection of ready-made and custom shoes and bags suggests they're up on fashion. Even better, prices are comparable with neighboring shops. ✉ G/F, 173 Wong Nai Chung Rd., Happy Valley ☎ 2577–2383 Ⓜ Causeway Bay.

Kow Hoo Shoe Company. If you like shoes made the old-fashioned way, then Kow Hoo, one of Hong Kong's oldest (circa 1946), is for you. They also do great cowboy boots—there's nothing like knee-high calfskin. ✉ 2/ F, Prince's Bldg., 10 Chater Rd., Central ☎ 2523–0489 Ⓜ Central.

Kwanpen. Famous for its crocodile bags and shoes, Kwanpen has acted as a manufacturer for famous brands since 1938, as well as being a stand-alone retailer. They also use ostrich and leather. ✉ Pacific Place, 88 Queensway, Admiralty ☎ 2918–9199 ⊕ www.kwanpen.com Ⓜ Admiralty.

Ladyplace. Their prices on French Sole brand ballerinas will have you doing pirouettes. In the United States, the ballet flats by British designer Jane Winkworth sell for about US$160. At Ladyplace, they're HK$895—or about US$115—a pair. While you're here, browse through the second-hand shoes and apparel by famous fashion labels, all at discounted prices. ⊠ *1/F, World Trust Tower, 50 Stanley St., Central* ☎ *2854–2321* ⊕ *www.ladyplace.com* Ⓜ *Central.*

Lianca. This is one of those unique places that makes you want to buy something even if there's nothing you need. Lianca, first and foremost a manufacturer, sells well-made leather bags, wallets, frames, key chains, and home accessories in timeless, simple designs. It's an un-branded way to be stylish. ⊠ *Basement, 27 Staunton St., entrance on Graham St., SoHo, Central* ☎ *2139–2989* ⊕ *www.lianca.com.hk* Ⓜ *Central.*

★ **LIII LIII Shoes.** Possibly the best made and most fashionable custom shoe makers in Hong Kong, the Chan brothers have also become the most arrogant. Prices have tripled over the last few years (to between HK$1,300 and HK$2,300 for high heels), but the excellent shoes and good bags keep pulling customers back. Despite the attitude, they will re-do shoes if you're unhappy with the results. ⊠ *Admiralty Centre, 18 Harcourt Rd., Wan Chai* ☎ *2865–3989* Ⓜ *Admiralty.*

Mayer Shoes. Since the 1960s, Mayer has been making excellent custom order shoes and accessories in leather, lizard, crocodile, and ostrich. Go to them for the classic pieces for which they became famous rather than this season's it-bag. Prices start at about US$200 up. ⊠ *Mandarin Oriental, 5 Connaught Rd., Central* ☎ *2524–3317* Ⓜ *Central.*

Milan Station. Even if you're willing to shell out for an Hermès Kelly bag, how can anyone expect you to survive the waitlist? Milan Station resells the it-bags of yesterday that have been retrieved from Hong Kong's fickle fashionistas. Inexplicably, the shop entrances were designed to look like MTR stations. The concept has been so successful, unimaginatively named copycats have sprung up such as Paris Station. Discounts vary according to brand and trends, but the merchandise is in good condition. ⊠ *G/F, Percival House, 77–83 Percival St., Causeway Bay* ☎ *2504–0128, 2730—8037 customer service* ⊕ *www.milanstation. net* Ⓜ *Causeway Bay* ⊠ *G/F, 26 Wellington St., Central* ⊠ *G/F, Pakpolee Commercial Centre, 1A–1K Sai Yeung Choi St., Mong Kok, Kowloon* Ⓜ *Mong Kok* ⊠ *G/F, 81 Chatham Rd., Tsim Sha Tsui, Kowloon* Ⓜ *Tsim Sha Tsui.*

Mischa Designs. Designer Michelle Lai's bags are handmade from Japanese brocade obis (sashes) and kimonos from the 1920s to the 1950s. Clutch bags such as the Dumpling or any of the reversible styles could make even the most unremarkable outfit look noteworthy. Keep an eye out for bigger totes made of obis paired with leather. The designs are sold by appointment or at Sharon Rocks fashion jewelry showroom. ☎ *2546–0342* ⊕ *www.mischadesigns.com* ⊠ *Sharon Rocks, 11/F Yu Yuet Lai Bldg., 43–55 Wyndham St., Central* ☎ *2523–9333 or 6199–4145* ⊕ *www.sharonrocks.com* Ⓜ *Central.*

Noven Shoes & Handbags. At this reliable shoe and bag maker in the valley, styles range from gaudy to good, all for about HK$400 per pair. Custom-made boots take three weeks—longer than shoes and bags. ⊠ *G/*

F, 163 Wong Nai Chung Rd., Happy Valley ☎ *2577–8323.*

On Pedder. The art installation–style window displays will draw you into this stunning boutique. Designed as a giant jewel box, the store's brand directory reads like a fashion editor's wish list of world-famous shoe, bag, accessory, and jewelry designers. You might see the same brands at Lane Crawford—that's because they're sister companies. For the same aesthetics at lower prices, check out trendy younger sibling **Pedder Red** (✉ The Gateway, Harbour City, Canton Rd., Tsim Sha Tsui, Kowloon Ⓜ Tsim Sha Tsui). ✉ *G/F, Wheelock House, 20 Pedder St., Central* ☎ *2118–3388, 2118–0130 for branch information* Ⓜ *Central.*

> **FIX IT & FORGET IT**
>
> Shoe troubles? For basic services the shoe-repair chains in MTR stations or hotels can help. But for special cases (mauled Manolos, for instance) head straight to the **Top Shoes Repair & Lock Centre** (✉ G/F, 35 Queen's Rd. Central, Central ☎ 2530–0978 Ⓜ Central)

★ **Perfect Shoes & Handbags Co., Ltd.** One of the best shoe shops in Happy Valley is known to Hong Kongers yet still a well-kept secret. Don't let the address confuse you, this is the beginning of the Wong Nai Chung Road strip of shoe shops. ✉ *G/F, 4 Leighton Rd., Causeway Bay* ☎ *2577–1771* Ⓜ *Causeway Bay.*

Prestige Shoe Co. Ltd. Like the Happy Valley shoemakers, Prestige does fashion-forward, acceptable quality, reasonably priced shoes. Unlike its valley brethren it's more convenient, with several locations around town. ✉ *G/F, 66 Percival St., Causeway Bay* ☎ *2783–8100* Ⓜ *Causeway Bay* ✉ *World Wide House, 19 Des Voeux Rd. Central, Central* Ⓜ *Central.*

★ **Rabeanco.** Hong Kong–based Rabeanco has a reasonably priced line of beautiful, quality leather bags in contemporary but never flashy or absurd designs. Buy yours now before the world discovers them. ✉ *G/F, 33 Sharp St. E, Causeway Bay* ☎ *2577–9221, 2245–5085 customer service and branch information* ⊕ *www.rabeanco.com* Ⓜ *Causeway Bay* ✉ *L1, Man Yee Arcade, 68 Des Voeux Rd., Central* Ⓜ *Central* ✉ *G/ F, Hong Kong Pacific Centre, 28 Hankow Rd., Tsim Sha Tsui, Kowloon* Ⓜ *Tsim Sha Tsui.*

Right Choice Export Fashion Co. Take a moment to look past the plastic stilettos worthy of an exotic dancer, and you might just discover unfathomably cheap yet stylish shoes (if they'll only last one season). The sandals are especially pretty and can cost as little as HK$60. Look for shops like this near most market streets. ✉ *G/F, 187 Fa Yuen St., Mong Kok, Kowloon* ☎ *2394–6953* Ⓜ *Prince Edward.*

Sam Wo. A veteran of this area, Sam Wo sells fashion-inspired leather bags at low prices and without the branding. You'll need a keen eye to spot the must-haves amid all the must-nots. See neighboring stalls for closer interpretations of branded bags. ✉ *Basement, 41–47 Queen's Rd. Central, Central* ☎ *2524–0970* Ⓜ *Central.*

Fodor'sChoice
★ **Tef Tef.** This shop has exquisite, statement-making bags by Hong Kong–based designer Tomoko Okamura. The collection is handmade with Chinese metalwork, vintage Japanese fabrics, Thai silks, and bamboo. Of all the artisanal Asian fabric bags, these are the best. They're

sold in various locations, including the Green Lantern (where you'll also get the best prices). ⊠ *G/F, 72 Peel St., SoHo, Central* ☎ *2526–0277* ⊕ *www.teftef.com.hk.*

Tailor-Made Clothing

CHINESE CLOTHING TAILORS

Chinese clothing has the potential to look incredibly chic or embarrassingly trashy. At the street level, it's easy to find a bargain *cheongsam,* though standard cuts don't allow for western hips and curves. Similarly, the market variety of men's jackets with Mandarin collars (lower) or Mao collars (higher) can look cheap. Rely on these experts for classic, tailor-made Chinese clothing.

Blanc de Chine. Blanc de Chine has catered to high society and celebrities, such as actor Jackie Chan, for years. That's easy when you're housed on the second floor of an old colonial building (just upstairs from Shanghai Tang) and you rely on word of mouth. The small, refined tailoring shop neatly displays exquisite fabrics. Next door is the Blanc de Chine boutique filled with lovely ready-made womenswear, menswear, and home accessories. With newer stores in New York and Beijing, it appears the word is getting out. Items here are extravagances, but they're worth every penny. ⊠ *Pedder Bldg., 12 Pedder St., Central* ☎ *2104–7934* ⊕ *www.blancdechine.com* Ⓜ *Central.*

Linva Tailors. It's one of the best of the old-fashioned *cheongsam* tailors, in operation since the 1960s. Master tailor, Mr. Leung, takes clients through the entire process and reveals a surprising number of variations in style. Prices are affordable, but vary according to fabric, which ranges from basics to special brocades and beautifully embroidered silks. ⊠ *38 Cochrane St., Central* ☎ *2544–2456* Ⓜ *Central.*

★ **Shanghai Tang—Imperial Tailors.** Upscale Chinese lifestyle brand, Shanghai Tang, has the Imperial Tailors service in select stores, including the Central flagship. A fabulous interior evokes the charm of 1930s Shanghai, and gives an indication of what to expect in terms of craftsmanship and price. From silk to velvet, brocade to voile, fabrics are displayed on the side walls, along with examples of fine tailoring. The expert tailors here can make conservative or contemporary versions of the *cheongsam.* Men can also have a Chinese *tang* suit made to order. ⊠ *G/F, 12 Pedder St., Central* ☎ *2525–7333* ⊕ *www.shanghaitang.com* Ⓜ *Central.*

MEN'S TAILORS

A-Man Hing Cheong Co., Ltd. People often gasp at the very mention of A-Man Hing Cheong in the Mandarin Oriental Hotel. For some it symbolizes the ultimate in fine tailoring with a reputation that extends back to its founding in 1898. For others it's the lofty prices that elicit a reaction. Regardless, this is a trustworthy source of European-cut suits, custom shirts, and excellent service. ⊠ *Mezzanine, Mandarin Oriental, 5 Connaught Rd., Central* ☎ *2522–3336* Ⓜ *Central.*

Ascot Chang. This self-titled "gentleman's shirtmaker" makes it easy to find the perfect shirt, even if you could get a better deal in a less prominent shop. Ascot Chang has upheld exacting Shanghainese tailoring traditions in Hong Kong since 1955, and now has stores in New York, Beverly

Continued on page 164

IT SUITS YOU

No trip to Hong Kong would be complete without a visit to one of its world-famous tailors, as many celebrities and dignitaries can attest. In often humble, fabric-cluttered settings, customer records contain the measurements of notables such as Jude Law, Kate Moss, David Bowie, Luciano Pavarotti, and Queen Elizabeth II.

Prince Charles, who has his pick of Savile Row craftsmen, placed a few orders while in the territory for the 1997 handover. When Bill Clinton passed through, word has it that tailors were up until 4 AM to accommodate him.

Like some of their international clientele, who often make up a third of their total business, a handful of tailors are famous themselves. They even go on world tours for their fans. Picking the right tailor can be daunting in a city where the phone book lists about 500 of them. A good suit will last for 20 years if cared for correctly. A bad one will probably leave your closet only for its trip to the thrift store. All the more reason to make thoughtful, educated choices.

TIP

The special economic zone of Shenzhen on the mainland, just a train ride away, is known for competitively priced and speedy tailoring. Quality doesn't always measure up, though, so buyer beware.

5 STEPS TO SIZING THINGS UP

If you've ever owned a custom-made garment, you understand the joy of clothes crafted to fit your every measurement. In Hong Kong, prices rival exclusive ready-to-wear brands.

Hong Kong is best known for men's tailoring, but whether you're looking for a classic men's business suit or an evening gown, these steps will help you size things up.

1. SET YOUR STYLE

Be clear about what you want. Bring samples—a favorite piece of clothing or magazine photos. Also, Hong Kong tailors are trained in classic, structured garments. Straying from these could lead to disappointment. There are three basic suit styles. Experienced tailors can advise on the best one for your shape.

The **American cut** is considered traditional by some, shapeless by others. Its jacket has notched lapels, a center vent, and two or three buttons. The trousers are lean, with flat fronts. The **British cut** also has notched lapels and two- or three-button jackets, but it features side vents and pleated trousers. The double-breasted **Italian cut** has wide lapels and pleated trousers—a look in remission these days.

2. CHOOSE YOUR FABRIC

You're getting a deal on workmanship, so consider splurging on, say, a luxurious blend of cashmere, mink, and wool. When having something copied, though, choose a fabric similar to the original. And buy for the climate you live in, not the climate of your tailor. (How often will you wear seersucker in Alaska?) Take your time selecting: fabric is the main factor affecting cost.

Examine fabric on a large scale. Small swatches are deceiving. Those strong pinstripes might be elegant on a tiny card, but a full suit of them could make you look like an extra from *The Godfather*.

3. MEASURE UP

Meticulous measuring is the mark of a superior craftsman, so be patient. And for accuracy, stand as you normally would (you can't suck in that gut forever). Tailors often record your information so you can have more garments sent to you without returning to Hong Kong. Still, double check measurements at home before each order.

4. PLACE YOUR ORDER

Consider ordering two pairs of trousers per suit. They wear faster than jackets, and alternating between two will help them last longer.

Most tailors require a deposit of 30%–50% of the total cost. Request a receipt detailing price, fabric, style, measurements, fittings, and production schedule. Also ask for a swatch to compare with the final product.

5. GET FIT

There should be at least two fittings. The first is usually for major alterations. Subsequent fittings are supposed to be for minor adjustments, but don't settle for less than perfect: keep sending it back until they get it right.

Bring the right clothes, such as a dress shirt and appropriate shoes, to try on a suit. Having someone you trust at the final fitting helps ensure you haven't overlooked anything.

Try jackets buttoned and unbuttoned. Examine every detail. Are shoulder seams puckered or smooth? Do patterns meet? Is the collar too loose or tight? (About two fingers' space is right.)

FINDING A TAILOR

- As soon as you arrive, visit established tailors to compare workmanship and cost.

- Ask if the work is bespoke (made from scratch) or made-to-measure (based on existing patterns but handmade according to your measurements).

- You get what you pay for. Assume the workmanship and fabric will match the price.

- A fine suit requires six or more days to create. That said, be wary but not dismissive of "24-hour tailors." Hong Kong's most famous craftsmen have turned out suits in a day.

4

IT SUITS YOU

MEN'S TAILORING

Although most tailors can accommodate women—and a few even focus on womenswear (see listings)—Hong Kong tailors are best known for men's suits and shirts. Many shirtmakers also do pajamas, boxer shorts, and women's shirts. To help you with all the options, here are some basics.

JACKETS

Buttons: Plastic buttons can make exquisite tailoring look cheap. Select natural materials like horn. (No two natural buttons will be exactly alike.) Ask for extras, too.

Cuffs: The rule is the number of buttons on each cuff should match the total number on the front of the jacket.

Double- or Single-Breasted: Single-breasted jackets are more versatile: you can dress them up or down and wear them open or buttoned. Two buttons are most popular, but single-breasted jackets can have from one to four.

Lining: The interior (sleeves and pockets, too) should be lined with a beautifully stitched, high-quality fabric like silk. The lining affects both how the jacket falls and how readily it glides on and off.

Pockets: Standard jackets have straight pockets; modern designs have slanted ones. Both can be a slot style or have flaps, which may add girth. A small ticket pocket above a standard pocket is a nice touch.

Stitching: Handstitched lapels subtly show off fine tailoring; the discerning request hand-stitched buttonholes as well. At the first fitting, stitches should be snug and free of any fraying.

Vent: The vent was created to allow cavalry officers to sit in their saddles comfortably. Although you probably won't go riding in your suit, don't skip the vent. Unvented jackets simply aren't flattering.

SHIRTS

Back: The back can be plain or have a box, side, or inverted pleat.

Collars: Some are straight (pointed), others are rounded. Ask for removable stays; cleaning with them inside a collar causes points to fray. The English collar has a semi-cutaway style; a tab collar has a strip of fabric holding it in place. Button-down collars are more casual.

Cuffs: Cuffs should just show from beneath jacket sleeves. Styles include rounded, square, or angled with one or two buttons. The elegant French (or double) cuff is worn with cufflinks.

Fit: Tailors can make shirts snug or baggy, depending on your taste, and still avoid the ballooned look of mass-produced garments.

Front: You can choose a plain front or one with a placket. Pockets (optional) can go on the left or right and be monogrammed.

TROUSERS

Hems: Some argue cuffless or flat hems are formal; others consider them casual—even costume-like. It's your call. To accommodate shoes, hems are slightly shorter at the front.

Length: Prescribed lengths differ by style, but socks should remain hidden, and trousers should cover half to two-thirds of the shoe.

Pleats: Younger generations prefer flat-front trousers. Traditionalists like single or double pleats, which are roomier in the hips and thighs.

Pockets: Pockets cut on the diagonal are standard, but you can opt for horizontal or vertical designs. One or two (more casual) back pockets, with or without flaps, are also options.

Waist Details: You can request waist adjusters (internal buttons and straps that let you adjust the waist by about 2 inches) or waistband buttons for suspenders.

	Save	Splurge	Break the Bank
SUITS	HK$2,800 (Yuen's Tailor and Jantzen Tailor); HK$3,000 (Sam's Tailor)	HK$4,500 (Mode Elegante); HK$5,800 (Ascot Chang)	HK$8,000–HK$17,000 (A-Man Hing Cheong)
SHIRTS	HK$300 (Yuen's Tailor); HK$350 (Sam's Tailor).	HK$500 (Mode Elegante)	HK$650–HK$4,000 (Ascot Chang, HK$1,000 is average); HK$800–HK$1,800 (A-Man Hing Cheong).

Hills, Manila, and Shanghai, in addition to offering online ordering and regular American tours. The focus here is on the fit and details, from 22 stitches per inch to collar linings crafted to maintain their shape. Among the countless fabrics, Swiss 200s two-ply Egyptian cotton by Alumo is one of the most coveted and expensive. Like many shirtmakers, Ascot Chang does pajamas, robes, boxer shorts, and women's blouses, too. It also has developed ready-made lines of shirts, T-shirts, neckties, and other accessories. ✉ *Prince's Bldg., 10 Chater Rd., Central* ☎ *2523–3663* ⊕ *www.ascotchang.com* Ⓜ *Central* ✉ *IFC Mall, 8 Finance St., Central* Ⓜ *Central* ✉ *Peninsula Hong Kong, Salisbury Rd., Tsim Sha Tsui, Kowloon* Ⓜ *Tsim Sha Tsui* ✉ *New World Centre (InterContinental Hong Kong), 18–24 Salisbury Rd., Tsim Sha Tsui, Kowloon* Ⓜ *Tsim Sha Tsui.*

David's Shirts Ltd. Like so many of its competitors, the popular David's Shirts has global reach and even a branch in New York City. But customers still enjoy the personalized service of a smaller business supervised by David Chu himself since 1961. All the work is done in-house by Shanghainese tailors with at least 20 years' experience each. There are more than 6,000 imported European fabrics to choose from, each prewashed. Examples of shirts, suits, and accessories—including 30 collar, 12 cuff, and 10 pocket styles—help you choose. Single-needle tailoring, French seams, 22 stitches per inch, handpicked, double-stitched shell buttons, German interlining—it's all here. Your details, down to which side you wear your wristwatch, are kept on file should you wish to use their mail-order service in the future. ✉ *G/F, Wing Lee Bldg., 33 Kimberley Rd.,, Tsim Sha Tsui, Kowloon* ☎ *2367–9556* ⊕ *www.davidsshirts.com* ✉ *Mezzanine, Mandarin Oriental, 5 Connaught Rd., Central* Ⓜ *Central.*

Jantzen Tailor. You'll have to push past a lively crowd and eclectic shops in a mall preferred by Filipina domestic helpers to get to Jantzen. Catering to expatriate bankers since 1972, this reputable yet reasonable tailor specializes in classic shirts; it also makes suits and women's garments. The comprehensive Web site displays their commitment to quality, such as hand-sewn button shanks, Gygil interlining, and Coats brand thread. ✉ *2/F World Wide House, 19 Des Voeux Rd., Central* ☎ *2570–5901* ⊕ *www.jantzentailor.com* Ⓜ *Central.*

Maxwell's Clothiers Ltd. After you've found a handful of reputable, high-quality tailors, one way to choose between them is price. Maxwell's is known for its competitive rates. It's also a wonderful place to have favorite shirts and suits copied and for straightforward, structured women's shirts and suits. It was founded by third-generation tailor Ken Maxwell in 1961, and follows Shanghai tailoring traditions while also providing the fabled 24-hour suit upon request. The showroom and workshop are in Kowloon, but son, Andy, and his team take appointments in the United States, Canada, and Europe twice annually. The motto of this family business is, "Simply let the garment do the talking." ✉ *7/F, Han Hing Mansion, 38–40 Hankow Rd., Tsim Sha Tsui, Kowloon* ☎ *2366–6705* ⊕ *www.maxwellsclothiers.com* Ⓜ *Tsim Sha Tsui.*

Raj Mirpuri. This establishment is best known for its Seven-Fold Tie. Most ties are made of several pieces of fabric and lined to give the illusion of weight. The Seven-Fold Tie is handmade from a single piece of silk that's folded seven times for a luxurious finish inspired by Renaissance craftsmanship. Raj Mirpuri further differentiates itself with bespoke (truly tailored to your measurements) rather than made-to-measure (based on an existing pattern) tailoring, with prices to match. They make suits, shirts, and accessories for men and women, and have stores in London, Geneva, and Zurich. ⊠ *8/F Star House, 3 Salisbury Rd., Tsim Sha Tsui, Kowloon* ☎ *2317–0804* ⊕ *www.mirpuri.com* Ⓜ *Tsim Sha Tsui.*

FodorśChoice ★ **Sam's Tailor.** Unlike many famous Hong Kong tailors, you won't find the legendary Sam's in a chic hotel or sleek mall. But don't be fooled. These digs in humble Burlington House, a tailoring hub, have hosted everyone from U.S. presidents (back as far as Richard Nixon) to performers such as the Black Eyed Peas, Kylie Minogue, and Blondie. This former uniform tailor to the British troops once even made a suit for Prince Charles in a record hour and 52 minutes. The men's and women's tailor does accept 24-hour suit or shirt orders, but will take about two days if you're not in a hurry. Founded by Naraindas Melwani in the 1950s, "Sam" is now his son, Manu Melwani, who runs the show with the help of his own son, Roshan, and about 55 tailors behind the scenes. In 2004 Sam's introduced a computerized bodysuit that takes measurements without subjecting you to the tape measure. (Actually, they now use a combination of both.) These tailors also make annual trips to Europe and North America. (Schedule updates are listed on the Web site). ⊠ *Burlington House, 90–94 Nathan Rd., Tsim Sha Tsui, Kowloon* ☎ *2367–9423* ⊕ *www.samstailor.com* Ⓜ *Tsim Sha Tsui.*

W. W. Chan & Sons Tailors Ltd. Chan is known for excellent quality suits and shirts, classic cuts, and has an array of fine European fabrics. It's comforting to know that you'll be measured and fitted by the same master tailor from start to finish. The Kowloon headquarters features a mirrored, hexagonal changing room so you can check every angle. Tailors from here travel to the United States several times a year to fill orders for their customers; if you have a suit made here and leave your address, they'll let you know when they plan to visit. ⊠ *2/F Burlington House, 92–94 Nathan Rd., Tsim Sha Tsui, Kowloon* ☎ *2366–9738* ⊕ *www.wwchan.com* Ⓜ *Tsim Sha Tsui.*

Yuen's Tailor. Need a kilt? This is where the Hong Kong Highlanders Reel Club comes for custom-made kilts. The Yuen repertoire, however, extends to well-made suits and shirts. The tiny shop is on an unimpressive gray walkway and is filled from floor to ceiling with sumptuous European fabrics. It's a good place to have clothes copied; prices are competitive. ⊠ *2/F, Escalator Link Alley, 80 Des Voeux Rd., Central* ☎ *2854–9649* Ⓜ *Central.*

WOMEN'S TAILORS

Brides and Gowns. Hong Kong used to take the cake when it came to meringuelike bridal confections. Brides and Gowns has led the way in providing sleek, chic options, with expert patternmakers and tailors on staff. International designers include Augusta Jones and Mariana Hardwick. Evening, bridal, and bridesmaid dresses, *cheongsams,* and accessories are all on display in the elegant bridal salon. ⊠ *8/F, Asia Pacific Centre, 8 Wyndham St., Central* ☎ *2873–5558* ⊕ *www.bridesandgowns.com* Ⓜ *Central.*

Irene Fashions. In 1987 the women's division of noted men's tailor, W. W. Chan, branched off and was renamed Irene Fashions. You can expect the same level of expertise and a large selection of fine fabrics. Experienced at translating ideas and pictures into clothing, in-house designers will sketch and help you develop concepts. Like its parent company, Irene promises the same tailor will take you through the entire process, and most of the work is done on-site. ⊠ *Burlington House, 92–94 Nathan Rd., Tsim Sha Tsui, Kowloon* 🕾 *2367–5588* ⊕ *www.wwchan.com* Ⓜ *Tsim Sha Tsui.*

Irene Fashions. In addition to having the same name as the W. W. Chan women's division, this Irene Fashions promises much of the same guidance and workmanship. But don't confuse this popular Central tailoress with her Kowloon side counterpart; the two are *not* related. Slightly more well-known, this tailor attracts many expatriate women in search of everything from suits to evening wear. Service in the cluttered atmosphere may be brusque, but it's only because they know what they're talking about. ⊠ *Tung Chai Bldg., 86–90 Wellington St., Central* 🕾 *2850–5635* Ⓜ *Central.*

Margaret Court Tailoress. A name frequently passed on by expert Hong Kong shoppers, Margaret Wong's tailoring services span women's daywear to bridal gowns to Chinese *cheongsams*. Prices tend to be in the midrange. ⊠ *8/F, Block A, Winner Bldg., 27–37 D'Aguilar St. Central* 🕾 *2525–5596* ⊕ *www.margaret-court.com.hk* Ⓜ *Central.*

Mode Elegante. Don't be deterred by the somewhat dated mannequins in the windows. Mode Elegante is a favorite source for custom-made suits among women and men in the know. Tailors here specialize in European cuts. You'll have your choice of fabrics from the United Kingdom, Italy, and elsewhere. Your records are put on file so you can place orders from abroad. They'll even ship the completed garment to you almost anywhere on the planet. Alternatively, you can make an appointment with director Gary Zee, one of Hong Kong's traveling tailors who makes regular visits to North America, Europe, and Japan. ⊠ *Peninsula Hong Kong, Salisbury Rd., Tsim Sha Tsui, Kowloon* 🕾 *2366–8153* ⊕ *www.modeelegante.com* Ⓜ *Tsim Sha Tsui.*

Perfect Dress Alteration (aka Ann & Bon). Hong Kong's tai tais bring their couture here for adjustments, as evidenced by the Chanel, Escada, and Versace bags hanging overhead in this cluttered little workshop buzzing with the sound of sewing machines. Although primarily known for alterations, they also offer tailoring services for women. ⊠ *2/F, Melbourne Plaza, 33 Queen's Rd., Central* 🕾 *2522–8838* Ⓜ *Central.*

Siriporn. Visible from the Midlevels Escalator and one of the most highly recommended Thai tailors in town, they're known for an acute sense of aesthetics, reasonable prices, and brightly colored Thai silks. They're also capable of crafting subtle garments to please minimalists. ⊠ *1/F, Merlin Bldg., 30–34 Cochrane St., Central* 🕾 *2866–6668* Ⓜ *Central.*

Teneel. The fume-filled thoroughfare that leads to Teneel doesn't exactly inspire confidence or put you in the mood to talk about evening wear, but you should persist. Teneel Chan is experienced in women's wear, particularly gowns. Although some of her creations are on the garish side (think T-shirts adorned with expletives in Swarovski crystals), clear direction will put her on the right track. Even better, her prices are low. Remember to ask about delivery times as more complicated work could take two or more weeks. ⊠ *G/F, 28C Canal Rd. E, Causeway Bay* 🕾 *2832–2981* Ⓜ *Causeway Bay.*

Where to Eat

WORD OF MOUTH

"Don't miss a meal at Café Deco [atop Victoria Peak]. We booked a window table about four weeks in advance. It was well worth the effort, as the view at night over the city is amazing. The food was terrific (expensive of course). We particularly enjoyed the lobster thermidor." —Gordon

By Robin
Goldstein

Stand your ground when faced with a barrage of 16-stroke Chinese characters. Don't flee from the gruesome goose hanging in the window or wince at the steaming cauldron of innards, the swinging knots of gnarled intestine, or the rows of webbed duck feet that announce the corner restaurant's offerings.

Be bold at the sight of a vicious cleaver beheading a roast suckling pig. If you do, you'll find that the resulting crackles of pork fat and tender slices of meat—served with rice and some glistening greens—taste better than anything at the western-theme restaurant or pan-Chinese chain down the street. You know the one. It has the English-language menu and the empty tables.

Besides losing your culinary inhibitions, what's the best way to have a memorable meal in Hong Kong? First, choose a restaurant that's full rather than empty. Then check out what's on everyone else's plate. Don't be shy about pointing to an interesting dish at your neighbor's table. This is often the best way to order, as many local specialties don't appear on the English version of the menu.

The pointing method of ordering will come in handy when you visit the plethora of small, brightly lit dives, many open into the wee hours, that specialize either in noodle soups or roast meats. At noodle-centric restaurants, fish ball soup with ramen noodles is an excellent choice and the goose, suckling pig, honeyed pork, and soy-sauce chicken are good bets at the roast meat shops. Combination plates, with a sampling of meats and some greens on a bed of white rice, is a foolproof way to go. Must-try condiments at either type of restaurant include chili sauce (which usually comes in little side dishes) and a vinegar soy sauce.

Whether Cantonese, traditional Italian or French, or celebrity-chef chic, most of the pricier restaurants lie within five-star hotels. While you shouldn't let these places monopolize your culinary exposure to Hong Kong, some are really world class. And of course, Hong Kong is the world's epicenter of dim sum, and while you're here you must have at least one dim sum breakfast or lunch in a teahouse. Those steaming bamboo baskets you see conceal delicious dumplings, buns, and pastries—all as comforting as they are exotic.

HONG KONG ISLAND

Western

The restaurants listed in this section (the Western district) are all in a neighborhood known as SoHo (the area *so*uth of *Ho*llywood Road), which is a few minutes' walk uphill from Central. SoHo spreads mainly along Elgin Street, Staunton Street, and Old Bailey Street, and is accessible by the long, outdoor Midlevels Escalator. The emphasis in SoHo is generally on foreign cuisines, including Spanish, Italian, Indian, Argentinian, Cuban, Cajun, French, Portuguese, and Russian. Quality and authenticity of the food varies, and (as seems to be the case in every SoHo in the world) trendiness can get the better of some of these joints—but the area is worth a visit to experience the SoHo atmosphere.

Cantonese

$-$$ ✕ **Jing Cheng Xiao Chu.** You'll have to take a taxi to the quiet Sai Ying Pun residential neighborhood to sample the delights of this private kitchen, which, unlike most of Hong Kong's many so-called "speakeasy restaurants," is actually licensed. The chef, who goes by "Master Law," takes orders in advance for dishes from all over China, which might include chicken in a farmer's bucket, jumbo shrimp in sweet sauce, or Ningbo pine-nut fish. The restaurant also pitches a health-food angle, but as is generally the case in Hong Kong, it's dubious. This will take you well off the tourist track, and delightfully so. ✉ *92 High St., Sai Ying Pun, Western* ☎ *2291–0289* ▭ *No credit cards.*

Malaysian

¢ ✕ **Katong Laksa.** Not many tourists wind up spending much time in Sheung Wan, but if you do, it's worth trying one of the many new Malaysian noodle shops in the area. This bright little Singaporean-Malaysian restaurant is one such place, and it makes a great lunch stop. Try the Straits noodle dishes such as laksa, the restaurant's namesake, or anything including shrimp. Service is more than welcoming. ✉ *8 Mercer St., Sheung Wan, Western* ☎ *2543–4008* ▭ *No credit cards* Ⓜ *Sheung Wan.*

Northern Chinese

$$-$$$ ✕ **Shui Hu Ju.** It's hard to character-
Fodor's Choice ize the cuisine of this evocative and
★ romantic theme restaurant whose influence comes from the north of China. You'll find Shanghainese, Cantonese, and Sichuan dishes on

> **SPICY SZECHUAN**
>
> Though it is more commonly known as *Sichuan* these days, the cooking style still features an eye-watering array of chilis and the ingredients are cooked slowly for an integrated flavor—the opposite of Cantonese food. Szechuan rice, bamboo, wheat, river fish, shellfish, chicken, and pork dishes are all prepared with plenty of salt, anise, fennel seed, chili, and coriander.

HONG KONG DINING PLANNER

Ancient Chinese Secrets

If you keep an open mind about food, you can lose yourself in the magic of a cuisine whose traditions have been braising for millennia. It, like many of Hong Kong's residents, has its roots in Guangdong (Canton) Province. Cantonese cooks believe that the secret to bringing out the natural flavors of food is to cook it quickly at very high temperatures. The resulting dishes are then served and eaten immediately.

Share & Share Alike

In China food is meant to be shared. Instead of ordering individual main dishes, it's usual for those around a table—whether 2 or 12 people—to get several. Four people eating together, for example, might order a whole or half chicken, another type of meat, a fish dish, a vegetable, and fried noodles—all of which would be placed on the table's lazy Susan so everyone can reach. Portions and prices may be altered according to the number of diners.

Silverware is common in Hong Kong, but what better place to practice your chopstick skills? Feel free to take food from communal plates with your own chopsticks; just be sure to use the ends that you haven't put into your mouth. It's also polite to serve others this way.

Time to Eat

Locals eat lunch between noon and 1:30 PM; dinner is around 8. Dim sum begins as early as 10 AM. Reservations aren't usually necessary except during Chinese holidays or at of-the-moment or high-end hotel restaurants like Alain Ducasse's SPOON or the Caprice. There are certain classic Hong Kong preparations (e.g., beggar's chicken, whose preparation in a clay pot takes hours) that require reserving not just a table, but the dish itself. Do so at least 24 hours out.

You'll also need reservations for a meal at one of the so-called private kitchens—unlicensed culinary speakeasies, which are often the city's hottest tickets. Book several days ahead, and if possible, join forces with other people. Some private kitchens only take reservations for parties of four, six, or eight.

Got Kids?

Café Deco atop Victoria Peak has games and other attractions to keep the little ones occupied, and the buffet at café TOO in the Island Shangri-La hotel is not only entertaining, but also has something for even the pickiest eaters. The same is true of the 300-seat international food court known as Café Kool in the Kowloon Shangri-La.

Dan Ryan's, in the Admiralty district, and some other western-style restaurants have children's meals, but Cantonese restaurants do not. That said, everyone helps themselves from a selection of dishes, so you can create your own child-size portions.

You'll see children at all but the most upscale restaurants. On Sunday, which is traditionally family day, you'll even see kids at the fanciest places, too. Regardless of where you're dining, don't be surprised if indulgent parents allow their children to run around freely.

Cru or Brew?

Markups on wine are high, and wine lists are often uninspired—or even inappropriate. French reds have a caché in Hong Kong, which is strange given the emphasis on seafood. Lists often have a glut of heavy Bordeaux blends and are devoid of better-matched dry rosés or light, acidic whites. Unless you're at a high-end French or Italian restaurant, stick with the traditional accompaniments to Cantonese food—tea or beer. If you must have wine, look for a mid-price white Burgundy or an Australian white. And we're sad to say it, but avoid Chinese wines at all costs. Even the best are undrinkable.

Tea is the dinner drink of choice, but Hong Kong likes its beer—before, during, or after dinner. It's generally light stuff, like Heineken, the locally brewed San Miguel (the company hails from Portugal), or a Chinese lager such as the crisp, immensely popular Tsing Tao. There's a plethora of English and Irish pubs with Guinness and Harp on tap. When it's time to hit the karaoke bars or discotheques, though, people switch to whiskey. It's generally drunk on the rocks or mixed with sweetened, iced, green tea. Beware: this local concoction goes down very easily. But then, that's the idea.

Check, Please!

The ranges in our chart reflect actual prices of main courses on dinner menus (unless dinner isn't served). That said, the custom of sharing dishes affects the ultimate cost of your dinner. Further, we exclude outrageously expensive dishes—abalone, bird's nest soup, shark's fin soup—and seafood at market prices when we assign ranges.

Don't be shocked when the bill shows that you've been charged for everything, including tea, rice, and those side dishes placed automatically on your table. Tips are expected (10% is average), even if the bill includes a service charge, which *won't* go to the waitstaff.

What's Your Pleasure?

■ **Dim Sum:** Che's, Dim Sum, Yung Kee

■ **Power Lunch:** Amber, Caprice, Pétrus

■ **To Be the Lone Westerner:** Guangdong Barbecue Restaurant, Hay Hay, Hing Fat Restaurant

■ **To See-and-Be-Seen:** dragon-i, Isola, Opia

■ **Classic Cantonese:** Cuisine Cuisine, Lung King Heen, Yan Toh Heen

■ **Western Cravings:** SPOON, Steak House, Toscana

■ **Flopping-Fresh Fish:** JW's California, Tung Kee Seafood Restaurant, Victoria City Seafood

■ **Restaurant Speakeasies:** Bo Innovation, Da Ping Huo, Yellow Door Kitchen

■ **Great Views:** Aqua, One Harbour Road, Oyster & Wine Bar

■ **Fodor's Choices ($$–$$$$):** Hutong, Lung King Heen, Shui Hu Ju, Toscana, VEDA, Yan Toh Heen

■ **Fodor's Choices ($–$$):** Che's Cantonese Restaurant, Dim Sum, Yellow Door Kitchen

WHAT IT COSTS In HK$

	$$$$	$$$	$$	$	¢
AT DINNER	over $300	$200–$300	$100–$200	$50–$100	under $50

Prices are per person for a main course at dinner and exclude the customary 10% service charge.

the menu; perhaps the epicenter of inspiration is the last of those, with successful versions of dishes such as deep-fried chicken with hot chilies. Good, too, is crispy mutton. Ultimately, though, Shui Hu Ju's atmosphere is an even greater draw than the food: heavy antique doors welcome you into an intimate, lacquered-wood space that will make you feel as though you've just walked into a Zhang Yimou movie. It's expensive, but it's a Hong Kong experience not to be missed. ⊠ *68 Peel St., SoHo, Western* ☎ *2869–6927* ⊕ *www.aqua.com.hk* ⊟ *AE, DC, MC, V* ☺ *No lunch* Ⓜ *Central.*

Sichuan

$$ ✕ **Da Ping Huo.** If you can find the semi-hidden door to this restaurant speakeasy, one of Hong Kong's famed private kitchens, the rewards will be great indeed. It will begin with a 14-course meal that will take you on a spicy tour of the Sichuan province, and end with live Chinese opera, courtesy of the chef. The menu varies day to day—it's whatever the chef feels like preparing—so leave your food phobias and quirks at the door, especially if those phobias include a burning mouth: this is some of the spiciest food in town. ⊠ *49 Hollywood Rd., SoHo, Western* ☎ *2559–1317* ⊟ *AE, MC, V* ☺ *No lunch* Ⓜ *Central.*

$–$$ ✕ **Yellow Door Kitchen.** A sunny, casual Sichuan private kitchen (unlicensed Fodor'sChoice restaurant), the Yellow Door is still one of the most talked-about places
★ to eat in SoHo, even though it's been open since 2002. The space is downhome and personal, with good food and good feelings. Many of the spices and ingredients are shipped in from Sichuan province to create such wonders as bean curd and meat cooked in spicy Sichuan sauce and a memorable stuffed Hangzhou-style "8-treasure duck," which is stuffed with sticky rice and braised. The HK$250 set dinner, including eight starters, six mains, and dessert, is a great value. ⊠ *6/F, 37 Cochrane St., SoHo, Western* ☎ *2858–6555* ⊕ *www.yellowdoorkitchen.com. hk* ⊟ *AE, DC, MC, V* ☺ *Closed Sun. No lunch Sat.* Ⓜ *Central.*

Thai

$–$$ ✕ **Soho Spice.** As with a lot of restaurants in SoHo, the foremost emphasis at this restaurant is on design: a stone-walled garden out back with tables and trees just oozes with feng shui—it's an excellent alfresco choice—and floor-to-ceiling glass doors allow the light and greenery to enliven the minimalist indoor room as well. The Thai-Vietnamese fare isn't the most impressive in town, but it's a good choice if you're in the area; try the green papaya and mango salad, or red curry duck. ⊠ *47B Elgin St., SoHo, Western* ☎ *2521–1600* ⊕ *www. diningconcepts.com.hk* ⊟ *AE, DC, MC, V.*

> **ABOVE-IT-ALL DINING**
>
> Central is the place to catch the tram up to the legendary Victoria Peak. A meal in a restaurant at the city's highest point has to be on everyone's itinerary. The trip is justified many times over on clear days when the views from the top (and en route) are unparalleled. When the clouds are thick and low, though, you won't be able to see a thing—you'll just hear the sounds of the city beneath you.

Central

One of Hong Kong's busiest areas is particularly crazy at lunchtime, when office workers crowd the streets and eateries. Most restaurants have set lunches—generally good values—with speedy service, so everyone gets in and out within an hour. At night the norm is either a formal dinner or a quick bite followed by many drinks, especially in Central's nightlife center, a warren of cobbled backstreets called Lan Kwai Fong. If you want to sample the expat party scene, you might want to eat elsewhere and head to LKF after dinner; restaurants in this district tend to have a contrived quality, with stylized themes and menus along with relatively steep prices. They remind us more of places in Las Vegas or Times Square rather than in the gateway to China.

Cantonese

$$$$ ✕ **Lung King Heen.** It's made a serious case for being the best Cantonese
FodorsChoice restaurant in Hong Kong—and consequently, the world. Where other
★ contenders tend to get too caught up in prestige dishes, and hotel restaurants in name-brand chefs, here there's a complete focus on taste. When you try a little lobster-and-scallop dumpling, or a dish of house-made XO sauce that is this divine, you will be forced to reevaluate your entire conception of Chinese cuisine. ⊠ *Four Seasons Hotel, 8 Finance St. Central* ☎ *3196–8888* ⊕ *www.fourseasons.com* ⌲ *Reservations essential* ⊟ *AE, DC, MC, V* Ⓜ *Central.*

$$–$$$ ✕ **Cuisine Cuisine.** The dramatic structures that make up the International Finance Centre complex, dominated by IFC One, Hong Kong's tallest skyscraper, have become a hotbed of ambitious new restaurants—almost all of which have harbor views. This Cantonese restaurant is one of the best, already gaining praise for its traditional menu albeit with some nouvelle liberties such as sautéed sea whelk sliced into the shape of a flower and balanced above four cherry tomatoes au gratin. Other winners are chicken baked with rock salt in an age-old method, and deep-fried crispy duck breast stuffed with minced chicken and crabmeat. ⊠ *3101–3107, Podium Level 3, International Finance Center Mall, Central* ☎ *2393–3393* ⊕ *www.cuisinecuisine.hk* ⊟ *AE, DC, MC, V* Ⓜ *Central.*

¢–$$ ✕ **Yung Kee.** Since 1950 this massive eatery has served Cantonese food amid riotous decor and writhing gold dragons. Convenient to both hotels and businesses, Yung Kee specializes in roast goose with beautifully crisp skin, but the place is equally well known for dim sum. More adventurous palates may wish to check out the meltingly tender thousand-year-old eggs with ginger. Among the good seafood offerings are sautéed fillet of pomfret with chili and black-bean sauce, or braised garoupa. ⊠ *32–40 Wellington St., Central* ☎ *2522–1624* ⊕ *www.yungkee.com.hk* ⊟ *AE, DC, MC, V* Ⓜ *Central.*

¢ ✕ **Mak's Noodles Limited.** Mak's looks like any other Hong Kong

> **WORD OF MOUTH**
>
> "At Yung Kee, the service was quick, which was just as well because this restuarant must be one of the coldest places I've ever eaten (and I'm from Scotland!). The a/c was so high that our meal was spoiled."   –jab64000

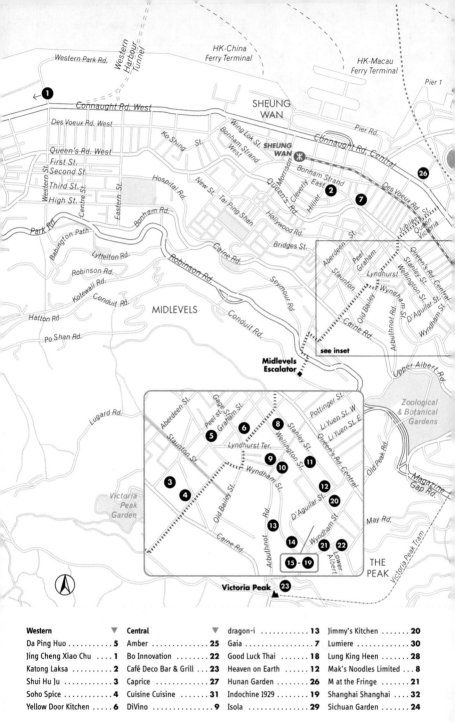

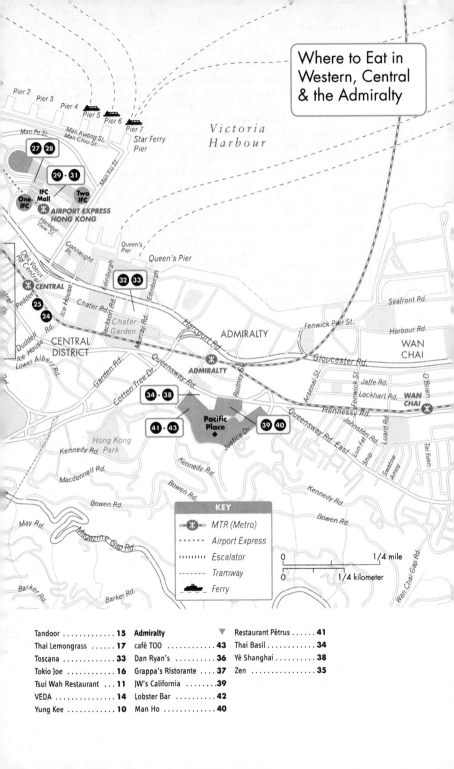

Where to Eat in Western, Central & the Admiralty

KEY

- MTR (Metro)
- Airport Express
- Escalator
- Tramway
- Ferry

0 ——— 1/4 mile
0 ——— 1/4 kilometer

noodle shop, but it's one of the best known in town, with a reputation that belies its humble decor. The staff is attentive, and the menu includes some particularly inventive dishes, such as tasty pork-chutney noodles. The real test of a good noodle shop, however, is its wontons, and here they're fresh, delicate, and filled with whole shrimp. And don't miss the *sui kau*, filled with minced chicken and shrimp. ✉ *77 Wellington St., Central* ☎ *2854–3810* ▭ *No credit cards* Ⓜ *Central.*

¢ ✕ **Tsui Wah Restaurant.** Looking for a hearty meal in Central doesn't mean you have to spend a fortune—especially not if you head here first. Join the locals and order milk tea, and then move on to the extensive menu, which ranges from toasted sandwiches to noodles, fried rice, and Malaysian curries. Although it's not quite what typical Hong Kongers would make at home, it's as close as you can come to Chinese comfort food. Noodles and fried rice are some of the safest bets for timid palates. There's also a wide range of set meals with very reasonable prices. ✉ *15D–19 Wellington St., Central* ☎ *2525–6338* ⊕ *www. tsuiwahrestaurant.com* ▭ *No credit cards* Ⓜ *Central.*

Contemporary

★ $$$$ ✕ **Amber.** When the Landmark Mandarin Oriental hotel opened in 2005 its aim was to be seen as the preeminent hotel on Hong Kong Island. It only made sense, therefore, that it would contain a flagship power-lunch restaurant that aspires to a similar level of impeccable, modern style. At his best, chef Richard Ekkebus shows shades of true genius, as when he serves a gentle bisque of New Zealand scampi daringly paired with chicken-liver custard, unexpected but passionate bedfellows. Amber also excels with desserts, for instance a crisp hazelnut and Caraibe chocolate bar served with a "moccachino." Prices are high, but so is the ambition—and the wavelike amber sculpture that soars like a grandiose pipe organ above the room. ✉ *Landmark Mandarin Oriental Hotel, 15 Queen's Rd., Central* ☎ *2132–0066* ▭ *AE, DC, MC, V* Ⓜ *Central.*

$$$$ ✕ **Bo Innovation.** One of the most deservedly renowned of Hong Kong's "private kitchens," Bo Innovation is a little gem that serves a kind of Japanese-Chinese-French fusion. It feels more upscale than most speakeasies, with sleek lines, dim lighting, and an open kitchen. The food, likewise, is unusually original. Chef-renaissance man Alvin Leung has a particular way with foie gras, which seems to make its way into most dishes in some way or another. Don't be shocked if it winds up paired with toro sashimi—two rich softnesses blending into one. And if you engage in a conversation with Alvin, you might end up learning something about musical acoustics—or wines from Burgundy. ✉ *UG/F, 32— 38 Ice House, Central* ☎ *2850–8371* ⊕ *www.boinnovation.com* ☖ *Reservations essential* ▭ *AE, MC, V* ☉ *Closed Sun. No lunch Sat.* Ⓜ *Central.*

★ $$–$$$ ✕ **M at the Fringe.** When Michelle Garnaut opened M at the Fringe in 1989, the idea of a high-end restaurant that fused various culinary traditions, and was not affiliated to any hotel, was completely novel to Hong Kong. Although the concept is no longer unusual, the restaurant is still excellent, and its menu continues to defy categorization, at once embracing French, European, Turkish, Lebanese, and Italian cuisines. The common denominator, says Garnaut, is "simple, good, down-to-earth food that I like to eat and cook," from homemade sausages and her trademark slow-cooked lamb, to antipasto or meze platters, suckling pig, and creamy fish pie. Her pavlova is legendary, but try it amid the grand dessert platter of eight bite-size desserts. ✉ *1/F, South Block, 2 Lower Albert Rd., Central* ☎ *2877–4000* ⊕ *www.m-restaurantgroup.com* ✎ *Reservations essential* ☐ *AE, MC, V* ⊗ *No lunch weekends* Ⓜ *Central.*

Eclectic

♻ **$$–$$$$** ✕ **Café Deco Bar & Grill.** As at most restaurants that cater to captive audiences, dining up at the Peak is a crapshoot. This huge eatery in the Peak Galleria mall—at this writing, the only one with real views—is no exception: you come for the views, not the food. The best strategy might be to come here in time for sunset, hit Café Deco just for drinks and appetizers, and enjoy the vistas; then head down to the city for dinner. The overambitious menu, which haphazardly traverses five or six continents, is dramatically prepared by chefs in open kitchens (which will, at least, amuse the kids). Oysters are good and the pizza is okay, but you should avoid the insipid Southeast Asian fare and overpriced steaks. When you book (and you must), be sure to request a table with a view, as many tables in the place have none, which defeats the purpose of coming. ✉ *1st level, Peak Galleria, 118 Peak Rd., The Peak, Central* ☎ *2849–5111* ⊕ *www.cafedecogroup.com* ✎ *Reservations essential* ☐ *AE, DC, MC, V.*

> ### WORD OF MOUTH
>
> "Café Deco is definitely tourist oriented and very noisy. But the view from a window table is divine."
> –Paul

$$–$$$$ ✕ **Jimmy's Kitchen.** One of the oldest restaurants in Hong Kong, Jimmy's opened in 1928 and has been catering to a loyal clientele of mostly Old China Hands ever since. The setting is shamelessly colonial, with dark-wood booths and brass fittings. The menu features comfort food as charmingly old-fashioned as the place itself: everything from corned beef and cabbage to a traditional mixed grill. Other specialties include borscht, goulash, and bangers and mash, plus Asian selections ranging from curry to fried rice. Homey desserts include bread-and-butter pudding. ✉ *South China Bldg., 1–3 Wyndham St., basement, Central* ☎ *2526–5293* ☐ *AE, DC, MC, V* Ⓜ *Central.*

French

★ **$$$$** ✕ **Caprice.** The Four Seasons spared no expense in creating this stunning space, bringing in well-known designers and feng shui masters, which has resulted in a private dining room that is quite possibly one of the most spectacular in the world: you sit next to an indoor garden, looking through the entire open kitchen, floor-to-ceiling glass, and the great harbor beyond. Chef Vincent Thierry sets himself apart with the details: beside an expertly roasted Dover sole whose texture strikes an ideal balance of softness and resilience sit a few modest-looking asparagus shoots sautéed in butter, quietly approaching perfection. Reserve well in advance, even for lunch. ⊠ *Four Seasons Hotel, 8 Finance St., Central* ☎ *3196–8888* ⊕ *www.fourseasons.com* ⌁ *Reservations essential* ⊟ *AE, DC, MC, V* Ⓜ *Central.*

Hunan

$–$$ ✕ **Hunan Garden.** The spicy-hot Hunan cuisine here is served in a serene setting, with live Chinese classical music as accompaniment on certain evenings. Crispy fried-fish "butterflies" (thinly sliced carp pieces deep-fried and dipped in a very sweet coating) make a delicious appetizer. The spicy fried chicken with chili may well set your mouth on fire; if you like things milder, stick with the codfish fillet with fried minced beans—the chewy and nutty bean paste goes perfectly with the fillet's soft texture. For an authentic experience try the warm Shaoxing wine; request lemon slices with the wine for a zestier aroma. ⊠ *3/F, The Forum, Exchange Sq., Connaught Rd., Central* ☎ *2868–2880* ⊟ *AE, DC, MC, V* Ⓜ *Central.*

Indian

$$–$$$ ✕ **VEDA.** Hong Kong's only "new wave" Indian restaurant is a culinary
Fodor's Choice   journey to the best of India's regional cuisines, presented in a refresh-
★   ingly modern style. The low-lighted rooms are comfortable, modern, and chic, and the staff couldn't be nicer. Chef Rajiv Singh Gulshan is a master of his craft, from his spectacular breads to the groundbreaking main courses like venison with Himalayan berry chutney, tandoori lobster, and Anjou pigeon with caramelized onion and mango puree. At the same time, traditional dishes like rogan josh (stewed lamb) are handled with an expert touch. The lunch buffet is a remarkable value. Reservations are necessary on weekends. ⊠ *8 Arbuthnot Rd., Central* ☎ *2868–5885* ⊕ *www.veda.com.hk* ⊟ *AE, DC, MC, V* Ⓜ *Central.*

$–$$ ✕ **Tandoor.** One of Hong Kong's oldest Indian restaurants is back in a new Lan Kwai Fong location, with a renewed sense of adventure for those seeking more than standard fare. The classy curry house has long been a favorite among the business community, and the lunch buffet gives you the most value for your money. Chef Anil Khurana's exceptional dishes include spicy prawns and lamb with fresh fenugreek leaves. A live band performs traditional Indian music in the evening. ⊠ *1/F, Lyndhurst Tower, Lan Kwai Fong, 1 Lyndhurst Terr., Central* ☎ *2845–2262* ⊕ *www.hktandoor.com* ⊟ *AE, DC, MC, V* Ⓜ *Central.*

Italian

$$$$ ✕ **Toscana.** One of the best Italian restaurants in Asia, Toscana is not con-
Fodor's Choice   tent to serve just the classics, as many Hong Kong Italian joints, however
★   fancy, are wont to do. Rather, Umberto Bombana's cuisine is something more exciting, more artistic. He begins by flying just about every ingredient in from Italy, right down to the eggs. Then, the master chef embarks upon inspired flights of fancy. Delicately seared foie gras might meet up with Sicilian lemon, or a dish of pasta that distills the sweetest essence from scampi (a sweet Adriatic shellfish) yet seamlessly marries it to tomato. All this is served up in a room that is sumptuous and elegant without being stuffy—equally suited for a business lunch or a romantic dinner. ⊠ *Ritz-Carlton, 3 Connaught Rd., Central* ☎ *2532–2062* ⊕ *www.*

ritzcarlton.com ⊟ *AE, DC, MC, V* ☉ *Closed Sun.* Ⓜ *Central.*

$$–$$$ ✕ **DiVino.** This ultracool wine bar feels like something straight out of Milan, bringing with it small plates for casual snacking and mixed platters ideal for sharing. Not surprisingly, it's popular with the drinks-after-work crowd—and you

WORD OF MOUTH

"Quite popular with the after-work crowd, DiVino makes for an energizing start to a big night out in Hong Kong."   –Nicole

get complimentary savory treats with your wine from 6 to 8 PM. But don't underestimate the cuisine: the tailor-made cold-cut platters, for starters, are superb. The cheese board is served with crusty, oven-warm bread. Heavier pasta main courses include gnocchi with lamb and mushroom sauce. The place also stays open for revelry late into the evening. ⊠ *Shop 1, 73 Wyndham St., Central* ☎ *2167–8883* ⊕ *www.divino.com. hk* ⊟ *AE, DC, MC, V* ☉ *Closed Sun. No lunch Sat.* Ⓜ *Central.*

$$–$$$ ✕ **Gaia.** Even if you find the concept here—a re-creation of Rome's Spanish steps—cheesy it's hard to argue with the alfresco seating at this trendy wine bar and restaurant. You should venture indoors only if you can put up with the loud investment bankers. The authentic pan-Italian fare includes pappardelle in a Sangiovese-marinated rabbit ragout, and a simple *fritto misto,* the classic combination of fried fish, calamari, and shrimp. ⊠ *G/F, The Piazza, Grand Millennium Plaza, 181 Queen's Rd., Central* ☎ *2167–8200* ⊕ *www.gaiaristorante.com* ⊟ *AE, DC, MC, V* Ⓜ *Sheung Wan.*

$$–$$$ ✕ **Isola.** In the shadow of the world's sixth-tallest building, flowing Isola is everything that the new Hong Kong is all about, especially the outdoor seats, which are set amid an urban jungle of concrete, manicured glass, and potted trees, in front of the open harbor. But Isola's regional Italian cuisine is also shockingly authentic, with selections like chestnut-and-mushroom ravioli with pumpkin, thyme, and sage sauce; simple and well-executed stone-baked pizzas; or roasted langoustines wrapped in *lardo di collonnata,* a delicious type of pork fat. Even so, Isola is as much of a nighttime bar scene as anything else, and it's worth coming just to sample cocktails and take in the soaring room. ⊠ *Levels 3 & 4, International Finance Center Mall, Central* ☎ *2383–8765* ⊕ *www.isolabarandgrill.com* ⊟ *AE, DC, MC, V* Ⓜ *Central.*

Japanese

$$$–$$$$ ✕ **dragon-i.** If you can stomach the scene at this top of the scenesters, an evening at Dragon-I can be a memorable experience. The hip, "orientalist" interior is a window into the world of Hong Kong's Beautiful People. A velvet rope shows up at some point each evening, and the models all put in an appearance on Wednesday nights (and along follows everyone else). Happily, the Japanese fusion food and sushi generally keeps up—just don't come with lofty expectations, and be prepared to spend a lot for small portions. Dim sum lunch on the terrace (an exception to the general Japanese culinary theme) is a lower-impact way to go. ⊠ *UG/F, The Centrium, 60 Wyndham St., Central* ☎ *3110–1222* ⊕ *www.dragon-i.com.hk* ☌ *Reservations essential* ⊟ *AE, DC, MC, V* ☉ *Closed Sun.* Ⓜ *Central.*

$$–$$$$ ✕ **Tokio Joe.** This funky casual Japanese joint in Lan Kwai Fong serves "user-friendly Japanese food" with attentive and courteous finesse, yet without intimidating formality. The interior is fun—beautiful ceramic pots line faux-fur walls. Chefs work in a central bar area, and lend a wonderfully contemporary twist to some classic dishes. Selections include spicy toro tartare, kelp-grilled sea bass, and battered tempura shrimp. Ask for a sake recommendation. For dessert, try homemade sesame ice cream. ✉ *16 Lan Kwai Fong, Lan Kwai Fong, Central* ☎ *2525–1889* ⊕ *www.lankwaifong.com* ⌕ *Reservations essential* ▤ *AE, DC, MC, V* ⊘ *No dinner Sun.* Ⓜ *Central.*

Shanghainese

★ **$$$–$$$$** ✕ **Shanghai Shanghai.** This retro-Chinese restaurant with art deco touches, stained glass, discreet private rooms, and wooden booths captures the mood of 1930s Shanghai. The menu ranges from simple Shanghainese midnight snacks and cold appetizers, such as mock goose and smoked fish, to pricey delicacies such as abalone. After 9 PM the lights dim and a chanteuse croons favorites requested by diners. The intimate restaurant has become a hot spot for affluent Chinese reminiscing about the good old days. ✉ *Ritz-Carlton Hotel, 3 Connaught Rd., Central* ☎ *2877–6666* ⌕ *Reservations essential* ▤ *AE, DC, MC, V* ⊘ *Closed Sun.* Ⓜ *Central.*

¢–$$ ✕ **Heaven on Earth.** There are some Hong Kong moments when all you feel like is a simple bowl of spicy noodles, but you aren't in the mood for the sensory barrage and language-barrier antics associated with the neighborhood noodle shops. That's where Heaven on Earth, which used to be just a bar and still feels like a sleek cocktail lounge, comes in. It's a modern, dimly lighted, but relatively inexpensive place for Shanghainese noodle and dumpling dishes that nudge toward originality but don't cross familiar bounds. Lunch specials at HK$30—HK$35 are a particular bargain. ✉ *Basement, Century Sq., 1–13 D'Aguilar St., Central* ☎ *2537 8083* ⊕ *www.kingparrot.com* ▤ *AE, MC, V* Ⓜ *Central.*

Sichuan

$$–$$$ ✕ **Lumiere.** Modern, sexy Lumiere, in the IFC Mall, bills itself as a "Szechuan Bistro and Bar," and its menu blends Sichuan and South American cuisines. Although main courses are Sichuan in inspiration, like spicy jumbo crab claws, the starters include ceviche. Mongolian mutton slices also get high marks, as does the unique cocktail list at the long bar, which overlooks the harbor. Drinks are classified into "fruity," "creamy," and "sweet-and-sour," and also categorized by strength. Here, too, there's South America to thank, as in a "Caipiritini"—or, if you prefer, there's always the 1970 Pétrus. ✉ *3101–3107, Podium Level 3, International Finance Center Mall, Central* ☎ *2393–3393* ⊕ *www.cuisinecuisine.hk* ▤ *AE, DC, MC, V* Ⓜ *Central.*

$–$$ ✕ **Sichuan Garden.** This spacious restaurant is renowned for its exotic Sichuan delicacies such as smoked duck in camphor wood and tea leaves. The interior is not posh, and the lighting is too bright, but the food is the real deal. Fried sliced mutton with spring onion and sesame pockets is a menu highlight; to eat this delicacy you stuff the warm sesame pocket with the tender fried meat and make your own Sichuan-style mutton sandwich. Friendly and attentive service adds to the overall score. ⊠ *The Landmark, 3/F, Gloucester Tower, Central* ☎ *2521–4433* 🖃 *AE, DC, MC, V* Ⓜ *Central.*

Thai

$–$$$ ✕ **Thai Lemongrass.** Regional Thai cuisine is served with a modern twist in this relaxed and comfortable Lan Kwai Fong restaurant with large windows providing some natural light. The menu highlights dishes from three different regions of Thailand. Your gourmet tour could include grilled, whole, freshwater fish and herbs cooked in banana leaves with coriander-chili-lime sauce (north and northeast); sizzling seafood mousse with light red curry and coconut milk, or roast duck in red curry (Central Plains); or Thai barbecued lamb cutlets (south). ⊠ *30–32 D'Aguilar St., California Tower, Lan Kwai Fong, Central* ☎ *2905–1688* ⊕ *www. lankwaifong.com* 🖃 *AE, DC, MC, V* ⊘ *No lunch Sun.* Ⓜ *Central.*

¢–$$ ✕ **Good Luck Thai.** If you're around Lan Kwai Fong at mealtime but don't feel like spending a fortune, this Thai spot is one of your best options. Tucked in a dead-end street, the hole-in-the-wall offers hearty and unpretentious Thai food with very friendly prices and service. Pad Thai, grilled chicken, and diced beef wrapped in lettuce are just some of the favorites here. Enjoy the alfresco seating as you watch the world go by. If you're into the boisterous expat scene, the nearby bars and pubs are great choices for a pre-meal aperitif and after-dinner drinks. ⊠ *13 Wing Wah La., G/F, Lan Kwai Fong, Central* ☎ *2877–2971* ⊕ *www. lankwaifong.com* 🖃 *No credit cards* ⊘ *Closed Sun.* Ⓜ *Central.*

Vietnamese

$–$$$ ✕ **Indochine 1929.** It's touristy and it caters to westerners, but this second-floor Vietnamese restaurant in the heart of the Lan Kwai Fong nightstrip is fun, too, transporting you to a French plantation veranda in colonial Indochina, surrounded by old maps, antique fans, and lamps. Most of the spices used are

> **WORD OF MOUTH**
>
> "The elevator at Indochine 1929 whisks you back to French Indochina, where you dine in style on scrumptious Vietnamese cuisine."   –HR

imported from Vietnam, even if they're employed less liberally than they would be over there. Highlights include soft-shell crab, grilled beef salad, and fried fish Hanoi style (using northern spices). Unfortunately, in classic LKF form, service is distracted, sometimes even rude—maybe they're sick of listening to all the raucous foreigners. ⊠ *2/F, California Tower, 30–32 D'Aguilar St., Lan Kwai Fong, Central* ☎ *2869–7399* ⊕ *www.lkfe.com* 🖃 *AE, DC, MC, V* ⊘ *No lunch Sun.* Ⓜ *Central.*

Admiralty

Since this is essentially an office area, wedged between Central and Wan Chai and made up of a series of large shopping malls, much of the food is aimed at meeting the lunch needs of workers and shoppers. A major cinema and several good restaurants in the Pacific Place mall, however, make it a convenient destination for dinner as well. Admiralty is also home to several large hotels, which is part of why the area, along with Lan Kwai Fong and Tsim Sha Tsui, has one of Hong Kong's highest concentrations of western restaurants. Not that that's necessarily a good thing.

American

☕ $-$$$ ✕ **Dan Ryan's.** If, after a few days of goose web and thousand-year egg, you have a sudden burger craving, this is the place. You'll find good approximations of the kind expats dream about when they think of the States. The popular bar and grill is often standing room only, so call ahead for a table. Apart from burgers and beer, the menu offers a smattering of international dishes—pasta and the like—but we recommend that you stay away from anything complicated (and certainly anything with fish) and stick to the simple, rib-sticking fare, served up without fuss or formality. ✉ *114 Pacific Pl., 88 Queensway, Admiralty* ☎ *2845–4600* ⊕ *www.danryans.com* ⌦ *Reservations essential* ⊟ *AE, DC, MC, V* Ⓜ *Admiralty.*

Cantonese

$$-$$$$ ✕ **Man Ho.** The big, open, banquet-style room with the rows of round tables is the most authentic format for Cantonese high dining, and in a city full of flashy, postmodern restaurants, it's nice to see the JW Marriott's flagship Chinese dining room still wedded to tradition. The same can be said for the food: it's high-end and well-executed, but you won't find fusion here. This is a good place to try abalone (such as braised chicken with fresh abalone in a casserole), fresh fish (pan-fried garoupa in soy sauce has a wonderfully delicate flavor), and Cantonese classics like the impossibly light, roast crispy suckling pig, with its skin the consistency of a wafer—it's one of the best in the city. ✉ *JW Marriott Hotel, Pacific Place, 88 Queensway, Admiralty* ☎ *2841–3899* ⊕ *http://marriott.com* ⊟ *AE, DC, MC, V* Ⓜ *Admiralty.*

$$-$$$ ✕ **Zen.** The dim sum is a highlight at this upscale nouvelle Cantonese eatery, part of a group of chic London restaurants of the same name. Recommended small dishes include deep-fried boneless chicken wings stuffed with glutinous rice, and deep-fried shrimp with chili and garlic. More familiar Cantonese dishes are delicately prepared and

> **WORD OF MOUTH**
>
> "A local recommended dim sum at Zen. We found a short menu of very traditional items, but everything we had was very good and cooked to order."   –Doris

presented. Service is flawless, and the decor is contemporary, with dramatic hanging lights and a central waterfall. ✉ *Lower Level, The Mall, Pacific Place 1, 88 Queensway, Admiralty* ☎ *2845–4555* ⊟ *AE, DC, MC, V* Ⓜ *Admiralty.*

Contemporary

★ $$$-$$$$ ✕ **JW's California.** Lobster and raw fish are the draw at this sleek, trendy flagship of the JW Marriott Hotel. Slide up to the sushi bar and leave your fate in the hands of the virtuoso sushi chef, who serves up pricey but artistic plates of sushi and sashimi made with incredibly fresh fish. At the restaurant itself, the JW's Taster Plate introduces the appetizers, and then there's the lobster. You might also try salmon with artichokes and chorizo, spring lamb done "three ways" (cutlet, confit, and liver), and finish with the Napa Valley dessert sampler of chocolate Napoleon, peanut butter mousse, and a raspberry tart. ⊠ *5/F, JW Marriott Hotel, Pacific Place, 88 Queensway, Admiralty* ☎ *2841–3899* ⊕ *http://marriott.com* ▤ *AE, DC, MC, V* Ⓜ *Admiralty.*

Ⓒ **$$–$$$$** ✕ **café TOO.** It'll amuse the buffet-loving kids, at least: the innovative café TOO introduces all-day dining and drama with seven separate cooking "theaters" and a brigade of 30 chefs. The liveliness and bustle make it a good place to stop for breakfast or lunch. Take your pick from seafood, sushi, and sashimi; Peking duck and dim sum; a carving station for roasts, poultry, and game; noodles and pastas; and pizzas, curries, tandooris, antipasto, cured meats, salads, or sandwiches. You can even have a late-night snack here from 10:30 PM to midnight. ⊠ *7/F, Island Shangri-La, Pacific Place, Supreme Court Rd., Admiralty* ☎ *2820–8571* ⊕ *www.shangri-la.com* ▤ *AE, DC, MC, V* Ⓜ *Admiralty.*

French

★ **$$$$** ✕ **Restaurant Pétrus.** Commanding breathtaking views atop the Island Shangri-La, Restaurant Pétrus scales the upper Hong Kong heights of prestige, formality, and price. This is one of the city's few flagship hotel restaurants that have not attempted to reinvent themselves as fusion; sometimes traditional French haute cuisine is what you want. Likewise, the design of the place is in the old-school restaurant-as-ballroom mode. The kitchen has a particularly good way with (surprise!) foie gras, and the wine list is memorable, with verticals of Chateau Pétrus among the roughly 1,000 celebrated vintages. ⊠ *56/F, Island Shangri-La, Pacific Place, Supreme Court Rd., Admiralty* ☎ *2820–8590* ⊕ *www.shangri-la.com* ⌂ *Reservations essential* 🏛 *Jacket required* ▤ *AE, DC, MC, V* Ⓜ *Admiralty.*

Italian

$$–$$$ ✕ **Grappa's Ristorante.** Don't let the location of this restaurant put you off. Once inside, you can turn your back on the mall surroundings and let the kindly staff serve you superb Italian food. The endless selection of pastas can prolong your decision making, but the food is well worth it. Pan-fried foie gras makes an excellent kickoff, and osso buco, smothered in a rich flavorful sauce, is a dish you shouldn't miss. Game hen stuffed with sun-dried tomatoes, garlic, and fresh rosemary tastes as good as it sounds. With good coffee and a range of bottled beers, Grappa's is equally useful for a quick pick-me-up or a post-shopping rendezvous. ⊠ *132 Pacific Place, 88 Queensway, Admiralty* ☎ *2868–0086* ⊕ *www.elgrande.com.hk* ▤ *AE, DC, MC, V* Ⓜ *Admiralty.*

> **WORD OF MOUTH**
>
> "There is no better way to take a break from shopping than a bite at Grappa's."   –Ryan

Seafood

$$–$$$$ ✕ **Lobster Bar.** The giant tropical-fish tank at the entrance sets the scene here. As the name suggests, lobster is the featured ingredient, whipped into soups, stuffed into appetizers, and presented in full glory in numerous entrées. Lobster bisque is creamy yet light, with great chunks of meat at the bottom. The seafood platter—half a lobster thermidor, whole grilled langoustine, shrimps, baked oysters, creamy scallops, crab cakes, black cod—doesn't disappoint. Decorated in blue and gold, with mahogany timbers, leather upholstery, and the sparkle of stained glass, the restaurant has a vibe that is at once formal and cozy—and as such, the place is also great for before- or after-dinner drinks at the bar. ⊠ *Island Shangri-La, Pacific Place, Supreme Court Rd., lobby level, Admiralty* ☎ *2877–3838 Ext. 8560* ⊕ *www.shangri-la.com* ⌕ *Reservations essential* ⊟ *AE, DC, MC, V* Ⓜ *Admiralty.*

Shanghainese

$$–$$$$ ✕ **Yè Shanghai.** This nostalgic replica of old Shanghai is part of a chain expanding across Asia. The old-fashioned setting includes 1950s furnishings and ceiling fans. First there are the dumplings: an exemplary version of steamed pork soup dumplings, for instance; then, entrées like pork knuckle braised in sweet soy sauce, or braised meatballs ("lion's head"). For dessert, try the Shanghai staple, deep-fried egg white stuffed with banana and mashed red-bean paste. Reserve early for comfortable booth seats or window tables. A band plays Chinese oldies on Thursday, Friday, and Saturday nights. ⊠ *Level 3, Pacific Place, 88 Queensway, Admiralty* ☎ *2918–9833* ⊕ *www.elite-concepts.com* ⊟ *AE, DC, MC, V* Ⓜ *Admiralty.*

Thai

$–$$ ✕ **Thai Basil.** At this smart mall restaurant at the entrance to Pacific Place, the chef artfully presents Asian creations with a contemporary twist. Innovative dishes include mussels wok-fried in green curry, sting ray salad with green mango, and green papaya and crispy fish. Also highly recommended in winter is the braised lamb shank. The homemade ice-cream selection is eclectic with flavors from ginger to honeycomb. For a price, you can watch your dinner being created at an exclusive table called the Kitchen. ⊠ *Lower G/F, Shop 005, Pacific Place, Admiralty* ☎ *2537–4682* ⊟ *AE, DC, MC, V* Ⓜ *Admiralty.*

> **WORD OF MOUTH**
>
> "Thai Basil's dishes have great flavors, and the desserts are wonderful. A tad expensive but I would definitely go again."   –Jude

Wan Chai

At lunchtime Wan Chai is just another jumble of people, but after dark it comes into its own. This is Hong Kong's prime nightlife district, its long roads lined with fluorescent lights and jam-packed with taxis and lively crowds of people. The range of dining options is extreme—from five-star luxury to noodle-shop dives open into the wee hours. On the ground-floor level along main drags, in part because of the western

CLOSE UP

At Least the Sex Is Good

IT MAKES SENSE that soup made from shark's fin—said to be an aphrodisiac—costs so much. Only the promise of increased virility would lead someone to pay HK$1,000 or more for a bowl of the stuff. It actually consists of cartilage from the great beast's pectal, dorsal, and lower tail fins that has been skinned, dried, and reconstituted in a rich stock form. This cartilage has almost no taste on its own and is virtually indistinguishable from *tun fun* (cellophane) noodles that are used to create "mock shark's fin soup."

Selling shark's fins is a big business, and Hong Kong is said to be responsible for 50% of the global trade. The soup is a fixture at banquets, weddings, and state dinners here. Love potion, elixir,

vitality booster, or not, at the very least the dish is high in protein. Recently, however, conservation groups have pointed out that it's also high in mercury. But of even greater concern is the practice of "finning." Since shark meat as a whole isn't valuable, fishermen often clip the fins and dump the rest of the animal back into the sea.

So, is eating shark's fin soup a not-to-be-missed Hong Kong experience or a morally reprehensible act? Well, we don't need to take sides in the debate to warn you away from it. Let us repeat: the shark's fin cartilage *has no taste*. This makes it—and bird's nest soup, that other tasteless Cantonese delicacy—one of the biggest wastes of money in the culinary universe.

nightlife influence, you're far more likely to find a mediocre pan-European tapas bar hawking happy-hour specials than a brilliant, innovative Asian restaurant. To find the best local places you have to head to the upper floors or hit the side streets.

Cantonese

$$$–$$$$ ✕ **Dynasty.** Dining on haute Cantonese cuisine at the highest Chinese restaurant in Hong Kong, with panoramic views over Victoria Harbor, is indeed a memorable experience. The chef, Tam Sek Lun, is famed for adapting family-style recipes into works of art. The menu changes with the seasons and leans heavily toward fresh seafood, plus luxurious temptations like bird's nest and shark's fin—although not everyone believes those items are necessarily worth the money, here or anywhere else. Lunchtime dim sum is recommended. ✉ *3/F, Renaissance Harbour View, 1 Harbour Rd., Wan Chai* ☎ *2802–8888 Ext. 6971* ⊕ *http://marriott.com* ⊟ *AE, DC, MC, V* Ⓜ *Wan Chai.*

$$–$$$$ ✕ **One Harbour Road.** It's hard to say what's more impressive at the Grand Hyatt's Cantonese showpiece—the interior design (two terraced indoor levels, the sound of rushing water, and an incredible sense of space and motion), or the view over the harbor from the restaurant's floor-to-ceiling windows, which dominates the experience of every table on both levels of the restaurant. Unlike many harborside establishments, you don't need a window seat to catch the view. And the Cantonese cuisine is tra-

ditional but excellent—for best results, order from among the rotating seasonal dishes. ⊠ *8/F, Grand Hyatt Hotel, 1 Harbour Rd., Wan Chai* 🕾 *2584–7938* ⊕ *http://hongkong.grand.hyatt.com* ⊟ *AE, DC, MC, V* Ⓜ *Wan Chai.*

$–$$ ✕ **Che's Cantonese Restaurant.** Smartly dressed locals-in-the-know
Fodor'sChoice   head for this casually elegant dim sum specialist, which is in the
★   middle of the downtown bustle yet well concealed on the fourth floor of an office building. From the elevator, you'll step into a classy Cantonese world. It's hard to find a single better dim sum dish than Che's crispy pork buns, whose sugary baked pastry conceals the brilliant saltiness of stewed pork within. Other dim sum to try include pan-fried turnip cake; rich, tender braised duck web (foot) in abalone sauce; and a refreshing dessert of cold pomelo and sago with mango juice for a calming end to an exciting meal. ⊠ *4/F, The Broadway, 54–62 Lockhart Rd., Wan Chai* 🕾 *2528–1123* ⊟ *AE, DC, MC, V* Ⓜ *Wan Chai.*

¢   ✕ **Hay Hay.** The best food in Hong Kong can hide out in the dingiest storefronts, and nowhere is this more true than at Hay Hay, a restaurant whose business card contains not a word of English. Surprisingly, though, there's an English menu lurking somewhere in the back office, but you shouldn't bother with it. Instead, just point to what looks good on other tables—it's likely to be a delicious plate of rice, sweet, tender roast goose or pork, and greens; or an exemplary noodle soup with slices of roast meat resting on top. Apply the hot sauce liberally, and don't expect the staff to speak a word of English. ⊠ *72–86 Lockhart Rd., corner of Ward St., Wan Chai* 🕾 *2143–6183* ⊟ *No credit cards* Ⓜ *Wan Chai.*

Indonesian
★ **$$**   ✕ **Bebek Bengil 3** (Dirty Duck Diner). Inspired by a tiny but legendary institution in Bali, this re-creation in the heart of Wan Chai similarly specializes in crispy duck, marinated for 36 hours in an age-old recipe of spices. The seating is sala-style (at a low table, sitting on pillows on the floor), on an outside terrace overlooking bustling Lockhart Road. Familiar Indonesian dishes like *nasi lemak* (spicy fried rice with egg and anchovies) and beef *rendang* are on the menu. Finish with drinks at BB's lively sister establishment on the ground floor, the Klong Bar & Grill. ⊠ *5/F, The Broadway, 54–62 Lockhart Rd., Wan Chai* 🕾 *2217–8000* ⊕ *www.elite-concepts.com* ⊟ *AE, DC, MC, V* Ⓜ *Wan Chai.*

Shanghainese
$$ ✕ **Gitone Fine Arts.** This pottery-studio-cum-restaurant-speakeasy has acquired quite a following since its 1995 opening. An artistic couple runs the studio and gallery, and turn it into a cozy, unlicensed "private dining" restaurant at night. The menu varies completely from day to day, but there are generally both Shanghainese and Cantonese options. Go for the Shanghai-style meal, as this is the specialty—it will include up to 16 small courses making up a long night of adventurous tasting. The pork leg braised in sweet soy, when available, is outstanding; it's a

Shanghainese classic. Booking is absolutely essential, and unless you get lucky on a particular night, you must have at least a group of four. ⊠ *1/F, 100 Queen's Road E, Wan Chai* ☎ *9025–7777* ⚱ *Reservations essential* ▤ *AE, DC, MC, V* Ⓜ *Wan Chai.*

Seafood

★ **$–$$$$** ✕ **Victoria City Seafood.** This perennially popular restaurant excels at Cantonese dim sum, Shanghainese, and seafood. It's a big, bright, banquet-style space, generally packed with large groups. Not to be missed are the spectacular soup dumplings with hairy crab roe; steamed blood with leek and egg tarts; and stir-fried rice rolls with XO sauce. Seafood, which you select live from the tank, might include whitebait in chili sauce, steamed prawns in vinegar sauce, whole local garoupa with ginger, or crab cooked with fried garlic. There's an Admiralty branch, too. ⊠ *Sun Hung Kai Center, 30 Harbour Rd., Wan Chai* ☎ *2827–9938* ✉ *5/F Citic Tower, 1 Tim Mei Ave., Admiralty* ☎ *2877–2211* ▤ *AE, DC, MC, V* Ⓜ *Wan Chai.*

Thai

$$–$$$$ ✕ **JJ's.** For years, JJ's was one of the hottest tickets in town for live music and revelry, with a particular following among expats. Then, after Hong Kong's economic downturn, it closed, but has since reopened and is as good as ever. A visit here is first and foremost about the atmosphere and the music; with nooks, crannies, dark wood, and twisting staircases, the place feels akin to a dim Parisian artists' haunt, but with live bands. There's a Thai menu that's more creative than the norm, and a large cocktail list, including a truly luxurious concoction of caviar over frozen vodka. ⊠ *Grand Hyatt Hotel, 1 Harbour Rd., Wan Chai* ☎ *2584–7662* ⊕ *http://hongkong.grand.hyatt.com* ▤ *AE, DC, MC, V* Ⓜ *Wan Chai.*

SHANGHAI STYLE

Shanghai's culinary traditions favor seafood, but the city is also famous for its great varieties of buns and dumplings. Rich-flavored Shanghainese hairy crabs are winter favorites; sautéed freshwater shrimp are also a staple. Many dishes are fried and can be a bit greasy.

5

Causeway Bay

With a series of large Japanese department stores and numerous shopping malls, Causeway Bay is one of Hong Kong's busiest shopping districts, and becomes a real cultural phenomenon on Saturday afternoons. Adjoining Causeway Bay on its southern edge is Happy Valley, where the density of the population can be overwhelming. Several pubs are in the vicinity, but they're not concentrated on one strip; likewise, there are several good restaurants, but they can be hard for the uninitiated to find. Times Square, a huge, modern shopping mall, has four floors of restaurants in one of its towers, serving international cuisines including Korean, French, steak, and regional Chinese.

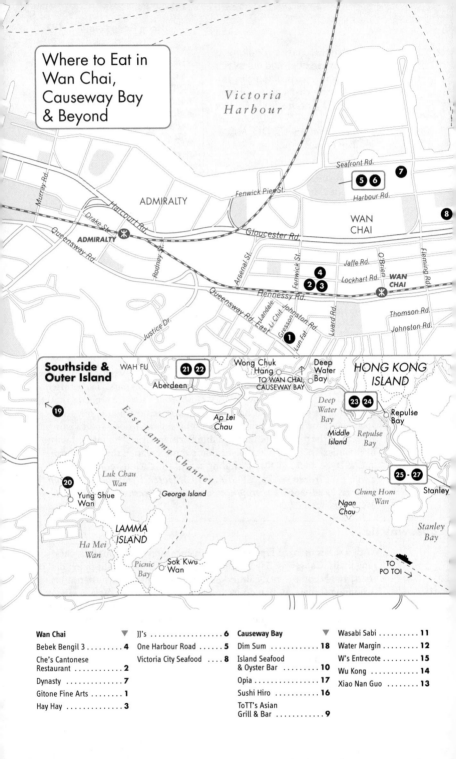

Where to Eat in Wan Chai, Causeway Bay & Beyond

Victoria Harbour

ADMIRALTY

WAN CHAI

WAN CHAI

Southside & Outer Island

HONG KONG ISLAND

WAH FU

Aberdeen

East Lamma Channel

Ap Lei Chau

Deep Water Bay

Middle Island

Repulse Bay

Repulse Bay

Stanley

Yung Shue Wan

Luk Chau Wan

George Island

Chung Hom Wan

Ngan Chau

Stanley Bay

Ha Mei Wan

LAMMA ISLAND

Picnic Bay

Sok Kwu Wan

TO PO TOI

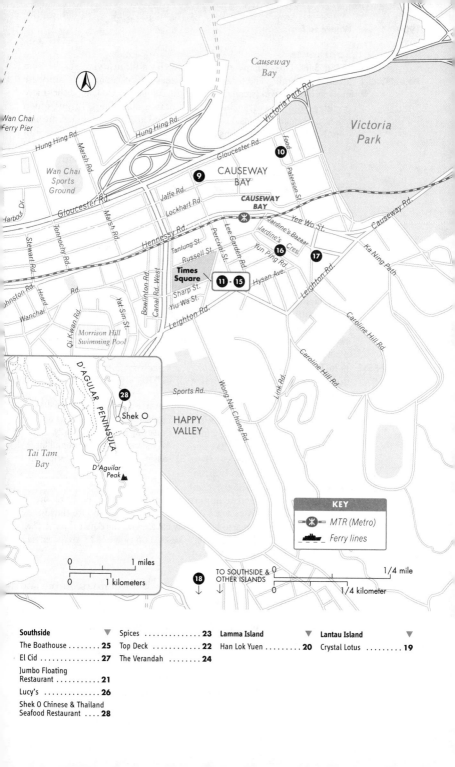

Cantonese

$–$$ ✕ **Dim Sum.** This elegant jewel breaks with tradition and serves dim sum
Fodor'sChoice all day and night. The original menu goes beyond common Cantonese
★ morsels like *har gau* (steamed shrimp dumplings), embracing dishes more
popular in the north, including chili prawn dumplings, Beijing onion
cakes, and steamed buns. Lobster bisque and abalone dumplings are also
popular. Lunch reservations are not taken on weekends, so there's always a long line. Arrive early, or admire the antique telephones and old
Chinese posters while you wait. Even if it feels somewhat contrived, it's
worth it. ✉ *63 Sing Woo Rd., Happy Valley, Causeway Bay* ☎ *2834–8893*
🍽 *AE, DC, MC, V* Ⓜ *Causeway Bay.*

Contemporary

★ **$$$$** ✕ **Opia.** The Philippe Starck–designed Jia Hotel is one of Hong Kong's
hottest, hippest spots, whether to eat, drink, or stay. Opia is its restaurant. Sip a smooth cocktail in the bar-lounge before being seated for dinner at one of the minimalist tables, and keep in mind that the place doesn't
really get going until 9 PM or so. The culinary theme is Australian, but
that won't help you predict what's on the menu: it might be better dubbed
Euro-Japanese-Thai, with dishes like yellowfin tuna sashimi with bonito
panna cotta and Wagyu red beef curry with pumpkin. DJs spin on
Wednesday and weekends. ✉ *UG/F, 1–5 Irving St., Causeway Bay*
☎ *3196–9000* ⊕ *www.jiahongkong.com* ✍ *Reservations essential*
🍽 *AE, MC, V* Ⓜ *Causeway Bay.*

$$–$$$$ ✕ **ToTT's Asian Grill & Bar.** The funky
interior—zebra-stripe chairs, a
central oval bar, and designer table-
ware—is matched by the East-
meets-West cuisine at this restaurant
on top of the Excelsior hotel, which
looks down on Causeway Bay and
the marina. It's one of the very best
dinner views in town, with a fun,
lively vibe to boot. Best on the menu

are steaks, with excellent imported meat cooked properly to order;
there's also an extensive wine list. Live music kicks in late during the
evening, offering a chance to burn a few calories on the dance floor. ✉ *Ex-
celsior Hotel, 281 Gloucester Rd., Causeway Bay* ☎ *2837–6786* 🍽 *AE,
DC, MC, V* Ⓜ *Causeway Bay.*

Japanese

$$$–$$$$ ✕ **Wasabi Sabi.** Panes of glass glowing in shades of red escort you into
a world full of columns of golden light draped from the ceiling, round
black banquettes, and swiveling red sofas—the interior of Wasabi Sabi
transports you far away from the shopping mall outside. The Japanese
creations served here seem also to come from another realm: from the
carpaccio of sea bream with wasabi red tea jelly, to a memorable sea urchin
custard, they are delightfully original, reaching far beyond sushi and
sashimi. ✉ *13/F Times Sq., 1 Matheson Rd., Causeway Bay* ☎ *2506–0009*
⊕ *www.aqua.com.hk* 🍽 *AE, DC, MC, V* Ⓜ *Causeway Bay.*

★ **$$–$$$** ✕ **Sushi Hiro.** Uni (sea urchin). Shirako (blowfish sperm). O-toro (the fattiest of fatty tuna). If these words make you drool, then you should make a beeline for Sushi Hiro, buried within an office building, and quite possibly the best place for raw fish in Hong Kong. The minimalist interior stays faithful to Japanese style, unlike some more opulent Hong Kong restaurants. But what really draws in the Japanese crowd is the freshness of the fish, which you can watch being filleted in front of you at the sushi bar. And by high-end sushi standards, Hiro is relatively inexpensive. ⌧ *10/F Henry House, 42 Yun Ping Rd., Causeway Bay* ☎ *2882–8752* ▭ *AE, DC, MC, V* Ⓜ *Causeway Bay.*

Northern Chinese

$$ ✕ **Water Margin.** Care to spend an evening along the ancient Silk Road? Water Margin, a beautiful, immensely popular restaurant done up in dark wood, stone, and red hanging lanterns—is as close as you'll get to it in Hong Kong. The meal begins with kimchee—the north of China is close to Korea—and continues with daring preparations of pig's throat, jellyfish, and braised lotus root. Steamed scallops in pumpkin puree would be a great winter dish if only Hong Kong had winter. ⌧ *Food Forum, 12/F Times Sq., 1 Matheson Rd., Causeway Bay* ☎ *3102–0088* ⊕ *www. aqua.com.hk* ▭ *AE, DC, MC, V* Ⓜ *Causeway Bay.*

Seafood

$$–$$$ ✕ **Island Seafood & Oyster Bar.** Tucked into a Causeway Bay shopping area that was once Hong Kong's food street, this laid-back spot is drawing foodies back. The deliciously fresh oysters come in several varieties from around the world; pick them as creamy or firm

> **WORD OF MOUTH**
>
> "If you make reservations at Island Seafood, be sure and ask if table No. 1 is available. Its location is perfect." –Lowell Thomas

as you like from the oyster bar, where the staff will happily make suggestions and serve the sexy mollusk on ice, or cooked hot to your liking. Read the chalkboard for daily specials, which are bound to include seafood and meat. ⌧ *Shop C, Towning Mansion, 50–56 Paterson St., Causeway Bay* ☎ *2915–7110* ▭ *AE, DC, MC, V* Ⓜ *Causeway Bay.*

Shanghainese

$–$$ ✕ **Wu Kong.** At the intersection of Nathan Road and Peking Road, this big basement dining room serves first-rate Shanghainese fare at reasonable prices. Pigeon in wine sauce is an excellent appetizer. Goose wrapped in crispy bean curd skin is delicious and authentic, as is the fish smothered in a sweet-and-sour sauce. The Shanghai-style doughnut on the dessert menu is a deep-fried sweet ball whipped up with fluffy egg whites and stuffed with red bean and banana. ⌧ *12/F, Food Forum, Times Sq., Causeway Bay* ☎ *2506–1018* ▭ *AE, DC, MC, V* Ⓜ *Causeway Bay.*

¢–$ ✕ **Xiao Nan Guo.** First, a disclosure: this is a chain restaurant. But in this case it's not a bad thing, since it's part of a Shanghai chain, and you want your Shanghainese food to be authentic. In the years since it came to Hong Kong, Xiao Nan Guo has developed a serious following, particularly for

The Dim Sum Experience

DIM SUM RESTAURANTS have always been associated with noise, so don't be dissuaded by the boisterous throngs of locals gathered around large round tables. At one time, big metal carts filled with bamboo baskets were pushed around the restaurant by ladies who would shout out the names of the dishes and stamp a mark onto a table's check when they ordered a basket of this or that. This is still the typical dim sum experience outside of China, but in Hong Kong, most restaurants require you to order off a form, creating a more sedate dining experience. Thankfully, many places offer English-translated order forms or menus, although you should ask your waiter about daily specials that might not appear in translation, as those are often some of the most exciting dim sum options. And never forget that most basic principle of Hong Kong ordering: simply point to something you see at a nearby table.

Although dim sum comes in small portions, it's still intended for sharing between three or four people. When all is said and done, a group can expect to try about 10 or 12 dishes, but don't order more than one of any single item. Most dim sum restaurants prepare between 15 and 100 varieties of the more than 2,000 kinds of dim sum in the Cantonese repertoire, daily. These can be buns, crêpes, cakes, pastries, or rice; they can be filled with beef, shrimp, pork, chicken, bean paste, or vegetables; and they can be bamboo-steamed, panfried, baked, or deep-fried. More esoteric offerings vary vastly from place to place. Abandon any squeamish tendencies and try at least one or two

unusual plates, like duck web in abalone sauce, liver dumplings, or dried pork bellies.

You'll be able to find dim sum from before dawn to around 5 or 6 PM, but it's most popular for breakfast (from about 7:30 to 10 AM) and lunch (from about 11:30 AM to 2:30 PM). Dim sum is served everywhere from local teahouses to high-concept restaurants, but it's often best at casually elegant, blandly decorated midrange spots that cater to Chinese families.

The following is a guide to some of our favorite common dim sum items, but don't let it narrow your mind. It's almost impossible to find a bite of dim sum that's anything less than delicious, and the more unique house specialties can often be the best.

BUNS

- **Cha siu so:** baked barbecued pork pastry buns; they're less common than the steamed cha siu bao, but arguably even better.

- **Cha siu bao:** steamed barbecued pork buns are an absolute must. With the combination of soft and chewy textures and sweet and salty tastes, you might forget to remove the paper underneath before eating.

DUMPLINGS

- **Ha gow:** steamed dumplings with a light translucent wrap that conceals shrimp and bamboo shoots.

- **Siu mai:** steamed pork dumplings are the most common dumplings and you'll find them everywhere; some are stuffed with shrimp.

MEATS

- **Ngau yuk:** steamed beef balls, like meatballs, placed on top of thin bean-

curd skins; not the most flavorful option, but a good one for kids or picky eaters.

- **Pie gwat:** bite-sized pieces of succulent pork spare ribs in a black bean and chili pepper sauce.

RICE CREATIONS

- **Ha cheong fun:** shrimp-filled rice rolls, whose dough is made in a rice-noodle style; the thick, flat rice rolls are drowned in soy sauce. Other versions include ngau yuk cheong fun (beef filled) and cha siu cheong fun (barbecued pork filled; if available, these are not to be missed).

- **Ho yip fan:** delicious sticky rice, which is usually cooked with chopped Chinese mushrooms, Chinese preserved sausage, and dried shrimp, and wrapped and steamed in a lotus leaf to keep it moist (don't eat the leaf).

DON'T BE AFRAID OF. . .

- **Woo tao go:** a glutinous pan fried taro cake, sweet enough for dessert but eaten as a savory dish, with delicate undertones that come from preserved Chinese sausage, preserved pork belly, and dried shrimp. Another version of this is lau bak go, which is made with turnip instead of taro.

- **Foong jow:** marinated chicken feet, whose smooth, soft texture is unlike any other. Once you get past the idea that you're sucking the cartilage off a foot, the sensation is wonderful.

SWEETS

- **Dan taht:** tarts with a custard filling, generally served for dessert. These sweet pastries are a Macau specialty.

- **Mong gwor bo deen:** mango pudding that has a consistently glassy texture and is not too sweet.

dim sum. The feeling is casual and unpretentious, with a bright, expansive, bustling dining room lined with round tables. The focus is really on the food: soup dumplings are excellent, as you'd expect, but don't forget about the fatty "Lion's Head" meatballs, or the pork belly. ⊠ *Shop 1201, 12/F Times Sq., 1 Matheson Rd., Causeway Bay* ☎ *2506–0009* ⊠ *Shop 1201, 12/F Times Sq., 1 Matheson Rd., Causeway Bay* ☎ *2874–8899* ⊕ *www.aqua.com.hk* ⊟ *AE, DC, MC, V* ⊘ *No lunch* Ⓜ *Causeway Bay.*

Steak House

$$–$$$ ✕ **W's Entrecote.** W's is a dining dictatorship: you can order steak, steak, or steak. Your only choices have to do with size and cooking time. Some call this the best steak in town, and the price includes a salad and as many fries as you can eat. The wine list is French, as is the interior: red-and-white-check tablecloths and French posters. Service is attentive and friendly, and it's a good place for a family meal. If you come with children and want to share a portion, just ask and the waiters will happily help you. Perched at the top of bustling Times Square, it's ideal for a bout of protein replenishment after battling the crowds. ⊠ *13/F, 1303 Times Sq., Causeway Bay* ☎ *2506–0133* ⊟ *AE, DC, MC, V* Ⓜ *Causeway Bay.*

Southside

The south side of Hong Kong Island is a string of beaches, rocky coves, and luxury developments; and Repulse Bay, 20 minutes away by bus from Central, is comprised of all three. Popular on weekends and in summer, the beach here is one of the best on the island. The Repulse Bay complex also has a number of good restaurants and shops, along with corporate apartments (housing for business travelers). The fastest way to get to this area is by taxi, though taking a bus is much cheaper.

A visit to Stanley Village reveals another side of Hong Kong, with a much slower pace of life than the one you see in the city. After exploring the market, historical sights, and beaches, take a leisurely meal at one of the top-notch restaurants scattered around, some of which have harbor views. Stanley is 30 minutes by bus or taxi from Central.

Also on the south side, Shek O is a tiny seaside village, but it has a few decent open-air restaurants. And once you've made the trek—the longest overland trip possible from Central—you'll need some sustenance. You can reach the village by bus or minibus from the Chai Wan MTR stop.

Contemporary

$$$ ✕ **The Verandah.** Step into another era here with champagne-cocktail trolleys, cool, granite floors, antique fans overhead, and palm trees waving through the arched teak windows. Tuxedoed waiters attend to your every whim at this unashamed celebration of the halcyon days of colonial rule, which serves an excellent Sunday brunch and afternoon tea daily. It really turns up trumps at night, though, when the chef whips up an impressive array of Continental dishes, from lobster to rack of lamb. The soufflé is a good way to finish. Even though it's expensive and full of tourists, it's a classic island experience. ⊠ *The Repulse Bay, 109 Repulse Bay Rd., Repulse Bay, Southside* ☎ *2292–2882* ⊕ *www.therepulsebay.com* ⊟ *AE, DC, MC, V.*

Eclectic

★ ✕ **Top Deck.** For a long time, the Jumbo Floating Restaurant and
☾ **$$–$$$$** Dragon Court were the only places to eat at Aberdeen's famed Jumbo Kingdom. But times change, and now there's Top Deck, a classier, less kitschy, if equally pricey alfresco option on the roof deck of the big boat, beneath a three-story pagoda. It has a vastly better view (and breeze) than the indoor restaurants beneath. If the weather permits, you should sit outdoors rather than at one of the few indoor tables. The menu is somewhat haphazard (Thai, Japanese, Indian, Italian, steak) but generally good. The raw bar is the best option, if you like seafood. There's a jazz band playing on Wednesday, and a Sunday brunch every week. ⊠ *Shum Wan Pier Path, Wong Chuk Hang, Aberdeen, Southside* ☎ *2552–3331* ⊕ *www.cafedecogroup.com* ⊟ *AE, MC, V* ☾ *Closed Mon.*

Mediterranean

$$–$$$ ✕ **The Boathouse.** The cozy Boathouse has a lovely view of the seafront, making it the perfect spot to hang out with friends and family. A bucket of mussels, served with nicely toasted garlic bread, goes down well with a glass of chilled white wine. Sandwiches and pastas are good bets for casual dining. And the delicious cobbler with wild berries will send you home happy. ⊠ *86–88 Stanley Main St., Southside, Stanley* ☎ *2813–4467* ⊟ *DC, MC, V.*

★ **$$** ✕ **Lucy's.** Laid-back, dark, and intimate, Lucy's has a dedicated following among locals. The food is fresh, lovingly presented, and unpretentious. Stilton, spinach, and walnuts in phyllo pastry make a perfect starter; for a main course,

> **WORD OF MOUTH**
>
> "Lucy's is perfect for lunch after a visit to Stanley Market."   –Paul

try the veal with polenta and Parma ham, or the deliciously light sea bass with pumpkin mash. And remember to leave room for Lucy's rich chocolate cake. ⊠ *G/F, 64 Stanley Main St., Southside, Stanley* ☎ *2813–9055* ⊟ *MC, V.*

Pan-Asian

$$ ✕ **Spices.** You can dine alfresco at Spices, surrounded by lawns and patios. And if the weather fails, there's an elegant interior to retreat to. The menu of classic Asian food flies from India to Japan and back again. Singaporean satay or Indonesian *kuwe udang goreng* (deep-fried prawn cakes) make good starters. Main courses include Indian tandoori plates, Vietnamese fried soft-shell crabs, Japanese beef *shogayaki* (panfried fillet with sake sauce), and Malaysian *char kwayt teow* (seafood fried noodles). Curry lovers can try different versions from India, Vietnam, Singapore, and Indonesia. ⊠ *The Repulse Bay, G/F, 109 Repulse Bay Rd., Southside* ☎ *2292–2821* ⊟ *AE, DC, MC, V.*

☼ ¢–$$ ✕ **Shek O Chinese & Thailand Seafood Restaurant.** Nothing particularly stands out about the food at this legendary restaurant—it's just such *fun.* On summer weekends, people arrive en masse and sit for hours despite the relentless heat. The curious hybrid cuisine ensures plenty of rice, noodle, and fish dishes. The *tom yung kung* (spicy prawn and coconut soup) is guaranteed to bring color to your cheeks; the green curry is a safe chicken choice; and the honey-fried squid is a popular choice. Eating here is a festive experience, and you can do it without breaking the bank. Note, however, that you have to spend more than HK$300 to use your credit cards. ⊠ *303 Shek O Village, main intersection, next to bus stop, Shek O, Southside* ☎ *2809–4426* ⚓ *Reservations essential* ⊟ *AE, DC, MC, V.*

Seafood

☼ $–$$$$ ✕ **Jumbo Floating Restaurant.** It's worth seeing, if only for the kitsch value: this is the floating restaurant you see on postcards. The Jumbo Kingdom is a huge, pagoda-shape vessel burning with a thousand lights at night. Don't come for the food—this is a sightseeing outing. There's also a "fine dining restaurant" called Dragon Court in the complex, but it's an even bigger waste of money than Jumbo, whose straightforward seafood menu is overpriced and underwhelming. Unless you must have Chinese seafood, you should dine at the open-air Top Deck instead. Shuttle ferries depart every two or three minutes; bring your camera. ⊠ *Shum Wan Pier Path, Wong Chuk Hang, Southside, Aberdeen* ☎ *2553–9111* ⊕ *www.jumbo.com.hk* ⊟ *AE, DC, MC, V.*

Spanish

$$–$$$ ✕ **El Cid.** It may feel a bit weird to have a Spanish fiesta at the former British Army Officers' quarters, but nevertheless, this restaurant is definitely worth a visit. Order a few tapas and a sangria or a bottle of Rioja, and remember to ask for a table with a sea view. Garlic prawns and stuffed mushrooms are some of the best choices on the tapas menu. ⊠ *Shop 102, 1/F, Murray House, Stanley Plaza, Southside, Stanley* ☎ *2899–0858* ⊟ *AE, DC, MC, V.*

OUTER ISLANDS

Lamma Island

Lamma Island is relatively easy to get to, with ferries leaving Central's pier almost hourly. Yung Shue Wan, where you disembark, has several local seafood restaurants, one or two western ones, and an odd assortment of shops.

Cantonese

☼ $–$$ ✕ **Han Lok Yuen.** Roast pigeon is the star at Han Lok Yuen. Everyone in Hong Kong makes a pilgrimage here at one time or another to try it, usually during a boat trip. Don't arrive too late, or you might miss out:

Continued on page 204

FOR ALL THE TEA IN CHINA

Legend has it that the first cup dates from 2737 BC, when Camellia sinensis leaves fell into water being boiled for Emperor Shenong. He loved the result, tea was born, and so were many traditions.

Historically, when a girl accepted a marriage proposal she drank tea, a gesture symbolizing fidelity (tea plants die if uprooted). Betrothal gifts were known as "tea gifts," engagements as "accepting tea," and marriages as "eating tea." Today the bride and groom kneel before their parents, offering cups of tea in thanks.

Serving tea is a sign of respect. Young people proffer it to their parents or grandparents; subordinates do the same for their bosses. Pouring tea also signifies submission, so it's a way to say you're sorry.

When you're served tea, show your thanks by tapping the table with your index and middle fingers.

And forget about adding milk or sugar. Not only is most Chinese tea best without it, but why dilute and sweeten a beverage long known by herbalists to be good for you? Even modern medicine acknowledges that tea's powerful antioxidants reduce the risk of cancer and heart disease. It's also thought to be such a good source of fluoride that Mao Zedong eschewed toothpaste for a green-tea rinse. Smiles, everyone.

DRINKING IN THE CULTURE

The way tea was prepared historically bears little resemblance to the steep-a-tea-bag method many westerners employ today. Tea originally came in bricks of compressed leaves bound with sheep's blood or manure. Chunks were broken, ground into a powder, and whisked into hot water. In the first tea manual, *Cha Jing (The Way of Tea)*, Tang-dynasty writer Lu Yu describes preparing powdered tea using 28 pieces of teaware, including big brewing pans and shallow drinking bowls.

The potters of Yixing (near Shanghai) gradually transformed wine vessels into small pots for steeping tea. Yixing pottery is ideal for brewing: its fine unglazed clay is highly porous, and if you always use the same kind of tea, the pot will take on its flavor.

Today the most elaborate Chinese tea service—which requires only two pots and enough cups for all involved—is called *gong fu cha* (skilled tea method). Although you can experience it at many teahouses, most people consider it too involved for every day. They simply brew their leaf tea in three-piece lidded cups, called *gaiwan*, tilting the lid as they drink so that it acts as a strainer.

THE CEREMONY

1 Rinse teapot with hot water.

2 Fill with black or oolong to one third of its height.

3 Half-fill teapot with hot water and empty immediately to rinse leaves.

4 Fill pot with hot water, let leaves steep for a minute; no bubbles should form.

5 Pour tea into small cups, moving the spout continuously over each, so all have the same strength of tea.

6 Pour the excess into a second teapot.

7 Using the same leaves, repeat the process up to five times, extending the steeping time slightly.

Gaiwan

TEA TIMELINE

Yunnan Pu-erh Tea Bricks

350 AD	"Tea" appears in Chinese dictionary.
618–1644	Tea falls into and out of favor at Chinese court.
7th c.	Tea introduced to Japan.
1610–1650	Dutch and Portuguese traders bring tea to Europe.
1662	British King Charles II marries Portugal's Catherine of Braganza, a tea addict. Tea craze sweeps the court.
1689	Tea taxation starts in Britain; peaks at 119%.

HOW TEA IS MADE

Chinese tea is grown on large plantations and nearly always picked by hand. Pluckers remove only the top two leaves. A skilled plucker can collect up to 35 kg (77 lbs) of leaves in a day; that's 9 kg (almost 20 lbs) of tea or 3,500 cups. After a week, new top leaves will have grown, and bushes can be plucked again. Climate and soil play an important role on a tea plantation, much as they do in a vineyard. But what really differentiates black, green, and oolong teas is the way leaves are processed.

Plucked leaves arrive at factory

Leaves left to wilt in warm, humid environment

STEAM
GREEN TEA: Steam leaves to prevent oxidation

OXIDATION
Leaves broken to encourage oxidation.
BLACK TEA: 4 hrs
OOLONG: 1-2 hrs

FIRING
(that is, dried in warm ovens or large woks)

GREEN TEA
Curled, packed flat, or rolled into pellets

OOLONG TEA
Formed/packed like green tea

BLACK TEA

WHITE TEA
Only new buds; processed like green tea

PU-ERH TEA
Green, black, and oolong are fermented and compressed

FLAVORED TEA
Flavorings added to black or oolong

Boston Tea Party

1773	Boston Tea Party: Americans dump 342 chests of tea into Boston Harbor, protesting British taxes.
1784	British tea taxes slashed; consumption soars.
1835	Tea cultivation starts in Assam, India.
1880s	India and Ceylon produce more tea than China.
1904	Englishman Richard Blechynden creates iced tea at St. Louis World's Fair.
1908	New York importer Thomas Sullivan sends clients samples in silk bags—the first tea bags.
2004	Chinese tea exports overtake India's for the first time since the 1880s.

TYPES OF TEA

Some teas are simply named for the region that produces them (Yunnan or Assam); others are evocatively named to reflect a particular blend. Some are transliterated (like Keemun); others translated (Iron Goddess of Mercy). Confused? Keep two things in mind. First, the universal word for tea comes from *one* Chinese character—pronounced either "te" (Xiamen dialect) or "cha" (Cantonese and Mandarin). Second, all types of tea come from *one* plant.

	BLACK	PU-ERH	GREEN
Overview	It's popular in the West so it makes up the bulk of China's tea exports. It has a fuller, heavier flavor than green tea, though this varies enormously according to type.	Pu-erh tea is green, black, or oolong that's fermented from a few months to 50 years and compressed into balls during aging. Pu-erh is popular in Hong Kong, where it's called Bo Lei.	Most tea grown and consumed in China is green. It's delicate, so allow the boiling water to cool for a minute before brewing to prevent "cooking" the tea.
Flavor	From light and fresh to rich and chocolatey	Rich, earthy	Light, aromatic
Color	Golden brown to dark mahogany	Reddish brown	Light straw-yellow to bright green
Caffeine per Serving	40 mg	20–40 mg	20 mg
Ideal Water Temperature	203°F	203°F	160°F
Steeping Time	3–5 mins.	3–5 mins.	1–2 mins.
Examples	Dian Hong (dark, chocolatey aftertaste; unlike other Chinese teas, can take milk). Keemun (Qi Men; mild, smoky; once used in English breakfast blends). Lapsang Souchong (dried over smoking pine; strong flavor). Yunnan Golden (full bodied, malty).	Buying Pu-erh is like buying wine: there are different producers and different vintages, and prices vary greatly.	Bi Luo Chun (Green Snail Spring; leaves rolled into pellets; rich, fragrant). Chun Mee (Eyebrow; pale yellow; floral). Hou Kui (Monkey Tea; nutty, sweet; flowery aftertaste). Long Ding (Dragon Mountain; sweet, minty). Long Jing (Dragon's Well; bright green; nutty).

Black
Green
White
Oolong
Flavored

	WHITE	OOLONG	FLAVORED
Overview	The rare white tea is made from the newest buds, picked unopened at day-break and processed like green tea. Small batches mean high prices. It's a tea for refined palates.	Halfway between green and black tea, this tea is more popular in China than elsewhere. The *gong fu cha* ceremony best reveals its complexities.	Petals, bark, and other natural ingredients are added to black or green tea to create these brews. Earl Grey is black tea scented with Bergamot (a recipe supposedly given to the tea's 18th-century namesake by a Mandarin). Jasmine tea is green tea dried with jasmine petals.
Flavor	Very subtle	Aromatic, lighter than black tea	
Color	Very pale yellow	Pale green to pale brown	
Caffeine per Serving	15 mg	30 mg	Others include lychee congou and rose congou: black tea dried with lychee juice or rose petals. Flavor, color, caffeine content, and ideal preparation depend on the tea component of the blend.
Ideal Water Temperature	185°F	203°F	
Steeping Time	4–15 mins.	1–9 mins.	
Examples	Bai Hao Yin Zhen (Silver Needle; finest white tea; sweet and very delicate, anti-toxin qualities). Bai Mu Dan (White Peony; smooth and refreshing).	Da Hong Pao (Scarlet Robe; the real stuff comes from only 4 bushes; full bodied, strongly floral). Tie Guan Yin (Iron Goddess of Mercy; legend has it a farmer repaired an iron statue of the goddess, who rewarded him with the tea bush shoot; prized; golden yellow; floral).	Don't confuse flavored teas with the caffeine-free herbal teas made from herbs, roots, and blossoms (e.g., chamomile, peppermint, rosehips, licorice, ginger).

LEAVES OF THE CITY

Tea in the morning; tea in the evening, tea at suppertime . . .

Get up early in Hong Kong, and you'll see old men shuffling along the streets with their pet birds in tow. The destination? A teahouse for some warm brew and chat with pals while their birds chirp away from cages hung nearby.

But tea isn't just for old-timers. Hot black tea comes free—usually in glass beakers that are constantly refilled—with all meals in Chinese restaurants. Pu-erh tea, which is known here as Bo Lei, is the beverage of choice at dim sum places. In fact, another way to say dim sum is *yum cha*, meaning "drink tea."

Afternoon tea is another local fixation. Forget cucumber sandwiches and petit fours. Here we're talking neighborhood joints with Formica tables, grumpy waiters, and menus only in Chinese. Most people go for *nai cha* made with evaporated milk. A really good cup is smooth, sweet, and hung with drops of fat. An even richer version, *cha chow*, is made with condensed milk. If *yuen yueng* (yin yang, half milk tea and half instant coffee) sounds a bit much, *ling-mun cha* (lemon tea) is also on hand. Don't forget to order buttered toast or *daan-ta* (custard tarts).

The bubble (or boba) tea craze is strong. These cold brews contain pearly balls of tapioca or coconut jelly. There's also been a return to traditional teas. Chains such as Chinese Urban Healing Tea serve healthy blends in MTR stations all over town—giving Starbucks a run for its money.

FLAGSTAFF HOUSE
MUSEUM OF TEA WARE

All that's good about British colonial architecture is exemplified in the simple white facade, wooden monsoon shutters, and colonnaded verandas of Flagstaff House. Over 600 pieces of delicate antique teaware from the Tang (618–907) through the Qing (1644–1911) dynasties fill rooms that once housed the commander of the

British forces. ■ **TIP→ Skip the lengthy, confusing tea-ceremony descriptions; concentrate on the porcelain itself.** Look out for the unadorned brownish-purple clay of the Yixing pots: unglazed, their beauty hinges on perfect form. There's a carved wooden booth on the first floor where you can listen to Chinese tea songs.

The best place to put your tea theory into practice is the **Lock Cha Tea Shop** (☎ 2801–7177 ⊕ www.lockcha.com), in the K.S. Lo Gallery annex of Flagstaff House. It's half shop, half teahouse, so you can sample brews before you buy. Friendly staffers prepare the tea gongfu style at carved rosewood tables. Try the Tie Guan Yin, a highly aromatic green tea. ✉ *Hong Kong Park, 10 Cotton Tree Dr., Admiralty* ☎ *2869–0690* ⊕ *www.lcsd.gov.hk* ✉ *Free* ☾ *Wed.–Mon. 10–5* Ⓜ *Admiralty MTR, Exit C1.* ■ **TIP→ The Hong Kong Tourist Board runs tea appreciation classes at Lock Cha Tea Shop—phone the shop to book a place.**

FOOK MING TONG

Staffers will brew you any of their range of teas at this classy store inside the IFC Mall. Look for books about tea, tea caddies and sets, and Yixing pots (some with hefty price tags). ✉ *IFC Mall, shop 3006, 8 Finance St., Central* ☎ *2295–0368* ⊕ *www.fookmingtong.com* Ⓜ *Hong Kong Station MTR, Exit F.*

PENINSULA HOTEL

The British haven't been in the tea business as long as the Chinese, but they know a thing or two about it. Afternoon tea in the soaring grand lobby of this icon is all very Noel Coward. A string quartet plays as liveried waiters pour from silver pots. Three tiers' worth of salmon sandwiches, petit fours, and Valrhona truffles will keep you munching for a while. There's clotted Devonshire cream for the airy scones—so popular the Pen makes 1,000 a day. All this comes to a snip of what a suite here costs: HK$340 for two. ✉ *Salisbury Rd., Tsim Sha Tsui, Kowloon* ☎ *2920–2888* ⊕ *www.peninsula.com* ✉ *AE, DC, MC, V* ☾ *Tea served daily 2–7* Ⓜ *Tsim Sha Tsui MTR, Exit E.*

■ **TIP→ You can't make reservations for tea at the Peninsula; to avoid lines come at 2 on the dot or after 5:30.**

TEA ALTERNATIVES

Green Tea Ice Cream. It's the dessert of choice at Genki, a popular local sushi chain. ✉ *Times Square Mall, Shop B222, 1 Matheson St., Causeway Bay* ☎ 2506-9366 Ⓜ *Causeway Bay MTR, Exit A.*

Earl Grey MarTEAni. Gin infused with Earl Grey tea is the basis of a signature cocktail at trendy RED Bar +Restaurant. ✉ *IFC Mall, shop 3082, 8 Finance St., Central* ☎ 8129-8882 Ⓜ *Hong Kong Station MTR, Exit F.*

Green Tea Frappuccino. The Starbucks take on green tea is everything the stuff normally isn't: creamy, sugary, and icy.

Green Tea Bread. It looks like something Shrek made, but tastes surprisingly wholesome. German-style bakery Das Gute might be on to something. ✉ *Times Square Mall, Shop B301, 1 Matheson St., Causeway Bay* ☎ 2506-9488 Ⓜ *Causeway Bay MTR, Exit A.*

the pigeon can be sold out by 8 PM on busy weekend nights, when booking in advance is usually essential. The kitchen also turns out an array of typical Chinese dishes to accompany the pigeon. Beautiful sea views make this institution popular with both locals and visitors alike. ⊠ *16–17 Hung Shing Ye, Yung Shue Wan* ☎ *2982–0680* ⊟ *AE, DC, MC, V* ⊗ *Closed Mon.*

Lantau Island

You'll wind up on Lantau Island if you're visiting Disneyland Hong. There are several restaurants within the Disneyland park itself, none of them distinguished. The best restaurants are found, rather, in the hotels.

Cantonese

$$$–$$$$ ✕ **Crystal Lotus.** The first thing you'll notice upon entering the Disneyland Hotel's flagship restaurant is also the most Disney-ish touch: a computer-animated koi pond, where electronic fish deftly avoid your feet, darting out of the way as you walk across. Once inside the glittering, crystal-studded yet warm and inviting space, you'll choose from a well-thought-out menu that's really more pan-Chinese than Cantonese, with careful preparations of dishes like barbecue fillets of eel glazed with Osmanthus honey, gently stewed king prawn with spicy Sichuan sauce, and perfectly executed XO seafood fried rice. If you wind up in Disneyland—perhaps on your way to or from the airport—this is by far the best way to dine (unless the kids demand a character meal at the Enchanted Garden in the hotel's lower level. ⊠ *Hong Kong Disneyland Hotel, Hong Kong Disneyland Lantau Island* ☎ *830–830* ⊕ *http://park. hongkongdisneyland.com* ⊟ *AE, DC, MC, V* Ⓜ *Disneyland Resort.*

KOWLOON

Parts of Kowloon are among the most densely populated areas on the planet, and support a corresponding abundance of restaurants. Many hotels, planted here for the view of Hong Kong Island (spectacular at night), also have excellent restaurants, though they're uniformly expensive. Some of the best food in Kowloon is served in backstreet eateries, where immigrants from Vietnam, Thailand, and elsewhere in Asia keep their native cooking skills sharp.

Tsim Sha Tsui, on Kowloon's tip, is crammed with shops and restaurants, from spots in luxury hotels to holes-in-the-wall. Starting from the Kowloon-side Star Ferry Terminal, the district embraces the most glittering end of the famous Nathan Road's "Golden Mile," snakes around the harbor front to Tsim Sha Tsui East, and extends to the end of Kowloon Park at Austin Road, marking the boundary of

---

WHAT IS BEIJINGESE?

This hearty fare is designed for the chilly climate of northern China—noodles, dumplings, and breads are more evident than rice. Peking duck is a perennial favorite. Firm flavors—such as garlic, ginger, and leek—are popular.

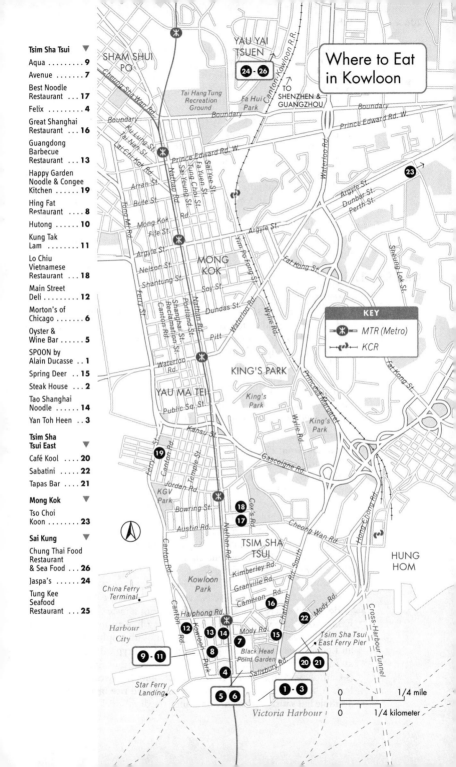

Where to Eat in Kowloon

KEY

✳ MTR (Metro)

•᠁• KCR

Jordan. The restaurants here are easily accessible from either the Tsim Sha Tsui MTR stop or Kowloon's Star Ferry Terminal. Beyond Chatham Road and south toward the Cross-Harbour Tunnel, Tsim Sha Tsui East is packed with high-end hotels with exquisite restaurants. The closest MTR stop is the Tsim Sha Tsui stop.

Locals go to Kowloon City, a 10-minute taxi ride north from Tsim Sha Tsui, adjoining Hong Kong's former international airport at Kai Tak, for casual, authentic, tasty meals at affordable prices. Renowned for its seafood restaurants and neighborhood hill-walking tracks, Sai Kung is off most tourist itineraries. Yet it's a town worth investigation, and it's really only a 20-minute taxi ride north of Tsim Sha Tsui (or you can take Minibus 1 from Choi Hung MTR). Many restaurants run adjoining seafood shops, so you can select a fresh catch from tanks and have it cooked to order—steamed, fried, sautéed, or deep-fried with salt and pepper. There are also lots of intimate, laid-back western restaurants serving delicious food.

Tsim Sha Tsui

Beijingese

$-$$ ✕ **Spring Deer.** With shades of pastel blue and green in a somber interior, and waiters in bland uniforms, this Peking duck specialist looks like something out of 1950s communist Beijing. The crowd, too, is hilariously old-school, which only adds to your duck experience. You'll see locals with noodle dishes, stir-fried wok meat dishes, and so forth, and they're good, but the Peking duck is the showstopper—it might be the best in town. Even the peanuts for snacking, which are boiled to a delectable softness, go above and beyond the call of duty. ⊠ *1/F, 42 Mody Rd., Tsim Sha Tsui, Kowloon* ☎ *2366–4012* ▤ *AE, DC, MC, V* Ⓜ *Tsim Tsa Shui.*

Cantonese

$$-$$$$ ✕ **Yan Toh Heen.** This Cantonese restaurant in the Hotel InterContinental sets formal elegance against expansive harbor views, and its food is
Fodor'sChoice at the top of its class in town. Exquisite is hardly the word for the place
★ settings, all handcrafted with green jade. Equally successful are dim sum, sautéed Wagyu beef with mushrooms and shishito pepper, and exemplary braised whole abalone in oyster sauce. The vast selection of seafood—the largest range in Hong Kong—which transcends the usual tank to offer such exotic fishes as maori and green wrasse and shellfish like red coral crab, cherrystone clam, and sea whelk. ⊠ *Lower Level, Hotel InterContinental Hong Kong, 18 Salisbury Rd., Tsim Sha Tsui, Kowloon* ☎ *2721–1211* ⊕ *www.ichotelsgroup.com* ⌫ *Reservations essential* ▤ *AE, DC, MC, V* ⋔ *No shorts* Ⓜ *Tsim Sha Tsui.*

$ ✕ **Happy Garden Noodle & Congee Kitchen.** For a taste of down-to-earth Hong Kong fare without the fear of feeling like an interloper in Chinese-only local joints, this is the place to go. With helpful waitresses and an English menu, this small place is great for a typical local breakfast, an easy lunch, and even a big dinner. A popular morning combination is Cantonese congee and a glutinous rice dumpling wrapped in a lotus leaf. A bowl of wonton soup or a plate of fried rice or noodles makes a simple but satisfying lunch. For dinner, the diced chicken with cashews and sweet-and-sour pork are delicious Cantonese staples. ⊠ *G/F, 72 Canton Rd., Tsim Sha Tsui, Kowloon* ☎ *2377–2603* ▭ *No credit cards* Ⓜ *Tsim Sha Tsui.*

¢ ✕ **Guangdong Barbecue Restaurant.** Of the many typical roast meat (Chinese barbecue) shops that line the streets of Tsim Sha Tsui, this is one of the most consistently popular, and deservedly so. Between the two rooms, the clanking plates, and the shouting in Cantonese, it can be bewildering at first; don't be put off if you're pushed out of the way by a server before being seated. Once seated, you can order from an English menu (you have to ask for it). The roast goose is delicious, as is the crispy roasted pig, soy sauce chicken, and honeyed roast pork. All are served with rice and greens. You might want to just order by pointing to someone else's plate if it looks appealing; and don't forget to pile on the chili sauce and other condiments. ⊠ *G/F, Hankow Bldg., 43 Hankow Rd., Tsim Sha Tsui, Kowloon* ☎ *2735–5151* ▭ *MC, V* Ⓜ *Tsim Sha Tsui.*

¢ ✕ **Hing Fat Restaurant.** There are so many simple roast meat and noodle soup shops in the area around lower Nathan Road that it can be hard to choose from among them. The popular Hing Fat is a reliable choice both for soup dumplings and for Cantonese-style roast meats—and the place is open all night, which is a definite plus. If you've made a long night of it, plop down here among the locals for late-night refueling within easy reach of the big Tsim Sha Tsui hotels. ⊠ *G/F, 8–10 Ashley Rd.,Tsim Sha Tsui, Kowloon* ☎ *2736–7788* ▭ *No credit cards* Ⓜ *Tsim Sha Tsui.*

Contemporary

★ $$$$ ✕ **SPOON by Alain Ducasse.** Even if culinary legend Alain Ducasse is not exactly presiding over this kitchen, his inspiration is felt at this sleek restaurant, especially in preparations such as steamed foie gras, which balances the richness of seared foie gras with the resilience of a cold terrine de foie gras. De-

> **WORD OF MOUTH**
>
> "SPOON is a great concept, beautifully done food, amazing view and wonderful staff. Could not ask for a better restaurant."   –Jenniene

spite the odd Asian flavor (seaweed pesto and shiitake mushrooms), the menu is contemporary French, liberally employing lobster, truffle, and other luxury ingredients with a keen sense of balance. The best, if priciest, way to go is the multicourse tasting menu. The tables overlooking the harbor provide a romantic setting—or reserve the kitchen-side chef's table for a completely different experience. ⊠ *Hotel InterContinental Hong Kong, 18 Salisbury Rd., lobby level, Tsim Sha Tsui, Kowloon* ☎ *2313–2256* ⊕ *www.ichotelsgroup.com* ⌁ *Reservations essential* ▭ *AE, DC, MC, V* Ⓜ *Tsim Sha Tsui.*

$$–$$$$ ✕ **Felix.** It's not for the faint of stomach, this Philippe Starck–designed, preposterously fashionable scene atop the Peninsula. The floor-to-ceiling walls do have breathtaking views of Hong Kong though, unless the blinds are drawn, as they sometimes are. The dinner menu, which might include Asian-influenced items such as misoyaki-marinated Atlantic cod or honeyed tempura prawns, is good but certainly overpriced. Most people come just for cocktails—or to try out the most celebrated pis-

soir in Asia, whose views across Tsim Sha Tsui are superior to those in the restaurant itself. ✉ *28/F, Peninsula Hong Kong, Salisbury Rd., Tsim Sha Tsui, Kowloon* ☎ *2366–6251 or 2315–3188* 🌐 *http://hongkong.peninsula.com* ✍ *Reservations essential* 💳 *AE, DC, MC, V* Ⓜ *Tsim Sha Tsui.*

WORD OF MOUTH

"The best High Tea in Hong Kong is at The Peninsula Hotel. Then again, once you have been to the Peninsula, nothing else will come close." -Brock

$$–$$$ ✕ **Avenue.** One of the places to see and be seen in Tsim Sha Tsui, trendy Avenue serves modern European cuisine in a crisp contemporary location overlooking the bustling Golden Mile of Nathan Road. Whitewashed walls and white-marble tile flooring are dramatically accented by unusually large and colorful abstract paintings and murals. Typical dishes include sautéed wild mushrooms, bursting with flavor; a refreshing crab-and-avocado salad with lemon mayonnaise; chunky, fresh roast cod; and a luscious crème blur dessert, a variation of crème brûlée, served with strawberries. ✉ *1/F, Holiday Inn Golden Mile, 50 Nathan Rd., Tsim Sha Tsui, Kowloon* ☎ *2315–1118* 🌐 *http://www.ichotelsgroup.com* 💳 *AE, DC, MC, V.*

Deli

$–$$ ✕ **Main Street Deli.** Inspired by New York's (now closed) Second Avenue Deli, with a tiled interior to match, Main Street Deli introduced traditional Big Apple neighborhood favorites to Hong Kong and found immediate popularity with visitors and locals alike. The chef even trained at the Second Avenue Deli, and continues to make lunch favorites such as hot dogs, bagels, and pastrami on rye and hot corned beef sandwiches. Brisket, meat loaf, and matzoh-ball soup satisfy homesick New Yorkers. Lemon meringue pie makes an ideal accompaniment to afternoon coffee. ✉ *G/F, Langham Hong Kong, 8 Peking Rd., Tsim Sha Tsui, Kowloon* ☎ *2375–1133* 🌐 *http://hongkong.langhamhotels.com* 💳 *AE, DC, MC, V* Ⓜ *Tsim Sha Tsui.*

Eclectic

$$–$$$ ✕ **Aqua.** Perhaps in reference to Hong Kong's many yoga studios, Tsim Sha Tsui's gracefully arching One Peking Road building seems to be doing a giant steel back bend. This trendy restaurant and bar is in the penthouse, and goes by many names (Aqua Tokyo, Aqua Roma, Aqua Spirit). Similarly, the chefs here wear many hats, for instance combining sashimi, crab tempura with crab roe miso, and a heavy risotto into one meal. The raw fish, flown in from Japan, is a better choice than the uninspired pasta, but the only thing really worth going to Aqua for is the superb view from the windows of the Hong Kong skyline. You might just stop in for a drink—the bar stays open until 2 AM, 3 on weekends. ✉ *Penthouse, 1 Peking Rd., Tsim Sha Tsui, Kowloon* ☎ *3427–2288* 🌐 *www.aqua.com.hk* 💳 *AE, DC, MC, V* ⊗ *No lunch* Ⓜ *Central.*

Northern Chinese

$$–$$$ Fodor'sChoice ★ ✕ **Hutong.** It's not hard to see why Hutong is one of the hottest tables in Hong Kong: it has some of the most imaginative food in town, yet it's completely Chinese. Meanwhile, its spot at the top of the dramatic

One Peking Road tower overlooks the entire festival of lights that is the Island skyline. Best among a sensational selection of northern Chinese creations are crispy de-boned lamb ribs, whose crackling skin conceals a deep, tender gaminess within. More subtle but equally special is Chinese spinach in a well-developed herbal ginseng broth, and delicate scallops with fresh pomelo. If you have just one meal in Hong Kong, make certain it's here. And remember to reserve well in advance. ⊠ *28/F, 1 Peking Rd., Tsim Sha Tsui* ☎ *3248–8342* ⊕ *www.aqua. com.hk* ⌕ *Reservations essential* ▭ *AE, DC, MC, V* ☉ *No lunch* Ⓜ *Tsim Sha Tsui.*

Seafood

$$–$$$$ ✕**Oyster & Wine Bar.** Atop the Sheraton Hong Kong Hotel & Towers, against the romantic backdrop of Hong Kong's twinkling harbor, this is the top spot in town for oyster-lovers. More than 30 varieties are flown in daily and kept alive on ice around the horseshoe oyster bar,

ready for shucking. Staff cheerfully explain the characteristics of the available oysters and guide you to ones to suit your taste. Also on the aphrodisiac menu is the San Francisco fisherman's stew, as well as clams, mussels, crab, and black cod. An extensive wine cellar lines the walls. ⊠ *Sheraton Hong Kong Hotel & Towers, 20 Nathan Rd., Tsim Sha Tsui, Kowloon* ☎ *2369–1111 Ext. 3145* ▭ *AE, DC, MC, V* ☉ *No lunch* Ⓜ *Tsim Sha Tsui.*

Shanghainese

$–$$$ ✕**Great Shanghai Restaurant.** It might be old and fairly dingy, but Great Shanghai is perfect if you prefer the bold flavors of Shanghainese food to the more delicate tastes of local Cantonese fare. Even if you don't feel ready for the sea blubber or braised turtle with sugar candy, you should at least consider one of the boneless eel dishes, the Shanghai-style yellow fish soup, the beggar's chicken (order in advance before noon for dinner), or the excellent spiced soy duck. For less adventurous palates there are more fundamental Shanghainese goodies such as sautéed river shrimp, Chinese cabbage with Yunnan ham, tasty fried noodles, or juicy dumplings. ⊠ *26–36 Prat Ave., Tsim Sha Tsui, Kowloon* ☎ *2366–8158* ▭ *AE, DC, MC, V* Ⓜ *Tsim Sha Tsui.*

¢–$ ✕**Best Noodle Restaurant.** Just beyond the northern boundary of Tsim Sha Tsui, on a side street off Nathan Road, near the Jordan MTR station, this humble place is popular among locals seeking a quick bowl of noodles or a simple, tasty Shanghainese dish. Try a dish of Shanghainese rice with vegetables, topped with your choice of meat, or the fried noodles, soup noodles, and sweet spareribs. ⊠ *105 Austin Rd., Jordan, Kowloon* ☎ *2369–0086* ▭ *No credit cards* Ⓜ *Tsim Sha Tsui.*

¢ ✕**Tao Shanghai Noodle.** Near the Tsim Sha Tsui MTR and shopping area, this smart little joint has a great variety of northern Chinese dishes (think hot and spicy) and makes a nice spot for a quick lunch or snack. Chow down on a bowl of noodles or dumplings accompanied with a chilled soya drink, or sample the typical northern specialties such as braised bean curd or spicy diced chicken. It's cramped and crowded, but the staff is friendly and accommodating. ⊠ *Shop A, G/F, 44 Hankow Rd., Tsim Sha Tsui, Kowloon* ☎ *2367–9011* ⊟ *No credit cards* Ⓜ *Tsim Sha Tsui.*

Steak House

$$$$ ✕ **Morton's of Chicago.** Some might argue that the outpost of an American steak-house chain would not be the appropriate place for a break-the-bank meal in Hong Kong. And in many ways they'd be right. On the other hand, Morton's does what it does so well—and so consistently—that it can well satisfy the steak craving that can sometimes arise when you're in faraway places. The meat is world-class: most flavorful is the New York strip; the filet mignon is juicy and tender; and the porterhouse, for sharing, combines the best of both worlds. ⊠ *3/F and 4/F, Sheraton Hotel, 20 Nathan Rd., Tsim Sha Tsui* ☎ *2732–2343* ⊕ *www.mortons.com* ⊟ *AE, DC, MC, V* Ⓜ *Central.*

★ **$$$–$$$$** ✕ **Steak House.** This restaurant with its lively, informal din, salad buffet, and gleaming harbor views, serves the best steak in the city. After being seated, you are made to choose from among 10 steak knives, 12 mustards, and eight kinds of rock salt—gimmicky, but fun. But the main event is of course the meat: wagyu steaks come from Australia, are aged for more than a year, and the results are shockingly tender, buttery, and flavorful. Other delicious cuts are flown in from the United States; and all of it is lovingly seared on Hong Kong's only charcoal grill. There isn't a jacket-and-tie policy but note that shorts are not allowed. ⊠ *Hotel InterContinental Hong Kong, 18 Salisbury Rd., Tsim Sha Tsui, Kowloon* ☎ *2721–1211* ⊕ *www.ichotelsgroup.com* ⌕ *Reservations essential* ⊟ *AE, DC, MC, V* Ⓜ *Tsim Sha Tsui.*

Vegetarian

¢–$$ ✕ **Kung Tak Lam.** Health-conscious diners will appreciate this simple Shanghainese vegetarian food. The interior is light and airy, in keeping with the ultramodern One Peking Road tower feel. Still, it's the food that makes this place so popular. The menu revels in its vegetarianism, rather than trying to emulate meat; highlights include the Golden Treasure Cold Platter, which includes delicious sweet gluten with mushrooms; the Shanghai-style cold noodles with seven different sauces; and gentle bean curd dumplings. Good, too, are the sweet panfried cakes. Set-price meals are incredibly cheap, but beware the high prices on the à-la-carte menu, which can add up. ⊠ *7/F, 1 Peking Rd., Tsim Sha Tsui, Kowloon* ☎ *2312–7800* ⊟ *AE, DC, MC, V* Ⓜ *Tsim Sha Tsui.*

Vietnamese

$–$$ ✕ **Lo Chiu Vietnamese Restaurant.** The spartan interior may not impress you at first glance, but pay no heed since what you're here for is the hearty authentic food. Take your time and try not to burn your tongue on the sizzling hot and wonderfully flavorsome lemongrass chicken wings. Deep-fried sugarcane with minced shrimp is sweet and juicy. There are also a good variety of noodles and vermicelli served in soup or with fish sauce. A bottle of imported French beer is just the thing to wash it all down. ⊠ *Shop 1, G/F, Diamond Court, 10–12 Hillwood Rd., Tsim Sha Tsui, Kowloon* ☎ *2314–7983 or 2314–9211* ⊟ *MC, V* Ⓜ *Tsim Sha Tsui.*

Tsim Sha Tsui East

Eclectic

☾ **$$–$$$** ✕**Café Kool.** This 300-seat international food court has something fun for the whole family, with entertainment provided by chefs in six "show kitchens" focusing on cuisines from around the world. Take your pick from the salad counter; a seafood station; pasta, paella, risotto, and carvery from the western kitchen; dishes from all over Asia; tandoories and curries from the Indian counter; and fresh soufflés, crepes, and even liquid chocolate from Hong Kong's only chocolate fountain at the dessert station. Good-value, all-you-can-eat buffets are served up to midnight. A deli sells take-out food and gourmet gifts. ⊠ *Kowloon Shangri-La, 64 Mody Rd., Tsim Sha Tsui East, Kowloon* ☏ *2733–8753* ⊕ *www. shangri-la.com* ⊟ *AE, DC, MC, V* Ⓜ *Tsim Sha Tsui.*

Italian

$$–$$$$ ✕**Sabatini.** Run by the Sabatini family, who also have restaurants in Rome, Japan, and Singapore, this small corner of Italy with sponge-painted walls and wooden furnishings is in the Royal Garden's atrium. It has a cult following among those who crave authentic Italian cuisine. Linguine Sabatini, the house specialty, is prepared according to the original Roman recipe in a fresh-tomato-and-garlic marinara sauce, served with an array of luscious seafood. For dessert, try homemade tiramisu or refreshing wild-berry pudding. ⊠ *3/F, Royal Garden, 69 Mody Rd., Tsim Sha Tsui East, Kowloon* ☏ *2733–2000* ⊕ *www.rghk.com.hk* ⚑ *Reservations essential* ⊟ *AE, DC, MC, V* Ⓜ *Tsim Sha Tsui.*

Spanish

$–$$ ✕**Tapas Bar.** International tapas meet New World wines at this upbeat venue in the Kowloon Shangri-La Hotel. Chefs work in an open kitchen, where a tandoor oven regularly produces freshly baked bread to go with the little dishes. Typical Spanish tapas like whitebait, sardines, and chorizo sausage are served, but there are also dips from around the world, a smorgasbord of olives, sushi-style tuna, and potato-wrapped shrimp—plus a global oyster selection. ⊠ *1/F, Kowloon Shangri-La, 64 Mody Rd., Tsim Sha Tsui East, Kowloon* ☏ *2733–8750* ⊕ *www.shangri-la. com* ⊟ *AE, DC, MC, V* Ⓜ *Tsim Sha Tsui.*

Mong Kok

Cantonese

¢—$ ✕**Tso Choi Koon.** If you have a delicate constitution, or prefer fine food, take a pass on this home-style Cantonese restaurant. Tso Choi (which translates as rough dishes) is not everyone's cup of tea. Tripe lovers and haggis fans, however, might like to try the Chinese versions of some of their favorites: fried pig tripe, fried pig brain (served as an omelet), double-boiled pig brain . . . you get the idea. The older Hong Kong generation still likes this stuff; younger folks may demur. The wary can still opt for creamy congee, fried chicken, or a fish fillet. ⊠ *17–19A Nga Tsin Wai Rd., Mong Kok, Kowloon* ☏ *2383–7170* ⊟ *No credit cards* Ⓜ *Mong Kok.*

Sai Kung

Eclectic

$–$$ ✗ **Jaspa's.** What could be better than heading straight to a cozy restaurant after a day out in the countryside? The food here is always delicious and filling, perfect after a day walking in the hills or enjoying the water and sun. Whether sitting out on the terrace or indoors, a satisfying dinner is

guaranteed. The goat cheese parcel makes a delectable starter, and the chicken fajitas arrive on your table sizzling hot. Pasta with bay bugs (large crayfish) and lamb chops is also delicious. ⊠ *13 Sha Tsui Path, Sai Kung, Kowloon* ☎ *2792–6388* ▭ *AE, MC, V* Ⓜ *Hung Hau.*

Seafood

$$–$$$ ✗ **Tung Kee Seafood Restaurant.** Lobsters, slipper lobsters, clams, abalone, crabs, prawns, fish, and everything else from the deep blue sea is here for the tasting on Sai Kung's picturesque harborside. Crustaceans and fish are quickly cooked by steaming and wok-frying and are presented whole, leaving no doubt as to the freshness of your food. A quick look inside the tank is like a lesson in marine biology. Pick your favorites, and leave the rest to the chef. Then just prepare yourself for a feast *de la mer.* ⊠ *96–102 Man Nin St., Sai Kung, Kowloon* ☎ *2792–7453* ▭ *AE, DC, MC, V* Ⓜ *Hang Hau.*

¢–$$ ✗ **Chung Thai Food Restaurant & Sea Food.** As its name suggests, this seafood corner is best known for both Chinese and Thai cooking, prepared separately by chefs of both nationalities. Those with a taste for spice can try the Thai-fried crabs with curry or fried prawns with chili; otherwise, pick any seafood you like from the store next door, and the chef will prepare it to order. Steaming is one good way to go, but ask the restaurant's advice for each type of fish individually. Prices depend on the type and weight of the seafood you choose. ⊠ *93 Man Nin St., Sai Kung, Kowloon* ☎ *2792–1481* ✉ *Seafood shop, 5 Siu Yat Bldg., Hoi Pong Sq., Sai Kung, Kowloon* ☎ *2792–8172* ▭ *MC, V* Ⓜ *Hang Hau.*

After Dark

Carnegie's Pub, Wan Chai

WORD OF MOUTH

"We went to Hong Kong a few days before making our way back to the States. The nightlife and the shopping there was great! We had so much fun and met wonderful people from around the world . . . everywhere we went."

—amc

By Eva Chui
Loiterton

A riot of neon, heralding frenetic after-hours action, announces Hong Kong's nightlife districts. Hectic workdays make way for an even busier nighttime scene. Clubs and bars fill to capacity, evening markets pack in shoppers looking for bargains, restaurants welcome diners, cinemas pop corn as fast as they can, and theaters and concert halls prepare for full houses.

The neighborhoods of Wan Chai, Lan Kwai Fong and SoHo are packed with bars, pubs, and nightclubs that cater to everyone from the hippest trendsetters, to bankers ready to spend their bonuses, and more laid-back crowds out for a pint. Partying in Hong Kong is a way of life; it starts at the beginning of the week with a drink or two after work, progressing to serious bar hopping, and clubbing if it's the weekend. Work hard, play harder is the motto here and people follow it seriously.

Because each district has so much to offer, and since they're all quite close to each other, it's perfectly normal to pop into two or three bars before heading to a nightclub . . . or two, depending on how late you party. At the other end of the spectrum, the city's arts and culture is equally lively, with innovative music, dance, and theater. There are small independent productions as well as large-scale concerts that take to the stage across the territory every weekend. You simply cannot go home without a Hong Kong nightlife story to tell!

HONG KONG ISLAND

Central

Hong Kong is proud of its own *très* chic SoHo—SOuth of HOllywood Road—a small warren of streets between Central and Midlevels. This area is filled with commensurately priced cosmopolitan restaurants ranging from Middle Eastern and Portuguese to Vietnamese and Italian, as well as a handful of bars. Below SoHo is the infamous Lan Kwai Fong, a hillside section around Central's D'Aguilar Street that has many good bistros and a large selection of bars. Along with the drink-swinging hordes, busloads of Japanese and mainland Chinese tourist offload here on their tour—not to enjoy a beverage, but only to have their picture taken underneath the LAN KWAI FONG street sign.

Bars

Barco. Had enough of the crowds and looking for a quiet drink and conversation that you can actually hear? Barco is the place. One of many small drinking holes popping up in SoHo, it's cozy, with a small lounge area and a courtyard in the back. ☒ *42 Staunton St., SoHo, Central* ☎ *2857–4478* ☞ *Closes 1* AM.

★ **California.** Set in a semi-basement, but with large open windows at the top so the crowds in Lan Kwai Fong can easily peer down, California is a slice of the West Coast for homesick expats or Western visitors looking for a more familiar environment. It's a mini-institution, having survived the notoriously high turnover rate in the area, and remains one of the busiest bars in Lan Kwai Fong. ☒ *32–34 D'Aguilar St., Lan Kwai Fong, Central* ☎ *2521–1345* ☞ *Closes 3* AM.

D'Apartment. Visit the library, lounge, or even the bedroom in this hip basement "apartment." The tiny library is dimly lighted and stacked with real books, but there's no chance of dozing off with the music blaring in the next room. The bedroom has a lush bedlike sofa to laze on, and, don't worry, there are no neighbors to complain about the racket. ☒ *California Entertainment Bldg., 34–36 D'Aguilar St., basement, Lan Kwai Fong, Central* ☎ *2523–2002* ☞ *Closes 3* AM.

F.I.N.D.S. The name of this red-hot bar comes from the first letters of Finland, Iceland, Norway, Denmark, and Sweden. In keeping with the theme, the light-blue-and-white interior is also kept quite cold at this Scandinavian ice bar, but the crowds that frequent it are anything but icy. There's a large terrace to escape the smoke-filled haze indoors, and from here you can check out the crowds in Lan Kwai Fong. About 30 premium vodkas are served, or you can try one of the many house cocktails with corny names such as the Edvard Munch, made with lime aquavit and ginger wine. ☒ *2/F, LKF Tower, 33 Wyndham St., entrance of D'Aguilar St., Central* ☎ *2522–9318* ☞ *Closes 3* AM.

Goccia. The beautiful people flock to this cool bar (with a restaurant upstairs) and it's packed wall to wall most nights. *Goccia*—"drop" in Italian—occupies a long room on the ground floor, and if it had a VIP table, it would have to be one by the window facing the street where you can see and be seen. ☒ *73 Wyndham St., Central* ☎ *2167–8181* ☞ *Closes 3* AM.

Insomnia. It's *almost* open 24/7 (closing for only three hours 6–9 AM), hence the name. Live music is what really draws people here; there's a small stage and a dance floor at the back, but you'll have to fight your way there on weekends through the perfumed women and suited men. You might have more breathing room if you stay near the front bar, by the arched windows. ☒ *38–44 D'Aguilar St., Lan Kwai Fong, Central* ☎ *2525–0957.*

La Dolce Vita. Crowds at this tiny bar, beneath its sister restaurant **Post 97** and next to its other sibling **Club 97**, often spill onto the pavement. One of the first modern bars to pop up when the area gained popular-

HONG KONG
AFTER DARK PLANNER

Mug or Martini Glass

Lively pubs proliferate in Hong Kong. Some serve cheap drinks in a modest setting, while others are pricier and more elegant. They help ease homesickness for British expats by serving up fish-and-chips while airing rugby and football matches. Trivia quiz games have taken many of the Hong Kong pubs by storm. Pub-hopping in Wan Chai is best enjoyed by the energetic and the easy-to-please—or those trying to immortalize Suzie Wong.

Hong Kong's licensed designer bars provide some diversion from the staid pubs. Sophisticated and elegant cocktail bars are the norm at luxury hotels; some offer live music (usually Filipino trios with a female singer; occasionally international acts) in a gleaming setting with a small dance floor.

Whether because of the transient nature of the city or hardworking lifestyles, which leave little time for relationships, there's a rampant singles scene at most bars. Happy hours typically run from late afternoon to early evening, with most places offering two drinks for the price of one. Remember to request a window seat when making reservations.

Members Only

Many clubs have a "members-only" policy, but don't let this deter you. Usually this just means that you're required to pay a cover charge before gaining entry. And although most clubs and discos levy a cover charge, this fee usually includes a complimentary drink.

Hot Picks

Best Neighborhood to Let Loose: Lan Kwai Fong

Best Drink with a View: Aqua

Best Disco Room: Felix

Best Irish Export: Delaney's

Best Music Club Venue: Fringe Club

Hostesses with the Mostest: Club BBoss

Nightlife Savvy

For listings and quirky reviews of all that's on, pick up *Hong Kong Magazine,* distributed free in Central's bars and cafés each Thursday. The nightlife coverage in *BC Magazine* is almost as extensive. Another good source of nightlife and cultural information is the daily newspaper, the *South China Morning Post.* The free monthly newspaper *City News* lists City Hall performances and events.

Tickets for most big cultural events are on sale through city-wide branches of **URBTIX** (☎ 2111-5999 ⊕ www.urbtix.gov.hk). **HK Ticketing** (☎ 3128–8288 ⊕ www.hkticketing.com) sells tickets to many shows.

Disco Dancing

There are nightclubs and discos to suit all tastes and prices. The thriving youth culture is best exemplified in these houses of dance, where young folks prance about in the latest fashions. Cover charges are high by U.S. standards; entrance to the smarter spots is usually HK$100 or more, though this usually entitles you to one or two drinks. If you prefer dance parties to discos, look for posters in Lan Kwai Fong and Wan Chai that herald the latest international DJ arriving in town to play for one night only.

Some bars and restaurants also hold weekly or monthly club nights, where music ranges from drum-and-bass to happy house. Although nightclubs are similar in some ways to discos, the ones listed here tend to be smaller and more intimate than their high-octane megaplex cousins.

Hostess Clubs

Hong Kong's many hostess clubs are clubs in name only. Some of these are multimillion-dollar operations with plush interiors with hundreds of hostess-companions working for them. Computerized time clocks on each table tabulate companionship charges; the costs are clearly detailed on cards, as are standard drink tabs. Dance floors here are often large, and they have one or more live bands and a lineup of both pop and cabaret singers.

The clubs also have dozens of luxuriously furnished private rooms, with partitioned lounges and the ubiquitous karaoke setup. Local and visiting businessmen adore these rooms—and the multilingual hostesses; business is so good that the clubs are willing to allow visitors *not* asking for companionship. The better clubs are on a par with music lounges in deluxe hotels, though they cost a little more. Their happy hours start in the afternoon, when many have a sort of tea-dance ambience, and continue through to mid-evening. Peak hours are 10 PM to 4 AM.

Many so-called hostess clubs, however, are in fact fronts for prostitution. In Wan Chai, for instance, hostess clubs are dotted among regular bars, too many to mention by name. But most, if not all of them are sad little places full of leering men watching girls with vacant expressions performing halfhearted pole dances dressed in leotards. These houses of prostitution are not the same as establishments such as the upmarket Club BBoss in Tsim Sha Tsui.

Better Safe than Sorry

All premises licensed to serve alcohol are supposedly subject to stringent fire, safety, and sanitary controls, although at times this is hard to believe, given the overcrowding at the hippest places. Think twice before succumbing to the city's raunchier hideaways. If you stumble into one, check out cover and hostess charges before you get too comfortable. Pay for each round of drinks as it's served (by cash rather than credit card), and never sign any blank checks.

Hong Kong is a surprisingly safe place, but as in every tourist destination the art of the tourist rip-off has been perfected. If you're unsure, visit places signposted as members of the Hong Kong Tourist Board (HKTB).

Stay Legal

You must be over 18 to buy alcohol. Drugs, obscene publications, and unlicensed gambling are ostensibly illegal. There's some consumer protection, but the generally helpful police, many of whom speak English, expect you to know the meaning of *caveat emptor* (buyer beware).

After the Party

The ever-reliable MTR shuts down at 1 AM, and taxis are your only way home after that. They can easily be flagged down on the street; when the light on the car roof is on, it's available for hire. If the cab has an "out of service" sign over its round "for hire" neon sign on the dashboard, it means it's a cross-harbor taxi.

ity, La Dolce Vita has a sleek interior and is a popular stomping ground for the name-dropping masses. ⊠ *9 Lan Kwai Fong, Lan Kwai Fong, Central* ☎ *2810–9333* ☞ *Closes 3* AM.

Le Jardin. For a gregarious, cosmopolitan vibe, check out this casual bar with its lovely outdoor terrace overlooking a not-so-lovely alley. It's a little hard to find, situated at the top of a flight of steps above Indian, Malaysian and Vietnamese restaurants below, but the leafy garden setting is worth it. ⊠ *1/F, 10 Wing Wah La., Central* ☎ *2526–2717* ☞ *Closes 3* AM.

Lux. The well-heeled drink martinis and designer beers at this swanky corner spot. It has a prime location in Lan Kwai Fong and is another great bar to people-watch; they also serve excellent food in booths at the back. ⊠ *U/F, California Tower, 30–32 D'Aguilar St., Lan Kwai Fong, Central* ☎ *2868–9538* ☞ *Closes 4* AM.

MO Bar. This plush bar in the Landmark Mandarin Oriental is where the banking set goes to relax. You'll pay top dollar for the martinis, but the striking interior makes it worthwhile. A huge red light circle dominates an entire wall, the "O" being a Chinese symbol of shared experience. There's also a drawbridge and an elevated lily pond, tilted at an angle to reflect light over the bar at night. ⊠ *The Landmark Mandarin Oriental Hotel, 15 Queen's Road Central, The Landmark, Central* ☎ *2132–0077* ☞ *Closes 2* AM.

RED Bar. Although its shopping mall location may not seem appealing at first, once you arrive at RED, you'll throw all your preconceived notions into the harbor. Situated on the roof of IFC Mall, RED has breathtaking views of Victoria Habour as well as the skyscrapers towering over Central and Western. There's also a restaurant here and it's part of Pure Fitness group of gyms. That's right, so after a session at the gym, grab some dinner, and then relax with a cocktail while watching the breathtaking sunset. You've earned it. ⊠ *Level 4, Two IFC, 8 Finance St., Central* ☎ *8129–8882* ☞ *Closes 2* AM.

Staunton's Wine Bar & Cafe. Adjacent to Hong Kong's famous outdoor escalator is this hip bistro-style café and bar. Partly alfresco, it's the perfect place to people-watch. You can come for a drink at night, or for coffee or a meal during the day. It's also a Sunday-morning favorite for nursing hangovers over brunch. ⊠ *10–12 Staunton St., SoHo, Central* ☎ *2973–6611* ☞ *Closes 3* AM.

Discos & Nightclubs

★ **C Club.** The upwardly mobile and occasionally some minor Hong Kong celebrities party here. There's a large dance floor, a flashy bar, and plenty of nooks to lounge in. But be warned: no sneakers, no shorts, no jeans. Weekends command a HK$200 door charge that includes one standard drink. ⊠ *32–34 D'Aguilar St., basement, Lan Kwai Fong, Central* ☎ *2526–1139* ☞ *Closes 4* AM.

Club 97. A glamorous and glitzy nightspot, Club 97 draws mobs of beautiful people. It started off life as a members-only club, but that rule has since been disregarded. The space is dominated by a circular bar in the center of the room, and has a small dance floor surrounded by cozy nooks. ⊠ *9–11 Lan Kwai Fong, Central* ☎ *2186–1897* ☞ *Closes 4* AM.

★ **dragon-i.** A place to prance, pose, and preen, dragon-i is owned by local party boy and social celebrity Gilbert Yeung. The entrance is marked

Lan Kwai Fong

A CURIOUS, L-SHAPE cobblestone lane in Central is the pulsating center of nightlife and dining in Hong Kong. Lan Kwai Fong, or just "the Fong," is a spot that really shines after the sun sets. You can start with a predinner drink at any number of bars, then enjoy some of the territory's finest dining, before stopping at a nightclub to boogie the night away.

For such a small warren, Lan Kwai Fong has an incredibly broad range of nightlife to offer, with more than 20 bars, restaurants, and clubs within just a few blocks. Since most of the ground-floor establishments spill out onto the pavement, there's an audible buzz about the place, lending it a festive air that's unmatched elsewhere in Hong Kong. Whether it's corporate financiers celebrating their latest million-dollar deals at California, La Dolce Vita, or Oscar's, or more humble office workers having drinks with their buddies at Le Jardin or Insomnia, there's a place here to suit everyone.

The same "something for everyone" motto extends to the plethora of upmarket restaurants in Lan Kwai Fong. From Asia, there are Chinese, Thai, Japanese, and Vietnamese restaurants, while European food can be found at French and Italian establishments. If your wallet's feeling a little light from your latest shopping expedition, take heed of the excited waiters waving to potential customers along Wing Wah Lane. Here you'll find rowdy Indian, Thai, and Malaysian restaurants that serve piping-hot dishes at reasonable prices.

Lan Kwai Fong used to be a hawkers' neighborhood before World War I I. Its modern success is largely due to

Canadian expatriate Allan Zeman, an eccentric figure who has been dubbed the "King of Lan Kwai Fong" by the local media. He opened his first North American-style restaurant here 20 years ago; today he not only owns dozens of other restaurants and bars, but also the buildings they're in. He claims to have about 100 restaurants, and although he doesn't actually own them all, he acts as the landlord for most of them. The Fong is now simply a hobby for Zeman, whose business empire includes everything from property development to fashion.

New Year's Eve on December 31 is undoubtedly the busiest time for Lan Kwai Fong. Thousands of people line the tiny area to celebrate and party. You'll notice a strong police presence moving the human traffic through the streets and keeping an eye out for any troublemakers. This is mainly to prevent another tragedy such as the one in the early 1990s when 21 people were crushed to death as a massive throng went out of control as they ushered in a new year. Now when large crowds are anticipated—usually New Year's Eve, Christmas Eve, and also Halloween—the police carefully monitor the number of people entering the area.

Call it progress or a type of survival-of-the-strongest evolution, but this trendy neighborhood has seen as many establishments open as those that have closed down. New spots are constantly in development, or old places under refurbishment. Regardless of the changes, Lan Kwai Fong is always alive with scores of people and places to be merry.

— Eva Chui Loiterton

6

by an enormous birdcage (filled with real budgies and canaries) made entirely of bamboo poles. Have a drink on the wonderful alfresco deck by the doorway or step inside the rich, red playroom, which doubles as a restaurant in the early evening. Take a trip to the bathroom to see arguably the biggest cubicles in Hong Kong, with floor-to-ceiling silver tiles and double-height mirrored ceilings. ⊠ *Upper G/F, The Centrium, 60 Wyndham St., Central* ☎ *3110–1222* ☞ *Closes 5 AM.*

★ **Drop.** Drop is where in celebrities party when they're in town—usually until the sun rises. It may take some effort to find, but that only adds an air of exclusivity to the speakeasy like location. The excellent martinis are their forte. And as with most popular clubs, this one doesn't get going until late. ⊠ *On Lok Mansion, 39–43 Hollywood Rd., basement, entrance off Cochrine St., Central* ☎ *2543–8856* ☞ *Closes 6 AM.*

The Edge. A young crowd flocks to this nightclub, situated directly beneath dragon-i. A rotating line-up of DJs keep the hip-hop throng coming back for more, especially on Saturday nights when people line up for hours to get in—it's arguably the biggest hip-hop night in town. ⊠ *G/ F, The Centrium, 60 Wyndham St., Central* ☎ *2523–6690* ☞ *Closes 2 AM Mon.–Wed.; 5 AM Thurs. and Fri.; 6 AM Sat.*

Hei Hei Club. Two Jacuzzis and a 2-foot pool aren't often found at nightclubs, but Hei Hei—"Double Happiness" in Chinese—encourages clubbers to bring their swimwear. But the Playboy Mansion it's not. The aquatic features are on two outdoor terraces; the rest of Hei Hei's 7,000 square feet is a bar and dance floor blasting hip-hop and R&B. ⊠ *3/F, On Hing Terr., Central* ☎ *2899–2068.*

Volar. Barking dogs and beefy bouncers front the entrance to Volar, a hugely popular nightclub. In a cavernous basement, different rooms feature the latest hip-hop, house, and tech-funk spun by a roster of international DJs. On weekends, the lines to enter are long, so unless you're a member, a model, or celebrity, be prepared to wait. ⊠ *B/F, 39–44 D'Aguilar St., Lan Kwai Fong, Central* ☎ *2810–1272.*

Gay & Lesbian Spots

Meilanfang Bar. Named after the most accomplished Peking Opera artist of the last century (on whom the film *Farewell My Concubine* was loosely based) Meilanfang is the newest gay bar in Central. How better to pay tribute to a man whose livelihood was made by impersonating females on stage (men commonly played female roles in Chinese opera), paving the way for present-day drag queens? Appropriately decked out in a riot of traditional bright Chinese opera colors, the bar is busy most nights, especially weekends. Locals called it "M Bar." ⊠ *14 On Wo La., Sheung Wan* ☎ *2152–2121* ☞ *Closes 1 AM.*

Propaganda. Off a quaint but steep cobblestone street, this is *the* most popular gay club in Hong Kong, with a near-monopoly on the scene (it's known as P P to the locals, Props to the expatriate lot). The art deco bar area has elegant booths and tables and soft lighting; on the other hand, the dance floor has lap poles on either side for go-go boys to flaunt their wares. It's pretty empty during the week; the crowds arrive well after midnight on weekends. The entrance fee of HK$180 on Friday and Saturday nights includes one standard drink. ⊠ *Lower G/F, 1 Hollywood Rd., Central* ☎ *2868–1316* ☞ *Closes 5:30 AM.*

Arts Spaces

Fringe Club. The pioneer of Hong Kong's alternative arts scene has been staging excellent independent productions since opening in 1983. The distinctive brown-and-white striped structure that houses it was built as a cold-storage warehouse in 1892. It was derelict when the Fringe took over; the painstaking renovation has earned awards. Light pours through huge windows into the street-level gallery, with its small, well-curated changing exhibitions.

The über-cool Volkswagen Fotogalerie is Hong Kong's only photographic space, and the Fringe's latest demonstration that it's one step ahead of the game. Downstairs, meat and cheese were once sold in the space that houses the Fringe Theatre. The lighting box of the smaller Studio Theatre was once a refrigeration unit, built to preserve not food but colonials' winter clothes from summer mildew. (Note that many Fringe productions are in Cantonese, so check the program carefully.) ⊠ *2 Lower Albert Rd., Central* ☎ *2521-7251, 3128-8288 box office, 2877-4000 M-at-the-Fringe* ⊕ *www.hkfringe.com.hk* ✉ *Galleries free* ⊙ *Art galleries and box office: Mon.-Sat. noon10 PM. Fotogalerie: Mon.-Thurs. noon-midnight, Fri. and Sat. noon3 AM. Fringe Gallery Bar: Mon.-Thurs. 3 PM-midnight, Fri. and Sat. 3 PM-3 AM* Ⓜ *Central MTR, Exit D2.*

Hong Kong Arts Centre. A hodge-podge of activities take place in this bleak concrete tower, financed with horse-racing profits donated by the Hong Kong Jockey Club. Intriguing contemporary art exhibitions are held in the 14th-floor Goethe Gallery, a white-cube space. Thematic cycles of art-house flicks run in the basement

Agnès b. Cinema. Community theater groups are behind much of the fare at the Shouson Theatre and smaller McAulay Studio, though international drama and dance troupes sometimes appear. Quality is hit-and-miss so check newspaper reviews for advice. Similarly erratic are the shows in the split-level Pao Galleries. From Wan Chai MTR cross the footbridge to Immigration Tower, then dog-leg left through the open plaza until you hit Harbour Road: the center is on the left. ⊠ *2 Harbour Road,, Wan Chai* ☎ *2582-0200, 2802-0088 Goethe Gallery* ⊕ *www.hkac.org.hk* ✉ *Free* ⊙ *Center: Daily 10-8. Goethe Gallery: weekdays 9-9, Sat. 2-6* Ⓜ *Wan Chai MTR, Exit C.*

Ma Tau Kok Cattle Depot. A former slaughterhouse in industrial To Kwa Wan—aka the middle of nowhere—has become a happening hub of independent art. The century-old brown-brick building looks like it would be more at home in northern England than Hong Kong. It's divvied up into spaces run by different groups. In July 1997—handover month—a group of young local artists formed the **Artists' Commune** (⊠ Unit 12 ☎ 2104-3322 ⊕ www. artistcommune.com ✉ Free ⊙ Tues.-Sun. 2-8), whose massive loftlike premises showcase offbeat works. Expect funky, well-curated pickings at **1aspace** (⊠ Unit 14 ☎ 2529-0087 ⊕ www.oneaspace. org.hk ✉ Free ⊙ Tues.-Sun 2-8), a cool, sleek gallery. The easiest way to get here is by taxi from Tsim Sha Tsui (around HK$50) or from Lok Fu MTR (around HK$35). ⊠ *63 Ma Tau Kok Rd., To Kwa Wan, Kowloon.*

— Victoria Patience

6

Late-Night Bites

WHEN THE LATE-NIGHT pub-crawl-rumbles strike, go to **Al's Diner** (✉ 39 D'Aguilar St., Lan Kwai Fong ☎ 2869–1869), which is open until 4 AM, serving hamburgers and fry-ups, along with good bagels and coffee in a music-filled, neon-lighted, chrome-plated diner space. You can exploit your inner frat-boy with a vodka-spiked Jell-O shot or a tequila Jell-O shot *with* the worm.

A perennial late-supper favorite is **Post 97** (✉ 1/F, 9 Lan Kwai Fong, Lan Kwai Fong ☎ 2810–9333), where the kitchen is open until 2 AM on Friday and Saturday. The all-day menu has consistently good grub from focaccias and salads to chicken wings and hearty breakfasts. Grab a window seat to peer down at the other late-night revelers of Lan Kwai Fong.

While locals head to **Tsui Wah** (✉ 15–19 Wellington St., Central ☎ 2525–6338), a large, three-story Chinese restaurant, at any time of the day, the late-night crowds are the happiest. Service is quick, there's a huge menu of typical Chinese fare such as fried rice and noodles, as well as Western dishes such as steak. It's noisy, smoky, has bright fluorescent lighting, and the crowds just keep on coming. You may even find the odd celebrity chowing down on beef brisket noodles at 2 AM. The place closes at 4 AM.

– Eva Chui Loiterton

Rice Bar. This friendly bar is no-smoking—an impressive move, and they still manage to keep the business coming in. Weekends are very crowded from midnight, and if you're willing to go topless, you'll be rewarded with free drinks. The owner also owns a gay café around the corner called Billy Boy. ✉ *33 Jervois St., Sheung Wan* ☎ *2851–4800* ☞ *Closes 3 AM.*

Music Clubs

The Cavern. Cover bands dressed up as Abba, the Monkees, and even Bruce Springsteen keep the crowds on their feet and singing at this bar. Pop music rules—the cheesier, the better. The place is impossible to miss, not only for its loud music, but for its bright, lolly-pop-color mural on the exterior wall, and tables on the pavement, straddling Lan Kwai Fong. ✉ *Shop 1, G/F, LKF Tower, 33 Wyndham St, entrance on D'Aguliar St., Central* ☎ *2121–8969* ☞ *Closes 4 AM.*

★ **Fringe Club.** The arts-minded mingle in this historic redbrick building that also houses the members-only Foreign Correspondents' Club. The Fringe is the headquarters for Hong Kong's alternative arts scene and normally stages live music twice a week. ✉ *2 Lower Albert Rd., Central* ☎ *2521–7251* ☞ *Closes 3 AM.*

Pubs

Globe. Between Lan Kwai Fong and SoHo, the Globe is one of the few laid-back places in the area to knock back a beer or two with down-to-earth folks. It's the local pub for homesick expats who live in the area. ✉ *39 Hollywood Rd., Central* ☎ *2543–1941* ☞ *Closes 2 AM.*

The Keg. As its name implies, beer and more beer is the beverage of choice at this small pub. Large wooden barrels serve as tables and the floors are covered with discarded peanut shells. All manner of sports coverage reigns on the TV screens. ✉ 52 D'Aguilar St., Lan Kwai Fong, Central ☎ 2810–0369 ☞ Closes 3 AM.

Wine Bars

Boca Tapas and Wine Bar. What better combination than delicious tapas and some lovely wine? The 80-bottle list has top Australian, Argentinean, Italian, and French wines and more. Boca—"mouth" in Spanish—has a diverse tapas menu, too, ranging from traditional chorizo and stuffed olives to Asian bites such as spicy spring rolls and satay sticks. ✉ 64 Peel St., SoHo, Central ☎ 2548–1717 ☞ Closes 2 AM.

Le Tire Bouchon. If you're planning an intimate encounter, try this little restaurant and wine bar, where fine wines by the glass accompany tasty bistro meals. The staff is friendly and warm and the wine list is extensive. ✉ 45A Graham St., Central ☎ 2523–5459 ☞ Closes 12:30 AM.

ARTFUL DATES

■ **Hong Kong City Fringe Festival (January):** Theater, dance, comedy, film, visual arts, new media—all these and more take place in venues across town. ⊕ www.hkfringe.com.hk.

■ **Hong Kong Arts Festival (February and March):** It draws some serious international names—past visitors have included Mikhail Baryshnikov, Pina Bausch, and José Carreras. The focus is on performing arts. ⊕ www.hk.artsfestival.org.

■ **Man Hong Kong International Literary Festival (March):** Asia's most important English-language literature festival prioritizes literature with an Asian focus. ⊕ www.festival.org.hk.

■ **Hong Kong International Film Festival (April):** Asian cinema accounts for many of the 200 new films shown in this festival. ⊕ www.hkiff.org.hk.

Wan Chai

Wan Chai is no longer the seedy area that inspired *The World of Suzie Wong*. The hostess bars are still here though, and "freelance" girls stalk the street corners. Tattoo parlors do a heavy trade in the early mornings when the inebriated, convinced it's a good idea at the time, get inked. Such establishments now share the streets with hip bars and pubs. But some things never change: the busiest Wan Chai nights are still when there's a navy ship in the harbor, on an R&R stopover.

Bars

★ **Brown.** Brown is comfy and homey for those who need to wind down from a hectic day (either working or shopping). High ceilings give the space an airy feel, and there are sink-down-and-chill sofas at the back. The small courtyard is a favorite for weekend brunches. ✉ 18A Sing Woo Rd., Happy Valley, ☎ 2891–8558 ☞ Closes 1:30 AM.

★ **1/5.** Walk upstairs through the narrow corridor with a mirrored ceiling to enter a large, dimly lighted bar with triple-height ceilings and brown velour lounge areas. In the hip Star Street area, this is the bar of choice for those who want an alternative to Lan Kwai Fong and SoHo. There are often international DJs spinning vinyl, and popular manicure and martini nights are held each Wednesday for HK$120. ✉ 1/F, Starcrest Bldg., 9 Star St., Wan Chai ☎ 2520–2515 ☞ Closes 3 AM.

Chinese Opera

THERE ARE 10 **Cantonese opera** troupes headquartered in Hong Kong, as well as many amateur singing groups. Some put on performances of "street opera" in, for example, the Temple Street Night Market almost every night, while others perform at temple fairs, in City Hall, or in playgrounds under the auspices of the Urban Council. Those unfamiliar with Chinese opera might find the sights and sounds of this highly complex and sophisticated art form a little strange. Every gesture has its own meaning; in fact, there are 50 gestures for the hand alone.

Props attached to the costumes are similarly intricate and are used in exceptional ways. For example, the principal female often has 5-foot-long pheasant-feather tails attached to her headdress; she shows anger by dropping the head and shaking it in a circular fashion so that the feathers move in a perfect circle. Surprise is shown by what's called "nodding the feathers." You can also "dance with the feathers" to show a mixture of anger and determination. Orchestral music punctuates the singing. It's best to attend with someone who can translate the gestures for you; or you can learn more at the Cantonese Opera Halls in the Hong Kong Heritage Museum.

The highly stylized **Peking opera** employs higher-pitched voices than Cantonese opera. Peking opera is an older form, more respected for its classical traditions; the meticulous training of the several troupes visiting Hong Kong from the People's Republic of China each year is well regarded. They perform in City Hall or at special temple ceremonies. You can get the latest programs from the Hong Kong Cultural Centre.

– Eva Chui Loiterton

Mes Amis. In the heart of Wan Chai, on the corner of Lockhart and Luard roads, Mes Amis is a friendly bar that also serves good food. Its corner setting and open bi-fold doors means that none of the action outside is missed, and vice versa—the patrons inside are on show for those on the street. ⊠ *83 Lockhart Rd., Wan Chai* ☎ *2527–6680* ☞ *Closes 6 AM.*

Klong Bar & Grill. Named after the many canals that intersect the Thai capital of Bangkok, Klong's ground-floor bar opens onto the street serving up tasty grilled snacks to go with Singha beers. Head upstairs to knock back more Singhas at the U-shape bar, or you can sit in booths or crossed-legged on the raised floor, Thai-style—shoes off, please. ⊠ *54–62 Lockhart Rd., Wan Chai* ☎ *2217–8330* ☞ *Closes 3 AM.*

Discos & Nightclubs

Boracay. This disco is a Hong Kong institution—its basement space isn't very large, but that doesn't stop the crowds from heading down there. The dance floor gets going in the wee hours, and keeps going. There's a bit of a sleaze factor here, but when it's late, who cares? ⊠ *Basement, 20 Luard Rd., Wan Chai* ☎ *2529–3461* ☞ *Closes 5 AM.*

Joe Bananas. Its reputation for all-night partying and general good times remains unchallenged. This disco and bar strictly excludes the military and people dressed too casually: no shorts, sneakers, or T-shirts (the only exception is the Rugby Sevens weekend when even Joe can't turn away the thirsty swarm). The wet T-shirt contest nights are obviously popular. Arrive before 11 PM to avoid the line. ⊠ *23 Luard Rd., Wan Chai* ☎ *2529–1811* ☞ *Closes 6 AM.*

Neptune Disco II. This is another late-night haunt for the dance-till-you-drop set. It's a basement location and is somewhat seedy—venture at your own risk. You have been warned. ⊠ *Basement, 98–108 Jaffe Rd., Wan Chai* ☎ *2865–2238* ☞ *Closes 7 AM.*

Tribeca. A "New York-style nightclub," Tribeca occupies the space that formerly housed Manhattan (is there a trend in names here?) and more recently Club Ing. Unlike many other nightclubs in Hong Kong, it has a huge space—one of the largest in the city—full of dance floors, bars, lounges, and the requisite VIP areas. The plush interior attempts to emulate a swanky nightclub in the Big Apple, and judging by the crowds who flock here, it's doing it well. ⊠ *4/F, Convention Plaza, 1 Harbour Rd., Wan Chai* ☎ *2836–3690* ☞ *Closes 4 AM.*

Music Club

JJs. Having had to close in 2003 after the SARS epidemic hit the Hong Kong economy, this famous hotel spot has once again thrown open its doors. The Music Room is renowned for having the best in-house hotel bands in town. It's also notorious for being a pickup joint and fellas, mind your wallets—not all the ladies are looking for love. ⊠ *Grand Hyatt Hotel, 1 Harbour Rd., Wan Chai* ☎ *2588–1234* ☞ *Closes 3 AM.*

Pubs

Carnegie's. Named after the Scotsman and steel baron Andrew Carnegie, whose family sailed to America in the late 1800s, this rock-and-roll bar lives up to its name. Although Carnegie himself probably didn't imagine bar-top dancing to classic rock tunes at an establishment bearing his name, the Scottish owners feel that the spirit of his love of music lives on regardless. ⊠ *53–55 Lockhart Rd., Wan Chai* ☎ *2866–6289* ☞ *Closes 4 AM.*

Horse & Groom. This friendly pub has a lot of charm, and plenty of regulars who come here to unwind after a day's work. ⊠ *161 Lockhart Rd., Wan Chai* ☎ *2507–2517* ☞ *Closes 3 AM.*

Old China Hand Hand. Once full of gritty booths and stark lighting, this pub now has a facade that opens onto the street, absorbing all the hustle and bustle of Lockhart Road. It's open 24/7, and has been here from time immemorial. The kitchen serves typical pub fare and is something of an institution for those wishing to sober up with greasy grub after a long night out. ⊠ *104 Lockhart Rd., Wan Chai* ☎ *2865–4378.*

Causeway Bay

Bar

Talk of the Town. At the Excelsior's bar, also known as ToTT's, you're treated to a 270-degree vista of Hong Kong Harbor. As you walk in, you're greeted with a riot of wacky interior features ranging from zebra-stripe lounges and multicolor chairs to what looks like color-by-numbers paintings and carpeting of questionable taste. ⊠ *34/F, The Excelsior, 281 Gloucester Rd., Causeway Bay* ☎ *2837–6786* ☞ *Closes 2 AM.*

CLOSE UP

Performance Places

City Hall. From Isaac Stern, Yo-Yo Ma, and the New York Phil to the Bee Gees; from the Royal Danish Ballet to the People's Liberation Army Comrade Dance Troupe, the offerings here are varied, but consistently excellent. Two buildings make up the chunky '60s complex, divided by a WW II memorial garden and shrine. The 1,500-seat concert hall and a smaller theater are in the low-rise block, as is Maxim's City Palace, a massive clattering restaurant with really good dim sum. The high-rise building has an exhibition space and a smaller recital hall as well as a public library and marriage registry office. Performances are usually held Friday and Saturday at 8 PM. ✉ *5 Edinburgh Pl., Central* ☎ *2921–2840, 2734–9009 box office* ⊕ *www.lcsd.gov.hk* ☼ *9–9; box office 10–8* Ⓜ *Central MTR, Exit K.*

Hong Kong Academy for Performing Arts. Many of Hong Kong's most talented performers studied at this academy's schools of drama, music, dance, television, and film. It also has five theaters and a gallery. Large-scale productions are staged in the huge Lyric Theatre and the smaller Drama Theatre; offerings are often in-the-round at the dinky Studio Theatre. The two concert halls host choice classical or traditional Chinese music performances. ■ TIP→ **When the weather's good, inquire about shows in the garden amphitheater.** ✉ *1 Gloucester Rd., Wan Chai* ☎ *2584–8580* ⊕ *www.hkapa.edu* ☼ *Box office Mon.–Sat. noon–6 PM* Ⓜ *Wan Chai MTR, Exit C.*

Hong Kong Cultural Centre. Superlatives abound here: the massive oval concert hall, which seats 2,000, is Asia's biggest; its 8,000-pipe Austrian organ is one of the world's largest. Only slightly smaller, the tiered Grand Theatre often hosts visiting Broadway musicals and opera and ballet productions. Cozier plays take place in the Studio Theatre. Look out for performances by the world-class **Hong Kong Philharmonic Orchestra** (☎ 2721–2030 ⊕ www.hkpo.com), which performs everything from classical to avant-garde to contemporary music by Chinese composers. Past soloists have included Vladimir Ashkenazy, Rudolf Firkusny, and Maureen Forrester. Exhibits are occasionally mounted in the atrium. ✉ *10 Salisbury Rd., Tsim Sha Tsui, Kowloon* ☎ *2734–2010, 2734–9009 box office* ⊕ *www.lcsd.gov.hk* ☼ *11–11; box office 10–9:30* Ⓜ *Tsim Sha Tsui MTR, Exit E.*

Kwai Tsing Theatre. It might be in the sticks, but it's a major player in the cultural scene. Sunlight pours into the atrium through a curving glass facade that looks onto a plaza where performances are often held. Inside, the 900-seat theater provides a much-needed middle ground between the massive spaces and tiny studio theaters at other venues. And if the likes of Phillip Glass and the Royal Shakespeare Company can schlep out here, 20 minutes from Central, to perform, you can certainly get out here to watch. ✉ *12 Hing Ning Rd., Kwai Chung, New Territories* ☎ *24080128, 2406–7505 box Office* ⊕ *www.lcsd.gov.hk* ☼ *Daily 9 AM–11 PM* Ⓜ *Kwai Fong MTR, Exit C.*

– Victoria Patience

Pub

Dickens Bar. For a reasonably priced hotel drinking hole, try the Excelsior's basement pub, which also has live music and shows football games via satellite TV. The food served up is hearty and goes down better with an ale or two. ✉ *281 Gloucester Rd., basement, Causeway Bay* ☎ *2837–6782* ☞ *Closes 2* AM.

Wine Bar

Juliette's. Classy, Juliette's is a cozy spot for chuppie (Hong Kong's Chinese yuppies) couples and corporate types relaxing after a busy day's trading. ✉ *6 Hoi Ping Rd., Causeway Bay* ☎ *2882–5460* ☞ *Closes 2* AM.

KOWLOON

Central and Wan Chai are undoubtedly the king and queen of nightlife in Hong Kong. If you're staying in a hotel, however, or having dinner on *the other side,* that is, Kowloon, a fun place in Tsim Sha Tsui for nightlife is an out-of-the-way strip called Knutsford Terrace.

Bars

6

Aqua. Felix at the Peninsula Hotel has had a stronghold in the sophisticated bar-with-a-view competition for years, but now its crown has been handed over to Aqua. Inside One Peking, an impressive curvaceous skyscraper dominating the Kowloon skyline, this very cool bar is on the mezzanine level of the top floor. The high ceilings and raking glass walls offer up unrivaled views of Hong Kong Island and the magical lights of the harbor filled with ferries and ships. ✉ *29th and 30th floors, One Peking, 1 Peking Rd., Tsim Sha Tsui, Kowloon* ☎ *3427–2288* ☞ *Closes 2* AM.

Bahama Mama's. You'll find tropical rhythms at the Caribbean-inspired bar, where world music plays and the kitsch props include a surfboard over the bar and the silhouette of a curvaceous woman showering behind a screen over the restroom entrance. ✉ *4–5 Knutsford Terr., Tsim Sha Tsui, Kowloon* ☎ *2368–2121* ☞ *Closes 4* AM.

Balalaika. Vodka is served in a -20°C (-36°F) room at this Russian-theme bar, but don't be alarmed at the freezing temperature—they provide you with fur coats and traditional Russian fur hats. Take your pick from the 15 varieties of vodka from five different countries. ✉ *2/F, 10 Knutsford Terr., Tsim Sha Tsui, Kowloon* ☎ *2312–6222* ☞ *Closes 1* AM.

The Bar. You'll certainly feel well taken care of at the Peninsula's lobby bar. Society watchers linger here; sit to the right of the hotel entrance to better observe the crème de la crème. ✉ *Peninsula Hotel, Salisbury Rd., Tsim Sha Tsui, Kowloon* ☎ *2920–2888* ☞ *Closes at midnight.*

FodorśChoice ★ **Felix.** High up in the Peninsula Hotel, this bar is immensely popular with visitors; it not only has a brilliant view of the island, but the interior was designed by the visionary Philippe Starck. Don't forget to check out the padded mini-disco room. Another memorable feature is the male urinals, situated right by glass windows overlooking the city. ✉ *28/F, the Peninsula Hong Kong, Salisbury Rd., Tsim Sha Tsui, Kowloon* ☎ *2920–2888* ☞ *Closes 2* AM.

Gripps. With spectacular harbor views from the ocean-liner level and a central bar modeled after a high-class London pub, this bar in the

Marco Polo draws the executive set, and, more recently, businessmen from mainland China and some tourists who stay at this hotel in the heart of Kowloon. ⊠ *6/F, Marco Polo Hongkong Hotel, Harbour City, Canton Rd., Tsim Sha Tsui, Kowloon* ☎ *2113–0088* ☞ *Closes 1* AM.

Sky Lounge. Ride the bubble elevator to this bar high up in the Sheraton in time for sunset, and you won't be disappointed. Once you're there, try one of their frozen fruit cocktails or the signature lychee martinis. ⊠ *18/F, Sheraton Hong Kong Hotel & Towers, 20 Nathan Rd., Tsim Sha Tsui, Kowloon* ☎ *2369–1111* ☞ *Closes 2* AM.

Hostess Clubs

Fodor'sChoice
★
Club BBoss. This is Hong Kong's grandest and most boisterous hostess club, tended by a staff of more than 1,000, and frequented by local company executives. If your VIP room is too far from the entrance, you can hire an electrified vintage Rolls-Royce and purr around an indoor roadway. Be warned that this is tycoon territory—a bottle of brandy can cost HK$18,000. ⊠ *Mandarin Plaza, Tsim Sha Tsui East, Kowloon* ☎ *2369–2883* ☞ *Closes 4* AM.

Club Kokusai. As its name implies, this place appeals to visitors from the Land of the Rising Yen. Interestingly, there's no karaoke here, just the shows—and girls, of course. ⊠ *81 Nathan Rd., Tsim Sha Tsui, Kowloon* ☎ *2367–6969* ☞ *Closes 3* AM.

New Era. Along the harbor is the former Club Deluxe, with its spacious and open dance floor and lounge area. Wannabe pop stars or visitors simply wishing to stretch their vocal cords can karaoke the night away. ⊠ *New World Centre, East wing, Level 3, Tsim Sha Tsui, Kowloon* ☎ *2721–0277* ☞ *Closes 1* AM.

Music Club

Ned Kelly's Last Stand. Come to this Aussie-managed haven in Kowloon for pub meals and, oddly enough, Dixieland jazz. Arrive before 10 PM to get a comfortable seat. ⊠ *11A Ashley Rd., Tsim Sha Tsui, Kowloon* ☎ *2376–0562* ☞ *Closes 2* AM.

Pubs

★ **Delaney's.** Both branches of the pioneer of Hong Kong Irish pubs have interiors that were made in Ireland and shipped to Hong Kong, and the mood is as authentic as the furnishings. There is Guinness and Delaney's ale (a specialty microbrew) on tap, corner snugs (small private rooms), and a menu of Irish food, plus a happy hour that runs from 5 to 9 PM daily. ⊠ *71–77 Peking Rd., basement, Tsim Sha Tsui, Kowloon* ☎ *2301–3980* ⊠ *G/F, 1 Capital Pl., 18 Luard Rd., Wan Chai* ☎ *2804–2880* ☞ *Closes 3* AM.

Just "M." The guess is that this curiously named pub stands for either "men" (but don't mistake it for a gay bar) or "money," but the owners playfully refuse to give up the mystery. The minimalist industrial design gives it a laid-back feel, and the small mezzanine level has large black couches to sink into. Karaoke kicks off after 2 AM. ⊠ *Shop 5, Podium Plaza, 5 Hanoi Rd., Tsim Sha Tsui, Kowloon* ☎ *2311–9188* ☞ *Closes 4* AM.

Where to Stay

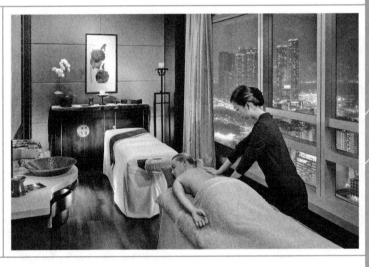

7

WORD OF MOUTH

"For $150 a night you can still get a decent hotel. As long as it's close to the MTR (subway), it's fine. Doesn't matter if it's in Mong Kok or Tsim Sha Tsui on the Kowloon side or Central or Causeway Bay on Hong Kong Island." —rkkwan

By Robin Goldstein

Hong Kong has a truly postmodern skyline—and the hotels to match. Space is at a premium, so rooms are often cramped and expensive. But they're also tricked out with cutting-edge conveniences and luxurious amenities.

Digs with rainfall-style showers, 42-inch plasma TVs, and iPod docks are more the rule than the exception. And it's hard to find a hotel without wireless Internet or a spa these days. Then there's that Hong Kong trademark—unparalleled harbor and skyline views.

Reserve well in advance, and plan to pay dearly. Hong Kong is now overrun as much by the new breed of vacationing upper-middle-class Mainlanders as by the international business set. Room shortages mean that the age of the under-US$100 hotel room is vanishing; top spots run US$500–$600.

Though hotel construction isn't happening fast enough to meet the demand, each month seems to see the opening of yet another megastar—among them the Four Seasons in Central and the Langham Place in Kowloon's up-and-coming Mong Kok district. Smaller, friendlier places—like Causeway Bay's groundbreaking Jia—have a discreet flashiness and all the amenities of larger hotels but none of the sky-scraping rooms or lobby malls that somehow seem dated. Central's Landmark Mandarin Oriental, on the other hand, might not be as trendy as the boutique places, but it's even more discreetly elite. Choose carefully, though: ever-increasing prices have turned some hotels into spectacular rip-offs.

HONG KONG ISLAND

Western

The Western district has several hotels in the lower Midlevels and Sheung Wan areas. These places are convenient to the Peak Tram, as well as to SoHo (South of Hollywood Road), one of Hong Kong's top nightlife areas. It also has that eclectic mix of international restaurants, boutiques, and bourgeois-bohemian development that seems common to areas dubbed "SoHo" around the world.

☾ **$$** 🏠 **Garden View YWCA.** Don't be put off by the name: this attractive
Fodor'sChoice cylindrical guesthouse on a hill overlooks the botanical gardens and
★ harbor, and its well-designed rooms make excellent use of small irregular shapes and emphasize each room's picture windows. If you want to do your own cooking, ask for one with a kitchenette (which will include a microwave oven); if not, the coffee shop serves European and Asian food. You can also use the swimming pool and gymnasium in the adjacent YWCA. Garden View is a five-minute drive (Bus 12A or Minibus 1A) from Central and a few minutes from the Peak tram station. ✉ *1 MacDonnell Rd., Midlevels, Western* ☎ *2877-3737* ⊕ *www.ywca.org.hk* ↝ *133 rooms* ♧ *Coffee shop, some kitchenettes, minibars, cable TV, in-room data ports, pool, gym, laundry service, in-room broadband, business services, no-smoking floors* ▭ *AE, DC, MC, V* Ⓜ *Central.*

★ **$$** 🏠 **Island Pacific Hotel.** There isn't much around this 29-story property way out to the west, and it has small rooms, but the windows are large and there are views aplenty of the city or the harbor. The Western Harbour Tunnel, which connects to the airport expressway, is nearby, as is the Hong Kong-Macau Ferry Terminal. There's a tram stop outside the hotel, and a ride to Central takes about 10 minutes. Service is somewhat lacking, and carpets and furnishing look frayed in some rooms, but it's still a good deal for the reasonable room rates. ✉ *152 Connaught Rd. W, Western* ☎ *2131-1188* ⊕ *www.islandpacifichotel. com.hk* ↝ *343 rooms, 7 suites* ♧ *Coffee shop, room service, in-room safes, minibars, cable TV with movies and video games, in-room broadband, pool, gym, bar, babysitting, laundry service, business services, meeting rooms, no-smoking floors* ▭ *AE, DC, MC, V* Ⓜ *Sheung Wan.*

★ **$-$$** 🏠 **Novotel Century Harbourview.** This modern hotel is surrounded by traditional Chinese streets full of stores selling antiques, herbal medicines, and bric-a-brac, seemingly unchanged with the passage of time. Rooms are small but have city or harbor views. A free shuttle bus takes you to the Airport Express Hong Kong Station and the HK Convention & Exhibition Centre. Biz Café in the lobby has Internet facilities and is open from early morning for breakfast to late night for supper and drinks. The rooftop pool and gym have panoramic views. ✉ *508 Queen's Rd. W, Western* ☎ *2974-1234* ⊕ *www.accorhotels.com/asia* ↝ *262 rooms, 12 suites* ♧ *Restaurant, coffee shop, room service, in-room safes, minibars, cable TV with movies, in-room broadband, pool, gym, massage, 2 bars, babysitting, laundry service, business services, meeting rooms, no-smoking floors* ▭ *AE, DC, MC, V* Ⓜ *Sheung Wan.*

$ 🏠 **Bishop Lei International House.**
Fodor'sChoice Owned and operated by the
★ Catholic diocese of Hong Kong, this guesthouse is up the Midlevels

> **7**

WORD OF MOUTH

"Bishop Lei is a fantastic value for Hong Kong. The location is great (about a 2-minute walk from the moving sidewalk), the bus is outside the door, the front desk staff are helpful, and it's about a 40-minute walk to the top of the Peak."   –Anna

HONG KONG
LODGING PLANNER

What's Your Pleasure?

■ **Unmatched skyline views:** Inter-Continental Hong Kong

■ **Boutique-hotel glam:** Jia

■ **Sci-fi technology:** Landmark Mandarin

■ **Cutting-edge comfort in a traditional 'hood:** Langham Place

■ **Inexpensive and well located:** Salisbury YMCA

■ **Overrated, overpriced:** The Peninsula

■ **Apartment-style living:** Ice House

■ **Breakfast with Mickey Mouse:** Hong Kong Disneyland Hotel

■ **Lobbies to get lost in:** JW Marriott, InterContinental Hong Kong, Grand Hyatt

■ **Fodor's Choices ($$$–$$$$):** Four Seasons, Harbour Plaza Hong Kong, Jia, InterContinental Hong Kong, Island Shangri-La, Landmark Mandarin Oriental, Mandarin Oriental, Renaissance Harbour View

■ **Fodor's Choices ($–$$):** Bishop Lei International House, Garden View YWCA, Langham Place, Salisbury YMCA

■ **Arguably Asia's best hotel:** Four Seasons

Location, Location, Location

Hong Kong has the business hubs as well as the nightlife areas of Lan Kwai Fong and SoHo. Kowloon is best for shopping. But thanks to three tunnels beneath Victoria Harbor, the scenic Star Ferry, and the Mass Transit Railway (MTR, or subway), it really doesn't matter whether you stay "Hong Kong side" or "Kowloon side." They're only minutes from each other. To give you an idea: the airport rail link whisks you over the Tsing Ma Suspension Bridge through Kowloon to Central in around 25 minutes; the ferry sails you between the two sides in eight minutes; and the MTR transports you in a brisk five minutes.

Lantau Island is home to the international airport and Disneyland Hong Kong. Look into staying here if you're arriving late, flying out early, or the kids demand Disney. If you want to stay in Hong Kong without breaking the bank, the Wan Chai district has some good budget options. Active and energized 24 hours a day, Causeway Bay is good for night owls who are on a budget or not.

ROOMS WITH A VIEW

Hotels in Tsim Sha Tsui (TST), on the Kowloon side, generally have the best views because it's across the harbor from the most distinctive area of skyline. Remember that silence speaks loudly; if your room (or hotel) isn't advertised as "harbor view," it's almost certainly not. And be wary of the nomenclature: rooms described as "peak view" have exactly the views you *don't* want—that is, back toward the hills rather than over the beautiful harbor.

Reservations & Rates

Book well in advance, especially for stays in March or September to early December, high seasons for conventions. Most hotels operate on the European plan (no meals included). All rooms have private baths unless indicated otherwise. We always list available facilities, but always ask what's included.

Apartment Rentals

If you're in town for a month or more, consider staying in a serviced apartment. It's expensive but you'll save something in the neighborhood of 50% compared with a month at a hotel.

Erba. Perhaps appropriately given the location (near SoHo), its ultramodern apartments are described as "New York–style." Think "feng shui." Then think browns and greens and wood and metal. ⊠ *284 Queen's Rd., Central* ☎ *2910–0700* ⊕ *www.erba.hk* Ⓜ *Central.*

Four Seasons Place. These modern, beautiful apartments are managed by the world-class Four Seasons Hong Kong, so renting here gets you access to the hotel's spa and gym facilities—and what facilities they are. ⊠ *International Finance Center 8 Finance St., Central* ☎ *3196–8228* ⊕ *www.fsphk.com* Ⓜ *Central.*

Hanlun Habitats. These economical studios and one-bedrooms have well-equipped kitchens and TVs just about everywhere you turn. A stay here gets you access to a nearby gym and puts you close to SoHo and Lan Kwai Fong. ⊠ *284 Queen's Rd., Central* ☎ *2868–0168* ⊕ *www.hanlunhabitats.com* Ⓜ *Central.*

Ovolo. Thanks to bold design elements and primary colors, these apartments look like bachelor pads. The location is convenient to nightlife and business areas. ⊠ *2 Arbuthnot Rd., Central* ☎ *3105–2600* ⊕ *www.ovolo.com.hk* Ⓜ *Central.*

Shama Causeway Bay. It's in Causeway Bay's centrally located Times Square complex. Its modern apartments have stereo systems and original Asian artwork. ⊠ *8 Russell St., Causeway Bay* ☎ *2522–3082* ⊕ *www.shama.com* Ⓜ *Causeway Bay.*

Executive Privilege

Most top hotels have a restricted-access executive floor or club. Breakfast and free cocktails are generally served in these clubs, which can range from modest rooms with a few tables, newspapers, and a fridge full of drinks, to a lavish daylong buffet and waiters pouring Dom Perignon (as at the InterContinental Hong Kong). The business facilities tend to include faxes, laser printing, special dedicated concierges, and so on.

Entry to these clubs and lounges is based on what category of room you book, although some hotels allow you simply to pay extra for access. And frequent guests often gain this privilege at large chains.

Childish Things

Many hotels allow children under a certain age to stay in their parents' room at no extra charge, but be sure to find out the cutoff age. The Marco Polo has lots of kid-friendly amenities including miniature bathrobes, mild shampoos, and rubber duckies. Hotels with large pools and rec facilities—the Peninsula, Ritz-Carlton, Grand Hyatt, Renaissance Harbour View, Salisbury YMCA, and Holiday Inn—are good. And of course hotels at Hong Kong Disneyland are the definition of kid-friendly.

7

WHAT IT COSTS In HK$

	$$$$	$$$	$$	$	¢
FOR 2 PEOPLE	over $3,000	$2,100–$3,000	$1,100–$2,100	$700–$1,100	under $700

Prices are for two people in a standard double room in high season, excluding 10% service charge and a 3% government tax.

Escalator at the top of SoHo. Rooms are quite small but functional, and half have harbor views. Although it's economically priced, there is a fully equipped business center, a workout room, a pool, and a restaurant serving Chinese and Western meals. ☒ *4 Robinson Rd., Midlevels, Western* ☎ *2868-0828* ⊕ *www.bishopleihtl.com.hk* ⇱ *104 rooms, 101 suites* ⊘ *Restaurant, in-room safes, minibars, cable TV, in-room broadband, pool, gym, babysitting, laundry service, business services, meeting rooms, no-smoking floors* ▭ *AE, DC, MC, V* Ⓜ *Central.*

Central

It's surprising that there are so few hotels in Central given that it's Hong Kong's financial hub, it's full of top restaurants, and it's home to the Lan Kwai Fong nightlife district. The hotels you do find, though, have top-notch service and marvelous skyline views. You get what you pay for, and here you'll pay for-and get-a lot. Unsurprisingly, you'll find many of Central's hotels full of Russian, Chinese, and Arab businessmen.

$$$$
Fodor'sChoice
★
Four Seasons. When the Four Seasons opened, in the shadow of the world's sixth-tallest building, there was a collective intake of breath: with the elegantly colorful Chinese-theme rooms and their more muted Western counterparts, the place displays equal levels of effortless modern style, yet they're not about trendy minimalism; the *smallest* of them is a roomy 500 square feet. World-class linens, feng shui elevator banks, heated infinity pools, tropical rain showers, 42-inch plasma TVs, skyline-view hot-rock massages in the city's most cutting-edge spa, clairvoyant service, fantastic restaurants . . . and this list doesn't even include the holistic effect of staying in a place that's redefining the world's very notion of an urban luxury hotel. ☒ *International Finance Center, 8 Finance Rd., Central* ☎ *3196-8888* ⊕ *www.fourseasons.com* ⇱ *345 rooms, 54 suites* ⊘ *5 restaurants, room service, minibars, cable TV with movies, in-room DVDs, Wi-Fi, in-room stereos, 2 pools, gym, spa, room service, health club, hair salon, shops, hot tub, massage, sauna, 3 bars, lounge, dry cleaning, laundry service, concierge, business services, meeting rooms* ▭ *AE, DC, MC, V* Ⓜ *Sheung Wan.*

$$$$
Fodor'sChoice
★
Landmark Mandarin Oriental. Hong Kong hotels are like computers: every year, the new technology outdoes the old by such a staggering margin that you're left wondering why anyone would stick by their old models. The design of this boutique-size hotel is dazzling, and a complete departure from the Mandarin's standard MO. The three room types are named for their square footage; the midrange L600 is the most interesting, with a round bathroom fascinatingly placed at the center of the space. Everything from iPod docks to surround-sound speakers are controlled through your TV remote, and the 21,000-square-foot spa has Turkish baths and tropical-rain saunas. And all of this is implausibly concealed within the financial mitochondrion of the city. ☒ *15 Queen's Rd., Central* ☎ *2132-0188* ⊕ *www.mandarinoriental.com/landmark* ⇱ *113 rooms* ⊘ *3 restaurants, room service, minibars, cable TV with*

movies, in-room DVDs, Wi-Fi, in-room stereos, pool, gym, health club, hot tub, massage, shop, spa, sauna, bar, lounge, dry cleaning, laundry service, concierge, business services ▭ *AE, DC, MC, V* Ⓜ *Central.*

$$$$ 🏨 **Mandarin Oriental Hong Kong.** In September 2006, the legendary
Fodor'sChoice Mandarin, which has served the international elite since 1963, completed
★ a top-to-bottom renovation that included the installation of one of the
city's most elaborate spas. Five new categories of rooms, from "study"
to "harbour," span a wider price range than ever before. All have been
updated to a space-age standard: flat-panel LCDs, iPod docks, Hermès
toiletries. On the 25th floor, rising high above the Central skyline, are
renowned chef Pierre Gagnaire's restaurant and the panoramic M Bar.
✉ *5 Connaught Rd., Central* ☎ *2522-0111* ⊕ *www.mandarin-oriental.
com* 🛏 *434 rooms, 68 suites* ⚬ *6 restaurants, room service, in-room
safes, minibars, cable TV with movies, in-room data ports, indoor pool,
gym, health club, hair salon, hot tub, sauna, spa, 4 bars, dry cleaning,
laundry service, concierge, WiFi, business services, meeting rooms, no-
smoking floors* ▭ *AE, DC, MC, V* Ⓜ *Central.*

★ **$$$-$$$$** 🏨 **Ritz-Carlton.** Refined elegance and superb hospitality are signatures
of the Ritz-Carlton. Although gilt-frame mirrors and crystal chandeliers
evoke old-world Europe, the design does give the occasional nod to Asia.
Service is in the stratosphere, as you'd expect from a Ritz-Carlton, and
every room has either a harbor view or a Peak-and-skyscraper view. The
upper club floors have a private concierge, and a lounge with free food
and drinks all day long, where you'll likely see elite business deals being
transacted in hushed tones. The small lobby is less impressive than
those of its peers, but on the flip side, its location, right aside Central's
main plaza, is unbeatable. ✉ *3 Connaught Rd., Central* ☎ *2877-6666,
800/241-3333 in U.S.* ⊕ *www.ritzcarlton.com/hotels/hong_kong* 🛏 *187
rooms, 29 suites* ⚬ *6 restaurants, room service, in-room safes, minibars,
cable TV with movies, in-room DVDs, Wi-Fi, pool, gym, health club,
hot tub, massage, sauna, bar, lounge, shop, babysitting, dry cleaning,
laundry service, concierge, business services, meeting rooms, no-smok-
ing floors* ▭ *AE, DC, MC, V* Ⓜ *Central.*

★ ♨ **$-$$** 🏨 **Ice House.** Consider yourself lucky to be alive at the right time: the apart-
hotel accommodation concept has finally hit Hong Kong, and at the Ice
House, it's done right. These chic, modern studio apartments are available to rent by the day or week, not just by the month (which, by the way,
is quite reasonable at around HK$14,000). Sunlight is plentiful, and the
glass cube showers are an amusing touch. The location is excellent, next
to the Foreign Correspondents' Club and Lan Kwai Fong, and there's free
unlimited broadband, a dedicated phone line, and other business amenities. There's housekeeping service every day but Sunday. If you want to
feel like you have a place of your own in town, the Ice House is a unique
option. ✉ *38 Ice House St., Central* ☎ *2836-7333* ⊕ *www.icehouse.com.
hk* 🛏 *30 rooms* ⚬ *Kitchenettes, minibars, cable TV, in-room broadband, laundry service, business services* ▭ *AE, DC, MC, V.*

Admiralty

You might think that because Admiralty is not in the center of the city's
financial nerve, you'd save a few cents on a hotel here. You'd be wrong.

7

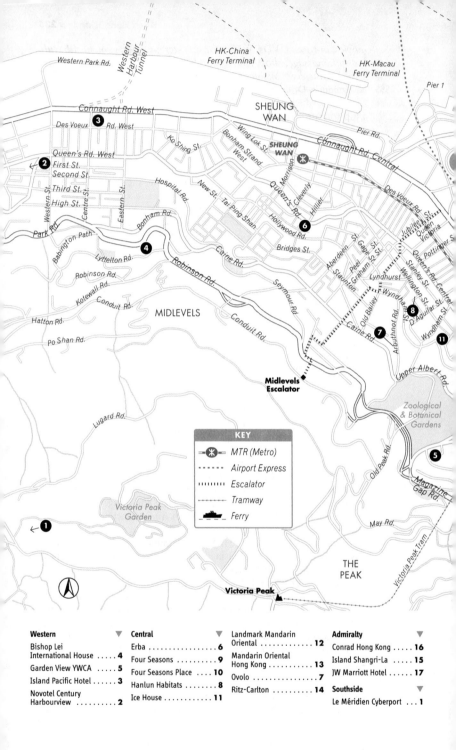

Western ▼

Bishop Lei
International House **4**

Garden View YWCA **5**

Island Pacific Hotel **3**

Novotel Century
Harbourview **2**

Central ▼

Erba **6**

Four Seasons **9**

Four Seasons Place **10**

Hanlun Habitats **8**

Ice House **11**

Landmark Mandarin
Oriental **12**

Mandarin Oriental
Hong Kong **13**

Ovolo **7**

Ritz-Carlton **14**

Admiralty ▼

Conrad Hong Kong **16**

Island Shangri-La **15**

JW Marriott Hotel **17**

Southside ▼

Le Méridien Cyberport ... **1**

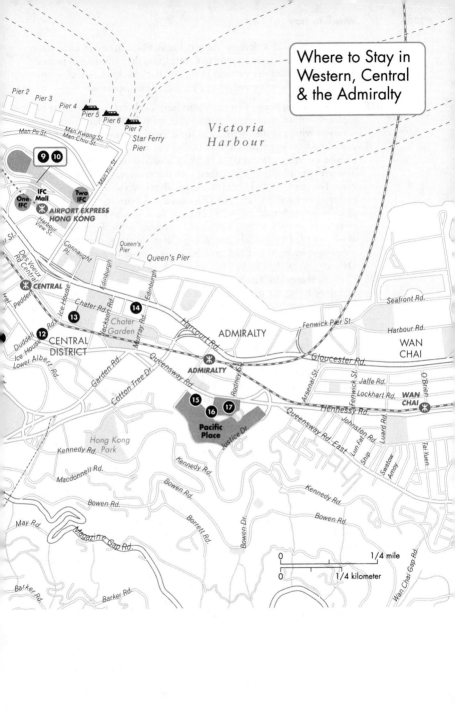

Victoria
Harbour

Pier 2
Pier 3
Pier 4
Pier 5
Pier 6
Pier 7
Star Ferry
Pier

Man Po St.
Man Kwong St.
Man Chiu St.
Man Yiu St.

9 **10**

One-
IFC
IFC
Mall
Two
IFC

AIRPORT EXPRESS
HONG KONG

Harbour
View St.

Connaught
Pl.

Queen's
Pier

Queen's Pier

Des Voeux
Rd Central

CENTRAL

Edinburgh

Edinburgh

Seafront Rd.

Pedder

Ice House

Chater Rd.

14

Harbour Rd.

Ice House

13

Jackson Rd.

Chater
Garden

Murray Rd.

Harcourt Rd.

ADMIRALTY

Fenwick Pier St.

WAN
CHAI

Duddell

12

CENTRAL
DISTRICT

Ice House

Lower Albert Rd.

Gloucester Rd.

ADMIRALTY

Garden Rd.

Queensway Rd.

Rodney Rd.

Arsenal St.

WAN
CHAI

Cotton Tree Dr.

Jaffe Rd.

Fenwick St.

Lockhart Rd.

O'Brien

15

17

Queensway Rd. East

Hennessy Rd.

Johnston Rd.

Lun Fat St.

Luard Rd.

Ship St.

Swatow

Amoy

Tai Yuen

16

Pacific
Place

Justice Dr.

Hong Kong
Park

Kennedy Rd.

Kennedy Rd.

Macdonnell Rd.

Bowen Rd.

Kennedy Rd.

May Rd.

Bowen Rd.

Borrett Rd.

Bowen Dr.

Bowen Rd.

Magazine Gap Rd.

Barker Rd.

Barker Rd.

Wan Chai Gap Rd.

0   1/4 mile
0   1/4 kilometer

Admiralty hotels, particularly those in Pacific Place, are every bit as classy and expensive as the big names in Central, and they soar just as proudly. You get great skyline, Victoria Peak, and harbor views as well as myriad (although Westernized) shopping and dining options.

$$$$ ☷ **Conrad Hong Kong.** This luxurious business hotel occupies part of a gleaming-white, oval-shape tower rising from Pacific Place, an upscale complex with a multistory mall at the edge of Central. Rooms are spacious and have dramatic views of the harbor and city; all have irons and ironing boards, coffee and tea facilities, and high-speed Internet access. The five executive floors have their own private elevator and lounge and gym. The pool, tucked beneath an apocalyptic skyscraper-scape, is legendary. ✉ *Pacific Place, 88 Queensway, Admiralty* ☎ *2521-3838* ⊕ *www.conradhotels.com* ⥅ *467 rooms, 46 suites* ⚒ *4 restaurants, room service, in-room fax, in-room safes, minibars, cable TV with movies, Wi-Fi, pool, health club, bar, lounge, dry cleaning, laundry service, concierge, business services, meeting rooms, no-smoking floors* ▭ *AE, DC, MC, V* Ⓜ *Admiralty.*

$$$$
Fodor'sChoice
★
☷ **Island Shangri-La.** This trademark elliptical building has become an icon of Hong Kong, as has *The Great Motherland of China,* the world's largest Chinese landscape painting, housed in a 16-story glass-top atrium with elevators soaring up and down. The lobby of the deluxe hotel, affectionately known to locals as the "Island Shang," sparkles with more than 780 dazzling Austrian crystal chandeliers hanging from high ceilings and huge, sunlighted windows. Take the elevator up from the 39th floor and see the mainland's misty mountains drift by. Rooms are some of the largest on Hong Kong Island and have magnificent views; all have large desks and all-in-one bedside

> **WORD OF MOUTH**
>
> "Everything, without exception, was absolutely perfect at the Island Shangri-La. I cannot imagine a hotel doing better!" —Yves

control panels. For very upscale dining there's the scenic, formal French eatery Pétrus on the top floor, or for Chinese food, the classy Summer Palace. ✉ *Supreme Court Rd., 2 Pacific Pl., Admiralty* ☎ *2877-3838, 800/942-5050 in U.S.* ⊕ *www.shangri-la.com* ⥅ *531 rooms, 34 suites* ⚒ *4 restaurants, room service, in-room safes, minibars, cable TV with movies, in-room DVDs, Wi-Fi, pool, gym, health club, hair salon, hot tub, massage, sauna, spa, steam room, 3 lounges, shops, babysitting, dry cleaning, laundry service, concierge, business services, meeting rooms, no-smoking floors* ▭ *AE, DC, MC, V* Ⓜ *Admiralty.*

★ ☾ $$$$ ☷ **JW Marriott Hotel.** With its spacious, sunlight-filled lobby with floor-to-ceiling windows revealing fantastic views of the harbor, you might be tempted to spend hours drinking tea or cocktails at this high-end Marriott. Rooms have harbor or mountain views, ample work space, and thoughtful amenities such as irons and ironing boards, complimentary coffee, tea, and mineral water, and high-speed Internet access. Suites have stereos and CD alarm clocks. There's a well-equipped 24-hour gym and an outdoor pool, and even tai chi lessons every Saturday. ✉ *Pacific Place, 88 Queensway, Admiralty* ☎ *2810-8366, 800/228-9290 in U.S.* ⊕ *www. marriott.com* ⥅ *577 rooms, 25 suites* ⚒ *4 restaurants, room service,* *in-room safes, minibars, cable TV with movies, Wi-Fi, pool, health club, spa, 3 bars, shop, babysitting, dry cleaning, laundry service, concierge, business services, meeting rooms, no-smoking floors* ⊟ *AE, DC, MC, V* Ⓜ *Admiralty.*

Lantau Island

The main advantage of staying on Lantau Island is its proximity to the airport. It's a good choice if you arrive late at night and don't want to put up with the chaos of the city on your first night, or on the back end of your trip if you have an early-morning flight. Otherwise, come to Lantau only if you seek a beach escape or if you finally succumb to your kids' Disney dreams (Mickey Mouse, after all, is plastered all over the Hong Kong metro).

★ ☺ 🖼 **Hong Kong Disneyland Hotel.** Modeled in Victorian style after the
$$$-$$$$ Grand Floridian in Florida's Walt Disney World Resort, this top-flight hotel is beautifully executed on every level, from the spacious rooms with balconies overlooking the sea to the Hidden-Mickey topiary gardens and grand, imposing ballrooms that wouldn't be out of place in a fairy-tale secret castle. There's a full daily schedule of activities, many aimed at children; and downstairs, Disney characters meet and greet guests during the enormous buffet breakfast—a good way to get your kids to forgive you for the three days you spent sampling the geese hanging from their necks in Mong Kok. Don't overlook Disneyland as a place to stay before or after your early-morning or late-night flight—it's minutes from the airport. ⊠ *Hong Kong Disneyland Resort, Lantau Island* 🕾 *1-830-830* ⊕ *www.hongkongdisneyland.com* ⬐ *400 rooms* ♿ *3 restaurants, room service, in-room safes, children's programs, minibars, cable TV with movies, in-room broadband, pool, gym, spa, health club, massage, 2 bars, lounge, shops, dry cleaning, laundry service, business services, meeting rooms* ⊟ *AE, DC, MC, V.*

$$$ 🖼 **Regal Airport Hotel.** Ideal for passengers in transit, this is one of the largest airport hotels in the world. It's some distance from the city, but the efficient high-speed rail system can have you on Hong Kong Island in around 25 minutes. It's also connected directly to the passenger terminal by an air-conditioned, moving walkway. Some rooms have terrific views of planes landing from afar; those with balconies overlook the hotel's two swimming pools

> **WORD OF MOUTH**
>
> "I found the Regal to be a very stylish, opulent, and relaxing haven after a very long day of flying."   –Brian

and feel like you're staying in a resort. The Grand Ballroom has space for up to 1,000 people and has simultaneous translation, video-conferencing capability, and a built-in stage. ⊠ *9 Cheong Ted Rd., Lantau Island* 🕾 *2286-8888* ⊕ *www.regalhotel.com* ⬐ *1,103 rooms, 27 suites* ♿ *7 restaurants, coffee shop, room service, in-room safes, minibars, cable TV with movies, WiFi, indoor-outdoor pool, exercise equipment, gym, bar, 2 lounges, shop, dry cleaning, laundry service, business services, meeting rooms, no-smoking floors* ⊟ *AE, DC, MC, V.*

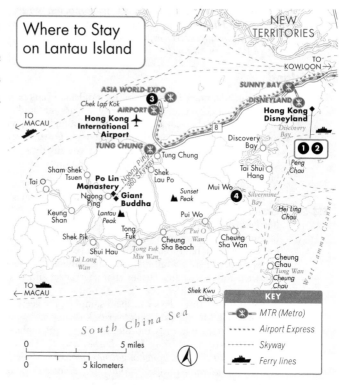

Where to Stay on Lantau Island

★ ☺ **$$** 🏨 **Disney's Hollywood Hotel.** Like its pricier sister, the Disneyland Hotel, Disney's Hollywood Hotel could theoretically be viewed simply as one of Asia's best airport hotels. But that would hardly do justice to the creativity and attention to detail that so brightly color every aspect of your stay here. The theme is the golden age of Hollywood, and if you're from the United States you'll smile at the loving display of Americana here, from the New York-theme restaurant to the art deco frontage of the cocktail lounge. Of course, this is Disneyland, and there are the Chef Mickey restaurants, too. Rooms are on the smaller side, and a bit more 'Goofy' than they are at the Disneyland Hotel, with perhaps even greater appeal for the children. ⊠ *Hong Kong Disneyland Resort, Lantau Island* ☎ *1-830-830* ⊕ *www.hongkongdisneyland.com* ⇗ *600 rooms* ☖ *3 restaurants, room service, in-room safes, children's programs, minibars, cable TV with movies, in-room broadband, pool, gym, spa, health club, massage, 2 bars, shops, dry cleaning, laundry service, business services, meeting rooms* ⊟ *AE, DC, MC, V.*

$ 🏨 **Silvermine Beach Hotel.** This bay-side resort in Mui Wo steers entirely clear of Hong Kong's sound and fury. It's a half hour by fast ferry from Hong Kong Island, then a five-minute walk from the pier. A pool is open in summer, and a tennis court, gym, and sauna are open year-round. Guest rooms are spacious (in spite of small bathrooms) and have tea- and coffee-making facilities. Public buses or taxis outside the hotel can take you to the airport as well as some of the island's attractions. ⊠ *D. D. 2, Lot 648 Silvermine Bay, Mui Wo, Lantau Island* ☎ *2984-8295* ⊕ *www.resort.com.hk* ⟿ *128 rooms, 2 suites* ⟳ *2 restaurants, cable TV, tennis court, pool, exercise equipment, gym, sauna, steam room, meeting rooms* ⊟ *AE, DC, MC, V.*

Wan Chai

Wan Chai, east of Central and Admiralty, was once a boozy sailor's dream. It still has plenty of nightlife (and the red-light activity to go with it) and everything from 24-hour noodle joints to hip new wine bars. At the same time, office high-rises and the Hong Kong Convention & Exhibition Centre, a Sydney Opera House-wannabe structure and the territory's most popular venue for large-scale conferences, draw businesspeople to the area. Thus Wan Chai has some prestigious business hotels: the Grand Hyatt rivals the shining stars of the IFC, Pacific Place, and Tsim Sha Tsui for CEO appeal; the Renaissance Harbour View isn't far behind. Surprisingly the area has also more budget hotels than neighboring districts.

★ ⟳ **$$$$** 🏨 **Grand Hyatt.** A ceiling painted by Italian artist Paola Dindo tops the Hyatt's art deco-style lobby, and black-and-white photographs of classic Chinese scenes hang on the walls. The elegant guest rooms have sweeping harbor views, many with interesting zigzag window frames; amenities include large interactive TVs with cordless keyboards. The One Harbour Road Cantonese restaurant is notable—as is JJ's nightclub and Thai restaurant—and the ground-floor breakfast buffet is a decadent feast. The Plateau spa has a Zen-like calm and there are extensive outdoor facilities. The hotel is especially convenient if you're spending time at the Hong Kong Convention & Exhibition Centre, which is connected to the building. ⊠ *1 Harbour Rd., Wan Chai* ☎ *2588-1234* ⊕ *www. hongkong.grand.hyatt.com* ⟿ *519 rooms, 51 suites* ⟳ *7 restaurants, room service, in-room safes, minibars, cable TV with movies, Wi-Fi, driving range, 2 tennis courts, pool, exercise equipment, gym, health club, hair salon, spa, 3 bars, lounge, nightclub, babysitting, dry cleaning, laundry service, concierge, business services, meeting rooms, no-smoking floors* ⊟ *AE, DC, MC, V* Ⓜ *Wan Chai.*

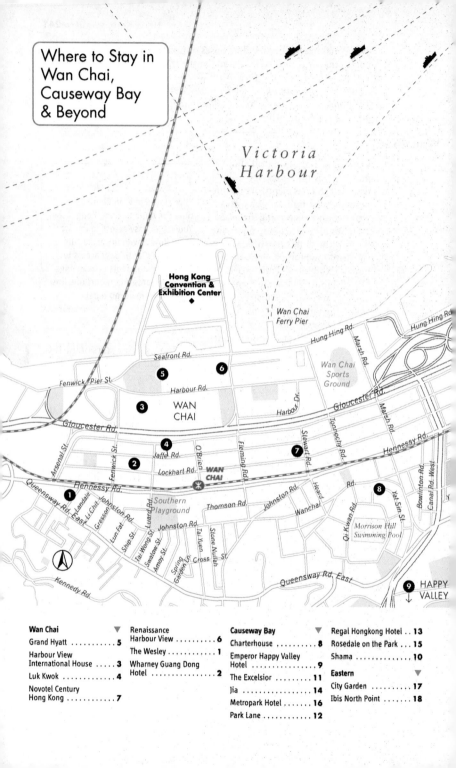

Where to Stay in Wan Chai, Causeway Bay & Beyond

Victoria Harbour

Hong Kong Convention & Exhibition Center

Wan Chai Ferry Pier

Seafront Rd.

Fenwick Pier St.

Harbour Rd.

WAN CHAI

Wan Chai Sports Ground

Gloucester Rd.

Harbour Dr.

Hung Hing Rd.

Marsh Rd.

Hung Hing Rd.

Arsenal St.

Gloucester Rd.

Jaffe Rd.

O'Brien

Fleming Rd.

Stewart Rd.

Tonnochy Rd.

Marsh Rd.

Hennessy Rd.

Lockhart Rd.

WAN CHAI

Hennessy Rd.

Heard

Rd.

Bowrington Rd.

Canal Rd. West

Queensway Rd. East

Landale

Li Chit

Johnston Rd.

Gresson St.

Lun fat

Ship St.

Southern Playground

Thomson Rd.

Johnston Rd.

Wanchai

Qi Kwan Rd.

Yat Sin St.

Tai Wong St.

Luard Rd.

Johnston Rd.

Swatow St.

Amoy St.

Spring Garden Ln.

Tai Yuen

Stone Nullah

Cross St.

St.

Morrison Hill Swimming Pool

Kennedy Rd.

Queensway Rd. East

HAPPY VALLEY

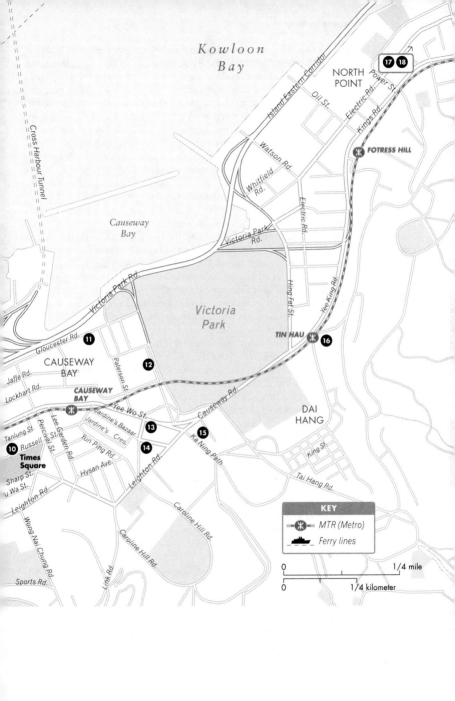

$$-$$$ ▦ **Luk Kwok.** This contemporary hotel and office tower designed by Hong Kong's leading architect, Remo Riva, replaced the Wan Chai landmark of the same name immortalized in Richard Mason's novel *The World of Suzie Wong*. The Luk Kwok's appeal, aside from its slightly kitschy classic Asian feel, is its proximity to the Hong Kong Convention & Exhibition Centre, the Academy for Performing Arts, and the Arts Centre. Guest rooms in the building's 19th to 29th floors are simply furnished, and the higher floors have mountain or city views. There's also a good Chinese restaurant. ⊠ *72 Gloucester Rd., Wan Chai* ☎ *2866-2166* ⊕ *www.lukkwokhotel.com* ⟳ *195 rooms, 2 suites* ⚴ *Restaurant, room service, in-room safes, minibars, cable TV with movies, in-room broadband, health club, lounge, dry cleaning, laundry service, concierge, business services, meeting rooms, babysitting, no-smoking floors* ⊟ *AE, DC, MC, V* Ⓜ *Wan Chai.*

☾ **$$-$$$**
Fodor'sChoice
★
▦ **Renaissance Harbour View.** Sharing the Hong Kong Convention & Exhibition Centre complex with the Grand Hyatt is this more modest but attractive hotel. Guest rooms are medium size with plenty of beveled-glass mirrors that reflect the modern decor. Many rooms have good harbor views and all have high-speed Internet access. Grounds are extensive and include a large outdoor pool, plus gardens, a playground, and jogging trails, which makes this a good place to stay if you are with children. The wonderfully scenic, soaring lobby lounge has a live jazz band in the evening and is a popular rendezvous spot for locals and visiting businesspeople. ⊠ *1 Harbour Rd., Wan Chai* ☎ *2802-8888* ⊕ *www. renaissancehotels.com* ⟳ *809 rooms, 53 suites* ⚴ *4 restaurants, room service, in-room fax, in-room safes, minibars, cable TV with movies, Wi-Fi, driving range, 2 tennis courts, pool, gym, health club, hair salon, sauna, 2 bars, shops, babysitting, playground, dry cleaning, laundry service, concierge, business services, meeting rooms, no-smoking floors* ⊟ *AE, DC, MC, V* Ⓜ *Wan Chai.*

$$ ▦ **Harbour View International House.** This waterfront YMCA property has small but relatively inexpensive rooms near the Wan Chai Star Ferry Pier. Rooms are not luxurious but have the basic amenities; the best ones face the harbor. The hotel is well placed if you want to attend cultural events in the evening: both the Arts Centre and the Academy for Performing Arts are next door. It's also just opposite the Hong Kong Convention & Exhibition Centre. The 16-story hostel provides free shuttle service to Causeway Bay and the Central Star Ferry. You can use the superb YMCA Kowloon facilities, just a short ferry ride away, for a small fee. ⊠ *4 Harbour Rd., Wan Chai* ☎ *2802-0111* ⊕ *www.harbour.ymca.org.hk* ⟳ *320 rooms* ⚴ *Restaurant, room service, minibars, cable TV, in-room broadband, babysitting, laundry service, concierge, business services, meeting rooms, no-smoking floor* ⊟ *AE, DC, MC, V* Ⓜ *Wan Chai.*

$-$$ ▦ **Novotel Century Hong Kong.** Ideal for conventioneers—a five-minute walk by covered overpass (a lifesaver in the steamy summer heat) from the convention center and the MTR—this 23-story hotel also has a well-equipped business center and executive floors. Rooms are modern and have wood furniture. The gym has an outdoor pool and a golf driving bay. Within the complex are a popular, independently run Shanghainese restaurant, a 24-hour coffee shop (in keeping with Wan Chai's reputation for nightlife), and a karaoke lounge. ⊠ *238 Jaffe Rd., Wan Chai*

☎ *2598-8888* ⊕ *www.accorhotels.com/asia* ⇶ *497 rooms, 19 suites* ౿ *2 restaurants, room service, in-room safes, minibars, cable TV with movies, Wi-Fi, pool, gym, health club, massage, 2 bars, dry cleaning, laundry service, concierge, business services, meeting rooms, no-smoking floor* ▱ *AE, DC, MC, V* Ⓜ *Wan Chai.*

$-$$ Ⓣ **Wharney Guang Dong Hotel.** A convenient base for Hong Kong island, this old-school Chinese-style hotel is one of the more affordable options in Wan Chai, especially if you manage to get a special rate on the Internet. Make sure you get a room in one of the upper floors because they're better furnished, though still rather small. A rooftop swimming pool and outdoor Jaccuzi are welcome surprises at this price point. ✉ *57-73 Lockhart Rd., Wan Chai* ☎ *2861-1000* ⊕ *www.gdhhotels.com* ⇶ *358 rooms* ౿ *Restaurant, room service, in-room safes, minibars, cable TV with movies, in-room broadband, pool, gym, sauna, spa, bar, lounge, nightclub, babysitting, dry cleaning, laundry service, concierge, business services, meeting rooms, no-smoking floors* ▱ *AE, DC, MC, V* Ⓜ *Wan Chai.*

$-$$ Ⓣ **The Wesley.** Built on the site of the old Soldiers & Sailors Home, this reasonably priced 21-story hotel is a short walk from the Hong Kong Convention & Exhibition Centre, the Academy for Performing Arts, and the MTR. The interior is Asian-kitschy; rooms are small but pleasant, and the more spacious corner "suites" have alcove work areas. There's no health center or pool on the premises, but long-staying guests can use the facilities at the Grand Plaza Apartments in Quarry Bay for a discounted fee. A tram stop is right outside the door, and Pacific Place and the bars of Wan Chai are close by. ✉ *22 Hennessy Rd., Wan Chai* ☎ *2866-6633* ⊕ *www.grandhotel.com.hk/wesley* ⇶ *251 rooms* ౿ *Restaurant, minibars, cable TV, in-room broadband, dry cleaning, laundry service, concierge, business services, babysitting, no-smoking floors* ▱ *AE, DC, MC, V* Ⓜ *Wan Chai.*

Causeway Bay

Causeway Bay is now such a hot spot that the city's upwardly mobile neighborhoods (West Kowloon and Mong Kok, for instance) are all imitating it. The brightly lighted district, whose 24-hour crowds defy all logic with their relentless energy, teems with restaurants, cinemas, shopping, and street life—especially in the area around Times Square. Why is Causeway Bay so up-and-coming? Location, for one: it's close to the convention center and Victoria Park, it's an easy hop to Wan Chai and Central, and the upper floors of its hotels still command beautiful water views. Happily, there are hotels here to suit a variety of budgets, although quarters can sometimes be cramped in the cheapest spots. Causeway Bay also includes Happy Valley, near the racetrack, and Hong Kong Stadium, the territory's largest sports facility.

★ **$$$-$$$$** Ⓣ **Park Lane.** With an imposing facade that wouldn't look out of place in London, this elegant hotel overlooks Victoria Park and backs onto one of Hong Kong Island's busiest shopping, entertainment, and business areas, Causeway Bay. There's a spacious and grand lobby and rooms have luxurious marble bathrooms, elegant handcrafted furniture, and marvelous views of the harbor, Victoria Park, or the city. The rooftop restaurant has a panoramic view and serves international cuisine with a touch of Asian flavor. The Premier Club floors have butler service. ⊠ *310 Gloucester Rd., Causeway Bay* ☎ *2293-8888* ⊕ *www.parklane.com.hk* 🛏 *759 rooms, 33 suites* ♨ *2 restaurants, room service, in-room safes, minibars, cable TV with movies, in-room broadband, gym, health club, hair salon, massage, sauna, spa, bar, shop, babysitting, dry cleaning, laundry service, concierge, business services, meeting rooms, no-smoking floor* ▤ *AE, DC, MC, V* Ⓜ *Causeway Bay.*

☺ **$$-$$$$** 🏨 **The Excelsior.** Despite its dated 1970s furnishings and interior, this hotel remains perennially popular with travelers, mainly because of its moderate prices compared with other higher-end hotels. But note that this is only true if you manage to find a special rate, on the Internet for instance. There's a lively English pub in the basement, which perhaps explains its popularity with British business travelers and British Airways crews. Some rooms are spacious with splendid sea views, and of the yachts and boats moored at the Hong Kong Yacht Club; other rooms are smaller and have street views. The location, adjacent to Victoria Park, is ideal for shopping and dining. ToTT's Asian Grill & Bar, on the top floor, has East-meets-West cuisine and live music. On a historical note, the hotel sits on the first plot of land auctioned by the British government when Hong Kong became a colony in 1841. ⊠ *281 Gloucester Rd., Causeway Bay* ☎ *2894-8888* ⊕ *www.excelsiorhongkong.com* 🛏 *863 rooms, 21 suites* ♨ *4 restaurants, room service, in-room safes, minibars, cable TV with movies, in-room broadband, 2 tennis courts, health club, hair salon, spa, 2 bars, lounge, shop, dry cleaning, laundry service, concierge, business services, meeting rooms, no-smoking floors* ▤ *AE, DC, MC, V* Ⓜ *Causeway Bay.*

> ### WORD OF MOUTH
>
> "I've stayed in Central and Kowloon as well, but much prefer Causeway Bay and stay there a couple of times a year. The Octopus is handy, and cabs to Central are relatively cheap. Causeway Bay is a safe and interesting area with a variety of shops, foodstuffs, people-watching, etc."
>
> –cjbryant

$$-$$$$ 🏨 **Regal Hongkong Hotel.** The reception area is quite small, but gilded elevators take you up to guest rooms with brightly colored bedspreads, furniture handcrafted by local artisans, and spacious bathrooms with triangular tubs. There are four executive floors. Restaurants include the top-floor Mediterranean Zeffirino's, which has a great view of Victoria Park. The peaceful rooftop pool and terrace also have impressive views. The hotel is close to the Hong Kong Stadium and the Happy Valley Racetrack, as well as the city's most popular shopping area, Causeway Bay. ⊠ *88 Yee Wo St., Causeway Bay* ☎ *2890-6633, 800/222-8888 in U.S.* ⊕ *www.regalhongkong.com* 🛏 *425 rooms, 30 suites* ♨ *3 restaurants, room service, in-room safes, minibars, cable TV, in-room broadband, pool, gym, health club, sauna, spa, bar, lounge, shops, dry cleaning, laun-*

dry service, concierge, business services, meeting rooms, no-smoking floor ▭ *AE, DC, MC, V* Ⓜ *Causeway Bay.*

$$-$$$
Fodor'sChoice
★
🖼 **Jia.** The first boutique hotel designed by Philippe Starck in Asia is a wonder to behold, beginning with the (see-and-be-) scene in the lobby, bar, and restaurant, making it one of the hippest places to drink or dine in town. Although the sculptural furniture and accompanying trendiness won't be everyone's cup of tea, this is still a groundbreaking concept that is helping to redefine the modern Hong Kong hotel landscape. For instance, it doesn't have rooms; rather, it has "apartments," with mini-kitchens, dining tables, and cookware. You can choose between smaller "studios" or the larger one-bedroom "suites," which have separate bedrooms. Will the design of this hotel feel "so 2006" 10 years hence? Perhaps. But for the moment, Jia is the place. ✉ *1-5 Irving St., Causeway Bay* ☎ *3196-9000* ⊕ *www.jiahongkong.com* ⤷ *54 rooms* ⌂ *Restaurant, room service, minibars, Wi-Fi, in-room stereos, in-room DVDs, kitchenettes, bar, lounge, dry cleaning, laundry service, meeting room, no-smoking rooms* ▭ *AE, DC, MC, V* Ⓜ *Causeway Bay.*

★ **$$-$$$** 🖼 **Metropark Hotel.** At this contemporary hotel with Euro-boutique flair you'll get a prime location and unobstructed views for a lower cost than many other hotels. Most rooms have extensive views of Victoria Park next door or the harbor through the floor-to-ceiling windows, and all rooms are equipped with high-speed Internet access. The tiny lobby leads into Vic's, a tapas bar; the trendy Café du Parc has French and Japanese fusion food. Free shuttle buses to and from the Hong Kong Convention & Exhibition Centre and the hub of Causeway Bay run throughout the day. ✉ *148 Tung Lo Wan Rd., Causeway Bay* ☎ *2600-1000* ⊕ *www.metroparkhotel.com* ⤷ *266 rooms, 56 suites* ⌂ *Restaurant, room service, in-room safes, minibars, cable TV, in-room broadband, pool, gym, sauna, spa, bar, babysitting, dry cleaning, laundry service, business services, meeting rooms, no-smoking floor* ▭ *AE, DC, MC, V* Ⓜ *Causeway Bay.*

★ **$$** 🖼 **Rosedale on the Park.** This "cyber boutique hotel," the first of its kind in Hong Kong, has lots of high-tech extras. All public areas have computers, and you can rent a printer, computer, or fax for use in your room, where you also have broadband Internet access and a cordless telephone that can be used anywhere on the property. Mobile phones are also available for rent during your stay. Although only the top few floors have park or stadium views, all rooms are bright and comfortable. Next to Victoria Park and only a five-minute walk to the MTR subway, it's a great location for shopping—and the price is one of the best values in the category. You're in Hong Kong, after all, so why not take advantage of all that technology? ✉ *8 Shelter St., Causeway Bay* ☎ *2127-8888* ⊕ *www.rosedale.com.hk* ⤷ *229 rooms, 45 suites* ⌂ *2 restaurants, room service, in-room safes, minibars, cable TV with movies, Wi-Fi, lounge, babysitting, dry cleaning, laundry service,*

7

business services, meeting rooms, no-smoking floors ▭ AE, DC, MC, V Ⓜ Causeway Bay.

$-$$ ▦ **Emperor Happy Valley Hotel.** Catering mainly to business and corporate travelers, this hotel is one of the few places to stay in the predominantly residential Happy Valley area. The Emperor is also the best deal in town for horse-racing fans, as it's a few minutes' walk from the Happy Valley Racetrack. It's also 5 to 10 minutes by taxi from the Causeway Bay shopping area. The public rooms have regal-looking, European furnishings, but the corridors are narrow and rooms are quite small. Look for Internet special "promotional rates" at less than half the rack rate, even during high season. ✉ 1A Wang Tak St., Happy Valley, Wan Chai ☎ 2893-3693 ⊕ www.emperorhotel.com.hk ⚲ 150 rooms, 2 suites ♤ 2 restaurants, room service, in-room safes, minibars, cable TV with movies, in-room broadband, bar, laundry service, concierge, no-smoking floor ▭ AE, DC, MC, V Ⓜ Wan Chai.

$ ▦ **Charterhouse.** This inexpensive hotel is more or less equidistant between Wan Chai and Causeway Bay, and quite close to Times Square. Rooms have wooden furnishings and pastel colors, although the junior suites feel quite a bit more modern than the regular rooms. There's no pool, and few luxurious touches, but the value for the location is excellent. ✉ 209-219 Wan Chai Rd., Causeway Bay ☎ 2833-5566 ⊕ www.charterhouse.com ⚲ 277 rooms ♤ Restaurant, room service, minibars, in-room safes, cable TV with movies, in-room broadband, gym, 2 bars, nightclub, dry cleaning, laundry service, meeting rooms ▭ AE, DC, MC, V Ⓜ Causeway Bay.

Eastern

Eastern is not the most popular hotel location in Hong Kong. Though connected by MTR, North Point lacks the energy of Hong Kong's bigger districts. It's notable, however, for its relatively reasonable prices, especially if you prefer to stay on the Hong Kong Island side of things rather than heading up to the farther-out areas of Kowloon, where budget hotels generally proliferate.

$$-$$$ ▦ **City Garden.** In a residential area in North Point and about a five-minute walk to the MTR, this hotel has the advantage of being easily accessible to the Eastern Corridor Expressway, which links Causeway Bay to Taikoo Shing and the eastern-harbor crossing. The rooms are small, but the service is efficient. The hotel caters to Asian tour groups and has a good Cantonese restaurant. The top 13 floors are recently renovated and designated as "Executive Rooms" at a much higher price. ✉ 9 City Garden Rd., North Point, Eastern ☎ 2887-2888 ⊕ www.citygarden.com.hk ⚲ 598 rooms, 15 suites ♤ 2 restaurants, room service, in-room safes, minibars, cable TV with movies, in-room broadband, pool, gym, health club, sauna, bar, babysitting, laundry service, business services, meeting rooms, no-smoking floors ▭ AE, DC, MC, V Ⓜ Fortress Hill.

$ ▦ **Ibis North Point.** In the increasingly developed eastern harbor-front area, this hotel is well located for business travelers who are working around Quarry Bay, but it's somewhat out of the way for vacationers. The prices might also be attractive to the budget-minded who want to stay on the Hong Kong side. Many rooms have harbor views, compensating for their small size, and have a full range of functional amenities. But don't expect plush linens or high-end service; this is bare-bones. ✉ *138 Java Rd., North Point, Eastern* ☎ *-2204-6618* ⊕ *www.accorhotels-asia. com* ↝ *275 rooms, 3 suites* ⚙ *Restaurant, room service, in-room safes, cable TV, Wi-Fi, in-room broadband, lounge, laundry service, business services* ▭ *AE, DC, MC, V* Ⓜ *Quarry Bay.*

Southside

The Southside of Hong Kong Island finally has a hotel, the Le Méridien Cyberport, which is on the waterfront of Telegraph Bay. Built as a high-tech business hub, Cyberport also has residential and leisure facilities, including the hotel and a commercial complex. More hotel and retail development is planned in the area, one of the many districts of Hong Kong that is enjoying an unprecedented boom.

★ $$$-$$$$ 🏨 **Le Méridien Cyberport.** This relatively small, boutique-style hotel is the first high-profile hotel to open in Hong Kong's Southside. It comes with high-tech amenities such as 42-inch plasma TVs and wireless Internet in all rooms, as well as hip bars and restaurants. Rooms are spacious; bathrooms have so-called "rain" showers, which have extra-large showerheads with many spouts that rain water down onto you. Each room also has a "soothing corner," where you'll find a stone bowl filled with fresh flower petals, essential oils, and floating candles. Most rooms have sea views, the rest look over the gardens or the pool. ✉ *100 Cyberport Rd., Cyberport, Southside* ☎ *2980-7778* ⊕ *www.starwoodhotels. com/lemeridien* ↝ *169 rooms, 4 suites* ⚙ *3 restaurants, room service, in-room safes, minibars, cable TV with movies and video games, Wi-Fi, pool, Jacuzzi, bicycles, bar, lounge, wine bar, shops, dry cleaning, laundry service, concierge, business services, meeting rooms, no-smoking rooms* ▭ *AE, DC, MC, V.*

KOWLOON

Hung Hom

Hung Hom, adjacent to Tsim Sha Tsui East, includes a noisy old residential area and a private-housing complex with cinemas, shops, and hotels. Its hotels are relatively new and tend to have lower prices than those in Tsim Sha Tsui and other better-known areas.

$$$-$$$$
Fodor'sChoice
★

🏨 **Harbour Plaza Hong Kong.** The opulent Harbour Plaza has one of the best harbor views in town. The atrium lobby is spacious with lounges on two levels. Rooms are large, comfortable, and contemporary. Dining options include a Japanese *robatayaki* grill restaurant and a lively pub called the Pit Stop. A scenic rooftop pool, a fitness center, and a spa are also on-

> **WORD OF MOUTH**
>
> "I prefer Kowloon—though I haven't stayed anyplace else. It's a shopping hub. We found the best shops were above the ground floor. Just look at the overhead signs."   –rhkkmk

site. Although it's in the residential area of Whampoa Gardens, which is out of the way of most of what you'll probably be up to, hotel shuttles run the 10- to 15-minute trip to Tsim Sha Tsui all day—and you'll get more bang for the buck because of the location. Close by is the railway station, with trains to China, and a ferry terminal for Hong Kong Island. ⊠ *20 Tak Fung St., Hung Hom, Kowloon* ☎ *2621-3188* ⊕ *www.harbour-plaza.com* ➥ *381 rooms, 30 suites* ⚴ *4 restaurants, room service, in-room safes, minibars, cable TV with movies, in-room broadband, pool, health club, hair salon, spa, lounge, pub, shop, babysitting, dry cleaning, laundry service, concierge, business services, meeting rooms, no-smoking floors* ▭ *AE, DC, MC, V.*

★ **$$-$$$** ▦ **Harbour Plaza Metropolis.** The Harbour Plaza Metropolis is an ideal place to stay if you're planning to travel by train into China. It's next to the Kowloon-Canton Hung Hom Railway Station, which has a direct link to Shenzhen and Guangzhou. It's also next to the Coliseum, where concerts and sports events take place. A shuttle bus to nearby Tsim Sha Tsui leaves every 20 minutes. Rooms are small and have showers only; most have harbor views. Restaurants include the Patio,

> ## WORD OF MOUTH
>
> "The Harbour Plaza has the best swimming pool in Hong Kong. It's an excellent hotel in spite of being a little out of the way."   –Grant

which serves Thai food alfresco along with panoramic harbor views. ⊠ *7 Metropolis Dr., Hung Hom, Kowloon* ☎ *3160-6888* ⊕ *www. harbour-plaza.com* ➥ *700 rooms, 100 suites* ⚴ *3 restaurants, in-room safes, minibars, cable TV with movies, in-room broadband, pool, gym, bar, lounge, shop, babysitting, dry cleaning, laundry service, business services, meeting rooms, no-smoking floors* ▭ *AE, DC, MC, V.*

Tsim Sha Tsui

This is Hong Kong's hotel heartland, with many of the city's best (the InterContinental Hong Kong, for instance) and most famous (the Peninsula) accommodations. The fabled Golden Mile of shopping on Nathan Road runs through Tsim Sha Tsui, and restaurants and stores fill the surrounding backstreets, striking an ideal mix of local Chinese joints and high-concept Western malls. Meanwhile, the area could hardly be more convenient to Central or Wan Chai, whether on the scenic Star Ferry or on a five-minute MTR ride. In addition, TST's waterfront has the best views of Hong Kong's skyline and nightly light-and-laser show. Many TST hotel rooms take full advantage of these Blade Runner panoramas.

$$$$ ▦ **InterContinental Hong Kong.** Perhaps one of the most attractive hotels **Fodor'sChoice** in Asia, the InterContinental Hong Kong is opulent inside while it of- ★ fers some of the finest views of the Hong Kong skyline outside. Simply coming here for a spectacularly conceived cocktail at 8 PM to take in the skyline light show is a memorable Hong Kong experience, perhaps equivalent to tea at the Peninsula. The lobby has a delicious airy qual-

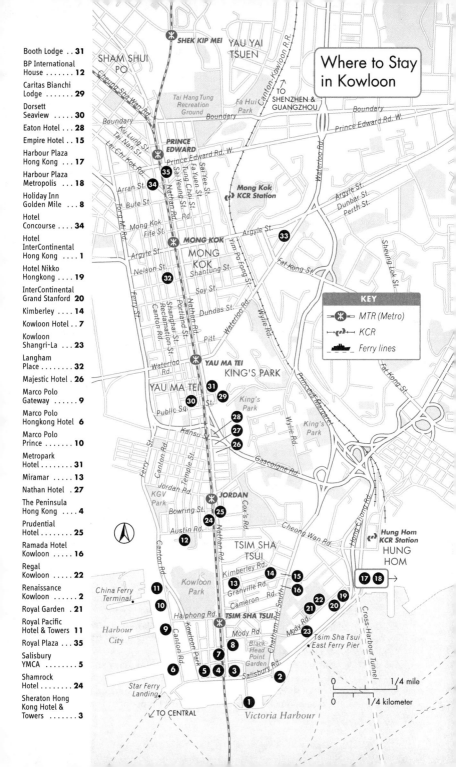

Where to Stay in Kowloon

SHEK KIP MEI

YAU YAI TSUEN

SHAM SHUI PO

TO SHENZHEN & GUANGZHOU

Tai Hang Tung Recreation Ground

Fa Hui Park

Boundary

Prince Edward Rd. W.

Boundary

Ku Lung St.

Tai Nan St.

Lai Chi Kok Rd.

Cheung Sha Wan Rd.

PRINCE EDWARD

Prince Edward Rd. W.

Canton-Kowloon R.R.

Waterloo Rd.

Argyle St.

Dunbar St.

Perth St.

Sheung Lok St.

Mong Kok KCR Station

Arran St.

Bute St.

Sai Yee St.

Fa Yuen St.

Tung Choi St.

Sai Yeung Choi St.

Nathan Rd.

Mong Kok Fife St.

MONG KOK

MONG KOK

Argyle St.

Fat Kong St.

Nelson St.

Shantung St.

Yim Po Fong St.

Soy St.

Ferry St.

Reclamation Rd.

Shanghai St.

Portland St.

Canton Rd.

Dundas St.

Pitt

Waterloo Rd.

Wylie Rd.

KEY

MTR (Metro)

KCR

Ferry lines

YAU MA TEI

KING'S PARK

YAU MA TEI

Public Sq.

King's Park

Kansu St.

Princess Margaret

Wylie Rd.

King's Park

Gascoigne Rd.

Jordan Rd.

KGV Park

Temple St.

Canton Rd.

Ferry St.

JORDAN

Cox's Rd.

Bowring St.

Cheong Wan Rd.

Hung Hom KCR Station

HUNG HOM

Austin Rd.

Nathan Rd.

TSIM SHA TSUI

Kimberley Rd.

Kowloon Park

Granville Rd.

Cameron Rd.

Chatham Rd. South

China Ferry Terminal

Haiphong Rd.

TSIM SHA TSUI

Mody Rd.

Black Head Point Garden

Mody Rd.

Tsim Sha Tsui East Ferry Pier

Harbour City

Canton Rd.

Kowloon Park

Salisbury Rd.

Cross-Harbour Tunnel

Star Ferry Landing

TO CENTRAL

Victoria Harbour

0   1/4 mile

0   1/4 kilometer

ity, and the impeccably modern rooms are just as exciting, with luxuriously large beds, desks with ergonomically designed chairs, and superlative showers in the bathrooms. Corner suites have 180-degree harbour views, Dom Perignon is the house champagne in the executive lounge, and the spa is worth e-mailing home about. The incredible restaurant lineup, meanwhile, is soon to include Nobu—to give Alain Ducasse a bit of company, perhaps. ⊠ *18 Salisbury Rd., Tsim Sha Tsui, Kowloon* ☎ *2721-1211, 800/327-0200 in U.S.* ⊕ *www.ichotelsgroup. com* ⮞ *495 rooms, 92 suites* ⚘ *5 restaurants, minibars, room service, cable TV with movies, Wi-Fi, pool, gym, health club, hot tub, sauna, spa, steam room, shop, babysitting, dry cleaning, laundry service, concierge, business services, meeting rooms, no-smoking floors* ▤ *AE, DC, MC, V* Ⓜ *Tsim Sha Tsui.*

$$$$ 🏨 **The Peninsula Hong Kong.** Established in 1928, the Peninsula has long been synonymous with impeccable taste and colonial glamour. And many people adore this hotel. But time may well have left this hotel behind. These days, the Pen's rooms just feel gaudy and overpriced, with stodgy, uncomfortable sofas, awkward desks, chandeliers, and outdated TV systems. The spa is decked out with faux-Roman statues that are all show without a sense of style. Even the hotel's famous Rolls-Royces feel dingy these days. And at about US$600 for the cheapest harbor-view room, it seems the only thing keeping up with the times is the price. There is still the famous high tea in the lobby bar, and if you must see this place, that might be the best reason to do it. ⊠ *Salisbury Rd., Tsim Sha Tsui, Kowloon* ☎ *2366-6251* ⊕ *www.peninsula.com* ⮞ *246 rooms, 54 suites* ⚘ *7 restaurants, room service, in-room fax, in-room safes, minibars, cable TV with movies, in-room VCRs, in-room broadband, pool, gym, health club, hair salon, hot tub, spa, bar, shops, babysitting, dry cleaning, laundry service, concierge, business services, meeting rooms, helipad, no-smoking floors* ▤ *AE, DC, MC, V* Ⓜ *Tsim Sha Tsui.*

★ $$$$ 🏨 **Sheraton Hong Kong Hotel & Towers.** Across the street from the Space Museum at the southern end of the fabled Golden Mile, the Sheraton is somewhat packed in on Nathan Road and so doesn't get as much light as some of its competition. But the lobby is filled with artwork and feels airy and expansive. Guest rooms are comfortable yet modern with flat-screen televisions, slick glass desktops, and glass washbowls in the bathrooms. There are harbor, city, or courtyard views from the rooms. Make your way to the rooftop pool and terrace via the exterior glass elevator. The sky lounge has a fantastic harbor view, and Someplace Else is a popular hangout at happy hour; the Oyster & Wine Bar is on the top floor. ⊠ *20 Nathan Rd., Tsim Sha Tsui, Kowloon* ☎ *2369-1111* ⊕ *www. sheraton.com* ⮞ *688 rooms, 94 suites* ⚘ *5 restaurants, room service, in-room safes, minibars, cable TV with movies, Wi-Fi, pool, health club, 3 lounges, shop, babysitting, dry cleaning, laundry service, concierge, business services, meeting rooms, no-smoking floors* ▤ *AE, DC, MC, V* Ⓜ *Tsim Sha Tsui.*

� $$$-$$$$ 🏨 **Marco Polo Hongkong Hotel.** Next to the Star Ferry and Cultural Centre and part of the wharf-side Harbour City complex, this is the largest and best of three Marco Polo hotels along the same street. Spacious rooms have special touches such as a choice of 11 types of pillows and, for children, miniature bathrobes, mild shampoos, and rubber ducks. The Continental Club floors include 24-hour butler service. All three hotels share the pool, gym, and spa that are at this location. The largest Oktoberfest in town takes place here, with more than 1,000 thigh-slapping, beer-swilling, fun-loving participants. ⊠ *Harbour City, Canton Rd., Tsim Sha Tsui, Kowloon* ☎ *2113-0088* ⊕ *www.marcopolohotels.com* ⊲ *621 rooms, 44 suites* ⧉ *7 restaurants, room service, in-room safes, minibars, cable TV with movies, in-room broadband, pool, gym, hair salon, spa, lounge, shops, babysitting, dry cleaning, laundry service, concierge, business services, meeting rooms, no-smoking floors* ⊟ *AE, DC, MC, V* Ⓜ *Tsim Sha Tsui.*

☾ **$$-$$$$** 🏨 **Holiday Inn Golden Mile.** On the Golden Mile of Nathan Road, the hub of Kowloon's business and shopping area, is this business-style hotel whose friendly service has ensured its popularity with tourists, business travelers, and locals for more than two decades. The cozy lobby lounge, from which an elegant staircase leads up to the lounge bar, has an East-meets-West theme. The medium-size rooms are designed for comfort and have a sofa and coffee table; the views, however, are not the best in town. The Avenue restaurant serves delicious contemporary European cuisine overlooking the neon sights and sounds of Tsim Sha Tsui's main artery. ⊠ *50 Nathan Rd., Tsim Sha Tsui, Kowloon* ☎ *2369-3111* ⊕ *golden-mile-hk.holiday-inn.com* ⊲ *597 rooms, 8 suites* ⧉ *3 restaurants, room service, in-room safes, minibars, cable TV with movies, Wi-Fi, pool, gym, health club, sauna, spa, bar, lounge, shop, babysitting, dry cleaning, laundry service, business services, meeting rooms, no-smoking rooms, no-smoking floors* ⊟ *AE, DC, MC, V* Ⓜ *Tsim Sha Tsui.*

$$$ 🏨 **Marco Polo Prince.** Like its neighboring Marco Polo namesakes in the Harbour City complex (the Hongkong and Gateway), the Prince is convenient to upscale shops, cinemas, and the restaurants and shops of Tsim Sha Tsui. It's also near the China Hong Kong Terminal, where ferries, boats, and buses depart for mainland China. Most of the small but comfortable rooms overlook expansive Kowloon Park, and some suites have views of Victoria Harbour. The Spice Market restaurant serves Southeast Asian buffets and an international menu. You can use the pool, gym, and spa at the Marco Polo Hongkong, a five-minute walk away. ⊠ *Harbour City, Canton Rd., Tsim Sha Tsui, Kowloon* ☎ *2113-1888* ⊕ *www.marcopolohotels.com* ⊲ *343 rooms, 51 suites* ⧉ *4 restaurants, snack bar, room service, in-room safes, minibars, cable TV with movies, in-room broadband, hair salon, bar, shop, babysitting, dry cleaning, laundry service, business services, meeting rooms, no-smoking floors* ⊟ *AE, DC, MC, V* Ⓜ *Tsim Sha Tsui.*

$$-$$$ 🏨 **Empire Hotel.** This midrange hotel in a round, modern skyscraper has a glittery Asian feel to it. The indoor swimming pool is housed in a giant atrium, and the spa services are excellent. Standard rooms are small but posh, decked out in that futuristic Hong Kong way; many of the windows look out onto the beautiful skyline. Be sure to ask for a room on an upper floor. The Kimberley Road location is right in the middle of things, and prices are well contained given the upmarket feel of the place and the extensive facilities. ⊠ *62 Kimberley Rd., Tsim Sha Tsui* ☎ *2865-3000* ⊕ *www.asiastandard.com* ⊲ *292 rooms, 23 suites* ⧉ *3 restau-*

rants, room service, in-room safes, minibars, cable TV with movies, Wi-Fi, in-room broadband, pool, gym, sauna, massage, bar, babysitting, dry cleaning, laundry service, concierge, business services, meeting rooms, no-smoking floors ⊟ AE, DC, MC, V Ⓜ Tsim Sha Tsui.

$$-$$$ 🏨 **Marco Polo Gateway.** This 16-story hotel, popular with Japanese tour groups, is in the shopping and commercial area along Canton Road and close to the Tsim Sha Tsui MTR station. The tastefully decorated rooms and suites have large windows and comfortable beds. The most notable restaurant is La Brasserie, serving French provincial cuisine in a typical brasserie style (long bar, dark wood, leather seats, red-checkered tablecloths). The business center is well supplied, and the staff is helpful. You can use the pool, gym, and spa at the nearby Marco Polo

> **WORD OF MOUTH**
>
> "We went back to Marco Polo a second time because of its great location and the comfortable room size. It's a bit on the expensive side, but you get what you pay for."   –Daniel & Cynthia

Hongkong Hotel. ✉ Harbour City, Canton Rd., Tsim Sha Tsui, Kowloon ☎ 2113-0888 ⊕ www.marcopolohotels.com ⤳ 377 rooms, 56 suites ♨ 3 restaurants, room service, in-room safes, minibars, cable TV with movies, in-room broadband, hair salon, bar, shops, babysitting, dry cleaning, laundry service, business services, meeting rooms, no-smoking floors ⊟ AE, DC, MC, V Ⓜ Tsim Sha Tsui.

$$-$$$ 🏨 **Miramar.** When it opened in 1948, the Miramar was owned by the Spanish Catholic Mission, which intended to use the structure to shelter missionaries expelled from China. As tourism blossomed here, the priests changed their plan and turned the premises into a hotel. At the top of the Golden Mile and across from Kowloon Park, the Miramar has a vast lobby with a dramatic stained-glass ceiling, functional rooms, and smiling service. Rooms are spacious but need some redecorating; moreover, noise from adjoining rooms and the commotion from busy Nathan Road just outside can be a problem. But you're close to both the Jordan and Tsim Sha Tsui MTR stations, and this is quite possibly one of the best values in the area. ✉ 118-130 Nathan Rd., Tsim Sha Tsui, Kowloon ☎ 2368-1111 ⊕ www.miramarhk.com ⤳ 512 rooms, 13 suites ♨ 3 restaurants, minibars, cable TV with movies, in-room broadband, indoor pool, bar, shop, babysitting, dry cleaning, laundry service, business services, meeting rooms, no-smoking floors ⊟ AE, DC, MC, V Ⓜ Tsim Sha Tsui.

☾ $$ 🏨 **BP International House.** Built by the Boy Scouts Association, this hotel next to Kowloon Park offers an excellent value for the money. A portrait of association founder Baron Robert Baden-Powell, hangs in the spacious modern lobby. The hostel-like rooms are small and spartan but have regular hotel amenities and panoramic views of Victoria Harbour and clear views of the busiest part of Kowloon. Ask to see your room before settling in, as some rooms are better than others. A multipurpose hall hosts exhibitions, conventions, and concerts, and the health club is one of the biggest in town. Another attraction for budget travelers is the self-service coin laundry. There are Internet terminals available for use. ✉ 8 Austin Rd., Jordan, Kowloon ☎ 2376-1111 ⊕ www.bpih.com.

hk ⟷ *529 rooms, 4 suites* ⌂ *2 restaurants, cable TV with movies, health club, spa, dry cleaning, laundry facilities, laundry service* ▭ *AE, DC, MC, V* Ⓜ *Jordan.*

$$ 🏨 **Kimberley.** On one of the colorful busy streets between Nathan Road and Tsim Sha Tsui East, this hotel has bright but extremely small rooms. Its health spa includes masseurs to ease away the aches and pains of shopping. Golf driving nets are available for those who can't kick the habit. The two main restaurants serve Cantonese and Japanese cuisines. There are Internet terminals for guests to use. ✉ *28 Kimberley Rd., Tsim Sha Tsui, Kowloon* ☎ *2723-3888* ⊕ *www.kimberleyhotel.com.hk* ⟷ *498 rooms, 48 suites* ⌂ *3 restaurants, room service, minibars, cable TV with movies, gym, health club, sauna, spa, bar, lounge, babysitting, laundry service, business services, meeting rooms* ▭ *AE, DC, MC, V* Ⓜ *Tsim Sha Tsui.*

$$ 🏨 **Kowloon Hotel.** The mirrored exterior and the chrome, glass, and marble lobby reflect the hotel's high-tech orientation. Kowloon means "nine dragons" in Cantonese, and is the theme here. Triangular windows and a pointed lobby ceiling, made from hundreds of handblown Venetianglass pyramids, represent dragons' teeth. The Kowloon is the lesser sibling to the adjacent Peninsula hotel, so you can sign up for services at the Pen and charge them to your room account here; similarly, all the facilities at the Peninsula are open to you. Rooms are small, but each has a computer with free Internet service and fax. Airline information is displayed in the lobby *and* in each room. ✉ *19-21 Nathan Rd., Tsim Sha Tsui, Kowloon* ☎ *2929-2888* ⊕ *www.harbour-plaza.com* ⟷ *730 rooms, 12 suites* ⌂ *3 restaurants, room service, in-room fax, minibars, cable TV with movies, in-room broadband, babysitting, dry cleaning, laundry service, business services, meeting room, no-smoking floors* ▭ *AE, DC, MC, V* Ⓜ *Tsim Sha Tsui.*

$$ 🏨 **Ramada Hotel Kowloon.** The Ramada is relatively small by Hong Kong standards, and tries to use its size to create a cozy, home-away-from-home feeling. There's a decorative fireplace in the lobby and comfortable rooms with natural wood furniture. The bar attracts young locals for drinks and karaoke. ✉ *73-75 Chatham Rd., Tsim Sha Tsui, Kowloon* ☎ *2311-1100* ⊕ *ramadahongkong.com* ⟷ *195 rooms, 10 suites* ⌂ *Restaurant, room service, in-room safes, minibars, cable TV with movies, Wi-Fi, bar, shops, babysitting, laundry service, business services, meeting room* ▭ *AE, DC, MC, V* Ⓜ *Tsim Sha Tsui.*

$$ 🏨 **Renaissance Kowloon.** Part of a large shopping complex, and now a member of the Marriott chain, this popular hotel on the Tsim Sha Tsui waterfront has perfect views of Hong Kong Island from its upper club floors, rivaled only by the adjacent hotel InterContinental Hong Kong, part of the same complex. Long escalators lead from the shopping area to the hotel's large second-floor lobby. The comfortable, modern guest rooms are homey and have plenty of space for working and relaxing. Greenery surrounds the outdoor pool, which stays open throughout the year. The Panorama restaurant, one of three in the hotel, has one of the best harbor views in town. ✉ *22 Salisbury Rd., Tsim Sha Tsui, Kowloon* ☎ *2369-4111* ⊕ *www.marriott.com* ⟷ *492 rooms, 53 suites* ⌂ *3 restaurants, room service, in-room safes, minibars, cable TV with* *movies, Wi-Fi, pool, gym, health club, hair salon, sauna, spa, lounge, babysitting, dry cleaning, laundry service, business services, meeting rooms, no-smoking floors* ⊟ *AE, DC, MC, V* Ⓜ *Tsim Sha Tsui.*

$-$$ 🏨 **Royal Pacific Hotel & Towers.** On the Tsim Sha Tsui waterfront, the Royal Pacific is part of the Hong Kong China City complex, which includes the terminal for ferries to mainland China. Guest rooms are arranged in two blocks, the hotel and tower wings. Tower-wing rooms have harbor views and are luxuriously furnished, while more inexpensive hotel-wing rooms have Kowloon street and park views and are smaller but just as attractive. The hotel connects to Kowloon Park by a footbridge and is close to shops and cinemas. ✉ *33 Canton Rd., Tsim Sha Tsui, Kowloon* ☎ *2736-1188* ⊕ *www.royalpacific.com.hk* 🛏 *641 rooms, 32 suites* ♨ *3 restaurants, room service, in-room safes, minibars, cable TV with movies, in-room broadband, gym, health club, sauna, spa, steam room, squash, bar, babysitting, dry cleaning, laundry service, business services, meeting rooms* ⊟ *AE, DC, MC, V* Ⓜ *Tsim Sha Tsui.*

🐾 **$-$$** 🏨 **Salisbury YMCA.** This upscale YMCA is Hong Kong's most popular
Fodor'sChoice and is great value for your money. Next to the Peninsula and opposite
★ the Cultural Centre, Space Museum, and Art Museum, it's in an excellent location for theater, art, and concert crawls. The pastel-color rooms have harbor views and broadband Internet access. The Y also has a chapel, a garden, a conference room with a built-in stage, a children's library, and excellent health and fitness facilities, which include a dance studio and even a climbing wall. Restaurants in the area are cheap and good, and the shopping is great. ✉ *41 Salisbury Rd., Tsim Sha Tsui, Kowloon* ☎ *2369-2211.* ⊕ *www.ymcahk.org. hk* 🛏 *303 rooms, 62 suites* ♨ *2 restaurants, room service, in-room safes, minibars, cable TV, in-room broadband, indoor pool, gym,*

> ### WORD OF MOUTH
>
> "Not a YMCA as such, but an excellent hotel. It offers good value for money, especially the (partial) harbor-view rooms. The Peninsula right next door charges much more for similar views. There's friendly service, modern rooms, and lots of facilities, including a pool. The location is also perfect—on the Kowloon side, close to the Star Ferry terminal and MTR."
> –F. Schubert

health club, hair salon, spa, squash, lounge, shops, babysitting, laundry facilities, business services, meeting room, no-smoking floors ⊟ *AE, DC, MC, V* Ⓜ *Tsim Sha Tsui.*

Tsim Sha Tsui East

Tsim Sha Tsui East is a grid of modern office blocks—many with restaurants or nightclubs—and luxury hotels. This area was created on land reclaimed from the harbor in the 1970s. A disadvantage of staying here is a somewhat longer walk to the MTR—Tsim Sha Tsui is generally the closest stop, but it's a bit of a hike from most of the establishments listed below.

★ **$$$-$$$$** 🏨 **Kowloon Shangri-La.** Catering mainly to business travelers, this up-scale hotel has a 24-hour business center with teleconferencing facil-ities as well as some strange features, such as the elevator carpets that are changed at midnight to indicate the day of the week. You'll feel like a tycoon in the posh lobby; the guest rooms all have magnificent harbor or city views, and although it doesn't have quite the glamour or services of the Island Shangri-La (or the accompanying sky-high prices) it's still a wonderful place to stay. Complimentary newspapers are delivered daily to your room; club rooms have combination fax/printer/copier/scanners, as well as in-room DVDs and even TVs in the bathroom. A wireless telephone system allows guests to receive calls throughout the hotel. Attention to detail and outstanding service, in a city where service is already tops, set this hotel apart. ⊠ *64 Mody Rd., Tsim Sha Tsui East, Kowloon* ☎ *2721-2111, 800/942-5050 in U.S.* ⊕ *www.shangri-la.com* ⇥ *700 rooms, 25 suites* ♨ *5 restau-rants, room service, in-room safes, minibars, cable TV with movies, Wi-Fi, indoor pool, gym, health club, hair salon, sauna, spa, bar, lounge, shops, babysitting, dry cleaning, laundry service, concierge, business services, meeting rooms, no-smoking floor* ⊟ *AE, DC, MC, V* Ⓜ *Tsim Sha Tsui.*

$$-$$$ 🏨 **Hotel Nikko Hongkong.** Part of the Japanese chain, this luxury har-bor-front hotel at the far end of Tsim Sha Tsui East attracts mostly Japa-nese travelers. The large, split-level atrium depicts a Japanese garden with water trickling between the greenery. The rooms and bathrooms are com-fortable and spacious; nearly 200 rooms have harbor views, and those on the executive floors are equipped with additional facilities such as tea- and coffeemakers. The Kyoto-inspired restaurant Sagano uses in-gredients imported from Japan. ⊠ *72 Mody Rd., Tsim Sha Tsui East, Kowloon* ☎ *2739-1111* ⊕ *www.hotelnikko.com.hk* ⇥ *445 rooms, 18 suites* ♨ *4 restaurants, room service, in-room safes, minibars, cable TV with movies, in-room broadband, pool, gym, health club, sauna, spa, 3 bars, shop, business services, meeting rooms, no-smoking floors* ⊟ *AE, DC, MC, V* Ⓜ *Tsim Sha Tsui.*

$$-$$$ 🏨 **InterContinental Grand Stanford Hong Kong.** More than half the rooms in this luxury hotel, the lesser sibling of the larger InterContinental Hong Kong in downtown Tsim Sha Tsui, have an unobstructed harbor view. The elegant lobby is spacious, the staff is helpful and friendly, and the modern comfortable rooms are decorated in warm earth tones with fine wood fittings and large desks. Executive rooms have a direct-line fax machine and amenities include trouser presses. The restaurants are well known locally, including Mistral (Italian), Belvedere (regional French), and Tiffany's New York Bar, which celebrates the Roaring 1920s with antique furniture, Tiffany-style glass ceilings, and a live band. ⊠ *70 Mody Rd., Tsim Sha Tsui East, Kowloon* ☎ *2721-5161* ⊕ *www.grandstanford. com* ⇥ *554 rooms, 25 suites* ♨ *4 restaurants, room service, in-room safes, minibars, cable TV with movies, in-room data ports, pool, gym, health club, sauna, spa, bar, shop, babysitting, dry cleaning, laundry ser-vice, business services, meeting rooms, no-smoking floors* ⊟ *AE, DC, MC, V* Ⓜ *Tsim Sha Tsui.*

$$-$$$ ▦ **Royal Garden.** A garden atrium with lush greenery and whispering running water rises from the ground floor to the Royal Garden's rooftop. Glass elevators, live classical music, trailing greenery, and trickling streams create a sense of serenity. The spacious comfortable rooms surround the atrium. Rooftop health facilities include an indoor-outdoor pool fashioned after an ancient Roman bath with fountains, a colorful sun mosaic, and underwater music. Its Sabatini restaurant is a sister establishment to the popular Rome. ✉ *69 Mody Rd., Tsim Sha Tsui East, Kowloon* ☎ *2721-5215* ⊕ *www.theroyalgardenhotel.com.hk* ⇨ *422 rooms, 17 suites* ⚲ *4 restaurants, room service, in-room safes, minibars, cable TV with movies, Wi-Fi, tennis court, indoor-outdoor pool, gym, health club, hair salon, sauna, spa, bar, pub, dance club, shop, babysitting, dry cleaning, laundry service, concierge, business services, meeting rooms, no-smoking floor* ▭ *AE, DC, MC, V* Ⓜ *Tsim Sha Tsui.*

$$ ▦ **Regal Kowloon.** If you're in the mood for a French experience, check in at the Regal. The lobby has an impressive tapestry, and Louis XVI-style furniture graces the guest rooms and one of the lounges. Rooms on the club floors have a more minimalist, modern two-tone appeal than the rest of the hotel would suggest. The French restaurant Maman serves home-style French cooking in a relaxed setting. Still, the hotel is starting to show its age, and it's a bit far from the lively and busy area of Tsim Sha Tsui. ✉ *71 Mody Rd., Tsim Sha Tsui East* ☎ *2722-1818* ⊕ *www.regalkowloon.com* ⇨ *543 rooms, 39 suites* ⚲ *4 restaurants, room service, in-room safes, minibars, cable TV with movies, Wi-Fi, gym, hair salon, sauna, 2 bars, lounge, shop, babysitting, dry cleaning, laundry service, concierge, business services, meeting rooms, no-smoking floor* ▭ *AE, DC, MC, V* Ⓜ *Tsim Sha Tsui.*

Yau Ma Tei & Mong Kok

Yau Ma Tei and Mong Kok are known for their noisy street life, bargain shopping, night markets, and cheap and cheerful dining. They also have older, smaller, more moderately priced hotels than Tsim Sha Tsui, often with small, less-than-peaceful rooms. Most of these hotels are on or near Nathan Road and many are good for travelers on budgets. This is an exciting part of Kowloon if you can handle the crowds, which don't seem to dwindle until about 10 PM. Don't be scared off by the fact that Mong Kok is crowded, has the city's red-light district, and is a known prowling ground for pickpockets. Just be aware of your surroundings. Excellent bus service and the MTR connect both Yau Ma Tei and Mong Kok to the center of Tsim Sha Tsui.

$$-$$$ ▦ **Eaton Hotel.** In a brick-red shopping and cinema complex in the middle of Nathan Road, the Eaton provides quick access to Hong Kong's bustling after-dark street scene: it's a stone's throw from the

> **WORD OF MOUTH**
>
> "I have recently stayed at Eaton's Club Deluxe Room, with a floor-to-ceiling window featuring 180-degree city view. The room was nice and the service was good too. I love the club lounge and the cafe on the ground floor."
>
> –Wilco Yeung

Temple Street Night Market. The modern rooms have all the necessities, including fast Internet access and business services. The top floor has a swimming pool and a gym. ⊠ *380 Nathan Rd., Yau Ma Tei, Kowloon* ☎ *2782-1818* ⊕ *www.eaton-hotel.com* ⇆ *459 rooms, 26 suites* ♿ *6 restaurants, room service, minibars, cable TV with movies, in-room broadband, pool, exercise equipment, gym, health club, bar, laundry service, business services, meeting rooms, no-smoking floor* ▭ *AE, DC, MC, V* Ⓜ *Jordan.*

$$-$$$ 🏨 **Langham Place.** When the Langham opened in March 2005 as part
Fodor's Choice of the new Langham Place Shopping Center, it ushered in a new era
★ of prestige and prominence for its once seedy, but still refreshingly un-Westernized Mong Kok neighborhood, full of bustling markets, characteristic noodle shops, and, yes, the occasional prostitute. Mao's Red Guards stand at attention at the entrance to this sleek, cyber-age hotel full of glass and steel; it's a great exemplar of that specific science-fiction feel that defines much of modern Hong Kong. The hotel's top three stories are consumed by the Chuan (Chinese spa), with panoramic city views to accompany treatments. The price is significantly lower than what you'd pay for such luxury elsewhere in town. ⊠ *555 Shanghai St., Mong Kok* ☎ *3552-3388* ⊕ *www.langhamhotels. com* ⇆ *665 rooms* ♿ *3 restaurants, room service, in-room safes, minibars, cable TV with movies, Wi-Fi, pool, gym, health club, massage, sauna, spa, bar, lounge, shops, dry cleaning, laundry service, concierge, business services, meeting rooms* ▭ *AE, DC, MC, V* Ⓜ *Mong Kok.*

$$ 🏨 **Dorsett Seaview Hotel.** High-rise buildings now block the Dorsett's sea view, but the location is still a good one if you want to see traditional Hong Kong. Guest rooms are very small; staff are friendly and efficient. The hotel is close to the Yau Ma Tei MTR as well as decent shopping; Shanghai Street is filled with shops selling everything from handmade kitchenware to temple offerings. The restaurant

> **WORD OF MOUTH**
>
> "Rooms at the Dorsett Seaview are very small; you won't be hosting cocktail parties in here. Exiting the hotel, the night market is right there. Lots of colour . . . a cheap and cheerful little hotel."
> –Richard

has bargain-priced buffets, especially for lunch. The hotel often gets very busy with tour groups and checkout can be chaotic. ⊠ *268 Shanghai St., Yau Ma Tei, Kowloon* ☎ *2782-0882* ⊕ *www.dorsettseaview. com.hk* ⇆ *255 rooms, 3 suites* ♿ *Restaurant, room service, minibars, cable TV with movies, bar, lounge, laundry service* ▭ *AE, DC, MC, V* Ⓜ *Yau Ma Tei.*

$$ 🏨 **Metropark Hotel Kowloon.** Just north of Nathan Road's major shopping area, the Metropark (formerly known as the Metropole) is a diner's delight. The on-site Chinese restaurant, House of Tang, is locally renowned for its Sichuanese resident master chefs, who serve authentic Sichuan and Cantonese food. The modern rooms are small and feel slightly dated, but they have a harmonious mélange of East and West furnishings, and the Mong Kok area, nearby, is a fun Chinese section of the city. The rooftop pool is a relaxing space to unwind. ⊠ *75 Waterloo Rd., Yau Ma Tei, Kowloon* ☎*2761-1711* ⊕*www.metropole.com.hk* ↩*479 rooms, 8 suites* ♨ *3 restaurants, room service, minibars, cable TV with movies, in-room broadband, pool, gym, health club, bar, laundry service, business services, meeting rooms* ▭ *AE, DC, MC, V* Ⓜ *Yau Ma Tei.*

$$ 🏨 **Majestic Hotel.** This hotel is on the site of the old Majestic Cinema on upper Nathan Road. The lobby is quite plain, and the sparsely decorated rooms have contemporary furniture; suites have fax machines. Facilities are minimal, with no pool or gym, and there's no restaurant— only a coffee shop and bar. The complex, though, has shops and a cinema, and plenty of restaurants, from Chinese food to Malaysian. The Jordan MTR is nearby. ⊠ *348 Nathan Rd., Yau Ma Tei, Kowloon* ☎ *2781-1333* ⊕ *www.majestichotel.com.hk* ↩ *380 rooms, 8 suites* ♨ *Coffee shop, room service, some in-room faxes, minibars, refrigerators, cable TV with movies, in-room broadband, bar, cinema, shop, laundry service, business services, meeting rooms, no-smoking floor* ▭ *AE, DC, MC, V* Ⓜ *Jordan.*

★ $$ 🏨 **Royal Plaza.** The Royal Plaza is easily accessible from either the adjacent Kowloon-Canton Railway station or the nearby Mong Kok MTR station. As part of the massive Grand Century Place complex, it's a shopper's delight. Rooms, which have views of Lion Rock and Kowloon, are elegant and modern and surprisingly quiet considering the busy location. The hotel itself offers a mix of restaurants, bars, and leisure facilities, including a ballroom and a large pool with underwater music. The garden allows seekers of solitude to contemplate the true meaning of Mong Kok in peace and quiet. ⊠ *193 Prince Edward Rd. W, Mong Kok, Kowloon* ☎ *2928-8822* ⊕ *www.royalplaza.com.hk* ↩ *469 rooms, 17 suites* ♨ *3 restaurants, room service, in-room safes, minibars, cable TV with movies, in-room broadband, indoor pool, gym, health club, sauna, spa, bar, laundry service, business services, meeting rooms* ▭ *AE, DC, MC, V* Ⓜ *Mong Kok.*

$-$$ 🏨 **Hotel Concourse.** One of Hong Kong's nicer low-to-moderately priced hotels, the Concourse is run by the China Travel Service. It's tucked away from Nathan Road but only a minute's walk from the Prince Edward MTR station in Mong Kok. Rooms have quite hard beds. The hotel is well placed for a glimpse of real, day-to-day life in Hong Kong. Loads of simple eateries dot the area, and the night markets are nearby. Most of the streets in Kowloon are busy and noisy and it's no different here, but it's relatively clean and safe. The hotel has both a Chinese and a pan-Asian restaurant. ⊠ *22 Lai Chi Kok Rd., Mong Kok, Kowloon* ☎ *2397-6683* ⊕ *www.hotelconcourse.com.hk* ↩ *425 rooms, 5 suites* ♨ *2 restaurants, coffee shop, room service, minibars, cable TV with movies, in-room broadband, bar, laundry service, business services, meeting rooms* ▭ *AE, DC, MC, V* Ⓜ *Prince Edward.*

$-$$ 🏨 **Prudential Hotel.** Rising from a busy corner on upper Nathan Road, above the Jordan MTR station, this hotel is a find if you're on a modest budget. The spacious rooms have views of bustling Nathan Road, with the neon-lighted shop signs and banners. The hotel shares a building with a lively shopping mall and has its own pool. Rooms on the five executive floors have tea- and coffeemakers. The lobby is small and not the most welcoming. ⊠ *222 Nathan Rd., Yau Ma Tei, Kowloon* ☎ *2311-8222* ⊕ *www.prudentialhotel.com* ⟿ *411 rooms, 21 suites* ⌂ *Coffee shop, room service, minibars, cable TV with movies, in-room broadband, pool, bar, shop, laundry service, business services, meeting rooms* ⊟ *AE, DC, MC, V* Ⓜ *Jordan.*

$ 🏨 **Nathan Hotel.** Popular with tour groups from both the East and the West, this busy hotel is near the Jordan MTR and just a stone's throw away from the street-market attractions of Mong Kok and Yau Ma Tei. Rooms are moderately sized and colorful, and include all the basic necessities. Keep in mind that if you stay here, you'll have to stomach the incredibly crowded streets and noise level in the area. ⊠ *378 Nathan Rd., Yau Ma Tei, Kowloon* ☎ *2388-5141* ⊕ *www.nathanhotel.com* ⟿ *190 rooms* ⌂ *Restaurant, room service, minibars, cable TV, bar, shop, laundry service, business services* ⊟ *AE, DC, MC, V* Ⓜ *Jordan.*

¢-$ 🏨 **Shamrock Hotel.** One of the oldest budget hotels on Nathan Road, the Shamrock opened its doors in the early 1960s. It's just north of Kowloon Park and steps from the Jordan MTR, putting it in the middle of all the 24-hour-a-day Yau Ma Tei action. Still, the northern location translates to better value than Tsim Sha Tsui, and rooms are a decent size for the price. The hotel also offers buffet-style dining from its in-house restaurant. ⊠ *223 Nathan Rd., Yau Ma Tei, Kowloon* ☎ *2735-2271* ⊕ *www.shamrockhotel.com.hk* ⟿ *157 rooms, 2 suites* ⌂ *Restaurant, room service, minibars, cable TV with movies, laundry service* ⊟ *AE, DC, MC, V* Ⓜ *Jordan.*

★ ¢ 🏨 **Booth Lodge.** This pleasant contemporary retreat, which is down a dead-end side street near the Jade Market, is operated by the Salvation Army. But contrary to the image that might conjure up for you, everything in this lodge looks bright and fresh, from the walls to the starched sheets on the double beds. The lobby is a study in minimalism and may resemble an office, but the Booth is a good value overall. The coffee shop serves mainly buffets, with a small outdoor balcony offering nice views. The Yau Ma Tei MTR is nearby. ⊠ *11 Wing Sing La., Yau Ma Tei, Kowloon* ☎ *2771-9266* ⊕ *boothlodge.salvation.org.hk* ⟿ *60 rooms* ⌂ *Restaurant, coffee shop, laundry service* ⊟ *AE, MC, V* Ⓜ *Yau Ma Tei.*

¢ 🏨 **Caritas Bianchi Lodge.** Rooms at this friendly hostel, operated by the Catholic Diocese of Hong Kong, are simple and modern and have basic facilities including TVs, minibars, air-conditioning, and private bathrooms. Just around the corner from busy Nathan Road, the lodge is also close to the Jade Market and the nightly Temple Street Market, but it offers peace and quiet due to its dead-end location. ⊠ *4 Cliff Rd., Yau Ma Tei, Kowloon* ☎ *2388-1111* ⊕ *www.caritas-chs.org.hk* ⟿ *88 rooms, 2 suites* ⌂ *Restaurant, minibars, cable TV, laundry service* ⊟ *AE, DC, MC, V* Ⓜ *Yau Ma Tei.*

Side Trip
to Macau

Largo do Senado, the main square, central Macau

WORD OF MOUTH

"We were more interested in sights than gambling, so we hopped a bus at the ferry terminal. We stepped off into a different country. The buildings were European, and the plazas were paved with black-and-white cobblestones in wave patterns. At the ruins of São Paulo we enjoyed the view and breeze. For lunch, we tried *bacalhau* (salt cod)—really good and not as salty as I'd imagined. Later, we saw some drying on a street sign. Do traffic fumes enhance the flavor?"   —Skedaddle

WELCOME TO MACAU

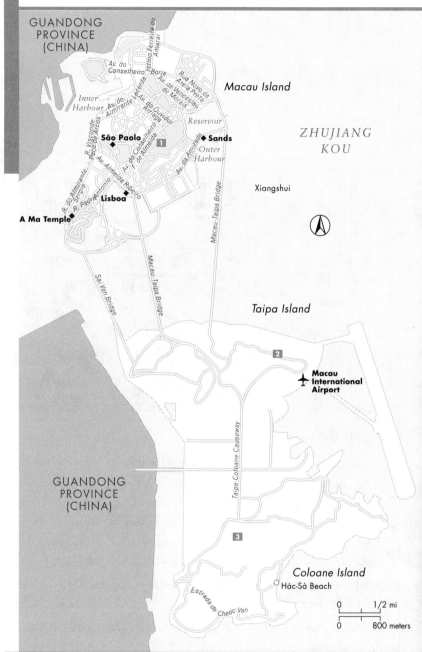

GUANDONG
PROVINCE
(CHINA)

Macau Island

*Inner
Harbour*

Av. do
Conselheiro Borja

Rua Nova da
Areia Preta

Istmo Ferreira do Amaral

Av. de Morais

Av. de Vences au

R. Visconde Paço de Arcos

Av. do Almirante Lacerda

Av. do Ouvidor Arriaga

Reservoir

São Paolo ◆

◆ Sands

1

*Outer
Harbour*

Av. do Conselheiro F. de Almeida

Av. Almeida Ribeiro

Av. da Almirade

*ZHUJIANG
KOU*

Xiangshui

Lisboa ◆

R. do Almirante Sergio

R. Padre Antonio

A Ma Temple ◆

Sai Van Bridge

Macau-Taipa Bridge

Macau-Taipa Bridge

Taipa Island

2

✈ **Macau
International
Airport**

Taipa-Coloane Causeway

GUANDONG
PROVINCE
(CHINA)

3

Coloane Island

○ Hàc-Sà Beach

Estrada de Cheoc Van

0		1/2 mi
0		800 meters

GETTING ORIENTED

Macau, a Special Administrative Region (SAR) of the People's Republic of China, is on the western bank of the Pearl River Delta, less than an hour from Hong Kong by hydrofoil. It consists of the Macau Peninsula and Taipa and Coloane islands. The newly reclaimed area of Cotai lies between Taipa and Coloane and virtually merges the two.

Most people visit Macau to gamble, eat cheap seafood, and shop without crowds. But don't overlook its timeless charms and unique culture, born from centuries of both Portuguese and Chinese influence.

1 Downtown Macau. You'll experience authentic Macau in a downtown square, with its European-style paving and sidewalk cafés as well as in a Buddhist temple, with its red lanterns and fragrant joss sticks. But perhaps even more authentic is that pink colonial Portuguese building that houses a Chinese herbal medicine shop.

2 Taipa Island. Although the Portuguese presence on Macau dates from the mid-1500s, Taipa wasn't occupied until the mid-1800s. The island remained a garrison and a pastoral retreat until the 1970s, when it was linked to Macau by bridge. Today parts retain a village feel and parts are crowded with soul-less high-rises.

3 Coloane Island. The 3-km (2-mi) causeway that once separated this island from Taipa has been bridged by a massive land-reclamation and development project that includes building casinos. Still, the larger island remains less populated and more intimate than Taipa. It's also known for its parks, beaches, and golf club.

TOP REASONS TO GO

★ **Ruins of São Paulo.** The church facade is a symbol of Macau. En route to it, sample regional cuisine and experience local charm in Senado Square.

★ **A-Ma Temple.** It's steeped in Macau's culture and history. Search for the Lucky Money Pool, then wash your hands in the blessed water before heading to the casinos.

★ **Place Your Bets.** Even if you don't gamble, take a peek inside the Lisboa, a Macau landmark, or the Sands, where you can also succumb to gluttony at 888 Las Vegas Buffet.

★ **Relax on Hàc-Sà Beach.** Sunbathe on charcoal gray sands before taking a stroll, heading out on Jet Skis, or feasting on seafood.

★ **Spaaahhh.** Macau's spas have ultraindulgent treatments and world-class facilities—with prices to match. But who cares? You're on vacation.

8

MACAU PLANNER

Travel Between Hong Kong & Macau

You can fly to Macau from Hong Kong by helicopter in less than 20 minutes. Even more affordable though not as fast is the hour-long ferry trip.

BY SEA

Ferries run every 15 minutes 24 hours a day with a reduced schedule from 1:30 AM to 7 AM. Prices for the three classes of tickets—economy, first, and super—run HK$142–HK$260. VIP cabins cost HK$1,650 and up. Weekday traffic is usually light, so you can buy tickets right before departure. Weekend tickets often sell out, so make reservations. You can do so up to 28 days in advance with travel agents and at most Hong Kong hotels and large MTR stations. You can also book by phone and pay with American Express, Diners Club, and Visa cards, but you must pick tickets up at least a half hour before departure.

Most ferries leave from Hong Kong's Shun Tak Centre (Sheung Wan MTR Station) in Central, though limited service is also available from Kowloon's Tsim Sha Tsui Ferry Terminal. In Macau all service is handled by the Macau Ferry Terminal. The trip takes 55 minutes one way. Buses and cabs await you on the Macau side.

Ferry Reservations & Turbojet Tickets (☎ 2859–3333 for schedules, 2921–6688 for bookings ⊕ www.turbojet. com.hk). **First Ferry** (✉ Shun Tak Centre, 200 Connaught Rd., Sheung Wan, Hong Kong ☎ 2131–8181 ⊕ www. nwff.com.hk).

BY AIR

International flights do come into Macau, but there are no flights from Hong Kong, which is only 10 minutes away by plane. There are, however, 16-minute helicopter flights between Hong Kong's Shun Tak Centre and the Macau Ferry Terminal; they leave every 30 minutes from 9:30 AM to 10:30 PM daily. Prices are HK$1,268 Monday to Thursday and HK$1,477 Friday to Sunday and holidays. Reservations are essential. **East Asia Airlines** (☎ 2108–9898 Shun Tak Centre, 853/727–288 Macau Terminal ⊕ www.helihongkong.com). **Macau International Airport** (☎ 853/861–111 ⊕ www.macau-airport. gov.mo).

The Basics

The Macau Government Tourist Office (MGTO) is well managed and generously funded.

MGTO (✉ Macau Ferry Terminal, Macau ☎ 853/726–416 ⊕ www. macautourism.gov.mo ✉ Shun Tak Centre, 200 Connaught Rd., Sheung Wan, Hong Kong ☎ 2857–2287).

PASSPORTS & VISAS

To enter Macau, Americans, Canadians, European Union citizens, and others only need a valid passport for stays of up to 20 days. Check the government's Web site (www.fsm. gov.mo) for more information.

CURRENCY

The currency is the pataca (abbreviated MOP) with a fixed exchange rate of MOP$1.032 to HKD$1—roughly MOP$8 to US$1. Patacas come in 10, 20, 50, 100, 500, and 1000 MOP banknotes plus 1, 5, and 10 MOP coins. 1 pataca is divided into 100 avos, which come in 10, 20, and 50 avos coins. Hong Kong dollars are accepted on a 1:1 basis.

LANGUAGE

Chinese and Portuguese are Macau's official languages. Both Cantonese and Mandarin are widely spoken. English is often used in commerce, but relying on it will be frustrating outside of tourist areas and with most taxi drivers.

By Hiram Chu

Enter the desperate, smoky atmosphere of a Chinese casino, where frumpy players bet an average of five times more than the typical Vegas gambler. Sit down next to grandmothers who smoke like chimneys while playing baccarat—the local game of choice—with visiting high-rollers. Then step out of the climate-controlled chill and into tropical air that embraces you like a warm, balmy hug. Welcome to Macau.

Follow the cobblestone paths of old town up a small hill to where the intersection of two alleys—Travessa de Dom Quixote and Travessa de Sancho Panca—is marked by a Buddhist temple. Sit beside a fountain or in a square and watch young children play as you listen to elderly Chinese and Portuguese converse about how it once was and what it's like now.

Stroll the black sands of Hàc-Sà Beach before feasting on a dinner of *bacalhau com natas* (dried codfish with a cream sauce), grilled African chicken, Chinese lobster with scallions, or firey prawns infused with Indian and Malaysian flavors. Wash everything down with *vinho verde,* the crisp young wine from northern Portugal. Top it all off with a *pastel de nata* (creamy egg tart) and dark, thick espresso.

The many contrasts in this tiny enclave of 450,000 people serve as reminders of how very different cultures have embraced one another's traditions for hundreds of years. Though Macau's population is 95% ethnic Chinese there are still vibrant pockets of Portuguese and Filipino expats. And some of the thousands of Eurasians—who consider themselves neither Portuguese nor Chinese, but something in between—can trace the intermarriage of their ancestors back a century or two.

SIGHTS & EXPERIENCES

Macau is a small place where, on a good day, you could drive from one end to the other in 15 minutes. This makes walking and bicycling the ideal ways to explore winding city streets, nature trails, and long stretches of beach. Most of Macau's population lives on the peninsula attached to mainland China. The region's most famous sights are here—Senado

Square, the Ruins of St. Paul's, A-Ma Temple—as are the luxury hotels and casinos. As in the older sections of Hong Kong, cramped older buildings stand comfortably next to gleaming new structures.

Downtown Macau

Chances are you'll arrive at the Macau Ferry Terminal after sailing from Hong Kong. There's not much to see within walking distance of the terminal, so hop into one of the waiting taxis, buses, or pedicabs and head directly to the historic center, less than 10 minutes away. The short stretch of road named Avenida Almeida Ribeiro, more commonly known as San Ma Lo, is Macau's commercial and cultural heart. The region's biggest and best casinos are minutes away in the Downtown peninsula area and next to the ferry terminal in the Outer Harbour area.

Get Fortified

Fodor'sChoice
★

Fortaleza da Guia. The Guia Fortress, built between 1622 and 1638 on Macau's highest hill, was key to protecting the Portuguese from invaders. You can walk the steep, winding road up to the fortress or take a five-minute cable car ride from the entrance of Flora Garden on Avenida Sidonio Pais. Once inside the fort, notice the gleaming white Guia Lighthouse (you can't go inside, but you can get a good look at the exterior) that's lighted every night. Next to it is the Guia Chapel, built by Clarist nuns to provide soldiers with religious services. The chapel is no longer used for services but restoration work in 1998 uncovered elaborate frescoes that mix Western and Chinese themes. They're best seen when the morning or afternoon sun floods the chapel.

The elegant yellow and white building with Mughal architectural influences built onto a slope of Guia Hill is the **Quartel dos Mouros** (Moorish Barracks). It now houses the Macau Maritime Administration but originally was constructed in 1874 for Indian police regimens brought into the region, a reminder of Macau's historic relationship with the Indian city of Goa. ⊠ *Guia Hill, Downtown* 🚃*Free* ⊙*Daily 9–5:30.*

Fortaleza do Monte (Mount Fortress). On the hill overlooking the ruins of São Paulo and affording great peninsular views, this renovated fort was built by the Jesuits in the early 17th century. In 1622 it was the site of Macau's most legendary battle, where a priest's lucky cannon shot hit an invading Dutch ship's powder supply, saving the day. The interior buildings were destroyed by fire in 1835, but the outer walls remain, along with several large cannons and artillery pieces. Next to the

> ### THE BIG BOSS
>
> Many mixed-blood Macanese are from old, established families, including Dr. Stanley Ho, Macau's biggest *taipan* (Chinese for "big boss"). Dr. Ho—and his gambling and tourism empire under the Sociedade de Jogos de Macau (SJM) umbrella—keeps the region afloat, providing more than 70% of the government's tax revenues. His interests include the boat that speeds you from Hong Kong to Macau, the hotel you stay at, the casino you lose money in, the one TV station you watch, and the electricity you use. Locals often quip, "Dr. Ho is richer than God and almost as powerful."

fort, exhibits at the **Macau Museum** (✉ 112 Praceta do Museu de Macau, Downtown ☎ 853/357–911) take you through Macau's history—from its origins to modern development. It's open Tuesday through Sunday 10–6, and admission is MOP$15. ✉ *Monte Hill, Downtown* ✉ *MOP$15; free entrance on the 15th of each month* ⊙ *Tues.–Sun. 10–6.*

Say a Little Prayer

Igreja de São Lourenço. St. Lawrence's Church was founded by Jesuits in 1560 and has been lovingly rebuilt several times. It overlooks the South China Sea amid pleasant, palm-shaded gardens. The interior will take your breath away thanks to elegant wood carvings, a baroque altar, and crystal chandeliers. The Macau International Music Festival holds a concert finale here each October. ✉ *Rua de São Lourenço, Downtown* ✉ *Free* ⊙ *Daily 10–4.*

Lin Fung Miu. Built around 1592, the Temple of the Lotus honors several Buddhist and Taoist deities, including Tin Hau (goddess of the sea), Kun Lam (goddess of mercy), and Kwan Tai (god of war and wealth). The front of the temple has awesome clay bas-reliefs of renowned figures from Chinese history and mythology. Inside are several halls, shrines, and courtyards. The temple is most famously known as a lodging place for Mandarins traveling from Guangzhou, and its most famous guest was Commissioner Lin Zexu, whose confiscation and destruction of British opium was largely responsible for the First Opium War. Today, June 3, the date of the opium confiscation, is celebrated as an antismoking day in China, where people abstain from smoking cigarettes with varying degrees of success. ✉ *Av. do Artur Tamagnini Barbosa at Estrada do Arco, Downtown* ☎ *No phone* ⊙ *Daily dawn–dusk.*

Fodor's Choice ★ **Ruínas de São Paulo** (Ruins of St. Paul's Church). Only the magnificent, towering facade, with its intricate carvings and bronze statues, remains from the original church. This widely adopted symbol of Macau was built between 1602 and 1640 by Jesuit priests and Japanese Christians. The church, an adjacent college, and Mount Fortress once formed East Asia's first western-style university and was collectively regarded as the Acropolis of Asia. Most of the structures were destroyed by fire in 1835, but the ruins remain popular with visitors, and there are snack bars and antiques and other shops at the foot of the site.

Behind the façade of São Paulo is the **Museum of Sacred Art,** which holds statues, crucifixes, and the bones of Japanese and Indo-Chinese Christian martyrs. There are also some intriguing Asian interpretations of Christian images, including samurai angels and a Chinese Virgin and child. The museum is free and open Sunday through Monday 9–6.

> ## WORLD HERITAGE
>
> In 2005 the "Historic Centre of Macao" was listed as China's 31st UNESCO World Heritage Site. The term "center" is misleading as the site is really a collection of churches, buildings, and neighborhoods that colorfully illustrate Macau's 400-year history. Included in it are China's oldest examples of western architecture and the region's most extensive concentration of missionary churches.

8

A BIT OF HISTORY

Macau's current economic surge mirrors a long history of ebb and flow. When trading began through the Silk Road, farmers from Guangdong and Fujian settled in the area. By 1557, the Portuguese had taken Macau and made it the first European colony in East Asia. Macau was known as "A Ma Gao" in honor of the patron goddess of sailors, A-Ma. The Portuguese adapted this Chinese name to "Macau" and for more than a century, the port thrived as the main intermediary in the trade between Asia and the rest of the world. Ships from Italy, Portugal, and Spain came here to buy and sell Chinese silks and tea, Japanese crafts, Indian spices, African ivory, and Brazilian gold.

In addition to international trade, Macau became an outpost for western religions. St Francis Xavier successfully converted large numbers of Japanese and Chinese to Christianity and used Macau as a base of operations. In the 1500s and 1600s, many churches were built, including an ambitious Christian college. Today in Macau, this religious legacy can be seen in the array of well-preserved churches.

Macau's age of prosperity ended in the 1800s when the Dutch and British gained control of most trading routes to East Asia. After the British victory over China in the 1814 Opium War, the huge, deep-water port of Hong Kong was established and Macau was relegated to a quiet, sleepy port town. Macau did, however, remain important to Chinese refugees of World War I and World War II and the Cultural Revolution. With the widespread introduction of legalized gambling in the 1960s, Macau became a freewheeling place, where gambling, espionage, and crime reigned in the long shadow of modern, wealthy Hong Kong.

Today, textile, furniture, electronics, and other exports join a world-class tourism industry (numbers are expected to surpass even Hong Kong's in less than five years) in making Macau prosperous. Just before the 1999 handover to the Chinese government, the Portuguese administration launched a staggering number of public works. A huge international airport was built on a reclaimed island, and two new bridges were built to connect Macau's two islands. These years also saw the construction of two artificial lakes in the Outer Harbor along the Praia Grande.

Yet another phase of development is under way to transform Macau into a location of choice for casinos and luxury resorts. The casino boom, closely followed by rapid growth in other businesses and a property bubble, has created tens of thousands of jobs. Europeans who left before the Chinese handover have been returning. Indeed it seems that a brand-new age of prosperity has dawned on Macau.

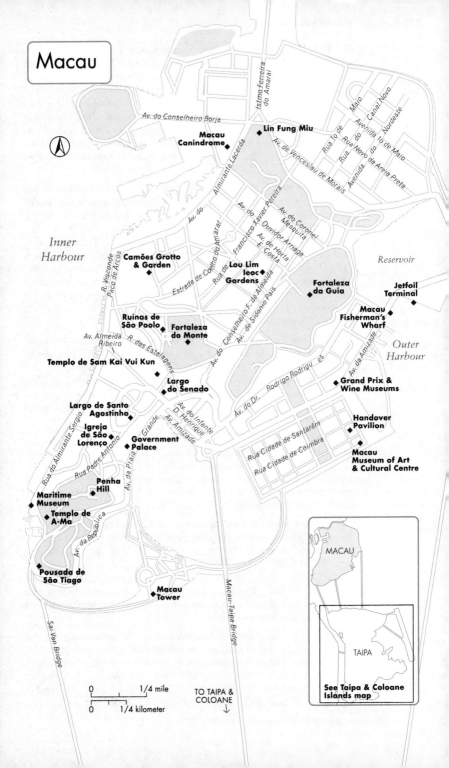

Macau

Av. do Conselheiro Borja

Lin Fung Miu

Macau Canindrome

Av. de Venceslau de Morais

Istmo Ferreira do Amaral

Rua 1o de Maio

Avenida 1o de Maio

Canal Novo

Rua Novo da Areia Preta

Avenida — Nordeste

Almirante Lacerda

Av. do Coronel Mesquita

Av. do

Av. do Ouvidor Arriaga

Av. do Francisco Xavier Pereira

Inner Harbour

Camões Grotto & Garden

Estrada de Coelho do Amaral

Rua de Coelho do Amaral

Lou Lim Ieoc Gardens

Av. de Horta

R.ª Costa

Av. do Conselheiro F. de Almeida

Av. de Sidónio Pais

Fortaleza da Guia

Reservoir

Jetfoil Terminal

R. Visconde Paço de Arcos

Ruínas de São Paolo

Fortaleza do Monte

Macau Fisherman's Wharf

Av. Almeida Ribeiro

R. das Estalagens

Templo de Sam Kai Vui Kun

Largo do Senado

Av. da Amizade

Av. do Dr. Rodrigo Rodrigues

Outer Harbour

Grand Prix & Wine Museums

Largo de Santo Agostinho

Av. do Infante D. Henrique

Av. da Amizade

Handover Pavilion

Igreja de São Lorenço

R. Grande

Government Palace

Rua Cidade de Santarém

Rua Cidade de Coimbra

Macau Museum of Art & Cultural Centre

Rua do Almirante Sérgio

Rua Padre Antonio

Av. da Praia

Penha Hill

Maritime Museum

Templo de A-Ma

Av. da República

Pousada de São Tiago

Macau Tower

Macau-Taipa Bridge

Sai Van Bridge

0 ————— 1/4 mile

0 ————— 1/4 kilometer

TO TAIPA & COLOANE ↓

MACAU

TAIPA

See Taipa & Coloane Islands map

The **Templo de Na Tcha** is a small Chinese temple that was built in 1888, during the Macauan plague. The hope was that Na Tcha Temple would appeal to a mythical Chinese character who granted wishes and could save lives. The **Troco das Antigas Muralhas de Defesa** (Section of the Old City Walls) is all that remains of Macau's original defensive barrier and borders the left side of the Na Tcha Temple. These crumbling yellow walls were built in the mid-16th century and illustrate the durability of *chunambo,* a local material made from compacted layers of clay, soil, sand, straw, crushed rocks, and oyster shells. ⊠ *Downtown* 🖃 *Free* 🕙 *Daily 8–5.*

Fodor'sChoice
★ **Templo de A-Ma** (A-Ma Temple). Properly called Ma Kok Temple but known to locals as simply A-Ma, it's thought to be Macau's oldest building. It's also one of the most picturesque. The structure has its origins in the Ming Dynasty (1368–1644), and was influenced by Confucianism, Taoism, and Buddhism as well as local religions. Vivid-red calligraphy on large boulders tells the story of the goddess A-Ma (also known as Tin Hau), the patron of fishermen. The entrance is obscured by overhanging trees; a small gate opens onto prayer halls, pavilions, and caves carved directly into the hillside. There's also a small on-site museum that contains temple artifacts. ⊠ *Rua de São Tiago da Barra, Largo da Barra, Downtown* 🕙 *Daily 7–6* 🖃 *Free.*

Templo de Sam Kai Vui Kun. Built in 1750, this temple is dedicated to Kuan Tai, the bearded, fierce-looking god of war and wealth in Chinese mythology. Statues of him and his two sons sit on an altar, and a steady stream of people come to pray and ask for support before they go wage battle in the casinos. May and June see festivals honoring Kuan Tai throughout Macau. ⊠ *Rua Sui do Mercado de São Domingo, Downtown* 🖃 *Free* 🕙 *Daily 8–6.*

Square Things Up

Largo de Santo Agostinho (St. Augustine Square). It was built in the image of traditional Portuguese squares. It's paved with black-and-white *azulejos* (tiles) laid out in wave patterns and lined with leafy overhanging trees and lots of wooden benches. It's easy to feel as if you're in a European village, far from South China.

One of the square's main structures is the **Teatro Dom Pedro V,** a European-style theater with an inviting green-and-white facade built in 1859. It's an important cultural landmark for Macanese and was regularly used until World War II, when it fell into disrepair. It was recently renovated by the Orient Foundation and the 300-seat venue once again hosts concerts, recitals, and important public events, which is the only time you can go inside. It does, however, have a garden that's open daily 10 AM to 11 PM, and admission is free.

Igreja de Santo Agostinho (St. Augustine's Church) dates from 1814 and has a grand, weathered exterior and a drafty interior with a high wood-beam ceiling. There's a magnificent stone altar with a statue of Christ on his knees, bearing the cross, with small crucifixes in silhouette on the hill behind him. The statue, called *Our Lord of Passos,* is carried in a procession through the streets of downtown on the first day of Lent.

READY, SET, GO!

Grand Prix racing, which began in Macau in 1953, is the region's most glamorous annual sporting event. During the third or fourth weekend of November, the city is pierced with the sound of supercharged engines testing the 6-km (4-mi) Guia Circuit, which follows city roads along the Outer Harbour to Guia Hill and around the reservoir. The route is as challenging as that of Monaco, with rapid gear changes demanded at the right-angle Statue Corner, the Doña Maria bend, and the Melco hairpin. Cars achieve speeds of 224 km/h (140 mph) on the straightaways, with the lap record approaching 2 minutes, 20 seconds. The premier event is the Formula Three Championship, with cars competing from around the world in what's now the official World Cup of Formula Three. Winners qualify for Formula One licenses. There are also races for motorcycles and production cars. If you plan to travel during this time, beware of the logistical disruption it causes, like re-routing of main roads and lack of hotel accommodation.

Fodor'sChoice ★ **Largo do Senado.** The charming Senado Square, Macau's hub for centuries, is lined with neoclassical-style colonial buildings painted bright pastels. Only pedestrians are allowed on its shiny black-and-white azulejos, and the alleys off it are packed with great restaurants and shops. Take your time wandering. There are plenty of benches on which to rest after all your shopping and sightseeing. Come back at night, when locals of all ages gather to chat, and the square is beautifully lighted.

8

The magnificent yellow **Igreja de São Domingo** (St. Dominick's Church) beckons you to take a closer look. You can do so for free each day from 10 to 6. After a recent restoration, it's again among Macau's most beautiful churches, with a cream-and-white interior that takes on a heavenly golden glow when lighted up for services. The church was originally a convent founded by Spanish Dominican friars in 1587. In 1822, China's first Portuguese newspaper, *The China Bee,* was published here. The church became a repository for sacred art in 1834 when convents were banned in Portugal.

The imposing white facade of **Santa Casa da Misericordia** is hard to ignore. Founded in 1569 by Dom Belchior, Macau's first bishop, the Holy House of Mercy is the China coast's oldest Christian charity, and it continues to take care of the poor with soup kitchens and health clinics as well as to provide housing for the elderly. The exterior is neoclassical but the interior is done in a contrasting opulent modern style. A reception room on the second floor contains paintings of benefactress Marta Merop. It's open daily 10–1 and 2–5:30; admission is MOP$8.

The neoclassical **Edificio do Leal Senado** (Senate Building) was built in 1784 as a municipal chamber and continues to be used by the government today. An elegant meeting room on the first floor opens onto a magnificent library based on one in the Mafra Convent in Portugal, with books neatly stacked on two levels of shelves reaching to the ceiling. A beautiful foyer and garden, open Tuesday through Sunday from 9 to 9, frequently host art and historical exhibitions. Admission is free.

■■■■■■■■■■
┌
│ **NEED A**
│ **BREAK?**
Macau's oldest restaurant, the no-frills **Fat Siu Lau** (✉ Rua de Felicidade, Downtown) is near the fountain at the top of Largo do Senado. It's a great place to try Macanese fare. For a slightly out-of-the-ordinary refreshment, step into the **Leiteria i Son** (☎ 853/573–638) milk bar at Largo do Senado 7—look for the small cow sign overhead. The decor is cafeteria-style spartan, but the bar whips up frothy glasses of fresh milk from its own dairy and blends them with all manner of juices: papaya, coconut, apricot. Your trip won't be complete unless you sample several items here.

Immerse Yourself in Culture

Grand Prix Museum. Exhibits here tell the stories of the best drivers from every year, but the highlights are the actual race cars that are on display. ✉ *431 Rua Luis Gonzaga Gomes, Downtown* ☎ *853/798–4108* ▤ *MOP$10* ☽ *Mon. and Wed.–Sun 10–6.*

Heritage Exhibition of a Traditional Pawn Shop. This impressive re-creation documents the important role that pawn shops have played in Macau for hundreds of years. ✉ *396 Av. Almeida Ribeiro, Downtown* ☎ *No phone* ▤ *MOP$5* ☽ *Daily, except 1st Mon. of month, 10:30–7.*

Macau Museum of Art. The large boxy MMA is as known for its curving, rectangular framed roof as it is for its calligraphy, painting, copperware, and international film collections. It's Macau's only art museum and has five floors of eastern and western works as well as important examples of ancient indigenous pottery found at Hàc-Sà Beach. Free guided tours are available. ✉ *Av. Xian Xing Hai, Downtown* ☎ *853/791–9814 or 853/791–9800* ⊕ *www.artmuseum.gov.mo* ▤ *MOP$5; free Sun.* ☽ *Tues.–Fri. 2–7, weekends 11–7.*

Maritime Museum. Across from the A-Ma temple, this museum is a great place to spend an interesting hour brushing up on seafaring history. The handsome white building looks like a ship, thanks to jutting white slats and porthole windows. A row of fountains out front soothes you almost as much as the calm, cool interior. Multimedia exhibits cover fishermen, merchants, and explorers from Portugal, South China, and Japan. Look for compasses, telescopes, and sections of ships. There's even a small aquarium gallery with local sea life. Try your hand at astronomic navigation—which sailors have used for thousands of years—by looking up at the top floor's nifty celestial dome ceiling. ✉ *Pier 1, Largo Senado Barra,*

DISCOUNT PASS

Macau has worked hard to preserve and promote its unique cultural history by renovating and restoring many sights. In addition, several museums have been built during the past decade. To make these museums even more accessible, the government offers the Macau Museum Pass, which entitles you to a single entry into each one. The cost is MOP$25, and you can pick one up at the MGTO.

Inner Harbour ☎ 853/595-481 ⊕ *www.museumaritimo.gov.mo* 🎫 *MOP$10, MOP$5 on Sun.* ☉ *Mon. and Wed.–Sun. 10–5:30.*

Wine Museum. In the same building as and beside the Grand Prix Museum, this museum has more than 1,100 wines on display; some are almost 200 years old. You'll learn about production techniques and the importance of *vinho* in Portuguese culture. Plus there are more than 50 varieties on hand for impromptu tastings. ✉ *431 Rua Luis Gonzaga Gomes, Downtown* ☎ 853/798-4188 🎫 *MOP$15* ☉ *Mon. and Wed.–Sun 10–6.*

Do Some Gardening

Camões Garden. Macau's most popular park is frequented from dawn to dusk by tai chi enthusiasts, lovers, students, and men huddled over Chinese chessboards with their caged songbirds nearby. The gardens, which were developed in the 18th century, are named after Luís de Camões, Portugal's greatest poet, who was banished to Macau for several years during the 16th century. A rocky niche shelters a bronze bust of the poet in the park's most famous and picturesque spot, Camões Grotto. At the grotto's entrance a bronze sculpture honors the friendship between Portugal and China. A wall of stone slabs is inscribed with poems by various contemporary writers praising Camões and Macau.

Alongside Camões Garden is a smaller park, the **Casa Garden,** originally the grounds of a merchant's estate. Today, the estate's villa, which was built in 1770, is the headquarters for the Orient Foundation, a private institution involved in community, cultural, and arts affairs. Some of its rooms contain historical and art exhibits; the basement has an art gallery. The grounds are lovingly landscaped with a variety of flora and bordered with a brick pathway. There's also a central pond stocked with lilypads and lotus flowers. ✉ *13 Praça Luis de Camões, Downtown* ☎ *554–699* ⊕ *www.macautourism.gov.mo* 🎫 *Free* ☉ *Weekdays 9:30–6.*

Lou Lim Ieoc Gardens. These beautiful gardens were built in the 19th century by a Chinese merchant named Lou Kau. Rock formations, water, vegetation, pavilions, and sunlight were all carefully considered when planning this garden. Balanced landscapes are the hallmark of Suzhou garden style. The government took possession and restored the grounds in the late 1970s so that today you can enjoy tranquil walks among delicate flowering bushes framed with bamboo groves and artificial hills. A large auditorium frequently hosts concerts and other events, most notably recitals during the annual International Music Festival. Adjacent to the gardens, a European-style edifice contains the **Macau Tea Culture House** (✉ 10 Estrada de Adolfo Loureiro, Downtown ☎ 853/827–103), a small (and free) museum with exhibits on the tea culture of Macau and China. It's open every day but Monday from 9 to 7. ✉ *Estrada de Adolfo Loureiro at Av. do Conselheiro Ferreira de Almeida, Downtown* ☎ *No phone* 🎫 *MOP$1; free Fri.* ☉ *Daily 8–6.*

Be Amused

★ **Macau Canidrome.** Asia's only greyhound track looks rundown and quaint compared to the pristine jockey club and the glitzy casinos, but it offers a true taste of Macau. It opened in 1932 and tends to attract a steady crowd of older gamblers several times a week for the slower-pace, lower-stakes gambling rush of betting on fast dogs chasing an electronic rabbit. Check out the parade of race dogs before each race. You can sit on benches in the open-air stadium, at tables in the air-conditioned restaurant, or in a luxury box seat. Remember to have a souvenir picture taken with one of the friendly retired greyhounds. Races are broadcast live and bets are accepted at many of Macau's casinos. ⊠ *Av. do Artur Tamagnini Barbosa at Av. General Castelo Branco, Downtown* ☎ *853/333–399* ⊕ *www. macauyydog.com* ✎ *Public stands: MOP$2. Private boxes: MOP$80.* ⊙ *Tues., Thurs., and weekends 6 PM–11 PM; first race at 7:30.*

🅒 **Macau Fisherman's Wharf.** This complex of amusements, shops, restaurants, and convention facilities is split into themed areas, including China's Tang Dynasty, a Middle East Bazaar, Tibet's Lhasa, African deserts, and ancient Rome. Each has unique dining and shopping options along with amusement rides for younger children. Crowds are thin, so the rides usually have no line. The whole area is a hodgepodge at best. Come if you have kids in tow. Otherwise skip it.

The Legend Wharf, which is done in a classical European architectural style, is home to restaurants, shops, and convention and hotel facilities. Keep an eye out for the strange costumed characters—a freaky stork, a human slinky—who walk around and pose for pictures. Several decent restaurants offer everything from Chinese and Macanese to German (there's even an Irish pub), but your fellow diners will all be visitors like you; locals rarely eat here. Your best bet is the high-energy aquatic stunt show at Da Gama Water World. Note, though, that the performance is short, tickets sell out fast, and there are few shows at night. ⊠ *Av. da Amizade at Av. Dr. Sun Yat-Sen, Downtown* ☎ *853/299–3300* ⊕ *www. fishermanswharf.com.mo* ✎ *Rides and shows MOP$10–MOP$100* ⊙ *Amusement rides daily 10–9. Restaurants daily 10–10.*

Fodor'sChoice **Macau Tower & Convention & Entertainment Centre.** Rising above every-
★ thing else in the city, the world's 10th largest free-standing tower (1,100 feet) recalls a similar structure in Auckland. And it should as both were designed by New Zealand architect Gordon Moller. A. J. Hackett, the extreme sports company, is another bit of Kiwi flavor at the tower. The company offers a variety of thrills, including the Mast Climb, which challenges the daring and strong of heart and body to make a two-hour climb 300 feet up the tower's mast for incomparable views of Macau and China. On the Ironwalk, you clamber up the tower's legs and shafts as if you were rock climbing. What's that? You prefer walking to climbing? Well then perhaps you could take the Skywalk, an open-air stroll around the tower's exterior—without any gates or handrails. Even more intense is the Skyjump, which is listed in the *Guinness Book of World Records* as the world's highest decelerator descent. You essentially bungee jump—free falling for 765 feet—while control wires prevent you from swinging into the tower. Prices range from MOP$233 for the Skywalk to MOP$688 for the Mast Climb. There are, however, discounts for groups and multiple experiences. Yikes! ⊠ *Largo da Torre de Macau, Downtown* ☎ *853/988–8656* ⊕ *www.macautower.com.mo.*

Taipa Island

The island directly south of peninsular Macau was once two small islands that were, over time, joined by deposits from the Pearl River Delta. It's connected to peninsular Macau by three long bridges. The region's two universities, its best hiking trails, and its international airport are all here.

Like downtown Macau, Taipa has been greatly developed in the past few years, yet it retains a visual balance between old Macau charm and modern sleekness. Try to visit on a weekend so you can shop for clothing and crafts in the traditional flea market that's held from the morning to evening in Taipa Village.

Live the Village Life

Fodor's Choice ★

Taipa Village. Its narrow, winding streets are packed with restaurants, bakeries, shop houses, temples, and other buildings with traditional South Chinese and Portuguese design elements. The aptly named Rua do Cunha (Food Street) has many great Chinese, Macanese, Portuguese, and Thai restaurants. Several shops sell homemade Macanese snacks, including steamed milk pudding, almond cakes, beef jerky, and coconut candy. A small public square hosts frequent music and dance performances by students and other local performers.

Atop a small hill overlooking Taipa Village, the beautiful **Carmel Gardens** (⊠ Rua da Cunha, Taipa) have a number of palm trees that provide great shade. Within the garden stands the brilliant white-and-yellow Nossa Senhora do Carmo (Church of Our Lady of Carmel), built in 1885 and featuring a handsome single-belfry tower. The gardens are open Monday and Wednesday through Sunday from 10 to 6. There's no admission fee.

Paths lead down from the Carmel Gardens to the **Taipa House Museums** (⊠ Av. da Praia, Carmo Zone, Taipa ☎ 853/827–103 or 853/827–527). These five sea-green houses were originally residences of wealthy local merchants and were converted into small museums and exhibition spaces. They were all fully restored shortly before the Macau handover and are interesting examples of Porto-Chinese architecture. Official receptions are often held here as are changing art exhibitions. The Venetian Casino and the Cotai complex construction block a once marvelous view of Coloane and the South China Sea. The museum is open Tuesday through Sunday, 10 to 6. Admission is MOP$5 every day but Sunday, when you can enter for free.

Vegetate

Po Tai Un Buddhist Monastery. The region's largest temple is part of a functioning monastery with several dozen monks. The classically designed structure has an ornate main prayer hall and central pavilions with sculptures, fish ponds, and banyan trees. Monks tend to the vegetable plots that supply the popular on-site vegetarian restaurant with all its ingredients. The monastery is next to the Macau Jockey Club and nearby the Four Faces Buddha statue. ⊠ *Estrada Almirante Marques Esparteiro, Taipa* ☎ *853/811–007* 🎟 *Free* ⊘ *Mon. and Wed.–Sun. 10–6.*

8

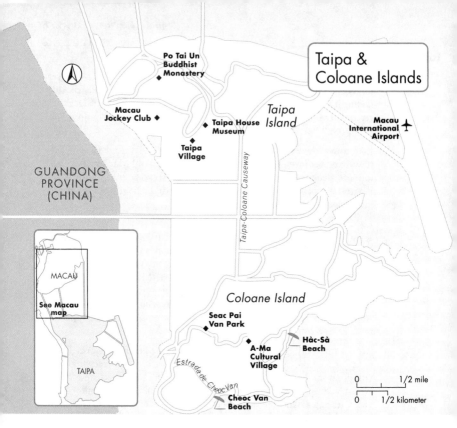

Horse Around

Macau Jockey Club. After Dr. Stanley Ho (who else?) bought the Macau Jockey Club (MJC) in 1991, he transformed what was a quiet trotting track into a lucrative, world-class racing facility. The MJC operates year-round, hosting an average of 100 races. A five-story, open-air grandstand accommodates as many as 15,000 spectators, and, of course, hundreds of private suites and VIP boxes for high rollers and celebrity visitors. All the facilities are top quality, and you can even get a great meal here. Horses have a comfortable lifestyle, too, with more than 1,250 air-conditioned stalls, an equine hospital, and an equine swimming pool. There's also a riding school for aspiring jockeys. Sand-track races are held weeknights at 7, and grass track races take place weekends at 2, except in summer when the heat and humidity forces all races to be held in the evenings. You can place bets at more than 80 stations throughout Macau and Hong Kong as well as through the Internet. If you opt to bet here, though, be sure to stop by the northeast exit to visit the large Four Face Buddha statue where you can say a short prayer for luck. ⊠ *Estrada Governador Albano de Oliveira, Taipa* ☎ *853/821–188* ⊕ *www.macauhorse.com* ⊡ *General admission is free, grandstand seating is MOP$20.*

Head for the Hills

Whether you prefer a leisurely walk though a park or conquering steep hills on foot or by bike, Taipa Island has the region's best trails. The rewards for heading up Taipa Grande and Taipa Pequena, the island's two largest hills, are majestic views. The Taipa Grande trail starts at Estrada Colonel Nicolau de Mesquita, near the United Chinese Cemetery. The Taipa Pequena trail starts at Estrada Lou Lim Ieoc (Lou Lim Gardens) behind the Hyatt Hotel. Be sure to wear rugged hiking shoes, use bug repellent, and, if possible, bring a mobile phone for emergency calls. The most popular place to rent bicycles is the shop at the bus stop outside the Civic and Municipal Affairs Bureau in Taipa Village on Largo Camões. Rates start from MOP$15 per hour, and trail maps are available.

Coloane Island

Centuries ago, Coloane was a wild place, where pirates hid in rocky caves and coves, awaiting their chance to strike at cargo ships on the Pearl River. Early in the 20th century, the local government sponsored a huge planting program to transform Coloane from a barren place to a green one. The results were spectacular—and enduring. Today this island is idyllic, with green hills and clean sandy beaches.

Once connected to Taipa Island by a thin isthmus, Coloane is now almost completely fused with Taipa via the huge Cotai reclaimed land project, where "Asia's Las Vegas" is being constructed and will be completed by 2010. Regardless of the recent development boom, Coloane remains the destination of choice for anyone seeking natural beauty and tranquility.

Wander the Town

★ **Coloane Village.** Quiet, relaxed Coloane Village is home to traditional Mediterranean-style houses painted in pastels as well as the baroque-style Chapel of St. Francis Xavier and the Taoist Tam Kung Temple. The surrounding small narrow alleys have surprises at every turn; among many things you may encounter are fishermen repairing their junks or a local baptism at the chapel.

The village's heart is a small square with a fountain with a bronze Cupid. The surrounding Macanese and Chinese open-air restaurants are among the region's best; some are the unheralded favorites of chefs visiting from Hong Kong and elsewhere in Asia.

Park It

FodorśChoice **A-Ma Cultural Village.** A path just south of Seac Pai Van Park leads to A-Ma Cultural Village, a huge complex built in a traditional Qing Dynasty style. It pays homage to Macau's namesake, the goddess of the sea. The vibrancy and color of the details in the bell and drum towers, the tiled roofs, and the carved marble altars are truly awe-inspiring. It's as if you've been transported back to the height of the Qing Empire and can now see temples in their true state of greatness. Other remarkable details include the striking rows of stairs leading to Tian Hou Palace at the entrance. Each row features painstaking detailed marble and stone carvings of auspicious Chinese symbols: a roaring tiger, double lions, five cranes, the double phoenix, and a splendid imperial dragon. The grounds here also have a recreational fishing zone and an arboretum with more than 100 species of local and exotic flora.

Behind A-Ma Cultural Village is the 560-foot-tall **Coloane Hill,** crowned by a gleaming white-marble statue of A-Ma (commemorating the year of Macau's handover), soaring 65 feet and visible from miles away. You can make the short hike up to the top or take one of the shuttle buses that leave from the foot of the hill every 30 minutes. ⊠ *Off Estrada de Seac Pai Van, Coloane* ☎ *Free* ☺ *Tues.–Sun. 8–6.*

☺ **Seac Pai Van Park** (Coloane Park). This large park has extensive gardens, ponds, and waterfalls, and a large walk-in aviary with more than 200 bird species chirping and flying about. There are lots of things of interest to children, including playgrounds, a mini zoo, and an interactive museum with exhibits on nature and agriculture.

Race enthusiasts and thrill seekers alike should head to the **Macau Kartodromo** (☎ 853/882–126) opposite Coloane Park. Traveling more than 73 kph (45 mph) on a professional course, these go-karts aren't for kids. Although you're guaranteed an intense, high-speed time, safety is taken seriously. Night racing with floodlights is offered Friday and Saturday. Prices are MOP\$100 for 10 minutes and MOP\$180 for 20 minutes. The course is open 10:30–7:30 Sunday through Thursday and 10–9 Friday and Saturday.

Worship the Sun
Hàc-Sà Beach and Cheoc Van Beach are Macau's two most accessible beaches and are usually crowded on the weekends.

Cheoc Van Beach is perfect for romantic walks. It's in a sheltered cove with a nice seafood restaurant to one side, the Marine Club with kayak rentals on the other side, and a charming pousada hotel overlooking the ocean. Be warned that there are lots of stray, though generally friendly, dogs on this beach.

☺ **Hàc-Sà** translated from the Chinese means "black sand" though the sands of the area's biggest beach are actually a deep gray. Playgrounds, picnic areas, and restaurants are all within walking distance. A sports complex has an Olympic-size swimming pool, tennis courts, and other sports facilities. Also nearby is the Hàc-Sà Reservoir BBQ park with picnic and barbecue facilities, boat rentals, and water sports outfitters.

CASINOS

The average gaming table in Macau grosses almost nine times the average one in Las Vegas, and the world's highest grossing casino, the legendary Lisboa, brings in more than \$7 million *per day.* Small wonder that international casino groups have swarmed the region, driving Macau's explosive double-digit growth during the past five years.

From the late 1960s until 2001, Macau native Dr. Stanley Ho owned all the casinos, helping him to become one of the world's wealthiest people. One of the first steps the Chinese government took after the 1999 handover was to break up Dr. Ho's monopoly and award casino licenses to several consortiums from Las Vegas. The grand plan to transform Macau from a quiet town that offered gambling into one of the world's top gaming destinations is well underway.

The Scene

Gambling is lightly regulated, so there are only a few things to remember. No one under age 18 is allowed into casinos. Most casinos use Hong Kong dollars in their gaming and not Macau patacas, but you can easily exchange currencies at cashiers. High- and no-limit VIP rooms are available on request. Minimum bets range from HK$50,000 to HK$100,000 per hand. You can get cash from credit cards and ATMs 24 hours a day, and every casino has a program to extend additional credit to frequent visitors. Most casinos don't have strict dress codes outside of their VIP rooms, but you're better off not wearing shorts or sleeveless shirts. Minimum bets for most tables are higher than those in Las Vegas, but there are lower limits for slots and video gambling.

The players here may not look sophisticated, but don't be fooled. Chinese men and women have long embraced gambling, so many of Macau's gamblers are truly hard-core. Average bets are in the hundreds per hand, and many people gamble until they're completely exhausted or completely broke, usually the latter.

Macau is also famous for gambling's sister industries of pawn shops, loan sharks, seedy saunas, and prostitution. This underbelly is hidden, though. You won't encounter such things unless you seek them out.

8

The Games

Macau's casinos are geared to Asian gamblers, so most tables are dedicated to baccarat, fan-tan, and Asian dice games. There are few blackjack, poker, or roulette tables.

Baccarat is by far the most popular game for Asian gamblers, so most casinos devote the majority of their floors to baccarat tables. Many Chinese gamblers believe that this is the fairest game so they tend to make larger bets on it compared to other games. You can bet on four items: the player's hand, the banker's hand, tie hand, and pair. Macau rules stipulate that you can't take the house, and there are maximum payouts, but you'll still see the biggest crowds and hear the loudest stirrings from the baccarat tables.

Big and Small (Dai-Siu) is a game based on guessing values of three dice under a covered glass canister. You can bet on values, number combinations, and most commonly, "big" value or "small" value. Hear the collective groan when three-of-a-kind turns up, and the house takes all.

Fan-tan is an ancient Chinese game that most Westerners have never heard of. The croupier (counter) plunges an inverted silver cup into a pile of porcelain buttons on the table. He then moves the cup containing a number of buttons to one side. After bets are placed the cup is lifted and the buttons are counted off in groups of four until either one, two, three, or four buttons are left at the end of the count. Cash bets are placed on the table on the numerals one, two, three, or four; odds or evens; corners; or divisions between numbers. This game is becoming less and less popular, though Lisboa and Sands still have several tables.

Pacapio is basically a Chinese version of Keno. Tickets are printed with 80 Chinese characters and you select 10 characters to bet on from a computerized draw of 20 characters. There are six locations for Pacapio betting, with the most popular one being the Lisboa Betting Centre. The game operates from 10 AM to 2 AM.

> ## ASIA'S VEGAS
>
> Sheldon Anderson, CEO of the Las Vegas Sands, is spearheading a $13 billion, multiple-phase to transform the Cotai Strip into "Asia's Las Vegas." The list of partners reads like an all-star roster of the hotel industry: Hilton, Conrad, Four Seasons, Sheraton, St. Regis, Shangri-la, Mandarin Oriental, Marriott. When finished, the Cotai Strip will have more than 20 luxury properties with a total of more than 6,000 gaming tables, 29,000 hotel rooms, and 4,000,000 square feet of retail space. As one businessman quipped, "Imagine the development Las Vegas underwent from 1975 to 2005; then compact that into 5 years."

Pai kao has been a popular Chinese game since the 19th century. It's played with dominoes and a revolving banker system where one player assumes the role of the house while the casino gets a percentage of all bets. The rules are relatively complicated, and the game is offered at the Lisboa and a few other casinos.

Roulette is played using the European wheel with a single "0," giving you a slightly better chance of winning over the American wheel with both a "0" and a "00" slot. You must exchange your cash or chips into special, roulette-only marker chips before playing and then exchange these chips back to casino chips when leaving the table. This game isn't very popular, so you'll find, at most, one or two live tables plus a handful of electronic tables in the larger casinos.

The Casinos

Cream of the Crop

Sands Macao Casino Hotel (✉ Largo de Monte Carlo 203, Downtown Macau ☎ 853/883–388 ⊕ www.sands.com.mo). **Mandarin Oriental Casino Hotel** (✉ 956-1110 Av. da Amizade, Downtown Macau ☎ 853/567–888 ⊕ www.mandarinoriental.com). **Wynn Macau** (✉ 6-8 Av. da Amizade, Downtown Macau ☎ 853/889–966 ⊕ www.wynnmacau.com). **Venetian Macao Resort Hotel** (✉ Cotai Strip, Macau ☎ 853/883–311 ⊕ www.venetianmacao.com).

Landmarks

Hotel Casino Lisboa (✉ 2-4 Av. de Lisboa, Downtown Macau ☎ 853/377–666 ⊕ www.hotelisboa.com). **Hyatt Regency Hotel Casino** (✉ 2 Estrata Almirante, Marques Esparteiro Taipa ☎ 853/831–537 ⊕ www.

macau.hyatt.com). **Jai Alai Casino** (✉ Jai Alai Building, Av. de Amizade, Downtown Macau ☎853/726–086). **Macau Jockey Club Casino** (✉ Grandview Hotel, Estrada Governador Albano de Oliveira 142, Taipa ☎ 853/ 837–788). **Golden Dragon Casino** (✉ Hotel Golden Dragon Rua de Malaca, Downtown Macau ☎ 853/727–979).

Fantasia

Greek Mythology Casino (✉ 889 Av. Padre Tomas Pereira, Taipa ☎ 853/ 831–111 ⊕ www.newcenturyhotel-macau.com). **Pharaoh's Palace Casino** (✉ The Landmark Hotel, Av. de Amizade 555, Downtown Macau ☎ 853/ 781–781).

WHERE TO EAT

Macau is legendary in the region for the diversity of its cuisine, which reflects the range of influences on its long history. There are a number of excellent Chinese restaurants, particularly Cantonese and Chiu Chow, which are particularly well known among Hong Kong residents. A large number of weekend Hong Kong travelers actually go to Macau just for dim sum, weekend brunches, and seafood feasts. In addition to more affordable prices, many people believe the ingredients are of higher quality, fresher, and there are fewer lines of people snaking out of the more popular places.

Macanese local cooking mirrors the colorful city, blending the flavors of East and West. For years this food was difficult to find outside private homes, but a few restaurants (such as Balicha O and Litoral) have stepped in to fill the gap. One of the most distinctive Macanese ingredients is the purple-grayish *balicha o,* a flavorful shrimp paste for which every family has its own special recipe. Another Macanese staple often served at lunch or dinner is *minchi,* a blend of ground pork or beef sautéed with onion, garlic, a bit of soy, and diced potatoes. In addition to these local favorites, you shouldn't miss the spicy and creamy Macanese interpretations of traditional Cantonese dishes such as baked prawns, braised abalone, and seafood stews.

Prices for both food and wine are, on the whole, reasonable, and a drinkable Portuguese wine often costs little more than a bottle of mineral water. Outside Chinese restaurants, the service trade is almost completely run by Filipinos, so ordering in English is rarely a problem—indeed, many Macanese have to order in English to make themselves understood. Meals are on a southern European schedule: long, leisurely lunches last from 1 to 3 PM and dinner doesn't begin until after 8, although it's possible to eat earlier. The majority of tourists don't arrive until Friday or Saturday, so weekday late-night dining options are limited after 10 PM. Most restaurants are open daily year-round, with perhaps a few days off around Chinese New Year (in late January to early February). Dress is casual, and reservations are rarely necessary except at the very finest restaurants, and even then only on weekends. The government tourism office produces an excellent magazine, *Eating Out in Macau,* which has an exhaustive listing of local dining spots. Most restaurants will add an automatic 10% service charge

8

and a tip of about 10% is expected where there is no automatic service charge added to the check.

		WHAT IT COSTS In Patacas			
	$$$$	**$$$**	**$$**	**$**	**¢**
AT DINNER	Over $300	$200–$300	$150–$200	$80–$150	Under $80

Prices are for two main courses, a small side dish, and two beverages at dinner and do not include the customary 10% service charge.

Cafés

¢ ✕ **Lord Stow's Bakery.** It's debatable who makes the best *pasteis de nata* (custard tarts) in Macau, since it's largely a question of personal taste, but there's no doubt that Lord Stow's Bakery is one of the best at marketing its tarts. The bakery is especially popular among English-speakers and Japanese tourists. Lord Andrew Stow is frequently in the bakery or the adjacent Lord Stow's Café and loves to greet fans of his egg tarts. ⊠ *Coloane Village Sq., Coloane* ☎ *853/882–534* ▭ *AE, DC, MC, V.*

¢ ✕ **Pastelaria Koi Kei.** When walking along the street toward the Ruins of St. Paul's Church, you will no doubt be accosted by dozens of aggressive salespeople trying to force samples of Macanese snacks into your hands. Don't be shy and have a taste or two because competition is fierce for the tourist dollar and they expect you to shop around. Along the street are several *pastelarias* (pastry shops) where you can buy traditional almond cakes, ginger candy, beef jerky, and egg rolls, but one of the oldest and best is Pastelaria Koi Kei. The Portuguese custards are excellent and especially popular among locals. You'll see lots of Hong Kong visitors hauling the bakery's distinctive tan bags, heavy with snacks, back home for friends and relatives. Koi Kei has branches throughout Macau. ⊠ *70–72 Rua Felcidade, base of Ruins of St. Paul's, Downtown, Macau* ☎ *853/938–102* ▭ *AE, DC, MC, V.*

FodorśChoice
★

Chinese

$$$$ ✕ **Chiu Chau.** This sumptuous restaurant in Macau serves the Chiu Chow–style cuisine from the northeast region of south China. Many Hong Kong and Thai Chinese have roots in Chiu Chow and revere the thick, strong soups, chicken in hot *chinjew* sauce (made from herbs and peppercorns), rich and crispy oyster omelets, and whole braised crab served here. The restaurant also serves top-quality shark's fin and abalone soup but be prepared to pay for it. ⊠ *Av. da Amizade, Hotel Lisboa, Downtown Peninsula, Macau* ☎ *853/712–549* ▭ *AE, DC, MC, V.*

$$$–$$$$ ✕ **Lua Azul.** An upscale alternative to standard dim sum restaurants, Lua Azul has traditional booth seating and round tables, with subtle lighting in a contemporary interior. It's usually full of well-heeled families, young and old. Waiters will make sure your table is never empty and your stomach is kept happy. Don't miss the deep-fried shrimp balls filled with hot broth. The dinner menu specializes in Huai Yang cuisine and you should check the rotating menu specials to see what delicacies are on offer that week. Weekends are particularly crowded so make reservations. ⊠ *Level 3 inside Macau Tower, Largo da Torre de Macau, Downtown Peninsula, Macau* ☎ *853/988–8700* ▭ *AE, DC, MC, V.*

$$$–$$$$ ✕ **Portas do Sol.** Originally a Portuguese restaurant (hence the name), Portas do Sol has been transformed into a destination for exquisite dim sum and Chinese cuisine. Tiny, sweet Shanghainese pork buns, turnip cakes, steamed rice-flour crepes, and soup dumplings are some of the traditional fare, and there are some innovative new creations that look like miniature jewels on the plate. For dessert, you can choose from a wide variety of Chinese sweets, including coconut milk sago pudding, double-boiled papaya with snow fungus, and sweet red bean porridge with ice cream. To accompany your meal there's a dinner cabaret show and ballroom dancing. Reservations are a good idea on weekends as this place fills up with Hong Kong and mainland visitors. ⌧ *Av. da Amizade, Hotel Lisboa, Downtown Peninsula, Macau* ☎ *853/377–666* ▭ *AE, DC, MC, V.*

$$ ✕ **Long Kei.** One of the oldest and most popular Cantonese restaurants in Macau, Long Kei is in busy Senado Square, in a handsome pink building a few meters from the fountain. The huge menu includes many daily specials printed only in Chinese; ask your waiter to translate, and he'll try his best. The restaurant is noisy and chaotic and makes no attempt at glamour or sophistication. The focus is the food, and for good reason, as it rarely disappoints. Be sure to sample the shrimp toast, congee, and the in-house roasted pork and chicken dishes. ⌧ *7B Largo do Senado, Downtown, Macau* ☎ *853/573–970* ▭ *AE, DC, MC, V.*

$$ ✕ **456 Shanghai Restaurant.** Those looking for refined Shanghainese food served in a chic space usually head here, and often in big boisterous groups. On the mezzanine level of the Lisboa Casino, you join other cheerful gamblers as they dine on famous house specialties, including steamed crabs, Shanghai dumplings, and quite possibly the best Beijing Duck in Macau. Make reservations on weekends. ⌧ *Av. da Amizade, Hotel Lisboa, Downtown Peninsula, Macau* ☎ *853/388–474* ▭ *AE, DC, MC, V.*

$ ✕ **Fat Siu Lau.** Well known to both locals and Hong Kong visitors, Fat

FodorsChoice Siu Lau has kept its customers coming back for more than 100 years

★ with delicious Macanese favorites and modern creations. For best results, try ordering whatever you see the chatty Cantonese stuffing themselves with on the surrounding tables, and you won't be disappointed! It will probably be whole curry crab, grilled prawns in a butter garlic sauce, and the famous roasted pigeon marinated in a secret marinade. A newly opened Fat Siu Lau 2 is on Macau Lan Kwai Fong Street and offers the same great food. Reservations are strongly recommended. ⌧ *Rua da Felicidade, Downtown, Macau* ☎ *853/573–580* ▭ *AE, DC, MC, V.*

Eclectic

$$$ ✕ **Os Gatos.** The Portuguese name "Os Gatos" means "cats" and sitting on the sunny outdoor terrace of the Pousada de São Tiago, a 17th-century fortress overlooking the South China Sea, you do feel like a feline basking in the afternoon sun. The large brick terrace is shaded by several leafy trees while the air-conditioned interior has hand-carved furniture and painted tiles from Portugal. The mixed Mediterranean, Italian, and Macanese dishes on the menu are straightforward and enjoyable, though somewhat disappointing when compared with the beautiful setting. There are good versions of seafood paella, baked crab with saffron and sage, and chicken piri-piri but the best deal is the afternoon tea set beginning at 3 PM. A popular buffet lunch and dinner is served daily. ⊠ *Pousada de São Tiago, Av. da República, Inner Harbour, Macau* ☎ *853/968–686* ▭ *AE, DC, MC, V.*

$$ ✕ **888 Las Vegas Buffet.** This buffet
Fodor'sChoice   is a gluttonous feast worthy of its
★   name, with more than 330 feet of Chinese, Japanese, Italian, Thai, and other assorted food options.

LOVE OF VINHO

Wine lovers should take full advantage of Macau's intimate love of *vinho*. Some restaurants have wine lists as thick as phone books. Most places list at least a couple of bottles of delicious Portuguese wine—usually a hearty red from the Dão region or a slightly sparkling *vinho verde* from the north.

A cornucopia of fresh seafood, roasted meats, breads, fruits, juices, and cakes are typical staples. Save room for the mountain of dessert choices ranging from pies to tarts to puddings and if you have a desire to bathe everything in thick, rich chocolate fondue, there is a continuously flowing chocolate fountain. If you're really hungry, this is one of the best dining values in town, and with dozens of open kitchens continually churning out fresh, quality food on a rotating menu, you're sure to leave several pounds heavier than when you came in. ⊠ *203 Largo de Monte Carlo, 3rd fl. Sands Casino, Outer Harbour, Macau* ☎ *853/983–8222* ▭ *AE, DC, MC, V.*

French

$$$$ ✕ **Robuchon a Galera.** A slice of Paris in the heart of Macau, this restaurant on the third floor of the Hotel Lisboa is a must, particularly if you just hit it big in the casino. The ornately detailed interior is heavy on dark woods, gold detailing, and has a lighted Swarovski crystal star field on the ceiling, gently twinkling above the rich velvets. The food concentrates on the natural flavors of fresh ingredients; signature dishes are a heavenly mille-feuille of tomato and crabmeat, duck breast with turnips and foie gras, and lamb served with creamy potato puree. But Robuchon's multicourse tasting menus, with more than a dozen dishes, are the best way to experience the restaurants' gastronomic offerings. Finish with selections from the excellent cheese trolley or dig into a warm molten chocolate cake. The wine list is as thick as an encyclopedia and includes some rare wines. ⊠ *Av. da Amizade, Hotel Lisboa, Downtown Peninsula, Macau* ☎ *853/377–666* ⌳ *Reservations essential* ▭ *AE, DC, MC, V.*

Italian

$$$ ✕ **Mezzaluna.** Reminiscent of a warm, luxurious Tuscan villa overlook-
Fodor'sChoice   ing lush landscaped greenery, this restaurant is perfect for romantic din-
★   ners. Tables are arranged around an open kitchen, allowing you to watch your food being prepared. The consistently excellent menu includes pasta with oven-baked cherry-stone clams, a rich sea urchin risotto with fava beans and tomato comfit, and, for some power dining, a dish of fusilli with bottarga and shrimp in lobster sauce. The crisp

pizzas are a rare treat in Macau, and the hot coffee soufflé is simply delicious. ⊠ *956–1110 Av. da Amizade, Mandarin Oriental Hotel, Outer Harbour, Macau* ☎ *853/567–888* ⊟ *AE, DC, MC, V* ☉ *Closed Mon.*

$$ ✕ **Pizzeria Toscana.** Despite the utilitarian name and location in the middle of a ferry pier parking lot, this is considered one of the best Italian restaurants in Macau. The owners have roots in Pisa and have created a warm, rustic interior to match the menu of refined comfort food on the menu. The *bresaola involtini* (air-cured beef with shredded Parmesan) and fresh salmon carpaccio antipasti are a tasty way to begin your meal; then try the grilled king prawns, homemade tortellini, and, of course, the perfect wood-fired pizzas. And you can finish your meal with the best cappuccinos in town. ⊠ *Av. da Amizade, opposite Macau Ferry Terminal, Outer Harbour, Macau* ☎ *853/726–637* ⌔ *Reservations essential* ⊟ *AE, DC, MC, V.*

Macanese

$$$ ✕ **Flamingo.** In a hot pink colonial-style building, with its lazy ceiling fans and palm trees, this restaurant has a wonderful setting for the Macanese and Mediterranean cuisine served here. Alfresco dining is a joy, with tables overlooking lush landscaped gardens and a duck pond, perhaps to remind you of the delicious signature dish: braised duck with thickened duck blood? Perhaps, but the rotating menu's best value lies in the mouthwatering seafood dishes, particularly stuffed crab, Macau sole, and spicy king prawns. Flamingo stands out in a crowded playing field with a strong combination of great food and attentive service. Reserve a table on weekends. ⊠ *2 Estrada de Almirante Joaquim Marques Esparteiro, Hyatt Regency Hotel, Taipa Island North* ☎ *853/831-2-34* ⊟ *AE, DC, MC, V.*

$$ ✕ **Litoral.** One of the most popular local restaurants, Litoral serves authentic Macanese dishes that are simple, straightforward, and deliciously satisfying. Tastefully decorated with whitewashed walls and dark-wood beams, must-try dishes include the tamarind pork with shrimp paste as well as codfish baked with potato and garlic and a creamy Portuguese green soup. For dessert, try the *bebinca de leite,* a coconut-milk custard, or the traditional egg pudding, *pudim abade de priscos.* You should make reservations if you're planning a weekend meal. ⊠ *261 Rua do Almirante Sergio, Inner Harbour, Macau* ☎ *853/967–878* ⊟ *AE, DC, MC, V.*

$$ ✕ **O Porto Interior.** Government officials and celebrities are often spotted here having quiet celebrations and enjoying the beautifully presented upmarket Macanese dishes and the daily set menu, which is one of the best deals in town. Come here for traditional Portuguese food that relies on meats, seafood, and heavy sauces, with excellent renditions of grilled prawns, African chicken, and various curries. It's the design, however, that makes the place so special, with an elegant two-story facade, brilliant white colonnades, and azulejo-tile Iberian arches complemented by marble steps and bridges. Minutes from the A-Ma temple and Maritime Museum, this is a great lunch or dinner spot after sightseeing. Reservations are a good idea on weekends. ⊠ *259B Rua do Almirante Sergio, Inner Harbour, Macau* ☎ *853/967–770* ⊟ *AE, DC, MC, V.*

8

$ ✕ **Sol Nascente.** This modest restaurant on the main road at the entrance to Taipa Village has proved a real winner, with a creative menu that has a modern take on Macanese food. It's simply furnished, but you don't need fancy surroundings to enjoy the succulent clams in coriander sauce or mussels stuffed with bread crumbs, spring onions, and garlic. Hearty main dishes include a thick Goan prawn curry, beef rice with chestnuts, and elegant desserts. The food and wine are relatively cheap, so this might be just the place to eat and drink the day away. ✉ *Edificio Chun Leong Garden, G/F, Av. Dr. Sun Yat-sen, Taipa Island South* ☎ *853/836–288* ▭ *AE, DC, MC, V.*

Portuguese

$$$$ ✕ **Restaurante Perola.** With its brilliant turquoise tiles, ironwork chandeliers, and dark wood, the sophisticated Perola evokes the seafaring heritage of Portugal and Macau. The emphasis is on the freshest seafood, and there are numerous imported Portuguese ingredients in the dishes. Here you can try an excellent *cataplana,* a savory stew of fish, shellfish, and pork served in a gleaming copper pot, as well as a tangy, juicy African chicken. Rich coffees and wines complement the sublime desserts, including Portuguese *serradura* (a layered dessert of cream and biscuits). ✉ *203 Largo de Monte Carlo, 3rd fl. Sands Casino, Outer Harbour, Macau* ☎ *853/883–377* ▭ *AE, DC, MC, V* ☽ *Closed Mon.*

$$$ ✕ **Clube Militar de Macau (The Macau Military Club).** Founded in 1870 as a private military club, the stately pink-and-white structure was restored in 1994 and reopened as a restaurant. The languid old-world atmosphere perfectly complements the extensive list of traditional Portuguese dishes offered, some of which aren't available anywhere else in Macau. Partridge pie, cold stuffed crab, *Bacalhau Dourado à Elvas* (a codfish specialty), and BBQ veal cutlets in a lemon-butter sauce are some outstanding choices among a strong menu. A Portuguese dessert platter and coffee are on offer after your meal. ✉ *975 Av. da Praia Grande, Downtown, Macau* ☎ *853/714–000* ▭ *AE, DC, MC, V.*

$$ ✕ **A Lorcha.** Vastly popular A Lorcha (the name means "wooden ship")
Fodor'sChoice celebrates the heritage of Macau as an important port with a maritime
★ theme for the menu. Don't miss the signature dish, Clams Lorcha Style, with tomato, beer, and garlic. Other classics include *feijoada* (pork and bean stew), steamed crab, and perfectly smoky and juicy fire-roasted chicken. Remember to save room for the excellent Portuguese desserts, such as thick mango pudding and sinfully dense serradura. Perfect for lunch or dinner after sightseeing at A-Ma Temple and the Maritime Museum next door. ✉ *289 Rua do Almirante Sergio, Inner Harbour, Macau* ☎ *853/313–195* ⚞ *Reservations essential* ▭ *AE, DC, MC, V* ☽ *Closed Tues.*

$$ ✕ **Fernando's.** Everyone in Hong Kong and Macau knows about Fer-
Fodor'sChoice nando's, but the vine-covered entrance close to Hàc-Sà Beach is diffi-
★ cult to spot. The open-air dining pavilion and bar have attracted beachgoers for years now and the enterprising Fernando has built a legendary reputation for his tiny Portuguese restaurant. The Portuguese menu focuses on seafood paired with homegrown vegetables and diners choose from among the actual bottles of Portuguese reds on display instead of a wine list. The informal nature of the restaurant fits in with the satis-

fying, home-style food such as grilled fish, baked chicken, and huge bowlfuls of spicy clams, all eaten with your fingers and washed down with crisp vinho verde (Portuguese green wine). And you'll be sweating as you eat since Fernando infamously has no air-conditioning. ☒ *9 Hàc-Sà Beach, Coloane Island South* ☏ *853/882–531* ☖ *Reservations not accepted* ▭ *No credit cards.*

$ ✕ **Afonso III.** After several years at the Hyatt Regency, Chef Afonso Carrao decided to open his own place and cook the way his grandmother did. The result is his modest café in the heart of downtown near Senado Square, with an intimate space downstairs with dark wood and stucco, and a more expansive upstairs. The food consists of simple, hearty, traditional dishes served in huge portions mostly to Portuguese expatriates and Macanese locals. Favorites include Afonso's Colido a Portuguesa (a tangy mix of meats and vegetables) and the thick vegetable soups, but your best bets are the daily specials, which invariably include *bacalhau* (Portuguese salted codfish), braised pork, or beef stew probably better than any other you'll taste in Macau. The wine list is extensive and comes in generous goblets or by the bottle. ☒ *11A Rua Central, Downtown, Macau* ☏ *853/586–272* ▭ *No credit cards* ☼ *Closed Sun.*

$ ✕ **Praia Grande.** The Praia Grande once had the best view of Macau's harbor but now sadly, just faces reclaimed land. Nevertheless, this classic Portuguese restaurant retains its Mediterranean beauty inside and outside, with a gleaming white facade opening into a dining room with graceful arches, terra-cotta floors, and wrought-iron furniture. The menu is creative, with dishes ranging from Portuguese dim sum, African chicken (in a peppery coconut broth), mussels in white wine, and pork and clams *cataplana* (in a stew of onions, tomatoes, and wine). The outdoor esplanade, with a serving kiosk and numerous umbrella-shaded tables, is ideal for alfresco dining and afternoon drinks. ☒ *10A Lobo d'Avila, Av. da Praia Grande, Downtown, Macau* ☏ *853/973–022* ▭ *AE, DC, MC, V.*

$ ✕ **Restaurante Espaco Lisboa.** A favorite among local Portuguese, this restaurant is in a converted two-story house with a small but pleasant outdoor balcony for alfresco dining overlooking the Coloane Village. Chef and owner Antonio Neves Coelho is often available to make recommendations, and prepares feasts that include savory Portuguese duck rice, boiled bacalhau with cabbage, and paper-thin slices of sweet, smoky pork cut imported

---

A COLONIAL FEAST

After centuries of Portuguese rule, it's not surprising that the Macanese like hearty Portuguese fare. Most restaurants serve the beloved *bacalhau* (salt cod) baked, boiled, grilled, deep-fried with potato, or stewed with onion, garlic, and eggs. Other common dishes include sardines, sausages, and soups such as *caldo verde* (vegetable soup). Giant prawns in a curry sauce recall the cuisine of Goa, India—another Portuguese colony. Indeed there are dishes drawn from throughout the colonial empire, including Brazilian *feijoada* (a stew of beans, pork, and vegetables) and Mozambique chicken, baked or grilled and seasoned with piri-piri chili, tangy spices, and coconut.

8

---

from Portugal. Finish the meal with homemade mango ice cream with a cherry flambé. There's an extensive wine list, with a focus on hearty Portuguese wines, which work in beautiful concert with the rich flavors of Antonio's home cooking. ⊠ *18 Rua das Gaivotas, Coloane Island West* 🕾 *853/882–226* 🖃 *AE, DC, MC, V.*

Steak

$$$$ ✕ **Copa Steakhouse.** The first traditional American steak house in
Fodor'sChoice Macau, the Copa has a selection of premium quality steaks and seafood,
★ along with a range of cigars and cocktails in an interior that looks like 1960s Las Vegas. A large fireplace pops and crackles during the winter months and blends in perfectly with the vintage chandeliers and celebrity photos hanging on the walls. Sip a cocktail at the bar near the grand piano, and get ready for your huge slabs of the beef, grilled to juicy perfection before your eyes in the open kitchen. Other dishes include sautéed sea scallops with crispy vegetable sushi, and for dessert, a sinfully rich crème brûlée. ⊠ *Sands Casino, 203 Largo de Monte Carlo, Outer Harbour, Macau* 🕾 *853/883–377* 🖃 *AE, DC, MC, V* ☯ *Closed Sun. No lunch.*

Thai

$$$ ✕ **Naam.** The Mandarin Oriental's Thai restaurant is set amid the hotel's landscaped tropical gardens. Start your meal off with a refreshing *yam som-o* (herbed pomelo salad with chicken and prawns) or aromatic *tom kha gai* (herbed coconut soup with chicken). Then move on to main courses like fried lobster with sweet basil and young peppercorns and the traditional favorite *moo phad bai ga praow* (spicy pork with chilies and hot basil leaves). For dessert, there's a melt-in-your-mouth *kluey thod krub bai toey* (deep-fried banana with pandanus sauce), or a sweet, chilled coconut custard in baby pumpkins. It's a popular lunch spot for local casino managers, and a hot ticket at dinnertime, so be sure to make reservations. ⊠ *Mandarin Oriental Hotel, 956–1110 Av. da Amizade, Outer Harbour, Macau* 🕾 *853/793–4818* ⌦ *Reservations essential* 🖃 *AE, DC, MC, V.*

WHERE TO STAY

Macau's primary industry is tourism and specifically the heavy weekend flow of tourists and gamblers from Hong Kong, Taiwan, China, and other parts of Asia and the Pacific Rim. In turn, this has led to many luxurious accommodations in a wide range of hotels, with spas, and restaurants to complement the glamour and excitement of the casinos. But although many luxury hotels cater to high-end travel, Macau also has hotels for travelers on a budget.

Higher-cost hotels often come with landscaped swimming pools, luxury spa and massage facilities, meeting rooms, fine restaurants, and guest rooms with deluxe beds and huge bathrooms. But you don't have to pay top dollar for many other places that have efficient service and comfortable accommodations, with air-conditioning, TVs, and good-size bathrooms. These are the most popular among those who come to gamble, as well as regular Hong Kong visitors, and budget tour groups. Note that in some of the lowest-priced hotels, staff speak limited English, so be patient. Some hotels may also have shared bathroom facilities.

For a true Macau experience, try staying in *pousadas,* which are state-owned historical buildings that have been restored and converted into hotel accommodations. You can sleep in a hand-carved mahogany bed in a former Portuguese fort and wake up to watch the sun rising on the South China sea, just as missionaries did in the past. The quality and price of a pousada can vary quite a bit, and advanced reservations are necessary as they all have very limited occupancy.

For both hotels and pousadas, bear in mind that Macau's heavy weekend traffic means that there are two distinct markets: weekday, from Monday to Thursday, and the popular weekend period. You can save up to 50% off the published rate if you book a room during the week. Call your hotel and ask about weekday deals and discounts.

WHAT IT COSTS In Patacas				
$$$$	**$$$**	**$$**	**$**	**¢**
FOR 2 PEOPLE Over $1,500	$1,000–1,500	$800–1,000	$300–800	Under $300

Prices are for two people in a standard double room on a typical Saturday night, not including 10% service charge and 5% tax.

Macau

★ **$$$$** 🏨 **Mandarin Oriental.** The Mandarin Oriental is synonymous with elegance and understated opulence, and its Macau location doesn't disappoint. This hotel is also widely known for deluxe treatments in the enormous spa complex next to the gorgeous, tropical swimming pool on the landscaped grounds. You'll feel like you're in a lush rain forest as you look out from the traditional Mediterranean architecture of the hotel. The hotel's restaurants and bars include the Bela Vista Bar, the intimate Mandarin Oriental Casino, and Naam Thai, the exquisite Thai restaurant popular with locals and visitors alike. ⊠ *956–1110 Av. da Amizade, Outer Harbour* ☎ *853/567–888, 2881–1988 in Hong Kong, 800/526–6566 in U.S.* ⊕ *www.mandarinoriental.com* ⌁ *407 rooms, 28 suites* ♿ *4 restaurants, café, room service, in-room safes, minibars, refrigerators, cable TV with movies, in-room data ports, 2 tennis courts, 2 pools, gym, hot tubs (indoor and outdoor), massage, sauna, spa, squash, bar, casino, children's programs (ages 3–12), dry cleaning, laundry service, business services, meeting rooms* ▭ *AE, DC, MC, V.*

★ **$$$$** 🏨 **Pousada de São Tiago.** The spirit of the structure's past life as a 17th-century fortress permeates every part of this romantic and charming lodging, making it an ideal location for a honeymoon or two. Your first sight is the front entrance, an ascending stone tunnel carved into the mountainside with water seeping through in quiet trickles, just as it has done for centuries. The location's namesake comes from a small chapel dedicated to São Tiago, the patron saint of the Portuguese army. Each room has imported Portuguese furniture and a careful balance between modern luxury and Portuguese charm. Note, though, that the service can be slow. The restaurant O Gatos has traditional Portuguese

CLOSE UP

Luxury Spas

MACAU IS WELL KNOWN FOR its casinos and restaurants, but it's also rapidly gaining a reputation for its luxury spa and sauna facilities, offering a huge range of treatments. Almost every luxury hotel has its own spa, with special packages and offers for hotel guests. Many visitors opt for spa treatments at luxury hotels, but Macau's independent spas have become a major force in recent years, offering equally exquisite service at lower prices than hotels. All spas offer services for couples, and provide a great opportunity to relax in a peaceful space with someone special.

Treatments begin at around MOP$700 and up for 90 minutes of service, and the following are some of the more impressive spa facilities available:

SPA PHILOSOPHY
This Chinese-theme spa treatment center has pollution-free, oxygenated air pumped throughout the complex and guests are offered a variety of treatments, including a Godiva chocolate skin nourishing program. ⊠ *Unit C D, 327–331 Av. Xian Xing Hai Nam On Garden, Outer Harbour,*

Macau ☎ *853/728–330* ⊕ *www. spaphilosophy.com.*

THE SPA AT THE MANDARIN ORIENTAL MACAU
The largest and most well-known spa in town takes advantage of the Mandarin's sumptuous Mediterranean architecture and lets in lots of natural sunlight for a bright and airy spa experience. More than 30 Chinese, European, Thai, and Japanese treatments are available, along with a separate boutique that sells the spa's beauty and skincare products. Reservations are essential. ⊠ *Mandarin Oriental Macau Hotel, 956–1110 Av. da Amizade, Outer Harbour, Macau* ☎ *853/728–330* ⊕ *www.spaphilosophy.com.*

NIRVANA SPA
The Nirvana has rooms decorated in Chinese, Thai, Balinese, and various other eastern themes. It has a variety of traditional massages available, as well as some more modern treatments. ⊠ *403 Av. da Praia Grande, G/F China Law Bldg., Downtown, Macau* ☎ *853/331–521.*

cuisine and an outdoor barbeque for grilled meats and vegetables in the summer. Sip an unforgettable cocktail on Cafe da Barra's terrace as the sun sets, painting the ocean waters a warm orange. ⊠ *Av. da República, Inner Harbour* ☎ *853/378–111, 2739–1216 in Hong Kong* ⊕ *www.saotiago.com.mo* 🖙 *20 rooms, 4 suites* ⚐ *Restaurant, room service, minibars, cable TV, pool, bar, dry cleaning, laundry service* ⊟ *AE, DC, MC, V.*

★ **$$$$** 🏨 **Sands Macau.** Casino tycoon Sheldon Anderson's first venture in Macau, the Sands is nothing if not luxurious. Spacious rooms have deep, soft carpets, comfortable, large beds, and huge marble bathrooms, and you get efficient, professional service from the smartly dressed staff, all of whom speak excellent English. You can opt for one of the 51 luxury suites, ranging in size from 1,000 to 8,000 square feet, with in-room hot tubs, a massage table for in-room service, karaoke rooms, plasma TVs, remote-control drapes and lighting, plus personal butler service to keep it all running smoothly. "VIP" guests also get high-limit gaming rooms, access to private limousines, jets, helicopters, and jetfoil service so they can travel in style. Dining options include the Copa Steakhouse and the large casino bar in the center of the main gaming room, where live bands perform nightly. ⊠ *Largo de Monte Carlo 203, Outer Harbour* ☎ *853/ 883–388* ⊕ *www.sands.com.mo* ⬥ *407 rooms, 28 suites* ⚮ *7 restaurants, room service, in-room safes, minibars, cable TV with movies, in-room broadband, tennis courts, 2 public pools plus private plunge pools, gyms, spa, sauna, squash, bar, casino, dry cleaning, laundry service, business services, meeting rooms* ▤ *AE, DC, MC, V.*

$$$ ▦ **Hotel Lisboa.** Macau's infamous landmark, with its distinctive, slightly bizarre architecture, rumored connections to organized crime, open prostitution, and no-limit VIP rooms, is in the heart of downtown Macau. No expense is spared, with plush custom-made carpets, luxurious beds, beautifully tiled bathrooms with Hermès toiletries, and hot tubs in every room. The lobby is a bit gaudy and ostentatious but always interesting because of the art on display from owner Dr. Stanley Ho's private collection. The multifloor casino remains one of the biggest in Macau, and the VIP rooms are legendary. But the Lisboa has more than just gambling, with high-end shopping arcades, extensive dining options, including the best French and Japanese restaurants in town, deluxe spa facilities, and a huge outdoor heated pool. ⊠ *Av. da Amizade, Downtown Peninsula* ☎ *853/577–666, 2559–1028, 800/969–130 in Hong Kong* ⊕ *www.hotelisboa.com* ⬥ *1,000 rooms, 100 suites* ⚮ *18 restaurants, room service, in-room safes, minibars, cable TV with movies, in-room broadband, tennis courts, gym, central pool, spa, sauna, squash, bar, casino, dry cleaning, laundry service, business services, meeting room* ▤ *AE, DC, MC, V.*

★ **$$** ▦ **Hotel Sintra.** Minutes from the Lisboa and Senado Square, the Hotel Sintra has carpeted rooms with soothing brown-and-cream color schemes and comfortable beds. The staff is smartly dressed and helpful, though their English can be inconsistent. Breakfast is a buffet spread that includes steamed breads, noodles and rice instead of traditional Western breakfast entrees. Facilities include a shopping arcade, and there are free shuttle buses from the Macau Ferry Terminal. ⊠ *Av. De D. Joao IV, Downtown Peninsula* ☎ *853/ 710–111* ⊕ *www.hotelsintra.com* ⬥ *112 rooms, 2 suites* ⚮ *4 restaurants, bar, room service, in-room safes, minibars, cable TV, sauna, shopping arcade, laundry service, banquet and conference facilities, shuttle bus* ▤ *AE, DC, MC, V.*

MACAU GOLF & COUNTRY CLUB

Unless you become a member, the only way to play a round of golf at the **Macau Golf & Country Club** is to stay at the Westin. The beautiful 18-hole, PGA Tour–level course has breathtaking sea views from atop a plateau. For more information, ⇨ Chapter 10, Golf. ⊠ *Westin, Resort, 1918 Estrada de Hàc-Sà, Coloane Island South* ☎ *853/871– 188* ⬥ *Greens fees: MOP$722 weekdays, MOP$1,444 weekends* ☉ *Daily 7 AM, call for tee times.*

8

$$ 🏨 **Kingsway Hotel.** In-room broadband and cable TV with movies make this moderately priced hotel on the Outer Harbour popular with Asian tour groups. The hotel's casino caters mostly to couples and groups on gambling-tour packages from Southeast Asia and the Philippines. ✉ *Rua Luis Gonzaga Gomes, Outer Harbour* ☎ *853/702–888, 2548–0989 in Hong Kong* ⊕ *www.hotelkingsway.com.mo* ⤵ *410 rooms* ⚭ *2 restaurants, minibars, cable TV with movies, sauna, casino* ▭ *AE, DC, MC, V.*

★ **$**   🏨 **Metropole Hotel.** The Metropole is the ideal hotel for budget travelers who don't mind no-frills accommodations in exchange for one of the best locations in the city. Minutes away from all of Macau's major casinos, shopping, and sightseeing, the Metropole provides friendly staff to compensate for minimalist guest rooms, a meager breakfast, and not many guest amenities apart from the free shuttle bus from the Macau Ferry Terminal. ✉ *Av. de Praia Grande 493–501, Downtown* ☎ *853/388–166* ⊕ *www.mctshmi.com* ⤵ *112 rooms, 2 suites* ⚭ *2 restaurants, room service, in-room safes, minibars, cable TV, laundry service, shuttle bus* ▭ *AE, DC, MC, V.*

Coloane

$$$$ 🏨 **Westin Resort.** Built into the side of a cliff, the Westin is surrounded
Fodor's Choice   by the black sands of Hàc-Sà Beach and lapping waves of the South China
★   Sea; this is where you truly get away from it all. Every room faces the ocean; the place glows as much because of the sunny tropical color scheme as because of the sunshine. The vast private terraces are ideal for alfresco dining and naps in the afternoon sun. Guests also receive access to Macau's only golf club, the PGA-standard, 18-hole Macau Golf and Country, which was built on the rocky cliffs and plateaus above the hotel. ✉ *Hàc-Sà Beach, Coloane Island South* ☎ *853/871–111 or 2803–2002, 800/228–3000 in Hong Kong* ⊕ *www.westin-macau.com* ⤵ *200 rooms, 8 suites* ⚭ *4 restaurants, room service, in-room safes, minibars, cable TV with movies, in-room data ports, driving range, 18-hole golf course, miniature golf, 8 tennis courts, 2 pools (1 indoor), health club, hot tubs (indoor and outdoor), massage, bicycles, badminton, squash, 2 bars, shops, babysitting, business services, meeting rooms, car rental, no-smoking rooms* ▭ *AE, DC, MC, V.*

★ **$$$$**   🏨 **Pousada de Coloane.** At Cheoc-Van Beach at the most southern tip of Coloane Island, Pousada de Coloane offers a quiet, natural setting, nestled within the lush hills and mountains of Macau's south. There are ample opportunities for kayaking, hiking, and swimming. A long winding path paved with Portuguese azulejo tiles leads you to the spacious terrace overlooking the beach and is ideal for outdoor wedding receptions and other celebrations. Facilities include a small pool, a comfortable fireplace, and a small bar in the restaurant. The Terrace restaurant offers traditional Portuguese, Macanese, and Chinese favorites cooked in a heavy, homestyle tradition served in generous portions to ensure you are full, but flavors can be bland. There are seafood restaurants down on the beach that you might consider trying instead. All 30 rooms have private double hot tubs, satellite TV, and balconies overlooking the beach, with the mountains of Mainland China in the distance. ✉ *Cheoc Van Beach, Coloane Island South* ☎ *853/882–143* ⊕ *www.hotelpcoloane.*

com.mo ⬦ *30 rooms, 10 suites* ⬦ *Restaurant, room service, minibars, cable TV, pool, bar, dry cleaning, laundry service, Internet room* ⊟ *AE, DC, MC, V.*

Taipa

★ **$$–$$$** 🏨 **Best Western Hotel Taipa.** In the heart of Taipa, the Best Western is a 10-minute taxi ride from the airport, and about the same distance from downtown Macau. The yellow facade is classic Portuguese design and marks the front entrance to the hotel where you'll pay relatively moderate prices for rooms that are comfortable, without any luxurious bells and whistles. The Restaurante Grande and Bar Grande are serviceable, but the Rua da Cunha, known as Souvenir and Food Street, offers a range of interesting local foods, snacks, and handicrafts and is less than a 10-minute walk away. The weekend Taipa Flea Market is also held near the Rua da Cunha. There's a free shuttle from the Macau Ferry Terminal. ⬦ *Estrada Governador Nobre Carvalho 822, Taipa Island North* ☎ *853/821–666* ⊕ *www.hoteltaipa.com* ⬦ *262 rooms* ⬦ *3 restaurants, bar, room service, in-room safes, minibars, cable TV, pool, gym, laundry service, dry cleaning, shuttle bus* ⊟ *AE, DC, MC, V.*

NIGHTLIFE

Old movies, countless novels, and gossip through the years have portrayed Macau's nightlife as a combustible mix of drugs, wild gambling, violent crime, and ladies of the night. Up until the 1999 handover back to mainland China, this image of Macau was mostly accurate and worked to drive away increasingly higher numbers of tourists.

Outside of the casinos and a few restaurants, today's Macau shuts down after 11 PM. You can slip into any dark, elegant lounge bar inside the larger hotels, and enjoy live music and expensive cocktails, but don't expect much energy or big crowds. And most late-night saunas are glorified brothels, with "workers" from China, Vietnam, Thailand, and Russia.

Nightclubs & Pubs

Macau's Lan Kwai Fong (⊠ Av. Dr. Sun Yat-Sen, Edificio Vista Magnifica Court, Outer Harbour) refers to a small collection of bars along a small stretch of street in the New Reclamation Area, within sight of the huge golden Guan Yin statue in Macau's harbor. Although it takes its name from the legendary bar area in Hong Kong, in reality, it's a bunch of nice, quiet bars to meet with friends or watch sports on a big-screen TV. A large number of expats come to this area to relax and drink in the evenings, but don't expect the wild times and thumping music you might find in the original LKF in Hong Kong. Go the way locals do and just hop into a cab and tell him "Lan Kwai Fong" and you'll be there in 10 minutes or less, no matter where you are in Macau.

Celluloid is the theme at the aptly named **Casablanca** (⊠ Ave. Dr. Sun Yat Sen, Outer Harbour ☎ 853/751–281), where posters pay homage to Marcello Mastroianni and Hong Kong director Wong Kar Wai. The opulent interior is not too dark, lined with plush red velvet curtains, and usually has a classic film playing soundlessly in the background.

The Embassy (✉ Mandarin Oriental, 956–1110 Av. da Amizade, Outer Harbour ☎ 567–888) bar is reminiscent of foreign correspondent clubs around the world. Portraits of ex–consuls general and indigenous souvenirs from far-flung countries abroad hang somberly on the walls while the quiet, upscale cliente drink expensive cocktails.

For live music spanning Latin American, jazz, and pop music styles, head to the **Green Spot** (✉ Emperor Hotel, Rue de Xangai, Downtown ☎ 853/788–666 or 781–888). The spacious mint-color lounge was opened by popular Hong Kong singer and Macau native Maria Cordeiro. She also owns the Green Spot in Hong Kong. Reservations are recommended for a table on weekends.

The Thirsty Gambler (✉ Fisherman's Wharf, Outer Harbour ☎ 853/972–878), is a spacious, traditional pub that evokes Dublin in the middle of Macau. On tap is Guinness and there are good renditions of traditional pub fare like ribs, wings, burgers, and fries.

SHOPPING

Macau, like Hong Kong, is a free port for most items, which leads to lower prices for electronics, jewelry, and clothing than other international cities. But coming from Hong Kong's intense shopping utopia, Macau seems like a poor country cousin. Currently, there are no Hong Kong–style megamalls here at all, and so shopping in Macau is a completely different experience, with a low-key atmosphere, small crowds, and compact areas. Commercial rents are not in the stratosphere as is the case in most Hong Kong shopping districts, so retail shops have had a longer history and look older. Sales staff aren't as pushy and persistent as in Hong Kong; their command of English isn't as good either.

Most of Macau's shops operate year-round with a short break in late January for Chinese New Year. Opening hours vary according to the type of shop, but most retail stores are open from 10 AM to 8 PM and later on weekends. Macau's major shopping district is along its main street, Avenida Almeida Ribeiro (more commonly known by its Chinese name, San Ma Lo); there are also shops in Mercadores and its side streets; in Cinco de Outubro; and the Rua do Campo. Shop names reflect Macau's Portuguese heritage, as in Pastelarias Mei Mun (Mei's Pastries), Relojoaria Tat On (Tat's Watches and Clocks), and Sapatarias João Leong (Leong's Shoes). For the best selection of traditional Chinese furniture, scroll paintings, porcelain, figurines, fans, silk robes, and lacquer ware, search the area around the ruins of St. Paul's, particularly Rua do São Antonio and Rua de São Paulo.

Macau also has its share of phony antiques, fake name-brand watches, and other rip-offs, so buyer beware: these "gray items" have no return or warranty policies. Shop around and compare prices. Get receipts and signed warranties for expensive items. Most shops accept all major credit cards, though specialty discount shops usually ask for cash. For most street vendors and some smaller stores, some friendly bargaining is expected; you should ask for the "best price," which ideally produces instant discounts of 10%–20%. The shopping mantra here, and in most of China, is "bargain hard, bargain often."

Department Stores

Originally a Japanese-owned department store, this failing shop was taken over by Stanley Ho's (who else?) and transformed into the most popular shopping destination for locals. Right next to the New Macau Maritime Ferry Terminal and the Jai Alai Casino, the **New Yaohan** (⊠ Av. de Amizade 1579, Outer Harbour) still calls itself "Macau's only department store" and has a good mix of shops selling household goods, clothing, jewelry, and beauty. There are also nice touches like on-site shoe repair centers, an extensive food court, a well-stocked grocery store, and popular bakery on the first floor. There's a major relocation scheduled for 2007 to make way for the construction of another Stanley Ho project, which will create one of the world's largest casino, hotel, and shopping complexes on New Yohan's current location.

The Grand Canal Shoppes (⊠ Av. Xian Xing Hai, Cotai Strip) is a jaw-dropping casino designed to look like Venice. It's an entire artificial city of 1,000,000 square feet, complete with cobblestone walkways, arched bridges, and working waterway canals manned by singing gondoliers. There are painstaking re-creations of Venice's treasures, and a generally festive atmosphere. And, of course, the shopping options are almost endless, with more than 350 retail shops, 20 restaurants, luxury spas, and an external lagoon capable of holding 10 blue whales. The Las Vegas Sands Corp., which manages the Grand Canal Shoppes, has taken no shortcuts with the shops either, signing exclusive boutiques and a mix of the biggest designer labels, such as LV, Gucci, and Prada, along with distinguished regional retailers.

Specialty Shops

Antiques & Traditional Crafts

It was said that in Old Macau, you could occasionally find treasures from the Ming dynasty buried among the bowls, carvings, and other old crafts in the island's many antiques shops. Those days are long gone but Macau continues to be a thriving hub for traditional Chinese arts, crafts, and even antiques and good reproductions. Try to get a professional appraisal before buying antiques, though, as Macau is famous for high-quality reproductions of Qing and Ming Dynasties. You can even see craftspeople at work making the new "antiques," particularly on the side streets of Tercena and Estalagens and the alleyways in front of the Ruins of St. Paul. Commonly sold pieces include lacquer screens, Chinese pottery, and huge wooden chests carved from solid mahogany, camphor wood, and redwood.

Asian Artifacts (✉ 25 Rua dos Negociantes, Coloane ☎ 881–022) specializes in detailed restorations of authentic antiques. Every piece features before and after pictures, a personal history, and a story from the friendly American owner. **Hong Hap** (✉ 170 Cinco de Outubro,) is a small, intimate shop where the owner, a font of information in Chinese and English, is involved with every piece on display. **Wing Tai** (✉ 1A Av. Almeida Ribeiro), a large, well-established antiques dealer in the heart of downtown, gives visitors a convenient introduction to Macau's variety of antique styles. A general rule of thumb when purchasing antiques is to bargain hard and bargain soft, and then bargain again.

Clothing & Accessories

Many clothing shops offer low and discounted prices on seasonal clothing for men, women, and children just like you would find in Hong Kong. The best bargains are found in off-season clothing, athletic shoes, and factory overruns. There's the usual assortment of fake brand-name clothing sold in street stalls, but the majority of these clothes can be found in larger discount stores and tend to be genuine overruns and dead stock from major labels such as Esprit, Banana Republic, Abercrombie & Fitch, GAP, and others. Major shopping areas include the small shops on Rua do Campoand around Mercadores. There are also bustling street markets that sell clothes on São Domingos (off Largo do Senado), Rua Cinco de Outubro, and Rua da Palha. Credit cards are accepted at most shops but street stalls only accept cash.

Jewelry shops—most directly across from casinos in the downtown area—sell luxury watches, pendants, and rings, some of which have been pawned by desperate gamblers. Prices are generally more reasonable than Hong Kong, and premiums for workmanship are much lower, so you can often find more affordable finished pieces. The price of the gold fluctuates with trading on the Hong Kong Gold Exchange, and each store will have an electronic display showing the current price of gold per *tael,* which is 1.2 troy ounces. Most Asian buyers prefer 24K gold and most shops prominently display 24K coins, bars, and crafts in their windows. Trusted Hong Kong stalwarts Chow Tai Fook and Chow Sang Sang have locations throughout Macau and are known for transparent pricing and knowledgeable staff with good English-language abilities, which is rare in small independent shops.

Wine

In tandem with rich, hearty Portuguese cooking, Macanese have also adopted a love for wine, and little-known Portuguese wines in particular. Wines from all over the world are readily available. The basement wine cellar at **Pavilions** (✉ 417–425 Avenida da Praia Grande, Downtown ☎ 853/374–026) has a wide and varied selection, especially from Portugal, France, and Chile. Although Hong Kong customs allows only one bottle per passenger, they don't vigorously enforce this rule, especially if you're discreet. Customs allows only one bottle of wine per passenger entering Hong Kong, but Pavilions will ship, a service that's only truly worthwhile for rare and expensive purchases.

MACAU ESSENTIALS

Transportation

For information on travel between Hong Kong and Macau, ⇨ the Macau Planner, at the start of the chapter.

AIR TRAVEL

The Macau International Airport is a 15-minute taxi ride from downtown.
Macau International Airport ☎ 853/861-111 for airport information, 853/396-5555 for Air Macau reservations ⊕ www.macau-airport.gov.mo.

BUS TRAVEL

Public buses are clean and affordable; trips to anywhere in the main peninsula cost MOP$2.50, service to Taipa Island is MOP$3.30, and service to Coloane and the airport is MOP$5. Buses require exact change upon boarding and detailed bus schedules are posted at all stops, though they are in Chinese and Portuguese only. Also available are replicas of 1920s London buses known as Tour Machines. They can be found at the Macau Ferry Terminal and the cost of one chartered bus for a party of up to nine people goes for MOP$300–MOP$380 per hour, depending on the time of day.

CAR RENTALS Avis Car Rental is the only choice in town for traditional car rentals. Cars go for MOP$450 to MOP$600 on weekdays and MOP$500 to MOP$650 on weekends. Book in advance for a discount, but as always, you must ask for it. Avis also has 15% discounts for selected frequent-flyer programs.

You can also rent *mokes,* motor vehicles that look like a jeep crossed with a British taxi. They're fun to drive and ideal for touring. Rates are MOP$350 for 24 hours, plus a whopping MOP$3,000 deposit but thankfully credit cards are accepted. The price includes third-party insurance, and the helpful staff will often give a discount if asked. Hotel packages also include special moke-rental deals and you can contact Happy Mokes for additional details.
Avis Rent A Car ☎ 853/336-789 in Macau, 2576-6831 in Hong Kong ⊕ www.avis. com. **Happy Mokes** ☎ 2523-5690 in Hong Kong, 853/831-212, 853/439-393 in Macau.

CAR TRAVEL

In contrast to Hong Kong's British system of driving on the left-hand side of the road, Macau has a system similar to the United States of driving on the right-hand side of the road. Add to this the fact that road signs are in Chinese and Portuguese only, and you have a recipe for very frustrated English speakers. Common sense and careful driving will help you get around most problems though. International driver's licenses are accepted in Macau.

PEDICABS

Tricycle-drawn two-seater carriages have been in business as long as Macau has had bicycles and paved roads. They cluster at the ferry ter-

8

minal and near hotels around town, their drivers hustling for customers and usually offering to serve as guides. It used to be a pleasure to hire a pedicab, but heavy traffic and construction projects detract from the experience. Macau's city center is not a congenial place for pedicabs, and the hilly districts are impossible. If you take one, you'll have to haggle; don't pay more than HK$30 for a trip to a nearby hotel.

TAXIS

Taxis are inexpensive and plentiful in Macau and the small geographic size of the region makes taxi rides an affordable luxury. The black cabs with cream-color roofs can be flagged on the street and the yellow cabs are radio taxis, which can be arranged through your hotel's concierge. All are metered, air-conditioned, and reasonably comfortable. Drivers often don't speak or read much English, so you should carry a bilingual map or name card for your destination in Chinese. The base charge is MOP$10 for the first 1¾ km (about 1¼ mi) and MOP$1 per additional 800 feet. Drivers don't expect a tip but will gladly accept one if offered. Expect to pay about MOP$15 for a trip from the ferry terminal to downtown Macau and MOP$20 from the airport.

Resources

TOURS

Two basic tours of Macau are available and you should choose according to how much time you want to spend and which sites you want to see. One covers mainland Macau and the most famous sites, with stops at the Chinese border, Kun Iam Temple, the ruins of St. Paul's, and Penha Hill. This type of tour lasts about 3½ hours. The other typical tour consists of a two-hour trip across the bridge to the islands of Taipa and Coloane to see old Chinese villages, lesser known temples, the main beaches, the Macau Jockey Club, and the Macau International Airport. Tours travel by liner bus or minibus, and prices vary between operators.

A comfortable way to tour is by chauffeur-driven minivan. A car with a maximum of four passengers costs HK$200 an hour with Avis and you can also charter a regular taxi for touring, though few drivers speak English or know sites well enough to provide good details. Depending on your bargaining prowess, the cost will be HK$50–HK$70 per hour.

Most travelers going to Macau on a day trip can book a tour with travel agents in Hong Kong, but it's not essential. If you do prearrange your trip, you'll have the convenience of transportation from Hong Kong to Macau all set, with your guide waiting in the arrival hall, which can be a real time-saver. There are several licensed tour operators in Macau and the ones listed below cater to English-speaking visitors.

🚩 Tour Operators **Able Tours** Also operates Grayline tours ⊠ Room 1015, Avenida da Amizade, Ferry Terminal, Macau ☎ 853/725-813. **Estoril Tours** ⊠ Shop 333, Shun Tak Centre, 200 Connaught Rd., 3/F, Central, Hong Kong ☎ 2559-1028 ⊕ www.estoril.com. **Sintra Tours** ⊠ Hotel Sintra, 58–62 Av. Dom João IV, Macau ☎ 853/710-361.

Side Trips to the Pearl River Delta

GUANGZHOU & SHENZEN

Pizhou Exhibition Hall, Guangzhou, Guangdong Province

WORD OF MOUTH

"My favorite 'local' activities are good inexpensive foot massages and adventurous eating."

—cjbryant

GETTING ORIENTED

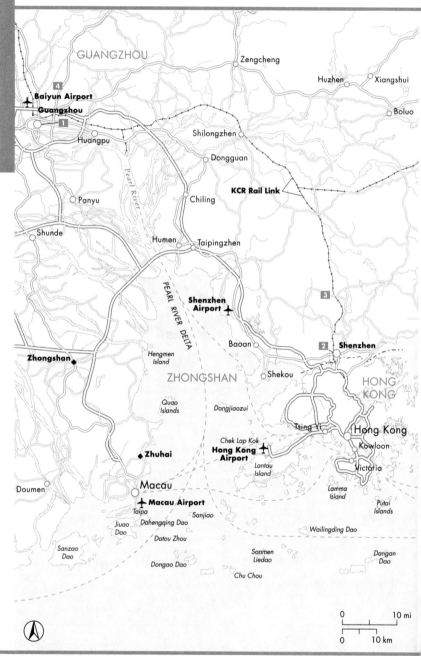

GETTING ORIENTED

The Pearl River Delta is a massive triangle. Guangzhou is at the top, Shenzhen on the east corner, and Zhuhai on the west. The area as a whole is just a bit too spread out for any one corner to make a good base of operations from which to explore the others. If you want to tour the Pearl River Delta, we recommend beginning at one corner and making your way around. Guangzhou is fairly dense, so leave yourself three days to soak it all in before heading down to Shenzhen. Though an amazing city, don't neglect the more bucolic spots just up the coast, including the ancient Dapeng Fortress. From Shenzhen's Shekou Harbor it's a one-hour ferry ride to Zhuhai, which takes less than a day to explore.

1 Colonial Shamian: During the late Qing Dynasty, Westerners weren't all that welcome, and those doing business were relegated to Shamian, a small island in the Pearl River. These colonial captains of industry built churches, banks, mansions, and hotels that are today beautifully restored.

2 Overseas Chinese Town: Culture's the name of the game in Shenzhen's Overseas Chinese Town (OCT District) area, and scattered around the neighborhood are an array of sculptures commissioned by the city fathers to "class up the joint." If you don't like your art alfresco, check out the rotating exhibits at the He Xiangning Art Museum.

3 Mission Hills: The Chinese are mad for golf, and nowhere else in the country is this passion as well-catered to as in the Pearl River Delta. If you've come to the middle kingdom to hit the links, the world-class Mission Hills Golf Club will blow your mind. (For details, ⇨ Chapter 10)

4 White Cloud Mountain: Climb to the top of Santailing Park, listen to the birds in Bird Spring Valley Park, and check out Jinye Pond, whose waters are said to be so clear that it acts as a mirror, clearly reflecting the surrounding mountains.

TOP REASONS TO GO

★ Feel the Buzz: This region is the undisputed engine driving China's current economic boom, and whether you're in Guangzhou or Shenzhen, you're sure to feel the buzz of this formerly Socialist nation on a serious capitalist joyride.

★ Explore the Ancient: Though thoroughly modern, the Pearl River Delta has by no means lost touch with its ancient roots. From the temples of Guangzhou to the Ming Dynasty–walled city of Dapeng in Shenzhen, a journey through the PRD is a journey through the centuries.

★ Soak up Some Colonial Splendor: Modern Guangzhou is rife with well-preserved examples of architecture dating to the 19th century, when European merchants amassed fortunes in the opium trade. Visit Shamian Island, where the buildings from which they once plied their trade still stand.

★ Shopping Sprees: In the mercantile capital of China, and maybe the world, it comes as no surprise that both Guangzhou and Shenzhen arouse the shopaholic in us all. Go on, indulge.

9

PEARL RIVER DELTA PLANNER

Whither the Weather?

When to go is a major question every traveler needs to ask themselves, and certainly in a place like the Pearl River Delta. Summer temperatures and humidity can make the area feel like the inside of a clothes dryer halfway through its cycle. Winter brings an all-pervading chill and dampness that sucks the joy from any endeavor, no matter how well planned. The spring and autumn is a good time to go, but is complicated by a few factors. Unless you have friends in the hotel industry (or with apartments in the city), don't visit Guangzhou during the annual spring trade fair, when prices of hotels skyrocket. And don't even think about traveling anywhere in China during the Golden Week holiday, which takes place annually from October 1 through 7. So what do we recommend? September, October (excluding Golden Week), and early to mid-November.

A Little Medicinal Shopping?

Guangzhou's Qingping Market has undergone a radical rebirth over the past few years. Once notorious as a filthy wet market from which weak-stomached travelers were advised to steer clear, this sprawling maze of shops and stalls has been transformed into a traditional Chinese–medicine market. On the grounds where caged cats, chickens, and turtles once awaited doom, a new mall has risen, one with wide aisles and escalators, and 100 or so stalls of varying sizes filled with merchants dealing in everything from acupuncture needles to zebra testicles.

Whether you choose to shop in the new mall or in the surrounding alleyways (still filled with shops of a less gentrified nature, offering both Chinese medicine and livestock), you're in for a serious *only in China* experience. How much are a pair of dried lizards on sticks really worth? How many ounces of dried sea horse are needed to make broth for a family of four? And how will you explain that sack full of dried geckos to the customs officer at home?

Cabaret, Chinese-Style

If you only go to one multimedia cabaret dinner–theater in Guangzhou, it has to be *The Magic Phantom* at Guangzhou's Mo Li Fang Theater. We mean this both as a recommendation and a literal statement, as this original, quirky, and very well-executed production is the only example of multimedia cabaret dinner–theater we've yet to come across in Guangzhou (or anywhere else in China).

Getting Around

Guangzhou is a chaotic city, famed for noise, crowds, and endless traffic jams—many a vacation hour has been wasted inside of taxicabs. Although taxis in Guangzhou are cheap and plentiful, traffic in the city is reaching nightmare proportions. One reason is because China's new middle class is currently in the midst of a love affair with automobile ownership, the likes of which hasn't been seen since 1950s America.

Many casual visitors are reluctant to take the Guangzhou metro, perhaps feeling that without the proper linguistic skills such a journey might be fraught with confusion. We think that this is a shame. The Guangzhou metro is quick, convenient, and a boon to day-trippers.

If you've decided to spend a day shunning automobiles—and we hope you do—ask your hotel concierge to give you an English subway map. For walking-tour-friendly neighborhoods, we recommend Dongshankou station. This is a lovely little area with plenty of shopping opportunities. Tree-lined streets just off the avenue are filled with enclosed gardens and old houses with traditional architecture.

The area surrounding the Linhex station is the most modern part of the city. This is a good neighborhood to walk around with your head tilted skyward. Of course, if you really want to continue on an anti-car trip, get off at Gongyuanqian station (where Lines 1 and 2 intersect) and walk to the Beijing Road Pedestrian Mall: the hip, trendy and car-free heart of young consumerism in Guangzhou.

What It Costs in Yuan

	$$$$	$$$	$$	$	¢
Restaurants	over Y165	Y100-Y165	Y50-Y99	Y25-Y49	under Y25
Hotels	over Y1,800	Y1,400-Y1,800	Y1,100-Y1,399	Y700-Y1,099	under Y700

Restaurant prices are for a main course, excluding tax and tips.
Hotel prices are for a standard double room, including taxes.

Ancient Days

Don't let the *Blade Runner*-like skyline fool you. China's newest city isn't all glass and steel. Though Shenzhen City is barely three decades old, the areas outside the city are resplendent with examples of ancient Chinese culture.

Like the rapidly disappearing hutong neighborhoods of Beijing, **Dapeng Fortress**—an ancient city—is a living museum, though in Dapeng's case the ancient quarter is located outside of the city proper. The old town contains homes, temples, shops, and courtyards that look pretty much the way they did when they were built over the course of the Ming (AD 1368–1644) and Qing (1644–1911) dynasties. For the most part, the residences are occupied, the shops are doing business, and the temples are active houses of worship. Dapeng's ancient city is surrounded by an old stone wall, and entered through a series of gates built at the cardinal points.

Likewise, the **Hakka Folk Customs Museum and Enclosures** are an amazingly well preserved example of a walled community that existed almost into the present day. Now more a museum than anything else—persecution of Hakkas went out of vogue after the collapse of the Qing Dynasty. The enclosures still stand as an excellent example of an ancient community built with defense in mind. The Hakkas built their homes inside of an exterior wall, complete with vertical-arrow slits for discouraging unwanted visitors. Many of the homes inside the fort are still furnished, and visitors may get the feeling that the original inhabitants have just popped out for a bit of hunting.

9

By Joshua
Samuel Brown

The Pearl River Delta is China's workshop, its fastest-growing, ever-changing, and most affluent region. It is the industrial engine powering China's meteoric economic rise—and it shows. Earth-at-night satellite photos give a telling view of Asia. Tokyo, Seoul, and Taiwan glow brightly, but it's the boomtown cities along the Pearl River Delta that burn brightest. You will find some of the greatest shopping, a flourishing nightlife, and a culinary scene, which less-prosperous regions can only dream of.

The Pear River Delta is also among China's most polluted regions, and this is saying a lot. From the southern suburbs of Guangzhou city to the northern edge of Shenzhen, industry stretches in all directions. As far as the eye can see, tens of thousands of factories churn out the lion's share of the world's consumer products. This hyper-industry has polluted the entire area's soil, water, and air so badly that in Hong Kong (on the region's southern tip) pollution is an overriding public concern. On a bad day, the air quality in Guangzhou can actually be described as *abusive*. On top of all of this, much of the region is noisy and chaotic.

So with all this in mind, why would the pleasure traveler even visit Pearl River Delta? The answers are myriad. History enthusiasts head to Guangzhou, Guangdong province's ancient capital, and the historic center of both Cantonese culture and the revolution that overthrew the last dynasty. Gourmands flock to both Guangzhou and Shenzhen to indulge in some of the best examples of Chinese cuisine—and increasingly, the world—at all price ranges. Culture vultures don't mind putting up with the pollution and chaos for a chance to visit the many temples, shrines, and museums scattered throughout the region. And shop-a-holics? A visit to the Pearl River Delta will quickly dismiss any lingering notions that China is still a nation bound by the tenets of Marx and Mao.

GUANGZHOU

Guangzhou (also known as Canton), the capital of Guangdong province, is both a modern boomtown and an ancient port city. This metropolis of over 7 million people has all the expected accoutrements of a competitive, modern Chinese city: Skyscrapers, heavy traffic, efficient metro, and serious crowds. Guangzhou is an old city with a long history. Exploring its riverfront, parks, temples, and markets, one is constantly reminded of the impact its irrepressible culture, language, and cuisine has made on the world.

The city has long been considered China's gateway to the West, and the Cantonese have a reputation for being China's most savvy entertainers. From the late 18th century, Western merchants set up trading houses in Guangzhou where they negotiated the purchase of tea.

In the early 20th century, Guangzhou was a hotbed of revolutionary zeal, first as the birthplace of the movement to overthrow the last dynasty (culminating in the 1911 Revolution), and then as a battleground between Nationalists and Communists in the years leading to the 1949 Communist revolution. Following the open-door policy of Deng Xiaoping in 1979, the port city was able to resume its role as a commercial gateway to China.

Rapid modernization during the 1980s and '90s has taken its toll not just on the environment but also on the pace of city life. On bad days the clouds of building-site dust, aggressive driving, shop touts, and persistent beggars can be overwhelming. But in Guangzhou's parks, temples, winding old-quarter backstreets, restaurants, river islets, and museums, the old city and a more refined way of life is never far away.

Exploring

9

Guangzhou is a massive, sprawling metropolis divided into several districts and many more neighborhoods. Roughly speaking, the city is divided in half by the Pearl River, which runs from east to west and separates the Haizhu District (a large island) from the districts in the north. Most of the explorations we're recommending will keep you north of the Pearl River, since this is where the majority of the more culturally edifying parts of Guangzhou lie.

Cultural Attractions

The Qingping Market has undergone a few changes over the past few years; the sprawling cluster of stalls was once infamous for its wet market, a hotbed of animal slaughter. Though it always had a good selection of general knickknacks, as well as a large section of goods of various apothicarial value (ginseng, fungi, and herbs, as well as more cruelly obtained items like bear bile and essence of tiger prostate), the wet market scared all but the heartiest visitors away. Fol-

CAUTION

Like any other urban area, Guangzhou has its fair share of pickpockets, so keep your wallet in a front pocket and your bags in front of you.

lowing SARS, the government decided to do away with the bloodier, less hygienic stalls. A large section of the old market was cleared away to make room for a shiny new mall-like structure with stalls dedicated to sales of traditional medicines. The funkier and older outdoor section of the market still exists off to one side, but for the most part items on sale are of the flora and not the fauna variety. Merchants of tiger claws and bear bile are still engaged in their cruel trade on the base of the bridge leading to Shamian Island. Even though most of these merchants are dressed Tibetan style (perhaps to engender the sympathy of foreigners?), the majority of them are Han Chinese engaged in a despicable trade.

Shamian Island. More than a century ago the mandarins of Guangzhou designated a 44-acre sandbank outside the city walls in the Pearl River as an enclave for foreign merchants. The foreigners had previously lived and done business in a row of houses known as the Thirteen Factories, near the present Shamian, but local resentment after the Opium Wars—sometimes leading to murderous attacks—made it prudent to confine them to a protected area, which was linked to the city by two bridges that were closed at 10 every night.

WORD OF MOUTH

"Shamian Island has a few interesting craft-type shops and colonial buildings."

–cjbryant

The island soon became a bustling township, as trading companies from Britain, the United States, France, Holland, Italy, Germany, Portugal, and Japan built stone mansions along the waterfront. With spacious gardens and private wharves, these served as homes, offices, and warehouses. There were churches for Catholics and Protestants, banks, a yacht club, football grounds, a cricket field, and the Victory hotel.

Shamian was attacked in the 1920s but survived until the 1949 Revolution when its mansions became government offices or apartment houses and the churches were turned into factories. In recent years, however, the island has resumed much of its old character. Many colonial buildings have been restored, and both churches have been beautifully renovated and reopened to worshippers. Worth visiting is **Our Lady of Lourdes Catholic Church** (⌂ Shamian Dajie at Yijie), with its cream-and-white neo-Gothic tower. A park with shady walks and benches has been created in the center of the island, where local residents come to chat with friends, walk around with their caged birds, or practice tai chi.

NEED A BREAK? Have an espresso in Chinese colonial splendor at the **Shamian Island Blenz** (⌂ 46 Shamian Ave.), across from **Customs Hotel** in a building dating back to the late Qing Dynasty. Comfy couches, strong coffee, and free Internet access are available in this old building that once housed Guangzhou's US Bank in the pre-revolutionary days. Right on the park, Blenz is a great place to watch people practice tai chi and traditional Chinese fan dancing.

Bright Filial Piety Temple (Guangxiao Si). This is the oldest Buddhist temple in Guangzhou and by far the most charming. The gilded wooden laughing Buddha sitting at the entrance adds to the temple's warm, welcoming atmosphere. A huge bronze incense burner, wreathed in joss-stick smoke, stands in the main courtyard. Beyond the main hall, noted for its ceiling of red-lacquer timbers, is another courtyard that contains several treasures, among them a small brick pagoda said to contain the tonsure hair of Hui-neng (the sixth patriarch of Chan Buddhism), and a couple of iron pagodas, which are the oldest of their kind in China. Above them spread the leafy branches of a myrobalan plum tree and a banyan, called Buddha's Tree because it is said Hui-neng became enlightened in its shade. ☒ *Corner of Renmin Bei and Guangxiao Lu, 2 blocks north of metro station Ximenkou* ☏ *Y5* ☉ *Daily 6:30–5* Ⓜ *Ximenkou.*

Chen Family Temple (Chen Jia Ci). The Chen family is one of the Pearl River Delta's oldest and biggest clans. In the late 19th century local members, who had become rich as merchants, decided to build a memorial temple. They invited contributions from the Chens—and kindred Chans—who had emigrated overseas. Money flowed in from 72 countries, and no expense was spared. One of the temple's

> **WORD OF MOUTH**
>
> "A very interesting book about China generally and the Guangdong area in particular is *God's Chinese Son: The Heavenly Kingdom of Hong Xiuquan,* by Jonathan D. Spence."
>
> –Cicerone

highlights is a huge and skillfully carved ridgepole frieze. It stretches 90 feet along the main roof and depicts scenes from the epic *Romance of Three Kingdoms,* with thousands of figures against a backdrop of ornate houses, monumental gates, and lush scenery. Elsewhere in the huge compound of pavilions and courtyards are friezes of delicately carved stone and wood, as well as fine iron castings and a dazzling altar covered with gold leaf. The temple also houses a folk-arts museum and shop. ☒ *7 Zhongshan Qi Lu* ☏ *Y5* ☉ *Daily 8:30–5* Ⓜ *Chengjia Ci.*

Huaisheng Mosque (Huaisheng Si Guang). In the cosmopolitan era of the Tang Dynasty (618–907) a Muslim missionary named Abu Wangus, said to be an uncle of the prophet Mohammed, came to southern China. He converted many Chinese to Islam and built this mosque in Guangzhou as their house of worship. His tomb in the northern part of the city has been a place of pilgrimage for visiting Muslims, but the mosque is his best-known memorial. A high wall encloses the mosque, which is dominated by the smooth, white minaret. Rising to 33 meters (108 feet), it can be climbed using an interior spiral staircase, and the views from the top—where a muezzin calls the faithful to prayer—are spectacular. ☒ *Guangta Lu, 3 blocks southwest of the Gongyuanqian metro station* ☏ *Free* ☉ *Sat.–Thurs. 8–5, except Muslim holy days* Ⓜ *Gongyuanqian.*

Guangxiao Temple (Guangxiao si). This impressively restored temple and city-gate complex, also known as the Five Celestials Shrine, was once the front gate for the wall that surrounded the city. The shrine and remaining sections of the wall in Yuexiu Park are the only pieces of old Guangzhou's fortifications still standing. The complex also has an impressive 3D model of how the city looked when the air was clean, the roads were filled with horse-drawn carts, and foreigners were confined

9

on pain of death to one small section of the city. ☒ *Renmin Bei Lu, 3 blocks north of the Ximenkou metro* 🕿 *10* ◷ *Daily 8–5* Ⓜ *Ximenkou.*

Six Banyan Temple (Liu Rong Si Hua Ta). Look at any ancient scroll painting or lithograph by early Western travelers, and you'll see two landmarks rising above old Guangzhou. One is the minaret of the mosque; the other is the 56-meter (184-foot) pagoda of the Six Banyan Temple. Still providing an excellent lookout, the pagoda appears to have nine stories, each with doorways and encircling balconies. Inside, however, there are 17 levels. Thanks to its arrangement of colored, carved roofs, it is popularly known as the Flowery Pagoda.

The temple was founded in the 5th century, but because of a series of fires, most of the existing buildings date from the 11th century. It was built by the Zen master Tanyu and is still a very active place of worship, with a community of monks and regular attendance by Zen Buddhists. It was originally called Purificatory Wisdom Temple but changed its name after a visit by the Song Dynasty poet Su Dongpo, who was so delighted by six banyan trees growing in the courtyard that he left an inscription with the characters for six banyans.
☒ *Haizhu Bei Lu, south of Yuexiu Park* 🕿 *Y10* ◷ *Daily 8–5.*

Parks & Museums

Guangdong Museum of Art is a major cultural establishment of the "new Canton," and regularly hosts the works of painters, sculptors, and other artists from around China and the world. An excellent sculpture garden surrounds the large complex with exhibitions both large and small. Located on Ersha Island, the Web site offers a map to help you find your way—so print it out before you go. ☒ *38 Yanyu Lu, Er Sha Island* 🕿 *020/ 8735–1468* ⊕ *www.GDMoA.org* ◷ *Tues.–Sun. 9–5.*

★ **Orchid Garden** (Lanpu). This garden offers a wonderfully convenient retreat from the noise and crowds of the city. It's spread over 20 acres, with paths that wind through groves of bamboo and tropical trees to a series of classic teahouses. Here you can sit and enjoy a wide variety of Chinese teas, brewed the traditional way. There are tables inside and on terraces that overlook the ponds. As for the orchids, there are 10,000 pots with more than 2,000 species of the flower, which present a magical sight when they bloom (peak time is May and June). ☒ *Jiefang Bei Lu* 🕿 *Y5* ◷ *Daily 8:30 AM–11 PM.*

> ## WORD OF MOUTH
>
> "There is a teahouse on a small island in the lake, and they had the most extensive assortment of high-end Xixing teapots I've seen anywhere. They also had quite an assortment of teas."
>
> –Kathie

★ **Tomb of the Southern Yue Kings.** Until recently only specialist historians realized that Guangzhou had once been a royal capital. In 1983 bulldozers clearing ground to build the China Hotel uncovered the intact tomb of Emperor Wen Di, who ruled Nan Yue (southern China) from 137 BC to 122 BC. The tomb was faithfully restored and its treasures placed in the adjoining **Nan Yue Museum.**

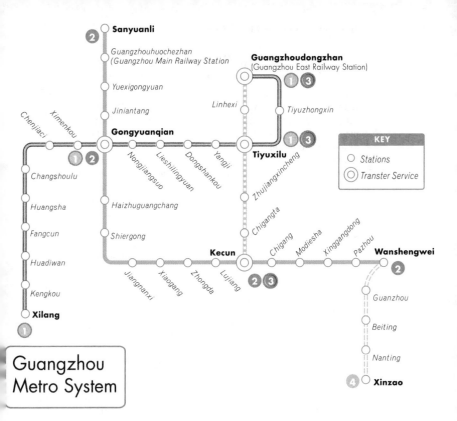

Guangzhou
Metro System

The tomb contained the skeletons of the king and 15 courtiers—guards, cooks, concubines, and a musician—who were buried alive to attend him in death. Also buried were several thousand funerary objects, clearly designed to show off the extraordinary accomplishments of the southern empire. The tomb itself—built entirely of stone slabs—is behind the museum and is remarkable for its compact size. ⊠ *867 Jiefang Bei Lu, around the corner from the China Hotel* ☎ Y15 ⊙ *Daily 9:30–5:30.*

★ ☾ **Yuexiu Park** (Yuexiu Gongyuan). To get away from the bustle, retreat into Yuexiu Park in the heart of town. The park covers 247 rolling acres and includes landscaped gardens, man-made lakes, recreational areas, and playgrounds. Children and adults get a kick out of the fish-feeding ponds.

Be sure to visit the famous **Five Rams Statue** (Wuyang Suxiang), which celebrates the legend of the five celestials who came to Guangzhou riding on goats to bring grains to the people. Guangzhou families like to take each other's photo in front of the statue before setting off to enjoy the park. ⊠ *Jiefang Bei Lu, across from China Hotel* ☎ Y5 ⊙ *Daily 6 AM–9 PM.*

Revolutionary Memorials

In the center of the city are memorials to people who changed Chinese history in the 20th century, using Guangzhou as a base of operations. The most famous were local boy Dr. Sun Yat-sen, who led the overthrow

Underground in Guangzhou

LIVING UP TO ITS MOTTO "gets you there on time," Guangzhou's subway system is cheap, clean, and (unlike Beijing's) reasonably efficient. Divided into four lines that span both sides of the Pearl River, most of the areas of interest to casual visitors are found on Lines 1 or 2 (the red and yellow lines on the maps).

The terminus of Line 1 is Guangzhoudongzhan, or Guangzhou East Train Station, which is where trains leave for Hong Kong. This area is also the heart of the Tienhe, Guangzhou's newest financial district. Gongyuanqian is the interchange for Lines 1 and 2. The most interesting temples and shrines are within walking distance of stations along Line 1, with signs in English pointing the way.

---

of the Qing Dynasty, and Communist Party–founders Mao Zedong and Zhou Enlai. There were many others, thousands of whom died in the struggles. All are recalled in different ways.

Mausoleum of the 72 Martyrs (Huanghua Gang Qishi'er Lieshi Mu). In a prelude to the successful revolution of 1911 a group of 88 revolutionaries staged the Guangzhou armed uprising, only to be defeated and executed by the authorities. Of those killed, 72 were buried here. Their memorial, built in 1918, incorporates a mixture of international symbols of freedom and democracy, including replicas of the Statue of Liberty. ⊠ *Xianlie Zhong Lu* 🚇 *Y10* ⊗ *Daily 6 AM–8:30 PM.*

Memorial Garden for the Martyrs (Lieshi Lingyuan). Built in 1957, this garden has been planted around a tumulus that contains the remains of 5,000 revolutionaries killed in the 1927 destruction of the Guangzhou Commune by the Nationalists. This was the execution site of many victims. On the grounds is the **Revolutionary Museum,** which displays pictures and memorabilia of Guangdong's 20th-century rebellions. ⊠ *Zhongshan San Lu* 🚇 *Y5* ⊗ *Daily 6 AM–9 PM.*

Sun Yat-sen Memorial Hall (Zhongshan Jinian Tang). Dr. Sun's Memorial Hall is a handsome pavilion that stands in a garden behind a bronze statue of the leader. Built in 1929–31 with funds mostly from overseas Chinese, the building is a classic octagon, with sweeping roofs of blue tiles over carved wooden eaves and verandas of red-lacquer columns. Inside is an auditorium with seating for 5,000 and a stage for plays, concerts, and ceremonial occasions. ⊠ *Dongfeng Zhong Lu* 🚇 *Y10* ⊗ *Daily 8–5:30.*

Tianhe-District Sights

The Tianhe District is Guangzhou's newly designated business and up-market residential area. It is the site of the new Guangzhou East Railway Station, the terminus for Hong Kong trains, a world-class sports stadium, and a growing number of office/apartment skyscrapers. Among the buildings is the 80-story **GITIC Plaza** which soars 396 meters (1,300 feet) and is China's second-tallest building. The **Guangzhou East Rail-**

way Station (⊠ Linhe Lu), with its vast entrance hall is worth a peak, even if you don't have a train to catch.

☺ A hub for most of Guangzhou's sporting events, the **Tianhe Stadium Complex** (⊠ Huanshi Dong Lu, East Guangzhou, Huanshi Dong Lu) has two indoor and two outdoor arenas that are equipped for international soccer matches, track-and-field competitions, as well as pop concerts and large-scale ceremonies. The complex is surrounded by a pleasantly landscaped park, with outdoor cafés and tree-shaded benches. The park includes a bowling center with 38 lanes and lots of video games.

Tours

The aptly named China Travel Service (CTS) (*see* Visitor Information *in* Pearl River Delta Essentials, *below*) is still the most trusted name in arranging tours throughout China. Their Web site ⊕ www.ctshk.com/english/index.htm has links to their many offices worldwide; they have 40 offices in Hong Kong, Kowloon, and the New Territories and can arrange just about any type of travel experience that might interest you in Guangzhou or the Pearl River Delta. CTS can also assist with visas and booking discount hotel rooms.

Where to Eat

For centuries Guangzhou has been known as a city of gourmands, and in the last decade, it has undergone a gastronomic renaissance the likes of which few cities will ever know. At the heart of this is commerce; as business travelers bring the ingredients, spices, and culinary traditions from their homes with them. Popping up alongside venerable Cantonese restaurants are eateries specializing in flavors from around the world. Guangzhou has more excellent Indian, Italian, Thai, and Vietnamese restaurants than you can shake a joss stick at, and owing to the recent influx of Middle Eastern traders, there are some parts of town where it's easier to find a falafel than a shrimp dumpling. Of course this isn't to say that Guangzhou's traditional delicacies have been usurped. Amazing seafood dishes and braised and barbecued meats are still available in delicious variety, and succulent dim sum still rules the roost as the city's hometown favorite.

$$$$ ✕ **Chiu Chou City.** The Landmark Canton hotel's Chiu Chou City has the reputation as one of Canton's more well-known culinary experiences and is often fairly crowded with locals looking for good regional cuisine. The decor is old-school Chinese-restaurant style, with large round tables and cloth-covered chairs, but if you like, or want to explore, Chiu Chou regional dishes, such as goose cooked in its own blood and dipped in white vinegar and chopped-garlic sauce, or the ever popular *yin-yang* soup (green vegetable soup and white congee soup served together to form a yin-and-yang symbol), this place might be for you. ⊠ *Landmark Canton hotel, 8 Qiao Guang Lu, Colonial Canton* ☎ *020/8335–5988* ▤ *AE, DC, MC, V.*

$$$$ ✕ **Connoisseur.** This premier restaurant feels like regency France with its arched columns and gilded capitals, gold-framed mirrors, lustrous drapes, and immaculate table settings. The resident French chef specializes in lamb and steak dishes. ✉ *Garden Hotel, 368 Huanshi Dong Lu, 3rd fl., Huanshi Road* ☎ 020/3964–3962 ▤ *AE, DC, MC, V* ⊗ *No lunch.*

$$$$ ✕ **The Roof.** With panoramic 18th-floor views, this restaurant oozes understated splendor. The menu offers seasonal specialties and classic staples, such as saddle of lamb marinated in mint and yogurt, fettuccine, scallops in saffron sauce, and prime cuts of U.S. beef. ✉ *China Hotel, Liuhua Lu, Station District* ☎ 020/8666–6888 Ext. 71892 ▤ *AE, DC, MC, V* ⊗ *Closed Sun. No lunch.*

$$$$ ✕ **Silk Road Grill Room.** This grill room in the White Swan Hotel is the place to see and be seen. The service is impeccable. You can choose between the set menu, which includes an appetizer, cold dish, soup, entrée, dessert, and drink (excluding wine), or à la carte. Highlight entrées include prime rib and sea-bass fillet. ✉ *White Swan Hotel, Yi Shamian Lu, Shamian Island* ☎ 020/8188–6968 ▤ *AE, DC, MC, V* ⚭ *Reservations essential* ⊗ *No lunch.*

$$$–$$$$ ✕ **La Seine.** This upscale restaurant on Er Sha Island offers a daily lunch
Fodor'sChoice buffet. Dinner highlights include classic French fare, such as beef ten-
★ derloin, escargot, and foie gras. An ideal place to eat before or after a show. ✉ *Xinghai Concert Hall, 33 Qing Bo Lu, Er Sha Island, close to Xinghai Concert Hall and Guangzhou Museum* ☎ 020/8735–2531 ⚭ *Reservations essential* ▤ *AE, DC, MC, V.*

$$$ ✕ **Lai Wan Market.** A re-creation of the old Canton waterfront, this theme restaurant has booths shaped like flower boats and small wooden stools at low counters. The Market is known for its dim sum and two kinds of rice, one made with pork, beef, fish, and seafood, the other with fish, beef, and pork liver. ✉ *Garden Hotel, 368 Huanshi Dong Lu, 2nd fl., Huanshi Road* ☎ 020/8333–8989 Ext. 3922 ▤ *AE, DC, MC, V.*

$$–$$$ ✕ **Banxi Restaurant.** On the edge of Liwan Lake, this restaurant has a series of teahouse rooms and landscaped gardens interconnected by zigzag paths and bridges that give the feel of a Taoist temple. One room is built on a floating houseboat. The food is as tasty as it looks with dishes such as scallop and crab soup and quail eggs cooked with shrimp roe on a bed of green vegetables. ✉ *151 Longjin Xi Lu, Liwan Park* ☎ 020/8181–5718 ▤ *AE, MC, V.*

$$–$$$ ✕ **Tang Yuan.** The location alone beats out most other restaurants in Guangzhou. It is in a faux colonial-style mansion on an island in Liuhuahu Park. Cuisine is pure old-school Cantonese, with expensive dishes like abalone and shark's fin soup being served alongside more rational staples like crispy fried pigeon, carbon-roasted mackerel, and stuffed garlic prawns. Naturally, there's plenty of dim sum, and the "Cantonese combo plate" features a variety of roasted meats sure to please carnivores. Although the food at Tang Yuan is excellent, most people come here for the opulence as well. Admission fee for the park is waived for guests of the restaurant, and a golf cart waits at the park's entrance on Liuhua Road to whisk diners to the restaurant's palatial front door. ✉ *Lihuahu Park, Dongfeng Xi Lu and Renmin Bei Lu, 2 blocks west of Yuexiu Gongyuan metro station* ☎ 020/8668–8863 ▤ *AE, DC, MC, V.*

$–$$$ ✕ **Datong Restaurant.** Occupying all eight stories of an old riverfront building, with an open terrace on the top floor, this is one of the city's veteran dining establishments. The restaurant is popular with locals all hours of the day, so arrive early to be guaranteed a seat. The atmosphere is chaotic and noisy, but the morning and afternoon dim sum and huge menu are well worth it. Famous dishes include stewed-chicken claws (delicious, by the way), crispy-skin chicken, and roasted *Xishi* duck. Probably not the best place for vegetarians. ⊠ *Nanfang Dasha, 63 Yanjiang Xi Lu, Colonial Canton* ☎ *020/8188–8988* ▤ *AE, DC, MC, V.*

$–$$$ ✕ **Dongjiang Seafood Restaurant.** There are two Dongjiang Seafood restaurants in Guangzhou. Both are renowned for their culinary excellence and authentic Canton decor, but we recommend the Pearl River location (on Qiao Guang and Yan Jiang roads). It features a seafood market where you can wander around and choose your own meal. The staff will try to steer you toward the most expensive items first, so make sure you check price beforehand. Some of our favorites include the braised duck stuffed with eight delicacies and glutinous rice, stuffed giant prawns, crab in black-bean sauce, and salt-roast chicken. ⊠ *No. 2 Qiao Guang Rd., Pearl River, 2 blocks SE of Haizhu Shichang metro* ☎ *020/ 8318–4901* ▤ *AE, DC, MC, V.*

$–$$$ ✕ **Guangzhou Restaurant.** One of the oldest eateries in the city, Guangzhou Restaurant was opened in 1936 and has a string of culinary awards. The setting is classic Canton, with courtyards of flowery bushes surrounded by dining rooms of various sizes. The food is reputed to be among the best in the city, with house specialties like "Eight Treasures," a mix of fowl, pork, and mushrooms served in a bowl made of winter melon. Other Cantonese dishes include duck feet stuffed with shrimp, roasted goose, and of course, dim sum. Meals here can be cheap or very expensive, depending on how exotic you're looking to get. ⊠ *2 Wenchang Nan Lu, Ancestral Guangzhou* ☎ *020/8138–8801* ▤ *AE, DC, MC, V.*

$–$$$ ✕ **Tao Tao Ju.** Prepare yourself for the garish decor, shouted conversations of fellow diners, and a menu comprised of enough weird animal parts to send vegetarians running. Tao Tao Ju (which, roughly translated, means "house of happiness") is one of the most revered traditional Cantonese restaurants in the city. Soups are a big thing here, and the menu (available in English) has many that you're unlikely to find elsewhere. The kudzu and snakehead soup is delicious, and they have over 200 varieties of dim sum. They're also open daily 6:30 AM to midnight, so it's a good place to stop for a late-night meal. ⊠ *20 Dishipu Lu, Shangxiajiu* ☎ *020/8139–6111* ▤ *AE, DC, MC, V.*

$$ ✕ **Back Street Jazz Bar & Restaurant.** Tall bamboo groves masks a spaceage interior of glass walls, sliding-metal doors, and Plexiglas walkways in this cantina attached to the Guangdong Art Museum. Food is pure world fusion, with dishes like deep fried salmon and lotus root, Thai chicken salad, and honey apple–foie gras. The softly lit red-neon bar serves mojitos, fruit martinis, and a wide selection of wines. Back Street has an in-house jazz band playing nightly from 10 until midnight, and often hosts international bands. ⊠ *38 Yanyu Lu, East Gate of the Guangdong Museum of Art, Ersha Island* ☎ *020/3839–9090* ▤ *AE, DC, MC, V.*

$–$$ ✕ **Lucy's.** With cuisines from so many cultures represented on its menu (Asian curries, mixed grills, Tex-Mex dishes, fish-and-chips, noodles, burgers, sandwiches, and much more), a UN–think tank could happily share a table. A favorite among foreigners, the outdoor dining area is lovely, and even the indoor dining area has a few trees growing through the roof. Take-out service is available. ⊠ *3 Shamian Nan Jie, 1 block from White Swan Hotel* ☎ *020/8121–5106* ▭ No credit cards.

$–$$ ✕ **A Thousand and One Nights.** Possibly due to its being part of a chain operating throughout China, this cavernous Middle Eastern restaurant gets written up a lot, and is crowded with Westerners on most nights. But despite the authentic Arabic decor, belly dancers, and menu filled with kebabs and babaghanoush, A Thousand and One Nights seems to be coasting on reputation, and Guangzhou has better Arab fare by far. But if you're at the China Hotel and don't feel like hopping in a taxi to the Nile, you could do worse than a meal here. ⊠ *899 Jie Fang Bei Rd., next to the China Hotel, Yuexiu Gongyuan metro* Ⓜ *Yuexiu Gongyuan* ☎ *020/3618–2280* ▭ *AE, DC, MC, V.*

$ ✕ **Da Chuan Japanese Food Restaurant.** This local eatery is located in a busy shopping area on Beijing Road. The best value is a sushi set meal, or you can dive into à la carte dishes plucked straight off the rotating sushi bar. ⊠ *294 Beijing Rd., 4th fl., Beijing Road Pedestrian Mall* ☎ *020/ 8319–0283* ▭ No credit cards.

$ ✕ **The Italian Restaurant.** This aptly named restaurant is a popular hangout for Western expats who work in the neighborhood. It offers a cheerful home-away-from-home feel, complete with flags from various countries hanging from the ceiling and beers from around the world. The food is inexpensive and good, with pizzas, pastas, and excellent brochette prepared by an Italian chef. The owner is an entrepreneur with a number of other restaurants and bars in the neighborhood. His reputation for catering to Western tastes is hardly undeserved. ⊠ *East Tower, Pearl Building, 3rd fl., 360 Huanshi Zhong Lu., 1 block west of Garden Hotel* ☎ *020/8586–6783* ▭ *AE, DC, MC, V* ☉ *Daily.*

$ ✕ **Nile Restaurant.** This lovely little three-story restaurant on the banks of the Pearl River serves excellent Middle Eastern food, including falafel, shwarma, and a variety of Middle Eastern salads. The Nile is worth noting for two reasons: the decor, including the uniforms worn by the waitstaff, is straight out of the movie *Cleopatra*; and the menu has a large number of vegetarian dishes, not always the easiest thing to find in Guangzhou. For our vegetarian friends, we recommend the lentil soup, babaghanoush, and the falafel salad. Nile also serves excellent breakfasts. ⊠ *31 Yanjian W. Rd., 2 blocks east of Shamian Island* ☎ *020/ 8101–2986* ▭ No credit cards ☉ *Daily.*

Where to Stay

The purpose of your visit to Guangzhou is likely to determine where you stay. Businesspeople increasingly choose the upcoming Tianhe District, close to Guangzhou East Railway Station and the city's growing thicket of office skyscrapers. Visitors are more likely to choose a hotel on the oasislike Shamian Island, in the heart of the city. Though traffic is still hellish, getting around is easier now than it has been in years past. Recently completed expressways and a growing underground-train system have vastly reduced cross-city travel time.

$$–$$$$ ⊞ **China Hotel.** Managed by Marriott, this hotel is part of a multicomplex that includes office and apartment blocks, a shopping mall big enough to get lost in, and a wide enough range of restaurants to satisfy any appetite. The hotel is favored by business travelers because it's connected to the metro and close to the Trade Fair Exhibition Hall. The 66-room executive floor has big private lounges, and the piano bar in the lobby offers champagne brunches. There's a walk-in humidor on the premises and the 4th-floor gym is open around the clock. ⊠ *Liuhua Lu, 510015* ☎ *020/8666–6888* ⤸ *1,013 rooms, 74 suites* ⚘ *4 restaurants, tennis court, pool, gym, nightclub, shops, piano bar, business services, in-room broadband, meeting room* ▤ *AE, DC, MC, V* Ⓜ *Yuexu Gongyuan metro.*

$$–$$$$
Fodor'sChoice
★
⊞ **Holiday Inn City Centre.** This centrally located hotel is bound to offer stiff competition to the Garden Hotel just down the road. The large tasteful rooms are arranged according to Chinese feng-shui principles. The top three executive floors have suites and a lounge–restaurant area with stellar views of smog-shrouded Guangzhou. In addition to all of its lovely facilities, the hotel also has enough meeting rooms to host a small Tony Robbins seminar. ⊠ *28 Guangming Lu, Overseas Chinese Village, Huanshi Dong Road, 510095* ☎ *020/6128–6868* ⊕ *www.guangzhou. holiday-inn.com* ⤸ *430 rooms, 38 suites* ⚘ *4 restaurants, pool, gym, lounge, business services, in-room broadband, meeting rooms, car rental, travel services* ▤ *AE, DC, MC, V.*

$$–$$$$ ⊞ **Holiday Inn Shifu.** The newest hotel in Guangzhou, and the only four-star hotel in popular tourist area Shangxiajiu, Holiday Inn Shifu is 14 stories, with rooms ranging in price from Y1,080 to Y2,680. There's a lovely rooftop pool and an adjacent bar with views of old Guangzhou. The Shifu is also a stone's throw from the newly renovated Qingping Market, which is a must-see for first-time visitors. ⊠ *No.188 Di Shi Fu Rd., Xiangxiajiu, 510140, signs from Changshou metro exit point the way* ☎ *020/8138–0088* ⤸ *280 rooms, 6 suites* ⚘ *2 restaurants, pool, gym, sauna, business services, in-room broadband, bar, meeting room* ▤ *AE, DC, MC, V* Ⓜ *Changshuo.*

$$–$$$$ ⊞ **White Swan Hotel.** Occupying a marvelous site on Shamian Island, beside the Pearl River, this huge luxury complex has landscaped gardens, two pools, a jogging track, and a separate gym and spa. Its presidential suite is just that: reserved for heads of state, it has been occupied by such luminaries as Richard Nixon and Kim Jong-il. Its restaurants are second to none; the windows of the elegant lobby bar and coffee shop frame the panorama of river traffic. ⊠ *Yi Shamian Lu, Shamian Island, Colonial Canton, 510133* ☎ *020/8188–6968, 852/2524–0192 in Hong Kong* ⊕ *www. whiteswanhotel.com* ⤸ *843 rooms, 92 suites* ⚘ *9 restaurants, 2 pools, gym, bar, shops, business services, in-room broadband, meeting rooms, travel services* ▤ *AE, DC, MC, V.*

> **WORD OF MOUTH**
>
> "The White Swan is a very fine hotel."
>
> –USNR

9

$–$$$$ 🏨 **Guangdong Victory Hotel.** Over the past few years, this Shamian Island hotel has undergone upgrades that have bumped it up from budget class. The two wings, both originally colonial guesthouses, have been beautifully renovated. The main building has a pink-and-white facade, an imposing portico, and twin domes on the roof, where you'll find a pool and an excellent sauna facility. Standard rooms are more than adequate, and the hotel still retains a fairly inexpensive dining room on the 1st floor. ⊠ *53 Yi Shamian Lu, Shamian Island, 510130* ☎ *020/8121–6688* ⊕ *www.gd-victory-hotel.com* ↘ *328 rooms* ⚬ *4 restaurants, dining room, pool, gym, sauna, business services, in-room broadband, meeting rooms* ⊟ *AE, DC, MC, V.*

Fodor'sChoice
★

> **TIGHTWAD TIP**
>
> All hotels in Guangzhou have in-room Internet access for those traveling with laptops. Although it's almost always free at the cheaper hotels, more expensive properties charge anywhere from Y100 to Y120 to "buy" a block of 24 hours of surfing time.

$$–$$$ 🏨 **Garden Hotel.** In the northern business suburbs, this huge, aging hotel is famous for its spectacular garden that includes an artificial hill, a waterfall, and pavilions. The cavernous lobby, decorated with enormous murals, has a bar–lounge set around an ornamental pool. Though long considered the standard of luxury in Guangzhou, other hotels are now giving the Garden a run for its money. ⊠ *368 Huanshi Dong Lu, Huanshi Road, 510064* ☎ *020/8333–8989* ⊕ *www.thegardenhotel.com.cn* ↘ *1,028 rooms, 63 suites* ⚬ *7 restaurants, 2 tennis courts, pool, gym, squash, bar, lounge, pub, shops, business services, in-room broadband, convention center* ⊟ *AE, DC, MC, V.*

$$–$$$ 🏨 **Tian Lun International Hotel.** A new, upscale boutique hotel located next to Guangzhou East Railway Station, offers large luxury rooms with a sleek edge. The colors are kept to soft blacks, grays, and beige. The buffet in the 2nd-floor café is beautifully arranged around a centerpiece of coral, and the high ceilings lend an air of sophistication. ⊠ *172 Linhe Lu Central, Tianhe District, 510610, next to Guangzhou East Railway Station* ☎ *020/8393–6388* ⊕ *www.tianlun-hotel.com* ↘ *382 rooms, 23 suites* ⚬ *2 restaurants, business services, in-room broadband, pool, gym, sauna* ⊟ *AE, DC, MC, V.*

$–$$$ 🏨 **Dong Fang.** Across from Liuhua Park and the trade-fair headquarters, this complex is built around a 22½-acre garden with pavilions, carp-filled pools, and rock gardens. The lobby is done up in a Renaissance motif, complete with Romanesque pillars and gold-and-white floor tiling. The shopping concourse has Chinese antiques and carpets. The hotel has recently added an 86,000-square-foot convention center. Discounts of up to 30% for rooms in the off-season are not unheard of. ⊠ *120 Liuhua Lu, 510016* ☎ *020/8666–9900, 852/2528–0555 in Hong Kong* ↘ *772 rooms, 114 suites* ⚬ *6 restaurants, gym, hair salon, spa, business services, in-room broadband, meeting room* ⊟ *AE, DC, MC, V.*

$–$$$ 🏨 **Guangdong International Hotel.** This 15-year-old towering hotel in the finance district is somewhat of an institution in Guangzhou, but it has a tired feel, as if the leap from state to private ownership hasn't been made in full. The hotel does have extensive recreation facilities and an indoor gym, as well as a large rooftop pool with an excellent view. For the money though, the nearby City Centre Holiday Inn is a better buy. ✉ *339 Huanshi Dong Lu, Huanshi Road, 510098* ☎ *020/8331–1888* ⇱ *603 rooms, 200 suites* ⚭ *3 restaurants, tennis court, pool, gym, bar, shops, business services, in-room broadband* ▤ *AE, DC, MC, V.*

$–$$$ ▥ **Landmark Canton.** Towering above Haizhu Square and the main bridge across the river, this hotel is in the heart of central Guangzhou. It's managed by China Travel Service of Hong Kong, so a lot of its guests tend to be Hong Kongers on holiday, but the hotel has its fair share of foreign guests as well. There's a great chocolate shop in the lobby, and a small but very pretty Chinese garden and carp pond in the courtyard. The Landmark's location allows it to boast that most guest rooms have great views of the river and city. ✉ *8 Qiao Guang Lu, 510115* ☎ *020/ 8335–5988* ⇱ *688 rooms, 103 suites* ⚭ *3 restaurants, pool, gym, bar, dance club, shops, business services, meeting room* ▤ *AE, DC, MC, V* Ⓜ *Haizhu Guangchang.*

¢–$ ▥ **Élan Hotel.** If you like cheap, funky, and hip little hotels, this is the spot for you. Guangzhou's first attempt at a boutique hotel has compact, Ikea-inspired rooms with bold color palettes and clean lines. Celine Dion muzak wafting through the hallways can be an annoyance, but the warm, cozy beds guarantee a restful sleep. The small 1st-floor restaurant serves cheap northeast Chinese food that is as authentic and tasty. ✉ *32 Zhan Qian Heng Rd., 510010, 2 blocks south of Guangzhou main railway station* ☎ *020/8622–1788* ⊕ *www.hotel-elan.com* ⇱ *76 rooms, 8 suites* ⚭ *Restaurant, business services, in-room broadband* ▤ *AE, DC, MC, V.*

¢ ▥ **The Customs Hotel.** This clean and inexpensive hotel has both character and an excellent location. The newly opened four-story establishment has an attractive colonial facade that blends well with the surrounding area. The bright interior surrounds an inner courtyard. Standard rooms are tastefully decorated with Republican-era furniture made of dark wood, though the suites seem more cluttered. If possible, get a room facing Shamian Avenue, the quiet, tree-lined street, which runs the length of the island. There is a karaoke bar and a lovely backyard garden. ✉ *No.35 Shamian Ave., Shamian Island, Colonial Guangzhou, 510130* ☎ *20/8110–2388* ⇱ *49 rooms, 7 suites* ⚭ *2 restaurants, gym, bar, business services, in-room broadband* ▤ *AE, DC, MC, V.*

¢ ▥ **HallBell De Fond.** This inexplicably named budget hotel is not a bad place for the price. However, a few of the rooms are a bit funky, the beds hard, and some of the wooden furniture seems rickety. We got the feeling that the hotel's clientele was primarily comprised of businesspeople on a strict budget, and patrons of the bar street below using the place for trysts. There are two common rooms with televisions, free Internet access, and the definite prospect of meeting interesting people. ✉ *16F Zhujiang Building, 358 Huanshi Dong Lu, Huanshi Road* ☎ *20/ 6122–4388* ⊕ *www.hallbell.com* ⇱ *50 rooms* ⚭ *Business services, in-room broadband* ▤ *MC, V.*

¢ ▥ **Shamian.** This is a great hotel for visitors on a budget. Its rooms are a little spartan and the lobby cramped, but it is clean and friendly and the location—right in the middle of Shamian Island—is second to none.

⊠ 52 Shamian Nan Jie, Shamian Island, 510130 ☎ 020/8121–8288 ⊕ www.gdshamianhotel.com ⟿ 58 rooms, 20 suites ⟜ Restaurant, business services ▭ AE, DC, MC, V.

¢–$ ▦ **Aiqun Hotel.** When it was built in the 1930s, this 16-story hotel was the tallest building in Pearl River Delta. Though it once hosted dignitaries of great importance during China's Republican era, these days this elegant art-deco hotel hosts visitors from around China and international travelers on a budget. Rooms are clean, comfortable, and tastefully furnished with rich mahogany, faux colonial-era furniture. The revolving restaurant on the 16th floor of the new wing offers great views of the surrounding area. *⊠ No.113 Yanjiang Rd., Pearl River District, 510120 ☎ 020/8186–6668 ⟿ 220 rooms, 20 suites ⟜ 4 restaurants, business services, meeting room, in-room broadband ▭ AE, DC, MC, V.*

Nightlife & the Arts

Though not as happening as Shanghai or Beijing, the Guangzhou nightlife scene is anything but boring. Western-style clubs vie for increasingly hip and knowledgeable crowds and invest serious money on international DJs and design. A wide variety of pubs, sports bars, coffee shops, and cafés have also sprung up. Bars tend to stay open until 2 AM; clubs continue to 5 AM.

Pubs & Bars

Bingjiang xilu (⊠ South of Shamian Island, across the Pearl River) is *the* street for barhopping. Very popular with a younger crowd, it has great views, and if you get bored with looking north across the river you can always cross the bridge to **Yanjiang Xilu** and drink at some of the bars on that side.

Huanshi Dong Lu and the area behind the Garden Hotel is popular with locals and expats (short- and long-term). Two favorites are **Gypsy** and **Cave,** both located on opposite ends of the Zhujiang Building. Cave has a distinct meat-market vibe and features nightly performances by a scantily clad woman whose specialty is dancing with snakes. Gypsy reeks of hashish and is much mellower.

The Paddy Field (⊠ 38 Huale Lu , behind Garden Hotel ☎ 020/8360–1379) makes you long for Ireland. There are darts, pints of Guinness and Kilkenny, and football matches on a massive screen.

Popular with foreigners and locals alike, **1920 Restaurant** (⊠ 183 Yanjiang Zhong Lu ☎ 020/8333–6156) serves up Bavarian food and imported wheat beers on a lovely outdoor patio. Meals start from Y30, beers from Y28.

The popular **Café Lounge** (⊠ China Hotel, lobby ☎ 020/8666–6888) has a mellow vibe, big comfortable bar stools, quiet tables for two, live music on weekends, and a fine selection of cigars.

The big attraction of the **Hare & Moon** (⊠ White Swan Hotel, Yi Shamian Lu, Shamian Island ☎ 020/8188–6968) is the panorama of the Pearl River as it flows past the picture windows.

Dance Clubs

Though normally thought of as inauspicious in Chinese culture, the number 4 is anything but at Guangzhou's newly renovated **Yes Club** (✉ 132 Dongfeng Xi Lu, across from Liuhua Lake Park ☎ 020 8136–8688 💲 Free), which actually has four separate clubs under one roof for four distinctly different clubbing experiences. **Super Yes** has techno and electronica, whereas **Mini Yes** offers house and break beat. **Funky Yes** offers a more eclectic mixture of R&B and hip hop, and **Club Yes** is a total chill-out zone, with softer music and lighting, and a fine selection of wine and cigars. Taken as a whole, the more than 6,000-square-foot megaclub is definitely the biggest in Guangzhou.

Baby Face (✉ 83 Changdi Da Ma Lu ☎ 020/8335–5771 💲 Y20) is where the stylish go to strike a pose. It fills up quickly on weekends with most tables reserved. Arrive early and be prepared to spend.

Deep Anger Music Power House (✉ 183 Yanjiang Lu ☎ 020/ 8317-7158 💲 Free ⊙ Daily 8 PM–2 AM) is a cool dance club located in a building that was a theater back in the days of Sun Yat-sen. Lounge lizards and history buffs will enjoy sipping a beer here.

> ### IN THE NEWS
>
> Some good publications to check out for regularly updated info on ongoing cultural happenings are *City Weekend's, City Guide, South China City Talk,* and *That's PRD.*

Art & Culture in Guangzhou

If you think Guangzhou's high culture begins and ends with Cantonese opera, think again, pilgrim—the art and performance scene here is vibrant, and getting more so every day. Even cynics who believe that Guangzhou's mainstream masses care more for dim sum than for dance are waking up to the fact that the city is undergoing a cultural broadening, as evidenced by the opening of small art spaces, more eclectic forms of theater, and more national attention being focused on the city's major museums. Of course, purists need not panic; the Cantonese opera has hardly disappeared.

Xinghai Concert Hall (✉ 33 Qing Bo Lu, Er Sha Island ☎ 020/8735–2222 Ext. 312 for English ⊕ www.concerthall.com.cn) is the home of the Guangzhou Symphony Orchestra, and puts on an amazing array of concerts featuring national and international performers. Their Web site, unfortunately, is only in Chinese, but your hotel should be able to call to find out what's going on. The concert hall is surrounded by a fantastic sculpture garden, and is next door to the Guangzhou Museum of Art, making the two an excellent mid-afternoon to evening trip.

Fodor'sChoice ★ **Mo Li Fang Theater** (✉ 292 Changdida Ma Lu ☎ 020/8132–2600 💲 Y 290 includes dinner) presents nightly performances of their original multimedia dinner–theater cabaret *The Magic Phantom,* combining elements of traditional Beijing Opera, Hong Kong Cinema, puppetry, karaoke, acrobatics, dancing, and computer animation. The play is in Putonghua, but the story is fairly simple: A young prince of the kingdom of Nanyue finds a magic ring that allows him to travel through time and space. His travels take him and his consort to Prohibition-era Chicago, Republican-era Shanghai, and outer space. As if this weren't enough to justify the price of admission, each member of the audience is served a pre-performance meal literally fit for a king, with eight separate and sumptuous dishes served in crystal bowls by waiters in full ancient costume. An evening well spent for all senses–see our front section for more about this terrific show, which begins at 7 PM nightly with matinees Saturdays and Sundays. Tickets are available at the box office, or through the front desk of most hotels.

Guang Ming Theatre (✉ 293 Nan Hua Zhong Lu ☎ 020/3415–4721) is a well-known place to catch Cantonese opera as well as other performances.

☺ **Guangdong Puppet Art Center** (✉ 21 Fenyuan St. ☎ 020/8431–0227) hosts live puppet shows every Saturday and Sunday at 10:30 AM and 3 PM.

Guangdong Modern Dance Company (✉ 13 Shuiyinhenglu, Shaheding ☎ 020/8704–9512 ⊕ www.gdmdc.com) is mainland China's first professional modern-dance company, and the troupe is regularly praised by publications as diverse and respected as the *New York Times* and the *Toronto Sun*. This theater is their home base, so if you're a fan of dance, check out their English-language Web site for a full performance schedule.

Galleries & Performance Spaces

Park 19 (✉ 19 Xiaogang Hauyuan, Jingnan Donglu ☎ 020/8425–2689 ⊕ www.park19.com ☉ Call for hours) is Guangzhou's newest and hippest art spot, which offers several floors of studio and performance space, and is definitely worth checking out. Call or check their Web site for current happenings and hours.

If eclectic art is your thing, then **Vitamin Creative Space** (✉ 29 Hengyi Jie, inside of Xinggang Cheng, Haizhu District ☎ 020/8429–6760) might be worth the trip. But be warned, it's located in the back of a semienclosed vegetable market and not easy to find even if you speak Chinese. Call first (the curator speaks English) and someone will escort you from in front of the market. Hours are somewhat erratic, but the art can be as wonderfully weird as anything you're likely to find in China.

Shopping

It's no surprise that the world's busiest manufacturing city offers an amazing array of shopping options. Whatever the item may be, if it's being sold chances are good that somebody's selling it in Guangzhou.

Malls & Markets

Shangxiajiu is a massive warren of old buildings and shops and considered the user-friendly heart of old Guangzhou. The half-mile main street is a pedestrian mall boasting nearly 250 shops and department stores. The buildings in Shangxiajiu are old, but the stores are the same ones as in "modern Guangzhou." Even though the overall decibel level hovers around deafening, the area isn't without its charms. Our favorite shops are the small storefronts offering dried-fruit samples, which are very addictive. The area draws a big, younger crowd, but there are a few quiet back alleys that keep it from feeling too overwhelming. There's also a wide variety of street stalls selling a large selection of delicious edibles. ✛ *Follow signs from Changshoulu metro.*

Beijing Road Pedestrian Mall (✉ Follow signs from Gongyuanqian metro) offers an interesting contrast to Shangxiajiu. Shangxiajiu offers new stores in old buildings, whereas Beijing Road makes no pretense at being anything other than a fully modern, neon-draped pedestrian mall, similar to Beijing's Wangfujing Street or Shanghai's Nanjing Street. Pedestrianized and open from around 10 AM until 10 PM, this is where city teenagers buy sensible, midrange Hong Kong–style clothes and increasingly garish local brands. Noisy and fun, the street is lined with cheap food stalls, cafés, and the ubiquitous fast-food chains like KFC and McDonald's.

Haizhu Plaza (✉ Haizhu Sq., north of Haizhu Bridge, Haizhu Ⓜ Guangchang metro ☉ Daily 10–6) is a massive, two-story flea and souvenir market where casual shoppers and wholesale buyers alike bargain for kitsch—think toys, faux antiques, and cultural revolution–themed knickknacks. Merchants keep calculators at hand for entering figures in the heat of negotiation, and vendors sell a variety of snacks from carts located by the exits.

The **Friendship Store** (✉ 369 Huanshi Dong Lu, across from the Garden Hotel) is an old stalwart, dating back from days of post-revolutionary China's earliest flirtation with capitalism. The Guangzhou Friendship Store occupies a five-story building with departments selling a wide range of designer wear, children's wear, luggage, and household appliances.

La Perle (✉ 367 Huanshi Dong Lu, across from the Garden Hotel ☉ Daily 10–10) is next to the Friendship Store, and a bit more upscale. They have genuine designer clothes at expensive rates, with shops such as Versace, Louis Vuitton, Polo, and Prada.

Antiques & Traditional Crafts

On Shamian Island, the area between the White Swan and Victory hotels has a number of small family-owned shops that sell paintings, carvings, pottery, knickknacks, and antiques.

Guangzhou Arts Centre (✉ 698 Renmin Bei Lu ☎ 020/8667–9898) has a fine selection of painted scrolls. **Guangzhou Ji Ya Zhai** (✉ 7 Xinwen Lu, Zhongshan Wulu ☎ 020/8333–0079) is a specialist in Chinese calligraphy and painting. The **South Jade Carving Factory** (✉ 15 Xia Jiu Lu, Shangxiajiu ☎ 020/8138–8040) offers a wide variety of jade and jadeite products at reasonable prices. On the 2nd floor visitors can watch jade being carved. The **White Swan Arcade** (✉ White Swan Hotel, Yi Shamian Lu, Shamian Island) has some of the city's finest upmarket specialty shops. They sell genuine Chinese antiques, traditional craft items, works of modern and classical art, Japanese kimonos and swords, jewelry, cameras, and books published in and about China.

Bookstore

Guangzhou Books Center (✉ 123 Tianhe Lu ☎ 020/3886–4208) is a chain with seven floors of books on every subject, including some bargain-priced art books in English. **Xinhua Bookstore** (✉ 276 Beijing Rd. ☎ 020/8333–2636) sells an extensive catalog of books on a wide range of subjects at very affordable prices.

Side Trip to White Cloud Mountain

17 km (10½ mi) north of Guangzhou.

White Cloud Mountain gets its name from the halo of clouds that, in the days before heavy pollution, appeared around the peak following a rainstorm. The mountain is part of a 28-square-km- (17-square-mi-) resort area and consists of 6 parks, 30 peaks, and myriad gullies. **Santailing Park** is home to the enormous Yuntai Garden, of interest to anybody with a thing for botany. **Fei'eling Park** has a nice sculpture garden, and **Luhu Park** is home to Jinye Pond, as pure and azure a body of water as you're likely to find within 100 miles. All in all, a trip to White Cloud Mountain is a good way to get out of the city—maybe for a day of hiking—without traveling too far. Buses 11 and 24 both stop here, though a taxi shouldn't set you back more than Y100. ⊠ *20Y* ☉ *Daily 9–5.*

To & from Guangzhou

120 km (74½ mi; 1½ hrs) northwest of Hong Kong.

Most travelers enter Guangzhou either by train or plane. Long-distance trains pull in at the Guangzhou East Station. This station is also on the metro line, so getting to your destination right off the train is a fairly simple matter. One-way tickets to or from Hong Kong cost between Y210 and Y250, and between Y130 and Y170 to Shenzhen.

Guangzhou is connected to Shenzhen (approximately 100 km [62 mi] to the south) by the aptly named Guangzhou–Shenzhen expressway. Buses from Guangzhou to Hong Kong leave from both the Guangzhou East Station and from major hotels such as the China and the Garden hotels, and cost about Y180. You can, in a pinch, get a taxi from the station to the Shenzhen–Hong Kong border, but be prepared to pay upward of Y400.

SHENZHEN

Shenzen may be China's youngest city, but this is one metropolis that's definitely come of age. A small farming town until 1980, Shenzhen was chosen by Deng Xiaoping as an incubator in which the seeds of China's economic reform were to be nurtured. The results are the stuff of legend; a quarter century later, Shenzhen is now China's richest, and, according to some, its most vibrant city.

Shenzhen is the wealthiest per capita of any Chinese city (a fact that irks second-place Shanghai to no end). As such, Shenzhen offers a vast variety of ways for the city's middle class and nouveau riche to be parted from their money.

Until recently, few visitors saw Shenzhen as a long-term destination in itself, choosing instead to think of China's youngest city as a place to pass through on the way from Hong Kong to Guangzhou. But over the last several years, this has changed as more expats choose to call Shenzhen home, and more travelers discover that the city is a unique destination in itself.

Exploring Shenzhen

Sprawling Shenzhen is composed of six districts. Luohu and Futian are the "downtown" districts, with most of the major shopping areas, financial districts, and hundreds of hotels. If beautiful beaches and Soviet-era aircraft carriers-cum-theme parks are your thing, you won't want to miss the Yantian district. Shekou District is an area extremely popular with locals and visitors alike for its waterfront dining and plethora of bars and restaurants. Nanshan is Shenzhen's arts and theme-park district. Surrounding these smaller districts like a misshapen croissant are Shenzhen's two largest (and least urban) districts: Bao'an to the east and Longgang to the west.

> ### UNDERGROUND SHENZEN
>
> Shenzhen's brand-new metro runs from the terminus at Luohu station to the Windows on the World Station in OCT. What's more, many stations have sculptures, murals, and other objets d'art The metro is cheap, easy to use, and has announcements in Chinese and English. Stored-value tickets are available at any station for Y100, and can be cashed in for any unused balance at the end of your trip.

Nanshan & Shekou

Nanshan is where you'll find Shenzhen's most stylish district, Huaqiao Cheng, or Overseas Chinese Town (often called the OCT District). Here you will find the **OCT park,** an urban expanse of greenery and sculpture (whose highlights include pieces like Fu Zhongwang's "Earth Gate," a Gothic-looking locked iron door buried in the ground, and French sculptor Bernar Vernet's *230.5,* a postmodern monument of forged steel that fits well with Shenzhen's industrious nature). There are two excellent museums, the **Hexiangning Museum of Contemporary Chinese Art,** and the more underground-feeling **OCAT** (Overseas Chinese Art Terminal). The OCT also has three popular theme parks.

Shekou was the first Special Economic Zone, marking the earliest baby step of modern China's transformation from state planned to market economy. Nowadays the neighborhood is best known for **Sea World Plaza,** a pedestrian mall featuring restaurants, bars, and a completely landlocked oceangoing vessel (now transformed into a bar, hotel, and nightclub complex), and the Shekou bar street.

Splendid China features China's 74 best-known historical and geographical sights collected and miniaturized to 1:15 scale. Built in 1991 and popularized by Deng Xiaoping (who stopped in for a photo op on his famous 1992 journey south promoting free enterprise), it is still a big draw with the patriotic camera-wielding masses, and not a few Westerners "doing China" in a day. The 74-acre site includes a waist-high

Continued on page 332

21ST ★

CENTURY
CHINA

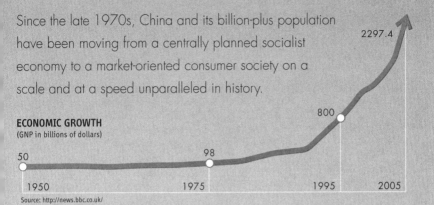

Since the late 1970s, China and its billion-plus population have been moving from a centrally planned socialist economy to a market-oriented consumer society on a scale and at a speed unparalleled in history.

ECONOMIC GROWTH
(GNP in billions of dollars)

2297.4

800

50

98

1950

1975

1995

2005

Source: http://news.bbc.co.uk/

9

SHANGHAI

BEIJING

A Chinese Century?

The SARS hiccup aside, China's economy has been red-hot since joining the World Trade Organization in 2001. One of the engines driving the global economy, it helped revive Japan's sagging economy and the slumping international shipping industry. Worldwide commodities markets have also been boosted by China's increasing hunger for everything from copper to coffee.

GDP-ANNUAL GROWTH RATE

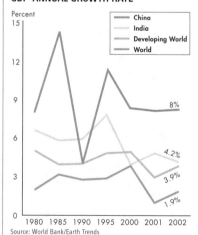

Percent

- China
- India
- Developing World
- World

8%
4.2%
3.9%
1.9%

1980 1985 1990 1995 2000 2001 2002

Source: World Bank/Earth Trends

The country that was long written off as just a cheap exporter is now a net importer. It's the fourth-largest economy in the world after the United States, Japan, and Germany, whose economies are growing at less than half the rate.

Such development is nothing short of remarkable, but national problems such as energy, the environment, and wealth inequality are threatening the country.

Internationally, it's how China and the United States cooperate on global issues, and how they manage their own complex relationship, that may have the greatest impact on the rest of the century. Since Nixon first opened the door in 1972, the two countries have managed to forge a working relationship. But Yuan revaluation, trade issues, energy supply (especially oil), and both countries' military role in the Asia-Pacific region are all issues that could sour this budding friendship.

(top) Architectural stars (or starchitects) like Rem Koolhaas, Li Hu, Paul Andreu, and Jacques Herzog and Pierre de Meuron (Olympic Stadium, above) are descending on Beijing for construction of state-of-the-art Olympic venues. (right) Hong Kong skyline.

HONG KONG

Fueling the Chinese Dream

China is now the number two energy consumer in the world, after the United States. Its consumption has exploded by an average of 5% yearly since 1998. This thirst for fuel is evident on roads all over the country. The land of the bicycle is now car-crazy. Three million vehicles were recently sold, and higher sales are predicted in the coming years.

Back in 2005, the country consumed 320 million tons of crude oil, roughly one-third of which was imported. It's expecting to import 500 million tons by 2020, two-thirds of its projected total imports.

Where will China get this oil? Much comes from countries with troubled relations with the west such as Iran and Sudan, but it is also working on importing more from traditional U.S. suppliers such as Saudi Arabia.

There's also a growing demand for electricity, 75% of which comes from coal. In the coming 25 years, the greenhouse gases produced by China's coal burning will probably exceed that of all industrial nations combined. And the country will continue to rely on coal for electricity in the years to come, despite large hydropower projects and a plan to increase the number of nuclear power plants.

Aside from developing clean, renewable energy sources, China needs to improve its poor energy efficiency—it uses nine times the energy Japan does to produce one GDP unit. But plans are being made to improve energy efficiency by 20% from 2006 to 2010.

WORLD OIL CONSUMPTION

USA 24.8%
Rest of the World 50.7%
China 7.9%
Japan 6.9%
Russia 3.5%
Germany 3.3%
India 2.9%

Source: http://www.nationmaster.com/

Can China Go Green?

A devastated environment is a major result of China's economic transformation. For example, because of deforestation around the capital, Beijing is threatened by the encroaching Gobi Desert, which dumped 300,000 tons of sand on the city in one week in 2006. Industrial carelessness and lack of regulation result in accidents such as the 50-mile benzene spill in a river near Harbin in late 2005.

Cities have been smoggy for decades because of pollution from factories, vehicles, and especially coal. But air quality is now becoming obscured by water issues. In mid-2006, the Water Resources Ministry reported that 320 million urban residents—more than the population of the United States—did not have access to clean drinking water.

Much of this is the result of a development-at-any-cost mentality, particularly in the wake of economic reform. Companies and factories, many of which are foreign-owned, have only recently had to deal with environmental laws— "scoff laws"—that are often circumvented by bribing local officials. And average citizens don't have freedom of speech or access to political tools to fight environmentally damaging projects.

Is the central government waking up? In 2006, the vice-chairman of China's increasingly outspoken State Environmental Protection Agency put it bluntly: "We will face tremendous problems if we do not change our development patterns."

Mind the Gap

China has come a long way from the days when everyone had an "iron rice bowl," or a state-appointed job that was basically guaranteed regardless of one's abilities or work performance.

Since 1980, the country has quadrupled per capita income and raised more than 220 million of its citizens out of poverty. A belt of prosperity is emerging along the coast, but hundreds of millions still live on less than $1 per day.

(left) Owning a car is the new Chinese dream. (top right) The Three Gorges Dam will be the largest in the world, supplying the hydroelectric power of 18 nuclear plants. (bottom right) China's cities are some of the most polluted in the world.

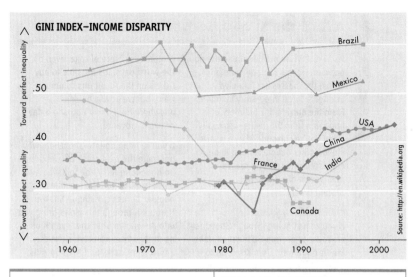

GINI INDEX—INCOME DISPARITY

Toward perfect inequality

.50

.40

Toward perfect equality

.30

Brazil

Mexico

USA

China

France

India

Canada

Source: http://en.wikipedia.org

1960 1970 1980 1990 2000

Economists use a statistical yardstick known as the Gini coefficient to measure wealth inequality in a society, with zero being perfect equality and one being perfect inequality. The World Bank estimates that China's national Gini coefficient rose from 0.30 to 0.45 from 1982, a 50% jump in two decades. In 2006, some academics estimated China's current Gini coefficient to be closer to, or even higher, than Latin America's 0.52.

As economic inequality has grown, so has discontent, particularly in rural areas. The country recorded 87,000 public protests in 2005, an increase of 11,000 over the year before.

Many of these protests are incited by the acts of local, particularly rural, officials whose corruption policies are sometimes beyond Beijing's sphere of influence.

Most protests are focused on specific incidents or officials rather than general dissent against the government, but the growing frequency of such events is not going unnoticed by the central government. In 2005, 8,400 officials were arrested on corruption-related charges.

CHINA IN NUMBERS

	CHINA	U.S.
Area in sq km:	9,560,960	9,631,420
Population	1.3 bil	300 mil
Men (15–64 yrs)	482 mil	100 mil
Women (15–64 yrs)	456 mil	101 mil
Population growth	0.59%	0.91%
Life expectancy: men	70.8	75
Life expectancy: women	74.6	80.8
GDP per head	$1,090	$37,240
Health spending, % GDP	5.8	14.6
Doctors per 1000 pop.	1.6	2.8
Hospital beds per 1000 pop.	1.6	3.0
Infant mortality rate per 1000 births	23.12	6.43
Education spending, % GDP	2.1	5.7
Adult literacy: men	95.1%	99%
Adult literacy: women	86.5%	99%
Internet users	111 mil	204 mil

Avoid the Luohu Border-Crossing Crush

AT LUOHU (the main border crossing between Hong Kong and mainland China) the masses are funneled through a large three-story building. From the outside this building looks huge, but from the inside—especially when you're surrounded by a quarter million other people waiting to be processed—the crossing can be reminiscent of a scene from *Soylent Green*.

ALTERNATIVE ROUTES

If you're just going through Shenzhen en-route to or from Guangzhou, take the through train from Kowloon to Guangzhou. The immigration line at the Guangzhou East station is a comparative piece of cake, even on the worst days. It's possible to buy tickets on the fly on this commuter train, but we advise booking anywhere from a few hours to a day or two in advance.

If you're heading into Shenzhen, why not trade the mad crush of Luohu for an hour-long ferry ride followed by a quick trip through the much less popular border crossing at Shekou Harbor? Although this won't bring you into downtown Shenzhen, you'll be no farther from attractions like the amusement parks and Mission Hills Golf Club.

Great Wall, a fun-size Forbidden City, and little Potala Palace. ⊠ *OCT District, Shenzhen* ☎ *0755/2660–0626* 🎫 *Y140* ⊙ *Daily 10–10* Ⓜ *Windows of the World metro station.*

⟳ **Windows of the World** gives a similar miniature makeover to 130 of the world's most famous landmarks and is China's biggest and busiest homegrown theme park. Divided into eight geographical areas interconnected by winding paths and a full-size monorail, it includes randomly scaled Taj Mahal, Mount Rushmore, Sydney Harbor Opera House, and a 100-meter- (328-foot-) high Eiffel Tower that can be seen from miles away. There is also a fireworks show at 9 PM on weekends and holidays which, for adults, is best viewed from across the street at the Crowne Plaza's rooftop V-Bar. ⊠ *OCT, Nanshan District, Shenzhen* ☎ *0755/ 2660–8000* ⊕ *www.szwwco.com* 🎫 *Y140* ⊙ *Daily 9 AM–10 PM* Ⓜ *Windows of the World metro station.*

Shenzhen is a great city for art lovers. In addition to its statue-filled Overseas Chinese Town Park, the OCT neighborhood is packed with other museums. The **He Xiangning Art Museum** is free on Friday and features contemporary and classical art from all over China. ⊠ *Shenzhen shi Huaqiaocheng Shennan Dadao 9013 hao, OCT, Nanshan District* ☎*0755/ 2660–4540* ⊙ *Tues.–Sun. 10–6* Ⓜ *Huaqiaocheng metro station.*

The **OCT Contemporary Art Terminal.** Shenzhen shi Huaqiaocheng Enping Lu is where you'll find works from the hippest artists from Beijing and beyond. ⊠ *OCT, Nanshan District* ☎ *0755/2691–6199* ⊙ *Call for hrs* Ⓜ *Huaqiaocheng metro station.*

Yantian, Longgang & Bao'an

Though these three districts make up the bulk of Shenzhen's land area, most casual visitors to the city never hear of them, let alone visit them. We think this is a pity, as it's these outer regions where you'll find both the prettiest scenery and the most culturally edifying places in the Pearl River Delta, not to mention China's most famous golf course, Mission Hills.

PLAY TIME

The theme parks in OCT could all be visited in a single day, but for the sake of sanity, we recommend only visiting two for the day. They are connected by an elevated monorail that costs Y20. Splendid China and Windows on the World have some "cultural" value, and Happy Kingdom is fun for kids.

Just east of Luohu, Yantian is Shenzhen's beach district. **Dameisha** and **Xiaomeisha** are two beaches adjacent to one another, which offer sun, surf, and strange statues of colorful winged men doing what appears to be beachfront tai chi. Dameisha is a public beach, whereas Xiaomeisha has a Y20 admission price. Both are about 40 minutes from Luohu by taxi. Yantian is also the home of **Minsk World,** a decommissioned Soviet-era aircraft carrier turned into a tourist attraction.

Minsk World. When a group of Shenzhen businessmen bought a decommissioned Soviet-era aircraft carrier in the late 1990s, Western intelligence agencies wondered if it was a military move by the Chinese. But the truth was revealed when these savvy entrepreneurs turned this massive warship into Minsk World, Shenzhen's most popular—and perhaps strangest—tourist attraction. Parked in perpetuity on the top deck of the ship (which is as long as three football fields placed end to end, and gets wickedly hot in the summer) are several Soviet fighter planes and helicopters. Every hour on the hour comely young ladies in military costumes perform a dance routine combining sensuality with martial flair and twirling rifles. A visit to Minsk World will be of greatest interest to military buffs. Even casual visitors should find it educational enough to warrant spending the afternoon. ✉ *Shatoujiao, Dapeng Bay, Yantian District, Shenzhen* 🖼 *Y110* ◔ *Daily 10–9.*

Longgang, Shenzen's ancient heart, is where you'll find the sights that belie the city's reputation as a place of new money and no history. **Dapeng Fortress** is a Ming Dynasty-era walled city where visitors can wander down narrow cobblestone streets and walk on parapets that were ancient even in the days of the last Qing empress. The **Hakka Folk Customs Museum and Enclosures** is another walled town. This one was built (and formerly occupied) by the Hakka—Han Chinese who are said to have migrated from north to south ages ago, bringing with them their own cuisine and traditions; not to mention peculair building design. Both of these slices of ancient China are about an hour away from the modern heart of Luohu by taxi.

Finally, the Bao'an District is famous for Mission Hills, the finest golf club in China and the largest in the world (according to the *Guinness Book of World Records*).

Dapeng Fortress was built over 600 years ago, and is an excellent example of a Ming Dynasty–military encampment (1368–1644). The fortress was originally built to resist Japanese pirates who'd been harassing the southern coastal areas of Guangdong. However, the fortress is best known as the site of the British Naval attack of September 4, 1839, in which British forces attacked China in what is widely considered the beginning of the Opium Wars. As local legend goes, Chinese troops in fishing boats, led by General Lai Enjue, defeated the better-equipped enemy. Today, visitors flock to the fortress to admire the inside of the walled town, which is replete with ornately carved beams and columns, with poetic couplets painted over each door. ⊠ *Pengcheng Village, Dapeng Town, Longgang District, Shenzhen* ☎ *No phone* ✆ *Y20* ☉ *Daily 10–9.*

Hakka Folk Customs Museum and Enclosures is actually a large series of concentric circular homes built inside of an exterior wall that basically turns the whole place into a large fort. Inside of the enclosure are a large number of old Hakka residences, some of which are still filled with tools and furniture left over from the Qing Dynasty. The site is somewhat feral; once you pass the ticket booth, you're pretty much on your own and free to stroll around the grounds and explore inside of the residences themselves, many of which seem to have been left in a mostly natural state. Although some restoration projects pretty things up to the point of making the site look unreal, the opposite is true here. Parts of the enclosures are so real as to seem downright spooky; visitors might get the feeling that the original inhabitants may return at any moment, crossbows cocked. ⊠ *Luoruihe Village, Longgang Township, Longgang District, Shenzhen* ☎ *0755/2883–5108* ✆ *Y20* ☉ *Daily 10–6.*

If you're interested in watching art in the making, spend an afternoon at the **Dafen Oil Painting Village,** a small town 20 minutes by taxi from Luohu, which employs thousands of artists painting everything from originals to copies of classics. Where do all those oil paintings you find in motels come from? Visit Dafen and you'll know. Be aware, opening hours are sporadic. ⊠ *Shen Hui Rd., Bu Ji St., Longgang District* ☎ *0755/8473—2622.*

Luohu & Futian

Though Luohu and Futian are the smallest districts in the city, for many it is this urban jungle of skyscrapers, markets, restaurants, and hotels that defines Shenzhen. Luohu (*Lo Wu* in Cantonese) is the area beginning right at the border crossing with Hong Kong. Jienshi Road is the street that ends at the border, and like many border areas, has more than just a bit of a rough feel about it. Single men walking on this road (which parallels the train tracks leading north to Guangzhou and south to Hong Kong) will be harassed by countless women shouting out "massage" and "missy" (ironically, this street also has a number of good, reputable massage parlors as well as a number of excellent restaurants).

Futian, Shenzhen's trading hub, is also where the Shenzhen's gourmands go for a night of gastronomic pleasure. The Zhenhua Road–restaurant district in Futian is where scores of excellent restaurants compete for the patronage of Shenzhen's very discriminating diners.

Where to Eat

Shenzhen is packed with people from other provinces, and its main culinary strength lies in this diversity. From the heavy mutton stews of Xinjiang to the spicy seafood dishes of Fujian, Shenzhen is home to thousands of restaurants existing not to please the fickle palates of visitors, but to alleviate the homesickness of people pining for native provinces left behind. Furthermore, over the past few years, Shenzhen has attracted a slew of restaurateurs from abroad, making the city a veritable culinary mecca, not merely for those with a taste for Chinese cuisine, but for international gourmands as well.

★ **$$$-$$$$** ✕ **Blue Italian Seafood & Grill.** Arguably one of the finest Italian restaurants in China, the decor, as the name suggests, is blue—blue walls, ceilings, and mellow indigo lighting. The food is expensive but worth every penny. If you're really in the mood for decadence, try the dessert tray—chocolates, pastries, and eight different types of mousse surround a caramelized sugar statue of David. ⊠ *Crowne Plaza hotel, 3rd fl., 9026 Shen Nan Rd., OCT District* ☎ *0755/2693–6888 Ext. 8022, 8023, or 8106* 🖃 *AE, DC, MC, V.*

$$-$$$ ✕ **Greenland Lounge.** This favorite is known for its international-style buffet and truly unique selection of Chinese teas. The glass-domed roof and smart-casual ambiance makes this a popular spot for Shenzhen's movers and shakers. ⊠ *Lobby, Pavilion Hotel, 4002 Huaqiang Rd. N, Futian District* ☎ *(0755) 8207–8888* 🖃 *AE, DC, MC, V.*

$$-$$$ ✕ **360.** The newest (and possibly brightest) star on the Shenzhen haute-
Fodor's Choice cuisine scene, 360 takes up the top two floors of the Shangri-La hotel,
★ and offers sumptuous dishes like homemade pasta with eggplant, zucchini, and pesto sauce and ginger-crusted-salmon fillet with couscous and lemon celery sauce. Ambiance is chic, and the view from any table in the house is breathtaking. For food, decor, and view we can't recommend this place highly enough. ⊠ *31st fl., Shangri-La hotel, 1002 Jianshi Rd., Luohu* ☎ *0755/ 8396–1380* 🖃 *AE, DC, MC, V* Ⓜ *Luohu metro.*

$-$$ ✕ **Sunday Chiu Chow King.** The dim sum and other Cantonese dishes are good, but what really sets this place apart is the excellent Chaozhou (or Chiu Chow) cuisine. The restaurant is well known on both sides of the border, and usually packed on the weekends with noisy diners from Hong Kong. Try the crispy fried tofu and steamed seafood balls, or the yin-yang soup (it's the soup that looks like a yin-and-yang symbol, made up of rice

9

ADVENTUROUS EATING

The Futian District's Zhen Hua Road, just two blocks north of the Hua Qiang metro station, is one of the few food streets that had not succumbed to the franchise blight of McDonald's and KFC. There are very few English menus and even less Western food, so be prepared to be adventurous. Two good choices are the North Sea Fishing Village Restaurant, whose waitstaff speak a bit of English, and has live seafood in tanks out front allowing diners point and choose, and Lao Yuan Zi, a restaurant with a definite *Crouching Tiger, Hidden Dragon* vibe.

CLOSE UP

To Your Health!

GOOD-BYE STARBUCKS, hello Wong Chun Loong! For decades the Loong-beverage franchise has dominated the Guangzhou scene, and for good reason. They serve drinks that are thirst-quenching, healthy, and taste good (sometimes). The most popular drink is *Huomaren*, a beverage made from crushed hemp seeds (it's the brown beverage displayed on the counter) and *yezi*, or coconut milk. A cup of either only costs Y2.

Wong Chun Loong also brews Chinese medicinal teas—some of the bitterest stuff you're ever likely to taste. If you'd like to try some, point to your throat and say *"wo gan mao"*–"I have a cold." If you're nice, they may give you a free piece of candy to cut the aftertaste.

There are about 800 branches in the city, so if you walk a few blocks in any direction, you're bound to stumble on one of them.

congee on one side and creamed spinach on the other, just point to the picture on the menu). All of these are Chaozhou specialty dishes. ⊠ *Jen Shi Rd. 1076, 9th–10th fls., Luohu, 2 blocks north of Shangri-La hotel* ☎ *0755/8231–0222* ▤ *V* Ⓜ *Luohu metro station.*

★ **$–$$** ✕ **Yokohama.** Here they offer excellent sushi with amazing views of the fishing boats and ferries of Shekou Harbor to the east, and the hills of Shekou to the north. Sashimi is the freshest around, and other dishes are the real deal. The clientele is mostly Japanese, which is always a good sign. Try a side dish of *oshinko* (traditional Japanese pickles)—unlike many lesser Japanese restaurants in China, Yokohama takes no short-cuts with its oshinko and offers eight different types. ⊠ *Shekou Harbor, Nanhai Hotel, 10th fl., Shekou District* ☎ *0755/2669–5557* ▤ *AE, DC, MC, V.*

$ ✕ **Little India.** This is definitely more than your average curry house. The Nepalese chef offers cuisine from both northern India and Nepal. The restaurant is especially known for its tandoori dishes, and for its selection of baked *nan* breads. Little India is also the only restaurant in the Sea World Plaza that offers hookahs, though they'll gently ask you to smoke on the outdoor pavilion during peak hours. ⊠ *Shop 73-74, Sea World Plaza, Shekou District* ☎ *0755/2685–2688* ▤ *MC, V.*

$–$$ ✕ **Shenzhen North Sea Restaurant.** This is a popular Shenzen franchise (there are two other locations) where diners can pick their own seafood from one of the tanks outside and have it cooked to order. The restaurant is known for its quality and freshness, and is busy on any given night. We've chosen the branch on the Zhen Hua Road food street simply because it's easy to find and a few of the waitresses understand a bit of English. ⊠ *79 Zhen Hua Rd., Futian District, 2 blocks north of the Huaqiang metro station* ☎ *0755/8322–1852* ▤ *MC, V.*

$ ✕ **Lao Yuan Zi.** They have Sichuan and Hunan food so spicy that scientists are looking into the connection between Lao Yuan Zi's cuisine and global warming. A favorite dish is the hotpot, made with fiery red chilies and a variety of meat and vegetables. A plethora of cold-vegetable dishes abound, as do meat, seafood, and vegetable dishes of all sorts. If you order the Sichuan hotpot, the best strategy is to keep a bowl of white rice close at hand; beer won't douse this fire fast enough. Be warned; this place can get rather noisy. ⊠ *1,2/F, Qi Che Building, at the intersection of Zhen Hua and Yan Nan Rds., Futian District, 2 blocks north of the Hua Qiang metro station* ☎ *020/8332–8400* ▤ *No credit cards.*

¢–$ ✕ **Foodfeast.** This is the only place in Shekou for genuine Hakka cuisine, including rich soups made with pork and bitter melon, serious Hakka-style dumplings, stewed clay-pot dishes and roasted chicken, duck, and fatty pork. Try the durian pancake, if you're a fan of the enormously smelly "king of fruits." (Durian's odor is so strong that it is sometimes banned from subways.) Foodfeast is unpretentious, the sort of place where Sun Yet-sen might have taken tea while plotting the revolution against the Manchu Dynasty. ⊠ *Sea World Hotel, 1st fl., Taizi Rd. #7, Shekou District* ☎ *0755/2540–4730* ▤ *No credit cards.*

Where to Stay

$$$$ ✕▦ **Crowne Plaza.** This hotel holds its own among the best hotels in

Fodor'sChoice Asia. Theme is pure Italian Renaissance, right down to the Venetian-

★ gondolier uniforms worn by the staff, and the wide spiral staircases and long hallways gives the place an M. C. Escher feel. The Crowne's swimming pool is the largest in Shenzhen, and extends from an indoor pool under a domed roof to a connected outdoor pool with a swim-up bar. One regular patron told us that she comes back "because anywhere you look in this hotel there's something interesting." The Crowne also has a number of excellent restaurants, including Blue, Marcos, and JK. ⊠ *OCT District, 9026 Shenzhen Rd. 518053, across from Windows on the World metro station* ☎ *0755/2693–6888* ⊕ *www.crowneplaza. com* ⇆ *340 rooms, 50 suites* ♨ *5 restaurants, pool, gym, sauna, 2 bars, business services, meeting room* ▤ *AE, DC, MC, V.*

$$$$ ✕▦ **The Pavilion.** With a great location in the heart of the Futian business district, and a gorgeous interior (check out the domed-glass roof over a central piano bar–teahouse), the Pavilion is one of the top international-class hotels in Shenzhen. Service is good, especially for a locally managed hotel, and most staff members speak English. In addition to the teahouse, the Pavilion has Western, Chinese, Korean, and Japanese restaurants, all very tastefully done-up. The meeting rooms have everything an international traveler could need. ⊠ *4002 Huaqiang Bei Lu, Futian District, 518028* ☎ *0755/ 8207–8888* ⊕ *www.pavilionhotel. com* ⇆ *297 rooms, 19 suites* ♨ *4 restaurants, pool, gym, sauna, business services, meeting room* ▤ *AE, DC, MC, V.*

$$$–$$$$ ✕▦ **Landmark Shenzhen.** Since completing its ambitious renovation program in 2006, The Landmark has become Shenzhen's first *all-suite* hotel; every room is a suite, boasting a 42-inch plasma television and extra-large bathrooms. In addition, the hotel has five excellent restaurants, including a wine and cigar bar with a walk-in humidor. However, what makes this hotel truly unique is its personalized butler service, managed by Robert Watson, director of the Guild of Professional English Butlers and the former principal tutor at the Lady Apsley School for But-

9

Sleeping on the Cheap

SPAS ARE A RECENT and much welcome trend in Shenzhen, and the city offers a number of excellent places to get soaked, sauna'd, and massaged to your heart's content. Although some of these places are thinly disguised houses of ill repute, many more cater to a higher class of clientele looking for a legitimate massage and sauna.

The way a Chinese sauna works is this: you check-in, lock up your belongings in a guarded locker room (you keep one key and the attendants keep the other), and have a shower and steam, and then soak as long as you like. Afterward, dressed in the spa's pajamas, you relax in a common area (usually well stocked with food and beverages, a couple of plasma-screen televisions piping in Hong Kong television, and comfortable chaise longues) until you're ready for your massage.

A well-known money-saving tip among Chinese travelers on overnight business is to check-in to one of these

places in the mid- to late evening and catch a few hours sleep in the common area after your massage. Your admission price—usually around Y200—entitles you to stick around until 9 AM the next day, and the common areas are generally pretty quiet after 2 AM (and guests are always provided blankets), making this a good strategy for anyone on a shoestring budget.

One such place in the Futian District that's both clean, cheerful, and co-ed is the **Shanshui Korean Spa** (⊠ No.1 Hua Fa Bei Lu,, Futian District, 2 blocks north of Hua Qiang metro station ☎ 0755/6135–8862). Shanshui (which means "mountain water") is a Korean-themed spa. Although the hot tubs in both areas are somewhat small, the spa offers a rather interesting co-ed dry-sauna filled with small, rounded stones, which visitors are meant to sink down into for a full-body experience. Y165 gets you a massage, full sauna privileges, a light snack, and night's stay should you be so inclined.

---

lers in London. As for amenities, this hotel basically has it all. If you're looking to experience the life of China's new elite, this is the place to do it. ⊠ 3018 Nanhu Lu, 3 blocks NE of Shenzhen main station, Shenzhen 518001 ☎ 0755/8217–2288 ⊕ www.szlandmark.com ⇌ 253 suites ♦ 5 restaurants, driving range, pool, gym, bar, shops, business services, meeting rooms ☐ AE, DC, MC, V.

★ $$$–$$$$ ✕🖫 **Shangri-La Shenzhen.** The location (practically straddling the border with Hong Kong) has made it a popular meeting place, and it's a city landmark. Rooms are first-class, hospitality is excellent, and the hotel features in-house wireless Internet and top-notch spa facilities. What really makes Shangri-La worth a visit is the newly renovated 360 Lounge and Restaurant, which takes up the top two floors of the hotel and offers a view of Shenzhen. The Shangri-La also has a number of other excellent restaurants, making it a good choice for first-time visitors who might not want to come into contact with the neighborhood's rougher edges. ⊠ 1002 Jianshe Lu, Luohu District, Shenzhen 518001, Luohu, east side of train station ☎ 0755/8233–0888 ⊕ www.shangri-la.com

553 rooms, 30 suites ⚘ *6 restaurants, pool, gym, hair salon, bar, shops, business services, meeting rooms* ▱ *AE, DC, MC, V.*

¢–$ ▦ **Cruise Inn.** Pearlescent tiled floors and stained-glass ceilings are the first thing you'll notice in the lobby of this newly opened hotel inside of the landlocked and permanently docked good ship *Minghua*, the central feature of Shekou's Sea World Plaza. Rooms are clean, comfortable, and nautically themed. The Romantic Sea View room has a waterbed and a view of the ocean and driving range; the Captain's Suite looks out over bar street, and has two plasma-screen televisions and a Jacuzzi. If a whimsical maritime *Alice in Wonderland*-style inn is what you're looking for, then look no further. ⊠ *Minghua Ship, Sea World, Shekou 518069* ☎ *0755/2682–5555* ⊕ *www.honlux.com* *110 rooms, 1 suite* ⚘ *3 restaurants, coffee shop, 2 bars, dance club, driving range, bicycles* ▱ *AE, DC, MC, V.*

¢–$ ✕▦ **Nan Hai.** This hotel's retro space-age exterior, featuring rounded balconies that look as if they might detach from the mother ship at any moment, is the first sight greeting visitors on the Hong Kong–Shekou ferry. Although one of Shenzhen's older luxury hotels, the Nan Hai still holds its own in the moderate- luxury class, offering a lobby piano bar, attractive rooms with balconies and sea views, and a number of excellent restaurants, including Yokohama. ⊠ *1 Gongye Yilu, Shekou 518069* ☎ *0755/2669–2888* ⊕ *www.nanhai-hotel.com* *358 rooms, 86 suites* ⚘ *5 restaurants, 2 tennis courts, pool, hair salon, piano bar, dance club, meeting rooms* ▱ *AE, DC, MC, V.*

¢–$$ ▦ **Shenzhen Sea View.** Staying in the OCT District but can't afford the Crowne Plaza? The nearby Sea View hotel is a good bet, albeit far less luxurious. Though rack prices are steep, discounts of up to 40% are usually available. The Sea View is clean, comfortable, has a water view, and thanks to its location across the street from the He Xiangning Art Museum, it is very popular with visiting artists. The 2nd-floor restaurant serves excellent Western food, and the 3rd-floor Cantonese restaurant is good for dim sum. ⊠ *No. 3-5 Guangqiao St., OCT, Nanshan District, Directly in front of Huaqiao Cheng metro* ☎ *0755/2660–2222* *446 rooms, 11 suites* ⚘ *2 restaurants, coffee shop, gym, sauna* ▱ *AE, DC, MC, V.*

¢–$ ▦ **Shanshui Trends Hotel.** This budget hotel in the Futian District appeals mostly to business travelers. With a round bed and view of the interior food court, the Romance Suite is a bit musty and distinctly unromantic. However, the Japanese Suite, with its wooden tub and traditional tatami-mats was much nicer. Shanshui Trends is a good deal for travelers on a shoestring, located in one of Shenzhen's most happening food districts. Discounts of up to 30% are available. ⊠ *No.1 Hua Fa Bei Lu,, Futian District, 2 blocks north of Hua Qiang metro station* ☎ *0755/ 6135–8802* *197 rooms, 2 suites* ⚘ *Spa, gym* ▱ *AE, DC, MC, V.*

Nightlife & Arts

Shenzhen's nightlife is so happening that it's not unusual to run into people—expats and Chinese—who've come in from Hong Kong and Guangzhou just to party. The two major happening nightlife centers in Shenzhen are the Luohu District and Shekou District (Luohu tends to be flashier and Shekou a bit more laid-back), but there are also a couple of cool spots in the OCT District as well.

Baby Face (✉ Beside Lushan Hotel, Luohu District ☎ 0755/9234–2565 ⊕ www.babyface.com.cn) is the Shenzhen branch of one of China's most popular nightspots, offering imported DJs, a late-night-party scene, and extremely chic clientele (so don't show up in sandals).

True Colors (✉ 3F Dongyuan Mansion, 1 Dongyuan Lu, Futian District ☎ 0755/8212–9333) has one of the coolest party scenes in Shenzhen and attracts top-name international DJs. Musical tastes range from trance to house, and the party usually doesn't break up until dawn.

PARTY LISTINGS

A great English-language Web site that lists the latest on what's happening in Shenzhen's ever-evolving party scene is ⊕ www.shenzhenparty.com.

V-Bar (✉ Crowne Plaza hotel, rooftop, OCT District ☎ 0755/2693–6888) is without a doubt the hottest nightspot in the OCT, featuring a live band, a holographic globe hovering over a circular bar, and a fireworks show on the weekends at 9 PM courtesy of the Windows on the World theme park across the street. The V-Bar is the only bar in town with an attached swimming pool.

Browns Wine Bar & Cigar House (✉ Portofino, OCT District, Shenzhen ☎ 0755/8608–2379) is the perfect, low-key place for quiet conversation over a bottle of wine and a Cuban cigar. Browns' has an admirable stock of vintage wines, cognacs, and Armagnacs, and a walk-in humidor to insure that all cigars are kept fresh. This is a good spot for those who appreciate old-money ambiance and fine cigars.

Soho Nightclub (✉ TaiZi Bar St, Shekou District ☎ 0755/2669–0148 or 0755/2669–2148) is the place in Shekou to dance, drink, and party. If you need a rest from dancing, be sure to slip out to the outdoor garden for a cocktail.

3 colors Bar (✉ Jing Yuan Building, 2nd fl., SongYuan Rd., Luohu District ☎ 0755/2588–7000) is a lively dance club that's very in with Shenzhen's gay crowd. It's a fun place so there's often a wide mix of people.

Er Ding Mu (✉ Jiang Nan Chun Hotel, 3rd fl., Ai Hua Rd. No.23, Futian District, at Nanyuan and Ai Hua Rds. ☎ 0755/8365–1879 or 131/4883–9798) is another popular gay club, offering a more relaxed spot for a mostly younger male crowd to unwind and hook up.

OUT IN SHENZHEN

One of the byproducts of China's rapid modernization has been the shedding of old taboos. While it's an overstatement to say being gay is no longer taboo, it is safe to say that the closet door has been opened in a big way. And no place is this more true than in Shenzhen, which has always prided itself as being ahead of the curve.

Shopping

The ever-upwardly mobile denizens of the city (not to mention bargain hunters from neighboring Hong Kong) are always looking for places to spend their hard-earned yuan, and from computer parts to fashion, shoes to cell phones, China's first city of capitalism pretty much has it all.

Dongmen Shopping Plaza (✉ Laojie Metro Station, Luohu District, Shenzhen ☎ No phone) is Shenzhen's oldest shopping area. It's a sprawling pedestrian plaza with both large shopping centers for name-brand watches, shoes, bags, cosmetics, and clothes, and plenty of smaller outdoor shops. Foot fetishists won't want to miss the huge **Dongmen Shoes City,** close to the east side of the plaza. If you're into people-watching, grab a glass of bubble-milk tea and soak up the sights—the plaza is like a low-rent version of the fashionista youth culture in Tokyo's Ginza.

CITIC City Plaza (✉ 1095 Shennan Rd., Futian, Shenzhen ☎ 0755/2594–1502 ⊙ Daily 10:30 AM to 10 PM Ⓜ Kexueguan metro station) offers upscale shopping for the time-conscious business traveler. Shops include Japanese department stores **Seibu and Jusco, Louis Vuitton, Polo,** and **Tommy Hilfiger.** There's also a food court on the lower level that's not a bad place to take a break over some coffee or a bowl of noodle soup.

Louhu Commercial City (Lo Wu) (✉Adjacent to the Hong Kong Border Crossing/Luohu metro station, Shenzhen ☎ No phone ⊙ Daily 10 AM–10 PM) is a venerable stalwart of Shenzhen mixed-bag shopping. On one hand, its location (straddling the Hong Kong–Shenzhen border) makes it a good place to do last-minute shopping for pirate DVDs, shoddy electronics, and phony versions of just about any name brand you can think of, and stalls selling semiprecious stones and feng-shui knickknacks on the 2nd floor are pretty cool. On the other hand, Luohu Commercial City has some of the most aggressive touts you're likely to find in Shenzhen. If having "DVD? Rolex watch?" shouted every 20 seconds doesn't bother you, this place might be worth the trip.

San Dao Plaza (✉ Jen Shi Rd. 1076, Luohu Shenzhen ☎ No phone ⊙ 9 AM–8 PM Ⓜ Luohu metro station). This four-story extravaganza is the area's best market for medicinal herbs, tea, and tea-related products. The top two floors contain a series of stalls where merchants sell a wide range of Chinese teas. Visitors are generally invited to *lai, he cha,* or come drink tea. Don't worry, it isn't considered rude to have a cup without buying anything, but if you're a tea aficionado you'll find it hard to leave empty-handed. Downstairs, there is also a large vegetable market and small shops selling traditional Chinese herbal medicines, incense, and religious items. If you speak a little Chinese, you can have your fortune told.

Side Trips to Zhongshan and Zhuhai

Two other cities worth visiting in the Pearl River Delta are Zhongshan and Zhuhai. Though some casual visitors might choose to spend more than one day in this region, both are small enough to be seen in an afternoon.

Zhongshan is 78 km (48 mi) from Guangzhou and 61 km (38 mi) northwest of Macau. Until recently it was a picturesque port, where a cantilever bridge over the Qi River was raised twice a day to allow small freighters to pass. Today, the old town has been all but obliterated by modern high-rises, and the surrounding farms are now factories. However, there are still a few spots of historical note worth seeing.

Zhongshan is the birthplace of Sun Yat-sen and home to the **Sun Yat-sen Memorial Hall** (✉ Sunwen Zhong Lu 🎟 Y10 ☉ Daily 8–4:50). Considered the father of the Chinese revolution that overthrew the corrupt Qing Dynasty, he is one of the few political figures respected on both sides of the Taiwan Straits.

The **Xishan Temple** (✉ Xishan Park 🎟 Y5 ☉ Daily 8–5) is a beautifully restored temple that's also worth a visit.

Probably the most popular spot in town is **Sunwen Xilu,** a pedestrian mall lined with dozens of restored buildings. At the end of the street is the lovely **Zhongshan Park,** where there is the seven-story Fufeng Pagoda (about the only thing in Zhongshan not named after Sun Yat-sen), and also the world's largest statue of . . . you guessed it, Sun Yat-sen.

Buses travel daily to Zhongshan from bus stations throughout the Pearl River Delta.

Bordering Macau, and a little over an hour away by ferry from Hong Kong and Shenzhen, most people don't see **Zhuhai** as a major destination in its own right. The city does, however, have a nice long coastline and many small offshore islands. Lover's Road, a 20-km (12½-mi) stretch of road hugging the shoreline, is Zhuhai's signature attraction, as beachside drives are a rarity in China. The road leads to the **Macau Crossing** and has enough bars and restaurants to draw a steady crowd of Macau partygoers. Near the Macau border, across from the bus station, is **Yingbin Street,** a popular shopping area. Cheap seafood restaurants stay open well after midnight and, thanks to a variety of hawkers, street musicians, and food stalls, it makes for a fascinating, if slightly earthy, evening stroll.

To & from Shenzhen

1 hr by express train, 2½ hrs by express bus (112 km [70 mi]) from Guangzhou. Walk across border from Hong Kong's Luohu KCR (Kowloon–Canton Railway) train station.

Tens of thousands of people cross from Hong Kong into Shenzhen (and back) daily, usually over the Luohu border crossing. Over the weekends, numbers can triple. Most visitors take the KCR train ⊕ www.kcrc.com from Kowloon to the crossing and walk into Shenzhen. A more expensive—but infinitely more pleasant—way is by taking the ferry from Hong Kong or Kowloon into Shekou Harbor. Here, immigration lines are a fraction of what they can be in Luohu. Shenzhen Party maintains an updated schedule for trains and ferries at ⊕ www.shenzhenparty.com/comingtoshenzhen/index.html.

The **Turbojet Company** (☎ 852/2921–6688 [#3 for English] ⊕ www. ctshk.com) runs regular ferries connecting Hong Kong, Shenzhen, Macau, and Zhuhai. Check their Web site for schedules and prices.

PEARL RIVER DELTA ESSENTIALS

Transportation

BY AIR

Guangzhou's new $2.4 billion international Baiyun Airport in Huada city opened in August 2004 and is expected to establish Guangzhou as a regional air hub connecting the city to 40 international destinations by 2007. The airport currently offers 10 flights per day to both Hong Kong (Y670) and Beijing (Y1,240) between 9 AM and 9 PM. It has direct flights to Paris, Los Angeles, Singapore, Bangkok, Sydney, Jakarta, and Phnom Penh and a number of cities in North America. The airport also serves 107 domestic flights to 77 Chinese cities. International airport tax is Y90, domestic departure tax is Y50.

Shenzhen Airport is very busy, with flights to 50 cities. There is commuter service by catamaran ferries and buses between the airport and Hong Kong. Bus service links the Shenzhen Railway Station, via Huaren Dasha, direct to Shenzhen Airport for Y25 (one-way). Zhuhai International Airport, the largest in size in China, despite its name operates only domestically, to 24 cities.

🛂 Airline & Contacts Civil Aviation Administration of China, CAAC represented by China Southern ✉ 181 Huanshi Lu, on left as you exit Guangzhou railway station (Guangzhou main station metro) ☎ 020/8668-2000, 24-hr hotline.

🛂 Airport Information Shenzhen Airport ☎ 0755/2777-7821. Zhuhai International Airport ☎ 0756/889-5494.

BY BOAT & FERRY

🛂 Boat & Ferry Information The **Turbojet Company** ☎ 852/2921-6688 (press 3 for English) ⊕ www.ctshk.com runs regular ferries connecting Hong Kong, Shenzhen, Macau, and Zhuhai. Check their Web site for schedules and prices. **Macau Ferry Terminal** ✉ Shun Tak Centre, Connaught Rd., Central ☎ 853/2546-3528.

BY BUS

Air-conditioned express buses crisscross most of the Pearl River Delta region several times a day. Most areas can be reached in only a few hours. Ask at your hotel for the closest bus station.

🛂 Bus Depots Guangdong Provincial Bus Station ✉ 145 Huanshi Xi Lu ☎ 020/8666-1297. Guangzhou Bus Station ✉ 158 Huanshi Xi Lu ☎ 020/8668-4259. Tianhe Bus Station ✉ Yuangang, Tianhe District ☎ 020/8774-1083. Shenzhen Luohu bus station ✉ 1st-2nd fls., East Plaza, Luohu District ☎ 755/8232-1670. Zhuhai Gongbei bus station ✉ No.1 Lianhua Rd., Gongbei District ☎ 756/888-8554. Zhongshan bus station ✉ Fuhua Rd., Shiqiben West District ☎ 760/863-3825.

🛂 Bus Information Citybus ☎ 852/2873-0818.

9

BY SUBWAY

Guangzhou's clean and efficient underground metro currently has two lines connecting 36 stations, including the new East and old Central railway stations. Tickets range from Y2 to Y7. Shenzhen's metro, the newest in China, has two lines, and tickets range between Y2 andY8.

🚺 Metro Information **Metro** ☎ 020/8310-6622 for information in English, 020/8310-6666.

BY TRAIN

Shenzhen can easily be reached from Hong Kong by taking the KCR light railway from Hong Kong's Kowloon Tong KCR station to Luohu Railway Station and then crossing over to Shenzhen on foot. Trains depart from Luohu to Hong Kong every five minutes.

Five express trains (Y234 first-class, Y190 second-class) depart daily for Guangzhou East Railway Station from Hong Kong's Kowloon Station. The trip takes about 1¼ hours. The last train back to Hong Kong leaves at 5:25 PM. Trains between Shenzhen's Luohu Railway Station and Guangzhou East Railway Station run every hour and cost between Y80 and Y100.

The best way to buy train tickets is either directly at the station, through your concierge, or through local travel agents.

🚺 Train Stations **Guangzhou East Railway Station** ✉ Lin Hezhong Rd., Tianhe District ☎ 020/6134-6222. **Guangzhou Railway Station** ✉ Huanshi Lu ☎ 020/6135-7222. **Shenzhen Railway Station** ✉ Luohu District ☎ 020/8232-8647.

Contacts & Resources

EMERGENCIES

In case of an emergency, contact your hotel manager for assistance. If you speak Chinese (or are traveling with someone who does), the following numbers may prove useful.

🚺 General Contacts **Police** ☎ 110, the **fire department** ☎ 119, and the **first-aid hotline** ☎ 120.

🚺 Hospitals **Shenzhen People's Hospital** ✉ Dongmen Rd. N, Shenzhen ☎ 0755/2553-3018 Ext. 2553 or 1387 (Outpatient Dept.).

INTERNET SERVICES

Most major hotels in town provide broadband Internet service in the rooms, though increasingly guests are expected to pay between Y50 and Y100 per day. If you still hanker for an Internet café, otherwise known as *wang ba,* they're scattered all over almost any Chinese city.

VISITOR INFORMATION

With more than 30 branches all over Hong Kong, and many offices around the world, China Travel Service is probably the best place to make travel-bookings arrangements in mainland China. They are open weekdays 9 AM to 7 PM, Saturday 9 AM to 5 PM, and Sunday and holidays 9:30 AM to 12:30 PM and 2 PM to 5 PM.

🚺 China Travel Services ✉ China Travel Bldg, ground floor, 77 Queen's Rd., Central District, Hong Kong ☎ 852/2851-1700 or 852/2522-0450 ⊕ www.ctshk.com/english/index.htm.

Golf

WORD OF MOUTH

"I would recommend that you try to get a game at Kau Sai Chau golf course near Sai Kung. It's relatively cheap, and you can make a nice day of it, as it is in a very picturesque area of HK. I've heard good reports, so just make sure you have a handicap card with you."

—geordie

By Hiram Chu   Tradition and modernity: golf courses in this region strike a perfectly harmonious balance of the two. In Shenzhen, a backdrop of towering skyscrapers and office buildings highlight the lush greenery and lychee trees that dot the course. Meanwhile, in Chung Shan, local laborers have sculpted tons of earth and soil by hand, without any heavy machinery, to create a traditional English course with gentle curves and a short, intimate layout. Wherever you decide to play, you can count on hours of high-quality, comfortable, and challenging golfing.

Join the Club
Perhaps because of its British legacy, Hong Kong has long been known as a club-oriented city: whether you're into golf, sailing, squash, or tennis, you'll find that members-only clubs have the best facilities. Several golf clubs have reciprocal privileges with other clubs outside Hong Kong. Visitors with reciprocal privileges at the Hong Kong Golf Club are allowed 14 free rounds of golf each year.

Near Hong Kong
Locals generally head to Hong Kong's only public course at Kau Sai Chau or to nearby Shenzhen, which is across the border in mainland China, to play golf; however, you need a Chinese visa to play in Shenzhen without spending an arm and a leg. Hong Kong's top clubs will also allow you to play their courses, but don t expect to spend much less than US$200.

South China Links
More affordable than the links at Hong Kong's prohibitively priced clubs, golf across the border in Southern China is a big draw for Hong Kong residents. Since the 1980s, golf has become a popular elite sport in China, and that is true nowhere more than in the Pearl River Delta, where dozens of full-service golf clubs with internationally recognized first-class courses have opened. Quite a few of them welcome nonmembers.

HONG KONG GOLF PLANNER

Practicalities

Border Crossing: The majority of clubs recommended here are in mainland China, so U.S. citizens will need to apply for a tourist visa to China *before* attempting a border crossing. Instant visas are not available for U.S. and U.K. citizens at the border itself. Instead, apply for a visa in Hong Kong, where the correct paperwork should be available quickly and easily. On the other hand, nationals of countries other than the United States and United Kingdom can obtain temporary five-day visas instantaneously at the China–Hong Kong border.

Getting to the Mainland

You can reach most of the Chinese mainland clubs easily from the Shenzhen–Hong Kong border crossing, itself easy to reach via train from Central. You have two choices from the Shenzhen–Hong Kong crossing: either negotiate with a taxi to take you to the club directly, or take a shuttle bus. Perhaps the easiest and fastest way is via taxi. If you do opt for a taxi ride, be sure to have your driver call ahead and get driving directions from the clubhouse. If you're concerned about language issues, you might consider writing down the name of the club on a piece of paper to show your driver.

About half the clubs have shuttle buses at the border crossing, but these buses can be slow and hard to find. Also, the shuttle buses are not free and may have different costs depending on whether you're a member of the club.

Golf

Not a Member? Unless stated otherwise all clubs listed welcome visitors. Additionally, there are several golf organizations in Hong Kong that welcome contact with tourists. Members of these organizations can be quite generous with invitations for visitors to play at members-only clubs. **Hong Kong Golf Association** (☎ 852/2504–8659 for general info ⊕ www.hkga.com). **Hong Kong Pro Golf** (☎ 852/2858–7777 ⊕ hkprogolf.com).

Reservations

Language difficulties may arise when dealing with clubs in mainland China. To be sure you're understood, consider faxing or e-mailing your desired tee times, reservations, and travel plans to the club.

Etiquette

Golfers in Hong Kong generally adhere to the same traditional rules and etiquette commonly found in the UK, U.S., and elsewhere. Golf etiquette in mainland China, though, may differ from what you are accustomed to.

From the moment you enter the parking lot you'll be inundated with eager helpers. In the locker rooms, expect waitstaff to stand next to you and fold your clothes, hand you towels, and help you with your shoes. If such service makes you uncomfortable, let the waitstaff know. Tips for caddies are appreciated (from Y50-100) but check with other players or the front desk for the going rate.

You'll notice that mobile phones are an omnipresent phenomena on most courses, with constant incoming calls and conversations accompanying every swing. This is the norm on most Chinese courses. Additionally, try to maintain a regular pace consistent with the group playing in front of you, since it is not considered appropriate to stand aside for faster-paced players in China.

10

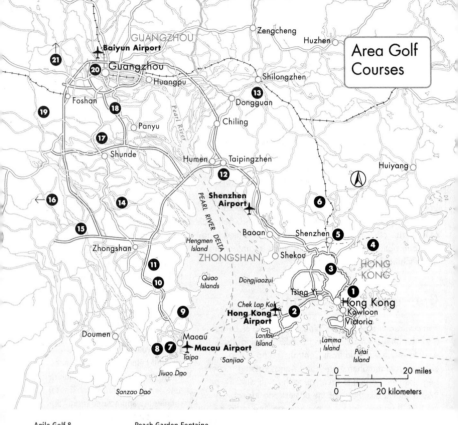

Area Golf Courses

TOP COURSES

Chung Shan Hot Springs Golf Club

Palmer Golf Design built this, the first modern course in China, in 1984. Local laborers moved tons of earth and soil by hand, without heavy machinery, and the resulting course has a traditional English feel with gentle curves and a shorter, intimate layout. A second course, longer and more challenging than the first, came courtesy of Jack Nicklaus in 1993, making this the only club in China with courses by both Palmer and Nicklaus. In contrast to the more glitzy contemporary courses commonly found in China, Chung Shan Hot Springs offers a more traditional golf experience—as it should, since it is the pioneer. Visitors are welcome weekdays; weekends and holidays are for members and guests only.

For travel from Hong Kong, take the train from Central to the Ferry Terminal at the Sheung Wan MTR station. Take the 70-minute Turbo-JET ferry to Jiuzhou Ferry Terminal in Zhuhai.

Regular shuttle service to and from the golf club is available at the ferry terminal or you can take a 40-minute taxi ride for about Y100; remember to negotiate hard on the price. Have the Chinese name written on a piece of paper or have the taxi driver call the golf club to confirm driving directions.

HIGHLIGHTS **The Chung Shan caddies are extremely knowledgable.** You can trust them for advice, as they are widely considered among the best in China.

Chung Shan's namesake hot springs are available for relaxation in the Spanish-style Hacienda clubhouse.

✉ *Sanxiang Town, Zhongshan, Guangdong, China 528463* ☎ *760/669–0055 Club, 852/2521–0377 Hong Kong office* ⊕ *www.cshsgc.com.cn* ☉ *Year-round, daily 6 AM–7 PM* ▭ *AE, DC, MC, V* ▨ *Y550 per round Palmer Course, Y440 per round Nicklaus Course; clubs Y120 Palmer Course, Y200 Nicklaus Course; Y220 cart* ⚑ *36 holes on 2 courses. Par 71 and 72. 5,929 yards on Palmer, 6,396 on Nicklaus.*

> **TIP**
>
> The Nicklaus course, perhaps the more difficult of the two, may require you to rely on the wisdom of your caddies for good course management. Water and bunker hazards abound, while tight dog-leg fairways call for carefully placed shots.

10

Dongguan Hillview Golf Club

Jim Engh and Global Golf Design have taken expansive fairways, picturesque hills, deep sands, and sharp sloping greens to create a shimmering jewel of a course just outside of Dongguan. The meticulously maintained fairways and greens of Hillview are a testament to the quality of the club. Experienced golfers with good iron games will find this to be a good workout and a real treat. The A and B courses are flood-lit for night play, and carts are available for all courses. High handicappers may not cope well with the tough carries required to avoid copious amounts of sand and water throughout the course, so use the forgiving tees to keep your shots on-line.

From Central, go to the China Hong Kong City Ferry Terminal on the Kowloon side of Hong Kong (TST MTR/Bus station) and take the one-hour TurboJET ferry to Fu Yong Ferry Terminal (Shenzhen).

Regular shuttle service to and from the golf club is available at the terminal or you can take a 30-minute taxi ride to the club.

HIGHLIGHTS **The C and D courses are dynamic and intimidating** with huge bunkers, plenty of water, and breaking greens. You'll need good iron play to succeed.

The A and B courses offer a slightly more subdued game, with fewer bunkers and water hazards. Still, mid- and low-handicap players will find a formidable challenge.

Enjoy the excellent club facilities, including a large sauna, a full bowling alley, and several squash courts.

⊠ *Ying Bin Rd., Fucheng District, Dongguan, Guangdong, China 523129* ☎ *769/2220–9998, 852/2229–8968, Club, 852/2527–3613 Hong Kong office* ⊕ *www.hillviewgolf.com* ⊘ *year-round, daily 6 AM–11 PM* ⊟ *AE, DC, MC, V* ☞ *Y750 Mon. and Tues., Y850 Wed. and Thurs.; Y1,450 weekends, green fees, caddie, and cart included for indicated prices; clubs Y250* ⚑ *36 holes on 4 courses. Par 72 on all courses. Courses A and B (Night Courses) 6,756 yards and C and D (Master Courses) 7,019.*

Hong Kong Golf Club Fanling

The Hong Kong Golf Club, established in 1889, owns two beautiful courses in Hong Kong: Deep Water Bay and Fanling. The Fanling location is the better of the two, widely considered the best golf course in Hong Kong. You can play any one of three courses. All take their names and design from St. Andrews in Scotland. The Old and New courses are walking courses, while Eden does allow carts. Visitors are welcome weekdays only and must register for tee times the day before play. The old course will reopen in late 2007, after extensive renovations.

For a slightly lower difficulty level, play the Palmer Course. It's shorter, with fewer bunkers and a less-demanding layout for a walking game. Straight and accurate shots win the day. Greens here are cut very short, leaving a smooth, fast surface for your putts, especially in the cooler and colder months.

You can reach Fanling quite easily from Hong Kong. Go to the Tsim Sha Tsui MTR station and board the KCR train bound for Luo Hu or Sheung Shui station. Get off at Sheng Shui and take a five-minute taxi ride to the clubhouse.

HIGHLIGHTS **Very fast greens, expansive fairways, and dense tree-filled layouts on all three courses** offer challenging yet enjoyable play for even the best golfers.

> **TIP**
>
> Tuesday is known as "Ladies Day." The club will be busy while groups of female players with handicaps compete, so call ahead to make sure you can get a tee time.

The Eden's signature finishing eighteenth hole is a tricky and rewarding challenge where you must carry a pond in front of the green while avoiding a line of protective bunkers.

✉ *Lot No. 1, Fan Kam Rd., New Territories, Sheung Shui, Hong Kong* ☎ *852/2670–1211* ⊕ *www.hkgolfclub.org* ☉ *Weekdays 9:30 AM–4:30 PM (except 1st Fri. of each month, when course stays open until 10 PM), weekends 9 AM–4:30 PM* ▭ *AE, DC, MC, V* 🏌 *HK$1,400 per round; clubs HK$250* ⛳ *54 holes on 3 courses. Par 70. 6,531 yards for New course.*

Hong Kong Jockey Club Kau Sai Chau

The Hong Kong Jockey Club spent HK$500 million to create the finest public golf course in Asia, and Gary Player's design took advantage of Kau Sai Chau Island's beautiful, mountainous terrain to offer players a challenging course at affordable prices. There's a 36.4 male–40.4 female handicap requirement to book tee times. 18-hole

TIPS
Kau Sai Chau stays busy year-round, so take advantage of the reservation hotline to book your reservation seven days in advance. You won't be able to book same-day tee times. Be sure to show up at least 20 minutes early.

and 9-hole courses are available for players of differing skill levels, but players with certified handicaps that meet the minimum requirement may bring nonhandicap players on the South Course. Non-HK residents may only play on weekdays.

This is one of the most convenient courses to reach from Hong Kong. Go to the Tsim Sha Tsui MTR station and board the KCR train bound for Luo Hu or Sheung Shui station. Get off at Sheng Shui station and take a five-minute taxi ride to the clubhouse.

HIGHLIGHTS **Low handicappers will find the North Course extremely challenging.** Playing the course's expansive terrain without a cart can be draining.

The South Course is a shorter, easier course, with wide fairways and tame playing surfaces. Beginners and high-handicap players will enjoy sharpening their skills here.

10

Hong Kong Jockey Club offers extensive practice facilities, including a 64-bay driving range, sand bunkers, chipping areas, and putting greens.

✉ *Kau Sai Chau, Sai Kung, New Territories, Hong Kong, China* ☎ *852/2791–3388* ⊕ *www.kscgolf.com* ☉ *Mon., Wed., and Thurs. 7 AM–8 PM, Tues. 1 AM–8 PM, Fri., Sat., and public holidays 7 AM–10 PM* ▭ *AE, DC, MC, V* 🏌 *HK$660 per round weekdays, HK$980 weekends; clubs HK$160* ⛳ *27 holes on 2 courses. Par 73 and 69. 6,692 yards on North course, 5,876 on South course.*

Mission Hills Golf Club

An assemblage of golf greats helped design this impressive golf complex, one of the world's largest, which has 10 courses and 180 holes. Nicklaus, Singh, Faldo, Norman, and Shorenstam have all lent their design skills (and names) to these courses. The club also has two top-notch hotels, service apartments, international restaurants, meeting rooms, and the renowned David Leadbetter Golf Academy. The Ozaki and Els courses are floodlit for night games, and tennis players will enjoy the 50-court Tennis Center.

Approximately 30–40 minutes from Hong Kong, Mission Hills provides shuttle bus service at the Sha Tian KCR station (Hong Kong) and at the Huanggang and Luohu Shenzhen–Hong Kong Border Crossings (China). Look for the Mission Hills staff in burgundy red uniforms. Departures to the Shenzhen clubhouse occur every 15 minutes and to the Dongguan Clubhouse every 30 minutes. Cost is HK$50 one-way.

HIGHLIGHTS **The huge Olazabal and Norman courses are among China's most beautiful and challenging,** so they require equal mastery of long and short games. Thick rough, deep bunkers, contoured doglegs, and a high slope will satisfy even the most jaded globe-trotting golfer.

The smaller Annika and Els courses present more modest challenges while offering an interesting game on attractive, well-designed layouts. They're perfect for mid-level players to gain confidence and beat a handicap with accurate shots.

The luxury resort facilities and outstanding restaurants are every bit as impressive as the golf course. Mission Hills has its own spa, massage, and wellness treatments as well as award-winning restaurants serving Asian and Western fare.

> **TIP**
>
> There are three different clubhouses, so be sure you know which course you're going to before you arrive. The newest courses (Norman, Annika, Leadbetter, Duval, and Olazabal) are at the Dongguang clubhouse, which is about 20 minutes past the regular clubhouse.

✉ *No. 1 Mission Hills Rd., Shenzhen, China 518110* ☎ *755/2802–0888 Club, 852/2826–0238 Hong Kong office* ⊕ *www.missionhillsgroup.com* ⊙ *Year-round, daily 6 AM–11 PM* ▭ *AE, DC, MC, V* ☒ *HK$1,400 per round. Rentals: clubs HK$250; ½-hr lesson HK$300* ⅃ *180 holes on 10 courses. For the World Cup Course (Jack Nicklaus): Par 72. 6,315 yards.*

Pine Valley Golf Club

Pine Valley is a quiet, sleepy golf club about an hour outside of Zhuhai, in the mountains bordering a local water reservoir. You can find a gorgeous view from the clubhouse balcony. The challenging course has impressive changes in terrain elevation and interesting approaches for almost every hole. This is an inviting course for low-handicap players and daring players. A thick grove of trees obscures your view on the 12th hole, but a straight 200-plus yard shot will set you up for a short iron play. The seventh hole requires a long carry over water, which can be tricky with active headwinds.

From Central, go to the Ferry Terminal at the Sheung Wan MTR station. Take the 70-minute TurboJET ferry to Jiuzhou Ferry Terminal in Zhuhai, China.

Regular shuttle service takes 55 minutes and is available from the ferry terminal, or you can take a 45-minute taxi ride to the club. Negotiate to about Y125 for the ride.

HIGHLIGHTS **The hills and mountains surrounding Pine Valley are well integrated into the course,** so elevation changes and upslope–downslope pairings are a major feature of play.

In addition to golf, the club features many other outdoor sporting activities, including a gun range, boating, hunting, and game farm facilities. Wandering ducks and geese are a common site on the grounds and playing field.

Pine Valley has a breathtaking view from the clubhouse balcony. The scene includes Zhuhai, the Zhuhai reservoir, and mountains.

⊠ *Quianwu Town, Doumen District, Zhuhai, Guangdong, China 519175* ☎ *756/557–3888* ⊕ *www.pinevalleyclub.com* ☉ *Year-round, daily 6 AM–sunset* ⊟ *AE, DC, MC, V* ⊠ *Y650–750 weekdays, Y1,280 weekends (includes locker, cart, and caddie); clubs Y250* ⚑ *18 holes on one course. Par 72. 7,050 yards.*

Shenzhen Golf Club

The Shenzhen Golf Club, opened in 1985, was one of the first golf clubs in China. An extensive redesign by the celebrated team of Nelson & Haworth in 2000 launched Shenzhen to a well-deserved place among the top courses in China. In the middle of Shenzhen's downtown, a backdrop of towering skyscrapers and office buildings highlight the lush greenery lining the fairways and the lychee trees that dot the grounds. Although you may hesitate at the club's exclusivity and high cost, it's a worthwhile treat for any golf enthusiast.

> **TIPS**
>
> The expansive, gentle rolling fairways at Shenzhen will tempt many players to power off the tee, but keep in mind the unforgiving greens and the danger of losing the ball into the dense fairway shrubbery and trees.

10

From Central, go to the Sheung Wan Ferry Terminal at the Sheung Wan MTR station. Take the 45-minute TurboJET ferry to Shekou Ferry Terminal in Shenzhen. Regular shuttle service to and from the golf club is available at the ferry terminal or you can take a 20- to 30-minute taxi ride to the club. You can also board the KCR train bound for Luo Hu station. Cross to the Shenzhen size of the border and take a 30-minute taxi ride to the club.

HIGHLIGHTS **One of the best clubs in China is also one of the closest clubs to HK,** a 30-minute ride from the Luo Hu station and Shenzhen-Hong Kong border, and 20 minutes from the Huanggang Shenzhen–Hong Kong border.

The course doesn't have a lot of rough, but the greens are unforgiving so take precautions against powering the ball into the groves of trees and shrubbery lining the fairways.

The club is next to one of Shenzhen's most popular tourist attractions, "Windows of the World," a theme park with miniature replicas of famous sites from China and elsewhere, including the Egyptian Pyramids, the Effiel Tower, and the Great Wall.

✉ *Shennan Rd., Fu Tian District, Shenzhen, Guangdong, China 518034* ☎ *755/8330–8888 Club, 852/2890–6321 Hong Kong office* ☉ *Year-round, daily 6 AM–6 PM* ☰ *AE, DC, MC, V* ⛳ *Y1,000 per round week-days, Y1,800 weekends; caddie Y190; clubs Y250* ⛳ *27 holes on 3 courses. Par 36 on all courses. A Course 3,532 yards, B Course 3,637 yards, C Course 3,542 yards.*

ALSO RECOMMENDED

Hong Kong

Clearwater Bay Golf and Country Club. Clearwater Peninsula's lush rolling hills form the backdrop for this challenging course with breathtaking views of the South China Sea. Accuracy and punching skill are essential here, especially if you hope to navigate the course's tight, small fairways successfully. Clearwater Bay has hosted Hong Kong's Amateur Golf Championships and PGA events on its championship course, which features a signature 14th hole that carries over a short cliff. Free shuttle buses are available from the Hang Hau MTR station. ✉ *139 Tai Au Mun Rd., Clearwater Bay* ☎ *852/–2719–1595, 852/2335–3885 for booking office* ⊕ *www.cwbgolf.org* ⛳ *HK$1,600–HK$1,800 per round (includes cart)* ⛳ *18 holes, with 9-hole executive course. Par 70. 6,115 yards* ☞ *Rental: clubs HK$300; shoes HK$50. Facilities: driving range, putting green, chipping area, rental clubs, pro shop, lessons, restaurant, pool, bar.*

Discovery Bay Golf Club. This course, accessible only via a 25-minute boat ride from Star Ferry Pier, lies on Lantau Island's hilly eastern coast. Robert Trent Jones Jr. skillfully incorporates the rugged landscape and high elevations to provide a challenging 27 holes with stunning views of Clearwater Bay, Discovery Bay, and Kowloon Peninsula. Nonmembers can play on the 18-hole course on Monday, Tuesday, and Thursday in the morning and early afternoons only; you can book as many as two days in advance. ✉ *Discovery Bay* ☎ *852/2987–7273* ⊕ *www.discoverybayhk. com* ⛳ *HK$1,400 per round* ⛳ *27 holes. Par 36. 3,348 yards* ☞ *Rental: clubs HK$160; cart HK$190; shoes HK$50. Facilities: driving range, putting green, chipping area, hand-pulled carts, rental clubs, pro shop, lessons, restaurant, bar.*

Macau

Macau Golf and Country Club. Each year Westin Resort hosts the Asian PGA Macau Open on their magnificent Links course. Well-maintained greens, tight fairways, and some big twists and turns keep even professional golfers swinging from the bunkers. Additionally, weather greatly affects play since much of the course borders on the South China Sea. This is the only golf club in Macau and is for members and guests of the Westin Resort only. To get here take any bus to Hàc-Sà station or a taxi ride to the Westin Resort. ✉ *Estrada De Hàc-Sà, Ilha De Coloane, Macau* ☎ *853/871–188* ⊕ *www.macaugolfandcountryclub.com*

HK$800 per round weekdays, HK$1,500 weekends ⚐ *18 holes. Par 71. 6,624 yards* ☞ *Rental: clubs Y250; shoes HK$50. Facilities: driving range, putting green, chipping area, hand-pulled carts, caddies, rental clubs, pro shop, lessons, restaurant, pool, bar.*

Southern China

GUANGZHOU
Fodor'sChoice
★
Guangzhou Luhu Golf & Country Club. Dave Thomas took advantage of the natural outcroppings and hilly landscape of Baiyun Mountain and Luhu Lake to create a sublime and challenging golf experience in the heart of Guangzhou. The personable staff here can accommodate your every need, from late-night tee times on a floodlighted 9-hole course, available for night games, to an extensive list of business services, including conference rooms. This course is your best bet for meetings and golf on the same day. To get here via public transit, take the KCR train from TST station to Guangzhou East train station, and from there take the free, 20-minute club shuttle buses or a one-way negotiated Y30 taxi ride. ✉ *Lujing Rd., Guangzhou, Guangdong, China 510095* ☎ *20/8350–7777* ⊕ *www.luhugolf.com* ✍ *Y1,180 weekdays per round, Y1,480 weekends (includes locker, cart, and caddie); clubs Y200; shoes Y35* ⚐ *18 holes, with 9-hole night course. Par 72. 6,831 yards* ☞ *Facilities: driving range, putting green, chipping area, hand-pulled carts, caddies, rental clubs, pro shop, golf academy, lessons, restaurant, pool, bar.*

Holiday Islands Golf Club. Though it's more than two hours northwest from the Shenzhen–Hong Kong border, China's newest course (opened in early 2006) has gained a sparkling reputation. Everything feels modern and well designed, from the huge clubhouse with its excellent waitstaff, to the upscale hotel rooms, to the pristine course. Generous but complex fairways mix with ample water features, making for moderately challenging play, particularly on the narrow green island on the signature fourth hole. Take the KCR train from TST station to Guangzhou East train station, and from there take the free, 60-minute club shuttle buses or a one-way negotiated Y160 taxi ride. ✉ *Huadou Developing Area, Qingcheng, Guangzhou, China 510830* ☎ *763/383–6666* ⊕ *www. bgy.com.cn* ✍ *Y500 per round weekdays, Y1,000 weekends* ⚐ *36 holes. Par 72. 7,338 yards* ☞ *Rental: clubs Y180; shoes Y35. Facilities: driving range, putting green, chipping area, hand-pulled carts, caddies, rental clubs, pro shop, lessons, restaurant, pool, bar.*

Lotus Hill Golf Club. Excellent service and modern facilities have long been a hallmark at this beautiful 18-hole championship course at the foot of Lian Hua Mountain, about one hour south of Guangzhou. It's a walking course with generous fairways, plentiful bunkers, and lots of water features. The signature 17th hole has an island green with a majestic rock formation as a backdrop. ✉ *Lotus Hill Town, Panyu District, Guangzhou, Guangdong, China 511440* ☎ *20/8486–6666* ⊕ *www. lotushillgolf.com* ✍ *Y770 weekdays per round, Y1,320 weekends (includes locker, cart, and caddie)* ⚐ *18 holes. Par 72. 6,865 yards* ☞ *Rental: clubs Y200; shoes Y30. Facilities: driving range, putting green, chipping area, caddies, rental clubs, pro shop, golf academy, lessons, restaurant, pool, bar.*

10

FOSHAN **Shunde Junan Country Garden Golf Club.** Wide fairways and gently sloping greens are the hallmark of this course about one hour west of
Guangzhou. The challenging, interesting emerald landscape feels like a
natural extension of the ecology park next door, and includes generous
fairways, doglegs, and gentle elevations. The clubhouse here offers some
fabulous interpretations of local Shunde seafood dishes, including whole
steamed mud carp and crab congee. Take the KCR train from TST station to Guangzhou East train station, and from there take the free, 55-
minute club shuttle buses or a one-way negotiated Y130 taxi ride.
⊠ *No.1 Cuihu Rd., Junan Town, Shunde District, Foshan, Guangdong, China 528234* ☏ *757/2538–3888* ⊕ *www.bgy.com.cn* ✍ *Y328
per round weekdays, Y1,000 weekends (includes locker)* ⚑ *18 holes.
Par 72. 7,018 yards* ⚲ *Rental: clubs Y150; shoes Y35. Facilities: driving range, putting green, chipping area, hand-pulled carts, caddies,
rental clubs, pro shop, lessons, restaurant, pool, bar.*

Peach Garden Fontaine Golf Club. You'll find this beautiful course,
opened in 2006, about 45 minutes southwest of Guangzhou. Designed
by Mark Hollinger of JMP, the course features wide fairways and little rough, which will entice long hitters. Accurate putters will delight
at the variety of green styles. The current 18 holes will be joined by a
9-hole night course by late 2007. Take the KCR train from TST station to Guangzhou East train station, and from there take the free, 50-
minute club shuttle buses or a one-way negotiated Y120 taxi ride.
⊠ *Nanguo Peach Garden, Nanhai District, Foshan, Guangdong, China
1518102* ☏ *757/ 8523–1888* ⊕ *www.peachgardengolf.com* ✍ *Y890
per round weekdays, Y1,290 weekends (includes locker, cart, and caddie)* ⚑ *18 holes, with 9-hole night course. Par 72. 7,236 yards* ⚲ *Rental:
clubs Y150; shoes Y30. Facilities: driving range, putting green, chipping area, hand-pulled carts, caddies, rental clubs, pro shop, golf academy, lessons, restaurant, pool, bar.*

ZUHAI **Zhuhai Golden Gulf Golf Club.** Colin Montgomerie designed this course,
which includes a Scottish-theme clubhouse and has brilliant emerald
greens with shimmering water bodies throughout. The terrain is mostly
flat, but plentiful bunkers and water hazards make for a challenging
18 holes, especially if the wind is up. Take the 1½ hour ferry from Hong
Kong (Sheung Wan Ferry Port) to Zhuhai (Jiuzhou Port) and from there
take the free, 30-minute club shuttle buses or a one-way negotiated Y100
taxi ride. ⊠ *Room 2105, Everbright International Trader Center, Jida
District, Zhuhai, Guangdong, China 519041* ☏ *756/ 763–1888* ⊕ *www.
zhggg.com* ✍ *Y800 per round weekdays, Y1,100 weekends (includes
locker, cart, and caddie)* ⚑ *27 holes. Par 72. 6,532 yards* ⚲ *Rental:
clubs Y250; shoes Y35. Facilities: driving range, putting green, chipping area, hand-pulled carts, caddies, rental clubs, pro shop, lessons,
restaurant, bar.*

SHUNDE CITY **Royal Orchid Golf Club.** The legendary British golfer Nick Faldo designed this walking course, but the low, rolling hills shouldn't be much
of a challenge for higher-caliber players. It's nicely manicured, and provides a clean, quiet environment about one hour south of Guangzhou.
Although this is a members-only course, travel agents and Hong Kong

golf associations should be able to help you get a tee time. ⊠ *Shunde Dadao, 105 State Rd., Beijiao Town, Shunde City, Guangdong, China 528311* ☎ *765/665–9888, 852/2377–2368 Hong Kong office* ⊕ *www. royal-orchidgolf.com* ✉ *Y600 per round weekdays, Y1,200 weekends (includes locker, cart, and caddie)* ⅃ *18 holes. Par 72. 6,831 yards* ☞ *Rental: clubs Y140; shoes Y35. Facilities: driving range, putting green, chipping area, hand-pulled carts, caddies, rental clubs, pro shop, golf academy, lessons, restaurant, pool, bar.*

ZHAOQING **Zhaoqing Resort and Golf Club.** This huge, scenic 7,300-yard championship course—designed by the illustrious Gary Player—lies in the middle of South China, about three hours west and slightly north from the Shenzhen–Hong Kong border. Plenty of fir trees, lakes, and bunkers mean you'll need to use careful, controlled shots. You won't have time to warm up, either: there's a treacherous stand of trees and a small brook flanking the left side of the signature first hole. Both beautiful and affordable, Zhaoqing deserves an overnight stay if you have time. For train service, take the KCR train from TST station to Guangzhou East train station, and from there take the free, 60-minute club shuttle buses or a one-way negotiated Y180 taxi ride. ⊠ *Huilong Town, Gaoyao City, Zhaoqing, Guangdong, China* ☎ *758/816–2168* ⊕ *www. zhaoqinggolf.com* ✉ *Y350 weekdays per round, Y600 weekends* ⅃ *18 holes, with 9-hole night course. Par 73. 7,300 yards* ☞ *Rental: clubs Y130; shoes Y30. Facilities: driving range, putting green, chipping area, hand-pulled carts, caddies, rental clubs, pro shop, restaurant, bar.*

ZHONGSHAN **Agile Golf & Country Club.** Boasting designs from two top U.S. companies, JMP Design and Schmidt-Curly Golf, these two distinct championship courses offer generous greens and fairways, impressive layouts, and rolling hills. The club is at the foot of a hill, right along the Chang Jiang Reservoir in Zhongshan. Prepare yourself for a challenge: the hilly front nine has plenty of doglegs and changes in elevation. The two courses are united by an excellent clubhouse with top-notch facilities. To get here, take the 1½ hour ferry from Hong Kong (Sheung Wan Ferry Port) to Zhuhai (Jiuzhou Port) and from there a one-way, 45-minute negotiated Y120 taxi ride. ⊠ *Changjiang Tourist Scenic Zone, Zhongshan, Guangdong, China 528404* ☎ *760/833–2868* ⊕ *www.agilegolf. com* ✉ *Y710 per round weekdays, Y1,595 weekends (includes locker, cart, and caddie)* ⅃ *36 holes. North course par 72, South course par 72. North course 7,037 yards* ☞ *Rental: clubs Y280; shoes Y35. Facilities: driving range, putting green, chipping area, caddies, rental clubs, pro shop, lessons, restaurant, pool, bar.*

DONGGUAN **Long Island Golf and Country Club.** Long Island requires a maximum handicap of 24 for men and 36 for women, and those that have these skills can experience a lush, picturesque and tree-filled layout on a 27-hole, USGA-standard course. The club also offers a deluxe short game practice course and floodlighting for night games. Use the KCR train from TST station to Luo Hu station, and from there cross the border to Shenzhen and take a one-way negotiated Y140 taxi ride. For members and guests only. ⊠ *Lotus Hill, Changan Town, Dongguan, Guangdong, China*

10

523846 ☎ 769/8531–3888 ⊕ *www.longislandgolfclub.com* ✉ *Y720 per round weekdays, Y1,320 weekends (includes locker, cart, and caddie)* 🏌 *18 holes, with 9-hole night course. Par 36. 3,505 yards* ☞ *Rental: clubs Y220; shoes Y50. Facilities: driving range, putting green, chipping area, hand-pulled carts, caddies, rental clubs, pro shop, golf academy, lessons, restaurant, pool, bar.*

JIANGMEN **Wuyi Fountain Palm Golf Club.** Nicklaus Design Golden Bear International Inc. brings its signature style of flat greens, wide fairways, and deep bunkers to South China. Approximately two hours from Hong Kong by ferry, the luxury club features spacious hotel rooms and excellent restaurants serving seafood and Western options. Delicate Jiangmen area seafood dishes are recommended. For members and guests only. ✉ *No. 60, Bei Huan Rd., Jiangmen, Guangdong, China 529000* ☎ *750/393–0777* ⊕ *www.wuyigolf.com* ✉ *Y400 per round weekdays, 800 weekends* 🏌 *27 holes. Par 72. 7,000 yards* ☞ *Rental: clubs Y150; shoes Y30. Facilities: driving range, putting green, chipping area, hand-pulled carts, caddies, rental clubs, pro shop, golf academy, lessons, restaurant, pool, bar.*

UNDERSTANDING HONG KONG

HONG KONG THEN & NOW

WITH ITS SOARING SKYSCRAPERS, futuristic fashions, and tomorrow's technology, Hong Kong may seem like it exists only in the here and now. So it may come as a surprise to hear that the area has been inhabited for thousands of years.

Hong Kong's history is inextricably linked to the sea: the original inhabitants were fisherfolk, and its strategic maritime position was what made it so attractive to the colonizing British. Even today, the newest and shiniest skyscrapers are built on land reclaimed from the harbor.

More than just a city, yet never quite a country, Hong Kong's desired and disputed territory has developed a unique character largely thanks to the great variety of people who made—and make—it their home.

Prehistory

In 2005 archaeologists uncovered 30,000-year-old stone artifacts on the Sai Kung Peninsula, evidence of Paleolithic peoples living in what is now Hong Kong. By 4,000 BC Neolithic fishing communities were scattered along the coast; by 1200–800 BC they could work bronze. Known as the Yueh, this Austro-Asiatic people were gradually assimilated by the Han Chinese settlers who trickled into the area during the first millennium AD.

Shopping & Settling

Hong Kong's reputation as a shoppers' paradise stretches back to the Tang Dynasty (618–907), when traders from China and the Middle East realized that its sheltered harbors were ideal places for boats to meet and exchange goods.

More Cantonese-speaking families from southern China began to arrive toward the end of the Song Dynasty (960–1279), notably the Tang, Hau, Pang, Liu, and Man families—known as the Five Great Clans—who built walled villages in different parts of the New Territories. Their descendants wield considerable clout in Hong Kong to this day. Despite having only just arrived, they gave themselves the name *boon dei* (meaning "local people" and usually rendered in English as Punti), and drove the territory's previous inhabitants to living on boats.

Political Unrest

With a population of fisherfolk, farmers, and pirates, it's not surprising that Hong Kong was seen as a barbarian backwater by members of the Beijing-based imperial court. They had to bite their tongues in 1276, however, when invading Mongols forced them to flee south. Nine-year-old emperor Duan Zong and his entourage briefly set up court in Hong Kong, but went to a watery grave during a battle in the Pearl River not long after.

There was more political upheaval a few centuries later. Hong Kong's inhabitants remained loyal to the Ming Dynasty (1368–1644) during its swansong, and so were punished by the victorious Qing Dynasty (1644–1911), which ordered a forced evacuation of the coastal population inland. When the ban was lifted several generations later, another ethnic group, the Hakka, also came to live in the area.

Did You Know? Hong Kong's contemporary mafia groups, the Triads, evolved from patriotic secret societies that swore allegiance to the Ming emperor and even participated in the defeat of the Qing Dynasty in 1911, when modern China was born.

Foreign Devils

European sailors seeking to trade with China began to arrive in the Pearl River Delta in the early 16th century. The Portuguese were the trailblazers, and were allowed to set up a legal trading post on Macau in 1557. The British showed their faces within a century, and soon European merchants could do business at

Guangzhou (Canton), where trade was strictly regulated. Merchants were only allowed in the city from November to May, and were forbidden from learning Chinese, leaving designated trading compounds, or bringing their families.

Foreign Mud

The Chinese initially had the upper hand in trade. Rich Europeans were desperate to get their hands on luxury goods like tea, porcelain, and silk, whereas the Chinese were unimpressed by the products European traders had to offer and insisted on payment in silver. This was problematic for the British, who used gold as their currency and had to buy their silver from Germany.

Looking for some other commodity to trade, they hit on opium, which the British East India Company could produce in large quantities in Bengal. The first shipment of what the Chinese came to call "foreign mud" was unloaded in 1773. Addiction spread so rapidly that by the mid-1830s more than 40,000 chests of the drug were being imported into China annually, despite the alarmed authorities' attempts to curb the trade.

The First Opium War

In 1839 the Chinese moved to zero-tolerance tactics. Hard-line official Lin Zexu cut off supplies of the British garrison at Guangzhou: the British were forced to hand over 20,000 chests of opium, which were publicly destroyed in Taiping. Trade was suspended, and China demanded Britain sign a treaty promising not to smuggle opium. Britain refused, and hostilities escalated rapidly into what would become known as the First Opium War. The British fleet proved itself tactically and technologically superior. They moved quickly up the coast to Shanghai, and eventually threatened Beijing, to the surprise and dismay of the emperor, who was forced to negotiate.

Did You Know? From the 15th century on, China had pretty much closed its doors to the outside world. This meant that their military and seafaring technology had stagnated while that of Europe flourished.

The British Move In

By 1841 negotiations between Britain and China were slowly ending hostilities. In January, British naval forces raised the Union Jack at Possession Point (between what are now Central and Sheung Wan), claiming Hong Kong Island as theirs. The occupation was made official with the Treaty of Nanjing, which ceded the island to Britain forever and opened five Chinese ports to foreign trade.

At the time, it took months to sail from China to Britain, so all the wheeling and dealing was done by envoys and navy officers, and the politicians got to hear about it all afterward. When British Prime Minister Lord Palmerston discovered Hong Kong was all he'd got out of the Opium War, he was distinctly unimpressed. "You have obtained a barren island with hardly a house upon it," he raged.

Did You Know? Excellent natural harbors and a source of fresh water were the reasons the British chose Hong Kong over other larger islands in the Pearl River Delta. The island's name was the result of a misunderstanding. *Heung gong,* meaning "fragrant harbor" was the name of a village near some incense mills on the island's southwest side. British sailors thought this was the name of the whole island, not just the village, and it stuck.

The Barren Rock Blooms

Merchants in Central didn't share his disdain. Traders bought lots along Queen's Road, then on the waterfront, to build stores and "godowns" (localspeak for warehouses). Meanwhile, the government was also hard at work constructing St. John's Cathedral, Central District Police Station, Government House, as well as extensive army barracks that have since been redeveloped.

Hong Kong's population began to swell: to the surprise of the British, thousands of

Chinese immigrants arrived and made their homes in the areas east (Wan Chai) and west (Sheung Wan) of the colonial center. The combined sea- and land-based populations in 1841 were around 6,000; within five years they'd hit 25,000. Numbers grew steadily as mainlanders fled the Taiping Rebellion (1851–64), the first of many conflicts to drive people over the border in one direction or the other.

Did You Know? Many of Hong Kong's most powerful companies date from the beginning of the colony—onetime opium smugglers Jardine Matheson is a famous example.

Another Unequal Treaty

The new commercial big shots weren't happy with how things in the colony were working, however. Many European trade ships still headed straight for Chinese ports, leaving Hong Kong–based companies out of the loop. So Britain began to push for more liberal trade terms with China, including legalizing opium sales. China rejected these and similar demands from France and the United States.

Things came to a head in 1856, when Chinese soldiers boarded the British schooner *Arrow,* supposedly in search of pirates. This faux pas led indirectly to the Second Opium War (1856–60). France joined the British cause, with naval support from Russia and the United States. Once again, European naval technology far outstripped that of China. By 1860 European forces had occupied Beijing, which forced China to capitulate and sign the Treaty of Beijing, handing over Kowloon and allowing the British to import opium into China. Hong Kong Harbor and all its naval approaches were now in British hands.

Life with the British

Although photos from the time show colonnaded arcades, polo grounds, and idyllic lawns stretching to the sea, Hong Kong was very much a country cousin to glam Shanghai, then the center of all the commercial and cultural action in southern China. There was no doubt that Hong Kong was on the right track, however: the economy thrived, and development began on Kowloon.

By 1865 the colony's population was at 122,000 and the new residential districts clearly reflected the British colonial obsession with class and race. Breezy, servant-filled mansions on Victoria Peak housed the rich elite; the Midlevels was the domain of less affluent Portuguese, Chinese, Jewish, and Parsi businessmen; while most of the Chinese were confined to ever-growing slums in Wan Chai and Sheung Wan. When the bubonic plague struck Hong Kong in the 1890s, overcrowding and poor sanitation in these shanty towns made their inhabitants easy victims—thousands died, and half the Chinese population returned to China.

Meanwhile, more and more Chinese-owned businesses were seeing success, yet even the well-to-do were discriminated against. Despite making up 90% of the population, Hong Kong Chinese were repeatedly denied the chance to participate in the colony's government.

A Growing Colony

In 1898 those in power felt Hong Kong and Kowloon were vulnerable to overland invasion. So they set about negotiating for more land from China, which offered more than they'd hoped for: all the land south of the Shenzhen River and 235 islands, a whopping 90% increase to Hong Kong's area. There was a catch, though. This land, known as the "new territories," was only on loan to Britain for 99 years—a lease that would end on June 30, 1997.

As the new century began, the economy boomed. Work began on public services like tramways, ferries, hospitals, gas and electric power plants, and the Kowloon–Canton Railway. Despite this, the living conditions of most of Hong Kong's Chinese would remain pitiful for decades. The 1911 Chinese Revolution and the decades of unrest and famine that followed it, however, meant that immigrants kept flooding in: by 1931 Hong Kong was home to 850,000.

Did You Know? One of Hong Kong's biggest infrastructure problems has always been fresh water. Leasing the New Territories eventually allowed several reservoirs to be built, but modern Hong Kong still relies on a pipeline from China for most of its water.

Bullets over Central

By 1938 Japanese forces controlled China's major cities, causing refugees to flood into Hong Kong in unprecedented numbers: by 1941 there were 1.6 million people in Hong Kong, half a million of them homeless. Japanese troops invaded Hong Kong eight hours after they bombed Pearl Harbor. They swept through the New Territories, taking control of Kowloon after three days of fighting.

The British government in London had long felt that defending Hong Kong against invasion was a hopeless task and thus a waste of money. Churchill ordered local forces to withstand as long as they could, but sent no reinforcements. War-scarred buildings and monuments at Central and Stanley are testament to the fighting. On Christmas Day 1941, however, Hong Kong became the first British colony to surrender to the Japanese. Governor Sir Mark Young crossed the harbor to sign the surrender in Room 336 of the Peninsula Hotel, where the Japanese had their headquarters.

Japanese Occupation

Living conditions on Hong Kong island had become horrific. Food, housing, fuel, and water shortages were massive, so the Japanese quickly sent Hong Kong's Chinese residents back to China. By the end of the war, the population was back down to 600,000. Life was grim for those left behind: thousands of local women were raped, and summary executions for trea-

son were common. Allied civilians were sent to concentration camps at Stanley and Sham Shui Po, and a former Allied barracks at Kowloon became prisons for male POWs. Many were eventually sent to do hard labor in Japan. Hong Kong dollars were replaced by reserve-less military yen, which led to massive inflation. Most business ground to a halt, streets were renamed, and Japanese became the main language in schools.

Did You Know? Upon the Japanese surrender in 1945, the United States suggested the United Nations return Hong Kong to China. When the highest-ranking British officials were released from prison, they were unaware of this and assumed control of Hong Kong until forces arrived from Sydney, and the colony remained British.

Postwar Boomtown

It didn't take Hong Kong long to get back on its feet. People poured once more over the border from China, and numbers swelled beyond belief after Mao Zedong's communist victory in 1949. Many of the new arrivals were Shanghainese businessmen eager to invest their capital. They took advantage of the labor glut and started building the light industries (textiles, plastics, and electronics) that would make the MADE IN HONG KONG tag world-famous.

Vast shanty towns housed most of Hong Kong's population through the 1950s. The government turned a blind eye to this until Christmas Day 1953, when a fire made more than 50,000 people homeless. This eventually sparked the creation of a massive public housing program—to this day, more than 60% of Hong Kong's population live in subsidized apartment blocks, owned by the world's largest landlord, the Hong Kong Housing Authority.

Did You Know? Hong Kong was able to recover from the war so quickly partly because it used dollars and not pounds sterling, making materials from the United States much more accessible.

The Shadow of the Cultural Revolution

By the '60s, Mao's Cultural Revolution was in full swing on the other side of the border, where Red Guards were killing millions and destroying most of China's heritage. The ripple effect led first to minor events like 1966's Star Ferry Riots, supposedly the reaction to a 10-cent increase in first-class Star Ferry fares. Deep-seated dissatisfaction with the colonial government emerged as a clearer reason for protest; strikes and demonstrations followed. By 1967, riots, bombs, and arson attacks had taken more than 50 lives, but the city's residents—many of whom had fled Mao's China—got fed up of the disturbances and things slowly settled down.

Social Change

Many of the changes that transformed Hong Kong into a world-class city were due to one man: Sir Murray MacLehose, governor between 1971 and 1981. He expanded the public housing program, introduced compulsory free high-school education, and established the Independent Commission Against Corruption (ICAC). Within a decade, Hong Kong's bribe-happy police force and public bodies were a thing of the past.

With Mao's death in 1978, China began to open up its economy. Hong Kong moved its factories over the border to cheaper Guangdong, and began to focus on the finance and service industries instead. The first skyscrapers on the Central waterfront were pointing in the direction everyone felt Hong Kong was heading: up and up.

China on Our Minds

By the early '80s, living standards had never been better, and the city's coffers never fuller. But one question had everyone in a flutter: what would happen in 1997, when the lease on the New Territories was up? After two years of behind-the-scenes political wrangling, Prime Minister Margaret Thatcher and Premier Deng Xiaoping agreed that all of Hong Kong would return to Chinese rule on July 1, 1997. Hong Kong would become a Special Administrative Region (SAR) of China, meaning its currency, economy, and legal system would remain the same for 50 years. Deng Xiaoping famously labeled this novel approach "One Country, Two Systems."

Did You Know? The 1984 Sino-British Joint Declaration provoked lots of bad feeling in Hong Kong. Residents were aggrieved about having had no say in their future. Britain's refusal to grant Hong Kong residents full British citizenship was another bone of contention.

The Demand for Democracy

Confidence in the future wavered. The economy kept growing, but so did lines outside the embassies of Canada, Australia, and the United States as many Hong Kong residents sought foreign passports, just in case. The situation exploded on June 4, 1989, when People's Liberation Army troops fired on pro-democracy protesters in Tiananmen Square. In Hong Kong, thousands filled the streets in protest, many weeping as they did. Thousands more left the country.

Hong Kong's residents had lived all their lives under the benign dictatorship of the British Government: no political parties, no elections, not even a constitution. The run-up to 1997 began to change this. A mini-constitution, the Basic Law, was drawn up in 1990; the city's first ever elections were held the year after—but voters could only choose a third of the legislative body. One of the Basic Law's long-term aims was full democracy for Hong Kong. Britain's last governor, Chris Patten, who arrived in 1992, spent a lot of time moving and shaking the democratic cause, provoking considerable wrath from China in the process. Many complain that Britain waited far too long to get the ball rolling: at present it still seems an impossible dream.

A New Order

At midnight on June 30, 1997, the world's eyes turned to Hong Kong. With much pomp and circumstance, Britain's richest colony was handed back to China. Press and audiences alike held their breath, wondering if—or hoping that—the PLA would goose-step through Central and randomly repress crowds. In the end, the change was anticlimactic and seamless. In fact, the huge economic crisis that hit Asia at the end of 1997 made far more impact on Hong Kong than the Handover. Government intervention in the stock market meant that the Hong Kong dollar remained stable, and the SAR wasn't as hard hit as other Asian economies. The floor finally fell out of the vastly overinflated property market, though, leaving many owners bankrupt.

Troubled Times

In late 1997 the first of many avian flu outbreaks swept the region. The government reacted slowly, and was lax about tightening up public health. Many feel this contributed to the territory's next—and much deadlier—epidemic: Severe Acute Respiratory Syndrome (SARS), in 2003. Three hundred people died, no one left home without a surgical mask, and the tourist industry almost collapsed.

The city emerged from the crisis much cleaner, but incredibly angry with the inefficient action of a government they hadn't even been allowed to choose. The final straw came later that year, when the government proposed Article 23, a highly unpopular national security bill affecting freedom of press and association. A whopping half million people—almost 10% of the population—came out to protest. The bill was indefinitely postponed and Chief Executive Tung Chee-hwa was given a public telling-off by Beijing. He eventually resigned in 2005, and was replaced by more popular Sir Donald Tsang, financial secretary from 1995 to 2001, under both the British and the Chinese administrations, then chief secretary from 2001 on. Political reform remains a serious concern for most Hong Kongers.

Did You Know? Hong Kong's political system is a complicated patchwork of parts. A largely pro-Beijing election committee of 800 people choose the chief executive, a pseudo-presidential figure. The chief executive appoints the 21 members of the executive council, a kind of cabinet. The legislation the executive council proposes must be passed by the single-chamber legislative council (so-called LegCo), made of 60 members who serve four-year terms. Half of the members are elected directly (there's universal suffrage for those over 18). The other half are elected by "functional constituencies," largely conservative, corporate-friendly groups that represent different occupational areas.

Essentials

PLANNING TOOLS, EXPERT INSIGHT, GREAT CONTACTS

There are planners, and there are those who fly by the seat of their pants. We happily place ourselves among the planners. Our writers and editors try to anticipate all the issues you may face before and during any journey, and then they do their research. This section is the product of their efforts. Use it to get excited about your trip to Hong Kong, to inform your travel planning, or to guide you on the road should the seat of your pants start to feel threadbare.

GETTING STARTED

We're proud of our Web site: Fodors.com is a great place to begin any journey. Scan Travel Wire for suggested itineraries, travel deals, restaurant and hotel openings, and other up-to-the-minute info. Check out Booking to research prices and book plane tickets, hotel rooms, rental cars, and packages. Head to Talk for on-the-ground pointers from travelers who frequent our message boards. You can also link to loads of other travel-related resources.

▌RESOURCES

ONLINE TRAVEL TOOLS

For a guide to what's happening in Hong Kong, check out the Hong Kong Tourist Board's (HKTB's) excellent site. For weather info, check out the Hong Kong Observatory. For political information plus news and interesting business links try the Hong Kong government site.

All About Hong Kong **Business in Hong Kong** ⊕ www.business.gov.hk: government-run site packed with advice. **Centamap** ⊕ www.centamap.com: online Hong Kong street maps so detailed they give street numbers and building names. **Hong Kong Government** ⊕ www.info.gov.hk. **Hong Kong Tourist Board** (HKTB) ⊕ www. discoverhongkong.com. **Hong Kong Weather** ⊕ www.weather.gov.hk

Cultural Activities **BC Magazine** ⊕ www. bcmagazine.net: ugly but searchable listings of all things cultural. **HK Magazine** ⊕ www. asia-city.com: online version of a quirky weekly rag with the lowdown on just about everything happening in town. **Hong Kong Film** ⊕ www.lovehkfilm.com: all you need to know about Hongkollywood. **Hong Kong Leisure and Cultural Services Department** ⊕ www.lcsd.gov.hk: access Web sites for all of Hong Kong's museums and parks through this government portal.

Currency Conversion **Google** ⊕ www. google.com does currency conversion. Just type in the amount you want to convert and an explanation of how you want it converted (e.g., "14 Swiss francs in dollars"), and then voilà. **Oanda.com** ⊕ www.oanda.com also allows you to print out a handy table with the current day's conversion rates. **XE.com** ⊕ www.xe.com is a good currency conversion Web site.

Local Insight **Eat Drink Hong Kong** ⊕ www. eatdrinkhongkong.com: excellent online guide to Hong Kong's bars and restaurants. **Gay Hong Kong** ⊕ www.gayhk.com: comprehensive guide to the local scene. **Geoexpat** ⊕ www.geoexpat.com: local know-how from Hong Kong's large expat community. **Hong Kong Outdoors** ⊕ www.hkoutdoors.com: the authority on hiking, camping, and all things wild in Hong Kong.

Newspapers **Hong Kong Standard** ⊕ www. thestandard.com.hk: English-language business paper. **South China Morning Post** ⊕ www.scmp.com: leading local English-language daily.

Time Zones **Timeanddate.com** ⊕ www. timeanddate.com/worldclock can help you figure out the correct time anywhere in the world.

Weather **Accuweather.com** ⊕ www. accuweather.com is an independent weather-forecasting service with especially good coverage of hurricanes. **Weather.com** ⊕ www. weather.com is the Web site for the Weather Channel.

▌THINGS TO CONSIDER

GOVERNMENT ADVISORIES

As different countries have different world-views, look at travel advisories from a range of governments to get more of a sense of what's going on out there. And be sure to parse the language carefully. For example, a warning to "avoid all travel" carries more weight than one urging you to "avoid nonessential travel," and both are much stronger than a plea to "exercise caution." A U.S. government travel warning is more permanent (though not necessarily more serious) than a so-called public announcement, which carries an expiration date.

The U.S. Department of State's Web site has more than just travel warnings and advisories. The consular information sheets issued for every country have general safety tips, entry requirements (though be sure to verify these with the country's embassy), and other useful details.

■ TIP➔ **Consider registering online with the State Department (https://travelregistration. state.gov/ibrs/), so the government will know to look for you should a crisis occur in the country you're visiting.**

Hong Kong is a highly safe place as far as crime goes. The only recent safety threats were health-related: the devastating Avian Flu and SARS outbreaks of 1997 and 2003. A massive awareness program stopped the spread of the illnesses, but it's worth checking to be sure there have been no new outbreaks.

General Information & Warnings U.S. Department of State ⊕ www.travel.state.gov.

GEAR

Appearances in Hong Kong are important. This is a city where suits are still *de rigueur* for meetings and business functions. Slop around in flip-flops and worn denims and you *will* feel there's a neon "tourist" sign over your head. Pack your nicer pairs of jeans or slacks for sightseeing—there are plenty of fake handbags around to dress them up with, come dinner.

From May through September it's seriously hot and sticky, but a/c in hotels, restaurants, and museums can be arctic—keep a crush-proof sweater or shawl in your day-pack. Don't forget your swimsuit and sunscreen; many large hotels have pools, and you may want to spend some time on one of Hong Kong's many beaches. In October, November, March, and April, a jacket or sweater should suffice, but from December through February bring a light overcoat, preferably waterproof. No self-respecting Hong Konger leaves home each morning without a folding umbrella, and nor should you. A packet of Kleenex

is another must: restrooms aren't known for their toilet paper stocks.

PASSPORTS & VISAS

Citizens of the United States need only a valid passport to enter Hong Kong for stays up to three months. It's best to have at least six months' validity on your passport before traveling to Asia. Upon arrival, officials at passport control will give you a Hong Kong entry slip. Keep this slip safe; you must present it with your passport for your return trip home. If you're planning to pop over the border into mainland China, you must first get a visa (⇨ *below*).

PASSPORTS

We're always surprised at how few Americans have passports—only 25% at this writing. This number is expected to grow in coming years, when it becomes impossible to reenter the United States from trips to neighboring Canada or Mexico without one. Remember this: a passport verifies both your identity and nationality—a great reason to have one.

U.S. passports are valid for 10 years. You must apply in person if you're getting a passport for the first time; if your previous passport was lost, stolen, or damaged; or if your previous passport has expired and was issued more than 15 years ago or when you were under 16. All children under 18 must appear in person to apply for or renew a passport. Both parents must accompany any child under 14 (or send a notarized statement with their permission) and provide proof of their relationship to the child.

There are 13 regional passport offices, as well as 7,000 passport acceptance facilities in post offices, public libraries, and other governmental offices. If you're re-

PACKING 101

Why do some people travel with a convoy of suitcases the size of large-screen TVs yet never have a thing to wear? How do others pack a duffle with a week's worth of outfits and supplies for every contingency? We realize that packing is a matter of style, but there's a lot to be said for traveling light. These tips will help you win the battle of the bulging bag.

MAKE A LIST. In a recent Fodor's survey, 29% of respondents said they make lists (and often pack) at least a week before a trip. You can use your list to pack and to repack at the end of your trip. Your list can also serve as record of the contents of your suitcase—in case it disappears in transit.

THINK IT THROUGH. What's the weather like? Is this a business trip? A cruise? A resort vacation? Going abroad? In some places traditions of dress may be more or less conservative than you're used to. As you create your itinerary, note possible outfits next to each activity (don't forget those shoes and accessories).

EDIT YOUR WARDROBE. Plan to wear everything twice (better yet, thrice) and to do laundry along the way. Stick to one basic look—urban chic, sporty casual, etc. Build around one or two neutrals and an accent (e.g., black, white, and olive green). Women can freshen looks by changing scarves or jewelry. For a week's trip, you can look smashing with three bottoms, four or five tops, a sweater, and a jacket you can wear alone or over the sweater.

BE PRACTICAL. Put comfortable shoes atop your list. (Did we need to tell you this?) Pack items that are lightweight, wrinkle-resistant, compact, and washable. (Or this?) Note that if you stack and then roll your clothes, they'll wrinkle less.

CHECK WEIGHT AND SIZE LIMITATIONS. In the United States you may be charged extra for checked bags weighing more than 50 pounds. Abroad some airlines don't allow you to check bags over 60 to 70 pounds, or they charge outrageous fees for every excess pound. Carry-on size limitations can be stringent, too.

BE PREPARED TO LUG IT YOURSELF. Unless you're on a guided tour or a cruise, select luggage that you can readily carry. Porters, like good butlers, are hard to find these days.

LOCK IT UP. Several companies sell TSA-approved locks (about $10) that can be unlocked by all U.S. security personnel. Alternatively, you can use plastic cable ties, which are sold at hardware stores in bundles.

TAG IT. Always tag your luggage; use your business address if you don't want people to know your home address. Put the same information (and a copy of your itinerary) inside your luggage, too.

DON'T CHECK VALUABLES. On U.S. flights, airlines are liable for only about $2,800 per person for bags. On international flights, the liability limit is around $635 per bag. But items like computers, cameras, and jewelry aren't covered. And though comprehensive travel policies may cover luggage, the liability limit is often a pittance. Your homeowner's policy may cover you sufficiently when you travel—or not. Why not just stash baubles and gizmos in your carry-on—right near those prescription meds?

REPORT PROBLEMS IMMEDIATELY. If your bags—or things inside them—are damaged or go astray, file a written claim with your airline before you leave the airport. If the airline is at fault, it may give you money for essentials until your luggage arrives. Most lost bags are found within 48 hours, so alert the airline to your whereabouts for two or three days. If your bag was opened for security reasons in the United States and something is missing, file a claim with the TSA.

newing a passport, you can do so by mail. Forms are available at passport acceptance facilities and online.

The cost to apply for a new passport is $97 for adults, $82 for children under 16; renewals are $67. Allow six weeks for processing, both for first-time passports and renewals. For an expediting fee of $60 you can reduce this time to about two weeks. If your trip is less than two weeks away, you can get a passport even more rapidly by going to a passport office with the necessary documentation. Private expediters can get things done in as little as 48 hours, but charge hefty fees.

■ TIP➔ **Before your trip, make two copies of your passport's data page (one for someone at home and another for you to carry separately). Or scan the page and e-mail it to someone at home and/or yourself.**

VISAS

A visa is essentially formal permission to enter a country. Visas allow countries to keep track of you and other visitors—and generate revenue (from application fees). You *always* need a visa to enter a foreign country; however, many countries routinely issue tourist visas on arrival, particularly to U.S. citizens. When your passport is stamped or scanned in the immigration line, you're actually being issued a visa. Sometimes you have to stand in a separate line and pay a small fee to get your stamp before going through immigration, but you can still do this at the airport on arrival. Getting a visa isn't always that easy. Some countries require that you arrange for one in advance of your trip. There's usually—but not always—a fee involved, and said fee may be nominal ($10 or less) or substantial ($100 or more).

If you must apply for a visa in advance, you can usually do it in person or by mail. When you apply by mail, you send your passport to a designated consulate, where your passport will be examined and the visa issued. Expediters—usually the same ones who handle expedited passport applications—can do all the work of ob-

> **INSPIRATION**
>
> Get in the mood for your trip with some great reads. **Epic Novels:** Timothy Mo's *An Insular Possession* and James Clavell's *Noble House.* **History 101:** *A History of Hong Kong* by Frank Welsh. **Classic Cultural Primer:** *Hong Kong* by Jan Morris. **Political Satire:** Larry Feign's comic book, *The World of Lily Wong.* **Reminiscence:** *Myself a Mandarin* by Austin Coates.

taining your visa for you; however, there's always an additional cost (often more than $50 per visa).

Most visas limit you to a single trip—basically during the actual dates of your planned vacation. Other visas allow you to visit as many times as you wish for a specific period of time. Remember that requirements change, sometimes at the drop of a hat, and the burden is on you to make sure that you have the appropriate visas. Otherwise, you'll be turned away at the airport or, worse, deported after you arrive in the country. No company or travel insurer gives refunds if your travel plans are disrupted because you didn't have the correct visa.

Travel agents in Hong Kong can issue visas to visit mainland China. Costs range from $25 for a visa issued within 2 to 3 working days to $65 for a same-day service. The same services cost $50 and $80 in the United States. Note: the visa application will ask your occupation. The Chinese don't look favorably on those who work in publishing or the media. People in these professions routinely state "teacher" under "occupation." Before you go, contact the embassy or consulate of the People's Republic of China to gauge the current mood. China Visa Information **Chinese Consulate** ☎ 212/244–9456 ⊕ www.nyconsulate. prchina.org. **Chinese Embassy** ☎ 202/338–6688 ⊕ www.china-embassy.org. **Visa to Asia** ⊕ www.visatoasia.com/china.html provides up-to-date information on visa applications for China.

Hong Kong General Information **Hong Kong Immigration Department** ☎ 2824-6111 ⊕ www.info.gov.hk/immd.
Hong Kong Travel Agents **Japan Travel Agency** ☎ 2368-9151 ⊕ www.jta.biz offer the quickest and most efficient visa service. **China Travel Service** ☎ 2315-7188 ⊕ www.ctshk. com has 22 branches all over Hong Kong.
U.S. Passport Information **U.S. Department of State** ☎ 877/487-2778 ⊕ http://travel. state.gov/passport.
U.S. Passport & Visa Expediters **A. Briggs Passport & Visa Expeditors** ☎ 800/806-0581 or 202/464-3000 ⊕ www.abriggs.com. **American Passport Express** ☎ 800/455-5166 or 603/559-9888 ⊕ www. americanpassport.com. **Passport Express** ☎ 800/362-8196 or 401/272-4612 ⊕ www. passportexpress.com. **Travel Document Systems** ☎ 800/874-5100 or 202/638-3800 ⊕ www.traveldocs.com. **Travel the World Visas** ☎ 866/886-8472 or 301/495-7700 ⊕ www.world-visa.com.

SHOTS & MEDICATIONS

It's a good idea to be immunized against typhoid and Hepatitis A and B before coming to Hong Kong. In winter, a flu vaccination is also smart, especially if you're infection-prone or are a senior citizen. (For more information *see* Health *under* On the Ground in Hong Kong, *below*.)
Health Warnings **National Centers for Disease Control & Prevention** (CDC) ☎ 877/394-8747 international travelers' health line ⊕ www.cdc.gov/travel. **World Health Organization** (WHO) ⊕ www.who.int.

TRIP INSURANCE

What kind of coverage do you honestly need? Do you even need trip insurance at all? Take a deep breath and read on.

We believe that comprehensive trip insurance is invaluable if you're booking an expensive or complicated trip (particularly to an isolated region) or if you're booking far in advance. Who knows what could happen six months down the road? But whether you get insurance has more to do with how comfortable you are assuming all that risk yourself.

Comprehensive travel policies typically cover trip-cancellation and interruption, letting you cancel or cut your trip short because of a personal emergency, illness, or, in some cases, acts of terrorism in your destination. Such policies also cover evacuation and medical care. Some also cover you for trip delays because of bad weather or mechanical problems as well as for lost or delayed baggage. Another type of coverage to look for is financial default—that is, when your trip is disrupted because a tour operator, airline, or cruise line goes out of business. Generally you must buy this when you book your trip or shortly thereafter, and it's only available to you if your operator isn't on a list of excluded companies.

If you're going abroad, at the very least buy medical-only coverage. Neither Medicare nor some private insurers cover medical expenses anywhere outside of the United States besides Mexico and Canada (including time aboard a cruise ship, even if it leaves from a U.S. port). Medical-only policies typically reimburse you for medical care (excluding that related to preexisting conditions) and hospitalization, and provide for evacuation. You still have to pay the bills and await reimbursement from the insurer, though.

■ TIP➔ Hong Kong has excellent public and private health care. Foreigners have to pay for both, so insurance is a good idea. Even for lesser complaints private doctors charge a fortune: head to a public hospital if money is tight. In an emergency you'll always receive treatment first and get the bill afterward— HK$570 is the standard ER charge.

Expect comprehensive travel insurance policies to cost about 4% to 7% of the total price of your trip (it's more like 12% if you're over age 70). A medical-only policy may or may not be cheaper than a comprehensive policy. Always read the fine print of your policy to make sure that you are covered for the risks that are of most concern to you. Compare several policies to make sure you're getting the best price and range of coverage available.

Trip Insurance Resources

INSURANCE COMPARISON SITES		
Insure My Trip.com		www.insuremytrip.com
Square Mouth.com		www.quotetravelinsurance.com
COMPREHENSIVE TRAVEL INSURERS		
Access America	866/807-3982	www.accessamerica.com
CSA Travel Protection	800/873-9855	www.csatravelprotection.com
HTH Worldwide	610/254-8700 or 888/243-2358	www.hthworldwide.com
Travelex Insurance	888/457-4602	www.travelex-insurance.com
Travel Guard International	715/345-0505 or 800/826-4919	www.travelguard.com
Travel Insured International	800/243-3174	www.travelinsured.com
MEDICAL-ONLY INSURERS		
International Medical Group	800/628-4664	www.imglobal.com
International SOS	215/942-8000 or 713/521-7611	www.internationalsos.com
Wallach & Company	800/237-6615 or 504/687-3166	www.wallach.com

BOOKING YOUR TRIP

Unless your cousin is a travel agent, you're probably among the millions of people who make most of their travel arrangements online.

But have you ever wondered just what the differences are between an online travel agent (a Web site through which you make reservations instead of going directly to the airline, hotel, or car-rental company), a discounter (a firm that does a high volume of business with a hotel chain or airline and accordingly gets good prices), a wholesaler (one that makes cheap reservations in bulk and then resells them to people like you), and an aggregator (one that compares all the offerings so you don't have to)? Is it truly better to book directly on an airline or hotel Web site? And when does a real live travel agent come in handy?

ONLINE

You really have to shop around. A travel wholesaler such as Hotels.com or Hotel-Club.net can be a source of good rates, as can discounters such as Hotwire or Priceline, particularly if you can bid for your hotel room or airfare. Indeed, such sites sometimes have deals that are unavailable elsewhere. They do, however, tend to work only with hotel chains (which makes them just plain useless for getting hotel reservations outside of major cities) or big airlines (so that often leaves out upstarts like jetBlue and some foreign carriers like Air India). Also, with discounters and wholesalers you must generally prepay, and everything is nonrefundable. And before you fork over the dough, be sure to check the terms and conditions, so you know what a given company will do for you if there's a problem and what you'll have to deal with on your own.

Booking engines like Expedia, Travelocity, and Orbitz are actually travel agents, albeit high-volume, online ones. And airline travel packagers like American Airlines Vacations and Virgin Vacations—well, they're travel agents, too. But they may still not work with all the world's hotels.

■ TIP→ **To be absolutely sure everything was processed correctly, confirm reservations made through online travel agents, discounters, and wholesalers directly with your hotel before leaving home.**

An aggregator site will search many sites and pull the best prices for airfares, hotels, and rental cars from them. Most aggregators compare the major travel-booking sites such as Expedia, Travelocity, and Orbitz; some also look at airline Web sites, though rarely the sites of smaller budget airlines. Some aggregators also compare other travel products, including complex packages—a good thing, as you can sometimes get the best overall deal by booking an air-and-hotel package.

WITH A TRAVEL AGENT

If you use an agent—brick-and-mortar or virtual—you'll pay a fee for the service. And know that the service you get from some online agents isn't comprehensive. For example Expedia and Travelocity don't search for prices on budget airlines like jetBlue, Southwest, or small foreign carriers. That said, some agents (online or not) *do* have access to fares that are difficult to find otherwise, and the savings can more than make up for any surcharge.

A knowledgeable brick-and-mortar travel agent can be a godsend if you're booking a cruise, a package trip that's not available to you directly, an air pass, or a complicated itinerary including several overseas flights. What's more, travel agents that specialize in a destination may have exclusive access to certain deals and insider information on things such as charter flights. Agents who specialize in types of travelers (senior citizens, gays and lesbians, naturists) or types of trips (cruises, luxury travel, safaris) can also be invaluable.

A top-notch agent planning your trip to Russia will make sure you get the correct

Online Booking Resources

AGGREGATORS		
Kayak	www.kayak.com	looks at cruises and vacation packages
Mobissimo	www.mobissimo.com	
Qixo	www.qixo.com	compares cruises, vacation packages, even travel insurance
Sidestep	www.sidestep.com	compares vacation packages and lists travel deals
Travelgrove	www.travelgrove.com	compares cruises and vacation packages
BOOKING ENGINES		
Cheap Tickets	www.cheaptickets.com	discounter
Expedia	www.expedia.com	large online agency that charges a booking fee for airline tickets
Hotwire	www.hotwire.com	discounter
lastminute.com	www.lastminute.com	specializes in last-minute travel; main site is for U.K. with link to U.S.
Luxury Link	www.luxurylink.com	auctions as well as offers on the high-end side of travel
Onetravel.com	www.onetravel.com	discounter for hotels, car rentals, airfares, and packages
Orbitz	www.orbitz.com	charges a booking fee for airline tickets but gives a clear breakdown of fees and taxes before you book
Priceline.com	www.priceline.com	discounter that also allows bidding
Travel.com	www.travel.com	compares its rates with those of other booking engines
Travelocity	www.travelocity.com	charges a booking fee for airline tickets but promises good problem resolution
ONLINE ACCOMMODATIONS		
Asia Hotels	www.asia-hotels.com	good selection of mid- to top-end hotels
Hong Kong Hotels Association	www.hkha.org	can often get you great deals, even at the last minute. They have a stand at the airport, too
Hotelbook.com	www.hotelbook.com	focuses on independent hotels world-wide
Hotel Club	www.hotelclub.net	good for major cities worldwide
Hotels.com	www.hotels.com	Expedia-owned wholesaler that offers rooms in hotels all over the world
Quikbook	www.quikbook.com	"pay when you stay" reservations that allow you to settle your bill at check-out, not when you book
OTHER RESOURCES		
Bidding For Travel	www.biddingfortravel.com	good place to figure out what you can get and for how much before you start bidding on, say, Priceline

10 WAYS TO SAVE

1. Nonrefundable is best. If saving money is more important than flexibility, then non-refundable tickets work. But you'll pay dearly (as much as $100) if you change your plans.

2. Comparison shop. Web sites and travel agents can have different arrangements with the airlines and offer different prices for exactly the same flights.

3. Beware those prices. Many airline Web sites—and most ads—show prices without taxes and surcharges. Don't buy until you know the full price.

4. Stay loyal. Stick with one or two frequent-flier programs. You'll rack up free trips faster and you'll accumulate more quickly the perks that make trips easier. On some airlines these include a special reservations number, early boarding, access to upgrades, and more roomy economy-class seating.

5. Watch those ticketing fees. Surcharges are usually added when you buy your ticket anywhere but on an airline Web site. (That includes by phone—even if you call the airline directly—and paper tickets regardless of how you book.)

6. Check early and often. Start looking for cheap fares up to a year in advance; keep checking till you find a good price.

7. Don't work alone. Some Web sites have tracking features that will e-mail you immediately when good deals are posted.

8. Jump on the good deals. Waiting even a few minutes might mean paying more.

9. Be flexible. Look for departures on Tuesday, Wednesday, and Thursday, typically the cheapest days to travel. Check on prices for departures at different times and to and from alternative airports.

10. Weigh your options. A cheaper flight might have a long layover rather than being nonstop, or it might land at a secondary airport, where your ground transportation costs might be higher.

visa application and complete it on time; the one booking your cruise may get you a cabin upgrade or arrange to have a bottle of champagne chilling in your cabin when you embark. And complain about the surcharges all you like, but when things don't work out the way you'd hoped, it's nice to have an agent to put things right.

■ TIP➡ Remember that Expedia, Travelocity, and Orbitz are travel agents, not just booking engines. To resolve any problems with a reservation made through these companies, contact them first.

Accommodation will probably be the most expensive item on your Hong Kong budget, so it's worth inquiring with travel agents as their rates are often better. That said, Hong Kong hasn't entirely recovered from its post-SARS tourism crisis, and in low season many hotels offer discounts on their Web sites. In a nutshell: shop around even more than usual.

Agent Resources **American Society of Travel Agents** ☎703/739-2782 ⊕www.travelsense.org.

■ AIRLINE TICKETS

Most domestic airline tickets are electronic; international tickets may be either electronic or paper. With an e-ticket the only thing you receive is an e-mailed receipt citing your itinerary and reservation and ticket numbers. The greatest advantage of an e-ticket is that if you lose your receipt, you can simply print out another copy or ask the airline to do it for you at check-in. You usually pay a surcharge (up to $50) to get a paper ticket, if you can get one at all. The sole advantage of a paper ticket is that it may be easier to endorse over to another airline if your flight is canceled and the airline with which you booked can't accommodate you on another flight.

■ TIP➡ Discount air passes that let you travel economically in a country or region must often be purchased before you leave home. In some cases you can only get them through a travel agent.

If you're planning to travel to several different Asian destinations, Cathay Pacific's All Asia pass is an excellent deal. For $1,500 you get a round-trip ticket from New York (JFK), Los Angeles, or San Francisco to Hong Kong, plus 21 days of unlimited travel to 17 other Asian cities. You can pay supplements to add on cities that aren't included and to extend the pass: $350 buys you up to 90 days. If you register for Cathay's online news, there's a $200 discount. If you just want to combine Hong Kong and one other Cathay destination, though, go for a regular ticket: the airline generally allows a free Hong Kong stopover.

The One World Alliance Visit Asia Pass might work out cheaper for three or four destinations. Cities are grouped into zones, and there's a flat rate for each zone. It doesn't include flights from the United States, however. Inquire through American Airlines, Cathay Pacific, or any other One World member.

Air Pass Info **All Asia Pass,** Cathay Pacific, ☎ 800/233-2742 ⊕ www.cathay-usa.com.

Visit Asia Pass One World Alliance ⊕ www.oneworld.com.

▮ RENTAL CARS

When you reserve a car, ask about cancellation penalties, taxes, drop-off charges (if you're planning to pick up the car in one city and leave it in another), and surcharges (for being under or over a certain age, for additional drivers, or for driving across state or country borders or beyond a specific distance from your point of rental). All these things can add substantially to your costs. Request car seats and extras such as GPS when you book.

Rates are sometimes—but not always—better if you book in advance or reserve through a rental agency's Web site. There are other reasons to book ahead, though: for popular destinations, during busy times of the year, or to ensure that you get certain types of cars (vans, SUVs, exotic sports cars).

▮ TIP➔ Make sure that a confirmed reservation guarantees you a car. Agencies some-

Car-Rental Resources

AUTOMOBILE ASSOCIATIONS		
American Automobile Association (AAA)	315/797-5000	www.aaa.com; most contact with the organization is through state and regional members
National Automobile Club	650/294-7000	www.thenac.com; membership is open to California residents only
LOCAL AGENCIES		
Hawk Rent-a-Car	2516-9822	www.hawkrentacar.com.hk has lots of models and prices; there are special rates for weekends and longer-term rentals
Parklane Limousine	2730-0662	www.hongkonglimo.com rents Mercedes with drivers
MAJOR AGENCIES		
Alamo	800/522-9696	www.alamo.com
Avis	800/331-1084	www.avis.com
Budget	800/472-3325	www.budget.com
Hertz	800/654-3001	www.hertz.com
National Car Rental	800/227-7368	www.nationalcar.com

10 WAYS TO SAVE

1. Beware of cheap rates. Those great rates aren't so great when you add in taxes, surcharges, and insurance. Such extras can double or triple the initial quote.

2. Rent weekly. Weekly rates are usually better than daily ones. Even if you only want to rent for five or six days, ask for the weekly rate; it may very well be cheaper than the daily rate for that period of time.

3. Don't forget the locals. Price local companies as well as the majors.

4. Airport rentals can cost more. Airports often add surcharges, which you can sometimes avoid by renting from an agency whose office is just off airport property.

5. Wholesalers can help. Investigate wholesalers, which don't own fleets but rent in bulk from firms that do, and which frequently offer better rates (note that you must usually pay for such rentals before leaving home).

6. Look for rate guarantees. With your rate locked in, you won't pay more, even if the price goes up in the local currency.

7. Fill up farther away. Avoid hefty refueling fees by filling the tank at a station well away from where you plan to turn in the car.

8. Pump it yourself. Don't buy the tank of gas that's in the car when you rent it unless you plan to do a lot of driving.

9. Get all your discounts. Find out whether a credit card you carry or organization or frequent-renter program to which you belong has a discount program. And confirm that such discounts really are a deal. You can often do better with special weekend or weekly rates offered by a rental agency.

10. Check out package rates. Adding a car rental onto your air/hotel vacation package may be cheaper than renting a car separately on your own.

times overbook, particularly for busy weekends and holiday periods.

Frankly, you'd be mad to rent a car on Hong Kong Island or Kowloon. Maniac drivers, traffic jams, and next to no parking make driving here severely stress-inducing. So why bother, when public transportation is excellent, and taxis inexpensive? If you must have your own wheels, consider hiring a driver; most top-end hotels arrange this. The minimum rental time is two hours, which will cost you HK$800–HK$1,000 (depending on car model); it's HK$400–HK$500 for each subsequent hour.

If you're determined to drive yourself, your driver's license is valid in Hong Kong if you're 18 to 70 years old (those over 70 must pass a physical examination before driving). You'll need an International Driver's Permit for long stays. Check the AAA Web site for more info as well as for IDPs ($10) themselves. Rental rates begin at HK$702 per day and HK$2,900 per week for an economy car with air-conditioning, automatic transmission, and unlimited mileage. Remember that you drive on the left in Hong Kong. Take traffic regulations seriously even if other drivers don't—the police are very ticket-happy.

CAR-RENTAL INSURANCE

Everyone who rents a car wonders whether the insurance that the rental companies offer is worth the expense. No one—including us—has a simple answer. It all depends on how much regular insurance you have, how comfortable you are with risk, and whether or not money is an issue.

If you own a car, your personal auto insurance may cover a rental to some degree, though not all policies protect you abroad; always read your policy's fine print. If you don't have auto insurance, then seriously consider buying the collision- or loss-damage waiver (CDW or LDW) from the car-rental company, which eliminates your liability for damage to the car. Some credit cards offer CDW coverage, but it's usually supplemental to your own insurance and rarely covers SUVs, minivans, luxury models, and the like. If your coverage is secondary, you may still be liable for loss-of-use costs from the car-rental company. But no credit-card insurance is valid unless you use that card for *all* transactions, from reserving to paying the final bill. All companies exclude car rental in some countries, so be sure to find out about the destination to which you are traveling.

■ TIP➜ Diners Club offers primary CDW coverage on all rentals reserved and paid for with the card. This means that Diners Club's company—not your own car insurance—pays in case of an accident. It *doesn't* mean your car-insurance company won't raise your rates once it discovers you had an accident.

Some countries require you to purchase CDW coverage or require car-rental companies to include it in quoted rates. Ask your rental company about issues like these in your destination. In most cases it's cheaper to add a supplemental CDW plan to your comprehensive travel-insurance policy (⇨ Trip Insurance *under* Things to Consider *in* Getting Started, *above*) than to purchase it from a rental company. That said, you don't want to pay for a supplement if you're required to buy insurance from the rental company.

Most car rental companies in Hong Kong include CDW, emergency service, and unlimited mileage (but hey, how far can you realistically go?).

■ TIP➜ You can decline the insurance from the rental company and purchase it through a third-party provider such as Travel Guard (www.travelguard.com)—$9 per day for $35,000 of coverage. That's sometimes just under half the price of the CDW offered by some car-rental companies.

▌VACATION PACKAGES

Packages *are not* guided excursions. Packages combine airfare, accommodations, and perhaps a rental car or other extras (theater tickets, guided excursions, boat trips, reserved entry to popular museums,

transit passes), but they let you do your own thing. During busy periods packages may be your only option, as flights and rooms may be sold out otherwise. Packages will definitely save you time. They can also save you money, particularly in peak seasons, but—and this is a really big "but"—you should price each part of the package separately to be sure. And be aware that prices advertised on Web sites and in newspapers rarely include service charges or taxes, which can up your costs by hundreds of dollars.

■ TIP➜ Some packages and cruises are sold only through travel agents. Don't always assume that you can get the best deal by booking everything yourself.

Each year consumers are stranded or lose their money when packagers—even large ones with excellent reputations—go out of business. How can you protect yourself? First, always pay with a credit card; if you have a problem, your credit-card company may help you resolve it. Second, buy trip insurance that covers default. Third, choose a company that belongs to the U.S. Tour Operators Association, whose members must set aside funds to cover defaults. Finally, choose a company that also participates in the Tour Operator Program of the American Society of Travel Agents (ASTA), which will act as mediator in any disputes. You can also check on the tour operator's reputation among travelers by posting an inquiry on one of the Fodors.com forums.

Given Hong Kong's high hotel prices, a package including your flight and accommodation might save you money. You really don't need a package for other activities, though—it's cheaper to book excursions through local companies (you can do this before your trip to be sure of a place on the day you want).

Organizations **American Society of Travel Agents** (ASTA) ☎ 703/739-2782 or 800/965-2782 ⊕ www.astanet.com. **United States Tour Operators Association** (USTOA) ☎ 212/599-6599 ⊕ www.ustoa.com.

▌GUIDED TOURS

Guided tours are a good option when you don't want to do it all yourself. You travel along with a group (sometimes large, sometimes small), stay in prebooked hotels, eat with your fellow travelers (the cost of meals sometimes included in the price of your tour, sometimes not), and follow a schedule. But not all guided tours are an if-it's-Tuesday-this-must-be-Belgium experience. A knowledgeable guide can take you places that you might never discover on your own, and you may be pushed to see more than you would have otherwise. Tours aren't for everyone, but they can be just the thing for trips to places where making travel arrangements is difficult or time-consuming (particularly when you don't speak the language). Whenever you book a guided tour, find out what's included and what isn't. A "land-only" tour includes all your travel (by bus, in most cases) in the destination, but not necessarily your flights to and from or even within it. Also, in most cases prices in tour brochures don't include fees and taxes. And remember that you'll be expected to tip your guide (in cash) at the end of the tour.

Few companies organize package trips only to Hong Kong. It's usually part of a bigger China or Asia multidestination package. Small groups and excellent guides are what Overseas Adventure Travel takes pride in. The company has three China packages, all ending in Hong Kong. China Focus Travel has several tours combining Hong Kong with other Chinese cities—they squeeze in a lot for your money. For something slightly more upscale, try Pacific Delight, which offers many China tours with a few days in Hong Kong.

Recommended Companies **China Focus Travel** ☎ 800/868-7244 ⊕ www.chinafocustravel.com. **Overseas Adventure Travel** ☎ 800/493-6824 ⊕ www.oattravel.com. **Pacific Delight** ☎ 800/221-7179 ⊕ www.pacificdelighttours.com.

▌CRUISES

Star Cruises has trips through southeast Asia that start from, or call at, Hong Kong. The crème de la crème of cruisers, Cunard, docks in Hong Kong on its round-the-world trips. Princess Cruises has a wide variety of packages that call in at Hong Kong and many other Asian destinations. Holland America has short China and Japan cruises as well as round-the-world options.

Cruise Lines **Cunard** ☎ 800/7CUNARD ⊕ www.cunard.com. **Holland America** ☎ 877/SAIL HAL ⊕ www.hollandamerica.com. **Princess Cruises** ☎ 800/PRINCESS ⊕ www.princess.com. **Star Cruises** ☎ 2317-7711 Hong Kong ⊕ www.starcruises.com.

TRANSPORTATION

Public transporation options are many and varied—all are good, too. Look into the "Octopus" stored-value card. It's used on all forms of public transport: you just swipe it over the ticket-gate sensor to deduct your fare, which will be cheaper than a regular one, by the way. You can buy an Octopus card in any MTR, KCR, or Airport Express Station. They cost HK$150, of which HK$50 is a refundable deposit, and the other HK$100 is for you to use. (If you return them in less than a month, you forfeit HK$7 of your deposit as a processing fee.) You charge them at any ticket counter, at speedy machines in stations, or at a 7-11 or Wellcome supermarket, where you can also use them to pay for purchases. Handy or what? **Octopus Cards** ☎ 2266–2222 ⊕ www. octopuscards.com.

▌ BY AIR

Flying time to Hong Kong is around 16½ hours direct from Newark/New York, 13½ hours direct from Los Angeles, or 12¼ hours direct from San Francisco. **Airlines & Airports Airline and Airport Links.com** ⊕ www.airlineandairportlinks.com has links to many of the world's airlines and airports. **Airline Security Issues Transportation Security Agency** ⊕ www.tsa.gov/public has answers for almost every question that might come up.

AIRPORTS

The sleek, sophisticated Hong Kong International Airport (HKG) is never called by its official name; it's universally referred to as Chek Lap Kok, which is where it's located. At almost a mile long, its Y-shape passenger terminal is the world's biggest.

Chek Lap Kok is one of the friendliest, most efficient airports around. Walkways connect the check-in and arrival halls with nearby gates. An electric train glides to gates at the end of the terminal. Restau-

rants, fast-food outlets, and bars abound—try Oliver's Super Sandwiches for snacks; Grappa's and Cafe Deco are both good bets for a bigger meal. Most eateries are open from 7 AM to 11 PM or midnight; only local chain Café de Coral in the east departures hall is open 24 hours.

There's Wi-Fi access all over the passenger terminal after check-in, but you have to pay for it. The Internet is free at the PCs in the Cyber Lounges near Gates 20 and 60. You can also surf the Net or make calls from the high-tech PowerPhones throughout the terminal.

If you're going to be overnighting at Chek Lap Kok, consider buying a package from the Plaza Premium Traveler's Lounge, near Gate 60. It has a rest area, showers, free 15-minute massages, Internet access, newspapers, and a 24-hour buffet—an overnight package costs HK$450. Note that there are no other public showers or spa or massage facilities at Chek Lap Kok.

Check in at least two hours before departing from Chek Lap Kok. If you're flying to anyplace but the United States and plan on taking the train to the airport, most major airlines let you use the In-Town check-in service at the Hong Kong or Kowloon Airport Express stations. You can check your bags up to 24 hours before your flight—a boon if you're flying at night and don't want to return to your hotel to look for your bags. The service closes 1½ hours before your flight-time. After September 11, 2001, carriers flying to the United States discontinued In-Town check-in indefinitely. Check with your carrier beforehand in case the rules have changed.

Airport tax is normally included in your ticket price. If it's not, hold on to HK$120 for the airport tax, payable on departure from the country. It's only levied on those 12 years and older and is waived for all transit and transfer passengers who arrive and leave on the same day. When you go through immigration, have your Hong

FLYING 101

Flying may not be as carefree as it once was, but there are some things you can do to make your trip smoother.

DON'T STAND IN A LINE. Buy an e-ticket, check in at an electronic kiosk, or—even better—check in on your airline's Web site before leaving home. Pack light and limit carry-on items to only the essentials.

ARRIVE WHEN YOU NEED TO. Research your airline's policy. It's usually at least an hour before domestic flights and two to three hours before international flights. But at some busy airports airlines have more stringent advance check-in requirements. Check the TSA Web site for security waiting times at major airports.

GET TO THE GATE. If you aren't at the gate at least 10 minutes before your flight is scheduled to take off (sometimes earlier), you won't be allowed to board.

DOUBLE-CHECK YOUR FLIGHT TIMES. Do this especially if you reserved far in advance. Airlines change schedules, and alerts may not reach you.

DON'T GO HUNGRY. Ask whether your airline offers anything to eat; even when it does, be prepared to pay.

GET THE SEAT YOU WANT. Often, you can pick a seat when you buy your ticket on an airline Web site. But it's not always a guarantee; the airline could change the plane after you book, so double-check. Avoid seats on the aisle directly across from the lavatories. Frequent fliers say those are even worse than back-row seats that don't recline.

GOT KIDS? Get info. Ask the airline about its children's menus, activities, and fares. Sometimes infants and toddlers fly free if they sit on a parent's lap, and older children fly for half price in their own seats. Also inquire about policies involving car seats; having one may limit where you can sit. And ask about seat-belt extenders for car seats. Note that you can't count on a flight attendant to automatically produce an extender; you may have to ask for one when you board.

CHECK YOUR SCHEDULING. Don't buy a ticket if there's less than an hour between connecting flights. Although schedules are padded, if anything goes wrong you might miss your connection. If you're traveling to an important function, depart a day early.

BRING PAPER. Even when using an e-ticket, always carry a hard copy of your receipt; you may need it to get your boarding pass, which most airports require to get past security.

COMPLAIN AT THE AIRPORT. If your baggage goes astray or your flight goes awry, complain before leaving the airport. Most carriers require this.

BEWARE OF OVERBOOKED FLIGHTS. If a flight is oversold, the gate agent will usually ask for volunteers and offer some sort of compensation for taking a different flight. If you're bumped from a flight involuntarily, the airline must give you some kind of compensation if an alternate flight can't be found within one hour.

KNOW YOUR RIGHTS. If your flight is delayed because of something within the airline's control (bad weather doesn't count), the airline must get you to your destination on the same day, even if they have to book you on another airline and in an upgraded class. Read the Contract of Carriage, which is usually buried on the airline's Web site.

BE PREPARED. The Boy Scout motto is especially important if you're traveling during a stormy season. To quickly adjust your plans, program a few numbers into your cell: your airline, an airport hotel or two, your destination hotel, your car service, and/or your travel agent.

Kong entry slip (given to you on arrival) ready to show officials along with your passport.

The arrivals hall is vast, so you might have trouble finding those who come to meet you. Each flight is allocated one of the two exit points, A and B, so stick with yours to avoid confusion.

Airport Information **Hong Kong International Airport** ☎ 852/2181-0000 ⊕ www.hkairport.com. **Plaza Premium Lounge** ☎ 852/2261-2068 ⊕ www.plaza-ppl.com.

GROUND TRANSPORTATION

The Airport Express train service is the quickest and most convenient way to and from the airport. Gleaming, high-speed trains whisk you to Kowloon in 19 minutes and Central in 24 minutes. Trains run every 12 minutes between 5:50 AM and 1:15 AM daily. There's plenty of luggage space, legroom, and comfortable seating with TV screens on the backs of the passenger seats showing tourist information and the latest news. Although it's the most expensive public transport option, the speed and efficiency make it well worth the extra cost.

The Airport Express station is connected to the MTR's Tung Chung, Kowloon and Central stations—the latter is via a long, underground walkway with no luggage carts, however. One-way or same-day return fare to or from Central is HK$100; from Kowloon, HK$90. Round-trip tickets valid for one month cost HK$180 for Central and HK$160 for Kowloon. The Airport Express also runs free shuttle buses every 12 minutes between major hotels and its Hong Kong and Kowloon stations—there are seven routes. To board, you must show your ticket, boarding pass, or Airport Express ticket.

Citybus runs five buses ("A" precedes the bus number) from Chek Lap Kok to popular destinations. They have fewer stops than regular buses, which have an "E" before their number, so are more expensive. Two useful routes are the A11, serving Central, Admiralty, Wan Chai, and Causeway Bay; and the A21, going to Tsim Sha

Tsui, Jordan, and Mong Kok. There's plenty of space and onboard announcements in English, so you won't miss your stop.

Several small shuttle buses with an "S" before their number run to nearby Tung Chung MTR station, where you can get the MTR to Central and Kowloon. The trains follow the airport express route, but are a little slower and ¼ of the cost.

Taxis from the airport are reliable and plentiful and cost around HK$340 for Hong Kong Island destinations and HK$270 for Kowloon destinations, plus HK$5 per piece of luggage. Two limo services in the arrivals hall, Parklane and Intercontinental, will run you into town in style. Depending on the zone and the type of car, limo rides from the airport range from HK$500 to HK$600.

GROUND TRANSPORTATION TO CENTRAL		
Transport Mode	Time	Cost
Airport Express	24 min.	HK$100
Citybus Line A (Airbus)	50 min.	HK$40
Citybus Line E (Regular)	70 min.	HK$21
Limo	45 min.	HK$500
Taxi	45 min.	HK$340
Tung Chung & MTR	10 min. + 35 min.	HK$3.50 + HK$23

GROUND TRANSPORTATION TO TSIM SHA TSUI		
Transport Mode	Time	Cost
Airport Express	19 min.	HK$90
Citybus Line A (Airbus)	45 min.	HK$33
Citybus Line E (Regular)	60 min.	HK$14
Limo	35 min.	HK$500
Taxi	35 min.	HK$270
Tung Chung & MTR	10 min. + 35 min.	HK$3.50 + HK$17

Airport Express ☎ 2881-8888 for MTR hotline ⊕ www.mtr.com.hk. **Citybus** ☎ 2873-0818 ⊕ www.citybus.com.hk. **Intercontinental Hire Car** ☎ 2261-2155 ⊕ www.trans-island.com.hk. **Parklane Limousine Service** ☎ 2261-0303 ⊕ www.hongkonglimo.com.

FLIGHTS

Cathay Pacific is Hong Kong's flagship carrier. It maintains high standards, with friendly service, good in-flight food, and an excellent track record for safety—all of which drive its prices higher than some of the other regional carriers. Cathay has nonstop flights from both Los Angeles and San Francisco on the west coast and from New York–JFK on the east, with connecting services to many other U.S. cities. Singapore Airlines is usually slightly less expensive and offers direct flights to San Francisco on the west coast and Newark on the east coast. Considerably less comfortable, Continental also frequently offers good price deals, and has a nonstop flight to Hong Kong from Newark Liberty International Airport. Several other airlines offer service from the United States to Hong Kong, sometimes with connections in Asia.

Airline Contacts **Cathay Pacific Airways** ☎ 800/233-2742 in U.S., 800/268-6868 in Canada, 2747-1888 in Hong Kong ⊕ www.cathay-usa.com. **China Airlines** ☎ 800/227-5118, 2868-2299 in Hong Kong ⊕ www.chinaairlines.com.hk. **Continental Airlines** ☎ 800/523-3273 for U.S. and Mexico reservations, 800/231-0856 for international reservations, 852/3198-5777 in Hong Kong. ⊕ www.continental.com. **Singapore Airlines** ☎ 800/742-3333 in U.S., 852/2520-2233 in Hong Kong ⊕ www.singaporeair.com.

BY BOAT & FERRY

With fabulous views of both sides of Hong Kong Harbor, the Star Ferry is so much more than just a boat. It's a Hong Kong landmark, and has been running across the harbor since 1888. Double-bowed, green-and-white vessels connect Central and Wan Chai with Kowloon in seven minutes daily from 6:30 AM to 11:30 PM; the ride costs HK$2.20 on the upper deck, making it the cheapest scenic tour in town.

New World First Ferry (NWFF) Services Ltd. runs nine routes from Central to the outlying islands of Lantau and Cheung Chau. Pick up printed schedules at the Hong Kong Tourist Board (HKTB) info centers at the Tsim Sha Tsui Star Ferry Concourse and in Causeway Bay MTR station; as well as through the HKTB Visitor Hot Line. Or, you can simply pick one up at the ferry ticket counters.

(For information about ferry service to Macau and locations in China, *see* Chapter 8, Macau *and* Chapter 9, Pearl River Delta.)

FERRY TRAVEL		
Line/Route	Travel Time	Fare
NWFF Central–Discovery Bay (Lantau)	25-30 min.	HK$27
NWFF Central–Cheung Chau	30-50 min.	HK$13.40–HK$16.70
NWFF Central–Mui Wo (Lantau)	30-50 min.	HK$13.40–HK$16.70
Star Ferry Central–Tsim Sha Tsui	7 min.	HK$2.20
Star Ferry Central–Wan Chai	8 min.	HK$2.20

HKTB Visitor Hot Line ☎ 2508-1234. **New World First Ferry** ☎ 2131-8181 ⊕ www.nwff.com.hk. **Star Ferry** ☎ 2367-7065 ⊕ www.starferry.com.hk.

▮ BY BUS

An efficient network of double-decker buses covers most of Hong Kong. Using them is a tricky business, though, as drivers don't usually speak English, and the route maps on bus shelters and company Web sites are so complex as to be off-putting. To compound this, there are several companies and no central Web site or pocket bus maps.

When determining bus direction, buses ending with the letter "L" will eventually connect to the Kowloon–Canton Railway; buses ending with the letter "M" connect to an MTR station; "As" go to the airport; and buses ending with the letter "X" are express.

Rattling along Hong Kong's roads at breakneck speed are numerous minibuses, which seat 16 people. They're cream with green or red roofs and display their route number and a fixed price prominently. They stop at designated spots, and you pay as you board. If you want to get off, shout "*Bah-see jam yau lok*" ("Next stop, please") to the driver and hold on tight as he screeches to a halt. Though slightly more expensive than buses, minibuses are quicker and more comfortable.

FARES

Double-decker bus fares range from HK$1.20 to HK$45; minibus fares from HK$2 to HK$20. For both you must pay exact change upon entering the bus. You can also use an Octopus card on both. **Bus Information Citybus** ☎ 2873-0818 ⊕ www.citybus.com.hk; Hong Kong Island, cross-harbor and airport routes. **Kowloon Motor Bus** (KMB) ☎ 2745-4466 ⊕ www. kmb.com.hk; mainly serves Kowloon and New Territories. **Long Win Bus Company** ☎ 2261-2791 ⊕ www.kmb.com.hk; serves north Lantau, including Tung Chung. **New World First Bus** ☎ 2136-8888 ⊕ www.nwfb. com.hk; runs services on Hong Kong Island and in New Kowloon. **Octopus Cards** ☎ 2266-2222 ⊕ www.octopuscards.com.

▌ BY CAR

We've said it before (under Car Rentals), and we'll say it again: the best advice we can give is don't drive in Hong Kong. Gasoline costs up to twice what it does in the United States, and parking is scarce *and* prohibitively expensive. What's more,

local bus and truck drivers seem to think slamming on their breaks (and sending their passengers flying forward) is the only way to stop—making it an exceptionally difficult city to drive in.

PARKING

There's next to no on-street parking in Central and Tsim Sha Tsui: if there isn't a sign that expressly states you *can* park (after paying a meter), assume you can't. Finding a space next to such a sign is nothing short of a miracle. Most people use multistory or mall parking garages, which cost around HK$7 per half hour. The Hong Kong traffic police are extremely vigilant and seem to take great pleasure in handing out copious parking tickets.

RULES OF THE ROAD

Cars drive on the left-hand side of the road in Hong Kong. Wearing a seat belt is obligatory in the front and back of private cars, and the standard speed limit is 50 kph (30 mph) unless road signs say otherwise. The Hong Kong Police spend a lot of time setting up photographic speed traps and handing out juicy fines for wannabe Schumachers. Likewise, using handheld cell phones while driving is forbidden. You can't make a right turn on a red light, and you should scrupulously obey lane markings regarding turns. Drunk driving is taken very seriously: the legal limit is 50mg of alcohol per 100ml of blood, and there are fines of up to HK$25,000 for those who disobey. You can get highly detailed information on Hong Kong's road rules online, at the Transport Department's Web site. **Road Rules Hong Kong Government Transport Department Road Safety Code** ⊕ http://www.td.gov.hk/road_safety/index.htm.

▌ BY SUBWAY

By far the best way to get around Hong Kong is on the Mass Transit Railway or MTR. There are five main lines: the Island Line runs along the north coast of Hong Kong Island; the Tsuen Wan line goes from Central under the harbor to Tsim Sha

Tsui then up to the western New Territories. Tsim Sha Tsui links to eastern New Kowloon via the Kwun Tong Line; also serving this area is the Tseung Kwan O Line, which crosses back over the harbor at Quarry Bay. Finally, the Tung Chung Line connects Central and west Kowloon with Tung Chung on Lantau, near the airport. [optional]

The MTR's highly modern trains are fast, clean, and very safe, as are the stations. Platforms and exits are clearly signposted, and all MTR areas are air-conditioned. Most stations have wheelchair access, and all have convenience stores and other shops or services. Trains run every 2–5 minutes between 6 AM and 1 AM daily. Station entrances are marked with a simple line symbol resembling a man with arms and legs outstretched.

FARES & SCHEDULES

You buy tickets from ticket machines (using coins or notes) or from English-speaking workers at the counters by the turnstile entrances. Fares are not zoned, but depend on which stations you're traveling between. There are no monthly or weekly tickets. If you're going to do more than one or two trips on the MTR (or any other form of transport), get yourself a rechargeable Octopus card. It saves you time lining up for tickets, and you get a discount on your fares, too.

Fares range from HK$4 to HK$26. The special Tourist MTR One-Day Pass (HK$50) allows you unlimited rides in a day. The three-day Airport Express Tourist Octopus (HK$220–HK$300) includes single journeys from–to the airport, unlimited MTR travel and HK$20 worth of trips on other transport.

HKTB Visitor Hot Line ☎ 2508-1234. **MTR** ☎ 2881-8888 ⊕ www.mtr.com.hk. **Octopus Cards** ☎ 2266-2222 ⊕ www.octopuscards.com.

▌ BY TAXI

During the day, heavy traffic means that taxis around Central and Tsim Sha Tsui aren't the way to go. Outside these areas, or after dark, they're much more useful. Drivers usually know the terrain well, but as many don't speak English, having your destination written in Chinese is a good idea. You can hail cabs on the street, provided it's a stopping area (i.e., not on double yellow lines). Note that it's sometimes hard to find a taxi around 4 PM when the drivers switch shifts.

Fares for the red taxis operating in urban areas start at HK$15 for the first 2 km (1½ mi), then HK$1.40 for each ⅕ km (⅒ mi) or minute of waiting time (so fares add up fast in bumper-to-bumper traffic). There's a surcharge of HK$5 for each piece of luggage you put in the trunk, and surcharges of HK$20 for the Cross-Harbour Tunnel, HK$40 for the Eastern Harbour Tunnel, and HK$50 for the Western Harbour Tunnel. The Tsing Ma Bridge surcharge is HK$30. The Aberdeen, Lion Rock, and Junk Bay tunnels also carry small surcharges (HK$5 to HK$10).

In the New Territories taxis are green; on Lantau they're blue. Fares are slightly lower than in urban areas, but while urban taxis may travel into rural zones, rural taxis can't cross into urban zones.

Backseat passengers must wear a seat belt or face a HK$5,000 fine. Most locals don't tip; however, if you do by rounding off the fare by a few Hong Kong dollars—you're sure to earn yourself a winning smile from your underpaid and overworked driver. Taxis are usually reliable, but if you have a problem, note the taxi's license number, which is usually on the dashboard, and call the Transport Complaints Unit.

In urban areas, it's as easy and safe to hail a cab on the street as to call one. There are hundreds of taxi companies and no central booking number, so it's usually best to get your hotel or restaurant to call a company they work with. Note that there's a HK$5 surcharge for phone bookings.

Complaints Transport Complaints Unit ☎ 2889-9999.

BY TRAIN

The ultra-efficient Kowloon–Canton Railway (KCR) connects Kowloon to the eastern and western New Territories. Trains run every 5–8 minutes, and connections to the MTR are usually quick. It's a commuter service and, like the MTR, has sparkling clean trains and stations—smoking and eating are forbidden in both. At this writing the KCR has three main lines, but there are all kinds of ambitious projects underway to extend its service network.

The KCR East Rail line has 13 stops on its journey from Tsim Sha Tsui East through urban Kowloon, Sha Tin, and Tai Po on its way to Lo Wu on the Chinese boundary. KCR East Rail is the fastest way to get to Shenzhen—it's a 40-minute trip from Tsim Sha Tsui to Lo Wu. The Tsim Sha Tsui terminus connects via a series of underground walkways with Tsim Sha Tsui MTR; you can also transfer to the MTR at Kowloon Tong.

The short Ma On Shan Rail service starts at Tai Wai (also on the East Rail line) and has eight stops in the northeastern New Territories. This line will one day be extended to pass through Tsim Sha Tsui.

KCR West Rail starts at Nam Cheong (also on the MTR) and stretches out through eight stops into Tuen Mun, in the western New Territories. Here West Rail connects with the weblike Light Rail Transit, an above ground train serving mainly residential and industrial areas in the western New Territories. KCR is currently building the tracks that will extend West Rail into Tsim Sha Tsui. It's also constructing a link to connect boundary-town Lok Ma Chau with both East and West Rail.

Fares range from HK$4.50 to HK$36.50; you can pay by Octopus card or buy tickets from sales counters or ticket machines. Train Information **Kowloon-Canton Railway Corporation** ☎ 2939-3399 ⊕ www.kcrc.com.

HKTB Visitor Hotline ☎ 2508-1234. **Octopus Cards** ☎ 2266-2222 ⊕ www.octopuscards.com.

BY TRAM

PEAK TRAM

It's Hong Kong's greatest misnomer—the Peak Tram is actually a funicular railway. Since 1888 it's been rattling the 1,207 feet up the hill from Central to Victoria Peak tram terminus. As well as a sizeable adrenaline rush, it offers fabulous panoramas. Both residents and tourists use it; most passengers board at the lower terminus between Garden Road and Cotton Tree Drive. (The tram has five stations.) The fare is HK$20 one-way, HK$30 round-trip, and it runs every 15 minutes between 7 AM and midnight daily. A shuttle bus runs between the lower terminus and the Star Ferry.

STREET TRAMS

Hong Kong Tramways runs old-fashioned double-decker trams along the north shore of Hong Kong Island. Routes start in Kennedy Town (in the west), and go all the way through Central, Wan Chai, Causeway Bay, North Point, and Quarry Bay to Shau Kei Wan. A branch line turns off in Wan Chai toward Happy Valley, where horse races are held in season.

Destinations are marked on the front of each tram; you board at the back and get off at the front, paying HK$2 (by Octopus or with exact change) as you leave. Avoid trams at rush hours, which are generally weekdays from 7:30 to 9 AM and 5 to 7 PM. Although trams move slowly, for short hops between Central and Western or Admiralty they can be quicker than the MTR. A leisurely top-deck ride from Western to Causeway Bay is a great city tour. Tram Information **Hong Kong Tramways** ☎ 2548-7102 ⊕ www.hktramways.com. **Octopus Cards** ☎ 2266-2222 ⊕ www. octopuscards.com. **Peak Tram** ☎ 2849-6754 ⊕ www.thepeak.com.hk.

ON THE GROUND

■ BUSINESS & TRADE SERVICES

BUSINESS CENTERS

Hong Kong has many business centers outside hotels, and some are considerably cheaper than hotel facilities. Others cost about the same but offer private desks (from HK$250 per hour for desk space to upward of HK$8,000 a month for an office). Amenities include a private address and phone-answering and -forwarding services. Many centers are affiliated with accountants and lawyers who can expedite company registration. Some will even process visas and wrap gifts for you.

Harbour International Business Centre provides typing, secretarial support, and office rentals. Reservations aren't required. The Executive Centre and Regus are two international business services companies with several office locations in Hong Kong. They provide secretarial services, meeting and conference facilities, and office rentals.

The American Chamber of Commerce can arrange a Breakfast Briefing Program at your hotel for a fee based on group size. The chamber hosts luncheons and seminars, and its Young Professionals Committee holds cocktail parties at least once a month. Facilities include a library and China trade services.

American Chamber of Commerce ✉ Bank of America Tower, 12 Harcourt Rd., Room 1904, Central ☎ 2526-0165 ⊕ www.amcham.org.hk. **The Executive Centre** ☎ 2297-0222 ⊕ www. executivecentre.com. **Harbour International Business Centre** ☎ 2529-0356 ⊕ www.hibc. com. **Regus** ☎ 2166-8000 ⊕ www.regus.hk.

CONVENTION CENTER

The Hong Kong Convention & Exhibition Centre is a state-of-the-art, 693,000-square-foot complex on the Wan Chai waterfront, capable of handling 140,000 visitors a day. There are five exhibition halls and two main convention halls; the section jutting into the harbor hosted the 1997 handover ceremony. One of Asia's largest complexes, the center houses two hotels, the 570-room Grand Hyatt and the 860-room Renaissance Harbour View; an apartment block; and a 54-story trade center–office building.

Hong Kong Convention & Exhibition Centre ✉ 1 Expo Dr., Wan Chai ☎ 2582-8888 ⊕ www.hkcec.com.hk.

MESSENGERS

Most business centers offer delivery service, and you can sometimes arrange a delivery through your hotel concierge. Couriers, including City-Link International, will pick up from your hotel, as will FedEx and DHL, who also have drop-off points all over Hong Kong. Price is based on weight and distance.

City-Link International Courier Co. Ltd. ☎ 2382-8289 ⊕ www.citylinkexpress.com. **DHL** ☎ 2400-3388 ⊕ www.dhl.com.hk. **Federal Express** ☎ 2730-3333 ⊕ www.fedex. com/hk_english.

TRADE INFORMATION

Hong Kong General Chamber of Commerce ☎ 2529-9229 ⊕ www.chamber.org.hk. **Hong Kong Trade Development Council** ☎ 2584-4333 ⊕ www.tdctrade.com. **Hong Kong Trade & Industry Department** ☎ 2392-2922 ⊕ www.tid.gov.hk. **Innovation & Technology Commission** ☎ 2737-2573 ⊕ www.itc.gov.hk.

TRANSLATION SERVICES

Language Line ☎ 2511-2677 ⊕ www. languageventure.com. **Polyglot Translations** ☎ 2851-7232 ⊕ www.polyglot.com.hk. **Translation Business** ☎ 2893-5000 ⊕ www. translationbusiness.com.hk.

■ COMMUNICATIONS

INTERNET

Hong Kong is an Internet-friendly place for those bearing laptops. All mid- to high-

LOCAL DO'S & TABOOS

CUSTOMS OF THE COUNTRY

Face is ever-important. Never say anything that will make people look bad, especially in front of superiors. Having said that, Hong Kongers call it as they see it—sometimes with an honesty that Westerners find brutal. You may be told how fat you're looking or that your mobile phone is a very old model. Take it in stride; it's not meant aggressively. Hong Kongers talk about money freely—how much they earn, how much their car costs—so don't be surprise to be asked about these things.

GREETINGS

Hong Kongers aren't touchy-feely. Stick to handshakes and low-key greetings.

SIGHTSEEING

By and large Hong Kongers are a rule-abiding bunch. Follow their lead and avoid jaywalking, eating on public transport, and feeding birds. Although you won't be banned from entering any sightseeing spots on grounds of dress, you'd do well to avoid overly skimpy or casual clothes.

Though common, smoking is officially banned in malls, banks, shops, and on public transportation. So far opposition has prevented it from being banned in restaurants and bars.

Hong Kong is *crowded;* pushing and nudging are common. It may be hard to accept, but it's not considered rude, so avoid reacting (even verbally) if you're shoved.

OUT ON THE TOWN

Meals are a communal event, so food in a Chinese restaurant is always shared. You usually have a small bowl or plate to transfer food from the center platters into. Although cutlery is common in Hong Kong, it won't hurt to brush up on your use of chopsticks.

It's fine to hold the bowl close to your mouth and shovel in the contents. Noisily slurping up soup and noodles is also the norm, as is belching when you're done. Covering the tablecloth in crumbs, drips, and even spat-out bones is a sign you've enjoyed your meal. Avoid leaving your chopsticks standing up in a bowl of rice—they look like the two incense sticks burned at funerals.

Hong Kongers dress quite smartly to eat out and go to the theater. Things get pretty glam at bars or clubs, too.

DOING BUSINESS

Make appointments well in advance and be punctual. Hong Kongers have a keen sense of hierarchy in the office: egalitarianism is often insulting. Let the tea lady get the tea and coffee—that's what she's there for. If you're visiting in a group, let the senior member lead proceedings.

Suits are the norm, regardless of the outside temperature. Local businesswomen are immaculately groomed, and avoid plunging necklines, heavy makeup or overly short skirts. Pants are acceptable.

Avoid being pushy or overly buddylike when negotiating: address people formally until invited to do otherwise, respect silences in conversation and don't hurry things or interrupt. When entertaining, locals may insist on paying: after a slight protest, accept, as this lets them gain face.

Business cards are a big deal: not having one is like not having a personality. If possible, have yours printed in English on one side and Chinese on the other (hotels can arrange this in a few hours). Proffer your cards with both hands, receive them in the same way, then read them carefully, and make an admiring comment.

Many gifts, including clocks and cutting implements, are considered unlucky. Money, high-quality sweets, and imported spirits are all acceptable. Go for showy wrapping, offer gifts with both hands, and don't expect them to be opened in your presence.

CON OR CONCIERGE?

Good hotel concierges are invaluable—for arranging transportation, getting reservations at the hottest restaurant, and scoring tickets for a sold-out show or entrée to an exclusive nightclub. They're in the know and well connected. That said, sometimes you have to take their advice with a grain of salt.

It's not uncommon for restaurants to ply concierges with free food and drink in exchange for steering diners their way. Indeed, European concierges often receive referral fees. Hotel chains usually have guidelines about what their concierges can accept. The best concierges, however, are above reproach. This is particularly true of those who belong to the prestigious international society of Les Clefs d'Or.

What can you expect of a concierge? At a typical tourist-class hotel you can expect him or her to give you the basics: to show you something on a map, make a standard restaurant reservation (particularly if you don't speak the language), or help you book a tour or airport transportation. In Asia concierges perform the vital service of writing out the name or address of your destination for you to give to a cab driver.

Savvy concierges at the finest hotels and resorts can arrange for just about any goods or service imaginable—and do so quickly. You should compensate them appropriately. A $10 tip is enough to show appreciation for a table at a hot restaurant. But the reward should really be much greater for tickets to that U2 concert that's been sold out for months or for those last-minute sixth-row-center seats for the hottest show in town.

end hotels have in-room Internet access; Wi-Fi is common both in hotels and in public places, including many cafés, bars, and restaurants. All business centers have high-speed access.

Laptops and Blackberries are so ubiquitous in Hong Kong that things get tough if you haven't got one. Internet cafés are practically nonexistent; the only place to check e-mail on the go is at one of the many branches of the Pacific Coffee Company—you can log on to one of their free terminals if you buy a coffee (HK$20–HK$30). **Cybercafes** ⊕ www.cybercafes.com lists more than 4,000 Internet cafés worldwide. **Pacific Coffee Company** ⊕ www.pacificcoffee.com.

PHONES

The good news is that you can now make a direct-dial telephone call from virtually any point on earth. The bad news? You can't always do so cheaply. Calling from a hotel is almost always the most expensive option; hotels usually add huge surcharges to all calls, particularly international ones. In some countries you can phone from call centers or even the post office. Calling cards usually keep costs to a minimum, but only if you purchase them locally. And then there are mobile phones (⇨ *below*), which are sometimes more prevalent—particularly in the developing world—than landlines; as expensive as mobile phone calls can be, they are still usually a much cheaper option than calling from your hotel.

Hong Kong was the first city in the world with a fully digitized local phone network, and the service is efficient and cheap. Even international calls are inexpensive relative to those in the United States. You can expect clear connections and helpful directory assistance. Don't hang up if you hear Cantonese when calling automated and prerecorded hotlines; English is usually the second or third language option. The country code for Hong Kong is 852; there are no local area codes.

CALLING WITHIN HONG KONG

Hong Kong phone numbers have eight digits: landline numbers usually start with a 2 (mobiles with a 9).

If you're old enough to talk in Hong Kong, you're old enough for a cell phone, which means public phones are dwindling. MTR stations still always have one or two: local calls to both land and cell lines cost HK$1 per 5 minutes. If you're planning to call abroad from a pay phone, buy a phone card. Convenience stores like 7-11 sell stored-value Hello cards (only for use at pay phones) and SmartCards (a PIN-activated card you can use from any phone). Some pay phones accept credit cards.

Restaurants and shopkeepers will usually let you use their phone for free, as the phone company doesn't charge for individual local calls. Many small stores keep their phone on the counter facing the street. Hotels may charge as much as HK$5 for a local call, though.

Dial 1081 for directory assistance from English-speaking operators. If a number is constantly busy and you think it might be out of order, call 109 and the operator will check the line. The operators are very helpful, if you talk slowly and clearly.

CALLING OUTSIDE HONG KONG

International rates from Hong Kong are reasonable, even more so between 9 PM and 8 AM. The international dial code is 001, then the country code. The country code is 1 for the United States. So to call the United States you dial 0011. You can dial direct from many hotel and business centers, but always with a hefty surcharge. Dial 10013 for international inquiries and for assistance with direct dialing. Dial 10010 for collect and operator-assisted calls to most countries, including the United States. Dial 10011 for credit-card, collect, and international conference calls. **Access Codes AT&T Direct** ☎ 800/96-1111. **MCI WorldPhone** ☎ 800/96-1121. **Sprint International Access** ☎ 800/96-1877.

MOBILE PHONES

If you have a multiband phone (some countries use different frequencies than what's used in the United States) and your service provider uses the world-standard GSM network (as do T-Mobile, Cingular, and Verizon), you can probably use your phone abroad. Roaming fees can be steep, however: 99¢ a minute is considered reasonable. And overseas you normally pay the toll charges for incoming calls. It's almost always cheaper to send a text message than to make a call, since text messages have a very low set fee (often less than 5¢).

If you just want to make local calls, consider buying a new SIM card (note that your provider may have to unlock your phone for you to use a different SIM card) and a prepaid service plan in the destination. You'll then have a local number and can make local calls at local rates. If your trip is extensive, you could also simply buy a new cell phone in your destination, as the initial cost will be offset over time.

■ TIP→ **If you travel internationally frequently, save one of your old mobile phones or buy a cheap one on the Internet; ask your cell phone company to unlock it for you, and take it with you as a travel phone, buying a new SIM card with pay-as-you-go service in each destination.**

Most GSM-compatible mobile handsets work in Hong Kong. If you can unlock your phone, buying a SIM card locally is the cheapest and easiest way to make calls. Local phone company PCCW sells them for around HK$200 from their "i-shops" all over town. Local calls cost around HK$0.50 a minute.

Otherwise, you can rent handsets from CSL (HK$35 a day) with prepaid SIM cards (HK$48–HK$180). There's a stand at the airport and shops all over town. If you're only in town for a day or two, this is a good-value option.

Cellular Abroad ☎ 800/287-5072 ⊕ www. cellularabroad.com rents and sells GMS phones and sells SIM cards that work in many countries. **CSL** ☎ 2512-3123 on Hong Kong Island, 2393-5597 in Kowloon ⊕ www.

one2free.com. **Mobal** ☎ 888/888-9162 ⊕ www.mobalrental.com rents mobiles and sells GSM phones (starting at $49) that will operate in 140 countries. Per-call rates vary throughout the world. **Planet Fone** ☎ 888/ 988-4777 ⊕ www.planetfone.com rents cell phones, but the per-minute rates are expensive. **PCCW** ☎ 2888-8888 ⊕ www.pccw.com.

▌ CUSTOMS & DUTIES

You're always allowed to bring goods of a certain value back home without having to pay any duty or import tax. But there's a limit on the amount of tobacco and liquor you can bring back duty-free, and some countries have separate limits for perfumes; for exact figures, check with your customs department. The values of so-called "duty-free" goods are included in these amounts. When you shop abroad, save all your receipts, as customs inspectors may ask to see them as well as the items you purchased. If the total value of your goods is more than the duty-free limit, you'll have to pay a tax (most often a flat percentage) on the value of everything beyond that limit.

Except for the usual prohibitions against narcotics, explosives, firearms, and ammunition and modest limits on alcohol, tobacco products, and perfume, you can bring anything you want into Hong Kong, including an unlimited amount of money. Nonresidents may bring in, duty-free, 200 cigarettes or 50 cigars or 250 grams of tobacco, and 1 liter of alcohol.

Information in Hong Kong **Hong Kong Customs & Excise Department** ☎ 2815-7711 ⊕ www.customs.gov.hk.

U.S. Information **U.S. Customs and Border Protection** ⊕ www.cbp.gov.

▌ ELECTRICITY

The current in Hong Kong is 220 volts, 50 cycles alternating current (AC), so most American appliances can't be used without a transformer. Most plugs are three square prongs, like British plugs, though

some use round prongs. You can buy adapters in just about every supermarket.

Consider making a small investment in a universal adapter, which has several types of plugs in one lightweight, compact unit. Most laptops and mobile phone chargers are dual voltage (i.e., they operate equally well on 110 and 220 volts), so require only an adapter. These days the same is true of small appliances such as hair dryers. Always check labels and manufacturer instructions to be sure. Don't use 110-volt outlets marked FOR SHAVERS ONLY for high-wattage appliances such as hair dryers.

Steve Kropla's Help for World Travelers ⊕ www.kropla.com has information on electrical and telephone plugs around the world. **Walkabout Travel Gear** ⊕ www. walkabouttravelgear.com has a good coverage of electricity under "adapters."

▌ EMERGENCIES

Locals and police are usually very helpful in emergencies. Most officers speak some English or will contact someone who does. For police, fire, and ambulance dial 999. There are 24-hour accident and emergency services at the Matilda, Caritas, Prince of Wales, and Queen Mary Hospitals. The Queen Mary and Adventist hospitals have 24-hour pharmacies; otherwise local chain Watson's has a pharmacy department at their shops throughout the city; they're usually open until 9 PM.

Consulate **U.S. Consulate General** ✉ 26 Garden Rd., Central ☎ 2523-9011 ⊕ www. usconsulate.org.hk.

General Emergency Contacts **Police, fire & ambulance** ☎ 999. **Hong Kong Police & Taxi Complaint Hotline** ☎ 2527-7177.

Hospitals & Clinics **Caritas Medical Centre** ✉ (public) 111 Wing Hong St., Sham Shui Po, Kowloon ☎ 3408-7911 ⊕ www.ha.org.hk. **Hong Kong Adventist Hospital** ✉ (private) 40 Stubbs Rd., Midlevels, Western ☎ 2574-6211 ⊕ www.hkah.org.hk. **Hong Kong Central Hospital** ✉ (private) 1 Lower Albert Rd., Central ☎ 2522-3141 ⊕ www.hkch.org. **Hong Kong Baptist Hospital** ✉ (private) 223 Waterloo Rd., Kowloon ☎ 2229-8888 ⊕ www.

hkbh.org.hk. **Matilda International Hospital** ✉ (private) 41 Mount Kellet Rd., The Peak, Central ☎ 2849-0111 ⊕ www.matilda.org. **Prince of Wales Hospital** ✉ (public) 30-32 Ngan Shing St., Sha Tin, New Territories ☎ 2632-2211 ⊕ www.ha.org.hk/pwh. **Queen Elizabeth Hospital** ✉ (public) 30 Gascoigne Rd., Yau Ma Tei, Kowloon ☎ 2958-8888. **Queen Mary Hospital** ✉ (public) 102 Pok Fu Lam Rd., Pok Fu Lam, Western ☎ 2855-3838 ⊕ www.ha.org.hk/qmh. Pharmacies **Watson's** ☎ 2868-4388.

∎ HEALTH

Water from government mains satisfies World Health Organization (WHO) standards, but bottled water tastes more pleasant. Expect to pay HK$10 to HK$12 for a 1½-liter bottle of purified water.

Condoms can help prevent most sexually transmitted diseases, but they aren't absolutely reliable and their quality varies from country to country. Speak with your physician and/or check the CDC or World Health Organization Web sites for health alerts, particularly if you're pregnant, traveling with children, or have a chronic illness.

For info on travel insurance, shots and medications, and medical-assistance companies *see* Shots & Medications *under* Things to Consider *in* Before You Go, *above*.

HONG KONG–SPECIFIC ISSUES Severe Acute Respiratory Syndrome (SARS), also known as atypical pneumonia, is a respiratory illness caused by a strain of coronavirus that was first reported in parts of Asia in early 2003. Symptoms include a fever greater than 100.4°F (38°C), shortness of breath, and other flulike symptoms. The disease is thought to spread by close person-to-person contact, particularly respiratory droplets and secretions transmitted through the eyes, nose, or mouth. To prevent SARS, the Hong Kong Health Department recommends maintaining good personal hygiene, washing hands frequently, and wearing a face mask in crowded public places. SARS hasn't returned to Hong Kong, but many experts believe that it or other contagious, upper-respiratory viruses will continue to be a seasonal health concern.

Avian Influenza, commonly known as Bird Flu, is a form of influenza that affects birds (including poultry) but can be passed to humans. It causes initial flu symptoms, followed by respiratory and organ failure. Although rare, it's often lethal: there've been three outbreaks in Hong Kong, causing a total of seven deaths. The Hong Kong Government now exercises strict control over poultry farms and markets, and there are signs all over town warning against contact with birds. Pay heed to them, and make sure that any poultry or eggs you consume are well-cooked.

Local Health Information **Department of Health Hotline** ☎ 2961-8968 ⊕ www.dh. gov.hk. **Traveller's Health Service** ☎ 2150-7235 ⊕ www.travelhealth.gov.hk.

OVER-THE-COUNTER REMEDIES You can find most familiar over-the-counter medications (like aspirin and ibuprofen) easily in pharmacies such as Watson's, and often in supermarkets and convenience stores, too. Acetaminophen—or Tylenol—is often known as paracetamol locally. Oral contraceptives are also available without prescription.

∎ HOURS OF OPERATION

Banks are open weekdays from 9 to 4:30 and Saturday from 9 to 12:30. Office hours are more or less the same as in the west: 9 to 5 or 6. Some offices are open from 9 to noon on Saturday. Lunch hour is 1 PM to 2 PM; don't be surprised if offices close during lunch. Museums and sights are usually open six days a week from 9 to 5. Each site picks a different day, usually a Monday or Tuesday, to close. Pharmacies are generally open from about 10 AM until about 9 PM. For a 24-hour pharmacy you need to go to the Queen Mary or Adventist hospitals. (⇨ Emergencies *above*).

HOLIDAYS

Major holidays in Hong Kong include: New Year's (first weekday in January), Chinese New Year (end of January/early February), Easter, Ching Ming (April 1), Labour Day (May 1), Dragon Boat Festival (late May/early June), Hong Kong SAR Establishment Day (July 1), Mid-Autumn Festival (late September/early October), National Day (October 1), and Christmas and Boxing Day (December 25 and 26). There are also other Chinese holidays throughout the year.

▌ MAIL

Hong Kong's postal system is excellent. Airmail letters to any place in the world should take three to eight days. The Kowloon Central Post Office and the General Post Office in Central are open 8 AM to 6 PM Monday through Saturday.

Letters sent from Hong Kong are thought of as going to one of two zones. Zone 1 includes China, Japan, Taiwan, South Korea, Southeast Asia, Indonesia, and Asia. Zone 2 is everywhere else. International airmail costs HK$2.40 or HK$3 for a letter or postcard weighing less than 20 grams mailed to a Zone 1 or 2 address, respectively. To send a letter within Hong Kong, the cost is HK$1.40. The post office also has an overnight express service called Speedpost.

Main Postal Branches **General Post Office** ✉ 2 Connaught Rd., Central ☎ 2921-2222 ⊕ www.hongkongpost.com. **Kowloon Central Post Office** ✉ 10 Middle Rd., Tsim Tsa Shui.

SHIPPING PACKAGES

Packages sent airmail to the United States often take two weeks. Airmail shipments to the United Kingdom—both packages and letters—arrive within three or five days, while mail to Australia often arrives in as little as three days.

You are probably best off shipping your own parcels instead of letting shop owners do this for you, both to save money and to ensure that you are actually shipping

yourself what you purchased and not a quick substitute—though most shop owners are honest and won't try to cheat you in this way. The workers at Hong Kong Post are extremely friendly and they will sell you all the packaging equipment you need, at unbelievably reasonable prices. Large international couriers in Hong Kong include DHL, Federal Express, and UPS.

Express Services **DHL** ☎ 2400-3388 ⊕ www.dhl.com.hk. **Federal Express** ☎ 2730-3333 ⊕ www.fedex.com/hk_english. **UPS** ☎ 2735-3535 ⊕ www.ups.com.

▌ MONEY

Cash and plastic are the way to go. Very few shops or restaurants accept U.S. dollars, so either change in bulk or draw Hong Kong dollars direct from an ATM. Traveler's checks aren't accepted in most shops, and can be a pain to cash—avoid them, if possible. Getting change for large bills isn't usually a problem.

SAMPLE PRICES

Item	Average Cost
Cup of Coffee/Tea	HK$28/HK$12
Glass of Wine	HK$40–HK$50
Glass of Beer	HK$45–HK$60
Sandwich	HK$25–HK$40
Fresh Juice from a Stall	HK$10
Bowl of Noodle Soup	HK$18
One-Mile Taxi Ride in Capital City	HK$15
Museum Admission	HK$10
Fake Louis Vuitton Purse	HK$40

Prices throughout this guide are given for adults. Substantially reduced fees are almost always available for children, students, and senior citizens.

▌ TIP➔ Banks never have every foreign currency on hand, and it may take as long as a week to order. If you're planning to exchange funds before leaving home, don't wait until the last minute.

ATMS & BANKS

Your own bank will probably charge a fee for using ATMs abroad; the foreign bank you use may also charge a fee. Nevertheless, you'll usually get a better rate of exchange at an ATM than you will at a currency-exchange office or even when changing money in a bank. And extracting funds as you need them is a safer option than carrying around a large amount of cash.

Reliable, safe ATMs are widely available throughout Hong Kong—some may carry the sign ETC instead of ATM. MTR stations are a good place to look if you're having trouble locating one. If your card was issued from a bank in an English-speaking country, the instructions on the ATM machine will appear in English. You can withdraw cash in multiples of HK$100.

■ TIP➜ PIN numbers with more than four digits are not recognized at ATMs in many countries. If yours has five or more, remember to change it before you leave.

CREDIT CARDS

Major credit cards are widely accepted in Hong Kong, though they may not be accepted at small shops, and in some shops you get better rates paying in cash. When adding tips to restaurant bills, be sure to write "HK$" and not just "$." Throughout this guide, the following abbreviations are used: **AE**, American Express; **DC**, Diners Club; **MC**, MasterCard; and **V**, Visa.

It's a good idea to inform your credit-card company before you travel, especially if you're going abroad and don't travel internationally very often. Otherwise, the credit-card company might put a hold on your card owing to unusual activity—not a good thing halfway through your trip. Record all your credit-card numbers—as well as the phone numbers to call if your cards are lost or stolen—in a safe place, so you're prepared should something go wrong. Both MasterCard and Visa have general numbers you can call

(collect if you're abroad) if your card is lost, but you're better off calling the number of your issuing bank, since MasterCard and Visa usually just transfer you to your bank; your bank's number is usually printed on your card.

If you plan to use your credit card for cash advances, you'll need to apply for a PIN at least two weeks before your trip. Although it's usually cheaper (and safer) to use a credit card abroad for large purchases (so you can cancel payments or be reimbursed if there's a problem), note that some credit-card companies *and* the banks that issue them add substantial percentages to all foreign transactions, whether they're in a foreign currency or not. Check on these fees before leaving home, so there won't be any surprises when you get the bill.

■ TIP➜ Before you charge something, ask the merchant whether he or she plans to do a dynamic currency conversion (DCC). In such a transaction the credit-card *processor* (shop, restaurant, or hotel, not Visa or MasterCard) converts the currency and charges you in dollars. In most cases you'll pay the merchant a 3% fee for this service in addition to any credit-card company and issuing-bank foreign-transaction surcharges.

Dynamic currency conversion programs are becoming increasingly widespread. Merchants who participate in them are supposed to ask whether you want to be charged in dollars or the local currency, but they don't always do so. And even if they do offer you a choice, they may well avoid mentioning the additional surcharges. The good news is that you *do* have a choice. And if this practice really gets your goat, you can avoid it entirely thanks to American Express; with its cards, DCC simply isn't an option.

Reporting Lost Cards American Express ☎ 800/992-3404 in U.S., 336/393-1111 collect from abroad ⊕ www.americanexpress.com. **Diners Club** ☎ 800/234-6377 in U.S., 303/799-1504 collect from abroad ⊕ www. dinersclub.com. **MasterCard** ☎ 800/622-7747 in U.S., 636/722-7111 collect from abroad ⊕ www.mastercard.com. **Visa** ☎ 800/847-

2911 in U.S., 410/581-9994 collect from abroad
⊕ www.visa.com.

CURRENCY & EXCHANGE

The only currency used is the Hong Kong dollar, divided into 100 cents. There are bronze-color coins for 10, 20, and 50 cents; silver-color ones for 1, 2, and 5 dollars; and chunky bimetallic 10-dollar pieces. There's also a green 10-dollar bill, as well as bills for HK$20 (blue-green), HK$50 (purple), HK$100 (red), HK$500 (brown), and HK$1,000 (yellow). Don't be surprised if two bills of the same value look different: three local banks (HSBC, Standard Chartered, and Bank of China) all issue bills and each has its own design. Although the image of Queen Elizabeth II doesn't appear on new coins, old ones bearing her image are still valid.

At this writing, there were approximately 7.8 Hong Kong dollars to 1 U.S. dollar. There are no currency restrictions in Hong Kong. You can exchange currency at the airport, in hotels, in banks, and through private money changers scattered through the tourist areas. Banks usually have the best rates, but as they charge a flat HK$50 fee for nonaccount holders, it's better to change large sums infrequently. Currency exchange offices have no fees, but they offset that with poor rates. Stick to ATMs wherever you can.

■ TIP→ **Even if a currency-exchange booth has a sign promising no commission, rest assured that there's some kind of huge, hidden fee. (Oh . . . that's right. The sign didn't say no *fee*.) And as for rates, you're almost always better off getting foreign currency at an ATM or exchanging money at a bank.**

TRAVELER'S CHECKS & CARDS

Some consider this the currency of the caveman, and it's true that fewer establishments accept traveler's checks these days. Nevertheless, they're a cheap and secure way to carry extra money, particularly on trips to urban areas. Both Citibank (under the Visa brand) and American Express issue traveler's checks in the United

States, but Amex is better known and more widely accepted; you can also avoid hefty surcharges by cashing Amex checks at Amex offices. Whatever you do, keep track of all the serial numbers in case the checks are lost or stolen. In Hong Kong, banks and some hotels will accept traveler's checks, but local restaurateurs and shop assistants won't be interested. It's best to change them into local currency at a bank.

American Express now offers a stored-value card called a Travelers Cheque Card, which you can use wherever American Express credit cards are accepted, including ATMs. The card can carry a minimum of $300 and a maximum of $2,700, and it's a very safe way to carry your funds. Although you can get replacement funds in 24 hours if your card is lost or stolen, it doesn't really strike us as a very good deal. In addition to a high initial cost ($14.95 to set up the card, plus $5 each time you "reload"), you still have to pay a 2% fee for each purchase in a foreign currency (similar to that of any credit card). Further, each time you use the card in an ATM you pay a transaction fee of $2.50 on top of the 2% transaction fee for the conversion—add it all up and it can be considerably more than you would pay when simply using your own ATM card. Regular traveler's checks are just as secure and cost less.
American Express ☎ 888/412-6945 in U.S., 801/945-9450 collect outside of U.S. to add value or speak to customer service ⊕ www.americanexpress.com.

∎ RESTROOMS

Hong Kong was once renowned for its lack of public restrooms, but things are improving. When sightseeing in the city, dip into malls or the lobby of big international hotels to use their facilities. Tipping attendants HK$2–HK$5 is the norm.

Many Westerners turn up their noses at squatter loos, but the well-maintained public ones are often cleaner than their Western equivalents, not to mention good for your thigh muscles. Since SARS and bird flu the government has been particularly active in keeping public facilities clean, but toilet paper is still hit-and-miss: bring your own tissues in case.

Find a Loo **The Bathroom Diaries** ⊕ www. thebathroomdiaries.com is flush with unsanitized info on restrooms the world over—each one located, reviewed, and rated.

▌ SAFETY

Hong Kong is an incredibly safe place—day and night. The police do a good job maintaining law and order, but there are still a few pickpockets about, especially in Tsim Sha Tsui. So exercise the same caution you would in any large city: be aware and avoid carrying large amounts of cash or valuables with you, and you should have no problems.

Nearly all consumer dissatisfaction in Hong Kong stems from the electronics retailers in Tsim Sha Tsui. Get some reference prices online before buying, and always check the contents of boxed items before you leave the shop.

▌ TIP➔ **Distribute your cash, credit cards, IDs, and other valuables between a deep front pocket, an inside jacket or vest pocket, and a hidden money pouch. Don't reach for the money pouch once you're in public.**

▌ TAXES

Hong Kong levies a 10% service charge and a 3% government tax on hotel rooms. There's no other sales tax or V.A.T.

▌ TIME

Hong Kong is 12 hours ahead of Eastern Standard Time and 7 hours ahead of Greenwich Mean Time. Remember during daylight savings time to add an hour to the time difference (so it's 13 hours ahead of EST and 8 hours ahead of GMT).

▌ TIPPING

Tipping isn't a big part of Hong Kong culture. That said, hotels are one of the few places where tips are expected. Hotels and major restaurants usually add a 10% service charge; however, in almost all cases, this money does not go to the waiters and waitresses. Add on up to 10% more for good service. Tipping restroom attendants is common, but it is generally not the custom to leave an additional tip in taxis and beauty salons, and unheard of in theaters and cinemas.

TIPPING GUIDELINES FOR HONG KONG	
Bartender	HK$10–HK$20 per round of drinks, depending on the number of drinks
Bellhop	HK$5–HK$20 per bag, depending on the level of the hotel
Hotel Concierge	HK$20–HK$50, more if he or she performs a service for you
Hotel Doorman	HK$5 if he helps you get a cab
Porter at Airport or Train Station	HK$2–HK$5 per bag
Waiter	5%–10% if service was good
Restroom Attendants	HK$2–HK$5

INDEX

PHOTO CREDITS

imilian Weinzierl/Alamy. 193, *Doug Scott/age fotostock*. 197 (top and bottom), *ImagineChina*. 198 (top), *Panorama/age fotostock*. 198 (bottom), *ImagineChina*. 199, *North Wind Picture Archives/Alamy*. 200 (top), *Christine Gonsalves/iStockphoto*. 200 (bottom left), *Profimedia CZ/Alamy*. 200 (bottom center), *TH Foto/Alamy*. 201 (right), *Sue Wilson/Alamy*. 202, *ImagineChina*. 203, *Richard T. Nowitz/age fotostock*. **Chapter 6: After Dark:** 213, *Picture Contact/Alamy*. 214, *Hong Kong Tourism Board*. **Chapter 7: Where to Stay:** 229, *Worldhotels*. 230, *Graham Uden*. **Chapter 8: Side Trip to Macau:** 263, *Iain Masterton/Alamy*. 265, *ImagineChina*. 267, *David Sanger Photography/Alamy*. **Chapter 9: Side Trips to the Pearl River Delta:** 301, *ImagineChina*. 303, *Wojtek Buss/age fotostock*. 304 (top), *Bruno Perousse/age fotostock*. 304 (bottom), *Doug Scott/age fotostock*. 306, *JTB Photo/Alamy*. 326-27, *SuperStock/age fotostock*. 328-29, *ImagineChina*. 330 (left and top right), *ImagineChina*. 330 (bottom right), *Bruno Perousse/age fotostock*. **Chapter 10: Golf:** 345, *Hong Kong Tourism Board*. 346, *Kau Sai Chau Public Golf Course*. **Color Section:** Taking the tram, Victoria Peak: *Hong Kong Tourism Board*. Star Ferry: *Hong Kong Tourism*. Cantonese Opera performers, Hong Kong Heritage Museum: *Sylvain Grandadam/age fotostock*. Tai Chi practitioners, Hong Kong Park: *Hemis/Alamy*. Wan Chai shopping street: *José Fuste Raga/age fotostock*. Buddha, Po Lin Monastery, Lantau Island: *Rough Guides/Alamy*. Flagstaff Museum of Tea Ware: *Pat Behnke/Alamy*. *Manpower* sculpture by Rosanna Li: *Grotto Fine Art Gallery*. Trams and taxis: *Hong Kong Tourism Board*. Avenue of the Stars, Kowloon waterfront: *Brad Mitchell/Alamy*. Hakka woman: *ImageState/Alamy*. Pacific Place mall: *Hong Kong Tourism Board*. Po Lin Monastery, Lantau Island: *Werner Otto/age fotostock*. Dancing girls: *Tim Graham/Alamy*. Sai Kung Peninsula, New Territories: *Hong Kong Tourism Board*. Chow Yun-Fat in *Crouching Tiger, Hidden Dragon*: *Pictorial Press Ltd/Alamy*. *Duk Ling* junk: *Hong Kong Tourism Board*.

NOTES

NOTES

NOTES

NOTES

NOTES

NOTES

NOTES

NOTES

ABOUT OUR WRITERS

Hiram Chu, who writes for several Chinese English-language publications, covered Macau and golf courses for this edition. He was born in San Francisco and spent his childhood listening to his parents' riveting tales of Mao's China. After studying at University of California–Davis, he decided to see the land of his ancestors. He loves the juxtaposition of modern society and ancient history and has spent several years in the metropolises of Guangzhou, Shenzhen, and Zhuhai.

Born in Hong Kong and raised in Australia, Eva Chui Loiterton returned to her birthplace in 1995 and for two years reported on arts and popular culture for *HK Magazine*. She then became a producer, first at News Corporation's Star TV and then at Walt Disney International Television. Currently she divides her time between writing and working in the TV and film industries. For this edition, she wrote On the Move, Sail Away, Beaches, Island Hopping, Hiking, Off to the Races, and Cinema Hong Kong in the Experience chapter; the Southside and New Territories sections of the Neighborhoods chapter; and all of the After Dark chapter.

Robin Goldstein, who covered Hong Kong restaurants and hotels, has also contributed to Fodor's guides on Thailand, Italy, Rome, Venice, Mexico, Cancún, Argentina, and Chile. Robin trained in cooking at the French Culinary Institute in New York City and has served as restaurant critic for the *New Haven Advocate* and *Metro New York*. He's also the founder and chief food critic of the *Fearless Critic* restaurant guide series; his latest title is the *Fearless Critic Austin Restaurant Guide*. Robin currently lives out of a suitcase, while his Yale law degree resides happily in a closet, collecting dust.

Victoria Patience—who grew up in Hong Kong, never stopped calling it home, and returns there regularly—once traveled by train all the way from Hong Kong to London, where she studied Spanish and Latin American literature. This led her to Buenos Aires, where she now lives and works as a freelance writer. Victoria penned the Cultural Sights chapter, the "All the Tea in China" article in Where to Eat, and the Hong Kong Then & Now and Essentials sections at the end of the book. She also wrote several Experience sections: the Planner, Top Attractions, Free Things to Do, Feasts & Fêtes, Feng Shui Structures, Peak Experience, To Your Health, and Very Amusing. In Neighborhoods, she covered Western, Central, Lantau, Wan Chai, and Kowloon. And in Shopping, her words help you plan; take you through the districts; and give you insight into department stores, markets, and malls.

Sofia A. Suárez runs her communications company, Fiorini Bassi, in Hong Kong, where she was born and raised. After studying in the United States and Italy, the Italian-Filipina moved to New York to work for Fairchild Publications. Sofia now contributes to various newspapers and magazines around the world, including the *South China Morning Post*, for which she writes weekly style and art columns. For this guide, Sofia put her fashion savvy to work on the "It Suits You" article and all the specialty-store reviews in the Shopping chapter.

We'd also like to thank writers Joshua Samuel Brown ("Spirituality in China" article, Cultural Sights chapter; the Pearl River Delta chapter); Elyse Singleton ("Markets" article, Shopping chapter); and Chris Horton ("21st Century China" article, Pearl River Delta chapter).